SECOND EDITION

Multinational Management

A STRATEGIC APPROACH

John B. Cullen
Washington State University

SOUTH-WESTERN

THOMSON LEARNING

Australia · Canada · Mexico · Singapore · Spain · United Kingdom · United States

Multinational Management: A Strategic Approach, 2e by John B. Cullen

Vice President/Publisher: Jack W. Calhoun
Executive Editor: John Szilagyi
Marketing Manager: Rob Bloom
Developmental Editor: Kelly Curtis/Ohlinger Publishing Services
Production Editor: Elizabeth A. Shipp
Media Technology Editor: Vicky True
Media Developmental Editor: Kristen Meere
Media Production Editor: Mark Sears
Manufacturing Coordinator: Sandee Milewski
Internal Design: Ramsdell Design/Cincinnati, OH
Cover Design: Ramsdell Design/Cincinnati, OH
Cover Image: © Catherine Karnow/CORBIS
Production House: Pre-Press Company, Inc.
Printer: R.R. Donnelley & Sons Company—Willard Manufacturing Division

Printed in the United States of America
2 3 4 5 04 03 02

For more information contact South-Western, 5191 Natorp Boulevard, Mason, Ohio, 45040 or find us on the Internet at http://www.swcollege.com

For permission to use material from this text or product, contact us by
• telephone: 1-800-730-2214
• fax: 1-800-730-2215
• web: http://www.thomsonrights.com

Library of Congress Cataloging-in-Publication Data
Cullen, John B. (John Brooks), 1948–
    Multinational management: a strategic approach / John B. Cullen.—2nd ed.
        p. cm.
    Includes bibliographical references and index.
    ISBN 0-324-05569-2
        1. International business enterprises—Management. I. Title.

HD62.4 .C85 2001
658'.049—dc21   2001020967

To *les deux*

J & J

Plan of the Book

Part 1: Foundations of Multinational Management

Chapter 1
Multinational Management in a Changing World

Chapter 2
Culture and Multinational Management

Chapter 3
International Negotiation and Cross-Cultural Communication

Chapter 4
Managing Ethical and Social Responsibility Challenges in Multinational Companies

Part 2: Strategy Content and Formulation for Multinational Companies

Chapter 5
Basic Strategies for the Multinational Company: Content and Formulation

Chapter 6
Multinational and Participation Strategies: Content and Formulation

Part 3: Management Processes in Strategy Implementation: Design Choices for Multinational Companies

Chapter 7
Organizational Designs for Multinational Companies

Chapter 8
International Strategic Alliances: Management and Design

Part 4: Multinational Strategy and Structure for E-Commerce and Small Businesses

Chapter 9
Multinational E-Commerce: Strategies and Structures

Chapter 10
Small Businesses as Multinational Companies: Overcoming Barriers and Finding Opportunities

Part 5: Management Processes in Strategy Implementation: Managing People in Multinational Companies

Chapter 11
International Human Resource Management

Chapter 12
National Differences in HRM: Knowing When and How to Adapt

Chapter 13
Motivation in Multinational Companies

Chapter 14
Leadership and Management Behavior in Multinational Companies

Part 6: Understanding Collaborators and Competitors: Comparative Strategic Management and Organizational Design

Chapter 15
Comparative Strategic Management and Organizational Design

BRIEF CONTENTS

CONTENTS

12: NATIONAL DIFFERENCES IN HRM: KNOWING WHEN AND HOW TO ADAPT   463

13: MOTIVATION IN MULTINATIONAL COMPANIES   502

PREFACE

Globalization is changing the nature of business education today. The process of globalization stems from a number of important factors including reduced trade barriers, multinational e-commerce, technological innovations, the growing similarity of customer needs, and the proliferation of transnational corporations, and it is strategy that defines this process. Developing and making strategic choices are the mainstay of successful decision making in our global environment. To help the reader develop the essential skills needed to formulate and implement these strategic moves, this text provides a thorough review and analysis of the latest research on international management.

Multinational Management: A Strategic Approach brings a distinctive method to the teaching and learning of international management, using a strategic perspective as a unifying theme to explore the global economy and the impact of managerial decisions. This text is the first international management text that uses this critical emphasis on strategic decision making as the cornerstone of its approach.

Successful multinational managers view the world as an integrated market where competition and collaboration evolve from almost anywhere and anyone. At the same time, these managers must appreciate the wide array of differences that exist in cultures and social institutions. To facilitate this orientation, this text explores not only a North American view of multinational management, but also looks at how companies throughout the world approach global competition. As such, the reader is not limited to understanding multinational management from the perspective of any one nation or group.

NEW TO THIS EDITION

While the entire text has been reworked to reflect current research and examples from the field of International Management, specific revisions to the text material include:

E-Business: The second edition features an entire chapter dedicated to multinational e-commerce strategies and structure. The chapter highlights the benefits and challenges of e-commerce for all types of multinational businesses.

Internet Activities: In the second edition Internet activities have been added to the end of *every* chapter to give learners an opportunity to apply Web resources to multinational management issues.

Diverse Examples: This edition extensively utilizes examples from regions outside of the Triad, including Africa, South America, Southeast Asia, and the Middle East.

Current: All chapters were updated to include the latest research, examples, and statistics in multinational management to create the most accurate and current presentation possible. Highlights include:

- the most current multinational management examples in the boxed features included in each chapter
- recent findings from Trompenaars' studies of national culture
- new findings on multinational leadership from GLOBE: The Global Leadership and Organizational Behavior Effectiveness Research Program
- prepublication information from the author's own research on trust within and between cultural groups
- five new integrating cases

PEDAGOGICAL APPROACH

Multinational Management: A Strategic Approach, Second Edition provides a thorough review and analysis of multinational management. In addition, this text includes several unique pedagogical learning tools:

Strategic Viewpoint: Although this is not a strategic management text, the strategic viewpoint provides a unifying theme that guides the reader through the material. Additionally, this theme highlights for students the process multinational companies engage in when deciding to compete in the global economy, and the management consequences of these strategic choices.

Comparative Management Issues: Multinational managers must learn to understand the strengths, weaknesses, and strategies of competitors from anywhere in the world. In addition, they must know when and how to adapt their organizational practices to accommodate local situations. The comparative nature of this text is designed to assist students in reorienting themselves to understand the complexities of other nations and cultures.

Reviews of Management Principles: The text contains several chapters that assume limited background knowledge in management. These topics include strategic management, organizational design, human resource management, and organizational behavior. For students with limited previous coursework or who need a review, each chapter provides background primers with a brief explanation of key concepts and ideas.

Small Business Applications: Unlike most international management texts, this book offers the multinational activities of small businesses a prominent position. An entire chapter focuses specifically on the problems and prospects for small businesses looking to become multinational competitors. Two of the integrating cases challenge students to apply the concepts and theories of small business management in the global environment.

KEY FEATURES

Internet Activities: All chapters include Internet activities that challenge students to use resources on the World Wide Web to locate international business information. Also, an extensive selection of Internet source information is listed at the end of each chapter. These include private corporations, government resources, and other valuable Web addresses.

Chapter Cases and Activities: The text divides major end-of-chapter projects between cases and activities. Eight chapters offer end-of-chapter cases, which give the learner the opportunity to apply text material to real life managerial problems. The remaining chapters feature detailed end-of-chapter experiential exercises or assignments that encourage the reader to apply text material to concrete problems. These exercises simulate the challenges that practicing multinational managers encounter on the job.

Integrating Cases: Each of the six parts offer a selection of full-length cases that require the integration of material from all preceding chapters. These cases were chosen to challenge the reader with the complexities of the global environment.

Extensive Examples: Throughout the text, there are many examples designed to enhance the text material and to show actual multinational management situations. These examples are illustrated in four different formats:

- *Preview Case in Point:* Brief cases open each chapter and focus the reader's interest on the chapter content.
- *Case in Point:* Include real life examples of multinational companies and discuss relevant topics in each chapter.
- *Multinational Management Challenge:* Explore decisions made by management staff using actual companies and situations.
- *Multinational Management Brief:* Each brief further explains or details an issue discussed in the text.

Models as Examples: To further explain key principles, extensive sets of models created by the author offer visual aides for students to draw upon as they study the material.

CONTENTS

The text is structured into six major parts. Part 1 is divided into four introductory chapters that provide essential background on the nature of multinational management. These chapters address the challenges facing managers in the new global economy, how national cultures affect management, international negotiation and communication, and managing ethical and social responsibility in multinational companies.

Part 2 includes two chapters that review how multinational companies formulate successful strategies to compete internationally. The first chapter provides a broad overview of strategic management with multinational implications. The second chapter focuses on the strategies required to "go international."

Part 3 addresses the management systems used to implement multinational strategies. Specifically, the first chapter of Part 3 considers how multinational companies design and structure their organizations to implement these strategies. The second chapter examines the management and design issues involved in building international strategic alliances.

Part 4 considers two specialized topics. One chapter, new to this edition, focuses on the strategies and structures of multinational e-commerce. Another chapter focuses on how the concepts discussed regarding multinational strategies and organizational design apply to smaller, entrepreneurial organizations.

Part 5 deals with strategy implementation at the level of the individual in the organization. Topics considered include international human resource practices, the adaptation of these practices across cultures, and motivation and leadership in multinational companies.

Finally, Part 6 explores how companies in different countries develop their own brands of strategic management and why different organization designs occur in various nations.

FOR INSTRUCTORS

Multinational Management offers the most learning and teaching intensive package for students and instructors. These supplements to the text give both students and instructors many options for learning and teaching the text content.

Instructor's Manual with Test Bank: This book offers instructional materials, a full test bank, and a full set of transparency masters. (ISBN: 0-324-05570-6)

PowerPoint™ Slide Presentations: The author has created more than 300 slides that illustrate the concepts of each chapter. These can be found on the Web site at http://cullen.swcollege.com.

Web Site: This strong Web site (http://cullen.swcollege.com) is updated by the author and offers a full set of PowerPoint slides, sample syllabi, teaching tips, and continuously updated Internet addresses, among other items.

FOR STUDENTS

Web Site: The same Web site offers students study questions and tips, key term definitions, and Internet sites and activities, among other learning aides.

ACKNOWLEDGMENTS

Numerous individuals helped make this book possible. Most of all, I must thank my wife, Jean Johnson, Associate Professor of Marketing at Washington State University and an experienced internationalist, for reading and commenting on all chapters. Her insights were invaluable, as was her suggestion to organize the book around the strategic management perspective. My daughter Jaye reluctantly gave up her access to the Internet when I needed to check a reference or read something online. She even occasionally sacrificed having sleepovers with her preteen friends when I had to work weekends to make deadlines.

This text would not be possible without the support of a team of professionals. My initial thanks go to Executive Editor John Szilagyi, the driver of South-Western's management list, who encouraged me to write the second edition. The commitment of Marketing Manager Rob Bloom to the first edition helped make this effort possible. For this edition, Theresa Curtis of Ohlinger Publishing Services managed the process of soliciting reviews of the first edition. Developmental Editor Kelly Curtis, also of Ohlinger Publishing Services, provided critical reviews of all chapters and diligently, but kindly, prodded me to keep on schedule. Jan Turner of the Pre-Press Company expediently managed copy editing and composition. Production Editor Libby Shipp at South-Western coordinated the team effort and put together a good-looking final product.

Colleagues Paul Huo of the University of Puget Sound and Steve Si of Bloomsburg University of Pennsylvania provided feedback on this text as they used the material in classrooms throughout the world. Praveen Parboteeah, University of Wisconsin-Whitewater, provided suggestions during the whole project and is the author of the Instructor's Manual.

Other colleagues who read and offered insightful comments on this edition include:

Carol Sánchez
Grand Valley State University

Raffaele DeVito
Emporia State University

David F. Martin
Murray State University

Anthony J. Avallone, Jr.
Point Loma Nazarene University

Gerry N. Muuka
Murray State University

Maru Etta-Nkwelle
Howard University

Gary Baker
Buena Vista University

Douglas M. Kline
Sam Houston State University

Michael J. Pisani
Texas A&M International University

Tracy A. Thompson
University of Washington, Tacoma

John B. Cullen

Chapter 1

Multinational Management in a Changing World

LEARNING OBJECTIVES
After reading this chapter you should be able to:

- **Define multinational management.**

- **Understand the characteristics of a multinational company.**

- **Understand the nature of the global economy and the key forces that drive globalization.**

- **Know the basic classification of the world's economies.**

- **Identify the characteristics of the next generation of multinational managers.**

<table>
<tr><td>

**Preview
Case in Point**

**Two Views of
Multinational
Opportunities**

</td><td>

"Somebody asked me a couple of years ago, 'Why do we spend so much time talking about the business outside of the United States?' and I said, 'That's because that's where most of the people live.' It's that simple. It's simply a fact of income."

—Donald R. Keough, past president and chief operating officer of Coca-Cola

Thirty-two-year-old Jorden Woods speaks five languages. He has lived in Japan, France, New York, and Hong Kong. Born in China, Excelle Liu was educated in the United States and worked as a marketing executive in Hong Kong. Together they founded a company called Global Sight. They are also new economy entrepreneurs with global mindsets.

Headquartered in San Jose, California, this 50-employee company helps firms globalize their Web sites. As companies build Web sites for multinational use, they must adjust content and language for different nations. Global Sight provides software and a staff of professional translators to expedite the process. Although just a small company, Global Sight's customers include such major players as HP, Cisco Systems, GE Information Services, Palm Computing, and Samsung. GE's Doug Erwin notes that Global Sight's software allows the Italian, French, and German versions of the company's TradeWeb site to be updated in several hours. Before using Global Sight, the process took three weeks. Although less than four years old in 2001, Global Sight has offices in London, Geneva, and Tokyo in addition to its four offices in the United States.

Sources: Based on Guttman 1992; *Frontier* 1999 and Globalsight 2001.

</td></tr>
</table>

As the Preview Case in Point shows, businesses of all sizes, whether from the old or new economy, increasingly see the entire world as a source of business opportunities. Why? Trade barriers are falling, and world trade among countries in goods and services is growing faster than domestic production. Thus, money is flowing more freely across national borders. Companies seek the best rates for financing anywhere in the world, and investors look for the best returns anywhere in the world. The Internet crosses national boundaries with the click of a mouse allowing even the smallest of businesses to go global immediately. All these processes represent a trend

Globalization

The worldwide trend of businesses expanding beyond their domestic boundaries.

known as **globalization**.

Globalization is the worldwide trend of businesses expanding beyond their domestic boundaries. Globalization means that the world is becoming one connected economy in which companies do business and compete anywhere and with anyone, regardless of national boundaries. In a global economy, any company from any country can become a competitor. Consequently, companies can no longer afford the luxury of assuming that success in their home market equates to long-term profitability—or even survival.

Companies that remain "domestic-only"—that is, companies that do business only within their own country—are already falling behind their multinational competitors. Consider the following observations regarding the world's biggest companies from *Business Week*'s Global 1000 rankings:

Since Business Week *first launched its ranking of the world's most valuable corporations in 1988, the global economy has been transformed. More countries are open to international trade and investment than ever before. Recent Global 1000 rankings are a barometer of such change. The rankings show investors clearly valuing global champions, particularly in the new economy technology industries, while shunning domestic also-rans. From the U.S. to Europe to Asia, the companies moving up the ranking are those that have become worldwide names in technology, manufacturing, and consumer goods. (Edmondson, Capell, Moore, & Burrows 2000; Symonds et al. 1996; Weber, Yang, Capell 1999)*

Consider the case of General Electric (BW Global 1000 #1). In 1993, only 16.5 percent of their sales came from outside of the United States. By the year 2000, international sales were over 30 percent. During the same period, Wal-Mart (BW Global 1000 #7) went from 0 percent to nearly 14 percent of sales from international operations. Few companies can match the Finnish cell phone maker Nokia (BW Global 1000 #9) with over 97 percent international sales (*Business Week Online* 2000a; *Business Week Online* 2000b).

Multinational management

The formulation of strategies and the design of management systems that successfully take advantage of international opportunities and respond to international threats.

What does this mean to the student of international business? With companies increasingly looking at global rather than domestic markets, managers of the next century will have little choice but to be multinational in outlook and strategies. Consequently, all students of business should have at least a basic background in multinational management. Simply put, **multinational management** is the formulation of strategies and the design of management systems that successfully take advantage of international opportunities and respond to international threats. Successful multinational managers are executives with the ability and motivation to meet and beat the challenges of multinational management. Later in the chapter you will learn more of the characteristics needed to be a successful multinational manager.

To provide you with basic background in multinational management, this book introduces you to the latest information on how managers throughout the world respond to the challenges of globalization. You will see how businesses, both large and small, deal with the complexities of national differences in cultures, economies, and political systems. You will learn how multinational managers use their understanding of these national differences to formulate strategies that maximize their companies' success in globalizing industries.

Because having good strategies is not enough to succeed in today's economy, you will learn how multinational managers carry out their multinational strategies. First, the book explains how managers design organizational and human resource systems for multinational companies. Second, the book shows how multinational managers develop motivational and leadership strategies that work in any national setting. In addition to these issues, you will see some of the challenges that multinational managers face in dealing with ethics and social responsibility in different national cultures.

To give you insights into the real world of multinational management, you will find four types of examples in this and the following chapters. *Preview Cases in Point* show you examples of how multinational companies are dealing with a key issue that is discussed in the chapter. *Cases in Point* give information on how actual multinational companies deal with the issues currently under review in the text. *Multinational Management Briefs* give you further detail and examples that extend the discussions in the chapters. *Multinational Management Challenges* describe problems and dilemmas faced by real multinational managers for which there is no easy answer.

Multinational management takes place in the multinational company. What is a multinational company? The next section gives a definition and brief introduction to the major players in multinational competition.

THE NATURE OF THE MULTINATIONAL COMPANY

Multinational company

Any company that engages in business functions beyond its domestic borders.

The **multinational company** is broadly defined as any company that engages in business functions beyond its domestic borders. This is a broad definition, which includes all types of companies, large and small, that engage in international business. Most multinational companies, however, are also multinational corporations—the companies are publicly owned through stocks. Most often, when you see references to MNCs in the popular business press, the reference is to multinational corporations. The largest multinationals are all public corporations. (Exhibit 1.1 lists the top thirty multinational corporations ranked by sales revenue.) Smaller multinational companies are often privately owned, but many of their business activities may be conducted outside their own country. Smaller, nonpublic multinational companies are also becoming increasingly important as it becomes more common for smaller organizations to compete globally.

What kinds of business activities might make a company multinational? The most apparent activity, of course, is international sales. When a company produces in its own country and sells in another, it engages in the simplest level of multinational activity. However, as you will see in much more detail later in the book, crossing national borders opens up more multinational options than simply selling internationally.

To introduce some of the multinational options, consider the following hypothetical U.S. company that produces and sells men's shirts. As a domestic-only company it can buy the dye, make the fabric, cut and sew the garment, and sell the shirt, all in the United States. However, the firm might not be able to compete successfully using this approach. The U.S. market may be stagnant, with competitive pricing and lower profit margins. Competitors might find higher-quality fabric or dye from overseas suppliers. Competitors might find lower production costs in low-wage countries, allowing them to offer lower prices. What can this company do?

As a multinational company, the firm might sell the shirt to overseas buyers in countries with less competition and higher prices. Several other multinational activities might increase its competitive strength. For example, this company might locate any of the steps in obtaining raw materials or completing production in another country. It might buy the highest-quality dye from Italy, use the lowest-cost, high-quality fabric producers in Hong Kong, and have the cutting and sewing done in Vietnam with very low labor costs. For any of these steps, the company might contract with local companies in another country or may own its own factories within another country. As you will see in later chapters, multinational companies must develop strategies and systems to accomplish all or some of the multinational business tasks of this hypothetical U.S. company.

Next, we will consider the forces that drive the new economic reality that faces the next generation of multinational managers and multinational companies.

THE GLOBALIZING ECONOMY:
A CHANGING ENVIRONMENT FOR BUSINESS

Several key trends drive the globalization of the world economy and, in turn, force businesses to become more multinational to survive and prosper. Some of the most important trends include falling borders, growing cross-border trade and investment, the rise of global products and global customers, the growing use of the

Exhibit 1.1 The Largest Companies in the World

Fortune Global 500 Rank (Revenues)	Business Week Global 1000 (Market Value)	Company Name	Main Industry	Headquarters Country	Revenues $ million	Market Value $ billion	Profit $ million	Profit Rank
1	124	General Motors	Automobiles	USA	176,558	44	6,002	14
2	7	Wal-Mart Stores	Retail	USA	166,809	257	5,377	19
3	5	Exxon Mobil	Energy sources	USA	163,881	290	7,910	5
4	89	Ford Motor	Automobiles	USA	162,558	58	7,237	12
5	97	Daimler-Chrysler	Automobiles	Germany/USA	159,986	54	6,129	13
6	476	Mitsui	Trading	Japan	118,555	11	321	>100
7	NA	Mitsubishi	Trading	Japan	117,766	NA	234	>100
8	21	Toyota Motor	Automobiles	Japan	115,671	171	3,653	39
9	1	General Electric	Electronics, electrical equipment	USA	111,630	520	10,717	1
10	NA	Itochu	Trading	Japan	109,069	NA	793	>100
11	10	Royal Dutch/Shell Group	Energy sources	Britain/Netherlands	105,366	214	8,584	3
12	NA	Sumitomo	Trading	Japan	99,860	NA	315	>100
13	15	Nippon Telegraph & Telephone	Telecom	Japan	97,658	189	609	>100
14	NA	Marubeni	Trading	Japan	95,796	NA	19	>100
15	93	AXA	Insurance	France	83,069	57	2,156	96
16	14	Intl. Business Machines	Computers	USA	87,548	192	57,712	8
17	12	BP Amoco	Energy sources	UK	83,566	208	5,008	>100
18	11	Citigroup	Finance	USA	82,005	210	9,867	23
19	355	Volkswagen	Automobiles	Germany	75,980	15	875	>100
20	NA	Nippon Life Insurance	Insurance	Japan	78,515	NA	3,405	45
21	53	Siemens	Electronics, electrical equipment	Germany	72,074	87	1,774	>100
22	52	Allianz	Insurance	Germany	70,305	87	2,382	77
23	133	Hitachi	Electrical & electronics	Japan	74,981	41	152	>100
24	112	Matsushita Electric Industrial	Appliances	Japan	68,404	49	896	>100
25	NA	Nissho Iwai	Trading	Japan	68,235	NA	92	>100
26	NA	U.S. Postal Service	Mail delivery	USA	62,726	NA	363	>100
27	92	ING Group	Insurance	Netherlands	62,492	57	5,250	21
28	36	AT&T	Telecom	USA	62,391	109	3,428	44
29	84	Philip Morris	Tobacco products	USA	61,751	60	7,675	10
30	58	Sony	Electrical & electronics	Japan	62,662	80	1,094	>100

Sources: Compiled with data from *Fortune* 2000; *Business Week Online* 2000a and *Forbes* 2000.

Exhibit 1.2 Selected Economies of the World

Developed Countries	% Change in GDP	Developing Countries							
		Four Tigers	% Change in GDP	Transition Economies	% Change in GDP	Others	% Change in GDP
Australia	4.2	Hong Kong	10.4	Czech Rep.	2.2	Argentina	0.8
Austria	3.8	Singapore	10.4	Hungary	4.6	Brazil	4.5
Belgium	4.4	South Korea	9.2	Poland	5.2	Chile	5.8
Britain	3.0	Taiwan	6.6	Russia	7.9	China	8.2
Canada	5.0					Colombia	3.1
Denmark	2.7	Baby Tigers	% Change in GDP			Greece	3.7
France	3.1					India	7.2
Germany	2.8	Malaysia	7.7			Israel	7.3
Italy	2.4	Indonesia	5.1			Mexico	7.0
Japan	1.4	Thailand	2.6			Philippines	4.8
Netherlands	3.4					Portugal	3.0
Spain	3.9					South Africa	4.5
Sweden	4.0					Turkey	7.4
Switzerland	3.6					Venezuela	3.3
United States	5.2						

Source: Adapted from *Economist* 2001.

Internet and sophisticated information technology, privatizations of companies formerly owned by governments, the emergence of new competitors in the world market, and the rise of global standards of quality and production.

Before discussing the key globalization trends that affect multinational managers and their companies, it is useful to look at some commonly used classifications of the world's countries. The classifications roughly indicate a country's gross domestic product (GDP) and the growth in GDP. The classifications are not exact but they simplify discussions of world trade and investments.

COUNTRIES OF THE WORLD: THE ARRIVED, THE COMING, AND THE STRUGGLING

Four tigers

The newly industrialized countries (NICs), including Hong Kong, Singapore, South Korea, and Taiwan.

Transition economies

Countries in the process of changing from government-controlled economic systems to capitalistic systems.

Exhibit 1.2 shows some divisions of the world's economies based roughly on classifications used by the United Nations and *The Economist*. Developed countries have mature economies with substantial per capita GDPs and international trade and investments. The developing countries, led by the **four tigers**, the newly industrialized countries (NICs) of Hong Kong, Singapore, South Korea, and Taiwan, have growing economies that, in spite of the setbacks of the Asian crisis in the late 1990s, many believe will be the future hot spots in the global economy. Other developing economies to watch are what the UN calls the **transition economies** of the Czech Republic, Hungary, Poland, and Russia and the developing economies of Indonesia, Malaysia, the Philippines, Vietnam, and Thailand.

Transition economies are countries in the process of changing from government-controlled, mostly Communist economic systems to market or capitalistic systems. The former systems relied on state-controlled organizations and centralized government control to run the economy. In the transition to free market and capitalistic systems, government-owned companies are converted to private ownership. The market and not the government then determines the success of companies.

Exhibit 1.3
The Globalizing
Economy

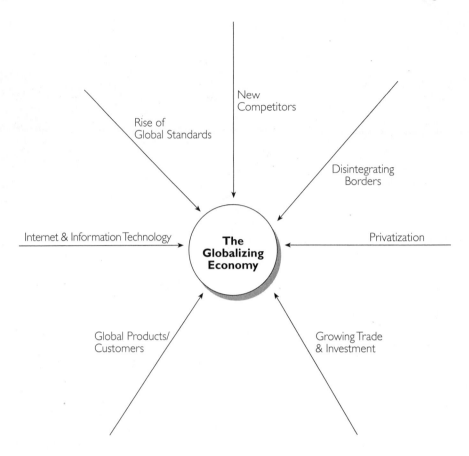

Several of these transition economies, such as Hungary, Poland, Estonia, and the
Czech Republic, have developed market economies that now qualify them for membership in the European Union (*Economist* 2000b; European Commission 2000).

**Less developed
countries (LDCs)**

*The poorest nations,
often plagued with
unstable political
regimes, high
unemployment, and
low worker skills.*

Less developed countries (LDCs) have yet to show much progress in the
evolving global economy. They are the poorest nations and are often plagued with
unstable political regimes, high unemployment, and unskilled workers. Most of these
countries are located in Central and South America, Africa, and the Middle East.

Led by Korea (in spite of the troubles of high profile Korean companies such as
Daewoo), Asian economies have bounced back from their deep slump in 1998
(*Economist* 2000a). As shown in Exhibit 1.2, their GDPs are back in the positive.
However, the Japanese and Taiwanese economies remain less vibrant than they were
in their early boom years. Some forecasters anticipate that more trouble may be in
store for certain Asian countries (*Economist* 2000d).

With this overview of the major economies of the world, we can now look
more closely at the driving forces of the new world economy. Exhibit 1.3 illustrates
these important forces. Each of these driving forces is discussed below.

BORDERS ARE DISINTEGRATING: THE WORLD TRADE ORGANIZATION AND FREE TRADE AREAS

In 1947, several nations began negotiating to limit worldwide tariffs and encourage
free trade. At that time, worldwide tariffs averaged 45 percent. Seven rounds of tariff negotiations reduced the average worldwide tariffs on manufactured goods from

General Agreement on Tariffs and Trade (GATT)

Tariff negotiations between several nations that reduced the average worldwide tariff on manufactured goods.

World Trade Organization (WTO)

A formal structure for continued negotiations to reduce trade barriers and a mechanism for settling trade disputes.

45 percent to less than 7 percent. These negotiations were known as **GATT**, the **General Agreement on Tariffs and Trade**.

Negotiations in Uruguay began in 1986 and ended in 1993 with agreements to reduce tariffs even further, liberalize trade in agriculture and services, and eliminate some nontariff barriers to international trade, such as excessive use of health regulations to keep out imports (*Economist* 1996b). The Uruguay talks also established the **World Trade Organization (WTO)** to succeed GATT. The WTO provides a formal structure for continued negotiations and for settling trade disputes among nations. There are now 140 nations in the WTO, up from 92 when the 1986 GATT talks began, including 29 of the UN-classified least developed countries. Thirty more countries, including Russia and China, seek WTO membership. Since 1995, tariffs on industrial products have fallen from an average of 6.3 percent to 3.8 percent (WTO 2000a).

In March 1997, trade ministers from countries representing 92 percent of world trade in information technology products agreed to end tariffs on trade in software, computer chips, telecommunications equipment, and computers. By the year 2005, this $500 billion a year trade should be mostly tariff free.

The immediate expected result is that with tariffs eliminated, high-tech exports to Europe from Asia and the United States should double. Developing countries, even those not party to the agreement, will likely also benefit. Prices should go down on products such as phones, faxes, and computers that are produced in tariff-free locations (WTO 2000a).

Is free trade working? The WTO thinks so and the data seems to support its conclusion. Since the early GATT agreements, world trade has grown at more than four times the output of the world's gross domestic product. This suggests that the world's economies are increasingly more intertwined and mutually stimulated.

There are, however, critics. Some argue that the WTO favors the developed nations, because it is more difficult for poorer nations to compete in a nonregulated world. Environmentalists note that free trade encourages large multinational companies to move environmentally damaging production to poorer and often environmentally sensitive countries. That is, commercial interests have priority over the environment, health, and safety. Labor unions see free trade leading to the migration of jobs from higher wage countries to lower wage countries. You can see the WTO's counter arguments on their Web site at: http://www.wto.org/.

The WTO is an evolving organization and its goal of free trade for all is still not achieved. Not all major world players are WTO members, and trade discussions continue over specific products. The next Multinational Management Brief describes the situation for China, not yet a member of the WTO.

Regional trade agreements

Agreements among nations in a particular region to reduce tariffs and develop similar technical and economic standards.

The WTO is not the only group encouraging the elimination of trade barriers. **Regional trade agreements** or free trade areas are agreements among groups of nations to reduce tariffs and develop similar technical and economic standards. Such agreements have usually led to more trade among the member nations. Some argue that these agreements are the first step toward complete globalization. Others criticize the agreements as benefiting only trade-group members and harmful for the poorer nations left out of the agreements (such as the Caribbean countries that are not members of NAFTA) (*Economist* 2000c; 1996a). From a practical point of view, regional agreements benefit world trade more than they hurt it. Although they do benefit member countries the most, such agreements are more politically manageable than worldwide trade agreements (Lubbers 1996).

By the end of the millennium, the number of regional trade agreements reached 139, more than double the number that existed in 1992 (WTO 2000a). In addition, more than 80 potential agreements are under consideration for approval

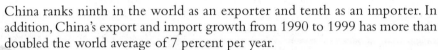

Multinational Management Brief
China in the WTO?

China ranks ninth in the world as an exporter and tenth as an importer. In addition, China's export and import growth from 1990 to 1999 has more than doubled the world average of 7 percent per year.

China, however, presents a problem for the WTO. The size and growth of China's trade almost require China to be part of any world trade agreements. For several years, China has been on the verge of WTO membership. However, China still has a semi-market economy with many restrictions that violate WTO regulations. These include the Chinese desire to protect "strategic" industries such as the automobile industry and Chinese trade restrictions such as import taxes, trade licenses, and import quotas and inspections. There are also questions regarding China's commitment to follow WTO regulations.

In addition, some members of the WTO, in particular the United States, see China's membership as determined by the Chinese record regarding human rights. However, the United States supports WTO membership for China and grants China the same trade access as it does to WTO members, although this status must be renewed each year.

Sources: Based on *Economist* 2000b; WTO 1997 and *European Report* 2000.

European Union (EU)

Austria, Belgium, Britain, Denmark, Finland, France, Germany, Greece, Ireland, Italy, Luxembourg, the Netherlands, Portugal, Spain, and Sweden, plus Norway and Switzerland in the related European Free Trade Area.

North American Free Trade Agreement (NAFTA)

A multilateral treaty that links the United States, Canada, and Mexico in an economic bloc that allows freer exchange of goods and services.

by the WTO (WTO 2000a). It should be noted that the majority of regional trade agreements came into existence after 1990 (WTO 2000; *Economist* 1996b).

The three largest groups account for nearly half of the world's trade. These groups are: the EU, NAFTA, and APEC (Bosheck 1996).

The **EU**, or **European Union**, includes Austria, Belgium, Britain, Denmark, Finland, France, Germany, Greece, Ireland, Italy, Luxembourg, the Netherlands, Portugal, Spain, and Sweden, plus Norway and Switzerland in the related European Free Trade Area. Current applicants, including many of the former Eastern Bloc countries, are Poland, Romania, the Czech Republic, Hungary, Bulgaria, Slovakia, Lithuania, Latvia, Slovenia, Estonia, Cyprus, and Malta.

Since 1992, the EU countries have allowed goods and services to move across borders without customs duties and quotas, and more recently, they adopted a unified currency called the European Economic and Monetary Union, or EMU.

The **North American Free Trade Agreement (NAFTA)** links the United States, Canada, and Mexico in an economic bloc that allows freer exchange of goods and services. After the agreement went into effect in the early 1990s, all three countries saw immediate increases in trade. However, the Mexican economy soon went into a tailspin, with inflation running as high as 45 percent (Boscheck 1996). Emergency loans from the United States helped stabilize the situation, and by 1996 Mexico had paid back the loans—before the due date. The next step for NAFTA may be FTAA or the Free Trade Area of Americas. This group will include not only the United States, Canada, and Mexico, but also most other Caribbean, Central American, and South American nations.

Exhibit 1.4
Who's Selling, Who's
Buying: The World's
Leading Exporters and
Importers

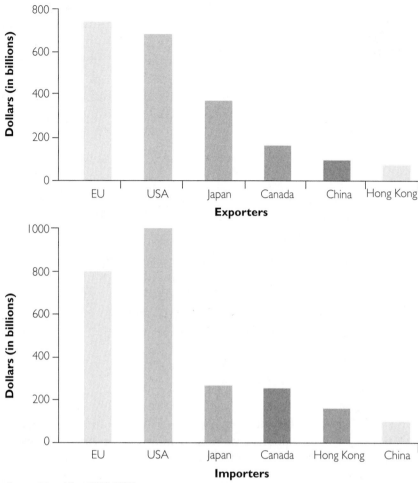

Source: Adapted from WTO 2000b.

Asia-Pacific Economic Cooperation (APEC)

A confederation of 19 nations with less specific agreements on trade facilitation in the Pacific region.

When compared with the EU or NAFTA, the **Asia-Pacific-Economic Cooperation (APEC)** is a looser confederation of nineteen nations with less specific agreements on trade facilitation. However, ultimate goals call for total free trade in the Pacific region by 2020 (*Economist* 1996a). Some of the major players in APEC include: China, the United States, Japan, Taiwan, South Korea, Hong Kong, Australia, Singapore, Thailand, and Malaysia.

SELL ANYWHERE, LOCATE ANYWHERE: TRADE AND FOREIGN INVESTMENT ARE GROWING

TRIAD

The world's dominant trading partners: European Union, United States, and Japan.

World trade among countries (imports and exports) has grown at an average rate of 6.5 percent per year between 1990 and 1999 (WTO 2000a). Exhibit 1.4 shows the leading exporting and importing countries based on data published by the WTO. Note that the combined countries of the EU now lead the United States in exporting. Exhibit 1.4 also shows that nearly half of the over $5 trillion in world trade is among the European Union, the United States, and Japan. This trading group is sometimes called the **TRIAD**. However, the developing economies of China, Korea, and Mexico are growing rapidly and are approaching Canada in trade volume.

Exhibit 1.5

Looking to the Future: Hot Growth Countries in Exports and Imports

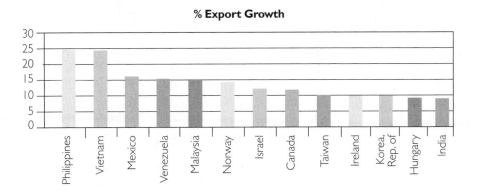

% Export Growth

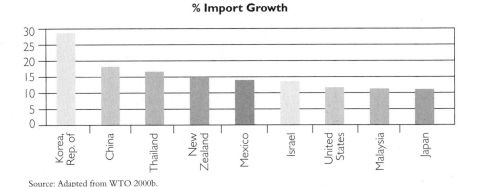

% Import Growth

Source: Adapted from WTO 2000b.

Hong Kong has a unique position as a world trade leader. Although now part of China, it retains a semi-independent status for trade. Note that only a small percentage of its import volume stays in this island city, and only a small percentage of its exports are produced in Hong Kong. Most of Hong Kong's imports come from other countries for eventual re-export to the rest of the world.

While the developed countries of the world continue to trade at approximately the world average, other economies are heating up. Where are the hot spots to which multinational managers must turn for future markets and future competitors?

LOOKING TO THE FUTURE: HOT GROWTH COUNTRIES IN EXPORTS AND IMPORTS

Exhibit 1.5 shows the leading countries in terms of import and export *growth*. Although many of these countries engage in international trade at substantially lower levels than the triad, their growth rates deserve attention. These countries all had at least $10 billion in exports in 1999 and a growth rate of at least one and one-half times the world average from 1998 to 1999.

Not only do multinational companies trade across borders with exports and imports, but they also build global networks that link R&D, supply, production, and sales units across the globe. The result is that cross-border ownership, called foreign direct investment, is on the rise, more than doubling between 1998 and 2000 (UNCTAD 2000a). **Foreign direct investment (FDI)** occurs when a multinational company from one country has an ownership position in an organizational unit located in another country. Fueled by cross-border mergers and acquisitions

Foreign direct investment (FDI)

Multinational firm's ownership, in part or in whole, of an operation in another country.

Exhibit 1.6 Who Owns the Most in Foreign Countries?

Rank	Company	Country	Industry	Assets Total ($ billion)	% Foreign	Total Employees	% Foreign Employees
1	General Electric	USA	Electronics	355.9	36%	293,000	44%
2	General Motors	USA	Motor vehicles	246.7	30%	396,000	29%
3	Royal Dutch Shell	UK/Netherlands	Petroleum	110.0	61%	102,000	60%
4	Ford	USA	Motor vehicles	237.5	25%	345,175	50%
5	Exxon	USA	Petroleum	70.0	72%	79,000	75%
6	Toyota	Japan	Motor vehicles	131.5	34%	183,879	62%
7	IBM	USA	Computers	86.1	51%	291,067	52%
8	BP AMOCO	UK	Petroleum	54.9	74%	98,900	80%
9	Daimler-Chrysler	Germany	Motor vehicles	159.7	23%	441,506	47%
10	Nestle	Switzerland	Food	41.1	87%	231,881	97%
11	Volkswagen	Germany	Motor vehicles	70.1	47%	297,916	48%
12	Unilever	UK/Netherlands	Food	35.8	92%	265,102	91%
13	Suez Lyonnaise Des Eau,	France	Diversified utility	84.6	37%	201,000	64%
14	Wal-Mart	USA	Retailing	50.0	60%	910,000	25%
15	ABB	Switzerland	Electrical equip.	32.9	88%	162,793	95%
16	Mobil	USA	Petroleum	42.8	65%	41,500	53%
17	Diageo Plc	UK	Beverages	46.3	60%	77,029	85%
18	Honda	Japan	Motor vehicles	41.8	63%	112,200	50%
19	Siemens	Germany	Electronics	66.8	37%	416,000	53%
20	Sony	Japan	Electronics	52.5	46%	173,000	59%
21	Renault SA	France	Motor vehicles	43.2	55%	138,321	67%
22	News Corp.	Australia	Media/pub.	33.6	68%	50,000	75%
23	BMW	Germany	Motor vehicles	35.7	64%	119,913	44%
24	Mitsubishi	Japan	Diversified	74.9	29%	11,650	31%
25	Nissan	Japan	Motor vehicles	57.2	38%	131,260	42%

Source: Adapted from data in UNCTAD 2000.

such as the merger of Chrysler and Daimler-Benz, cross-border ownership was especially high in the late 1990s. Foreign direct investment soared by nearly 32 percent between 1996 and 1999 and reached a record $800 billion in 1999 and 1.1 trillion in 2000 (UNCTAD 2000a; 2000b).

The large volume of cross-border ownership is due to the existence of an estimated 63,000 multinational corporations. These corporations have nearly 700,000 foreign affiliates with a combined worth of over $2 trillion (UNCTAD 2000b). Exhibit 1.6 lists the top 25 companies in the world by the size of their foreign-owned assets.

Who gives and who gets these investments in the global economy?

Honda Motor Company of Japan is a global producer of motorcycles and automobiles. In addition to its headquarters in Japan, Honda has R&D, production, and sales networks in four areas: Asia, Europe, Oceania, and the Americas. In total, there are 100 affiliated companies in 150 countries outside Japan engaged in marketing, R&D, and production.

Honda's FDI in Europe began in 1961 with marketing and service activities in Germany. In 1963, Honda started its first overseas production unit in Belgium. That company now manufactures only automobile parts but it was an invaluable experience for Honda. The company learned that it could use Western labor to produce for both local tastes and other world markets. Automobile production comes from two state-of-the-art plants in the UK.

Honda has taken advantage of the ease of trade among EU nations to integrate its European operations into one large network. In this network, some plants specialize in certain types of motorcycles for the whole European market. Plants in different countries produce different size models for the European market and other world locations. About 60 percent of the production is shipped outside Europe, primarily to the Middle East and Africa. Not all plants produce all components. Some plants also supply component parts to other plants in other countries. For example, Montessa Honda in Spain produces no engines. Most of its engines come from production sites in Italy and France. R&D takes place in Germany, the UK, and the recently completed motorcycle R&D unit in Italy.

Exhibit 1.7 shows the current links among Honda's operations in Europe and the founding date of each operation. There are also supply links to North and South America and Japan.

Exhibit 1.7 .The Honda Network in the EU

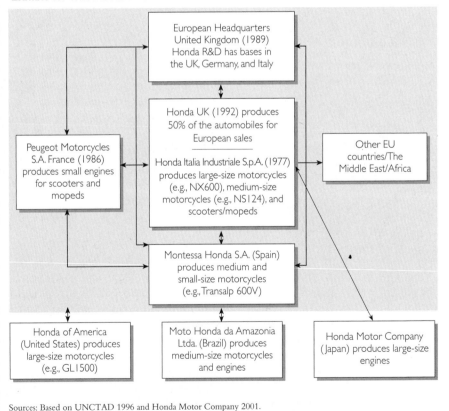

Sources: Based on UNCTAD 1996 and Honda Motor Company 2001.

Exhabit 1.8
High Stakes in China

Company	Stake	Major Activity
Royal/Dutch Shell	$4.5 billion	Petrochemical plant
BASF	$3.4 billion	Petrochemical plant
General Motors	$2 billion	Production plants and auto parts facilities
Motorola	$1.2 billion	Several joint ventures and a major wafer-production plant in planning
Volkswagen	$855 million	Two production plants with a total 400,000/year capacity
Coca-Cola	$500 million	16 bottling locations with more planned
AMOCO	$350 million	Oil production in the South China Sea
Ford	$250 million	Produces light trucks, vans, and components
United Technologies	$250 million	Otis makes escalators and elevators; Carrier makes air conditioners
Pepsico	$200 million	62 KFC franchises; 19 Pizza Huts; 12 bottling plants
Lucent Technologies	$150 million	Seven joint ventures in telecommunications
General Electric	$150 million	14 joint ventures for various products and 89% ownership of largest lighting manufacturer

Sources: Adapted from Schoenberger 1996 and *Economist* 1998.

By 2000, foreign investments in the developed countries reached approximately $899 billion (UNCTAD 2000a). The United States led all other countries as a recipient of investment. Multinational companies from the rest of the world invested a record $276 billion of FDI in their U.S. operations. The United Kingdom led in outward investment with its firms investing a record $199 billion in other countries, while FDI in the transitioning economies of central and eastern Europe reached an estimated $23 billion, increasing for the third consecutive year (UNCTAD 2000b).

As a whole, developing countries received $198 billion in foreign investments. The expected enlargement of the EU and the use by European firms of central and eastern Europe as low cost production sites stimulated increases in FDI in this area. The Czech Republic, Hungary, Poland, and the Russian Federation benefited most. However, the smallest 100 countries, most of which are LDCs, had minimal FDI. All of Africa, for example, received only 1.2 percent of FDI (UNCTAD 2000a; UNCTAD 2000b).

What does this mean for individual companies? Perhaps the most important implication is that multinational companies now manufacture and sell anywhere. Although the implications of this trend will be discussed in considerable detail in later chapters, the Case in Point on the previous page shows how Honda Motor of Japan uses FDI to create a European network of interrelated operations.

Although the triad countries dominate the bulk of world FDI, and will continue to do so in the immediate future, astute multinational managers are also looking to other areas of the world for future investments. Exhibit 1.8 shows some big investments by foreign companies whose officers hope eventually to gain handsomely in the world's fastest growing and most populous country. The following Multinational Management Brief shows how some major multinational companies are moving quickly to take advantage of opportunities in the transition economies.

Multinational Management Brief
US Steel Scores a First in Central Europe

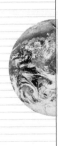

US Steel's acquisition of VSZ, a Slovak steel maker changes the competitive landscape in central Europe. It is the first takeover of a major steel company in this region. US Steel paid $450 million for VSZ and will build a new production line, at a cost of $70 million, capable of producing automotive-grade galvanized steel. The strategy is to supply the growing automobile manufacturing industry in central Europe. The acquisition will add 35 percent to US Steel's production capacity. VSZ is already a successful company supplying steel to the Skoda car plant in the Czech Republic. With US Steel's marketing and distribution strengths, this plant will compete with the major firms in Germany and Austria. Local companies in central Europe must take heed because they will need serious upgrading or foreign partners to survive.

Source: Based on Meth-Cohn 2000.

Although the developing countries may provide the great opportunities for multinational companies, they also are among the most risky locations in the world. We usually think of two types of risks in multinational business: economic and political. Political risk is anything a government might do (or not do) that might adversely affect a company. In extreme circumstances—and now very rarely—governments have expropriated or taken over foreign firms with little or no compensation. More often, though, a government's instability and the uncertainty of its reactions to foreign investment are most important. Economic risk considers all factors of a nation's economic climate that may affect a foreign investor. Government policies affect some of these factors such as mandating artificially high or low interest rates. Other factors, such as a volatile exchange rate, may respond to economic forces from outside the country. Exhibit 1.9 shows risk ratings for selected countries. These ratings combine economic and political risk.

Would you gamble your company on China? The Multinational Management Challenge on page 18 shows that Motorola thinks it's a good bet in the long term.

THE INTERNET AND INFORMATION TECHNOLOGY ARE MAKING IT ALL EASIER

The explosive growth in the Internet as well as in the capabilities of information technology increases the multinational company's ability to deal with a global economy. The Internet makes it easy for companies to go global since any Web site can be accessed by anyone in the world. Thus, companies and individuals can shop anywhere and sell anywhere. Consider some of these data. The global online population is nearing two million and expected to grow to one billion by 2005. There will be 47 million users in Latin America alone by 2003. The United States' lead in Internet use and e-commerce will end early in this decade. For example, global e-commerce in Europe alone will exceed the U.S. in spending on consumer products by 2002 (Internet Indicators 2000; OECD 2001).

Exhibit 1.9

Risk Ratings for
Selected Countries
(100 = Lowest Risk)

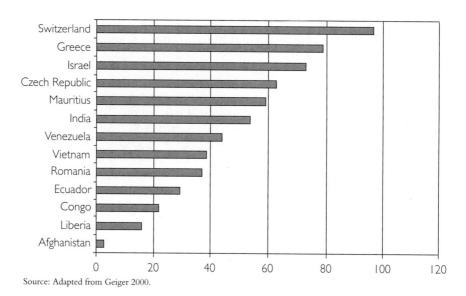

Source: Adapted from Geiger 2000.

Because of the importance of this growing trend, Chapter 9 in this book discusses the impact of the Internet on multinational management in detail.

Electronic communication (e-mail, the World Wide Web, etc.) allows multinational companies to communicate with company locations throughout the world. Information technology expands the global reach of an organization. Multinational companies can now monitor worldwide operations to an extent never before possible. Text and graphic information can flow to any part of the world nearly instantaneously. Headquarters, research and development, manufacturing, or sales can be located anywhere there is a computer. Because employees, suppliers, and customers are geographically dispersed, organizations are becoming virtual—linked by networks of computers. Information technology makes it all happen (Boudreau et al. 1998).

Information technology is also spurring a borderless financial market. Investors are going global, and companies of the future will get their financing not in local stock or bond markets but in global markets that seek the best companies worldwide. Consider this *Business Week* comment, which captures the feel of financial markets of the next century:

It's April 20, 2010, a fine spring day in Shanghai. You stroll up to a Citibank automated-teller machine along the Bund, insert your plastic card, and log on. A computer in Bombay greets you, and you get down to business. First, you shift 10,000 German marks [if German marks exist then] into today's special—an Australian-dollar certificate of deposit issued by GEC Capital in Rome. Equities are looking good, so you punch in an order for 500 shares of Teléfonos de México on the New York Stock Exchange. Then, at the press of a button, an account officer in South Dakota comes onto the screen to answer your questions about a loan for your factory in Argentina. (Javetski and Glasgall 1994)

The decreasing price and increasing sophistication of computer systems also affect globalization. Small companies can now have computer power that only the largest multinationals could have afforded just a few years ago. Similarly, cheap and readily available computer power allows companies in poorer nations to make technological gains previously reserved for the rich.

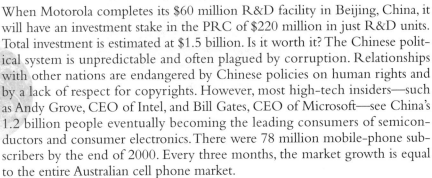

Multinational Management Challenge
The World's Biggest Electronics Market? Motorola's Big Gamble

When Motorola completes its $60 million R&D facility in Beijing, China, it will have an investment stake in the PRC of $220 million in just R&D units. Total investment is estimated at $1.5 billion. Is it worth it? The Chinese political system is unpredictable and often plagued by corruption. Relationships with other nations are endangered by Chinese policies on human rights and by a lack of respect for copyrights. However, most high-tech insiders—such as Andy Grove, CEO of Intel, and Bill Gates, CEO of Microsoft—see China's 1.2 billion people eventually becoming the leading consumers of semiconductors and consumer electronics. There were 78 million mobile-phone subscribers by the end of 2000. Every three months, the market growth is equal to the entire Australian cell phone market.

Motorola now has 6,100 Chinese employees making pagers and cell phones and packing semiconductors into housings for export and domestic use. Already, Motorola is getting almost 12 percent of its worldwide sales revenues from China (largely from pagers and cell phones), so the investments seem to be paying off. However, given the uncertainty of the Chinese political scene, not all shareholders feel that billion dollar investments in a developing nation are worthwhile. Moreover, although Nokia and Motorola continue a seesaw battle for top spot in the Chinese cell phone market, local competition is heating up. The Chinese government is encouraging local companies to compete with the foreigners. For example, Legend, the local PC maker that surpassed Dell as China's leading PC maker, is learning to make cell phones. Motorola's top managers counterargue that they have a longer-term view of China than some of their competitors do and that the heavy investments will pay off.

Sources: Based on Schoenberger 1996; Chang and Comparelli 2000; Motorola 2001 and Rohwer 2000.

The use of information technology and the Internet are also speeding up another globalization driver. Since many companies now use the Web to search for suppliers, it is easier to be a global customer.

THE RISE OF GLOBAL PRODUCTS AND GLOBAL CUSTOMERS

Although large differences still exist among countries in terms of national cultures and political and economic systems, the needs of customers for many products and services are growing more similar. For example, fast-food chains such as McDonald's, aircraft manufacturers such as Boeing, and automobile makers such as Toyota each have individual products that are quite similar and successful throughout the world. In industries where customers' needs are similar across national boundaries, global competition is more likely (Yip 1995).

Along with the rise of worldwide customer needs, a new type of customer is more common—the global customer. Global customers search the world for their supplies without regard for national boundaries. Price and quality affect the purchase decision more than nationality. At present, most global customers are com-

Case in Point

**The Global
Tennis Racquet**

In spite of the recent strength of the dollar, the author considered $270 for the Prince tennis racquet too steep in the Lille, France, sporting goods store. A quick check on the World Wide Web, however, showed me that the same racquet cost only $149 (plus $15 next-day air shipping) in the United States. It was also nice to see pictures of the racquet and read the evaluations.

Being a global shopper, I ordered the racquet by e-mail delivered to my U.S. address by next-day air. The racquet was then shipped by two-day air from Pullman, Wash., to Lille, France, for about $45 U.S. Import duty drove the total cost up to around $220—but I had my new racquet and saved around $50. Someday my electronic order will go directly to the Prince manufacturing plant in China. They will then ship it directly to me anywhere I happen to be in the world (avoiding the transportation costs from China to the Prince distribution center, from the distribution center to the mail-order house, from the mail-order company to my U.S. address, and then to France)—maybe without any tariffs at all.

The hope for these countries is that privatization will not only make their companies more globally competitive but will also attract foreign investors who can bring up-to-date technology and management practices. For multinational companies from other nations, the privatization in the developing world offers opportunities for bargain-basement investments. Buying formerly government-owned companies can be an easy way to gain access to new production facilities, often with local-government incentives such as several years of tax-free operations.

panies making industrial purchases. This explains why 70 percent of the global e-commerce comes from business-to-business transactions. However, with the globalization of mail-order businesses and the increased use of Web stores for purchasing consumer goods, including everything from athletic equipment to PCs, soon anyone can be a global customer. The preceding Case in Point may indicate the types of individual global purchasing that the future holds.

Similar customer needs and globally minded customers link economies because companies can produce one product for everybody and anyone can buy anything from anywhere. These trends will continue as developing nations become more than sources of cheap production and become the sources of the greatest consumer growth.

THE STATE IS GETTING OUT OF BUSINESS

Privatization

The sale of government-owned businesses to private investors.

Privatization is the sale of government-owned businesses to private investors usually through stock or direct sale to other companies. The total value of government sell-offs rose sharply in the 1990s, peaking at $160 billion in 1998, and currently maintaining that pace (Megginson 2000). Western Europe accounts for about one-third of yearly privatizations. The leading privatizers of the world are France and Britain, followed by Australia, Japan, Italy, and Germany. Sell-offs of formerly government-owned businesses averaged $5.4 billion a year for France and $4.8 for Britain (*Economist* 1997). From 1988–1998, Western Europe had 52 percent of the privatizations; Asia and the Pacific region had 23 percent; and Latin America had 15 percent. Currently, state-owned enterprises (SOEs) are largely obsolete in Spain, Portugal, and the United Kingdom (Megginson 2000).

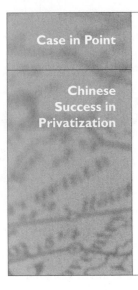

China's second-largest producer of TVs took its first step toward privatization. It listed its core consumer-electronics division on the Hong Kong stock market. Before this move, Panda split off its unprofitable military-communications division and formed a new entity, Nanjing Panda Electronics. The new company eliminated the cradle-to-grave employment system of the former state enterprise and opened itself to foreign investors. Motorola bought about $3 million of the stock in the initial public offering. Five years later, Panda, now PANDA International Communications System Co. Ltd., is a worldwide manufacturer and provider of electronics equipment. Over 70 million people in 40 countries use Panda products. Products include audiovisual equipment, multimedia computers, and personal communications devices. Recently, Panda formed a strategic alliance with the U.S. company BulletIN.net to bring wireless Internet services to China.

Sources: Based on *Fortune* 1996 and *Business Wire* 2000.

Two types of privatization are heating up the global economy—one in the developed world and another in the developing world. The developed countries are using privatization to make formerly government-controlled enterprises more competitive in the global economy. They represent the bulk of the dollar value of privatizations. These privatizations are driven by reductions in government trade protection, which often led government-owned organizations into complacency. Without protection from global competitors, newly privatized companies are forced to meet worldwide standards of quality and efficiency or face bankruptcy. When old government monopolies go public, foreign firms are often first in line to acquire the new organizations. For example, Ameritech Corp, one of the U.S. Baby Bells, was part of a consortium that purchased 49.9 percent of Belgacom, the privatized Belgian phone company (Javetski, Edmondson, and Echikson 1996).

The developing nations use privatizations to jump-start their economies or to speed the transition from a communist to a capitalist system. For example, the break from socialism was apparent when the former Soviet Union privatized the enormous SOEs: Lukoil (petroleum), Gazprom (natural gas), and Syzainvest (telecommunications). Foreign investment in Latin America hit record levels in 1999 and 2000 (UNCTAD 2000) due to opportunities for multinational firms to invest in local companies—Latin America had 70 percent of the privatizations of the developing nations in the late 1990s (World Bank 2000).

Multinational firms often acquire the best companies in the developing world. For example, when Bosnia's privatization program came online with 80 companies for sale in late 2000, Germany's Heidelberger Zement bought 51 percent of Cement Plant Kakanj, the country's biggest cement maker. This was the first company sold. It has a modern plant and a high demand for its high-quality cement. Experts agree, however, that it may be difficult to privatize the other companies. Like many operations from the transition economies in Russia and Eastern Europe, these old state companies are incapable of competing in the world economy. They have outdated equipment, poor management, and a bloated workforce, all vestiges of a time when they did not have to compete (Dizarevic 2000). However, privatizations that originate with stock offerings have also proven successful. The preceding Case in Point gives one story of a successful Chinese step toward privatization.

Exhibit 1.10 The Top 25 Emerging-Market Companies: 2000 (In millions of U.S. dollars)

Rank	Company	Country	Market Value	Sales	Profits	Assets
1	China Telecom (Hong Kong)	China	102,464	4,666	580	NA
2	Taiwan Semiconductor Mfg.	Taiwan	50,034	2,374	797	NA
3	Samsung Electronics	Korea	47,453	23,123	2,807	2,1877
4	Telefonos De Mexico (Telmex)	Mexico	36,383	10,112	2,638	18,759
5	United Microelectronics	Taiwan	32,954	946	341	NA
6	Sk Telecom	Korea	30,388	3,789	269	5,501
7	Petrobras	Brazil	24,463	16,224	963	31,060
8	Korea Telecom	Korea	23,218	8,490	339	NA
9	Anglo American	South Africa	17,711	NA	1,308	26,597
10	Korea Electric Power (Kepco)	Korea	17,171	13,737	1,300	56,795
11	Turkiye Is Bankasi	Turkey	15,487	NA	408	NA
12	Gazprom	Russia	14,796	6,063	−1,504	NA
13	Check Point Software Technologies	Israel	13,632	142	70	NA
14	Cathay Life Insurance	Taiwan	12,829	NA	NA	NA
15	Hindustan Lever	India	12,635	2,127	188	978
16	Hellenic Telecommunications Organization	Greece	12,349	3,018	659	NA
17	Asustek Computer	Taiwan	11,572	NA	NA	NA
18	Tenaga Nasional	Malaysia	11,339	3,199	204	11,510
19	Telekom Malaysia	Malaysia	10,984	2,061	216	6,795
20	Lukoil Holding	Russia	10,915	2,890	4	NA
21	Telecomunicacoes De Sao Paulo (Telesp)	Brazil	10,670	2,903	403	9,914
22	National Bank of Greece	Greece	10,620	NA	678	NA
23	Winbond Electronics	Taiwan	10,518	1,050	144	NA
24	Nan Ya Plastics	Taiwan	10,421	4,063	356	NA
25	Infosys Technologies	India	10,383	198	64	NA

Source: Adapted from *Businessweek Online* 2000b.

NEW COMPETITORS ARE EMERGING

The free-market reforms in emerging countries are creating a potential group of new competitors in the world market. Who are some of these companies to watch? Exhibit 1.10 shows the top 25 companies from the *Business Week* annual scoreboard of the top 200 emerging-market companies. At this point, Korean companies dominate the rankings with Korean Electric Power leading in market value and Samsung leading in sales and profits (*Business Week Online* 2000b).

Global trade has two important effects in developing new competitors. First, when the large multinationals use developing countries as low-wage platforms for high-tech assembly, they facilitate the transfer of technology. This means that workers and companies in developing countries often learn new skills when the large multinationals use them as sites for low-cost production and assembly. In countries

Case in Point

No Longer Local

Cemex S.A. de C.V. is the world's third largest cement company. This Mexican company has 56 plants in 30 countries. Cemex ranks fourth on the *World Investment Report*'s list of top 50 transnational corporations, based on size of foreign assets. Founded in the early 1900s, Cemex reached the number one rank in Mexico in the late 1980s. In the 1990s, the company went multinational. During the last decade, Cemex doubled its production capacity and tripled its revenues largely by acquiring companies outside of Mexico. They now own in part or completely 10 companies from other developing countries and three from developed countries.

Cemex CEO Lorenzo Zambrano is a technology enthusiast. Cemex has invested more than $200 million in a state-of-the-art computerized information system. This system gives managers real-time information on inventory, delivery schedules, quality records, and even oven temperatures at Cemex' operations in Spain, Venezuela, Colombia, Panama, the Philippines, Indonesia, and the United States. Most recently, Cemex tied their information system into Global Positioning Satellites that allow managers to find the shortest route to customers. Delivery time dropped from an average of three hours to 20 minutes. Cemex also uses Web technology to let customers make and track orders.

Sources: Based on UNCTAD 2000a; Smith 1999 and *Business Week Online* 2000c.

where the workers are well educated and motivated, the former assemblers often become the creators rather than the builders of advanced technologies. Second, aggressive multinational companies from emerging-market countries are also expanding beyond their own borders. Consider the Case in Point above for Cemex S.A. from Mexico. It shows not only how smaller competitors can grow to challenge any company but, also, how information and Web technology can be used successfully.

THE RISE OF GLOBAL STANDARDS

Increasingly, especially in technical industries, global product standards are common. For example, you can buy an AA battery anywhere in the world and it will fit in your flashlight. Why is this so? One driving factor is that, when a product standard is accepted globally or regionally, companies can make one or only a few versions of a product for the world market. This is much cheaper than making one hundred different versions for one hundred different countries. Component makers also benefit, since they can take advantage of the same efficiencies with fewer product designs.

Certainly there are still many diverse technical standards throughout the world. For example, Europe and North America have different formats for TVs and VCRs. Differences in electrical currents and plugs are common examples faced daily by international travelers. However, many electronic devices are now "smart" enough to overcome these differences. Power sources for computers, for example, often can adjust automatically for differences in voltage.

As new products are introduced into the world market, there is increasing competitive pressure to save money by developing one product for everyone. Thus the company that can establish its standard as dominant either regionally or worldwide has a tremendous strategic advantage. For example, Motorola of the United States is locked in a fierce competitive battle with Finland's Nokia and Sweden's Ericsson over setting the standard for the next generation of digital cell-phone technology.

Consistency in quality has also become a requirement of doing business in many countries. The International Organization for Standardization (ISO), in Geneva, Switzerland, has developed a set of technical standards known originally as ISO 9000, now called the **ISO 9000:2000** series (International Standards Organization 2001). There are also environmental protection standards known as ISO 14000.

ISO 9000:2000

The current name for the technical and quality standards of the International Organization for Standardization.

In 1992, ISO compliance became part of product-safety laws in many European countries. Many large European multinationals such as Germany's Siemens now require suppliers to be ISO-certified. As a result, in order to do business in the EU, the pressure is increasing for the United States and other countries to adopt ISO quality requirements and standardization (Levine 1992).

What type of managers will succeed in the global economy of the future? The next section addresses this question by describing some of the characteristics of the next generation of multinational managers.

THE NEXT GENERATION OF MULTINATIONAL MANAGERS

Consider what the experts say about the need for multinational managers and leaders:

It takes more than a lot of frequent flyer miles to become a global leader. Today's cosmopolitan executive must know what to do when competitive advantage is fleeting, when change becomes chaos, and when home base is the globe (Rhinesmith et al. 1989).

We need global leaders at a time when markets and companies are changing faster than the ability of leaders to reinvent themselves. We have a shortage of global leaders at a time when international exposure and experience are vital to business success. And we need internationally minded, globally literate leaders at a time when leadership styles are in transition around the world (Rosen, Digh, Singer, and Phillips 1999).

To become global leaders and keep pace with the dizzying rate of globalization, most managers will need additional strengths to meet its challenges. What traits and strengths will you need? According to some experts, the next generation of successful multinational managers must have the following characteristics (Beamish et al. 1994; Moran and Riesenberger 1994):

Global mindset

One that requires managers to "think globally, but act locally."

- *A global mindset:* A person with a **global mindset** understands that the world of business is changing rapidly and that the world is more interdependent in business transactions. A global mindset requires managers to "think globally, but act locally." This means that managers must see similarities in the global market while still being able to adapt to local conditions in any country. A global mindset is necessary for all employees, from the CEO to the rank and file, if a company is to support and implement a global strategic vision.
- *The ability to work with people from diverse backgrounds:* In the global economy, customers, partners, suppliers, and workers will often come from locations other than the company's home country. The next generation of multinational managers will build on their awareness of cultural differences to succeed in these cross-cultural relationships. Successful organizations will require all employees to work well with diverse groups of people.
- *A long-range perspective:* A short-term view seldom succeeds in the new global economy. Credited with responsibility for turning Motorola into a global player, former CEO Robert W. Galvin put a representative in Beijing more than

ten years ago. Now Motorola is the largest U.S. investor in China, with $1.2 billion in 1996 (Schoenberger 1996). Successful companies must be persistent to overcome the complexities of dealing with the international environment.

- *The ability to manage change and transition:* Although a long-term view favors survival in the global environment, the global economy is volatile and unpredictable. This will require leaders with the skills to effectively implement many organizational changes.
- *The ability to create systems for learning and changing organizations:* Organizations competing in the global economy will face rapidly changing and complex environments. These organizations will need to tap the talents of all employees concerning what is going on in the world and in the organization. They will need to coordinate complex interdependencies among business functions (e.g., marketing and manufacturing) across national boundaries. The next generation of multinational leaders will be responsible for building the organizations that can meet the needs of evolving strategies for global competition.
- *The talent to motivate all employees to achieve excellence:* The ability to motivate has always been a hallmark of leadership. In the next generation of organization, the leader will face additional challenges of motivation. Employees may come from any country and may live in any country. Leaders will face the motivational challenge of having employees identify with the organization rather than with their country. Leaders will also need to develop motivational strategies that transcend cultures.
- *Accomplished negotiating skills:* All business transactions require negotiation. However, leaders in the global economy will spend considerably more time negotiating cross-culturally. This will be more challenging as well as more necessary.
- *The willingness to seek overseas assignments:* The next generation of leaders will have significant international experiences. They will demonstrate management skills and success in more than one cultural environment.
- *An understanding of national cultures:* In spite of the pressures of globalization to treat the world as one market, large differences still exist among national cultures. No multinational leader or business can succeed without a deep understanding of the national cultures in which they do business. For the multinational managers, this will often require learning two or more additional languages as well as the nuances of local cultural differences.

Can you develop the skills necessary to be a successful multinational manager? One of the first tasks is to learn all you can about multinational management and international business. In the next section, we will discuss how this book can contribute to this goal.

MULTINATIONAL MANAGEMENT: A STRATEGIC APPROACH

Why should you study multinational management? In today's Internet connected world, you may have little choice but to be a multinational manager. Foreign competition and doing business in foreign markets are daily facts of life for today's managers. The study of multinational management helps prepare you to deal with this evolving global economy and to develop the skills necessary to succeed as a multinational manager. This book is intended to introduce some of the basic skills of multinational management.

This book takes a strategic approach to multinational management. It focuses on how multinational managers formulate and implement strategies to compete successfully in the global economy. Strategy is defined here as the maneuvers or activities that managers use to sustain and increase organizational performance. Strategy formulation is the process of choosing or crafting a strategy. Strategy implementation includes all the activities that managers and an organization must perform to achieve strategic objectives.

From the perspective of the multinational company and managers, strategies must include maneuvers that deal with operating in more than one country and culture. Thus, multinational strategy formulation takes on the added challenges of dealing with opportunities and competition located anywhere in the world. Similarly, multinational strategy implementation carries added challenges, including the need to develop complex management systems to carry out strategies that reach beyond domestic boundaries.

A fundamental assumption of the book is that successful multinational management requires managers to understand their potential competitors and collaborators (Hamel and Prahalad 1989). Consider:

When you understand your competitors and yourself, you will always win. (Sun Tzu, The Art of War.*)*

Multinational companies and managers must be prepared to compete with other firms from any country. In addition, they must be prepared to collaborate with companies and people from any country as suppliers, alliance partners, customers, and so on. To accomplish these tasks means that multinational managers must understand more than the basics of national culture. They must understand how people from different nations view organizational strategies and organizations. To provide such a background, this text devotes several chapters to comparative management—the comparison of management practices used by people from different nations.

Summary and Conclusions

This chapter provided you with key background information that supports the study of multinational management. The chapter defined multinational management and the multinational company. You saw examples of the world's largest multinationals. However, as the Preview Case in Point showed, companies of all sizes can be multinational.

Because we exist in a globalizing world, considerable attention has been devoted to the forces that drive globalization. These are key environmental issues that affect every multinational company and its managers. World trade and investments are growing rapidly, making all economies more linked and creating both opportunities and threats for both domestic and multinational companies. New competitors, strong and motivated, are coming from developing nations in Asia and the transitioning economies of eastern Europe. Customers, products, and standards are becoming more global. The increasing sophistication and lower cost of information technology fuel the development of global companies that can more easily manage worldwide operation.

Multinational managers of the next generation will need skills not always considered necessary for domestic-only managers. To give you some background on these skills, the chapter described key characteristics of successful multinational managers as identified by several experts. Perhaps the most encompassing characteristic is the global mindset. Managers with a global mindset understand the rapidly changing business and economic environment. They can see the world as an integrated market, yet appreciate and understand the wide array of differences in the world cultures and social institutions.

After reading this text, you should have the foundation for understanding the latest challenges and practices of multinational management. However, the field is dynamic, and your learning will never be complete. Successful multinational managers will view the understanding of their field as a lifelong endeavor.

Discussion Questions

1. Discuss how any company can become a multinational company. What are some of the options available to companies that allow them to use international markets and locations competitively?

2. Discuss some reasons why reductions in world trade barriers are driving the world toward a global economy.

3. Discuss the differences between foreign trade and foreign direct investment.

4. Discuss some of the advantages and disadvantages of setting up production in developing nations. Consider the benefits of market growth and the risk of the venture. Consider the position of Motorola discussed in the text. If you were the CEO, would you think that Motorola made the right move?

5. Look at the information on developing economies and hot competitors discussed in the text. Where do you think the next generation of world-class competitors will come from? Why?

6. Discuss the characteristics of a next generation multinational manager. How can you develop those characteristics through education and experience?

Chapter Internet Activity

As you will see throughout this text there are Internet Activities at the end of each chapter. These activities are designed to expand on important information as well as to enhance your knowledge and understanding of the management resources on the Web. Your instructor may assign these activities or you may choose to complete them on your own. However, while every effort has been made to ensure that the sites you are directed to are stable and live, the Internet is a rapidly changing environment in which it is hard to always keep pace.

One frustration in using the Web is address changes. A one-letter change and an address will not work. However, the majority of Web locations in this book are stable. If they do change, the location usually has a forwarding message telling where to go with one click. If you do find a location that does not work, don't give up. Use one of the search engines (e.g., Yahoo! or Excite) and you will likely find what you are looking for and more.

For the Internet Activity for this chapter, simply familiarize yourself with your Internet provider (whether this is a private company or your school's server). Log onto the Web and spend 30–60 minutes searching for multinational management information or resources. What did you find? Was it difficult to locate the information? Compile a list of resources for future use in this class or others.

Internet Sites

Selected Companies in the Chapter
ABB   http://www.abb.com
Daewoo   http://www.daewoous.com
Ford   http://www.ford.com
General Electric   http://www.ge.com
General Motors   http://www.gm.com/flash_homepage/
GlobalSight   http://www.globalsight.com
Honda   http://www.honda.com
Korean Electric   http://www.kepco.co.kr/ (in Korean)

Motorola   http://www.motorola.com
Nokia   http://www.nokiausa.com
Panda   http://www.irasia.com/listco/hk/nanjingpanda/index.htm
Prince   http://www.princesports.com
Samsung   http://www.samsung.com
Siemens   http://www.siemens.de

Hint: Looking for a job? Many companies list their job openings on their home pages. Some have online applications.

Find a Company

http://www.internationalist.com/business/   *Publicly traded companies around the world*

http://dir.yahoo.com/business_and_economy/ Companies/   *Find a company on the search engine Yahoo!*

Check Out Business Publications and Company Rankings for Multinational Companies

http://fortune.com/fortune/global500   *Global 500 data in user-selected formats*

http://businessweek.com   Business Week Online *with searchable articles from U.S. and International editions—America Online provides more complete access*

http://www.forbes.com   *Forbes International 800*

http://www.iht.com/   The International Herald Tribune

http://www.economist.com/   The Economist

http://www.shrm.org/hrmagazine/index.html   HRMagazine *contains hundreds of articles dealing with international HRM, many are online*

http://ibiblio.org/   *An index and WWW links to business journals and newspapers from around the world*

http://biztimes.asia1.com   Singapore Business Times

http://www.asia-inc.com   Asia Inc. Online

http://interactive.wsj.com   The Wall Street Journal's *online edition*

Look Up Statistics on International Business and Trade

http://unescostat.unesco.org/   *UNESCO's Statistical Yearbook*

http://ciber.bus.msu.edu/publication/mktptind. htm   *Market Potential Indicators for Emerging Markets*

http://www.worldbank.org/html/extpb/wdr95/ WDRENG.html   *World Bank World Development Report*

http://www.cia.gov/cia/di/products/index.html   *Handbook of International Economic Statistics*

http://www.imd.ch/index_4.cfm   *World Competitiveness Yearbook Published by the International Institute for Management Development*

http://www.wto.org/ *World Trade Organization*

http://www.unctad.org/en/enhome.htm   *UN Conference on Trade and Development—UNCTAD reports data on the behavior of transnational corporations*

http://www.census.gov/ftp/pub/ipc/www/idbnew. html   *International Data Base (IDB) US Census Bureau*

http://www.census.gov/   *Census Bureau: Statistical Agencies*

http://www.census.gov/foreign-trade/www/   *Foreign Trade Statistics—Main Page—Foreign Trade Division*

http://www.census.gov/ftp/pub/econ/www/wh0200. html   *Annual Trade Survey*

http://www.ciesin.org/IC/wbank/tde-home.html   *Trends in Developing Economies (TIDE) contains reports on the World Bank's borrowing countries*

Chapter Case: ABB in China: 1998

"I want to make ABB a company that encourages and demands innovation from all of its employees, and a company that creates the environment in which teamwork and innovation flourish," declares ABB's CEO Göran Lindahl. In seeking new growth, CEO Göran Lindahl is escaping the long shadow of his predecessor Percy Barnevik. The former CEO of ABB, Percy Barnevik, was argued to be one of the most successful international managers in Europe.

ABB, the world leader in electrical engineering, is a US$35 billion electrical engineering group, with companies all over the globe. It operates primarily in the fields of reliable and economical generation, transmission and distribution of electrical energy.[1] Much has been written about the worldwide company. In 1996 ABB was ranked in the top 40 listed by Fortune 500. Recently, the company announced its newest reorganization making it more up-to-date with the

Source: Suzanne Uhlen, Lund University, and Michael Lubatkin, University of Connecticut. Reprinted with permission. This case is to serve as a basis for class-room discussion rather than to illustrate either effective or ineffective handling of an administrative situation.

global world, as the current CEO, Göran Lindahl, expressed.[2] In 1997, Göran Lindahl took over from Percy Barnevik as CEO of the technology giant ABB, and is feeling the demanding market and shareholder pressures.

ABB has different priorities in different markets. Western Europe and North America are the company's biggest markets. However, the high-potential markets are the Middle East, Africa, Latin America and Asia. These markets are growing fast and ABB expects to have half of its customers in these regions not long into the next century. The priority is on building local manufacturing, engineering and other forms of added value. ABB wants to integrate these operations into the global networks to obtain full synergy effects and economies of scale.

During 1998 it was shown that the industrial production in OECD countries, in which ABB performs about 75 percent of its total business, continues to grow, although at a slower pace than the strong growth rates a year ago. Overall, industrial production in Europe is lower than a year ago, but still high compared with historical levels. Current economic activity in North America is slowing compared with the strong economy of recent years. In Latin America, high interest rates are delaying the financial closing of projects in an environment of reduced economic activity. The Indian economy is slowing due to reduced exports as a result of its strong currency compared with others in the region. Southeast Asia is gradually stabilizing at a low level, with reduced consumption and investments.

As a result of the ongoing economic uncertainty, overall global demand is forecast to remain soft in the near future. ABB expects to benefit with its well-established local presence around the world from higher demand in various industries and world markets. Appropriate cost cutting, continued selective tendering and successful working capital reduction programs are expected to continue contributing positively to the ABB Group results. The company recognizes the world to be rapidly changing and increasingly unpredictable. Efforts have paid off and the Group has taken its opportunities in Asia and positioned itself for future growth in what is seen to be "the world's most dynamic market over a long term—China."[3]

The interest in China is growing steadily and companies in Japan, the western European coun-

tries, the United States and elsewhere today view the Chinese market as having enormous potential. With a population of a billion and a growing economy, it seems to be worthwhile to gain a foothold in the market.[4] On the one hand, China represents a huge and largely untapped market. The Chinese market alone is potentially bigger than that of the United States, the European Community, and Japan combined! On the other hand, China's new firms are proving to be very competitive, and China's culture is quite different from that of the West. However, the Chinese market growth remains relatively good for enterprises such as Procter & Gamble, Motorola, Nestlé and ABB. This market acts as a lifeboat to many of worldwide companies suffering from the financial crisis in the rest of South East Asia. Nevertheless, discussions exist about China devaluating its currency, which might also drag China down into the crisis. Yet the country has not shown any visible scratches from the surrounding crisis. China seems to be unshakable and analysts are still valuing China as the country of the future.[5] Thus, the changes in China are creating both opportunities and threats for established worldwide companies. This is a country that, according to *Management Today*, will be one of the top 10 economies in the world by the year 2010.[6]

CHINESE INFLUENCE

China will enter the next century as the rising power in Asia after two decades of astonishing economic growth that has transformed the country and that has given rise to new challenges.[7]

Many cities in China have more than five million inhabitants. It is a country that has had a growing economy which cannot be compared to that of any other country during almost three decades.[8] It is argued that China is not like any other developing country, due to the rapid changes that are taking place in certain areas. In some areas, such as with home electronics,[9] the development has surpassed the development in Western countries, while in other areas, China lags far behind.

The Chinese culture and society is more than five thousand years old with a unique cultural heritage of philosophy, science and technology, societal structures and traditional administrative bureaucracy.[10] With this in mind it is no wonder, according to researchers, that conflicts often occur between Chinese and foreign cultures. This is caused by foreign managers being accustomed to other values and norms, some of which are not acceptable in China.[11]

In the current half-year reports from worldwide companies, a distinct trend is noticed, according to Dagens Industri.[12] The more focus that the companies have put on basic industry, the more the Asian crisis tends to affect these companies. However, China can save these companies and others, especially those companies operating in the business of infrastructure.[13] Now that the Cold War with China has ended, economic growth is stabilizing and the country is demanding a speedy reconstruction. The country has begun to enjoy unprecedented strategic latitude for the first time in 200 years, and it no longer faces the threat of aggression from superior powers.[14] This has enabled the country to focus on economic developments as the driving force of both its domestic and foreign policies. According to Professor Yahuda, China's leaders are basing their legitimacy on providing stability and continued high levels of prosperity. The need for economic development is fueled by many other factors, such as providing employment for a vast population that increases by some 15 million people a year. In addition, there are significant regional inequalities that can be addressed only by further economic development.[15]

China is expected to evolve into a hybrid system of authoritarianism, democracy, socialism, and capitalism. Also recognized are the internal problems the country faces, such as environmental disasters, political struggles, and tensions between the emerging entrepreneurial economy and the vast parts of China still under state control.[16] Today China receives the most direct investment and foreign aid of any developing country. Many companies are eager to establish their presence in China, which, it is argued, attracts more than its proportionate share of investments.[17] However, "westerners cannot expect to know how China will develop and need to expect that the Chinese will always be different from them. Instead of trying to change China, they should look for positive steps that take their differences into account."[18]

According to China's Premier, Zhu Rongji, China is indeed the largest market in the world. However, due to the problem of duplicate construction, there is a problem of oversupply in some areas. Nevertheless, the Premier states that the market is far from being saturated.[19] Since China opened up its doors to the outside world in the late 1970s, a large number of foreign investors have gained rich returns from their investments, yet some have ended in failure. Some guiding keys to ensuring successful business in China, according to *China Daily*, include:[20]

- Making long-term strategies for the Chinese market. Competition is intensifying and market exploitation needs time and patience. Foreign companies eager to get a quick return are usually disappointed at the results.
- Localizing staff. They are familiar with the local business environment.
- Being aware of changes in policies and regulation. China is in a process of transforming from a planned economy to a market economy. Various policies and regulations are being revised and replaced, while new ones are being issued. Foreign investors must keep informed of the ongoing changes.
- Undertake practical market research. Due to social, economic, and cultural differences, practical and down-to-earth market research is a must before and during investment in China.

CHINESE CULTURAL INFLUENCE

There is a consensus among several authors that China has a traditional respect for age, hierarchy and authority.[21] This originates from the Confucian concept of *li* (rite, proprietary), which plays an important role in maintaining a person's social position. *Li* can be seen today in the existing traditional bureaucracy and in vertical relationships concerning centralization of decision-making, and in corruption to some extent, which is acceptable in such a cultural context.[22]

Second, the family is viewed as an essential social unit and there is a strong tendency to promote the collective or the group. Members within the family or group must maintain harmonious relationships and these social relations are seen as more important than the individual.[23] Thus, the family or clan norms are adopted as the formal code of conduct, and members are bound to these standards. Other research found that in modern China, business and industrial enterprises were perceived as an extension of the family system.[24]

Third, the concept of "face" (*mianzi*) is seen as an important characteristic. As Ju noted, the general idea of *mianzi* is related to "a reputation achieved through getting on in life through success and ostentation."[25] *Mianzi* also serves to enhance harmony within the family or group, so that the positive is expressed publicly and any conflicts remain private.[26] Hong has found that the concept of mianzi still plays an important role in social relationships and organizational behavior.[27] However, Yuan points out that there are two sides to this concept.[28] The first includes the individual's moral character, and the strong fear of losing this limits the person's behavior. The second aspect of *mianzi* involves assertions about a person, which is not seen quite as seriously as the former type of loss of face.[29]

The importance of personal relations (*guanxi*) is the fourth characteristic. According to Hong, persons with guanxi usually share a common birthplace, lineage, surname or experience, such as attending the same school, working together or belonging to the same organization.[30] A comparative study of decision-making in China and Britain has revealed that Chinese managers use their personal *guanxi* more widely to exchange information, negotiate with planning authorities and accelerate decision-making processes than do managers from British firms.[31] As it is, the network transmits information, and because contacts and cooperation are built on trust, it is seen as very serious if that trust is broken. If a trust is broken, the whole network will soon know about the incident and it is maintained that the person involved will have a hard time doing business again.[32]

A company that has been doing business on the Chinese market since 1919 is ABB. At that time this was the first product delivery to China, and it was not until 1979 that ABB established its first permanent office. Almost 11 years later, the heart of almost every chairman of an energy company started to pound with excitement if it heard the words "Asia" and "electricity." There were billions to be had from the booming demand for electricity in Asia.[33] But in recent years, the emerging Asian market has slowed down due to the financial crisis in the area. At the moment it seems as if China is the only country not affected by this financial crisis, and consequently, there are many companies that are now trying to be successful in China.

ABB is argued to be a company with a good position on the Chinese market, due to good performance, delivery, autonomy and its good name. Today the company has 9 representative offices and 15 joint ventures, and the number of employees has grown in four years from approximately 1,000 to 6,000 employees in China.

LOCAL ROOTS

The strategy of ABB is to use its global strength to support the needs of its local customers around the world. However, in China, ABB has a fairly high import duty on its products, which limits how much the company can sell. The idea of setting up local production in China was to increase the market share, as most Chinese customers do not have foreign currency[34] and are consequently forced to buy locally produced goods with the local currency. Furthermore, the reason for ABB to localize in China was not to achieve lower production costs, as some locally supplied components are actually more expensive in China than elsewhere. It was rather to be closer to the local market, and therefore facilitate a few local modifications to the products and provide shorter delivery times to the customer.

The phase "think global, act local" is said to reflect ABB's fundamental idea of strong local companies working together across borders to gain economies of scale in many areas.[35] In spite of ABB's claims to respond swiftly and surely to market conditions,[36] some of the products in China are not truly adapted to the local market. Most of the products are designed for the IEC—international standard association based in Europe. The company manufactures products that have to be tested according to different norms and standards. For example, North America ABB follows the ANSI-standard, and Canada ABB follows the CSA-standard.

However, some of ABB's products would not pass a type test based on the Chinese standards. That is not because the quality is too low; on the contrary, the quality of ABB products is sometimes too high. The quality of some of the products has evolved far beyond the requirements of Chinese standards; therefore these ABB products cannot meet local Chinese standards. The Chinese standards are based on what the local manufacturer can produce, because the country does not have much other information. As one manager at ABB in China stated,

We are not going to redesign our products in order to meet the standards, for the obvious reasons: Why should we take our quality out? Why shall we take the advances out? It does become an issue from time to time. Chinese are very risk averse, if we have not done the type test in China. It is more to cover themselves in case something goes wrong.

Some managers feel that when ABB tries to adapt the products to the Chinese local standard, there is a negative response. The customer regards Western standards as superior and are actually asking for the superior product. The Chinese customers are seen as tough and sometimes demand more tests than ABB's products have gone through. Another reason put forward is insufficient feasibility studies when setting up new joint ventures in China. This delays the work when new information has to be collected about the market conditions. This aspect originates from the speed of changes in China and the difficulty for the company to catch up with what is going on.

However, when the so-called "type tests" of the product have been done, the company cannot change the design, due to the high costs involved in this test. Some criticism has been heard that ABB should adapt more to the Chinese situation, which the company cannot respond to concerning the technical design, because then the tests have to be done all over again. Of course, it is different from product to product; for some of the products, as one manager said,

We have to adapt to the configurations the customers have a demand for, because they have an option—go to the competitor.

Still in most cases, the local ABB companies in China are not allowed to change the products other than according to agreements with the licensee. The reason for that is that the technology partners[37] have the overall view of the quality and performance. The ABB corporation definitely does not want to have different product performance from different countries. The products must have the same descriptions, so that they are seen as the same product all over the world. Consequently the local ABB company can only do a few modifications to the standard product for the specific customer and cannot change the tech-

nology involved. The technology partners have a few alternatives that meet the demands of the Chinese customers, and these products are also tested, but do not necessarily meet the Chinese standards.

The local ABB company tries to follow the ABB Group's policy, to be close to the customer and responsive to his or her needs.[38] In China, however, contracts are not commonly used, and this frequently obstructs satisfying many customer demands.

They keep on saying this is China and you should adapt to the Chinese way: Ok, if you want to buy a Chinese product that's fine, but this is our product— here are the terms and conditions. You can't just give in to that; otherwise you will kill your company, because they expect you to accept unlimited liability and lifetime warranty, and the risks to which you would expose your company would eventually lead to its shutting down, so you just cannot do that.

ABB feels that to be close to the customer is the best guarantee that local requirements are met.[39] However, the headquarters in Zurich has also set up some rules about the kind of contracts that the local subsidiaries shall sign worldwide. In China contracts are something rather new, and many Chinese customers do not want it that way. The consequence is that some ABB companies in China do not use the standard ABB contract and are actually responsive to the customers' needs. When another ABB company comes to the same customer to set up a standard contract, the customer will refer them to the previous ABB company who did not seem to find the contract necessary. The question asked by the confused customer is said to be,

Why do you then have to use a standard contract when the other ABB didn't?

PROFIT CENTERS

ABB's strategy is to take full advantage of its economies of scale and at the same time be represented by national companies in many home markets where some 5,000 entrepreneurial profit centers are attentive to every local customer. These companies are independent and have to stand on their own economically. The individual company's profit can easily be compared to revenue. The individual ABB company is measured on its own performance and needs. It is recognized that the profit centers are efficient for decentralization and that the organization can act relatively fast. This enables the company to be sensitive and responsive to potential problems. Each company has a fair amount of autonomy, making the individual company flexible. Even though ABB brochures state that the strategy of having profit centers enables the easy transfer of know-how across borders,[40] the direction is pretty much one way—from the technology partners, Business Areas and Country level to the subsidiary—rather than a two-way exchange.

Nevertheless, some conflicts of interest have occurred because the local ABB company and all other licensees are more or less dependent on their licensors in Europe.[41] In the local ABB company's case, one of their technology partners is measured like the others, on performance and profit. If it gives the local ABB company support, it will cost the former money, and likewise, if it sells the local ABB company components, it wants to make a profit. The consequence is that it is charging the local ABB company 25–100 percent over and above the cost of its parts.

So in the end you end up calling them as little as possible and we end up buying parts from local suppliers that probably we should not buy from local suppliers. And we reduce our quality. They have great profit figures, we have some profit figures but there are some real serious problems along the way.

The technology partner argues that the prices are high because first it has to buy from its supplier and then sell to the local ABB company. This makes the products more expensive. The technology partners also pay for the "type tests" and all the product development.[42]

Conflicts of this sort have been occurring for a long time within ABB, but nobody has yet found a solution. It is difficult for a company like ABB, which is working with so many different products, markets, and in different cultures, to have anything other than sole profit centers. If the profit centers did not aim for a profit when selling within the ABB Group, then the companies would no longer be independent companies. Being independent is seen as a strength, and therefore it would be against the laws of nature if the companies were not always aiming for a profit.

Nonetheless, between these independent companies with profit centers there are some extreme examples:

Our partner in Y-country was selling the finished product in China before. Now he sells the parts to the joint venture in China and wants to charge more for the parts than he did for the finished product, and that is because it is in his interest and he will be evaluated on his performance. If he does not do that, his profits will be too low and he will be blamed for it. So he has got to do what he has got to do. That is what he is motivated to do and that is what he is going to do.

To some extent the technology partners are selling indirectly to the Chinese market using non-official agents to avoid a high import tax and the high market price that exists on the Chinese market. ABB China is trying to force ABB companies to use only two official channels for ABB goods into the Chinese market—the locally produced by the local ABB company and the directly imported from a technology partner.

STRUCTURE

ABB is a huge enterprise with dispersed business areas, which encompass the three segments: Power Generation, Transmission & Distribution and Industrial Building systems. However, this recently has been changed and divided into six segments. Before the reorganization, every country had its national ABB head office, dealing with all the company business in that particular country. The other dimension of the matrix structure reflects the clustering of the activities of the enterprise into 36 Business Areas (or BAs). Each Business Area represents a distinct worldwide product market. Simplified, each BA is responsible for worldwide market allocation and the development of a worldwide technical strategy for that specific product line. Additional responsibilities for the BA are to coordinate who shall supply or deliver where, and also to work as a referee in potential disagreements between companies within the ABB Group.

However, in China, as in most developing countries, there is no BA in place and the decision-power of the country management is consequently closer at hand. The power of the decision-making tends to rest more heavily on the country level than on the BA level. Disagreements between licensees in Western countries and subsidiaries in China have been, and are occurring, due to different business orientations. The local subsidiary in China has two or more licensors in western countries, from which they buy components. Some of the licensees sold these components themselves before the local subsidiary was set up in China. In some cases the licensee feels that the market in China was taken from them and that they therefore can compensate for potentially lost sales only by charging the Chinese subsidiary a higher cost. Consequently, if the disagreeing partner seeks the BA as a referee in this kind of case, the following happens and is explained by one manager:

The BA are looking at the global business—we can increase our global business if we set up a joint venture in China. But the technology partner can't increase their business if we set up a joint venture in China. If we set up a joint venture in China the technology partner wants to increase its business also, they are going to do some work, and of course want something for it. The BA is really powerless to push those along.

To date, the licensors have been paying for all the technology development, which is the reason for charging a higher price for the components they are selling. Since the enterprise is divided into 5,000 profit centers and because each of these profit centers wants a profit when selling a component or product, there have been some shortcomings in the coordination and cooperation between the licensors and the local Chinese subsidiary.

The licensor in X-country makes the same breakers that the local ABB company does and faces the same problems with quality. For example, in Germany, they do not inform their licensee in China, who will also run into the same problem with quality in the near future. The problem is also discussed at the local ABB company, but if it suggests changes to the licensor, the licensor will evaluate on the basis of benefits to itself. Since they are going to invest their own resources, they are, of course, going to invest in areas beneficial to themselves first, or else charge the local ABB company extra. The consequences are thus summarized as follows:

We have had some things that would really help us here in China. But I don't even bother, because I know the reaction.

Over 80 percent of what the Centers of Excellence produce is going to be exported,[43] making it important that the partners of the licensor manage the contemporary challenges and opportunities that can emerge. However, the BA divides the world markets into different areas in which the specific ABB companies are to be a first source.[44] Between some of the licensors and the local ABB company, this has resulted in certain disputes. For example,

We are responsible for the Peoples Republic of China's market and are supposed to be the sole source (or rather first source) because we have the expertise for this market. Our technology partner in X-country quotes into this market on a regular basis, does not inform us, and competes against us, and takes orders at a lower price. This can destroy our position in the marketplace.

According to the licensor, it does not quote in the local ABB company's market because a customer with foreign currency will prefer imported products. The licensor argues that it does not go into the Chinese market and offer its products, but does get inquiries from ABB in Hong Kong and deliver to it. Hong Kong sells the products directly to the Chinese customer after having increased the original price several times higher in China than in Europe. It is a decision of the ABB China management that the Hong Kong coordinated sales force shall sell the local ABB company's products on the Chinese market among imported products and locally joint venture produced products. It helps to have sales coordination when deciding whether the products should be imported or not.

The technology is owned today by the Centers of Excellence in Europe or so-called licensors who pay for all the product development. ABB has chosen these licensees to be responsible for the company's world source of this specific technology. These units are responsible for developing new products and look after the quality. They arrange technical seminars about the technology, and by keeping special technology parts at only their factory. The strategic decision to keep special parts and the drawings of these parts at only one chosen factory enables the company to secure itself against competitors copying its products. Consequently, these parts will not be localized or purchased in China. However, for one products group (THS) there has been an organizational change, including the establishment of a unit called CHTET, which shall now own all new technology that is developed and also pay for the product development. This change now involves all product groups.

MULTICULTURAL

The current fashion, exemplified by ABB, is for the firms to be "multicultural multinationals" and be very sensitive to national differences.[45] Barnevik did debate that a culturally diverse set of managers can be a source of strength. According to Barnevik, managers should not try to eradicate these differences and establish a uniform managerial culture. Rather, they should seek to understand these cultural differences, to empathize with the views of people from different cultures, and to make compromises for such differences. Barnevik believes that the advantage of building a culturally diverse cadre of global managers is to improve the quality of managerial decision making.[46]

ABB in China is typified by a culturally diverse set of managers with a mixture of managerial ideas, derived from the different managers' national backgrounds, different values, and different methods of working. It then depends on which stage in personal development the manager has reached if he or she is going to be influenced and absorb the new climate. Or as one manager said,

If you are close to being retired you might not change so much, there isn't much point. But you can't work in the same way as you do at home—it just wouldn't work.

According to another manager, ABB is a very international company with a great deal of influence from Scandinavian culture. However, it is a mixture of many cultures and it really depends on where the ABB company is located. In China the ABB culture is influenced by Chinese culture, by the environmental circumstances and by the laws. It is stricter in China than it is, for example, in Europe, because there are more rules. In spite of that, the managers do not feel that the result is a subculture of the ABB culture, rather a mixture of managers from different cultures—"we are a multidomestic company."

However, the top level of the ABB management is seen to be far away from the daily life at the subsidiary level in China, such as at the Local ABB company. Or as one manager expressed, "between that level and here, it's like the Pacific Ocean." All the managers agree that what the top level, including Barnevik and Lindahl,[47] says sounds very good and that is how it should be. Some managers continued the discussion and expressed this difference:

Sounds like I'm working for a different ABB than these guys are. What they talk about is really good and that is how it should be. But then when I sit back and go into the daily work and say that's not at all how it is. Somewhere along the line something gets lost between the theory and ideas at that level which is quite good. But when you get down to the working level and have to make it work something really gets lost along the way.

EXPATRIATES

It is the BA with its worldwide networks that recommends, after suggestions from local offices, who is going to be sent as an expatriate to China or any other country. Thereafter, it is a cooperation between the BA and the country level, but it is the latter that finally decides which potential foreign expatriate is appropriate. However, it is important that an expatriate be able to fit into the system when coming to China with the high costs involved in being there. It is estimated that an expatriate costs the company about $0.25 million a year, due to the high taxes the company is paying to have a foreign employee.

ABB's identity is supported by a coordinating executive committee and an elite cadre of 500 global managers, which the top management shifts through a series of foreign assignments. Their job is intended to knit the organization together, to transfer expertise around the world, and to expose the company's leadership to differing perspectives.[48]

However, ABB in China is not yet a closely tied country unit for several reasons. First, the expatriates come from the outside and most of their contacts are back in the home country. Most expatriates feel that the home office does not understand how difficult it can be to work abroad and that they need support. "Sometimes it just feels like I'm standing in the desert screaming," one expatriate expressed. The home office feels that the expatriates can be a burden because they need so much support. It is the home office, along with the BA, that selects candidates for foreign placement, even though it has brief or no knowledge, of how it is to work in that country. However, it would be impossible to have insights into how the working conditions are in the other operating countries.

Concerning growing a strong country unit, the expatriates are stationed in China on assignments for a relatively short time period, and are thus less able to build up informal networks. Few efforts are put into establishing an informal network, because the few contact persons the managers have today will eventually return home after a while and there is no formal way of contacting the replacing person. Of course, there is the formal LOTUS Notes®, which is a computer-based network with all managers worldwide included, but it is said to be deficient in building the preferred strong country unit within China. Finally, the managers do not feel they can offer the time to establish informal networks to be rebuilt due to the replacement of expatriates every two to three years. A worldwide policy within the company limits the expatriates to operating as such for not more than five years at a time. Executives have questioned this policy, saying that

It is during the first year you learn what is going on and get into your new clothes. During the second year you get to know the people and the system, the third year you apply what you learned and the fourth year you start to make some changes—and this is very specific for developing countries.

Three years ago the expatriates did not get any information or education about the country-specific situation before being sent out to ABB's subsidiaries in China. Today, when there are about 100 expatriates with 25 different nationalities in China, it has changed, but it is mostly up to the individual to collect material and prepare for the acclimatization. Within the worldwide corporation there is no policy of formal training before one is sent out as an expatriate; rather, it is up to the home office of the expatriates to prepare the managers for the foreign assignments. Some argue that "you could never prepare for the situation in China anyway, so any education wouldn't help." Others say that this has resulted in a lot of problems with the expatriates, which results in even higher costs for the company if the expatriate fails.

When the contract time as an expatriate is finished, he or she may feel unsure about placement for him or herself back home. Thus, it is important for the expatriate to have close contact with the home office and make use of the free trips home. In most cases the expatriates do not know what will happen when the contract expires and they are to return back home.

THE CHINESE CHALLENGE

According to ABB they prefer to send out managers with 10–15 years of experience. However, the task is difficult when the location may be in a rural area overseas and most managers with 10–15 years experience have families who are less likely to want to move to these areas. Sometimes a manager gets sent to China when the company does not want to fire him.

So instead they send the manager to where the pitfalls are greater and challenges bigger and potential risks are greater.

It is found throughout the research that most expatriates have strong feelings about living in and adapting to the new environment in China. Newly arrived expatriates seem to enjoy the respect they get from the Chinese, and several managers delightedly expressed,

I love it here, and how could you not, you get a lot of respect just because you're a foreigner and life is just pleasant.

Other expatriates that have stayed a bit longer disliked the situation to a great extent and a number of expatriates have asked to leave because their expectations about the situation in China have not been fulfilled.[49]

One country-specific situation is how to teach the Chinese employees to work in teams. The worldwide company ABB is especially focusing on creating an environment that fosters teamwork and promotes active participation among its employees.[50] This is a big challenge for Western managers (the expatriates) because the Chinese employees have a hard time working in a group, due to cultural and historical reasons. Some of the local ABB companies have failed in their attempt with team working, ad hoc groups and the like, because they have been in too much of a hurry. Or, as one manager said,

Here in China the management needs to encourage the teamwork a little bit, because it is a little against the culture and the nature of the people. This is not a question of lack of time for the managers, but I do not think we have the overall commitment to do it. Some of us feel strongly that we should, others that we can't.

Another consequence is expatriate management does not have the understanding or the commitment to teach local employees the company values, a situation that has resulted in unacceptable quality at some companies.

ABB has a great advantage in comparison to other worldwide companies due to its top priority of building deep local roots by hiring and training local managers who know their local markets.[51] Replacing expatriates with local Chinese employees, where the local employees are set to be successors to the expatriates after a certain number of years, shows the commitment to the philosophy of having a local profile. However, as the Chinese employees are coming from an extremely different system from the western expatriates, it takes quite a long time for the former to get exposed to western management practices. To ease this problem and to teach western management style, ABB China, among other companies, has recently set up an agreement with a business school in Beijing to arrange training for Chinese employees with good management potential. This is specific for ABB China because in developed countries the employees are responsible for their own development.[52] Recently ABB had its own school in Beijing for Chinese employees to learn ABB culture and management. Unfortunately, this school had to close due to the profit-center philosophy, where even the school had to charge the individual ABB companies for teaching their employees.

ABB is sending about 100 local Chinese employees to an ABB company in a Western country every year. After problems with several employees quitting after training, ABB has set up precautions with a service commitment. The employee (or new employer) has to pay back the training investment if he or she quits or that the employee signs an agreement that he or she will continue working for ABB for a certain number of years. The problem with local employees quitting after ABB's investment in training also has been experienced in India and Thailand. It is shown in the personnel turnover rate, approximately 22 percent

within ABB China, that many local employees are aiming for the experience of working for an international company such as ABB and then move on to a better-paying job.

However, by having local employees, the local ABB company is responsive to local conditions and sensitive to important cultural objectives such as the Chinese "guanxi."[53] It has been decided that the local employees should take care of the customer contact, since the expatriates are usually stationed for only a few years at one location and are consequently not able to build up strong connections with customers.

REORGANIZATION

The organization is decentralized based on delegated responsibility and the right to make decisions in order to respond quickly to customers' requirements. In the core of this complex organization are two principles: decentralization of responsibility and individual accountability. These principles have been very relevant in China, which is a relatively young country for ABB to be operating in.[54] Decentralization is highly developed and the expatriate[55] managers have a wide responsibility that would normally demand more than one specialist in a western company. However, in some instances the organization is criticized for being too centralized.

The changes in China happen very fast, and according to ABB brochures, the greatest efficiency gains lie in improving the way people work together.[56] Within the ABB China region, communication has its shortcomings. Companies with overlapping products or similar products do not exchange information to any large degree or coordinate their marketing strategies. On the technical side, communication is used frequently, which can be seen when a manager usually receives up to 100 e-mails per day from other ABB employees. However, tactics for building up effective informal communication are lacking between most ABB companies operating in China. The distances are large, and accordingly, a meeting demands greater efforts than in almost any other country in the world.

According to the former CEO, Percy Barnevik, the purpose with the matrix organization is to make the company more bottom heavy than top heavy—"clean out the headquarters in

Zurich and send everybody out, have independent companies operating in an entrepreneurial manner," as one respondent mentioned. It is further maintained in the company brochures that these entrepreneurial business units have the freedom and motivation to run their own business with a sense of personal responsibility.[57]

However, the result from the matrix organization in China is ABB subsidiaries have ABB China's objectives (the country level) and the Business Areas' (BA) objectives to follow. ABB China is measuring how the different companies are performing within China. The BA, on the contrary, is measuring how the specific products are performing on a worldwide basis and what the profitability is for the products. Each BA has a financial controller, and each country level has one also.

Rarely are the two coordinated, or do they meet. So you end up with one set of objectives from each . . . Duplication! Which one shall you follow?

According to the ABB Mission Book, the roles in the two dimensions of the ABB matrix must be complementary.[58] It demands that both the individual company and the headquarter level are flexible and strive for extensive communication. This is the way to avoid the matrix interchange becoming cumbersome and slow. It is seen to be the only way to "reap the benefits of being global (economies of scale, technological strength, etc.) and of being multidomestic (a high degree of decentralization and local roots in the countries in which we operate)."

For many years ABB was widely regarded as an exemplary European company, yet it is undergoing a second major restructuring within four years. CEO Göran Lindahl says that restructuring is aimed at making the organization faster and more cost efficient.[59] Due to the demands of a more global market, there are reasons for getting rid of the regional structure and to concentrate more on the specific countries. The reorganization has basically dismantled one half of the matrix: the country management. Henceforth, the BAs will manage their businesses on a worldwide basis and there will no longer be the confusion caused by BA and country management setting different objectives. At the same time, segments are split up (many BAs form a segment) to make them more manageable (e.g., the Transmission and Distribution segment has

been split into two segments: Transmission and Distribution). To conclude, the general managers of the individual joint ventures and other units will have only one manager above them in the organization that has a global view of the business. In China, it also means the dismantling of the Hong Kong organization as well as the Asia Pacific organization.

According to Göran Lindahl, the reorganization is preparation for a much faster rate of change on the markets and for the company to be able to respond more effectively to the demands of globalization. It is seen as an aggressive strategy to create a platform for future growth.

FUTURE VISION

CEO Göran Lindahl was appointed in 1997 to be the new president and chief executive of ABB. His view of the future is that it can no longer be extrapolated, but can be forecast by creativity, imagination, ingenuity, innovation—action based not on what was, but on what could be. The corporate culture needs to be replaced by globalizing leadership and corporate values. ABB is focusing on this by creating a unified organization across national, cultural, and business borders.

On the path towards the next century, ABB is going to focus on several essential elements: a strong local presence; a fast and flexible organization; the best technology and products available; and excellent local managers who know the business culture, are able to cross national and business borders easily, and who can execute your strategy faster than the competition.[60]

We are living in a rapidly changing environment, and our competitors will not stand still. In the face of this great challenge and opportunity, enterprises that adapt quickly and meet customer needs will be the winner, and this is the ultimate goal of ABB.[61]

APPENDIX

Motorola

Motorola was involved in Russia and faced some problems with Glasnost and decline of the country. At that time the founder of the company, Galvin, realized that there was no future in Russia and declared that China was the country where the growth was to be. Consequently, Motorola established its first representative office in China in 1987 and has grown very fast ever since. Today, China generates more than 10 percent of Motorola's sales and the company has its major businesses in China.

Motorola has found that modernization in China happens quickly and all their competitors are present in the country. They still predict China to be the potential leader in Asia for their business. The customers also have high expectations on the products Motorola is offering, because the products are regarded to be very expensive. However, the problem the company is facing in China is that the company is growing too fast, or as expressed another way,

The problem we have is that Motorola is growing very fast and it is like chasing a speeding train and trying to catch up with it.

Presently, Motorola has 12,000 employees and 200 expatriates in China, where the goal is that Chinese successors will take over the jobs of the expatriates. The expatriates are sent out on assignments for two to three years, with the possibility of renewal with a one–two rotation, but limited to a maximum of six years as an expatriate. High demands are set on the expatriates, especially concerning the difficulties experienced teaching teamwork to local employees. This is very important within the company, since all the strategy planning is done in teams. When the contract time for the expatriate has expired, the following is expressed:

You have done your job when the time comes and you have left the company and everything is working smoothly, but if everything is falling apart, you are a failure as an expatriate and have not taught a successor.

However, progress has been made in developing the company's local employees. Motorola has set up training abroad. The training, nevertheless, is preferably held within China, with rotation assignments and training at Motorola University. This company university was set up in 1994 when the company found that the Chinese universities did not turn out sufficiently well trained students. Within the company there is, however, a requirement that every employee worldwide shall have at least 40 hours of training, which is exceeded in China. There must be a combination of good training and mentor development. Motorola ad-

mits that it does not provide enough training for foreign expatriates before they come to China.

You get more understanding if you look like a foreigner and make some mistakes than if you don't. Overseas Chinese are measured through other standards than other foreigners.

Some expatriates just cannot handle the situation in China. If an expatriate fails, it has to be handled with care, otherwise the person loses face when coming back to the home office. The company also has pointed out that it needs expatriates with 10–15 years of experience in order to teach the local employees the company values and to transfer company knowledge. However, the people that are willing to change addresses and move to China are the younger employees with less than five years of experience.

The expatriates are often responsible for transferring technology knowledge and helping start projects, especially the newly set-up Center of Excellence in Tianjin, where $750 million was invested. This was Motorola's first manufacturing research laboratory outside the United States. The company has invested $1.1 billion in China and has plans to invest another $1–1.5 million. Motorola has also set up two branches of worldwide training universities to educate customers, suppliers, and government officials, as well as its own employees. The invested money in China is from the earnings within the whole enterprise, with the motivation that the Chinese market is going to be huge. Sincere commitment has been made and the present CEO, Gary Tucker, expressed the following:

When Motorola has come to your country they never leave . . . We manufacture in China, because this is where our market is. We get wealth by going to a lot of countries around the world and then doing well in that country.

The expansion strategy in China is through joint ventures. However, it is important that the Chinese partners bring something of value, which means that the partners have to be approved by the CEO. The company has become "so decentralized that it has become bad" and that the company desires to reorganize more along customer than product lines. A practical reorganization has taken place to move everybody operating in Beijing to the same newly built headquarters. However, entrepreneurial activities are also of importance, but difficult, due to financial motivation and autonomy.

In China the products are localized with Chinese characters on the cellular phones and pagers. In 1987 Motorola started selling pagers and thought there would not be a big market because the telephone-net was not well established. The company invented codebooks, which enabled two-way communication. Fortunately this also worked in Hong Kong, Singapore, and Taiwan. After five years of operation in China, the company does not have deep roots in the market. Motorola has invested huge sums in sponsoring environmental protection, providing scholarships to students, building labs at universities, and donating money to primary schools in rural areas.[62]

The worldwide organization is a "pyramid," with the corporate on top and Business Units underneath—"then put the apex at the bottom." The Corporate office works as the glue that holds the organization together. In 1997 Motorola conducted a reorganization to better reflect the global nature of the business.[63] The coordination is safeguarded by this new formal structure. However, the informal information flow is better, but it is overused. The information flow is mostly through e-mails. A manager gets approximately 70–100 per day, of which less than 30 percent are really useful. Regarding communication, the following was expressed:

Some days it feels like we have all these opportunities and we do not really communicate.

All the controllers or general managers in the joint ventures get together quarterly to counsel, to solve problems and give support to each other. Information is encouraged, but no system is developed to track what is going on in all the six districts in China where the company is operating. Competition between the different units is a common problem Motorola is experiencing, which results in the customers getting confused. This is a problem that has no solution due to the matrix organization, or as expressed another way,

We do not have the answers, because if we are too centralized then we miss new opportunities. How do you encourage creativity and yet keep people from competing with each other?

What makes Motorola a worldwide company is a set of key common beliefs or guiding principles from the role model and father figure of the company, Galvin: "uncompromising integrity and constant respect for people—that is what makes us Motorola." This is the principal code of conduct that Motorola practices, and which the management has to reread and sign every two years.

Motorola notes it "obviously" has to change because it is operating in the Chinese market—for example, show face, build relations, and go to ceremonial meetings. It is essential that the partner is reliable, that the business makes sense, and that it is legal. However, Motorola always looks the same all over the world, but it is the expatriates and their families that have made an effort to adapt to the surrounding changes.

The challenge for Motorola is doing business in China. China is very difficult for a company like Motorola, or as said another way, Motorola has trouble in China

because they would like to control the system and everything takes a long time because they will make sure that you are not cheating. You must be able to work with all the people that come from different departments and to let them trust you. Ordinary things like getting water, electricity, etc., is a huge problem. Doing business in the Chinese system is a challenge and therefore creates pressure because you get frustrated.

Procter & Gamble

In August 1998 China's largest international employer had been in China for ten successful years. Procter and Gamble, or P&G, has approximately 5,000 employees and 100 expatriates spread in 11 joint ventures and wholly owned enterprises in the country. P&G was ranked this year on *Fortune* magazine's "World's Most Admired Companies" list. Currently, the biggest market for the company is China, where new companies are being established. However, before companies were established in China, a feasibility study was done. As with most other feasibility studies done in China, the information was outdated even though it was only one year old, and people were criticized for not having sufficient knowledge about the country's specific situation.

The expatriates sent to China for the P&G account are no more prepared for the situation, except for knowing that the company has a deep culture that will support them. Furthermore, a continuous effort exists within the company to put different cultural backgrounds together. Cultural values are also written down and are consistent all over the world. However, the different expatriates have a wide variety of cultural backgrounds, and their culture is colored by their management style. This mixture of management styles might confuse the local Chinese employees.

The main benefit gained for an expatriate is the one offered in the daily work. One exception is made, for the expatriate sales people, who get a whole year of orientation training and language training. In line with the localization demands, the number of expatriates is decreasing. Due to the high costs involved in having expatriates, who are mostly 3–4 levels up in the organization, one key strategy is to develop local employees. Everybody who is an expatriate for P&G has a sponsor back home, a contact. It is essential to keep contact with the sponsor so that it is not just a name on a paper, and people are encouraged to go back home once a year at the company's cost. There is no official limit in expatriate policy within the company; however, most expatriates are on a three-year contract. The expatriate network is not yet an issue; however the expatriates are said to be a very close group—"we are all in this together and we have a common vision."

The optimal goal for P&G is to develop the organization so that it can be a Chinese-run company. Today, everything is made in the Chinese P&G factories for internal use and the company opened up a research center in Beijing, in cooperation with a prominent university.[64] If the company has developed a good idea in China, the company will analyze how to re-apply the idea in the rest of the world.

Counterfeits are the greatest competition for the company and an extensive problem. However, not all the products from P&G are sold in China and the quality of the products sold is not as high as it is in Western countries. The Chinese customers are unable to pay for better value; nevertheless, the company is trying to offer a consistency of quality to Chinese consumers.

In the Chinese P&G organization, fewer layers are developed and the decision-making takes a shorter time within the organization. Because the company evolved very quickly and the market is so dynamic and changing, it has not had the time

to implement the layers—"only tried to understand the market." Consequently, the Chinese organization and structure are not the same as in other countries, but the Chinese organization is more efficient. P&G will implement some of the ideas from China in other countries. At the current time a reorganization is taking place within the world-wide P&G group where the organization is being changed along with the culture and reward system—all to make the company more flexible.[65]

As for the Chinese situation, *"guanxi"* is mentioned, which is difficult for the expatriates to establish, and consequently the company relies on the local staff. On the contrary, the local employees get an immense amount of education at P&G's own school. Also, some of the company's expatriates have an explicit responsibility to deal with company principles, values, and all the technical specifics for P&G. The company falls short with the expatriates, because "they are so into running the business that sometimes the coaching of the locals is not possible."

One of the challenges Procter & Gamble faces in China is the difficulty in dealing with the government. The company has dealt with this by searching for a sophisticated government-relations manager who shall report not only to the head of operations in China but also to the chief executive of the company.[66]

Nestlé

In the beginning of the 1980s China asked the world's largest food company—Nestlé—to come and build "milk streets" in the country. China was unfamiliar with how to produce milk and turned to Nestlé, whose core business is actually milk powder. From that time the company has grown strongly in China and now has almost 4,000 employees, where 200 of them are foreign expatriates.

Today Nestlé is regarded as having come from Swiss roots and turned into a transnational corporation.[67] Nestlé is argued to have its foundation in its history for being locally adaptive. During the first world war, Nestlé gave its local managers increasing independence to avoid disruptions in distribution.[68] This resulted in a great deal of Nestlé's operations being established at other locations than its headquarters in Switzerland. Another cause was the company's belief that the consumers' tastes were very local and that there were no synergy effects to be gained by standardizing the products. However, in 1993 the company started to rethink its belief in localization, due to the increasing competition in the industry. Nestlé has acquired several local brands, influenced by its own country's culture, causing Nestlé to standardize where it is possible.[69]

However, although the company is growing in China, it is not always selling products with as much margin as desired. The downside is that they must have lower margins in order to be competitive, which might not always be profitable. On the question, "Why does Nestlé have to be in China?", the following was expressed:

It is because China is a large country and if you have a company that is present in more than 100 countries, you see it as a must for all international companies to be present there. We supply all over the world and it is our obligation to bring food to the people—which is the Company's priority.

Nestlé entered China with a long-term strategy to focus on the long-run perspective. Nestlé's overall approach is stated to be "Think global and act local!" The Company's strategy is guided by several fundamental principles, such as the following:

Nestlé's existing products will grow through innovation and renovation while maintaining a balance in geographic activities and product lines.[70]

With regard to the local Chinese employees, they receive a few days of Nestlé education to learn about the Nestlé culture, but the expatriates have less training going to another country. It is up to the home country to decide if it is necessary to train expatriates before sending them on an often three-year foreign assignment. However the leadership talent is highly valued within the company and consequently Nestlé has developed courses for this. The managers can independently develop their leadership talent without any connection with the specific company style or culture. Community centers have been developed to help expatriates with their contacts, supporting these expatriates psychologically and even offering language training.

In 1997 Nestlé's *The Basic Nestlé Management and Leadership Principles* was published, aimed to make "the Nestlé spirit" of the company generally known throughout the organization by discussing, seminars, and courses.[71] According to the CEO of Nestlé China, Theo Klauser, this publication is the key factor in Nestlé's corporate culture and started the company's international expansion 130 years ago.[72]

Within the organization of Nestlé China, the company has developed a specific structure, due to the joint-venture configuration. The information flow is easy and smooth between these regions, thanks to the company concentrating its activities in only three regions in China. However, communication is said to be on a high level; yet, it is not even necessary to get all levels involved. As an example, only one unit in China takes care of all the marketing. At the same time, each Nestlé company in China is responsible for its own turn-over rate, which creates the flexible and decentralized company Nestlé is today. Quite unique for a world-wide company, Nestlé does not have any external e-mail network, believed to concentrate the flow of information within the company.

A major challenge indicated for Nestlé in China is in building long relationships to establish Nestlé as the leading food company. Difficulties are to bring the products to a more acceptable level in terms of profitability. Legal difficulties are also more important than in any other country. Other challenges are the issues concerning change, about which the following was expressed:

Change happens every couple of months here, that is how the environment is, a lot of employees come from other more stable countries and sometimes find it difficult with all the changes. Change is how things are in China—it is normal. It is when something doesn't change, that is when you get worried! It is expected to change! Different from other countries where changes can be difficult to get.

CASE ENDNOTES

1. *100 years of experience ensures peak technology today,* ABB STAL AB, Finspong.

2. *Dagens Industri,* August 13, 1998, p. 25.

3. Ibid.

4. Usunier, Jean-Claude, *Marketing across Cultures.*

5. *Dagens Industri,* July 2, 1998.

6. *Management Today,* April 1996, by David Smith, p. 49.

7. Ahlquist, Magnus as editor, *The recruiter's guide to China,* by preface of Professor Michael Yahuda.

8. *Bizniz,* Sept. 30, 1997.

9. Examples include VCD-player, CD-ROM player, mobile telephones, beepers, and video cameras.

10. Garten, Jeffrey E., "Opening the Doors for Business in China," *Harvard Business Review,* May–June, 1998, pp. 160–172.

11. *Månadens Affärer,* Nov. 11, 1996, searched through AFFÄRSDATA via http://www.ad.se/bibsam/.

12. *Dagens Industri,* August 19, 1998, searched through AFFÄRSDATA via http://www.ad.se/bibsam/.

13. Ibid.

14. Ahlquist, Magnus as editor, *The recruiter's guide to China,* by preface of Professor Michael Yahuda.

15. Ibid.

16. Garten, Jeffrey E., "Opening the Doors for Business in China," *Harvard Business Review,* May–June, 1998, pp. 167–171.

17. See a recent report from *The Economist,* www.economist.com, in October 1998.

18. Hong Yung Lee, "The implications of reform for ideology, state and society in China," *Journal of International Affairs,* vol. 39, no. 2, pp. 77–90.

19. An interview with Premier Zhu Rongji in *China Daily,* March 20, 1998, p. 2.

20. *China Daily, Business Weekly,* Vol. 18, No. 5479, March 29–April 4, 1998, p. 2.

21. Hoon-Halbauer, Sing Keow, *Management of Sino-Foreign Joint Ventures;* Yuan Lu, *Management Decision-Making in Chinese Enterprises.*

22. Ibid.

23. Ma, Jun, *Intergovernal relations and economic management in China.*

24. Laaksonen, Oiva, *Management in China during and after Mao in enterprises, government, and party.*

25. Ju, Yanan, *Understanding China,* p. 45.

26. Hwang, Quanyu, *Business decision making in China.*

27. Hong Yung Lee, "The implications of reform for ideology, state and society in China," *Journal of International Affairs,* Vol. 39, No. 2, pp. 77–90.

28. Yuan Lu, *Management decision-making in Chinese enterprises.*

29. Yuan Lu, *Management decision-making in Chinese enterprises.*

30. Hong Yung Lee, "The implications of reform for ideology, state and society in China," *Journal of International Affairs,* Vol. 39, No. 2, pp. 77–90.

31. Yuan Lu, *Management decision-making in Chinese enterprises.*

32. *Månadens Affärer,* Nov. 11, 1996.

33. *The Economist,* Oct. 28, 1995, searched from http://www.economist.com.

34. Due to China still being a quite closed country, Chinese people are not able to obtain foreign currency, other than in very limited amounts.

35. ABB, "The art of being Local," ABB Corporate Communications, Ltd., printed in Switzerland.

36. ABB Brochure, "You can rely on the power of ABB." ABB Asea Brown Boveri, Ltd., Department CC-C, Zurich.

37. Technology partner (in this case) = Center of Excellence (CE), = Licensors.

38. ABB's Mission, Values, and Policies.

39. HV Switchgear, ABB, ABB Business Area H. V. Switchgear, Printed in Switzerland.

40. ABB Asea Brown Boveri, Ltd., You can rely on the power of ABB, Department CC-C, Zurich.

41. Licensing is defined here as a form of external production where the owner of technology or proprietary right (licensor) agrees to transfer this to a joint venture in China which is responsible for local production (licensee).

42. During the study this has changed to some degree, due to a unit called CHTET being introduced.

43. http://www.abb.se/swg/switchgear/index.htm in November 1997.

44. First source = you are the first source, but if you cannot meet the customers' requirements, the second source steps in.

45. *The Economist,* Jan. 6, 1996, searched from http://www.economist.com.

46. Ibid.

47. Göran Lindahl is the present CEO, Chairman of the Board.

48. *The Economist,* Jan. 6, 1996, searched from http://www.economist.com.

49. There are two types of common, but false, expectations expatriates have when coming to China. Either they believe they are going to make a lot of money or they are going to experience the old Chinese culture—a culture that, most of the time, does not correspond to the culture of today in China.

50. ABB's Mission, Values, and Policies, Zurich, 1991.

51. ABB, "The art of being Local," ABB Corporate Communications, Ltd., printed in Switzerland.

52. ABB's Mission, Values, and Policies, Zurich, 1991.

53. *Guanxi* = connections, relations.

54. ABB set up its first office, a representative office, in 1979.

55. An expatriate is a person who has a working placement outside the home country.

56. ABB Asea Brown Boveri, Ltd., *You can rely on the power of ABB,* Department CC-C, Zurich.

57. ABB Asea Brown Boveri, Ltd., *You can rely on the power of ABB,* Department CC-C, Zurich.

58. ABB's Mission, Values, and Policies.

59. *Dagens Industri,* August 13, 1998, p. 25.

60. "Meeting the Challenges of the Future," Presentation given to the Executives Club of Chicago, October 16, 1997.

61. ABB, "Leading the way in efficient and reliable supply of electric power," ABB Transmission and Distribution, Ltd., Hong Kong.

62. Garten, Jeffrey E., "Opening the Doors for Business in China," *Harvard Business Review,* May–June, 1998, pp. 174–175.

63. Motorola Annual Report, 1997.

64. Qinghua University.

65. Procter & Gamble Annual Report, 1998.

66. Garten, Jeffrey E., "Opening the Doors for Business in China," *Harvard Business Review,* May–June, 1998, pp. 173–175.

67. http://www.Nestlé.com/html/home.html, September 1998.

68. Quelch, J. A., & Hoff, E. J., "Customizing Global Marketing," *Harvard Business Review,* 1986, May–June, No. 3, pp. 59–60.

69. Brorsson, Skarsten, Torstensson, *Marknadsföring på den inre markanden— Standardisering eller Anpassning,* Thesis at Lund University, 1993.

70. http://www.Nestlé.com/html/h2h.html, in September 1998.

71. Nestlé Management Report, 1997.

72. Interview with CEO of Nestlé China, Theo Klauser, *Metro,* July 1998, p. 27.

References

Beamish, Paul J., Peter Killing, Donald J. Lecraw, and Allen J. Morrison. 1994. *International Management*.

Boscheck, Ralph. 1996. "Managed trade and regional preference." In IMD, *World Competitiveness Yearbook 1996*, 333–44. Lausanne, Switzerland: Institute for Management Development.

Boudreau, Marie-Claude, Karen D. Loch, Daniel Robey, and Detmar Straud. 1998. "Going global: Using information technology to advance the competitiveness of the virtual transnational organization." *The Academy of Management Executive*, 12, 120–4.

Business Week Online. 2000a. "The Business Week Global 1,000," July 10, chart.

———. 2000b. "The top 200 emerging market companies." July 10, chart.

———. 2000c. "Keeping the concrete and the cash flowing." September 18.

———. 1999. "The Business Week Global 1,000," August 28.

Business Wire. 2000. "BulletIN.net and PANDA team to bring wireless Internet services to China." December 7.

Chang, Allen T., and Peter Comparelli. 2000. "Back on top." http://www.asia-inc.com, April.

Dizarevic, Eldar. 2000. "Hot cakes." *Business Central Europe*, http://www.bcemag.com, December.

Economist. 2001. "Markets and data, weekly indicators." http://www.economist.com, January 9.

———. 2000a. "Let the good times roll." http://www.economist.com, April 13.

———. 2000b. "Not so fast." http://www.economist.com, October 5.

———. 2000c. "Responsible regionalism." http://www.economist.com, December 2.

———. 2000d. "The future that might have been." http://www.economist.com, December 14.

———. 1998. "Stalling in China." http://www.economist.com, April 18.

———. 1997. "Privatization." March 22, 143.

———. 1996a. "Spoiling world trade." December 7, 15–16.

———. 1996b. "All free traders now?" December 7, 23–25.

Edmondson, Gail, Kerry Capell, Pamela L. Moore, and Peter Burrows. 2000. "See the world, erase its borders." *Businessweek Online*, August 28.

European Commission. 2000. *Enlargement Strategy Paper*. Bruxelles.

European Report. 2000. "EU/China: Lamy warns Beijing over WTO talks." http://www.findarticles.com, October 4.

Forbes. 2000. "Forbes international 800 2000." http://www.Forbes.com.

Fortune. 2000. "Fortune Global 500 2000." http://www.fortune.com/fortune/global500.

———. 1996. "Could this be a Chinese Sony?" May 27, 122.

Frontier. 1999. "Taking in the sites." http://www.businessweek.com/smallbiz, November 30.

Geiger, Keri. 2000. *Euromoney*, September, http://www.euromoney.com.

GlobalSight. 2001. http://www.globalsight.com.

Guttman, Robert J. 1992. "Coca-Cola president Donald Keough." *Europe*, May, 30–32.

Hamel, Cary, and C. K. Prahalad. 1989. "Strategic intent." *Harvard Business Review*, May-June, 63–76.

Honda Motor Company. 2001. http://www.world.honda.com/Europe.

International Standards Organization. 2001. http://www.iso.ch.

Internet Indicators. 2000. http://www.internetindicators.com.

Javetski, Bill, and William Glasgall. 1994. "Borderless finance: fuel for growth." *Business Week*, November 18, 40–50.

Javetski, Bill, Gail Edmondson, and William Echikson. 1996. "Believing in Europe: U.S. companies are plowing billions into the Old World—and shaking up its business practices in the process." *Business Week*, International Edition—Europe, cover story, October 7.

Levine, Jonathan B. 1992. "Want EC business? You have two choices." *Business Week*, October 19, 58–59.

Lubbers, R. F. M. 1996. "Globalization: an exploration." *Nijenrode Management Review*, 1.

Megginson, William. 2000. "Privatization." *Foreign Policy*, http://www.findarticles.com, Spring.

Meth-Cohn, Delia. 2000. "Does US Steel threaten the region's steel firms?" *Business Central Europe*, http://www.bcemag.com, December.

Moran, Robert T., and John R. Riesenberger. 1994. *The Global Challenge*. London: McGraw-Hill.

Motorola. 2001. http://www.motorola.com.

OECD. 2001. http://www.oecd.org.

Rhinesmith, Steven H., John N. Williamson, David M. Ehlen, and Denise S. Maxwell. 1989. "Developing leaders for the global enterprise." *Training and Development Journal*, April, 25–34.

Rohwer, Jim. 2000. "China's coming telecom battle." *Fortune*, November 27, 209–211.

Rosen, Robert H., Patricia Digh, Mashall Singer, and Carl Phillips. 1999. *Global Literacies: Lessons on Business Leaders and National Cultures*. Riverside, NJ: Simon & Schuster.

Schoenberger, Karl. 1996. "Motorola bets big on China." *Fortune*, May 27, 116–24.

Smith, Geri. 1999. "Concrete benefits from a plunge into cyberspace." http://businessweekonline.com, April 29.

Symonds, William C., Brian Bremmer, Stewart Toy, and Karen Lowry Miller. 1996. "The *Business Week* Global 1000, the globetrotters take over." July 8.

UNCTAD (UN Conference on Trade and Development). 2000a. *World Investment Report*. New York and Geneva: United Nations.

———. 2000b. "World FDI flows exceed US$ 1.1 trillion in 2000." UNCTAD Press Release, December 7.

———. 1996a. "Global foreign direct investment flows reach $325 billion in 1995, an all-time high, says UNCTAD." UNCTAD Press release, June 4.

———. 1996b. "Foreign direct investment soars 40 percent as corporations become more global." Press release, September 24.

World Bank. 2000. *Global Development Finance*. Washington, DC: World Bank.

WTO (World Trade Organization). 2000a. *Annual Report (2000)*. Geneva: World Trade Organization.

———. 2000b. *International Statistics 2000*. Geneva: World Trade Organization.

———. 1997. "After two outstanding years, world trade growth in 1996 returned to earlier levels." Press release, April 4.

Weber, Joseph, Catherine Yang, and Kerry Capell. 1999. "The biggest influence on this year's ranking? You guessed it: The Internet." *Businessweek Online*. July 12.

Yip, George S. 1995. *Total Global Strategy*, Englewood Cliffs: Prentice Hall.

Chapter 2

Culture and Multinational Management

LEARNING OBJECTIVES
After reading this chapter you should
be able to:

- **Define culture and understand the
  basic components of culture.**

- **Identify instances of cultural
  stereotyping and ethnocentrism.**

- **Understand how various levels of
  culture influence multinational
  operations.**

- **Apply the Hofstede and 7d models to
  diagnose and understand the impact of
  cultural differences on management
  processes.**

- **Appreciate the complex differences
  among cultures and use these
  differences for building better
  organizations.**

**Preview
Case in Point**

This poem by Rudyard Kipling, "We and They," captures some of the feelings associated with intercultural experiences.

**Different and
the Same—
Explorations
in Culture**

Father, Mother, and Me
Sister and Auntie say
All the people like us are We,
And everyone else is They.
And They live over the sea
While we live over the way,
But—would you believe it?—They look upon We
As only a sort of They!

We eat pork and beef
With cow-horn-handled knives.
They who gobble Their rice off a leaf
Are horrified out of Their lives;
While They who live up a tree,
Feast on grubs and clay,
(Isn't it scandalous?) look upon We
As a simply disgusting They!

We eat kitcheny food.
We have doors that latch.
They drink milk and blood
Under an open thatch. We have doctors to fee.
They have wizards to pay.
And (impudent heathen!) They look upon We
As a quite impossible They!

All good people agree,
And all good people say,
All nice people, like us, are We
And everyone else is They:
But if you cross over the sea,
Instead of over the way,
You may end by (think of it!) looking on We
As only a sort of They!

Source: Rudyard Kipling, "We and They."

The Preview Case in Point shows the feelings that many people have when they meet people from other cultures. They see behavior that they have trouble understanding. They see, hear, smell, and taste things that are strange and unpredictable. However, in today's business world, these seemingly strange people are often your customers, employees, suppliers, and business partners.

To remain competitive and to flourish in the complex and fast-changing world of multinational business, multinational managers must look worldwide not only for potential markets but also for sources of high-quality and less expensive raw materials and labor. Even managers who never leave their home country will deal with markets and a workforce whose cultural background is increasingly diverse. Those managers with the skills to understand and adapt to different cultures are better positioned to succeed in these endeavors and to compete successfully in the world market.

Conducting business with people from other cultures will never be as easy as doing business at home. However, you can improve the chances of success at cross-cultural business interactions by learning more about the nature of culture and its effects on business practices.

Throughout this text you will be exposed to numerous cultural differences in management practices from countries around the world. To help you better understand these cultural underpinnings of management, this chapter considers two basic questions: (1) What is culture? (2) How does culture affect management and organizations? The next chapter also considers the impact of cultural differences on business, but from the perspective of culture's effects on negotiation and communication. Later chapters show how an understanding of cultural differences in management practices can contribute to the more effective management of multinational organizations.

WHAT IS CULTURE?

Culture

The pervasive and shared beliefs, norms, and values that guide the everyday life of a group.

Cultural norms

Prescribed and proscribed behaviors, telling us what we can do and what we cannot do.

Cultural values

Values that tell us such things as what is good, what is beautiful, what is holy, and what are legitimate goals for life.

Cultural beliefs

Our understandings about what is true.

Cultural symbols

These may be physical, such as national flags or holy artifacts. In the workplace, office size and location can serve as cultural symbols.

Cultural stories

These include such things as nursery rhymes and traditional legends.

Culture is a concept borrowed from cultural anthropology. Anthropologists believe that cultures provide solutions to problems of adaptation to the environment. Eskimos, for example, have by necessity a large number of words to deal with the nature of snow. Culture helps people become attached to their society. It tells us who we are and to what groups we belong. Culture provides mechanisms for continuation of the group. For example, culture determines how children are educated and tells us whom to marry and when. Culture pervades most areas of our life, determining, for example, how we should dress and what we should eat.

Anthropologists have numerous and subtle different definitions of culture (Kroeber and Kluckhohn 1952). However, for the purposes of this book, with its focus on comparative and multinational management, culture is defined as the pervasive and shared beliefs, norms, and values that guide the everyday life of a group. These beliefs, norms, and values are expressed to current group members and passed on to future group members through cultural rituals, stories, and symbols.

Cultural norms both prescribe and proscribe behaviors. That is, they tell us what we can do and what we cannot do. For example, norms prescribe when and whom we can marry, and what clothes we can or cannot wear to a funeral or to the office. **Cultural values** tell us such things as what is good, what is beautiful, what is holy, and what are legitimate goals for life. **Cultural beliefs** represent our understandings about what is true. For example, most people in the United States accept the scientific method as a valid way of discovering facts. In contrast, other cultures may have the belief that fact can only be revealed by God.

Cultural symbols, stories, and rituals communicate the norms, values, and beliefs of a society or a group to its members. Each generation passes its culture to the next generation by symbols, stories and rituals. A particular culture is continuously reinforced when people see symbols, hear stories, and engage in rituals.

Rituals include ceremonies such as baptism, graduation, as well as the tricks played on a new worker or the pledge to a sorority or fraternity. Stories include such things as nursery rhymes and traditional legends (such as the U.S. legend that George Washington could not tell a lie). Symbols may be physical, such as national flags or holy artifacts. In the workplace, office size and location can serve as a cultural symbol. North American managers, for example, use large offices with physical barriers such as outer offices as symbols to communicate their power. In contrast, Japanese managers avoid physical barriers. They prefer instead to locate their

Cultural rituals

Ceremonies such as baptism, graduation, or the tricks played on a new worker, or the pledge to a sorority or fraternity.

Pervasive

The idea that culture affects almost everything we do, everything we see, and everything we feel and believe.

Front stage of culture

The easily observable aspect of culture.

Back stage of culture

Aspects of culture that are understood only by insiders or members of the culture.

Shared cultural values, norms, and beliefs

The idea that people in different cultural groups have similar views of the world.

desks where they are surrounded by coworkers and remain at the center of communication networks.

Culture is **pervasive** in societies. It affects almost everything we do, everything we see, and everything we feel and believe. Pick any aspect of your life and it is likely affected by culture. What you sleep on, what you eat, what clothes you wear, how you address your family members and boss, whether you believe that old age is good or bad, what your toilet looks like, all respond to cultural differences. In each of these areas, societies develop pervasive cultural norms, values, and beliefs to assist their members in adapting to their environments.

Although culture is pervasive, not all aspects of culture are directly observable, especially to the outsider. We can see overt behaviors such as the Japanese executive's bow or the robust handshake of the North American. This easily observable aspect of culture is called the **front stage of culture** (Goffman 1959). As in a play, it is what we see on stage—but it does not necessarily reflect people's thoughts and emotions.

Only insiders or members of the culture understand other aspects of culture. These aspects are called the **back stage of culture**. For example, when the Japanese businessman tells his U.S. colleague that something "is difficult" and twists his head a little to one side, he is really saying something else: "It is impossible, but I don't want to say 'no' directly." To understand this deeper meaning of culture, you must go beyond simple observation and view the world through the eyes of the members of a particular culture. This usually happens only when you live in a culture for some time and learn to speak the language of that culture.

Because culture affects so many aspects of our lives, many of the core values, norms, and beliefs about what should happen in everyday life are taken for granted. That is, people do not consciously think about how culture affects their behavior and attitudes. They just do what they believe is "right and natural" (see the Preview Case in Point). Even the members of a specific society may have little awareness as to why they behave in a particular manner in their culture.

Another key component of the definition of culture is that **cultural values, norms, and beliefs** must be **shared** by a group of people: The group must accept that, for the most part, the norms, values, and beliefs of their group are correct and compelling (Terpstra and David 1991). "Correct and compelling" means that, although people in any culture do not all behave the same way all the time, behaviors are predictable most of the time. Imagine, for example, the chaos that would exist if we did not have norms to guide our driving. For example, when driving on two-lane roads in Ireland, drivers routinely pass slower vehicles even when faced with oncoming traffic. Unlike in the United States, oncoming drivers expect this tactic and routinely move to the breakdown lane. Although this norm is different from that in the United States, the majority of people manage to drive around without running into each other.

For the multinational manager, the importance of understanding and dealing with cultural differences is unavoidable. To succeed cross-culturally, multinational managers must learn as much as they can about the important cultural norms, values, and beliefs of the societies in which they work. They must also learn to recognize the important symbols, values, and rituals of a culture. Such knowledge helps the multinational manager understand the "why" behind the behavior of their customers, workers, and colleagues. The following Case in Point shows how one U.S. company faced a challenge caused by a lack of cultural sensitivity to local religious beliefs and rituals.

The next section expands our discussion of culture by looking at how the various levels of culture affect the multinational manager in the business world.

Case in Point

A Cultural Misunderstanding

Thom McAn is a shoe company that recently began operations in Bangladesh. When the firm's shoes first went on sale, a riotous protest occurred, resulting in injury to more than fifty people. Why?

The Thom McAn signature, which appears in a nearly illegible imprint on the sole of each shoe, looked similar to the Arabic script for "Allah" (God). In the Muslim world, the foot and especially the sole of the foot is considered unclean. For example, you should not show the sole of your shoes to guests. In this case, it looked as if Thom McAn was desecrating the name of God by asking the Bangladeshis to walk on it.

Source: Based on Morrison, Conaway, and Borden 1996.

LEVELS OF CULTURE

Levels of culture

These include national, business, and occupational and organizational culture.

The international businessperson needs to be aware of three **levels of culture** that may influence multinational operations. These include national culture, business culture, and the occupational and organizational cultures. Exhibit 2.1 shows the levels of culture that affect multinational management.

NATIONAL CULTURE

National culture

The dominant culture within the political boundaries of the nation-state.

National culture is the dominant culture within the political boundaries of the nation-state. The dominant national culture usually represents the culture of the people with the greatest population or the greatest political or economic power. Formal education is generally taught, and business is usually conducted, in the language of the dominant culture.

Political boundaries, however, do not necessarily reflect cultural boundaries. Many countries, such as Canada and Singapore, have more than one major cultural group within their political boundaries. Moreover, even states with relatively homogeneous cultures have various subcultures, representing regional and rural/urban cultural differences that affect business transactions.

Most business takes place within the political boundaries of the nation-state. As such, the dominant culture of the nation-state has the greatest effect on interna-

Exhibit 2.1
Levels of Culture in Multinational Management

Multinational Management Brief
Chinese Business Culture in Singapore and Indonesia

Chinese is the dominant culture in Singapore. Chinese control the majority of businesses and dominate business transactions. However, the government makes strong efforts to integrate the minority cultures. The majority of the people in Singapore are Chinese (77 percent). Most of the remaining population is Malay and Indian. The majority of the Chinese are Buddhists or atheists, while nearly all the Malays are Muslim. Chinese, Malay, Tamil, and English are all official languages.

The situation is quite different in Indonesia. Ethnic Chinese control the business culture even though they are a small minority. They make up only 5 percent of the population of 224 million, but control 75 percent of the wealth. This discrepancy in wealth creates ethnic tensions that this year resulted in labor riots and in the mid-1960s resulted in the looting of Chinese businesses and the massacre of thousands.

Sources: Adapted from *Central Intelligence Agency World Fact Book* 2000 and Shari 1994.

tional business. In particular, the dominant national culture usually influences not only the language of business transactions but also the nature and types of laws that govern businesses. Consider the Multinational Management Brief above, regarding the complex situation for Singapore.

All major social institutions—religious beliefs, education, the family, politics, law, and economics—are closely intertwined with national culture. The family and educational system serve as the major transmitters of cultural heritage. Cultural norms, values, and beliefs are passed on through what individuals learn at home and in school. Political and economic systems evolve within the constraints of national culture. For example, cultures with strong beliefs regarding the differences among the social classes may evolve into a centralized, paternalistic political system. The laws and legal system of a country reflect in a formal way the cultural norms that guide behavior. Religion is closely intertwined with culture in the sense that it prescribes and proscribes beliefs, values, and norms for everyday actions. Each religion has its own principles that guide behavior. Buddhists, for example, must abstain from lying, killing, stealing, and sexual wrongdoing. Christians are guided by principles in the Bible that prohibit similar behavior, and Muslims follow the Koran and its guidelines for living.

A detailed description of how each social institution relates to national culture is beyond the scope of this chapter. However, sections throughout the text show how various social institutions combine with culture to affect local business practices and multinational operations.

BUSINESS CULTURE

To a large degree, when multinational managers express concern with the impact of culture on international operations, they focus on how national cultures influence business operations. They ask, "How do the _____ (Germans, Indians, Japanese, Koreans, South Americans, Africans, Israelis, etc.) do business?" What

Case in Point

Mexican Business Culture

The majority of businesses in Mexico are small and owned and run by families. Even the larger businesses often have strong family ties. Because of the traditionally paternalistic nature of these organizations, jobs often go to family members and trusted friends of family members. Although education and training do count for getting a management job, to a large degree positions are assigned based on relationships with the corporate family. Loyalty to one's superior is a major factor in promotions.

The technical requirements of producing a product (e.g., production efficiency) do not dominate the administration and structure of the organization. Being sensitive to the needs of one's colleagues and subordinates and maintaining relationships often are higher priorities. Managers often base their decisions on custom and intuition rather than on formal analyses. An ideal workplace is free of excessive stress resulting from competition or conflict.

In Mexican business culture, work is considered a necessary evil, not the focus of life. Work provides support for life, family, and leisure. Unlike the Americans to the north, the "normal" person balances the demands of work and leisure.

Sources: Based on Gomes 1993 and Kras 1995.

Business culture

Norms, values, and beliefs that pertain to all aspects of doing business in a culture.

concerns these managers is the **business culture**. More than cultural differences in business etiquette, business culture represents norms, values, and beliefs that pertain to all aspects of doing business in a culture (Terpstra and David 1991). Business cultures tell people the correct, acceptable ways to conduct business in a society.

Each national culture contains its own business culture. However, business cultures are not separate from the broader national culture. Rather, the more pervasive national culture constrains and guides the development of business culture in a society. In any society, business closely interweaves with the broader culture's values, norms, and beliefs. Examples include the priorities given to age and seniority, the role expectations for women with their family, and expectations concerning how superiors should behave toward subordinates.

At a very broad level, business culture, as a reflection of national culture, influences all aspects of work and organizational life. This includes how managers select and promote employees, lead and motivate their subordinates, structure their organizations, select and formulate their strategies, and negotiate with other businesspeople. Much of what you read in this book will help you understand how national and business cultures affect organizations and management. The preceding Case in Point, on Mexican business culture, describes some of the practices considered typical in that culture.

Business culture also guides everyday business interactions, and the business cultures of different nations vary widely in the codes of conduct that represent proper business etiquette. What to wear to a meeting, when and how to use business cards, whether to shake hands or embrace are examples of business etiquette that vary according to national cultures.

Understanding the basic business etiquette of a business culture is a minimal requirement for the multinational manager. In Germany, "Show up half an hour late [for a business meeting] and it makes no matter how bad the traffic and how tight your schedule. You've likely lost the appointment and may have a tough time get-

Case in Point

Some Aspects of Business Etiquette in Germany and Japan

Business etiquette in both Germany and Japan is more formal than in the United States. Conservative dress in dark business suits and formal polite interactions are the norm. People seldom use first names. The Germans prefer honorific titles (e.g., "Herr [Mister] Doctor"). The Japanese prefer the suffix *san*, as in *Tanaka-san*, as a polite form of address.

Business cards are expected in Germany, but they are essential in Japan. The Japanese use business cards (*meishi*) as a form of introduction. Business cards help the Japanese place an individual in the appropriate context, in terms of both the prestige of one's company and one's position in the company. The Japanese may study you and your *meishi* for several minutes without any other interaction. Many Westerners may find this use of time disconcerting and wonder what is happening.

The Germans keep separate business and family lives. They seldom conduct business after 5 P.M. In contrast, the Japanese workday will run to sundown and after that, eating and drinking with colleagues and business partners will continue to 10 or 11 P.M. Because of this cultural expectation, a Japanese wife might be embarrassed if her husband, the manager, routinely came home at 6. This would suggest he was rejected by his colleagues. In Japan, expect to be entertained after business hours. The formality of the office often breaks down in ritualized drinking, as the Japanese view this as a way to really understand you in a relaxed situation. At 9 the next morning, however, all the formality of the day before will return.

Source: Based on *Craighead's International Business, Travel, and Relocation Guide 2000.*

ting another" (*Craighead's International Business, Travel, and Relocation Guide 2000*). The preceding Case in Point, dealing with Germany and Japan, describes essential elements of business etiquette for doing business in these countries.

OCCUPATIONAL CULTURE AND ORGANIZATIONAL CULTURE

Although differences in national and business cultures usually present challenges to the multinational manager, distinct cultures also develop around work roles and organizations. These are called the occupational and organizational cultures.

Different occupational groups, such as physicians, lawyers, accountants, and craftspeople, have distinct cultures, called **occupational cultures**. Occupational cultures are the norms, values, beliefs, and expected ways of behaving for people in the same occupational group, regardless of what organization they work for.

Occupational cultures

Distinct cultures of occupational groups such as physicians, lawyers, accountants, and craftspeople.

In spite of the importance of national and business cultures, the multinational manager cannot ignore differences in occupational cultures. To demonstrate this point, a study by Hofstede (1980), which included over forty different national cultures, found that people with similar jobs often had very similar cultural values. Moreover, the people from the different occupational groups were often more similar to one another than to people from their own national cultures.

The existence of an occupational culture is more prevalent for professional and technical occupations, such as physicians. This distinction occurs because professionals have similar educational backgrounds and have access to the free flow of technical information across national boundaries.

During the last decade, managers and academics realized that the concept of culture also applied to individual organizations. Differences in organizational cultures seemed to answer questions such as why two organizations with similar structures and strategies have different performance levels and why the merger of two otherwise successful companies failed. In particular, the idea of an organizational culture helps us understand how organizations are affected by more than their formally designed systems, such as the organizational structure.

Organizational culture

The norms, values, and beliefs concerning the organization shared by members of the organization.

Vijay Sathe defined **organizational culture** as "the set of important understandings (often unstated) that members of a community share in common" (Sathe 1985, 6). Edgar Schein of MIT added that these assumptions, values, and beliefs concerning the organization are discovered and created when members learn to cope with external and internal problems, such as developing a strategy or the criteria for allocating organizational rewards. When coping strategies—such as Hewlett-Packard's "management by wandering around"—work successfully, they are taught to new members as "the correct way to perceive, think, and feel in relation to those problems" (Schein 1985).

Seldom do organizations have only one organizational culture, nor perhaps should they. Because organizational subunits (divisions, departments, etc.) all face different situations, most develop distinct subcultures. Subunits may retain many of the overall characteristics of the parent company, but, for example, few would expect an R&D department to have the same culture as a manufacturing plant.

CAVEATS AND CAUTIONS

Although understanding the cultures of the people and organizations with which you work is crucial for international business success, multinational managers in particular must realize that cultures provide only broad guidelines for behavior. Cultures do not determine exactly how each individual behaves, thinks, acts, and feels. Assuming that all people within one culture behave, believe, feel, and act the same is known as **stereotyping**.

Stereotyping

When one assumes that all people within a culture behave, believe, feel, and act the same.

However, using the cultural stereotype—the typical way people act—to understand another culture is not necessarily wrong, *if* it is used carefully. Broad generalization about a culture can serve as a starting point for understanding the complexities of cultural differences. Most books on "How to do business with the _____ " (name a culture) use stereotypical cultural generalizations. After considering such information, however, the multinational manager must realize that organizational and occupational cultures differ within any national context and that individuals vary widely within each level of culture.

Consequently, management functions such as planning, organizational design, and personnel management must account for differences in occupational and organizational cultures as well as in national culture. Similarly, successful leadership, motivation, and development of individual employees must adjust for expectations based not only on all levels of culture, but also on the unique characteristics of each employee.

Ethnocentrism

When people from one culture believe that theirs are the only correct norms, values, and beliefs.

Cultural relativism

A philosophical position arguing that all cultures, no matter how different, are correct and moral for the people of those cultures.

Perhaps the greatest danger facing the multinational manager regarding culture is **ethnocentrism**. Ethnocentrism occurs when people from one culture believe that theirs are the only correct norms, values, and beliefs. The ethnocentric person may look down on people from other cultures, and may consider people from other cultural groups backward, dirty, weird, stupid, and so on. To offset the tendency of ethnocentrism, many anthropologists believe that one can understand another culture only if one adopts the position of **cultural relativism**. This is the

Multinational Management Challenge
Can Cultural Adaptation Go Too Far?

Eric Bouvier was executive assistant to the managing director of a Korean and French joint venture between a major European pharmaceutical company and a small but growing Korean pharmaceutical. Bouvier spoke fluent Korean and seved the company well as a cultural bridge between director Pascale Comont and Young Lim, his Korean counterpart.

After two years on the job, Comont became concerned about changes in Bouvier's behavior. Bouvier was no longer acting French. After his marriage to a Korean woman, he no longer socialized with his French expatriate colleagues, preferring instead to go to local bars with the Korean managers after work. In addition, whenever a disagreement arose between Comont and the Korean management team, Bouvier would side with the Koreans. He would simply tell Comont, "It's just the Korean way."

Although Comont initially found this behavior only mildly irritating, the issue came to a head over a personnel decision. When Comont fired a Korean manager for incompetence, Bouvier and Lim secretly had the man transferred to another division of the Korean parent company. When confronted with this situation, Bouvier simply explained it was his "moral duty to take care of subordinates—to protect their family and their reputation." As Comont pondered what to do, he wondered whether the issue of cultural sensitivity had gone too far.

Source: Based on Yoshino, in Beauchamp 1989.

philosophical stance that all cultures, no matter how different, are correct and moral for the people of those cultures.

Few multinational managers, however, are so ethnocentric that they fail to realize that people from other cultures just do things differently. Rather, the danger is a subtle ethnocentrism. Managers may find it difficult to remain entirely neutral in response to other cultures. For example, things such as the variations in pace of work in other countries, the unwillingness of subordinates to take responsibility, and practices such as bribery often frustrate North American managers. Early in an overseas assignment, especially, managers must be wary of judging subordinates in terms of the manager's own cultural values. "Why don't they do it right, as we do?" is a common ethnocentric reaction.

The preceding Multinational Management Challenge shows that it is not always easy for the multinational manager to determine how sensitive to be to other cultures. The U.S. manager in this case is seen by his boss as overidentifying with Korean culture and not identifying enough with the culture of the parent organization.

CULTURAL DIFFERENCES AND BASIC VALUES: TWO DIAGNOSTIC MODELS TO AID THE MULTINATIONAL MANAGER

Multinational managers face a complex array of cultures that challenge their ability to manage. The following sections describe two popular models that can help you understand the important ways in which national and business cultures differ and thereby help you manage successfully in the various cultures in which you do business.

Hofstede model of national culture

A cultural model mainly based on differences in values and beliefs regarding work goals.

The Dutch scientist Geert Hofstede introduced the first model in the early 1980s. Management scholars now use it extensively as a way of understanding cultural differences. We call this the **Hofstede model of national culture**. Hofstede developed his cultural model primarily based on differences in values and beliefs regarding work goals. Thus, it has easily identifiable implications for business by providing a clear link between national and business cultures. It also serves an important role as a basis for extensive research on cross-cultural management. You will see later in the text numerous examples of Hofstede's ideas providing the background to understand differences in management practices.

7d culture model

A seven dimension cultural model based on beliefs regarding how people relate to each other, how people manage time, and how people deal with nature.

The second model is more recent. Created by Fons Trompenaars, this model of culture is called the **7d culture model** since it represents seven dimensions of culture. This model comes from extensive and continuing cross-national research by Fons Trompenaars and his colleagues (Trompenaars and Hampden-Turner 1998; 2000).

Both models equip managers with the basic tools necessary to analyze the cultures in which they do business. Both approaches provide useful terms to help you understand the complexities of different cultural values. By using these models, you will develop an initial understanding of important cultural differences and key cultural traits.

The next section provides more detail on the Hofstede model followed by a section describing the 7d model.

HOFSTEDE'S MODEL OF NATIONAL CULTURE

To describe national cultures, Hofstede (1991) uses five dimensions of basic cultural values. These values address issues of:

1. Expectations regarding equality among people, called "power distance"
2. Typical reactions to situations considered different and dangerous, called "uncertainty avoidance"
3. The relationship between the individual and the group in society, called "individualism"
4. Expectations regarding gender roles, called "masculinity"
5. A basic orientation toward time, called "long-term orientation"

Hofstede identified four of these cultural value dimensions in a study of thirty-nine IBM subsidiaries throughout the world (Hofstede 1980). Later research by Hofstede and others added to the number of countries studied and introduced the fifth dimension, long-term orientation (Hofstede 1991; Hofstede and Bond 1988).

Research on the long-term orientation dimension was unique. Rather than using survey questions developed by Western researchers, Michael Bond and several Chinese colleagues developed a new survey based on questions developed by Asian researchers reflecting Confucian values. Hofstede and Bond have related the long-term orientation to the recent economic growth in the mini-dragons of the rising Asian economies (Hofstede and Bond 1988).

HOFSTEDE'S CULTURAL MODEL APPLIED TO ORGANIZATIONS AND MANAGEMENT

The following section defines Hofstede's dimensions of national culture and adapts and extends this work (Hofstede 1980, 1991) to show how cultural values affect numerous management practices in different cultures. The management practices considered in the discussion of Hofstede's model include:

1. Human resources management
   a. Management selection (how people are chosen for jobs)
   b. Training (what the focus of job training is)
   c. Evaluation and promotion (what counts to get ahead)
   d. Remuneration (what accounts for differences in pay)
2. Leadership styles (how leaders behave)
3. Motivational assumptions (beliefs regarding how people respond to work)
4. Decision making and organizational design (how managers structure their organizations and make decisions)
5. Strategy (effects of culture on selecting and implementing strategies)

First, we consider power distance followed by discussions of the other dimensions noted previously.

POWER DISTANCE

Power distance

Expectations regarding equality among people.

Power distance concerns how cultures deal with inequality. It focuses on (1) the norms that tell superiors (bosses, leaders, and so on) how much they can determine the behavior of their subordinates and (2) the values and beliefs that superiors and subordinates are fundamentally different kinds of people.

High power distance countries have norms, values, and beliefs such as (Hofstede 1980):

- Inequality is fundamentally good.
- Everyone has a place; some are high, some are low.
- Most people should be dependent on a leader.
- The powerful are entitled to privileges.
- The powerful should not hide their power.

Organizations in countries high on power distance use management systems and processes that reflect a strong concern with hierarchy. As shown later in the chapter with Exhibit 2.7, Latin American, Latin European, and Asian countries demonstrate the highest levels of power distance.

The concern for hierarchy and inequality in organizations is rooted in early socialization in the family and school. In high power distance cultures, children are expected to be obedient to parents and elders. This deference continues as long as parents are alive. When children enter school, teachers assume the role of dominance. Children must show extreme respect and seldom challenge a teacher's authority. Later in life, organizations assume many of the roles of parents and teachers.

In high power distance countries, the ideal people for a managerial job come from a high social class and/or have graduated from an elite university. These characteristics define the person as having the intrinsic or built-in qualities of a leader. Who you are in terms of elite associations is more important than past performance. Leaders and subordinates expect large wage differences between management and workers.

The basic motivational assumption in high power distance countries is that people dislike work and try to avoid it. Consequently, managers believe that they must adopt a Theory X leadership style; that is, they must be authoritarian, must force workers to perform, and must supervise their subordinates closely. Similarly, employee training emphasizes compliance (following orders) and trustworthiness.

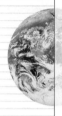

Multinational Management Brief
Respect and Power in Mexico vs. Respect and Fair Play in the United States

In describing Mexican business culture, a high power distance culture, Marc J. Erlich (1993, 18), a psychologist who works with U.S. businesses in Mexico, noted:

Within Mexican society, there is a tendency to respect those in power. The boss's respectability is manifested by maintaining a definite social distance, through an unwillingness to delegate.

Fair play, shared responsibility, and playing by the rules are characteristics of respect for the [North] American. Respect is earned, not given. North of the border, the ability to be one of the team reflects responsibilty.

The U.S. executive frequently perceives Mexican submission to authority as a lack of resolve and an unfortunate passivity. The Mexican will typically view the U.S. executive's insistence on fair play and desire to delegate as an inability to accept the power associated with position.

Source: Based on Erlich 1993.

Organizational structures and systems match the assumptions regarding leadership and motivation. Decision making is centralized. Those at the top make most of the decisions. The close supervision of workers requires many supervisors and a tall organizational pyramid (an organization with many levels). Strategic decisions in high power distance countries are influenced by the need to maintain and support those in power.

Exhibit 2.2 Management Implications of Power Distance

Management Processes	Low Power Distance	High Power Distance
Human Resources Management		
Management Selection	Educational achievement	Social class; elite education
Training	For autonomy	For conformity/obedience
Evaluations/Promotion	Performance	Compliance; trustworthiness
Remuneration	Small wage difference between management and worker	Large wage difference between management and worker
Leadership Styles	Participative; less direct supervision	Theory X; authoritarian, with close supervision
Motivational Assumptions	People like work; extrinsic and intrinsic rewards	Assume people dislike work; coercion
Decision Making/ Organizational Design	Decentralized; flat pyramids; small proportion of supervisors	Tall pyramids; large proportion of supervisors
Strategy Issues	Varied	Crafted to support the power elite or government

Sources: Adapted from Hofstede 1980; Hofstede 1991 and Hofstede in Pucik, Tichy, and Barnett 1993b.

Belgium ranks in the top 10 percent (91st percentile) on Hofstede's uncertainty avoidance dimension. As a result, one expects Belgian organizations to have many of the characteristics for high uncertainty avoidance, as shown in Exhibit 2.4. This seems true even for Belgium's universities.

At the University of Leuven, an old Belgian university, three lights stand over a professor's door: green, yellow, and red. Students wishing to see their professor must ring a bell and wait for an appropriate response. Green means come in; yellow means wait a few minutes; and red means go away. There is no ambiguity in these situations. Students do not have to interpret the situation to see if the professor is busy. In contrast, most students from the United States, a low uncertainty avoidance country (21st percentile), would probably find this degree of formality impersonal at best and perhaps even insulting.

Source: Based on Gannon and Associates 1994.

The preceding Multinational Management Brief describes how differences in power distance affect specific U.S. and Mexican business practices.

Exhibit 2.2 gives a summary of these managerial implications for power distance. The next section considers uncertainty avoidance.

UNCERTAINTY AVOIDANCE

Uncertainty avoidance relates to norms, values, and beliefs regarding a tolerance for ambiguity. A higher uncertainty avoidance culture seeks to structure social systems (politics, education, and business) where order and predictability are paramount, and rules and regulations dominate. In such a culture, risky situations create stress and upset people. Consequently, people avoid behaviors such as changing jobs.

High uncertainty avoidance countries have norms, values, and beliefs such as (Hofstede 1980):

Uncertainty avoidance

How people react to what is different and dangerous.

- Conflict should be avoided.
- Deviant people and ideas should not be tolerated.
- Laws are very important and should be followed.
- Experts and authorities are usually correct.
- Consensus is important.

The business cultures in countries high on uncertainty avoidance have management systems and processes that make organizations and employees dependable and predictable. People in such cultures react with stress and anxiety when the rules of behavior are not clear in organizational settings. Generally, Nordic and Anglo countries are low on uncertainty avoidance, while Latin European and Latin American countries are high. As the preceding Case in Point shows, Belgian students have little uncertainty when deciding whether to enter their professors' offices.

In high uncertainty avoidance cultures, entry-level people are chosen for their potential fit with and loyalty to the organization. Managers follow the logic, "If people are like me, come from my town or my family, then I understand them and trust them more." This minimizes interpersonal conflict, reduces potential employee turnover, and makes people more predictable.

In some cultures, uncertainty regarding employees is further reduced by selecting and promoting people with specialized expertise. Employers seek out people who will be loyal and committed to them and to the organization. Later, seniority, long-term commitment to the organization, and expertise in the area of management become the prime basis for promotion and payment. Both managers and employees believe that loyalty to the organization is a virtue and that conflict and competition should be avoided.

Task-directed leaders give clear and explicit directions to subordinates. This reduces ambiguity regarding job expectations. The boss tells workers exactly what to do. Task-directed leaders are the preferred leaders in high uncertainty avoidance cultures. Such leaders make subordinates less anxious, since subordinates know exactly what is expected of them. Similarly, organizations in these cultures have many written rules and procedures. Like the situation produced by the task-directed leader, extensive rules and procedures tell employees exactly what the organization expects of them. Consequently, employees believe that these rules should not be broken.

In contrast, leaders in low uncertainty avoidance cultures favor more flexibility and allow subordinates more choices on the job. The design of their organizations also builds in more freedom. There are fewer rules and regulations. There are also more subordinates per manager, which results in less supervision and greater autonomy for workers.

People in high uncertainty avoidance cultures do not like risk, and they often fear failure. As decision makers, they are conservative. Thus, it is unlikely that individual managers choose risky strategies for their organizations. Hofstede (1991) notes, however, that low or high uncertainty avoidance does not necessarily relate to success. Innovations may be more likely in weak uncertainty avoidance countries like the United States, but implementation of innovations may be more likely in high uncertainty avoidance countries such as Japan.

Exhibit 2.3 summarizes the managerial implications of uncertainty avoidance.

Exhibit 2.3 Management Implications of Uncertainty Avoidance

Management Processes	High Uncertainty Avoidance	Low Uncertainty Avoidance
Human Resource Management		
Management Selection	Seniority; expected loyalty	Past job performance; education
Training	Specialized	Training to adapt
Evaluation/Promotion	Seniority; expertise; loyalty	Objective individual performance data; job switching for promotions
Remuneration	Based on seniority or expertise	Based on performance
Leadership Styles	Task oriented	Nondirective; person-oriented; flexible
Motivational Assumptions	People seek security, avoid competition	People are self-motivated, competitive
Decision Making/ Organizational Design	Larger organization; tall hierarchy; formalized; many standardized procedures	Smaller organizations; flat hierarchy; less formalized, with fewer written rules and standardized procedures
Strategy Issues	Averse to risk	Risk taking

Sources: Adapted from Hofstede 1980; Hofstede 1991 and Hofstede in Pucik, Tichy, and Barnett 1993b.

INDIVIDUALISM/COLLECTIVISM

Individualism

The relationship between the individual and the group in society.

Collectivism

A set of cultural values that views people largely in terms of the groups to which they belong.

The values, norms, and beliefs associated with **individualism** focus on the relationship between the individual and the group. Individualistic cultures view people as unique. People are valued in terms of their own achievements, status, and other unique characteristics.

The cultural values associated with individualism are often discussed with the opposing set of values, called **collectivism**. Collectivist cultures view people largely in terms of the groups to which they belong. Social groups such as family, social class, organization, and team all take precedence over the individual.

Countries high on individualism have norms, values, and beliefs such as (Hofstede 1980):

- People are responsible for themselves.
- Individual achievement is ideal.
- People need not be emotionally dependent on organizations or groups.

In contrast, collectivist countries have norms, values, and beliefs such as (Hofstede 1980):

- One's identity is based on group membership.
- Group decision making is best.
- Groups protect individuals in exchange for their loyalty to the group.

Countries with low individualism have collectivist norms, values, and beliefs that influence a variety of managerial practices. Organizations in collectivist cultures tend to select managers who belong to favored groups. Most often, the favored group is the extended family and friends of the extended family. Being a relative or someone known by the family becomes more important than an individual's personal qualifications. In contrast, people in highly individualistic societies, such as the United States (the most individualistic society by Hofstede's measurement), often view favoritism toward family and friends as unfair and perhaps illegal. In such societies, most believe that job selection should be based on universalistic qualification. Universalistic qualification means that the same qualifications apply universally to all candidates. The cultural belief is that open competition allows the most qualified individual to get the job.

Organizations in collectivist cultures base promotions mostly on seniority and age. People tend to move up the organizational hierarchy by being promoted with their age cohort (people of the same age). People feel that a major reward for working is being taken care of by their organizations, a type of organizational paternalism. The senior managers in the organization act as father figures. Unlike individualistic societies, where people expect extrinsic rewards such as money and promotions, managers in collectivist societies use "a call to duty" as an emotional appeal to work for the good of the group.

In some collectivist cultures, older senior managers ultimately make important decisions. Such collectivist cultures also tend to rank high on power distance. However, other collectivist cultures prefer group decision making. Two factors favor greater participation and influence on decision making by people throughout the organization. First, because people in the organization are family members or trusted friends, privileged information flows up and down the organizational hierarchy. Second, as an extended family or at least a close-knit group, there is pressure to account for the feelings and desires of all members. However, because of the

Multinational Mangagement Brief
The Chinese Family Business

Chinese businesspeople outside the People's Republic of China, whom Hofstede calls "the overseas Chinese," have demonstrated highly performing businesses in Taiwan, Hong Kong, and Singapore, as well as throughout the world. Many of their organizations, however, lack all the trappings of modern management. They tend to be feudal (i.e., dominated by the entrepreneur father), family owned, and small, and have few if any professional managers. Most focus on only one product, and cooperation with networks of other small organizations is based on personal family friendships.

There are seldom any formal systems within or between organizations—only networks of people guided roughly by Confucian ethics. For example, in the father-dominated family firm, Confucian ethics dictate that the son must show respect and obdience to the father and the father must protect and show consideration for the son. In a practical sense, this means that the father will dominate organizational decision making. The son in turn as he gets older may be given considerations such as managing a new firm venture. However, on inheriting the family firm, brothers may engage in more horizontal decision making because their family obligations are less vertical.

Sources: Based on Hofstede 1993a and Syu in Marcic and Puffer (eds.) 1994.

---

need to take into account the input or feelings of group members, strategic decision making in collectivist cultures can be slow.

The effects of collectivism on some aspects of the Chinese family business are described in the preceding Multinational Management Brief.

Exhibit 2.4 summarizes the managerial implications of high individualism vs. collectivist (low individualism) norms, values, and beliefs.

MASCULINITY

Different cultural expectations for men and women occur in all societies. In all cultures, men and women receive different socialization and usually perform different roles. A variety of studies show that, in most—but certainly not all—cultures, male socialization has a greater emphasis on achievement motivation and self-reliance. In contrast, the socialization of women emphasizes nurturance and responsibility (Hofstede 1980).

Masculinity

Tendency of a society to emphasize traditional gender roles.

As a cultural dimension, **masculinity** represents the overall tendency of a culture to support the traditional masculine orientation. That is, higher masculinity means that the business culture of a society takes on traditional masculine values, such as emphases on advancement and earnings. However, within each culture there remain gender differences in values and attitudes.

High masculinity countries have norms, values, and beliefs such as (Hofstede 1980):

* Gender roles should be clearly distinguished.
* Men are assertive and dominant.

Exhibit 2.4 Management Implications of Individualism

Management Processes	Low Individualism	High Individualism
Human Resources Management		
Management Selection	Group membership; school or university	Universalistic based on individual traits
Training	Focus on company-based skills	General skills for individual achievement
Evaluation/Promotion	Slow, with group; seniority	Based on individual performance
Remuneration	Based on group membership/ organizational paternalism	Extrinsic rewards (money, promotion) based on market value
Leadership Styles	Appeals to duty and commitment	Individual rewards and punishments based on performance
Motivational Assumptions	Moral involvement	Calculative; individual cost/benefit
Decision Making/ Organizational Design	Group; slow; preference for larger organizations	Individual responsibility; preference for smaller organizations

Sources: Adapted from Hofstede 1980; Hofstede 1991 and Hofstede in Pucik, Tichy, and Barnett 1993b.

- Machismo or exaggerated maleness in men is good.
- People—especially men—should be decisive.
- Work takes priority over other duties, such as family.
- Advancement, success, and money are important.

In highly masculine societies, jobs are clearly defined by gender. There are men's jobs and women's jobs. Men usually choose jobs that are associated with long-term careers. Women usually choose jobs that are associated with short-term employment, before marriage and children. However, smaller families, delayed childbirth, pressure for dual-career earnings, and changing national cultural values may be eroding traditional views of masculinity. Consider the cases for working women in Japan and Sweden as described in the following Multinational Management Brief.

In addition to clear work-related roles based on gender, work in masculine cultures tends to be very central and important to people, especially men. In cultures like Japan, men often take assignments for over a year in other cities or other countries, while other family members remain at home.

In the high masculinity culture, recognition on the job is considered a prime motivator. People work long hours, often work more than five days a week, and take short vacations. In most low masculinity countries, in contrast, work typically has less centrality. People take more time off, take longer vacations, and emphasize the quality of life. There are, however, some exceptions. In the highly masculine Mexican culture, for example, gender differences are strong but work is less central. The cultural value is that people "work to live."

In masculine cultures, managers act decisively. They avoid the appearance of intuitive decision making, which is often regarded as feminine. They prefer to work in large organizations and they emphasize performance and growth in strategic decision making.

Exhibit 2.5 shows the major effects of high masculinity on work and organizations. The next section deals with the impact of long-term orientation on work and organizations.

Multinational Management Brief
Working Women in Japan and Sweden: Contrasts in Cultural Masculinity

Japan, the highest-ranking masculine culture, now faces a challenge to its traditional cultural values regarding masculinity and the role of women. Japanese companies expect that most women, even college graduates, will quit their jobs by the age of twenty-five. Women occupy most of the part-time jobs and have less access to the fabled lifetime employment than do men. However, with the slowdown in the Japanese economy, many women are not leaving as expected. The popular Japanese press now has many stories about companies who "have problems with their women." Such phraseology reflects the conflict of changing values regarding masculinity in Japan. Although there are traditional cultural expectations about what women "should" do regarding work and family, there is no legal or accepted way to force Japanese women to leave their jobs when they choose to remain employed.

Perhaps because of strong norms of equality, the Nordic countries rank lowest in masculinity. In contrast to masculine Japan, where support for working women, such as day care, is rare, the Swedish government provides day care to all who need it. Since over 85 percent of Swedish women work outside the home, day care is essential. In addition, with the birth of a child, one year of parental leave is available for both parents. Approximately 20 percent of the men take this option.

Source: Based in part on Gannon and Associates 1994.

Exhibit 2.5 Management Implications of Masculinity

Management Processes	Low Masculinity	High Masculinity
Human Resources Management		
Management Selection	Independent of gender, school ties less important; androgyny	Jobs gender identified; school performance and ties important
Training	Job oriented	Career oriented
Evaluation/Promotion	Job performance, with less gender-based assignments	Continues gender tracking
Remuneration	Less salary difference between levels; more time off	More salary preferred to fewer hours
Leadership Styles	More participative	More Theory X; authoritarian
Motivational Assumptions	Emphasis on quality of life, time off, vacations; work not central	Emphasis on performance and growth; excelling to be best; work central to life; job recognition important
Decision Making/ Organizational Design	Intuitive/group; smaller organizations	Decisive/individual; larger organization preferred

Sources: Adapted from Hofstede 1980; Hofstede 1991 and Hofstede in Pucik, Tichy, and Barnett 1993b.

LONG-TERM ORIENTATION

Long-term orientation

A basic orientation toward time that values patience.

Limited by the more recent discovery of the **long-term** (Confucian) **orientation**, Hofstede and others have produced less research on how this orientation relates to work and organizations. Consequently, the discussion on this issue is more speculative than some of the observations stated previously.

Because of the need to be sensitive to social relationships, managers in cultures high on the long-term orientation are selected based on the fit of their personal and educational characteristics to the company. A prospective employee's particular skills have less importance in the hiring decision than they do in cultures with short-term orientation. Training and socialization for a long-term commitment to the organization compensate for any initial weaknesses in work-related skills. Organizations in cultures with short-term orientation, in contrast, must focus immediately on usable skills. Managers do not assume that employees will remain with the company and cannot be assured of a return on any investment in employee training and socialization.

In short-term oriented cultures, leaders use short-term rewards that focus on pay and rapid promotion. Employees in long-term cultures value security, and leaders work on developing social obligations.

Hofstede (1991) notes that Western cultures, which tend to have short-term orientations, value logical analysis in their approach to organizational decisions. Managers believe in logically analyzing the situation for their company and following up with a solid game plan. In contrast, Eastern cultures, which rank highest on long-term orientation, value synthesis in organizational decisions. Synthesis does not search for the correct answer or strategy. Rather, synthesis takes apparently conflicting points of view and logic and seeks practical solutions. Not surprisingly, organizations in short-term oriented cultures are designed and managed purposefully to respond to immediate pressures from the environment. Managers often use quick layoffs of "excess" employees to adjust to shrinking demand for products. Organizations in long-term oriented cultures are designed first to manage internal social relationships. The assumption is that good social relationships eventually lead to successful organizations. The difference between long- and short-term cultures is apparent in the goals companies set in strategic decision making. Managers in countries such as the United States want immediate financial returns. They are most comfortable with fast, measurable success. Countries with more long-term orientations do not ignore financial objectives but prioritize growth and long-term paybacks. The long time horizons allow managers to experiment and seek success by developing their "game plans" as they go along. In the following Multinational Management Brief you can see how goals differ between U.S. and Japanese firms.

Exhibit 2.6 summarizes the managerial implications of long-term (Confucian) orientation.

To apply Hofstede's model to specific countries look at Exhibit 2.7. It displays the percentile ranks of selected countries on five of Hofstede's dimensions of national culture.

To interpret this exhibit you need to understand percentiles. The percentiles shown in the exhibit tell you the percentage of countries that rank below each country. For example, the United States has the highest scores on individualism, so its percentile rank tells you that 100 percent of the countries are equal to or below the United States on individualism. A percentile rank of 75 percent tells you that 75 percent of the other countries have equal or lower ranks on a cultural dimension.

Multinational Management Brief
U.S. and Japanese Strategic Goals

One study of the top firms in Japan and the United States showed distinct differences between the companies in terms of goals. Although firms from both countries considered financial performance important, the Japanese emphasized additional goals that would affect long-term financial performance. In addition, because Japanese stockholders also emphasize long-term investments, the Japanese companies face little pressurre to respond to immediate stockholder gains. Consider these rankings with regard to strategic goals for U.S. Fortune 500 firms and their Japanese equivalents:

Goals	U.S.	Japan
Return on Investment	1	2
Stockholder Gain	2	9
Increase Market Share	3	1
Introduction of New Products	7	3

Source: Based on Kagono et al. 1985.

Exhibit 2.6 Management Implications of Long-Term Orientation

Management Processes	Short-Term Orientation	Long-Term Orientation
Human Resources Management		
Management Selection	Objective skill assessment for immediate use to company	Fit of personal and background characteristics
Training	Limited to immediate company needs	Investment in long-term employment skills
Evaluation/Promotion	Fast; based on skill contributions	Slow; develop skills and loyalty
Remuneration	Pay, promotions	Security
Leadership Styles	Use incentives for economic advancement	Build social obligations
Motivational Assumptions	Immediate rewards necessary	Subordinate immediate gratification for long-term individual and company goals
Decision Making/ Organizational Design	Logical analyses of problems; design for logic of company situation	Synthesis to reach consensus; design for social relationships
Strategy Issues	Fast; measurable payback	Long-term profits and growth; incrementalism

Sources: Adapted from Hofstede 1980; Hofstede 1991 and Hofstede in Pucik, Tichy, and Barnett 1993b.

Exhibit 2.7 Percentile Ranks for Hofstede's Cultural Dimensions for Selected Countries by Cultural Cluster
(100 = highest; 50 = middle)

Cultural Group/Country	Power Distance	Uncertainty Avoidance	Individualism	Masculinity	Long-Term Orientation
Anglo:					
Australia	25	32	98	72	48
Canada	28	24	93	57	19
Great Britain	21	12	96	84	27
United States	30	21	100	74	35
Arab:					
Arab	89	51	52	58	n/a
Far Eastern:					
China	89	44	39	54	100
Hong Kong	73	8	32	67	96
Singapore	77	2	26	49	69
Taiwan	46	53	19	41	92
Germanic:					
Austria	2	56	68	98	n/a
Germany	21	47	74	84	48
Netherlands	26	36	93	6	65
Switzerland	17	40	75	93	n/a
Latin America:					
Argentina	35	78	59	63	n/a
Colombia	70	64	9	80	n/a
Mexico	92	68	42	91	n/a
Venezuela	92	61	8	96	n/a
Latin European:					
Belgium	64	92	87	60	n/a
France	73	78	82	35	n/a
Italy	38	58	89	93	n/a
Spain	43	78	64	31	n/a
Near Eastern:					
Greece	50	100	45	67	n/a
Iran	46	42	57	35	n/a
Turkey	67	71	49	41	n/a
Nordic:					
Denmark	6	6	85	8	n/a
Finland	15	42	70	13	n/a
Norway	12	30	77	4	n/a
Sweden	12	8	82	2	58
Independent:					
Brazil	75	61	52	51	81
India	82	17	62	63	71
Israel	4	66	66	47	n/a
Japan	32	89	55	100	n/a

Sources: Adapted from Hofstede 1980; Hofstede 1991; Hofstede in Pucik, Tichy, and Barnett 1993b and Ronen and Shenkar 1985.

Country clusters

Groups of countries with similar cultural patterns.

To simplify generalizations from Hofstede's data, the table groups countries by **country clusters** (Ronen and Shenkar 1985). Country clusters are groups of countries, such as North American, Latin American, and Latin European, with roughly similar cultural patterns. Although cultures differ within these broad classifications, such summaries are useful for condensing cultural information. They are also useful to predict likely cultural traits when specific information is not available on a national culture.

Next, we consider the model of culture used by Trompenaars and his colleagues. You will see that this model is similar in some respects to Hofstede's but it contains more dimensions and deals with a broader array of countries.

7d CULTURAL DIMENSIONS MODEL

The 7d cultural model builds on traditional anthropological approaches to understanding culture. That is, anthropologists argue that culture comes into existence because all humans must solve basic problems of survival (Kluckhohn and Strodtbeck 1961). These challenges include how people relate to others such as family members, supervisors, friends, and fellow workers; how people deal with the passage of time; and how people relate to their environment. All cultures develop ways to confront these basic problems. However, the solutions are not the same, which is why cultures differ significantly.

Five of the seven dimensions of the 7d cultural model deal with the challenges of how people relate to each other. Each dimension is a continuum or range of cultural differences. The five dimensions that deal with relationships among people include:

1. Universalism versus particularism: the choice of dealing with other people based on rules or based on personal relationships.
2. Collectivism versus individualism: the focus on group membership versus individual characteristics.
3. Neutral versus affective: the range of feelings outwardly expressed in the society.
4. Diffuse versus specific: the types of involvement people have with each other ranging from all aspects of life to specific components.
5. Achievement versus ascription: the assignment of status in the society based on performance (e.g., college graduation) versus assignment based on heritage.

The two final dimensions deal with how a culture manages time and how it deals with nature. They include:

6. Past, present, future, or a mixture: the orientation of the society to the past, present, or future or some combination of the three.
7. "Control of" versus "accommodation with" nature: nature viewed as something to be controlled versus something to be accepted.

Exhibit 2.8 gives a summary of the 7d model and the issues addressed by each dimension. The following sections define the dimensions and show their managerial applications.

Universalism

Dealing with other people based on rules.

Particularism

Dealing with other people based on personal relationships.

UNIVERSALISM VERSUS PARTICULARISM

Universalism and **particularism** pertain to how people from a culture treat each other based on equally applied rules versus personal relationships. In a universalistic culture, the "right" way to treat people is based on abstract principles such as the rules of law, religion, or cultural principles such as "Do unto others as you would have

Exhibit 2.8
The 7d Model
of Culture

Cultural Dimension	Critical Question
Relationships with People:	
Universalism vs. Particularism	Do we consider rules or relationships more important?
Individualism vs. Collectivism	Do we act mostly as individuals or as groups?
Specific vs. Diffuse	How extensively are we involved with the lives of other people?
Neutral vs. Affective	Are we free to express our emotions or are we restrained?
Achievement vs. Ascription	Do we achieve status through accomplishment or is it part of our situation in life (e.g., gender, age, social class)?
Perspective on Time:	
Sequential vs. Synchronic	Do we do tasks in sequence or several tasks at once?
Relationship with the Environment:	
Internal vs. External Control	Do we control the environment or does it control us?

Source: Adapted from Trompenaars and Hampden-Turner 1998.

them do unto you." Thus, universalism suggests that there are rules or appropriate and acceptable ways of doing things and we look to those precise guides in all situations.

In contrast, in particularistic cultures, rules represent only a rough guide to life. Each judgment represents a unique situation and the "right" way of behaving must take into account who the person is and their relationship to the one doing the judgment. In particularistic cultures rules may be in place and fully recognized but people expect exceptions to be made for friends, family relations, and others. The focus is on situation-to-situation judgments and the exceptional nature of circumstances as they change (Trompenaars 1994; Trompenaars and Hampden-Turner 1998).

In developing his 7d model, Trompenaars uses dilemmas that show the contrasts in cultural values. Consider the following dilemma and the different cultural assumptions that people use to make the "right" choice.

One of the dilemmas used to show differences between universalistic and particularistic cultures concerns the story of a motorist hitting a pedestrian while going 35 miles per hour in a 20 miles per hour zone. The driver's lawyer notes that if a witness says the driver was only going 20 mph, the judge will be lenient. The question is: should a friend who is a witness be expected to or feel obligated to testify to the lower speed? In universalistic cultures such as the United States and Switzerland, over 93 percent say no—the principle of telling the truth supercedes friendship. In particularistic cultures such as South Korea, Nepal, and Venezuela, close to 40 percent say yes—friendship supercedes the law (Trompenaars and Hampden-Turner 1998).

No culture is purely universalistic or particularistic. However, the tendency to lean in one direction or the other influences business practices and relationships between business partners from different cultures. In particular, more universalistic cultures tend to use contracts and law as a basis for business. Managers from such cultures often have difficulty when written documents are ignored and the personal

Exhibit 2.9

Universalism versus Particularism: Differences and Managerial Implications

Universalism					Particularism
USA	UK	Czech Rep.	Nigeria	Mexico	South Korea

Differences

Focus on rules	Focus on relationships
Contracts difficult to break	Contracts easy to modify
Trustworthy people honor their word	Trustworthy people adapt to each other's needs based on trust
Belief is in only one reality	Reality is relative to each person's situation
"Deals" are obligations	"Deals" are flexible to the situation and the person

Managerial Implications

Use procedures applied to all	Use informal networks to create understanding
Formalize business practices	Make changes subtly and privately
Treat all cases similarly	Treat each case based on its unique circumstances
Announce changes publicly	

Source: Adapted from Trompenaars and Hampden-Turner 1998.

relationships between partners become paramount. Consequently, managers from universalistic cultures doing business in particularistic cultures must be sensitive to building relationships. However, managers from particularistic cultures must make efforts to realize that the emphasis on law and contract does not mean a distrust of the business partner in a universalistic culture.

Exhibit 2.9 gives a brief description of universalism and particularism as cultural dimensions and shows the managerial implications for doing business in each cultural context.

INDIVIDUALISM VERSUS COLLECTIVISM

In the preceding sections, we examined Hofstede's view of individualism and collectivism. The 7d model considers the same distinctions. That is, in collectivist societies people are defined by their group memberships including family, organization, and community. Responsibility, achievement, and rewards are often group-based. In individualistic societies, people are trained from childhood to be independent, and each person assumes individual responsibility for success or failure.

Although the 7d view of individualism is similar to Hofstede's in its concept, the rankings of countries do not match exactly. One explanation for this difference may be that Trompenaars' ranking comes from more recent data. Another reason is that the 7d model uses a different methodology than Hofstede and captures more subtle aspects of the individualism–collectivism continuum.

One of the questions that Trompenaars used to look at cultural differences in individualism asked about typical organizations in each country. One choice represented organizations where individual work and individual credit were common. The other choice represented group work and group credit. In the more collectivist societies such as India and Mexico, less than 45 percent of the workers said that their jobs involved individual work with individual credit. Somewhat surprising was the finding that the former Eastern Bloc countries of the Czech Republic, Russia, Hungary, and Bulgaria were the most individualistic in their organizations, ranking ahead of the United States.

Exhibit 2.10

Individualism versus Collectivism: Differences and Managerial Implications

Individualism				Collectivism
Czech Rep.	UK	Nigeria	Egypt	Japan

Differences

Focus on "me" or "I"	Focus on "we"
Individual achievement and responsibility	Group achievement and responsibility
Individual decision making	Decision making by groups

Managerial Implications

Use individual incentives such as pay for performance	Focus on group morale and cohesiveness
Plan for turnover	Expect low turnover
Provide for individual initiative	Set group goals

Source: Adapted from Trompenaars and Hampden-Turner 1998.

Exhibit 2.10 gives a brief description of the individualism and collectivism cultural dimensions and the managerial implications of doing business in each cultural context.

NEUTRAL VERSUS AFFECTIVE

Neutral versus affective

The acceptability of expressing emotions.

The **neutral versus affective** dimension of the 7d model concerns the acceptability of expressing emotions. In cultures with a more neutral orientation, people expect that interactions are objective and detached. The focus is more on the task and less on the emotional nature of the interaction. People emphasize achieving objectives without the messy interference of emotions. In contrast, in cultures with a more affective orientation, all forms of emotion are appropriate in almost every situation. Expressions of anger, laughter, gesturing, and a range of emotional outbursts are considered normal and acceptable. The natural and preferred way is to find an immediate outlet for emotions (Trompenaars 1994; Trompenaars and Hampden-Turner 1998).

You can test yourself on this dimension by responding to one of Trompenaars' dilemmas. How would you respond in a negotiation if your partner called your proposal insane? People from neutral cultures will attempt to hide their emotional reactions to this insult. Revelation of the hurt would show weakness and vulnerability. People from affective cultures would react immediately and show they are insulted. They realize that such a reaction shows that they are insulted, but believe their partner should know this. This is expected behavior and is not viewed negatively by people in an affective culture (Trompenaars and Hampden-Turner 1998, 79).

Exhibit 2.11 gives a brief description of the neutral versus affective cultural dimension and the managerial implications of doing business within each cultural context.

SPECIFIC VERSUS DIFFUSE

Specific versus diffuse

The extent to which all aspects of an individual's life are involved in their work relationships.

The cultural dimension, **specific versus diffuse**, addresses the extent to which an individual's life is involved in their work relationships. In a specific oriented culture, business is segregated from other parts of life. People in business-exchange relationships and work relationships know each other, but the knowledge is very limited and for very specific purposes. In such societies, written contracts

Exhibit 2.11
Neutral versus
Affective: Differences
and Managerial
Implications

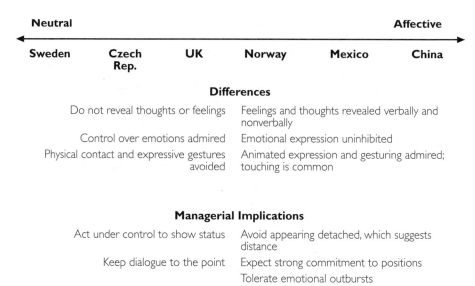

Neutral ←———————————————————————————————→ **Affective**

| Sweden | Czech Rep. | UK | Norway | Mexico | China |

Differences

Do not reveal thoughts or feelings	Feelings and thoughts revealed verbally and nonverbally
Control over emotions admired	Emotional expression uninhibited
Physical contact and expressive gestures avoided	Animated expression and gesturing admired; touching is common

Managerial Implications

Act under control to show status	Avoid appearing detached, which suggests distance
Keep dialogue to the point	Expect strong commitment to positions
	Tolerate emotional outbursts

Source: Adapted from Trompenaars and Hampden-Turner 1998.

frequently prescribe and delineate such relationships. Conversely, in diffuse-oriented cultures, business relationships are more encompassing and involving. In diffuse-oriented cultures, the preference is for an involvement of multiple areas and levels of life simultaneously; truly private and segregated spaces in life are quite small. In doing business, the parties come to know each other personally and more thoroughly, and become acquainted with each other across a variety of life's dimensions and levels (Trompenaars 1994; Trompenaars and Hampden-Turner 1998).

The example Trompenaars uses to test the differences between specific and diffuse cultures concerns a boss who asks a subordinate to help him paint his house. In specific cultures, most people believe that the worker has no obligation to help his boss because the boss has no authority over him outside of work. In diffuse cultures, in contrast, people feel an obligation to help the boss in any way possible although it is beyond the requirement of the job (Trompenaars and Hampden-Turner 1998).

Exhibit 2.12 gives a brief description of the specific versus diffuse cultural dimension and the managerial implications of doing business in each cultural context.

ACHIEVEMENT VERSUS ASCRIPTION

Achievement versus ascription

How a society grants or gives status.

The dimension identified as **achievement versus ascription** addresses the manner by which a particular society accords or gives status. In achievement-oriented cultures, people earn status by their performance and accomplishments. In contrast, when a culture bases status on ascription, one's inherent characteristics or associations define status. For example, ascription-oriented societies often assign people status based on schools or universities attended or a person's age. Ascribed status does not require any justification. It simply exists. In such cultures, titles and their frequent usage play a large part in interactions (Trompenaars 1994; Trompenaars and Hampden-Turner 1998).

Exhibit 2.13 gives a brief description of the achievement versus ascription cultural dimension and the managerial implications of doing business in each cultural context.

To better understand this cultural dimension, consider the Multinational Management Challenge on page 72. It describes a situation of culture clash for a young woman manager from an achievement-oriented society when working in an ascription-oriented society.

Exhibit 2.12
Specific versus Diffuse:
Differences and
Managerial Implications

Specific					Diffuse
Sweden	Czech Rep.	UK	Norway	Mexico	China

Differences

Direct in relationships	Indirect and subtle in relationships
Blunt and precise in communication	Ambiguous or evasive in communication
Principled moral reasoning	Situation-based moral decision making

Managerial Implications

Use of objectives and standards	Attempt continuous improvement
Separate private and business lives	Mix private and business lives
Give clear and precise directions	Use ambiguous directions to give employees latitude

Source: Adapted from Trompenaars and Hampden-Turner 1998.

Exhibit 2.13
Achievement versus
Ascription: Differences
and Managerial
Implications

Achievement					Ascription
Norway	Ireland	Austria	Japan	Hong Kong	Argentina

Differences

Use title only when relevant	Use of titles common and expected
Superiors earn respect through job performance	Respect for superior shows commitment to organization
Mixture of age and gender in management	Background and age main qualification for management

Managerial Implications

Emphasize rewards and respect based on skills and accomplishments	Emphasize seniority
Senior-level managers defer to technical and functional specialists	Use personal power of superior for rewards
	Emphasize the chain of command

Source: Adapted from Trompenaars and Hampden-Turner 1998.

TIME ORIENTATION

To coordinate any business, managers must have some shared understanding of time. Experts on culture find vast differences in how people deal with time and these differences become apparent when people from different cultures engage in business exchanges. One dimension of time of importance to managers is the time horizon. The **time horizon** concerns the way cultures deal with the past, present, future, and the boundaries among these time zones. Mexicans and the Chinese, for example, have long time horizons and distinct boundaries among the time zones (Trompenaars and Hampden-Turner 1998). Exhibit 2.14 summarizes the cultural characteristics of different time horizons. It also gives some managerial implications based on this cultural dimension.

In future-oriented societies, such as the United States, organizational change is considered necessary and beneficial. The static organization is the dying organization. For both people and organizations, one assumes that competition stimulates higher performance. It is assumed that individuals can influence the future. Both managers and workers assume that hard work now can lead to future success.

Time horizon

The way cultures deal with the past, present, and future.

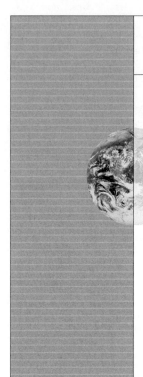

Multinational Management Challenge
Achievement-Based Management in an Ascription-Based Culture

What happens when young and previously successful managers from achievement-oriented Western societies find themselves in an ascription-based culture? Ms. Moore, a successful 34-year-old woman manager from a U.S. company, takes a promotion as director of marketing in Ankara, Turkey. She has international experience in Britain and is confident that she can replicate her success at winning the support and trust of her subordinates and colleagues.

Within a few months, Ms. Moore finds her authority eroding. Hasan, a 63-year-old Turk, gradually and consciously takes over her authority as the boss and becomes the driving force behind marketing projects. Although everyone recognizes that Ms. Moore's marketing knowledge is much greater than Hasan's, her attempts to manage her function meets with increased resistance. The company follows Hasan's direction although results are not satisfactory. Later, Ms. Moore learns that her predecessor, a U.S. man her age was fired for "failure to command local managers."

If you were sending a young, female manager to this assignment, what strategies would you recommend?

Source: Based on Trompenaars and Hampden-Turner 1998.

Exhibit 2.14
Time Horizon: Differences and Managerial Implications

Past/Present → **Future**

| **Hong Kong** | **Israel** | **Russia** | **Korea** | **Hong Kong** |

Differences

Past	Present	Future
Communication references history and origins of country, business, and family	Enjoy the moment	Communication refers to potential achievements
Respect for past glory and elders	Planning seldom results in execution	Planning important
History provides a context for present actions	Immediate impact most important	Potential for future advantage emphasized

Managerial Implications

Past and Present	Future
Emphasize and be sensitive to history and tradition	Motivate by emphasis on opportunities
Avoid strict deadlines for completion of tasks	Set specific deadlines

Source: Adapted from Trompenaars and Hampden-Turner 1998.

In past-oriented societies, people often assume that life follows a preordained course based on traditions or the will of God. As such, strategic planning for the organization has little importance. A changing organization is suspicious to both employees and society. Stability is revered. Within these organizations, it is thought that senior people make the best decisions because they have the authority and wisdom to know the right way. Symbols and rituals dominate the organizational culture.

To consider your own time horizon, ask: how long ago your past started and ended; how long ago your present started and ended; and, when your future will start and end. Trompenaars uses similar questions to measure the time horizons of different cultural groups (Trompenaars and Hampden-Turner 1998).

INTERNAL VERSUS EXTERNAL CONTROL

Internal versus external control

Beliefs regarding whether one controls one's own fate.

The cultural dimension of **internal versus external control** concerns beliefs regarding control over one's fate. This cultural dimension is perhaps best reflected in how people interact with their natural environment. Does nature dominate us or do we dominate nature?

To measure this dimension, Trompenaars and his colleagues present managers with the following options: "It is worthwhile trying to control important natural forces, like the weather" and "Nature should take its course and we just have to accept it the way it comes and do the best we can" (Trompenaars and Hampden-Turner 1998). Arabic countries such as Bahrain, Egypt, and Kuwait are the most fatalistic with less than 20 percent of managers choosing the control over nature option. This contrasts with over 50 percent of the managers from Spain and Cuba who choose the control over nature option.

Exhibit 2.15 summarizes the internal versus external cultural dimension and its managerial implications.

Differences in the cultural values regarding relationships with nature can affect how organizations and managers approach strategic and operational problems. In cultures where it is believed that nature dominates people, managers are likely to be fatalistic. They believe that situations must be accepted and reacted to rather than changed. In such cultures, people do not emphasize planning and scheduling. Work schedules must adjust to other priorities, such as family.

In contrast, where cultural values support the notion that people dominate nature, managers tend to be proactive. They believe that situations can be changed. Strategic plans and operations reflect the belief that obstacles can be conquered.

Exhibit 2.15

Internal versus External Control: Differences and Managerial Implications

Internal Control ←   → **External Control**

Poland	Brazil	Greece	Ethiopia	China

Differences

Dominate the environment	Emphasis on compromise
Show convictions	Harmony and adjustment is good
Focus on self or own group	Adaptation to cycles

Managerial Implications

Emphasize authority	Emphasize patience
Dominate subordinates	Build and maintain relationships with subordinates, equals, and superiors
	Emphasize win-win relationships

Source: Adapted from Trompenaars and Hampden-Turner 1998.

What works is what is important. Organizations focus on using concrete data that suggest the best way to solve problems.

This section concludes our examination of the 7d view of culture. Similar to Exhibit 2.7 for the Hofstede model, Exhibit 2.16 gives percentile rankings for these dimensions for selected countries.

In the next section we will discuss new information on a dimension of culture not considered by the major models, but generally recognized as key for conducting multinational business transactions.

PROPENSITY TO TRUST: A CULTURAL DIMENSION OF INCREASING IMPORTANCE

A growing concern of multinational businesspeople is the development of trusting relationships with business partners including strategic alliance partners, suppliers, distributors, and customers. Consequently, managers and academic researchers have begun to investigate differences among cultures in terms of how and when people trust each other (Johnson and Cullen 2000).

The common hypothesis is that individualistic societies, with their focus on self-interested behavior rather than what benefits the group (Triandis 1995), have values that allow one person to take advantage of another person (Williamson 1996). Symbolic statements such as "let the buyer beware" seem to support this cultural value in societies such as the United States. Alternatively, people often presume that collectivist cultures with their strong in-group ties and long-term relationships have a stronger predisposition for trusting each other, especially toward in-group members. Such logic leads some trust theorists to hypothesize that people from individualistic cultures enter relationships expecting opportunism and thus have low trust expectations (Downey, Cannon, and Mullen 1998).

However, the evidence from research (e.g., Yamagishi, Cook, and Watabe 1998) suggests the opposite. That is, it seems that people from individualistic cultures are more predisposed to trust others than people from collectivist cultures. For example, U.S. Americans, representing a highly individualistic culture, tend to have significantly higher levels for trust of other people than do the Japanese, representing a highly collectivist culture (Yamagishi, Cook, and Watabe 1998).

Recent research by the World Values Study Group (1994; Inglehart, Basañez, and Moreno 1998) provides perhaps the most comprehensive information, in terms of number of countries considered, on cultural values regarding trust. The World Values Survey (WVS) contains interview data on 45 societies (not all of which are nation-states) and is based on national sampling of adults 18 and over with a total sample of nearly 90,000 individuals.

To provide additional information of cross-cultural differences in trust, the author reanalyzed the original WVS data focusing on questions related to trust. As an indicator of general predisposition to trust, the WVS asked respondents whether they agreed with the statement: "Generally speaking, would you say that most people can be trusted or that you can't be too careful in dealing with people?" The dichotomous response categories were: "Most people can be trusted" and "Can't be too careful." Exhibit 2.17 shows the percentage of respondents in each society responding, "Most people can be trusted."

Nordic countries had the highest levels of trust. The United States ranked ahead of the more collectivist countries of Japan and South Korea. This was surprising because the business practices of these two countries are often characterized as

Exhibit 2.16 Percentile Ranks for the 7d Model Cultural Dimensions for Selected Countries

	Universalism	Individualism	Neutral	Specific	Achievement	Past Orientation	Future Orientation	Internal Control
Argentina	n/a	n/a	21	n/a	8	n/a	n/a	59
Australia	n/a	71	69	73	84	32	n/a	78
Austria	n/a	n/a	90	60	3	n/a	n/a	63
Belgium	n/a	52	46	n/a	n/a	n/a	n/a	43
Brazil	n/a	19	46	n/a	34	18	n/a	73
Bulgaria	n/a	84	81	n/a	29	n/a	n/a	20
Canada	95	74	77	80	92	n/a	47	88
China	26	26	85	3	58	82	89	2
Cuba	n/a	n/a	4	n/a	11	n/a	n/a	98
Czech Rep.	16	100	56	37	45	n/a	84	n/a
Denmark	n/a	61	33	70	82	n/a	n/a	80
Egypt	n/a	10	2	n/a	n/a	n/a	n/a	n/a
Ethiopia	n/a	n/a	100	97	37	n/a	n/a	24
Finland	n/a	58	50	63	76	n/a	n/a	39
France	63	n/a	25	53	71	77	74	90
Germany	n/a	35	35	n/a	61	64	53	34
Greece	42	32	38	40	55	n/a	n/a	51
Hong Kong	n/a	n/a	92	87	13	100	100	29
Hungary	79	94	58	23	47	n/a	n/a	n/a
India	21	16	83	27	18	9	39	27
Indonesia	47	n/a	85	17	n/a	36	39	32
Ireland	84	48	23	n/a	95	n/a	n/a	71
Italy	n/a	n/a	31	n/a	66	n/a	16	43
Japan	58	6	98	57	53	59	63	n/a
Kenya	n/a	n/a	n/a	n/a	26	n/a	n/a	17
Malaysia	n/a	29	25	43	n/a	n/a	n/a	n/a
Mexico	n/a	13	50	n/a	63	n/a	n/a	n/a
Netherlands	n/a	55	63	93	n/a	41	32	54
Nigeria	53	81	69	13	n/a	n/a	n/a	76
Norway	n/a	n/a	44	50	100	23	n/a	95
Pakistan	n/a	42	n/a	n/a	n/a	n/a	n/a	n/a
Philippines	n/a	n/a	15	33	21	n/a	n/a	n/a
Poland	37	87	96	90	39	27	n/a	100
Portugal	n/a	39	67	n/a	74	n/a	n/a	46
Romania	68	90	n/a	n/a	n/a	n/a	n/a	n/a
Russia	5	97	17	10	42	50	11	12
Korea	11	n/a	n/a	n/a	24	91	79	61
Singapore	32	23	69	47	68	73	5	10
Spain	n/a	68	4	n/a	32	55	n/a	93
Sweden	89	45	63	100	79	86	68	22
Switzerland	100	n/a	29	67	50	68	58	' 49
Thailand	n/a	n/a	58	n/a	16	n/a	n/a	56
UK	74	65	n/a	83	87	45	26	68
USA	n/a	77	54	77	97	14	21	66

Source: Computed from data reported in Trompenaars and Hampden-Turner 1998.

Exhibit 2.17
Levels of General
Trust in People

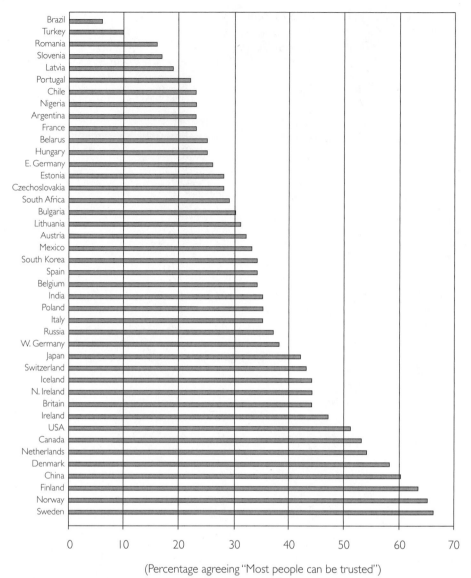

(Percentage agreeing "Most people can be trusted")

Source: Computed from data made available in World Values Study Group. 1994: *World Values Survey, 1981–1984 and 1990–1993 (Computer file), ICPSR version.* Ann Arbor: Institute for Social Research.

based on trust more than legal contracts. However, China, another collectivist society, had levels of general trust similar to the Nordic countries.

This somewhat surprising summary of cultural differences in people's propensity to trust reveals that some common stereotypes regarding cultures may be false. It also shows that cross-cultural business interactions often begin with invalid assumptions regarding the nature of people.

After reading the forgoing sections on cultural models and cultural differences in trust, you should have acquired two skills. First, you can apply the models and your knowledge of trust to diagnose and understand the basic cultural values of a society. Second, you can apply this information to assess how the characteristics of a particular culture affect business operations. Later chapters will build on your knowledge of culture and the concepts introduced here.

Summary and Conclusions

After completing this chapter you should know that culture has a variety of levels that affect multinational managers and organizations. However, you should also realize that the descriptions and examples of cultural effects on management are broad illustrations. No one book or chapter could do justice to the immense variety of cultures that exist in the world. This chapter hopes only to sensitize readers to the extremely complex and subtle influences that culture has on management and organizations.

The models of cultural values proposed by Trompenaars and his colleagues and by Hofstede provide basic concepts for analyzing cultural differences. They are tools to help you understand a culture and to help you adjust business practices to various cultural environments.

The most successful multinational managers will realize that understanding a different culture is

a never-ending learning process. They will prepare for their international assignments by studying all that they can about the country in which they will work. This includes the study of more than business etiquette. Understanding the national culture as well as important historical, social, esthetic, political, and economic trends builds a foundation. They will study the language. Few can really get behind the front stage of culture without speaking the local language. Finally, they will be sensitive and observant, continually adjusting their behavior to what works locally.

In this chapter, you received only a brief introduction. As you read later chapters, especially those with a comparative focus, you will broaden your understanding of cultural differences. You will also learn to seek advantage in differences and to avoid looking at culture as a potential obstacle to successful multinational operations.

Discussion Questions

1. Identify five cultural rituals, stories, or symbols from your native culture. Examples might include national holidays, the country's flag, nursery rhymes, childhood traditional stories, and sayings, such as "A stitch in time saves nine." Discuss how each of these communicates cultural values, norms, and beliefs.

2. Define and contrast back stage and front stage culture. Discuss how someone not familiar with your culture could misunderstand a front stage behavior.

3. Discuss several ways that stereotyping and ethnocentrism limit successful multinational management.

4. Define levels of culture and discuss the interrelationships among the levels.

5. Compare and contrast Hofstede's model of culture with the 7d model. Which do you think is more valuable for managers and why?

6. Pick three countries from Exhibits 2.7 and 2.16. Summarize and discuss the managerial implications of cultural differences by applying the Hofstede and 7d models.

Chapter Internet Activity

Fons Trompenaars provides an Internet site for his consulting firm, which specializes in applying the 7d model to help companies manage cross-cultural interactions. This site also provides several minicases

dealing with the 7d cultural dilemmas. Go to the 7d site at http://www.7d-culture.nl/ and test yourself on the 7d model.

Internet Sites

Selected Companies in the Chapter
Hewlett-Packard   http://www.hp.com
University of Leuven   http://db.cs.utwente.nl

Country Background Information
http://www.odci.gov/cia/publications/factbook/index.
   html   *The CIA's World Factbook Master Home Page.*
   Includes background information on country geography,
   people, government, economy, communications, and
   defense forces.
http://www.webofculture.com/   *The Web of Culture.*
   Articles on cultural differences.

http://lcweb2.loc.gov/frd/cs/cshome.html   *Country*
   Studies/Area Handbooks. Country background on
   political, economic, and social institutions.
http://dir.yahoo.com/Society_and_Culture/
   An index of cultural information from
   the Yahoo! search engine.
http://www.craighead.com/   *Cultural background*
   relevant to business for numerous countries; hard copy
   of the reports are available in most university libraries;
   Internet site has limited country information
   for free.

Chapter Activity: A Briefing Paper

Step 1. Read the following scenario.

You are a recent college graduate and a junior level executive in a midsize multinational firm. Your CEO will depart next week on a one-month business trip to meet potential joint-venture partners in Saudi Arabia, Poland, Hong Kong, Germany, Greece, and Brazil. Because of your expertise in international business, the CEO has asked you to prepare a cultural brief dealing with the national and business cultures where she will be visiting. She does not want to make any cultural faux pas. She expects a high-quality oral and written presentation. Since this is your first major assignment, it is important that you perform well. First impressions are lasting, and your job may depend on it.

Step 2. Your instructor will divide the class into six groups and assign each group at least one country.
Step 3. Using sources on the World Wide Web and in the library, research general cultural issues such as (but not limited to) basic cultural norms, values, and beliefs that may affect work (e. g., attitudes toward work in general, the role of the family in work, food and diet, the role of religion, language). Research specific business cultural issues such as expectations regarding dress, appointments, business entertaining, business cards, titles and forms of address, greetings, gestures, gift giving, language of business, interaction styles, time for deals to close, and the potential reactions to a woman executive.
Step 4. Present your findings to the class.

References

Central Intelligence Agency. 2000. http://www.odci.gov/cia/publications/factbook.

Craighead's International Business, Travel, and Relocation Guide 2000. Detroit: Gale Research.

Downey, P. M., J. P. Cannon, and M. R. Mullen. 1998. "Understanding the influence of national culture on the development of trust." *Academy of Management Journal,* 23 (3), 601–20.

Erlich, Marc J. 1993. "Making sense of the bicultural workplace." *Business Mexico,* August.

Gannon, Martin J., and Associates. 1994. *Understanding Global Cultures.* Thousand Oaks, Calif.: Sage.

Goffman, Erving. 1959. *The Presentation of Self in Everyday Life.* Englewood Cliffs, N. J.: Prentice-Hall.

Gomes, J. Eduardo Aguilar. 1993. "Mexican corporate culture." *Business Mexico,* August, 8, 9, 38.

Hofstede, Geert. 1980. *Culture's Consequences: International Differences in Work-Related Values.* London: Sage.

———. 1991. *Cultures and Organizations: Software of the Mind.* London: McGraw-Hill.

———. 1993a. "Cultural constraints in management theories." *Academy of Management Executive* 7:1.

———. 1993b. "Cultural dimensions in people management." In Vladimir Pucik, Noel M. Tichy, and Carole K. Barnett, *Globalizing Management.* New York: Wiley, 139–58.

———, and Michael Harris Bond. 1988. "The Confucian connection: From cultural roots to economic growth." *Organizational Dynamics* 16:4, 4–21.

Inglehart, R., M. Basañez, and A. Moreno. 1998. *Human Values and Beliefs: A Cross-Cultural Sourcebook*. Ann Arbor: University of Michigan Press.

Johnson, Jean L., and John B. Cullen. 2000. "The bases and dynamics of trust in cross-culture exchange relationships." In M. J. Gannon and K. L. Newman, (editors), *Handbook of Cross-Cultural Management*. London: Blackwell. Chapter 18.

Kagono, T., I. Nonaka, K. Sakakibara, and A. Okumura. 1985. *Strategic vs. Evolutionary Management: A U.S. Japan Comparison of Strategy and Organization*. Amsterdam: North-Holland.

Kipling, Rudyard. 1990. "We and They." In Craig Storti, *The Art of Crossing Cultures*. Yarmouth, Maine: Intercultural Press, 91–92.

Kluckhohn, Florence, and F. L. Strodtbeck. 1961. *Variations in Value Orientations*. New York: Harper and Row.

Kras, Eva S. 1995. *Management in Two Cultures*. Yarmouth, Maine: Intercultural Press.

Kroeber, A. L., and C. Kluckhohn. 1952. "Culture: a critical review of concepts and definitions." *Papers of the Peabody Museum of American Archaeology and Ethnology* 47:1.

Morrison, Terri, Wayne A. Conaway, and George A. Borden. 1996. "Kiss, bow or shake hands?" www.biztravel.com.

Ronen, S., and O. Shenkar. 1985. "Clustering countries on attitudinal dimensions: a review and synthesis." *Academy of Management Review*, September.

Sathe, Vijay. 1985. *Culture and Related Corporate Realities*. Homewood, Ill.: Irwin.

Schein, Edgar H. 1985. *Organizational Culture and Leadership*. San Francisco: Jossey-Bass.

Shari, Michael. 1994. "Selling family secrets." *Asia, Inc.*, December.

Syu, Agnes. 1994. "A linkage between Confucianism and the Chinese family firm in the Republic of China." In *Management International*, edited by Dorothy Marcic and Sheila M. Puffer. Minneapolis: West.

Terpstra, Vern, and Kenneth David. 1991. *The Cultural Environment of International Business*. Cincinnati, Ohio: South-Western.

Triandis, H.C. 1995. *Individualism and Collectivism*. Boulder, CO: Westview.

Trompenaars, Fons. 1994. *Riding the Waves of Culture: Understanding Diversity in Global Business*. Chicago: Irwin.

_____, and Charles Hampden-Turner. 1998. *Riding the Waves of Culture: Understanding Cultural Diversity in Global Business*. New York: McGraw-Hill.

_____. 2000. http://www.7d-culture.nl/.

Williamson, O. E. 1996. *The Mechanisms of Governance*. New York: The Free Press.

World Values Study Group. 1994. *World Values Survey, 1981–1984 and 1990–1993, (Computer file) ICPSR version*. Ann Arbor: Institute for Social Research.

Yamagishi, T., K. S. Cook, and M. Watabe. 1998 "Uncertainty, trust, and commitment formation in the United States and Japan." *American Journal of Sociology*, 104 (July), 195–94.

Yoshino, Michael. 1989. "John Higgins: An American goes native in Japan." In Tom L. Beauchamp, *Case Studies in Business, Society, and Ethics*. Englewood Cliffs, N.J.: Prentice-Hall, 234–39.

Chapter 3

International Negotiation and Cross-Cultural Communication

LEARNING OBJECTIVES
After reading this chapter you should be able to:

- **Understand the basics of spoken and nonverbal communication that may influence cross-cultural management and negotiation.**

- **Understand the basic international negotiation processes from preparation to closing the deal.**

- **Understand the basic tactics of international negotiation.**

- **Recognize and respond to "dirty tricks" in international negotiations.**

- **Know the differences between the problem-solving and competitive approaches to international negotiation.**

- **Identify the personal characteristics of the successful international negotiator.**

Preview Case in Point **A Deal that Failed**	When Kiel AG, a Swiss multinational conglomerate, discovered Georgia-based Edwards Engineering Inc. (EEI) for sale, Kiel's management felt that they had found the right company to acquire in the United States. There was a construction boom in the southeastern United States that Kiel viewed as a strategic opportunity. Moreover, EEI was a successful company, whose founder, Tom Edwards, was close to retirement and willing to sell. Kiel made an initial offer close to the asking price, and the outlook for the purchase looked positive. Kiel president Herbert Kiel even came to the United States to conduct the negotiations personally. However, after four difficult days of negotiation, the Kiel team went home and talks ended. What happened? In a typical U.S. American way, Edwards was open and friendly in the negotiations. He was eager to sell the business. He was direct and forthright about the strengths and weaknesses of his business. He made every effort to provide information requested and to adjust his proposals to Kiel's positions. But the U.S. style didn't work. Edwards confused the Swiss. They approached the negotiations in a formal and measured way. They perceived Edwards' openness as dangerous and untrustworthy. They responded by asking to review documents and by hiring a major U.S. accounting firm to audit the EEI books. Edwards, on the other hand, found the audit insulting and time consuming. He was annoyed by Kiel's continuously polite but unresponsive answers to his proposals. Ultimately, neither side played the negotiation game the way the other expected. Distrust grew and an otherwise good deal ended in failure. Sources: Based on Bryan and Buck 1989 and Whately 1994.

International negotiation is the process of making business deals across national and cultural boundaries. International negotiation precedes any multinational business project. However, as we have just seen in the Preview Case in Point, without successful negotiation and the accompanying cross-cultural communication, there are seldom successful business transactions.

Consider some of the following examples where the successful outcome of the business opportunity depends on successful international negotiations. Companies that sell overseas must negotiate with foreign distributors and sales organizations. Companies that participate in international joint ventures must negotiate a contact to establish the alliance. Companies that receive raw materials from international sources must negotiate with local suppliers to provide raw materials at an acceptable cost. Companies that set up manufacturing operations in other countries often must negotiate with foreign governments to get necessary permissions. Finally, as in this chapter's Preview Case in Point, companies that wish to acquire businesses in other countries must negotiate successfully with the current owners.

This chapter provides a survey of the basic processes that guide international negotiation: successful preparation, building relationships with foreign partners, using persuasion tactics, gaining concessions, and reaching a final agreement. We will also consider how to identify and avoid the common "dirty tricks" of negotiators, and what personal characteristics make a good international negotiator.

Successful communication across cultures is a prerequisite for international negotiation and for managing people from other cultures. Consequently, to identify some of the pitfalls of cross-cultural communication in negotiations and in cross-cultural management, the first section of this chapter provides a summary of important cross-cultural communication issues. After reading this first section, you will better understand the communication challenges involved in cross-cultural negotiation.

THE BASICS OF CROSS-CULTURAL COMMUNICATION

Successful negotiation requires successful communication. Thus, successful international negotiation requires successful cross-cultural communication. Negotiators must understand (or have interpreted) not only the written and oral language of their counterparts but also other components of culturally different communication styles. Mistakes in cross-cultural communication often go unnoticed by the communicator, but these mistakes can do damage to international relationships and negotiations. Mistakes or misinterpretations of the subtle gestures of hand and face, the use of silence, what is said or not said, and the intricacies of dealing with age and status often prove pitfalls for the multinational businessperson.

To help you negotiate and communicate more successfully in your role as a multinational manager, we will review some of the major issues in cross-cultural communication. These include the relationship between language and culture, differences between high and low context cultures, cultural differences in communication styles, nonverbal communication through body movements and the use of personal space, when and how to use interpreters, how to speak to nonnative speakers of your language, and how to avoid cross-cultural communication errors based on faulty attributions.

LANGUAGE AND CULTURE

There are approximately three thousand basic languages in the world, with many dialects (Terpstra and David 1991). Language is so essential to culture that many consider linguistic groups synonymous with cultural groups. Multinational managers should also note that many countries—Canada and Belgium, for example—have more than one national language. Even within political boundaries, these national languages often represent quite diverse cultural groups regarding communication and negotiation styles. In addition, the choice of the wrong language may touch on areas of extreme cultural sensitivity.

Whorf hypothesis

Theory that language determines the nature of culture.

The interrelationship between language and culture is so strong that some experts suggest that a society's language determines the nature of its culture. This is known as the **Whorf hypothesis**, developed by the anthropologist and linguist Benjamin Lee Whorf (1965). Whorf argued that words provide the concepts for understanding the world. According to Whorf, all languages have limited sets of words. These restricted word sets in turn constrain the ability of the users to understand or conceptualize the world. Since language structures the way we think about what we see, it determines cultural patterns.

In his famous and, at the time, futuristic novel, *1984*, George Orwell used Whorf's premise that those who controlled the available vocabulary would control the world. Not all experts agree with Whorf, and some argue the opposite. Culture comes first and requires the development of certain concepts and thus certain words. However, no one debates that there is a close interrelationship between language and culture.

HIGH- AND LOW-CONTEXT LANGUAGES

Low-context language

One in which people state things directly and explicitly.

High-context language

One in which people state things indirectly and implicitly.

The anthropologist Edward T. Hall (1976) identified an important distinction among the world's languages based on whether communication is explicit or implicit. Hall focused on how different cultures use the context or the situation in which communication takes place to understand what people are saying. Languages in which people state things directly and explicitly are called **low context**. The words provide most of the meaning. You do not have to understand the situation in which the words are used. Languages in which people state things indirectly and implicitly are called **high context**. In the high-context language, communications have multiple meanings that one can interpret only by reading the situation in which the communication occurs. So important are the ideas of high and low context that many people refer to the entire culture as being high or low context.

Most northern European languages, including German, English, and the Scandinavian languages, are low context. People use explicit words to communicate direct meaning. Thus, for example, if a German manager says Yes, she means Yes. In addition, most Western cultures attach a positive value to clear and direct communication. This is particularly apparent in negotiations, where low-context languages allow clear statements concerning what a negotiator wants out of the relationship.

In contrast, Asian and Arabic languages are among the most high context in the world. In Asian languages, often what is left unsaid is just as important as what is said. Silent periods and the use of incomplete sentences require a person to interpret what the communicator does not say by reading the situation. Arabic introduces interpretation into the language with an opposite tack. Extensive imprecise verbal and nonverbal communication produces an interaction where reading the situation is necessary for understanding. Exhibit 3.1 shows a ranking of languages by their degrees of high and low context.

Communication between high- and low-context people is a challenge for multinational operators. Translated words, that to a low-context speaker have explicit meanings, may have a multitude of meanings to a high-context speaker. For example, Japanese speech is full of words that encourage a speaker to continue and to repeat the message, often in a slightly different way. One of these words, *hai*, literally "yes" in English, means "yes" in the English sense only if other components of the situation also mean "yes." *Hai* can also mean: "Yes, I hear you," "Yes, say it again," "Yes, give me more information," "Yes, please continue with the conversation," or "Yes, I don't really want to say No but it should be obvious to you that the answer is No." Such difficulties in translation suggest that, when negotiations take place between high- and low-context cultures, it is important that both sides realize that communication may have errors. Moreover, even good translations may require contextual interpretations for effective communication.

BASIC COMMUNICATION STYLES

Direct communication

Communication that comes to the point and lacks ambiguity.

In addition to high- and low-context language use, other cultural differences in communication can influence cross-cultural interactions and negotiations. In some cultures, people speak very directly. That is, they tend to state opinions and ask questions that come right to the point and lack ambiguity. This is called **direct communication**. In contrast, in some societies, people consider directly asking a question or stating an opinion impolite. In indirect communication, people attempt to state their opinions or ask questions by implied meaning. Successful and polite communication allows the receiver to understand a statement without the

Exhibit 3.1   Country Differences in High-Context and Low-Context Communication

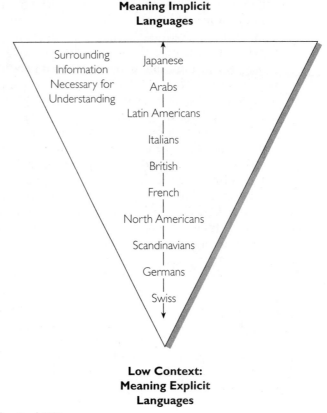

**High Context:
Meaning Implicit
Languages**

Surrounding
Information
Necessary for
Understanding

Japanese

Arabs

Latin Americans

Italians

British

French

North Americans

Scandinavians

Germans

Swiss

**Low Context:
Meaning Explicit
Languages**

Source: Adapted from Rosch 1987.

communicator stating directly his or her intentions. Consider the direct communicator who asks: "Will we reach a deal tonight?" Consider the response of the indirect communicator who says: "Tonight we will go to a superb restaurant, which best represents our national cuisine." This usually means "I am not ready to do business with you until I get to know you better." Exhibit 3.2 shows a ranking of direct communication styles for several countries.

Another cultural trait of communication style that often affects or surprises those communicating with U.S. Americans is the degree of **formal communication** expected. As you can see in Exhibit 3.2, U.S. Americans are among the least formal in communication. The casual use of first names, informal dress, and the dispensing of titles characterize U.S. communication styles when compared to the rest of the world. Most other cultures communicate, especially in business settings, with more formality. They take care to acknowledge rank and titles when addressing each other. There is also more formality of dress for men and women and sensitivity to ceremony and procedures in social interactions. In many countries, for example, adult men never wear short pants unless engaged in an exercise or sports activity.

At several points, we have noted that communication is more than verbal interaction. The next section provides background on the essential areas of nonverbal communication. Multinational managers and negotiators must be aware of cultural differences in both verbal and nonverbal communications.

Formal communication

Communication that acknowledges rank, titles, and ceremony in prescribed social interaction.

Exhibit 3.2
Cultural Differences in
Communication Styles

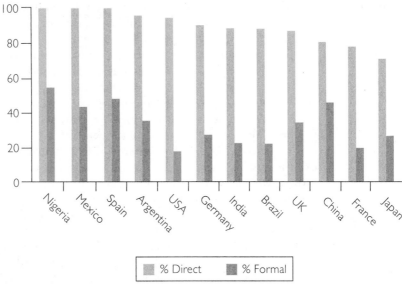

Source: Adapted from Salacuse 1998.

NONVERBAL COMMUNICATION

**Nonverbal
communication**

*Face-to-face
communication
that is not oral.*

Nonverbal communication means communicating without words. Often it is not necessary to say something orally to communicate with someone. People gesture, they smile, they gaze into another's eyes, they hug, they kiss—they engage in a whole array of behaviors that supplement or enhance spoken communication. The types of nonverbal communication considered here are body movements (called kinesics), the use of personal space (called proxemics), and touching.

KINESICS

Kinesics

*Communication
through body
movements.*

Kinesics means communicating through body movements. Every culture uses body posture, facial expressions, hand gestures, and movement to communicate nonverbally. Most Asian cultures, for example, use bowing to indicate respect for older people or people of higher status. The person of lesser status must bow at a lower angle than the person of higher status.

It is easy to misinterpret the meanings of body movements in another culture. As with oral communication, there is no universal code for what body movements mean in all societies. For example, U.S. Americans communicate a relaxed atmosphere by "putting their feet up." The manager with his or her feet on the desk is saying, "I am relaxing, and you can, too." However, people from many other cultures consider such behavior rude or even insulting. Most German managers would consider putting one's feet up on the desk uncivilized. Showing the soles of the feet is among the most outrageous insults to most Arabs (Ferraro 1994).

Facial expressions occur in every human interaction. People smile, frown, squint, sneer, and engage in a range of facial movements. Some scholars argue that some facial expressions are biological and do not vary across cultures. For example, the quick raising and lowering of eyebrows when people greet each other seems to occur in many different cultural settings (Eibel-Eibesfeldt 1971). In addition, people born deaf and/or blind have most of the common facial expressions, suggesting that at least some expressions are inborn (Ferraro 1994).

Body posture relates to the way people stand, walk, and sit. Each culture encourages and discourages different body postures in different situations. A trip on a Japanese subway, for example, will quickly reveal the proper way of sitting—straight forward, legs together, head slightly down, and (for women) handbag placed squarely on lap. Cultural norms determine whether people slouch, stand, or sit erect, and the speed and cadence of the walking gait.

All cultures use hand gestures to embellish and add emphasis to oral communication. Some cultures use expressive gestures, while other cultures use subtle gestures. The same gestures often mean different things in different societies, a common source of embarrassment for international communicators. For example, the gesture with the thumb and forefinger joined in a circle means okay in North America and money in Japan, and is obscene in Brazil. The thumbs-up gesture means everything is going well for North Americans and many Europeans, but is a rude gesture in Australia and West Africa. Even the "V" for victory sign made with two fingers held upward, popularized by the British prime minister, Winston Churchill, during World War II, has a rude meaning for the British and the French if the palm is facing inward. Nodding the head means "Yes" in most of the world, but it means "No" in Bulgaria (Axtell 1991; Chaney and Martin 1995).

The important point to remember for international negotiators and multinational managers is that it is easy to misinterpret gestures. A safe communication strategy minimizes the use of gestures. You should use only those gestures that you understand well. Eventually, as you get to know a culture better, acceptable and appropriate gestures will become second nature.

PROXEMICS

Proxemics

The use of space to communicate.

Proxemics focuses on how people use space to communicate. According to some experts on communication by space, all the basic senses allow people to perceive and sense differences in space (Hall and Hall 1990). Sight, smell, hearing, and touch all react to differences in space. Naturally, there are large cultural differences in how people react to the sounds, sights, smells, and personal contact associated with space. Each culture has appropriate distances for various levels of communication, and most people are uncomfortable if those distances are ignored. Violations of space may even be considered offensive.

The personal bubble of space around each individual may range from nine inches to over twenty inches. North Americans are most comfortable with twenty inches, while groups from Latin and Arab cultures generally prefer a closer spacing. It is not uncommon to see a North American continuously backing up to maintain his or her "comfortable" twenty inches when interacting with someone from the Middle East or Latin America.

Personal space may also affect the design of offices. In the following Multinational Management Brief, we see in Exhibit 3.3 a typical Japanese office, where the desks are in contact and managers work closely together. In contrast, Germans are even more protective of their personal office space than North Americans. They prefer heavy office furniture that people cannot move to get too close and invade their personal space. A German newspaper editor stationed in the United States was highly intolerant of the U.S. American habit of moving chairs closer in certain social situations. He finally reacted by having his visitor's chair bolted to the floor. This kept people at a comfortable and "proper" distance (Ferraro 1994).

Multinational Management Brief
The Typical Japanese Office

In the typical Japanese office, space is shared so that the workers and managers are all within hearing distance of each other. Unlike the typical U.S. office, the Japanese version has no separate rooms or partitions that divide the work area. Standard office desks are placed back to back and side by side. Workers often share the same phone and computer.

The closeness with colleagues provides a feeling of comfort for the Japanese that many Westerners find unnerving. Unlike most Westerners, the Japanese see no need for privacy during phone conversations or discussions with coworkers, or when concentrating on their work. In the reverse cultural situation, many Japanese salarymen who have expatriate assignments in the United States or Europe find the compartmentalization of buildings very uncomfortable.

Exhibit 3.3 shows the layout of a typical Japanese office with the placement of a manager (Kachoo), first-line supervisors, and workers.

Exhibit 3.3 Seating in a Typical Japanese Office

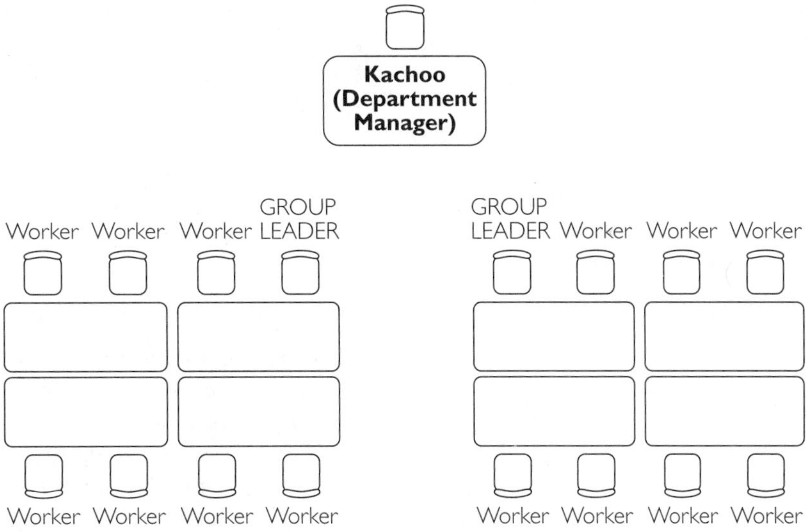

TOUCH

Touching

Basic form of human interaction, including shaking hands, embracing, or kissing when greeting one another.

Touching is related to proxemics and is a basic form of human interaction. In greeting one another, people may shake hands, embrace, or kiss. In routine interaction, people may touch or pat each other in a variety of ways. The type of touching deemed appropriate is deeply rooted in cultural values. For example, Russian men often kiss other men outside their family as a form of greeting. Brazilian men hug in greeting. Japanese schoolgirls routinely walk holding hands with other girls, although touching among strangers is less accepted. In some cultures, people expect

Multinational Management Brief
The EU's Boom Market for Linguists

The growth of the European Union places an increasing demand on the necessity of using interpreters. European Union's offices throughout Europe have more than three thousand full-time interpreters dealing with everything from trademarks to police work. EU staff translators earn between $47,000 and $150,000 a year. The going rate for business interpreters is $520 per day. To become an interpreter for the EU, one must pass an extremely difficult written and oral exam called a "concours." The pay is good, but interpreters spend half their time on the road and are often blamed for mistakes in negotiations. Along with their linguistic prowess, the best interpreters also have expertise in other fields; some are lawyers, engineers, and scientists.

Source: Based on Oster 1994.

a firm handshake, whereas in other cultures, the handshake is limp. Generally, Latin European and Latin American cultures accept more touching than do Germanic, Anglo, or Scandinavian cultures.

This section concludes our discussion of some basic forms of nonverbal communication. The following section builds on your knowledge of the cultural differences in communication. It deals with three practical issues in cross-cultural business communications: when to use interpreters, how to speak with someone whose language is not your own, and how to recognize and avoid incorrectly applying one's own cultural assumptions to people's motivations.

PRACTICAL ISSUES IN CROSS-CULTURAL BUSINESS COMMUNICATION

Cross-cultural negotiations and communications nearly always face a language barrier. One or both sides of the interaction must communicate in a foreign language. The international manager is always at an advantage if he or she speaks more than one language fluently. U.S. Americans are among the worst when it comes to learning a second language. Europeans, in contrast, are much more likely to be bilingual or multilingual. U.S. businesspeople are fortunate that English is the most common language of business. However, even if English is the local business language and one speaks English, communication and understanding of the local culture always improve if one speaks the local language. As such, an important preparation for any international assignment is gaining at least rudimentary skills in the language of the country.

USING INTERPRETERS

The increasing globalization of business means that the multilingual person is a valuable addition to any company. The preceding Multinational Management Brief describes the rising need for interpreters for business purposes in the multilingual European Union. With the gradual elimination of restrictions for doing business in Europe, nearly everyone who conducts business in Europe will need to communicate with people who speak another language.

Interpreter's role

To ensure the accuracy and common understanding of written and oral agreements.

To make sure that all parties understand agreements, international negotiation often requires the use of interpreters. The **interpreter's role** is to provide a simultaneous translation of a foreign language while a person speaks. This requires greater linguistic skills than speaking a language or translating written documents. Good interpreters not only are bilingual, but also have the technical knowledge and vocabulary to deal with technical details common in business transactions.

Even if some of the negotiators understand or speak both languages, it is often a good idea to use interpreters. It detracts from a team member's negotiation task if he or she must also serve as the negotiation team's interpreter. In addition, even if all members of the negotiating team are competent speakers of both languages, professional interpreters can be present to ensure the accuracy and common understanding of written and oral agreements.

To simplify the increasing diversity of languages in business organizations, some multinational companies use one language as the corporate tongue. Increasingly, this language is English, since it is the most common second language. Examples of companies using English include Philips Electronics and DHL Worldwide Express. Using English allows these companies a more consistent corporate culture, while dealing with the linguistic diversity of their employees and customers. However, even these major multinational companies have permanent translators on staff to manage such issues as interaction with the international press, translation of local product information, and negotiations with other companies.

Although the use of company-wide languages simplifies some of the multinational's communication problems, it creates other linguistic challenges. One of the greatest challenges is communicating with nonnative speakers. The next section gives practical suggestions on how to communicate with nonnative speakers.

COMMUNICATION WITH NONNATIVE SPEAKERS

In the multinational organization, it is very likely that you will be speaking with and writing to employees, customers, and business associates in their second or even third language. The following Case in Point shows how Caterpillar Tractor uses limited written English to provide one set of instructions to people who service Caterpillar equipment all over the world. In speaking with people using a nonnative language, communications scholars recommend several techniques. These techniques make communication easier and more accurate (Harris and Moran 1991):

- *Use the most common words with their most common meanings:* A good source of these words is a book for a beginning language course.
- *Select words with few alternative meanings:* If this is impossible, use the word with its most common meaning.
- *Strictly follow basic rules of grammar:* Follow these rules more than you would with native speakers.
- *Speak with clear breaks between words:* It is often difficult for a nonnative speaker to hear distinct words, especially when there is background noise.
- *Avoid "sports" words or words borrowed from literature:* In U.S. English, for example, phrases such as "he struck out" should be avoided.
- *Avoid words or expressions that are pictures:* Some words or expressions, such as "knee deep in the big muddy" in U.S. English, require listeners to have a mental image of the picture to understand.

Case in Point	Caterpillar is the world's leading manufacturer of construction equipment. As a major multinational company, Caterpillar must repair and maintain its products throughout the world. To avoid dozens of translations of its complex repair and parts manuals, Caterpillar adopted a 30-lesson course in reading English. There is no speaking. The vocabulary is limited to 800 words, including only 70 verbs and 450 nouns. The course teaches only the English necessary to read Caterpillar manuals.
The Caterpillar Functional-English Program	Source: Based on Terpstra and David 1991.

- *Avoid slang:* Slang is often based on age and region. The nonnative speaker may have learned the language from people from other regions. For example, British English slang is quite different from U.S. English slang.
- *Mimic the cultural flavor of the nonnative speaker's language:* For example, use more flowery communication with Spanish-speaking listeners than with Germans.
- *Summarize:* Paraphrase and repeat basic ideas.
- *Test your communication success:* Do not ask, "Did you understand?" Instead, ask your listener what he or she heard. Ask them to paraphrase what you have said.
- *When your counterpart does not understand:* Repeat the basic ideas using different words. Use more common nouns and verbs.

A multinational manager meets with all forms of verbal and nonverbal communication styles. Successful international communicators maintain flexibility and humor in adjusting to local communication patterns. Part of this adjustment comes from avoiding false or incorrect assumptions regarding the intentions of communicators. A considerable amount of communication is taken for granted and therefore a simple gesture or word (even if translated) can be misinterpreted. The next section shows how you can avoid this common error.

AVOIDING ATTRIBUTION ERRORS

Attribution

Process by which people interpret the meaning and intent of spoken words or nonverbal exchanges.

Attribution is the process by which we interpret the meaning and intent of spoken words or nonverbal exchanges based on our own cultural expectations. In our own culture, without thinking, we know what a certain body movement or word tells us about a person's intentions and motivations. That is, we attribute a meaning to the communication based on our taken-for-granted cultural expectations. In our own culture, we need not think about these attributions. They are the basis of our everyday communication and understanding.

However, the main danger in cross-cultural communication comes from the ease of making mistakes of attribution. Applying our own cultural interpretations, we can easily misjudge the meaning of a touch, a gaze, a period of silence, or an ambiguous word. This is a common error because it is difficult, if not impossible, to process communications without being influenced by our own cultural framework. Even bilingual people may not understand perfectly how to view the world through the eyes of another culture.

The safest strategy in cross-cultural communication and negotiation begins with observation and guarded interpretations. Watch carefully what people from the other culture do in their interpersonal exchanges. Realize that one cannot always attach the same meanings to verbal and nonverbal interactions. Unless you are bilingual, it is often a good idea to avoid subtleties of a foreign language. For example, do not swear or use familiar (personal) words. Avoid complex nonverbal behaviors unless one understands their meanings explicitly.

Sensitivity to cross-cultural communication provides a solid foundation for a multinational negotiator. Next, building on the foundation of your understanding of the basic issues of cross-cultural communication, the chapter provides you with the essential background to develop your knowledge of international negotiations and prepare you to negotiate in the global business environment.

INTERNATIONAL NEGOTIATION

International negotiation is more complex than domestic negotiation. Differences in national cultures and differences in political, legal, and economic systems often separate potential business partners. Consequently, most international negotiators find it necessary to modify the negotiation styles of their home country. If they wish to succeed in the multinational arena, they must develop a style of international negotiation based on the flexible application of sound negotiating principles. The next section develops your understanding of basic negotiating principles by describing the steps in a successful international negotiation.

STEPS IN INTERNATIONAL NEGOTIATIONS

Negotiation steps

Preparation, building the relationship, exchanging information, first offer, persuasion, concessions, and agreement.

Most experts recognize that the process of international negotiation includes several steps (Adler 1991; Graham and Herberger 1983). Although each international negotiation is unique and may combine two or more steps or repeat some, the negotiation process involves five steps leading to the final step, an agreement. The **negotiation steps** include preparation, building the relationship, exchanging information and the first offer, persuasion, concessions, and the agreement. Most important for international negotiation is preparation. The culturally naïve negotiator almost always fails to bring home an adequate agreement.

Exhibit 3.4 shows the negotiation steps. They are discussed in detail next.

STEP 1: PREPARATION

A winning international-negotiating strategy requires significant preparation. Ahead of time, the well-prepared international negotiator gathers extensive information on the negotiation issues, on the setting in which the negotiation will take place, and on the firm and people involved. Experts on international negotiation identify numerous essential questions and issues to consider before the negotiation (Copeland and Griggs 1985; Salacuse 1991). These include:

- *Determine if the negotiation is possible:* To begin the negotiation process, you must believe that you have at least some areas of agreement with your negotiating counterparts.
- *Know exactly what your company wants from the negotiation:* What does the company hope to achieve in the negotiation? What are the minimally acceptable conditions of an agreement?
- *Know the other side:* Can the other organization deliver what your company wants? What are the goals of the other side? Is the other side dealing with any competitors and do the competitors have any advantages?
- *Send the proper team:* Do the negotiators have the appropriate knowledge of the technical details, sufficient experience in negotiations, language abilities, and

Exhibit 3.4 Steps in International Negotiations

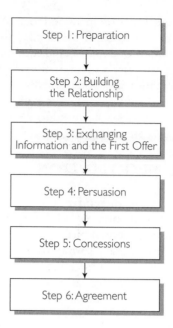

knowledge of the country and its culture? Have they prepared as a team? What authority do they have?

- *Agenda:* Is there an agreed-upon agenda? Can it lead somewhere the company does not want to go?
- *Prepare for a long negotiation:* Avoid being rushed to accept a disadvantageous solution. Know when you must leave, but don't tell the other side.
- *Environment:* Is the team familiar with the physical environment where the negotiations will take place? When will the team arrive? What support is necessary on site? What is the language of negotiation? Are interpreters necessary?
- *Strategy:* Plan a strategy but remain flexible. What are the principal issues? What are the opening moves?

The successful international negotiator not only prepares for the substance of the negotiation (e. g., technical details, company needs) but also does extensive research on the nature and negotiation styles of the foreign culture. For example, a study of successful U.S. negotiations with the Japanese found that careful preparations led to high-quality negotiations. Preparations that improved negotiations included reading books on Japanese business culture, hiring experts to train the negotiation teams, and practicing in simulated negotiations (Tung 1984).

While it is impossible to understand the negotiating styles of all the world's cultures, managers can anticipate certain differences among cultures in key negotiating processes. This section identifies some of the issues in negotiation most likely affected by cultural differences. These include cultural differences in the goals of the negotiation, the personal styles of the negotiators, the communication styles of the negotiators, the negotiators' sensitivity to timing and pacing of the negotiation, forms of agreement typical in the society, and the common types of organization of negotiating teams. The examples from different countries discussed next show the extreme differences in these areas (based on Salacuse 1991). Consider the following examples realizing that many countries fall in between these cases.

- *Negotiation goal—signing the contract or forming a relationship:* Most Chinese and Japanese businesspeople consider as the prime objective of negotiation the formation of relationships. A negotiation may produce signed agreements. However, the signed paper represents only the formal expression of the relationship between the companies, and sometimes of the personal relationships between the individual negotiators. The contract exists only as an initial step in the relationship, one that may lead to longer-term mutual benefits. In more legalistic societies, such as the United States, the detailed, signed contract is the most important goal of the negotiation. Commitment is less personally binding but relies instead on the force of law. The sanctity of the contract is a valued legal principle in U.S. courts.
- *Formal or informal personal communication style:* Business cultures differ widely on the acceptability of informal styles. Australians, like U.S. Americans, easily adapt to using first names and having informal conversations. As shown earlier in Exhibit 3.2, Nigerian, Spanish, and Chinese negotiators, however, react negatively to the informality of using first names among short-term business acquaintances.
- *Direct or indirect communication style:* The extent to which communication is direct and verbal, rather than indirect and nonverbal, varies widely by culture, as we saw in the section on communication. The rules of politeness and styles of interaction in different cultures encourage or restrict the ability of negotiators to come directly to the point. For example, the Japanese will seldom say "No" directly. Instead, if something "is very difficult," it is probably impossible. Conversely, a speaker of a more explicit language might interpret such aversion to direct speech as an effort to hide something.
- *Sensitivity to time—low or high:* The pace of negotiation and the time given to each phase of negotiation intertwine with the objective of the negotiation. That is, when a negotiator feels obliged to build a relationship as part of the deal, it takes much longer than simply trying to get a signed contract.
- *Forms of agreement—specific or general:* A negotiated agreement may consist of general principles or very detailed documents that attempt to anticipate all possible outcomes of the relationship. In many countries, Japan for example, the preferred contract states only general principles and not detailed rules and obligations. The Japanese argue that, since it is impossible to foresee all possible contingencies, a detailed agreement is dangerous and unnerving. The contract may obligate someone to do something that eventually becomes impossible due to unforeseen circumstances. In contrast, broad agreements, preferably based on strong personal relationships, allow for fair adjustments if circumstances change. Pressing for legalistic, detailed coverage of all contingencies, as is typical of U.S. Americans, leads many people from other cultures to believe that their U.S. partners have little trust in the relationship. Exhibit 3.5 shows the differences among nations in cultural preferences for a broad or detailed contractual agreement.
- *Team organization—a team or one leader:* The senior U.S. negotiator often has, within specified boundaries, the final authority to make commitments for his or her company and to close the deal. This style of organization fits the U.S. mode of more rapid negotiations to reach a signed contract. In international negotiations, a small U.S. negotiation team with one leader faces a much larger team where the true decision maker might not be present or, if present, might say very little. Russians, Japanese, and Chinese prefer large teams and rely more on consensus decision making.

Exhibit 3.5 Cultural Differences in Preference for Broad Agreements

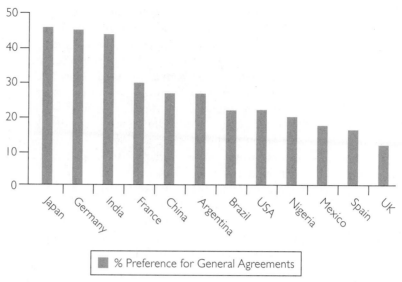

% Preference for General Agreements

Source: Adapted from Salacuse 1998.

Lack of preparation for cultural differences in international negotiations can lead to many problems. For example, the negotiating style typical of the highly individualistic U.S. culture seldom works well in more collectivist cultures. Both U.S. managers and managers from other cultures negotiating with the United States should prepare to avoid some of the pitfalls of the U.S. negotiating style. Exhibit 3.6 contrasts some common U.S. negotiating characteristics with those from other national cultures. U.S. negotiators have what John Graham and Roy Herberger (1983) call the "John Wayne" style of negotiation. As Exhibit 3.6 shows, U.S. negotiators are independent, aggressive, and direct. Although this style makes sense in the individualistic U.S. culture, it contrasts sharply with other negotiating styles from nations with other cultural values and norms. The Multinational Management Brief on page 96 shows what to expect in negotiations with Arabs.

After thorough preparation, a negotiator is ready to begin direct communication with his or her negotiating partners. In the next section, we will see how these interactions evolve in the negotiation process.

STEP 2: BUILDING THE RELATIONSHIP

Building a relationship

The first stage of the actual negotiation process, when negotiators concentrate on social and interpersonal matters.

After initial planning, the first stage of the actual negotiating process begins with **building a relationship** between the negotiating parties. At this stage, negotiators do not focus on the business issues. Rather, they concentrate on social and interpersonal matters. Negotiation partners get to know each other personally. They develop opinions regarding the personality characteristics of the negotiators: what they are really like, what their real goals are, and whether they can really be trusted.

This phase of the negotiation process often takes place at a location different from the formal negotiation place. The first step in a Japanese negotiation, for example, often occurs by drinking tea in a room outside the formal office. Only the exchange of business cards and small talk takes place during this encounter. In most countries, including Japan, restaurants, bars, and cultural tours often provide the context for relationship-building activities.

Exhibit 3.6 Preparation: Understanding Negotiators from Other Countries

U.S. Negotiation Style	Rationale	Contrasting Negotiation Style	Rationale
"I can go it alone"	Why spend the money for more people than necessary?	*Bring a team*	More people provide social pressure
"Just call me John"	Formalities are unnecessary	*Be extremely formal*	Rank and status count in language
"Pardon my French"	Why bother? English is the international language	*Understand English but use interpreters anyway*	Gives extra time to listen and formulate responses
"Get to the point"	Why beat around the bush?	*Build the personal relationship and exchange information first*	Personal relationships and trust are more important than contracts
"Lay your cards on the table"	Give and expect honest information up front	*Don't reveal the real position at first*	A bit of trickery or avoiding saying No is okay
"Don't just sit there, speak up"	Long periods of silence are unacceptable	*Long periods of silence, especially in response to an impasse*	Time is necessary to react
"One thing at a time"	A final agreement is a sum of agreements on each issue	*A holistic approach with all points open for discussion until the end*	Issues are always interconnected
"A deal is a deal"	A commitment is final down to the last detail	*Today's commitment can be voided if tomorrow's circumstances are different*	Negotiation partners must understand that absolutes are impossible and things change
"I don't need to check with the home office"	Negotiators should have the authority to make the deal	*I must check with the home office first*	To complete the negotiation, you have to convince not only me but also my boss, on another continent

Source: Adapted from Graham and Herberger 1983.

The duration and importance of the relationship-building stage vary widely by national culture. U.S. negotiators are notorious in their attempts to "get down to business" after brief and perfunctory socializing. German negotiators also get to the point quickly. When foreign negotiators bring up issues not related directly to the negotiation objective, U.S. negotiators often view this as a waste of time and an inefficient use of company resources. The pressure on U.S. managers is to get to the point, make the deal, and come home—particularly when they are overseas. International travel and hotels are costly, and many U.S. companies believe that a manager's time is better spent at home, getting on with implementing the negotiated deal.

The goal of U.S. negotiators is to get the details of the agreement on a written contract. This contract has specific requirements and specific due dates. As such, from this perspective, there is little need to develop personal relationships. In the U.S. legal view, "The partner must agree to a legally binding document." Other legal systems, however, do not see the contract as binding in its detail. For example, for many Chinese managers, a contract provides only the foundation on which to build the relationship, with details to be worked out later. As with most Asian societies, the Chinese believe that investing the time to build personal relationships must come first.

Multinational Management Brief
What to expect when negotiating with Arabs

There are five key characteristics of negotiations with people from Arab nations. These include:

(1) *Arabs look at the world as subjective:* Reality is based on perception not on facts. A common frustration for Westerners is that logical flaws in arguments have less impact than expected. If the facts do not fit someone's beliefs, then that person may reject the facts and consider only his or her own view of the situation. In particular, personal honor is more important than fact.

(2) *The type of relationship expected:* A good personal relationship is the most important foundation of doing business with Arabs.

(3) *Information on family and connections:* Social connections and networks are crucial in the highly personalized Arab societies. This should not be interpreted as useless information but, rather, it may represent the key to finalizing a business deal.

(4) *Persuasion:* For Arab negotiators, personalized arguments are more effective than logical arguments. Emphasis on friendship and personal appeals for consideration are common. Showing emotion by raising the voice, repeating points with enthusiasm or even pounding the table is acceptable. Emotional argument shows the sincerity of the concern.

(5) *The time required to complete the process:* From the perspective of Western business people, negotiations with Arab business partners take considerable time. Time is not fixed for Arabs. There are not fixed beginings and endings of events. Everyone expects delays.

Source: Based on Nydell 1997.

Building a good relationship among the negotiating parties provides a foundation for working out an eventual deal. Even in individualistic societies such as the United States, personal trust among negotiators is important. However, a business negotiation must eventually specify who is going to do what, when, and for what price. Thus, the next section shows how negotiators begin to address these issues.

STEP 3: EXCHANGING INFORMATION AND THE FIRST OFFER

Task-related information

Actual details of the proposed agreement.

First offer

First proposal by parties of what they expect from the agreement.

At this stage in the negotiation, both parties exchange information on their needs for the agreement. Parties exchange information that is **task-related information**. It pertains to the actual details of the proposed agreement. Typically, both sides make a formal presentation of what they desire out of the relationship. They present issues such as the quantity, characteristics, and price of a product. Both sides usually present their **first offer**. This is their first proposal of what they expect from the agreement.

At this stage, national and business cultures influence what information is given and requested; how the information is presented; and how close the initial offer is to the actually expected or hoped-for specifications in the agreement. Exhibit 3.7 shows a comparison among different nations regarding information exchange and first-offer strategies. Note, for example, the difference between the typical U.S. initial negotiation point (off the "real" goal by 5 to 10 percent) and the more extreme starting points used by Arab negotiators.

Exhibit 3.7 Information Exchange and First-Offer Strategies

	Arabs	**Japanese**	**Mexicans**	**Russians**	**U.S. Americans**
Information Exchange	Focus is on information about the relationship and less on technological details	Extensive requests for technical information	Focus is on information about the relationships and less on technical details	Great attention to detail	Information is given directly and briefly, often with a multimedia presentation
First-Offer or Counteroffer	20 to 50% off goal	10 to 20% off goal	Fair for both parties and close to goal	Extreme and purposefully unfair	5 to 10% off goal

Source: Adapted from Chaney and Martin 1995 and Yale 1992.

After the first offer, the core of the negotiation begins. Negotiators move beyond first-offer strategies and attempt to reach accord on the actual nature of the agreement. The next section outlines some of the tactics used after both sides make initial offers.

STEP 4: PERSUASION

Persuasion

Stage when each side in the negotiation attempts to get the other side to agree to its position.

In the **persuasion** stage, each side in the negotiation attempts to get the other side to agree to its position. This is the heart of the negotiation process. Numerous tactics are available to international negotiators. While all negotiators use somewhat similar tactics to argue for their side, their emphasis and mix of tactics vary according to their cultural background. We will review two general types of tactics here, standard verbal and nonverbal negotiation tactics and some of the "dirty tricks" of international negotiation.

Verbal and Nonverbal Negotiation Tactics

Verbal negotiation tactics

Promises, threats, recommendations, warnings, rewards, punishments, normative appeals, commitments, self-disclosures, questions, commands, "No" (refusals), interruptions.

John L. Graham, an expert on international negotiations, identifies several **verbal negotiation tactics** common in international negotiations (Graham 1985). These include:

- *Promise:* If you do something for me, I will do something for you.
- *Threat:* If you do something I don't like, I will do something you don't like.
- *Recommendation:* If you do something I desire, good things will happen to you (e.g., people will buy your product).
- *Warning:* If you do something I don't like, bad things will happen to you (e.g., other companies will know you cannot do business here).
- *Reward:* I am going to do something beneficial for you (without conditions).
- *Punishment:* I am going to do something you will dislike—without conditions (e.g., end the negotiations immediately).
- *Normative appeal:* This is the way we do or do not do business here (e.g., "You must learn the Japanese way").
- *Commitment:* I agree to do something specific (e.g., meet a delivery date).
- *Self-disclosure:* I will tell you something about myself or my company to show you why we need to close the deal.
- *Question:* I ask you something about your company or yourself.
- *Command:* This is an order that you must follow.
- *Refusal:* Just saying no.
- *Interruption:* I talk when you talk.

Exhibit 3.8 Frequencies of Verbal Negotiating Behaviors: A Comparison of Brazilian, U.S., and Japanese Negotiators (in half-hour bargaining session)

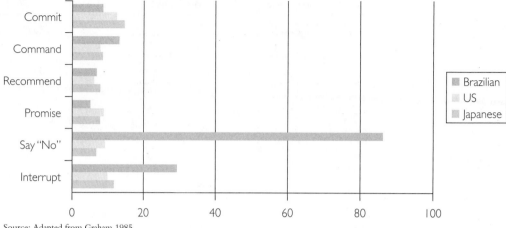

Source: Adapted from Graham 1985.

Exhibit 3. 8 shows examples of cultural differences in these verbal negotiating tactics among Japanese, U.S., and Brazilian negotiators.

Cultural differences in nonverbal communication styles also influences negotiations. **Nonverbal communication** through such things as body posture, facial expression, hand gestures, and the use of personal space are a natural part of any international negotiation. For example, a hand gesture or a facial expression might be a subtle way to indicate agreement or disagreement with a proposal. In addition, foreign nonverbal communication might also create (purposely or not) situations that make a negotiator uncomfortable. For example, people from cultures with a comfortable speaking distance of one meter might have difficulty concentrating on negotiations when someone stands inside their comfort range.

Earlier in this chapter you learned that the interpretation of nonverbal communication is difficult for people of different cultural backgrounds. For example, in dealings with the Japanese, a proposal might be met with downcast eyes and no response. U.S. negotiators often interpret the Japanese silence as a rejection of the proposal. The Japanese, however, take whatever time they need to think and formulate a proper response. Unlike most U.S. negotiators, they feel no pressure to fill the gaps in conversation. Stressed by the silence, U.S. negotiators may continue to talk, causing the Japanese to hesitate even more. Feeling that their position is rejected, U.S. negotiators often offer unnecessary concessions (Adler 1991).

While many Asian societies use silence to communicate that they are still deliberating, other cultures allow hardly any time for introspection. Consider that one study found that, in thirty minutes of negotiation, the Japanese had over five periods of complete silence of ten seconds or longer, nearly twice as many as U.S. negotiators. Brazilians, on the other hand, were never silent for more than ten seconds (Graham 1985).

The more direct tactics of negotiation are often supplemented by tactics that not all people consider fair. The next section shows you some of these tactics and possible responses.

"Dirty Tricks" in International Negotiations

There are many tactics in both international and domestic negotiations that people use to gain an upper hand. All negotiators want to get the best deal for their com-

Nonverbal communication

Face-to-face communication that is not oral.

Dirty tricks

Negotiation tactics that pressure opponents to accept unfair or undesirable agreements or concessions.

pany, and they use a range of ploys or tactics to get what they want. However, people from different cultures consider some negotiating tactics **dirty tricks**. "Dirty tricks" are negotiation tactics that pressure opponents to accept unfair or undesirable agreements or concessions (Adler 1991).

The nature of cross-cultural negotiation makes the perception of dirty tricks almost unavoidable. Cultures differ on the norms and values that determine acceptable strategies for negotiation. As compared to U.S. Americans, Brazilians, for example, expect more deception and truth stretching during the initial stages of negotiation (Graham 1985).

In many countries, differing from the situation typical for U.S. negotiators, the negotiating team lacks the authority to complete a contract. Just when one party believes the deal is final, the other party responds by saying that "higher authority" must approve the contract before the deal is complete. The "agreement" often comes back with modifications, psychologically pressuring the other side to accept numerous "minor" modifications.

Some examples of common ploys in international negotiations (that some may consider dirty tricks) follow, with possible response tactics (from Adler 1991; Fisher and Ury 1981; Kublin 1995):

- *Deliberate deception:* Negotiators present flagrant untruths either in the facts they offer or in their intentions for the negotiation. For example, one foreign negotiating team spent a week in a hotel pursuing a deal, only to find out later that they were part of a negotiating dirty trick played by the local company. The local company was already negotiating in earnest with another foreign company. They had brought in the second foreign company only to scare the negotiators from the first foreign company.

  Possible response: Point out directly what you believe is happening.

- *Stalling:* Negotiators wait until the last minute before the international negotiating team plans to go home. They then push for quick concessions to close the deal.

  Possible responses: Do not reveal when you plan to leave. When asked, say, "As long as it takes." Alternatively, state when you will leave, with or without the deal.

- *Escalating authority:* Negotiators make an agreement then reveal that it must be approved by senior managers or the government. The objective is to put the other team under psychological pressure to make more concessions.

  Possible response: Clarify decision-making authority early in the negotiating process.

- *Good-guy, bad-guy routine:* One negotiator acts agreeable and friendly, while his or her partner makes outrageous or unreasonable demands. The "good guy" suggests that only a small concession will appease the unreasonable "bad guy."

  Possible response: Do not make any concessions. Ignore the ploy and focus on mutual benefits of the potential agreement.

- *You are wealthy and we are poor:* Often used by negotiators from developing countries, this tactic attempts to make concessions seem trivial. Smaller companies may also use this tactic when dealing with larger companies.

  Possible response: Ignore the ploy and focus on mutual benefits of potential agreement.

- *Old friends:* Negotiators act as if the companies and their negotiators have long-enduring friendships. They feign hurt feelings if their counterparts disagree or do not agree to their requests.

  Possible response: Keep a psychological distance that reflects the true nature of the relationship.

Successful international negotiators recognize and deal with dirty tricks and other ploys used in negotiations. Besides the possible strategies just noted, experts suggest four general responses to dirty tricks (Adler 1991). First, avoid using the tricks yourself. This encourages negotiating counterparts to be more forthright. Second, point out the dirty tricks or ploys when they are used. This discourages the use of dirty tricks later in the negotiation. Third, be ready to walk out of the negotiation if the other side fails to play fairly. This may involve some cost, but it is probably better than a bad deal for your company. Fourth, realize that ethical systems differ by culture, and understand that your opponents may not feel that they are really doing something wrong or immoral.

Although negotiators use a variety of tactics to argue their points, the goal remains to make a business deal. In the next section, we will examine the final steps in negotiation that bring the process to a successful conclusion.

STEPS 5 AND 6: CONCESSIONS AND AGREEMENT

Final agreement

Signed contract, agreeable to all sides.

Successful negotiations result in the **final agreement**. The final agreement is the signed contract, agreeable to all sides. It must be consistent with the chosen legal system or systems. The safest contracts are legally binding in the legal systems of all the signers. Most importantly, people from different national and business cultures must understand the contract in principle. This means that partners must have a true commitment to the terms of the agreement, beyond whatever legal stipulations exist.

Concession making

Process requiring each side to relax some of its demands to meet the other party's needs.

For most negotiations to reach a final agreement, each side must make some concessions. **Concession making** requires that each side relax certain demands to meet the other party's needs. It usually means giving in on the points of less importance to you to achieve your major objectives in negotiating the potential deal.

Sequential approach

Each side reciprocates concessions made by the other side.

Styles of concession making differ among cultures. None are necessarily the most successful. Experts (Adler 1991; Kublin 1995) point out that North American negotiators take a **sequential approach** to concession making. Each side reciprocates concessions made by the other side. North Americans have a norm of reciprocity, which means that one should meet a concession by the other party by making one's own concession. In many cultures, however, people consider "giving in" a sign of weakness and an encouragement to extract more concessions. In addition, in the typical U.S. negotiating strategy, partners consider each issue as a *separate* point. Negotiators expect each side to give and take on the individual issues in sequence. They complete the agreement when the sequential concession making resolves all issues.

Holistic approach

Each side makes very few, if any, concessions until the end of the negotiation.

In contrast, a **holistic approach** is more common in Asia. The parties make very few, if any, concessions during discussions of each point in a potential agreement. Only after all participants discuss all issues can concession making begin. When dealing with holistic negotiators, North Americans are often perplexed to learn that a point that they believed was negotiated previously arises again in final discussion of the overall package.

Approaches to the negotiating steps discussed vary not only by culture but also by a general philosophy regarding negotiating strategy. The next section discusses two approaches to negotiation along with their implications for international negotiations.

BASIC NEGOTIATING STRATEGIES

Competitive negotiation

Each side tries to give as little as possible and tries to "win" for its side.

Problem-solving negotiation

Negotiators seek out mutually satisfactory ground that is beneficial to both companies' interests.

There are two basic negotiating strategies, competitive negotiating and problem-solving negotiating (Kublin 1995). The competitive negotiator views the negotiation as a win–lose game. One side's gain must result in the other side's loss. Problem-solving negotiators, in contrast, search for possible win–win situations where the outcome of the negotiation is mutually satisfactory to both sides.

In **competitive negotiation**, each side tries to give as little as possible. They begin with high and often unreasonable demands. They make concessions only grudgingly. Competitive negotiators use dirty tricks and any plot that leads to their advantage. They spend more energy defending their positions while attempting to get the other side to make all the concessions.

Competitive negotiation seldom leads to long-term relationships built on mutual trust and commitment. Additionally, starting from inflexible positions often leads to outcomes that satisfy neither side. Thus, both sides develop negative attitudes toward each other, and often the "losers" seek revenge, reneging on the agreement when the opportunity arises.

The foremost tenet of **problem-solving negotiation** is separating *positions* from *interests* (Bazerman and Neale 1991). Problem-solving negotiation means that negotiators should not think of defending their company's position as the major goal of the negotiation. Rather, they should seek out mutually satisfactory ground that is beneficial to both companies' interests. Problem-solving negotiators avoid dirty tricks and use objective information whenever possible. They often find that actively seeking to please both sides results in the discovery of new ways to achieve mutual gains.

Exhibit 3.9 summarizes and contrasts how the competitive negotiator and the problem-solver differ in their approaches, as discussed earlier in the chapter.

In international negotiations, there are three important points regarding the use of competitive or problem-solving strategies.

First, in cross-cultural bargaining, the ease of misreading the other side's negotiation strategy increases dramatically. For example, the formal politeness used by many Asian negotiators may look like problem solving to U.S. negotiators. The tendency of Brazilian negotiators to talk or to exaggerate may look like competitive bargaining to people from cultures with ritual politeness. However, in either of the examples, culturally based rules of social interaction can mask either a highly inflexible position or a true openness to problem solving.

Second, cultural norms and values may predispose some negotiators to one of the approaches. Exhibit 3.10 shows some recent evidence from a cross-national study on cultural differences in the preference for a problem-solving negotiation style.

Third, most experts on international bargaining recommend a problem-solving negotiating strategy. They believe that problem solving leads to better long-term contracts and relationships. Problem solving is more likely to achieve the multinational's goals of mutual benefits from international trade. In contrast, competitive negotiations exacerbate the inevitable conflicts and misunderstandings that occur in cross-cultural interaction.

Superior products or services and good negotiations lead to good multinational business relationships. However, people must do the negotiating. In the next section, we will consider the characteristics of the successful international negotiator.

Exhibit 3.9

Competitive and
Problem-Solving
Negotiation in the
Negotiating Steps

Stages in Negotiation	Competitive Negotiating Strategy	Problem-Solving Negotiating Strategy
Preparation	Identify the economic or other benefits that the company needs from the deal. Know the position to defend.	Define the interests of the company. Prepare to overcome cross-cultural barriers to defining interests.
Relationship Building	Look for weaknesses in the other side. Find out as much as possible about your competition. Reveal as little as possible.	Separate the people in the negotiation from the problem. Change negotiators if necessary. Adapt to the other side's culture.
Information Exchange and First Offer	Give as little as possible. Give only task-related information. Make your position explicit.	Give and demand objective information that clarifies interests. Accept cultural differences in speed and type of information needs.
Persuasion	Use dirty tricks and any ploys that you think will work. Use pressure tactics.	Search for and invent new options that benefit the interests of both sides.
Concession	Begin with high initial demands. Make concessions slowly and grudgingly.	Search for mutually acceptable criteria. Accept cultural differences in starting position and in how and when concessions are made.
Agreement	Sign only if you win and get an iron-clad contract.	Sign when the interests of your company are met. Adapt to cultural differences in contracts.

Sources: Adapted from Adler 1991 and Kublin 1995.

THE SUCCESSFUL INTERNATIONAL NEGOTIATOR: PERSONAL CHARACTERISTICS

Personal success characteristics

Ability to tolerate ambiguous situations, flexibility, creativity, humor, stamina, empathy, and knowledge of a foreign language.

The successful international negotiator is comfortable in a multicultural environment and is skilled in interpersonal relationships. In addition, successful international negotiators have a variety of **personal success characteristics** that enhance their abilities to adjust to the stress of cross-cultural negotiations. These include (Kublin 1995):

• *Tolerance of ambiguity:* Even if they are familiar with the culture of their counterpart, an international negotiator is still a cultural bridge between people from different national and organizational cultures. Consequently, both the process of negotiation and the ultimate outcome are never entirely predictable. Individuals who take comfort in certainty of outcomes should probably avoid international negotiations. During the negotiation process, success requires that negotiators remain patient and nonjudgmental and "go with the flow."

Exhibit 3.10
Cultural Differences
in Preference for a
Problem-Solving
Negotiation Strategy

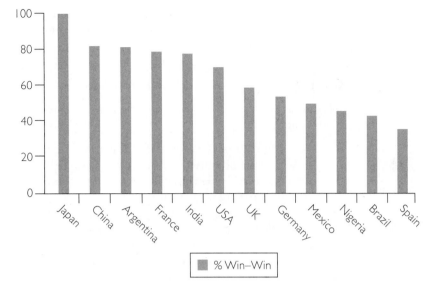

Source: Adapted from Salacuse 1998.

- *Flexibility and creativity:* The international negotiator must expect the unexpected. Explicit goals for the outcome may not work. Unanticipated proposals may be offered. Counterproposals may not come. Even the site of the negotiation may be entirely different from the planned location.
- *Humor:* Situations arise in intercultural exchanges that are sometimes embarrassing or humorous. Humor often breaks tension and allows both sides to deal with cultural ambiguities. For example, a U.S. businesswoman in Japan was shocked to see a lobster, which she was eating at the time, demonstrate its freshness by attempting to walk off the plate. Her Japanese hosts were much amused at her shock. She joined in their laughter as they teased her about eating more "active" food.
- *Stamina:* Long travel, jet lag, different foods, different climates, hotel living, and culture shock stress the physical stamina of even experienced international negotiators. Negotiators must overcome these physical challenges and still listen, analyze, observe, and socialize during the negotiation exchange. Only those negotiators with a strong constitution succeed.
- *Empathy:* Empathy means putting yourself in the place of your foreign colleagues—understanding the world from their perspective. This does not mean that a negotiator must agree with his or her counterpart on all issues. Rather, the empathic person must have a sincere concern for the feelings and perspectives of the other party. Empathy facilitates the negotiation because it softens the impact of interpersonal errors and cultural misunderstandings.
- *Curiosity:* Curiosity opens the door to new information. Managers with a genuine curiosity and respect concerning other cultures often discover subtleties that a more task-oriented negotiator misses.
- *Bilingualism:* Knowing the counterpart's language is an asset. However, sometimes linguistic ability alone is not enough. Even people who speak a language fluently may not understand significant aspects of a country's business culture. In particular, a good negotiator needs to understand how the business culture affects styles of negotiation.

This section completes our examination of the basics of international negotiation. In the next section, the major points are summarized.

STEPS IN, AND STYLES OF, NEGOTIATION, AND THE SUCCESSFUL NEGOTIATOR: SUMMARY OBSERVATIONS

Here are the major points to remember regarding the steps in international negotiation:

1. Few negotiations succeed without extensive preparation, both for the technical details of the potential relationship and for dealing with people who bring different cultural backgrounds to the negotiating process.
2. Building personal relationships is a key step in negotiation for most of the world. U.S. managers, in particular, must work harder on this step.
3. First offers may differ by cultural background, and managers must be aware of how their offers are viewed by people from other cultures.
4. There are many tactics in persuasion. Some of these may be considered dirty tricks. Good negotiators are prepared to deal with all tactics.
5. The processes surrounding giving and receiving concessions may be viewed quite differently by people from different nations. A good international negotiator knows how his or her counterpart views the concession-making process.
6. Culture and legal traditions influence the content and force of law regarding business contracts. An international negotiator should not assume that a signed contract means the same thing in all countries.
7. Competitive negotiation, with its use of dirty tricks and rigid positions, seldom leads to long-term relationships.
8. Problem-solving negotiation is more flexible and probably a more successful strategy for the international negotiator.
9. Individuals who engage in international negotiations must be flexible, empathic, and physically tough.

Summary and Conclusions

In this chapter, we examined the negotiating process and elements of cross-cultural communication in international business. The negotiating process involves preparation, building relationships with counterparts, persuading others to accept your reasonable goals through verbal and nonverbal negotiating tactics, making concessions, and finally, reaching an agreement. Successful negotiators prepare well and understand the steps of the negotiation processes. They also avoid the use of dirty tricks and competitive negotiating strategies.

The people who become successful negotiators are bilingual and have good cross-cultural communication skills. In addition, they are tolerant, flexible, empathic, and curious. They react to the stress of international negotiations with humor and stamina.

Oral cross-cultural communication demands that one learn the language or use interpreters, especially in complex negotiations. High-context languages also require that people learn to interpret situations that may not be apparent from analysis of the spoken component.

Nonverbal communications through body movements, proxemics, and touching vary widely for different cultural groups. International negotiators and managers must learn to interpret these behaviors in sensitive and empathic ways. This often requires looking at the world through the eyes of the other culture.

Avoiding attribution errors is a key to cross-cultural communication. International managers need sensitivity to their own behaviors and the behaviors of their foreign counterparts to avoid misinterpreting the meanings surrounding forms of communication. For example, a "dirty trick" in one culture may be a perfectly acceptable tactic in another culture.

Discussion Questions

1. Identify the steps in the negotiating process.

2. How does the U.S. "John Wayne" style of negotiation influence the steps in the negotiating processes?

3. Pick two countries and discuss the cultural differences in the ways people might use verbal negotiating tactics.

4. What is an attribution? How do attributions influence cross-cultural communication?

5. How can attributions influence the perception of "dirty tricks"?

6. Identify some cultural differences in body movements. How might these influence a negotiating session?

7. How might a manager successfully influence his or her subordinates in a high-context culture?

Chapter Internet Activity

NEGOTIATE ONLINE

With increasing use of electronic communication in multinational business, managers will need practice and skills for cross-cultural negotiation via the Internet. The InterNeg Group at Carleton and Concordia Universities and School of Business at McMaster University have online negotiation support systems for both practice and actual negotiations.

Go to either site and explore these systems at: http://www.business.carleton.ca/interneg/ or http://www.mcmaster.ca/home.html.

Each of these sites allows users to set up a negotiation and conduct the negotiation online. Your professor may suggest that you conduct the chapter negotiation exercise online.

Internet Sites

Selected Companies in the Chapter
Caterpillar Tractors   http://www.caterpillar.com/
Edwards Engineering Inc.   http://www.edwards-eng.com/
Kiel AG   http://www.stadtwerke-kiel.de/

Look at These Sites to Improve Your Knowledge of International Negotiations and Communication
http://www.lib.unc.edu/reference   *International Reference Sources from UNC Chapel Hill—includes foreign language dictionaries, maps, and atlases.*

http://www.berlitz.com   *Berlitz Language Homepage includes a culture quiz and helpful foreign phrases.*
http://rivendel.com/~ric/resources/dictionary.html   *A language dictionary and translator source.*
http://www.webofculture.com/   *Look here to find out what different gestures mean around the world.*
http://www.worldbiz.com/briefings.html   *Cultural background relevant to business for numerous countries.*

Chapter Activity: Negotiating an International Contract—A Simulation

Step 1: (1 minute) Read the following scenario.

This exercise simulates an international negotiation between *Sportique Shoes*, a North American manufacturer of athletic shoes, and *Tong Ltd.*, a shoe manufacturer from the fictitious Southeast Asian country of Poreadon. Both countries are members of the WTO. Because of increasing price competition in the shoe industry, *Sportique Shoes* is seeking a low-cost manufacturing facility overseas. In preliminary correspondence, *Tong Ltd.* has offered the lowest price. It is also common knowledge that Poreadon has a high quality and motivated workforce.

A negotiating team from *Sportique Shoes,* charged with the task of beginning negotiations, arrives today to negotiate with the *Tong Ltd.* management team for a contract to manufacture *Sportique's* shoes for the next year.

Step 2: (10 minutes) Your instructor will divide the class into two teams. One team will represent the management of *Sportique Shoes.* The other team will represent the management team of *Tong Ltd.* Go to separate rooms or separate parts of one classroom.

Independent of the two teams, four people will be assigned the roles of World Bankers (2) and Administrators (2). These four people do not participate in the negotiation; rather, they observe, keep time, manage the finances, and take notes on the progress of the negotiation.

The objective of both the *Sportique Shoes* team and the *Tong Ltd.* team is to achieve the best contract for their company.

Step 3: (15 minutes) Each team will receive a packet of materials from the instructor. Read the Timeline, Negotiation Tasks, Cultural Background, and Negotiation Roles at this time. Decide who will play what roles.

Step 4: (10 minutes) Read the general rules for the following simulation:

A. The contract must cover four points:
   1. Delivery dates for product shipments.
   2. Quantity to be delivered at each shipment.
   3. Price per 100 shoes manufactured.
   4. Penalties for lateness.

B. Finances
   1. Each team member must contribute $1.00 to each company's Capital Account. Your instructor may change or eliminate this requirement, depending on the particular circumstances of your course. The Capital Account is managed by each team's CFO.
   2. The CFO delivers 40 percent of each company's Capital Account to the World Bank. The World Bank will finance future operations and requires this payment as an indication of good faith negotiations. The World Bank calls this money your Good Faith Account.
   3. Forty percent of your Good Faith Account will be returned to each team after a successful contract is signed and delivered to your instructor. Should you fail to reach an accord in the time allocated, you will forfeit your entire Good Faith Account to the World Bank. It will be donated to a local charity. You may recover the additional 60 percent of your Good Faith Account by meeting certain objectives as stated in the Contract Negotiation Objectives.

C. General Contract Objectives and Financial Implications
   1. Each team should try to negotiate a contract that is consistent with its cultural values and economically favorable for its company.
   2. Long-term financial gains and losses can result from what you negotiate. As in real life, these are not completely certain to you during the negotiation. However, the closer you are to reaching your objectives, the more likely it is that you will gain in the negotiations. For each point of negotiation, there are ranges of possible outcomes—some are neutral and both teams win, and some result in financial gain for one or the other side. After you negotiate your contract, your instructor will inform you of the economic results of your negotiations. For each point on which a team gained a favorable outcome, the other team will contribute 10 percent of its remaining Capital Account to the other team's Capital Account. For each point on which the contract results in balanced out-

comes (you both win), the World Bank will contribute a flat fee of $1.00 to each company's Capital Account.

Step 5: (10 minutes) Read the Contract Negotiation Objectives provided by your instructor.

Step 6: (20 minutes) Plan a negotiation strategy with your team members.

Step 7: (10 minutes) Make a First Offer.

Step 8: (60 minutes) Negotiate!

Step 9: (30 minutes) World Bankers and Administrators balance accounts between teams. Entire group debriefs.

References

Adler, Nancy J. 1991. *International Dimensions of Organizational Behavior* (2d ed.). Boston: PWS-Kent.

Axtell, R. E. 1991. *Gestures*. New York: Wiley.

Bazerman, Max H., and Margaret A. Neale. 1991. *Negotiating Rationally*. New York: Free Press.

Bryan, Robert M., and Peter C. Buck. 1989. "When customs collide: the pitfalls of international acquisitions." *Financial Executive* 5:43–46.

Chaney, Lillian H., and Jeanette S. Martin. 1995. *Intercultural Business Communication*. Englewood Cliffs, N.J.: Prentice Hall.

Copeland, L., and L. Griggs. 1985. *Going International*. New York: Random House.

Eibel-Eibesfeldt, I. 1971. "Similarities and differences between cultures in expressive movement." In *Behavior and Environment: The Use of Space by Animals and Men*, edited by Robert E. Hinde, 297–312. London: Cambridge University Press.

Ferraro, Gary P. 1994. *The Cultural Dimension of International Business*. Englewood Cliffs, N.J.: Prentice Hall.

Fisher, Roger, and William Ury. 1981. *Getting to Yes*. New York: Penguin.

Graham, John L. 1985. "The influence of culture on the process of business negotiations: An exploratory study." *Journal of International Business Studies* 26:81–96.

———, and Roy A. Herberger, Jr. 1983. "Negotiators abroad—don't shoot from the hip." *Harvard Business Review* 61:160–68.

Hall, Edward T. 1976. *Beyond Culture*. Garden City, N.Y.: Anchor Press.

———, and Mildred Reed Hall. 1990. *Understanding Cultural Differences*. Yarmouth, Maine: Intercultural Press.

Harris, Philip R., and Robert T. Moran. 1991. *Managing Cultural Differences*. Houston: Gulf.

Kublin, Michael. 1995. *International Negotiating*. New York: International Business Press.

Nydell, Margaret K. 1997. *Understanding Arabs: A Guide for Westerners*. Yarmouth, Maine: Intercultural Press.

Oster, Patrick. 1994. "The new Europe: A boom market for linguists." *Business Week*, International Edition, May 9.

Rosch, Martin. 1987. "Communications: focal point of culture." *Management International Review*, 27, 4:60.

Salacuse, Jeswald W. 1998. "Ten ways that culture affects negotiating style: Some survey results." *Negotiation Journal*, July 221–40.

———. 1991. *Making Global Deals*. Boston: Houghton Mifflin.

Terpstra, Vern, and Kenneth David. 1991. *The Cultural Environment of International Business*. Cincinnati: South-Western.

Tung, Rosalie L. 1984. "How to negotiate with the Japanese." *California Management Review* 26:62–77.

Whately, Arthur. 1994. "International negotiation case." In *Management International*, edited by Dorothy Marcic and Sheila Puffer, 73–74. St. Paul: West.

Whorf, Benjamin Lee. 1965. *Language, Thought, and Reality*. New York: Wiley.

Yale, Richmond. 1992. *From Nyet to Da: Understanding the Russians*. Yarmouth, Maine: Intercultural Press.

Chapter 4

Managing Ethical and Social Responsibility Challenges in Multinational Companies

LEARNING OBJECTIVES
After reading this chapter you should
be able to:

- Know the definitions of international
business ethics and social responsibility.

- Understand some basic principles of
ethical philosophy relevant to business
ethics.

- Understand how social institutions and
national culture affect ethical decision
making and management.

- Understand the implications of using
ethical relativism and ethical
universalism in ethics management.

- Identify the basic principles and
consequences of the U.S. Foreign
Corrupt Practices Act.

- Understand how international
agreements affect international
business ethics.

- Understand the differences among
economic, legal, and ethical analyses of
business problems.

- Develop skills in international decision
making with ethical consequences.

Preview Case in Point	
The Growing Responsibility of Multi-nationals	How responsible are multinational managers for working conditions and the use of child labor in overseas production facilities? For example, is it the responsibility of the U.S. shoe or garment manufacturer to be concerned if its goods are produced by subcontractors (at the lowest competitive cost) using child-labor sweatshops in Asia? Is it the duty of retailers to worry about where and how the goods they sell were produced? Increasingly, such issues are becoming important to multinationals that source their production in the lowest-cost areas of the world. Such issues also attract public and governmental attention. The U.S. government even maintains a "no sweat" home page on the World Wide Web that identifies companies committed to not using sweatshops (http://www.dol.gov/dol/esa/public/nosweat/nosweat.htm).

In response to these issues, a growing number of U.S. multinationals actively monitor wages, working conditions, workers' rights, and safety in their production facilities—Levi, Nordstrom Inc., Wal-Mart Stores Inc., and Reebok International Ltd. Levi is among the most active. Levi routinely sends inspectors to Southeast Asia to inspect working conditions in factories from Indonesia to Bangladesh. Even over the objections of some senior managers and some board members, Levi CEO Robert D. Haas took action. He dropped two of the cheapest labor sites, China and Burma, from its manufacturing locations because of unsatisfactory working conditions.

Managing the ethical standards of its contract manufacturers is not easy for Levi or any other multinational. Governments in developing nations often react negatively to U.S. or European suggestions that local companies adopt Western labor standards. Such standards would cost money and erode the local competitive advantage in manufacturing costs. Skeptics also argue that standards such as Levi's are easily achieved or faked. Others, such as Larry Byrnes, director of the Council of Hemispheric Affairs in Washington, D.C., noted, "High-minded efforts usually evaporate because people with far less scruples decide to low-ball labor, and dictates of the market eliminate these ethical assays."

Sources: Based on Marion 1996 and Zachary 1994. |

The foregoing Preview Case in Point shows how Levi faced an ethical problem of increasing concern in multinational business. This chapter will review basic knowledge of business ethics and build on this knowledge to discuss ethical and social responsibilities unique to multinational management.

Managers at all levels face ethical issues every day. "If I fire a poorly performing employee, what will happen to his children?" "If we can get cheap child labor overseas, and it is legal there, should we use it because our competitors do?" "Should we refuse to give a bribe to an underpaid government official, and lose the contract to our competitor's weaker product?" Dealing with these and similar issues is not easy. However, with a better understanding of key ethical problems in multinational management, you can make more informed ethical judgments. This chapter will provide you with some of the background and skills required to deal with the ethical situations faced by multinational managers.

WHAT ARE INTERNATIONAL BUSINESS ETHICS AND SOCIAL RESPONSIBILITY?

Before one can understand the ethical dilemmas faced by multinational managers, one needs a working definition of business ethics. Most experts consider business ethics as one application of the broader concern for all ethical behavior and reasoning. In this broad sense, ethics pertain to behaviors or actions that affect people and their welfare. A decision by managers to knowingly sell a useful but dangerous product is an ethical decision. Ethics deal with the "oughts" of life—that is, the rules and values that determine what goals and actions people should follow when dealing with other human beings (Buchholz 1989).

Although economic logic (i.e., making money) dominates business decision making, most business decisions also have consequences for people (workers, suppliers, customers, society, etc.). Thus, ethical decision making permeates organizational life. For example, decisions such as those regarding product safety, layoffs, closing or relocating a plant, or the truthfulness of an advertisement have consequences for people. When managers make such decisions, they make decisions with ethical consequences—whether consciously or not.

However, it is important to remember that ethical questions seldom have clear or unambiguous answers that are accepted by all people. For example, it is possible to produce automobiles safer than those currently on the market. However, if such vehicles were required by law, they would be extremely expensive (meaning only the rich could drive); would probably result in smaller automobile-production plants (putting people out of work); would likely require larger engines (increasing oil consumption and pollution); and would likely reduce profits (violating the ethical responsibilities of the managers to stockholders). Thus, for the automobile manufacturers, there is always an ethical dilemma of whether a vehicle is sufficiently safe versus sufficiently affordable.

International business ethics

Those unique ethical problems faced by managers conducting business operations across national boundaries.

International business ethics pertain to those unique ethical problems faced by managers conducting business operations across national boundaries. International business ethics differ from domestic business ethics on two accounts. First, and perhaps most important, international business is more complex, because business is conducted cross-nationally. Different cultural values and institutional systems necessarily mean that people may not always agree on what one "ought" to do. Expatriate managers may face situations where local business practices violate their own culturally based sensibilities or their home-country laws. Second, the very large multinational companies often have powers and assets that equal those of some of the nations with which they deal. The managers in these large and powerful multinationals face challenging ethical dilemmas regarding how to use this power. The example of Levi shown in this chapter's Preview Case in Point illustrates how one CEO uses his company's assets in ways that benefit several stakeholders. These include the company and the people in the developing nations that produce Levi's products.

Social responsibility

Idea that businesses have a responsibility to society beyond making profits.

The concept of **social responsibility** is closely related to business ethics. Social responsibility refers to the idea that businesses have a responsibility to society beyond making profits. That is, social responsibility means that a company must take into account the welfare of other constituents (e.g., customers, suppliers) in addition to stockholders. While business ethics usually concern the ethical dilemmas faced by managers as individuals, social responsibility is usually concerned with the ethical consequences of policies and procedures of the company as an organization. Monitoring the working conditions of your suppliers, paying for the education of the children of workers, and donating money to the local community are examples of social responsibility in action.

Exhibit 4.1 Areas of Ethical and Social Responsibility Concerns for the Multinational Company

Stakeholder Affected	Ethical/Social Responsibility Issue	Example Problems for the MNC
Customers	Product safety	Should an MNC delete safety features to make a product more affordable for people in a poorer nation?
	Fair price	Should a sole supplier in a country take advantage of its monopoly?
	Proper disclosures and information	Should an MNC assume the cost of translating all its product information into other languages?
Stockholders	Fair return on investment	If a product is banned because it is unsafe in one country, should it be sold in countries where it is not banned to maintain profit margins?
Employees	Fair wages	Should a company pay more than market wages when such wages result in people living in poverty?
	Safety of working conditions	Should a company be responsible for the working conditions of its suppliers?
	Child labor	Should an MNC use child labor if it is legal in the host country?
	Discrimination by sex, race, color, or creed	Should a company assign a woman to a country where women are expected to remain separate from men in public?
Host Country	Impact on local economies	Should an MNC use transfer pricing and other internal accounting measures to reduce its actual tax base in a foreign country?
	Following local laws	Should an MNC follow local laws that violate home-country laws against discrimination?
	Impact on local social institutions	Should an MNC require its workers to work on religious holidays?
Society in General	Environmental protection	Is an MNC obligated to control its hazardous waste to a degree higher than local laws require?
	Raw-material depletion	Should MNCs deplete natural resources in countries that are willing to let them do so?

In practice, ethics and social responsibility are not easily distinguished. Usually, procedures and policies in a company regarding social responsibility reflect the ethical values and decisions of the top management team (Cullen, Victor, and Stephens 1989). For example, as shown in the Preview Case in Point, Levi's decision to engage in the socially responsible action of monitoring the working conditions of its suppliers reflects the ethical beliefs of Levi CEO Robert D. Haas regarding these issues.

The ethical and social-responsibility issues faced by multinational companies are complex and varied. Exhibit 4.1 identifies some of the stakeholders in the MNC and shows typical problems faced by the MNC that affect these stakeholders.

How can international managers deal with the constant ethical challenges such as those in Exhibit 4.1? To succeed and be profitable in a socially responsible fashion, MNC managers must weigh and balance the economic, legal, and ethical consequences of their decisions. The next sections discuss how managers must analyze situations with ethical consequences. The first section presents an overview of basic ethical philosophies used by managers as guides for ethical decision making. The second section deals with national differences in business ethics and social responsibility. In the third section we consider the development of transnational business ethics—an ethical system for the multinational that does not rely on the ethical principles and philosophies of any one country. In the final section, we consider the practical considerations of balancing the needs of the company and managerial actions with ethical consequences.

ETHICAL PHILOSOPHY

In this section, we examine two ways to consider your ethical decision making. The first comes from traditional ethical philosophy. The second is a contemporary philosophical view of how we can think about ethics.

TRADITIONAL VIEWS

Teleological ethical theory

One that suggests that the morality of an act or practice comes from its consequences.

Utilitarianism

Argument that what is good and moral comes from acts that produce the greatest good for the greatest number of people.

Deontological ethical theory

Focus on actions that, by themselves, have a good or bad morality regardless of the outcomes they produce.

Two basic systems of ethical reasoning dominate ethical philosophy. These are the teleological and the deontological.

In **teleological ethical theories**, the morality of an act or practice comes from its consequences. The most popular teleological theory is **utilitarianism**. Utilitarianism argues that what is good and moral comes from acts that produce the greatest good for the greatest number of people. For example, from a utilitarian perspective, one might argue that stealing a loaf of bread to feed a hungry family is moral because eating the bread is crucial for the family's survival.

In contrast to teleological ethical theories, **deontological ethical theories** do not focus on consequences. Rather, *actions by themselves have a good or bad morality regardless of the outcomes they produce.* For example, a person who chooses not to steal a loaf of bread because it is immoral to steal, even if people starve because of this action, behaves ethically according to some deontological arguments. In this case, the moral principle forbidding stealing, common in many religious doctrines, takes precedence over a bad outcome.

Some ethical philosophers who believe in deontological ethical theories argue that morality is intuitive and self-evident—that is, moral people just know what is right because it is obvious how an ethical person should behave. Other ethical philosophers argue that we cannot rely on intuition. Instead, we should follow an essential moral principle or value such as the Golden Rule or a concern for justice. Still other deontologists argue for a more comprehensive set of moral principles or rules that can guide our behavior, such as the Ten Commandments, the Koran, or the Bible (Buchholz 1989).

MORAL LANGUAGES

Another more contemporary way of looking at ethics, favored by Thomas Donaldson, an expert on international business ethics, broadens the rough distinction between teleological and deontological ethical theories. Donaldson argues that international business ethics is best understood by focusing on the "language of international corporate ethics" (Donaldson 1992a). According to Donaldson,

Moral languages

Description of the basic ways that people use to think about ethical decisions and to explain their ethical choices.

moral languages describe the basic ways that people use to think about ethical decisions and to explain their ethical choices. The six basic ethical languages identified by Donaldson include (Donaldson 1992a):

- *Virtue and vice:* This language identifies a person's good or virtuous properties and contrasts them with vices. For example, temperance might be contrasted with lust. People or groups who exhibit or who have virtuous characteristics are seen as ethical. It is not so important what results from an action, but rather the virtuous intent of the action.
- *Self-control:* This language emphasizes achieving perfection at controlling thoughts and actions, such as passion. It is apparent in Buddhist and Hindu views of the world but also appears in many Western traditions, such as in the philosophy of Plato and the control of "appetites."
- *Maximizing human welfare:* This is the basic language of the utilitarian view of ethics, emphasizing the greatest good for the greatest number of people. For example, using this language of ethical thought one might argue that exposing a few people to dangerous chemicals is okay if most people in the society benefit.
- *Avoiding harm:* Like the emphasis on the greatest good for the greatest number, this language of ethics also sees good or bad in the consequences of behavior or action. However, rather than maximizing benefits, it focuses on avoiding unpleasant outcomes or consequences. For example, one might argue: "If it doesn't hurt anyone, it's okay."
- *Rights/duties:* This language focuses on principles that guide ethical behaviors. The principles specify duties that are required, such as the duties of a parent to care for a child. The principles also specify the rights that people have, such as the right to free speech. According to Donaldson, the language of rights and duties fits well in a legal context.
- *Social contract:* The social-contract language structures ethics as a form of agreements among people. These agreements need not be written down but may be taken for granted by those concerned. In this sense, what is ethical is what the people in our culture or in our organization have come to agree is ethical.

The moral philosophies provide a language or structure for thinking about ethical decisions and dilemmas. They help the manager understand the philosophical bases for his or her decision making and the ethical or social-responsibility policies of a company. International managers face the additional challenge of understanding the cultural and institutional contexts surrounding their ethical decision making. The next section shows how culture and social institutions come into play in the complexities of ethical decision making.

NATIONAL DIFFERENCES IN BUSINESS ETHICS AND SOCIAL RESPONSIBILITY

As with most multinational business practices, national culture and social institutions also affect how businesses manage ethical behavior and social responsibility. Exhibit 4.2 gives a simple model of the relationships among national culture, social institutions, and business ethics.

Cultural norms and values influence important business practices—such as how women and minorities are treated on the job, attitudes toward gift giving and bribery, and expectations regarding conformity to written laws. Religion and the legal system are probably the key social institutions that affect what ethical issues are important in a society and how they are typically managed.

Exhibit 4.2 A Model of Institutional and Cultural Effects on Business Ethics Issues and Management

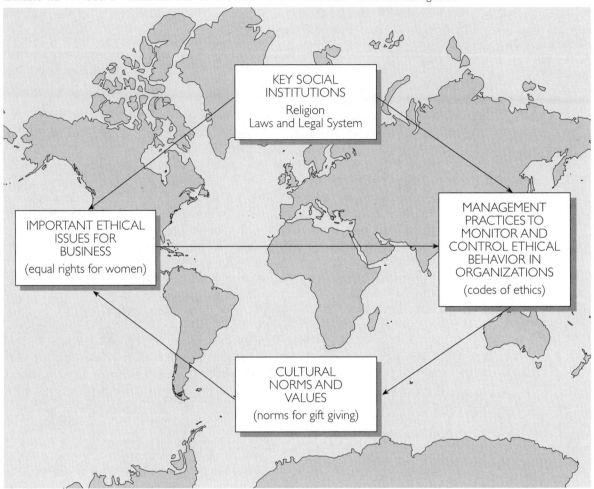

Unfortunately for the multinational manager, however, there is no comprehensive body of knowledge identifying exactly how national culture and social institutions affect business ethics and under what conditions. Instead, most of our knowledge comes from anecdotal evidence from practitioners and the few scientific studies that do exist. Thus, the multinational manager can often only infer from his or her knowledge of a country's social institutions and culture what ethical issues are important and how they are best managed.

To show how the national context affects business ethics, the text now gives some examples of international differences in business–ethics management. Exhibit 4.3 summarizes the results of one study on the ratings of ethical issues considered most important by senior U.S. and European executives (Schlegelmilch and Robertson 1995). Of course, a broader range of ethical issues or a larger sample of countries would produce more differences than those in the example here. However, although these managers all come from Western democracies, cultural differences and historical, legal, and political traditions influence which ethical issues managers deem important.

Why is the United States so different from the other countries on the ethics of HRM issues? U.S. cultural norms emphasize the value of individual freedom.

Exhibit 4.3 A Comparison of Key Ethical Issues Identified by Senior U.S. and EU Managers

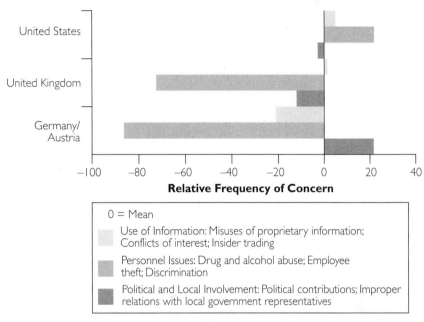

Source: Adapted from Schlegelmilch and Robertson 1995.

Compatible with these norms, the U.S. legal system has developed extensive prohibitions against discrimination and extensive laws regulating HRM issues. Consequently, U.S. managers ranked personnel issues as requiring the greatest concern for their ethics management.

Why are the German and Austrian managers more concerned with political issues? Perhaps because of recent legal and popular challenges to the historically close (and mutually self-serving) interactions between industry and political leaders, the German and Austrian managers have above-average concerns for ethical issues related to politics.

Although limited in national coverage, these examples show that, to identify key ethical issues in a society, multinational managers must be attuned to cultural, legal, and political traditions. These traditions affect people's beliefs concerning what ethical issues are important and, as you will see next, how they should be managed.

The techniques of managing ethical behavior in organizations also reflect cultural and institutional differences. Exhibit 4.4 shows the management techniques preferred by the same group of managers reported on in Exhibit 4.3. Consistent with their practice of a heavy emphasis on training, and in comparison to managers from other countries, Germans used training for ethical control most often and relied little on written policies. U.S. and British managers seemed to think that having the written policies was sufficient for ethics management.

Another example of cultural and institutional differences in ethics-management techniques comes from a study of the perceived benefits of using ethical codes (Becker and Fritzsche 1987). Ethical codes are popular techniques for controlling the ethical behaviors of employees. However, there are differences in the way managers from different societies perceive the use and effectiveness of the codes. Exhibit 4.5 provides an example of differences among U.S., German, and French managers regarding their beliefs about ethical codes.

Possibly because the French have a system of law based on specific written codes rather than law based on precedent (law determined by the history of court

Exhibit 4.4 The Management of Key Ethical Issues in U.S. and European Companies

Source: Adapted from Schlegelmilch and Robertson 1995.

Exhibit 4.5 National Differences in Beliefs Regarding Ethical Codes

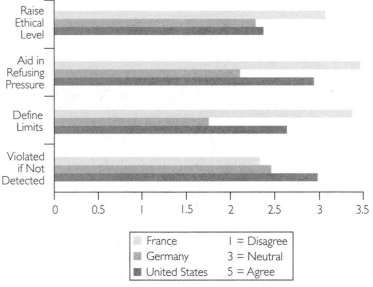

Source: Becker and Fritzsche 1987.

rulings) as in the United States, the French see the most benefits coming from written codes of ethics. In Exhibit 4.5, they rank highest among the three countries in managers' beliefs that codes raise ethical levels in the company, serve as an aid to point to when refusing to engage in unethical behavior, and help in defining the limits of behavior. The French managers rank lowest when asked whether they believe that people will violate the code when they can avoid detection or being caught. In contrast, German managers see codes as having little value, with generally neutral or negative reactions to the use of codes. U.S. managers fall between the French and Germans on most issues but more often believe that people will violate codes if they can avoid detection.

Aside from the effect of other social institutions on defining important ethical issues, religion can have a powerful impact on the nature of business ethics. Al-

---

Multinational Management Brief
The Koran in a Turkish Office

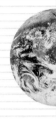

Although Turkey is a secular state, there is an increasing merger between the values espoused in the Koran and business practices. A voluntary group of executives, called the Musiad, try to combine Islamic teachings with Western business practices. The Musiad's eighteen hundred members pray the required five times a day. The group is male dominated, with only two women members. They follow the Muslim prohibition against charging *riba* (interest), and they feel it is a moral obligation to provide good pay and safe working conditions. The Musiad's ethics committee makes sure its members don't drink alcohol, avoid conspicuous consumption, and donate part of their income to charity. They believe that they must exercise a social responsibility to their society because they feel that the money they earn "isn't ours, and we'll be asked how we spent it when we get to the other world."

Source: Based on Doxey 1995.

---

though this is most apparent in states where there is a close relationship between a particular religious hierarchy and the government, religious values impact business ethics even in more secular states. For example, the Judeo-Christian traditions of values and beliefs regarding ethical behavior dominate the ethical philosophies of most Western countries. Similarly, as shown in the preceding Multinational Management Brief, other religious traditions can influence what people believe is good and correct actions at work.

Because of its extensive legal control over the management of ethical behaviors, the United States is unique in the world. The next section discusses a major law governing ethical behavior in international business that has possibly the greatest impact on U.S. multinational companies.

QUESTIONABLE PAYMENTS AND THE U.S. FOREIGN CORRUPT PRACTICES ACT

A particular ethical difficulty for many U.S. multinational companies revolves around the issue of bribery, or what some call questionable payments. In many societies, people routinely offer bribes or gifts to expedite government actions or to gain advantage in business deals. "Grease money" can speed importing or exporting of goods or cause customs agents to look the other way. A gift or a kickback may be expected for a purchasing agent to select your company's product over another. Words for these types of actions exist in all countries. For example, in Mexico the bribe is known as *mordida,* the bite; in France the *pot-de-vin,* jug of wine; in Germany, the "N.A.," an abbreviation of *nutzliche Abagabe,* the useful contribution; and in Japan, the *jeitinho,* the fix (Mendenhall, Punnet, and Ricks 1994).

Exhibit 4.6 shows estimates of the extent of bribery of public officials accepted from companies within leading exporting countries when doing business in emerging market economies. Emerging market economies included countries such as Indonesia, Poland, Nigeria, Colombia, and Russia. To create this "Bribe Payers

Exhibit 4.6 Levels of Bribery Paid by Leading Exporting Countries in Emerging Market Countries

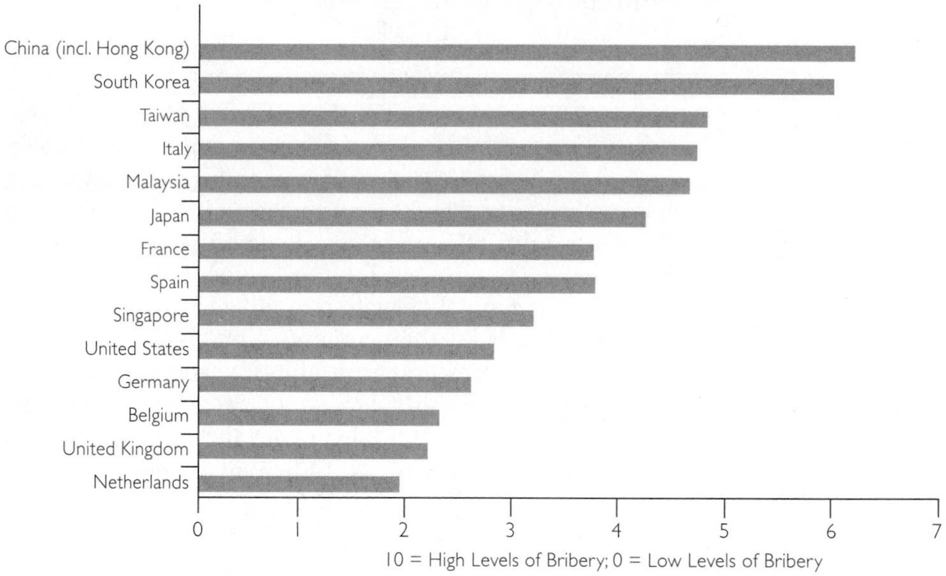

China (incl. Hong Kong)
South Korea
Taiwan
Italy
Malaysia
Japan
France
Spain
Singapore
United States
Germany
Belgium
United Kingdom
Netherlands

0   1   2   3   4   5   6   7

10 = High Levels of Bribery; 0 = Low Levels of Bribery

Source: Adapted from Transparency International 2000.

Index," Transparency International (2000) surveyed 770 business leaders in 14 developing economies asking: "in the business sectors with which you are familiar, please indicate whether companies from the following countries are very likely, quite likely or unlikely to pay bribes to win or retain business in this country." The results of this survey led Peter Eigen, Chairman of Transparency International, to conclude: "The scale of bribe-paying by international corporations in the developing countries of the world is massive" (Transparency International 2000).

As in the United States, most countries have formal laws forbidding such actions. However, because of wide differences among countries in legal traditions, enforcement varies greatly. The accepted amount of gift giving and entertainment associated with business transactions varies enormously. For example, even for academic-research grants, Japanese professors will budget as a legitimate expense about 20 percent of the grant for entertainment costs—something unheard of in U.S. academic research.

In 1977, in response to several investigations by U.S. government agencies, President Jimmy Carter signed the **Foreign Corrupt Practices Act**—commonly known as the **FCPA**. Exhibit 4.7 on pages 120–121, taken directly from the U.S. Code, shows excerpts from the FCPA.

Foreign Corrupt Practices Act (FCPA)

Forbids U.S. companies to make or offer illegal payments or gifts to officials of foreign governments for the sake of getting or retaining business.

The FCPA forbids U.S. companies to make or offer payments or gifts to foreign government officials for the sake of gaining or retaining business. However, the FCPA does not prohibit some forms of payments that may occur in international business. Payments made under duress to avoid injury or violence are acceptable. For example, in an unstable political environment, a company may pay local officials "bribes" to avoid harassment of its employees. Small payments that just encourage officials to do their legitimate and routine jobs are okay. Payments made that are lawful in a country are also acceptable. These "grease" payments must not seek illegal ends but just speed up or make possible normal business functions, such as necessary paperwork.

A tricky component of the FCPA for U.S. companies is the law's *reason-to-know* provision. The reason-to-know provision means that a firm is liable for bribes or questionable payments made by agents hired by the firm—even if members of the firm did not actually make the payments or see them made. To take advantage of a local person's knowledge of "how to get things done" in a country, U.S. multi-nationals often use local people as agents to conduct business. If it is common knowledge that these agents use part of their fees to bribe local officials to commit illegal acts, then the U.S. firm is breaking U.S. law. If, however, the U.S. firm has neither knowledge of the behavior of the agent nor any reason to expect illegal behavior from the agent, then the U.S. firm has no liability under the FCPA. A person is considered "knowing" if: the person actually knows an illegal bribe will be given, the person knows that the circumstances surrounding the situation make it likely that an illegal bribe will be given, or a person is aware of the high probability that an illegal act will occur.

Exhibit 4.7 also shows the types of penalties included in the FCPA. Note that penalties can be given to individuals as well as to companies and that individual fines cannot be paid by the company. In a recent case, a former executive from Lockheed Martin Corp. was convicted of bribing an Egyptian parliamentarian to facilitate the sale of three C-130 cargo planes. This individual now faces a sentence of eighteen months in prison and a $125,000 fine (Borrus, Toy, and Salz-Trautman 1995).

EFFECTS OF THE ETHICS GAP

Ethics gap

Idea that U.S. political and legal social institutions create greater coercive and normative pressures for U.S. businesses to follow ethical standards.

Legislation like the FCPA and the proliferation of ethical codes in U.S. corporations has caused some experts to argue that there is an **ethics gap** between the United States and the rest of the world. The ethics gap does not mean that the United States has a more ethical culture than other countries. Rather, it means that U.S. political and legal social institutions create greater coercive and normative pressure for U.S. businesses to follow ethical standards.

Does the FCPA hurt business? Soon after the passage of the FCPA, many business leaders felt that U.S. corporations would be at a competitive disadvantage when conducting business in countries prone to bribery. One early survey found that 78 percent of twelve hundred U.S. senior executives felt that the law put U.S. companies at a disadvantage (*Business Week* 1983). To address this question, several years after the law went into effect, John Graham (1983) looked at changes in the U.S. share of the import markets for the fifty-one countries that account for the majority of U.S. exports. Dividing the countries into two groups, one in which business practices traditionally allow bribery and the other in which bribery is frowned upon, they found no effect on U.S. overseas sales for either group.

However, more recent evidence suggests that, although the FCPA may not have caused U.S. businesses to fall behind, it has blocked some gains in export market share and extent of U.S. ownership in foreign countries. Harvard University economist James R. Hines Jr. estimates that U.S. direct investment in and exports to "corrupt" countries declined substantially when compared with competitors' investments in the same countries. U.S. Trade Representative Mickey Kantor estimates that successful use of bribery by companies from other countries costs the United States $45 billion a year. One study by the U.S. Commerce Department tracked one hundred business deals worth an estimated $45 billion, in which U.S. competitors used bribes. Eighty percent of the business went to the foreign competition (Borrus, Toy, and Salz-Trautman 1995; Koretz 1996). Such findings have encouraged some U.S. politicians and managers to pressure other nations to follow

Exhibit 4.7 Excerpts from the Foreign Corrupt Practices Act

Prohibited foreign trade practices

It shall be unlawful for *any domestic concern* or for any officer, director, employee, or agent of such domestic concern or any stockholder thereof acting on behalf of such domestic concern, to make use of the mails or any means or instrumentality of interstate commerce corruptly in furtherance of an offer, payment, promise to pay, or authorization of the payment of any money, or offer, gift, promise to give, or authorization of the giving of anything of value to any foreign official for purposes of—

A.   influencing any act or decision of such foreign official, political party, party official, or candidate in his or its official capacity, or

B.   inducing such foreign official, political party, party official, or candidate to do or omit to do any act in violation of the lawful duty of such foreign official, political party, party official, or candidate, or

C.   inducing such foreign official, political party, party official, or candidate to use his or its influence with a foreign government or instrumentality thereof to affect or influence any act or decision of such government or instrumentality, in order to assist such issuer in obtaining or retaining business for or with, or directing business to, any person.

Also prohibited is any offer, payment, promise to pay, or authorization of the payment of any money, or offer, gift, promise to give, or authorization of the giving of anything of value *when given to any person, while knowing* that all or a portion of such money or thing of value will be offered, given, or promised, directly or indirectly, to any foreign official, to any foreign political party or official thereof, or to any candidate for foreign political office, for purposes of A through C above.

Definitions

(1)   The term *"domestic concern"* means any individual who is a citizen, national, or resident of the United States; and any corporation, partnership, association, joint-stock company, business trust, unincorporated organization, or sole proprietorship which has its principal place of business in the United States, or which is organized under the laws of a State of the United States or a territory, possession, or commonwealth of the United States.

(2)   The term *"foreign official"* means any officer or employee of a foreign government or any department, agency, or instrumentality thereof, or any person acting in an official capacity for or on behalf of any such government or department, agency, or instrumentality.

(3)   A person's state of mind is *"knowing"* with respect to conduct, a circumstance, or a result if—
   (i)   such person is aware that such person is engaging in such conduct, that such circumstance exists, or that such result is substantially certain to occur; or
   (ii) such person has a firm belief that such circumstance exists or that such result is substantially certain to occur.
   Knowledge is established if a person is aware of a high probability of the existence of such circumstance, unless the person actually believes that such circumstance does not exist.

(continued)

U.S. rules. But should they? Consider some of these issues in the Multinational Management Challenge on page 122.

Growing international trade relationships have also resulted in calls for universal codes of ethics for the control of the ethical behavior of multinational companies and their employees. The following section discusses some of the current trends and proposals.

TOWARD TRANSNATIONAL ETHICS

Globalization dramatically increases contact among people with different ethical and cultural systems. This contact is creating pressure for ethical convergence and the development of transnational agreements among nations to govern business practices. For example, the Case in Point on page 123 shows that the battle against corrupt relationships between business and government is growing.

Next, we review some of the trends toward ethical convergence and transnational ethical agreements.

Exhibit 4.7 Excerpts from the Foreign Corrupt Practices Act *(continued)*

(4) The term *"routine government action"* means only an action which is ordinarily and commonly performed by a foreign official in such as obtaining permits, licenses, or other official documents to qualify a person to do business in a foreign country. The term "routine governmental action" does not include any decision by a foreign official whether, or on what terms, to award new business to or to continue business with a particular party, or any action taken by a foreign official involved in the decision-making process to encourage a decision to award new business to or continue business with a particular party.

(5) The term *"interstate commerce"* means trade, commerce, transportation, or communication among the several States, or between any foreign country and any State or between any State and any place or ship outside thereof.

Exceptions

A. Facilitating or expediting payment to a foreign official, political party, or party official the purpose of which is to expedite or *to secure the performance of a routine governmental action* by a foreign official, political party, or party official.

B. The payment, gift, offer, or promise of anything of value that was made, *was lawful under the written laws and regulations of the foreign official's, political party's, party official's, or candidate's country;* or

C. The payment, gift, offer, or promise of anything of value that was made, was a *reasonable and bona fide expenditure,* such as travel and lodging expenses, incurred by or on behalf of a foreign official, party, party official, or candidate and was directly related to the promotion, demonstration, or explanation of products or services; or the execution or performance of a contract with a foreign government or agency thereof.

Penalties

A. Any domestic concern that violates this section shall be fined not more than $2,000,000 and shall be subject to a civil penalty of not more than $10,000 imposed in an action brought by the Attorney General.

B. Any officer or director of a domestic concern, or stockholder acting on behalf of such domestic concern, who willfully violates this section shall be fined not more than $100,000, or imprisoned not more than 5 years, or both.

C. Any employee or agent of a domestic concern who is a United States citizen, national, or resident or is otherwise subject to the jurisdiction of the United States (other than an officer, director, or stockholder acting on behalf of such domestic concern), and who willfully violates this section, shall be fined not more than $100,000, or imprisoned not more than 5 years, or both.

D. Any officer, director, employee, or agent of a domestic concern, or stockholder acting on behalf of such domestic concern, who violates this section shall be subject to a civil penalty of not more than $10,000 imposed in an action brought by the Attorney General.

E. *Whenever a fine is imposed upon any officer, director, employee, agent, or stockholder of a domestic concern, such fine may not be paid, directly or indirectly, by such domestic concern.*

Source: *U.S. Code,* Title 15—Commerce and Trade, Chapter 2B—Securities Exchanges.

PRESSURES FOR ETHICAL CONVERGENCE

Ethical convergence

Refers to the growing pressures for multinational companies to follow the same rules in managing ethical behavior and social responsibility.

In spite of the wide differences in cultures and in social institutions, there are growing pressures for multinational companies to follow the same rules in managing ethical behavior and social responsibility. This is called **ethical convergence**. There are three basic reasons for ethical convergence.

1. The growth of international trade and trading blocs, such as NAFTA (North American Free Trade Act) and the EC, creates pressures to have common ethical practices that transcend national cultures and institutional differences. Predictable interactions and behaviors among trading partners from different countries make trade more efficient.

2. Interaction between trading partners creates pressure for imitating the business practices of other countries. As the people from different cultural backgrounds increase their interactions, exposure to varying ethical traditions encourages people to adjust to, imitate, and adopt new behaviors and attitudes.

Multinational Management Challenge
Should Other Countries Play by U.S. Rules?

The United States has the strictest legal standards regarding bribery in international trade and direct investment. The United States also has a strong culture of legal monitoring and sanctions. Other countries do not have these traditions. For example, in Germany, in spite of its reputation for law and order,
bribery is tax deductible. However, the deduction requires names to be
named. Moreover, some international executives consider U.S. views hypo-
critical and naive. As one Airbus executive noted: "Each time we win a deal,
it's because of dirty tricks. Each time Boeing wins, it's because of a better
product." Airbus points out, for example, that the Clinton administration often used the influence of the U.S. government to help Boeing get airplane-
manufacturing contracts from the national airlines of other countries. Airbus
doesn't believe that it is just for the United States to demand that everyone
follow its practices regarding bribery and then allow the prestige and influence of the U.S. government to influence business decisions.

Sources: Based on *Business Week Online* 1995 and Vogel 1992.

3. Companies that do business throughout the world have employees from varied
    cultural backgrounds who need common standards and rules regarding how to
    behave. As such, multinational companies, especially the transnationals, often
    rely on their corporate culture to provide consistent norms and values that gov-
    ern ethical issues.

    Not only is there a moral pressure to eliminate corrupt activity, but there is, in-
    creasingly, a financial pressure. Extensive corruption costs money, makes businesses
    less competitive internationally, and risks embarrassing scandals. The Case in Point
    on page 124 shows how pressures from the international financial community and
    the flight of investment capital from Germany pressured Germany to change its
    laws regarding insider trading.

PRESCRIPTIVE ETHICS FOR THE MULTINATIONAL

**Prescriptive ethics
for multinationals**

*Suggested guidelines for
the ethical behavior of
multinational
companies.*

Donaldson, an expert in international business ethics, argues that the three moral
languages of avoiding harm, rights/duties, and the social contract should guide
multinational companies. He advocates **prescriptive ethics for multinationals**;
that is, multinationals should engage in business practices that avoid negative consequences to their stakeholders (e.g., employees, the local environment). While multinationals retain basic rights, such as seeking a fair profit, these rights also imply duties, such as providing a fair wage to local employees. The multinational also has a
social contract between itself and its stakeholders. This contract, even if taken for
granted, defines the nature of the relationships. For example, when a multinational
enters a country, it accepts the social contract to follow local laws.

These three moral languages are the easiest to specify in written codes such as
contracts and international laws. Donaldson believes that these moral languages are
most appropriate for managing ethical behaviors among culturally heterogeneous

No nation is free from ethical violations in business practices. However, there are wide differences in how national legal systems prosecute violations and the degree to which the public tolerates ethical violations. Some evidence now suggests that there is a worldwide trend to clean up business practices, especially unethical business relationships with government. The growing power of shareholders challenges the once cozy relationship between business and government, from Paris to Seoul to Mexico City. Ordinary citizens, prosecutors, and the press are challenging the corporate elite and clamoring for more ethical corporate governance. Consider the following examples.

Investigators in Korea found that thirty-five Korean *chaebol* (conglomerate) gave approximately $369 million in bribes to former President Roh Tae Woo. Leading the bribery list were the chairmen of giant *chaebol* Samsung (with $32 million) and Daewoo (with $31 million in bribes). These exposures and the resultant severe sentences are expected to reduce illegal payoffs in Korea. Additionally, they may make Korean businesses more competitive as companies will now compete based on merit and avoid the excess costs of bribery.

In Germany, sixty-five former and current employees at Opel were investigated for taking bribes from Opel's suppliers. Over two hundred people from forty suppliers are suspects in a kickback scheme with Opel. One German prosecutor now estimates that inflated public-works contracts in Germany cost the government over $7 billion a year.

In France, Alcatel was accused of a $100 million overbilling of its largest customer, France Telecom. Alcatel's chairman quickly resigned, facing more investigations into abuse of corporate funds and personal fraud.

At the international level, the World Bank and the IMF have stopped lending or threatened to stop lending to countries such as Kenya, Nigeria, and Indonesia where corruption and bribery has stifled economic growth. Twenty-nine members of the OECD and five nonmembers signed a "bribery convention," which, like the U.S. Foreign Corrupt Practices Act, requires each country to make it a crime bribing a foreign office to win or retain business.

Sources: Based on Brull and Dawson 1995; *Economist* 1999; Edmondson et al. 1995 and Rossant 1995.

---

multinationals—that is, regardless of their national-culture background, companies can agree with their stakeholders on the basic rules of moral behavior (Donaldson 1989, 1992a).

For Donaldson's ideas to work, there must be a code of conduct to guide the multinationals that is independent of national boundaries. These codes must include prescriptive and proscriptive rules to guide multinational behavior. Prescriptive rules tell multinational managers and companies what they should do, while proscriptive rules tell them what they cannot do.

Some scholars argue that such ethical guides currently exist based on various international agreements and on the codes of international governing bodies, such as the United Nations and the International Labor Office (Frederick 1991; Getz 1990).

Exhibit 4.8 on page 125 summarizes ethical stipulations for the multinational derived from the following international sources:

- The United Nations Universal Declaration of Human Rights
- The United Nations Code of Conduct on Transnational Corporations

In 1995, Germany adopted for the first time laws that outlawed insider trading on the stock market. Insider trading is a criminal offense with punishments of up to five years. To monitor potential violators, German lawmakers approved the setup of the Federal Supervisory Office with broad powers to investigate potential violations. Before this time, only an informal code governed relationships with the bourses. Often key market data were released to insiders before the data became public. So extensive was the insider knowledge that the market often moved before the market-affecting data were released.

Pressure from U.S. securities regulators, international portfolio managers, and the European Union forced the issue for the Germans. International traders were skeptical of dealing with an insider market, and some big German companies began to go outside the country in search of capital.

Source: Based on Templeman and Javetski 1994.

- The European Convention on Human Rights
- The International Chamber of Commerce Guidelines for International Investment
- The Organization for Economic Cooperation and Development Guidelines for Multinational Enterprises
- The Helsinki Final Act
- The International Labor Office Tripartite Declarations of Principles Concerning Multinational Enterprises and Social Policy

The principles in the code of conduct for the multinational shown in Exhibit 4.8 have two basic supporting rationales. The first rationale comes from the basic deontological principles dealing with human rights, such as the right to work and the right to be safe. To a large degree, the international agreements specify the rights and duties of multinational companies that are presumed to be transcultural—that is, the basic ethical principles apply for all, regardless of a company's country of origin or its current business location. The second rationale for the types of issues addressed in the code comes from the history of experiences in international business interactions (Frederick 1991). For example, because multinationals often ignore the environmental impact of their operations in other countries, several international agreements specify the duties of the multinational regarding the environment.

In spite of the existence of extensive agreements and organizations governing multinational ethical behavior, there are several reasons why multinationals may not follow the ethical principles summarized in Exhibit 4.8 (Frederick 1991):

- *Governments make agreements:* Most international agreements are between governments and not the multinationals themselves. However, multinationals do fall under the jurisdiction of the governments involved in the pacts.
- *The agreements have only voluntary compliance:* Without an international enforcement agency, some argue that it is impossible to expect multinationals to follow any code of ethical behavior (Velasquez 1992).
- *Not all governments subscribe to the agreements:* Governments often reflect their own geopolitical interests and cultural and religious biases. Even if party to the agreements governing multinational-company behaviors, governments may choose to ignore them.

Exhibit 4.8 A Code of Conduct for the Multinational Company

Respect Basic Human Rights and Freedoms

- Respect fundamental human rights of life, liberty, security, and privacy
- Do not discriminate on the basis of race, color, gender, religion, language, ethnic origin, or political affiliation
- Respect personal freedoms (e.g., religion, opinion)
- Respect local cultural values and norms

Minimize Any Negative Impact on Local Economic Policies

- Conform to local economic and development policies
- Avoid adverse effects on currencies and balance of payments
- Follow policies regarding local equity participation
- Provide truthful information for accurate taxation
- Pay fair taxes
- Source raw materials locally
- Reinvest profits in local economy

Maintain High Standards of Local Political Involvement

- Avoid illegal involvement in local politics
- Don't pay bribes or other improper payments
- Do not interfere in local government internal relations

Transfer Technology

- Enhance the transfer of technology to developing nations
- Adapt technologies to local needs
- Conduct local R&D when possible
- Grant fair licenses to use technology

Protect the Environment

- Follow local environmental-protection laws
- Actively protect the environment
- Repair damage to the environment done by company operations
- Help develop local standards
- Provide accurate assessments of environmental impact of the company
- Provide complete disclosure of the environmental effects of operations
- Develop standards to monitor environmental effects

Consumer Protection

- Follow local consumer-protection laws
- Ensure accurate and proper safety disclosures

Employment Practices

- Follow relevant manpower policies and employment laws of host nation
- Help create jobs in needed areas
- Increase local employment opportunities and standards
- Provide local workers stable employment and job security
- Promote equal employment opportunities
- Give priority to local national residents when possible
- Provide training opportunities at all levels for local employees
- Promote local nationals to management positions
- Respect local collective-bargaining rights
- Cooperate with local collective-bargaining units
- Give notice of plant closings
- Do not use threat of leaving country in collective-bargaining dealings
- Provide income protection to terminated workers
- Match or improve local standards of employment
- Protect employees with adequate health and safety standards
- Provide employees information on job-related health hazards

Sources: Adapted from Getz 1990 and Frederick 1991.

- *Each of the agreements is an incomplete moral guide to the company:* It is probably impossible to arrive at an agreement that can cover all the ethical consequences of a firm's operations.

The following Multinational Management Brief discusses one of the more recent multinational agreements to manage ethics by stopping bribery.

Although the sources of agreements that govern the ethical behavior of multinational companies are diverse and not always enforceable, the agreements are useful. They provide a safe guide to ethical management for multinational companies' managers. It is likely that, if one follows the code of conduct shown in Exhibit 4.8, both in individual behavior and in guiding a company, one will generally be on safe ethical and legal ground in nearly all situations.

The next section concludes this chapter with a focus on ethical decision making for the individual multinational manager.

Multinational Management Brief
The OECD Anti-Bribery Convention: Will it Work?

The OECD's Anti-Bribery Convention attempts to eliminate bribery in international commerce. Modeled after the U.S. Foreign Corrupt Practices Act, the agreement criminalizes bribery and eliminates incentives to bribe such as tax deductions for payments to foreign officials. By the year 2000, 32 countries ratified the convention. Full text of the convention is available at: http://www.oecd.org/daf/nocorruption/report.htm.

Unfortunately, anti-bribery agreements at the national level may not always reach local operations. Transparency International (2000) reports that 45 percent of business executives of major multinationals located in leading emerging market countries answered "have not heard about it" in a recent survey. This finding raises the issue of whether such multinational agreements can lead to effective compliance.

Sources: Based on Organization for Economic Cooperation and Development (2000) and Transparency International (2000).

THE ETHICAL DILEMMA IN MULTINATIONAL MANAGEMENT: HOW WILL YOU DECIDE?

The potentially wide differences in ethical systems and in how ethics are managed create dilemmas for multinational managers. This section looks first at the issue of what ethical system one should use—your own country's or that of the host country. It concludes with a description of an ethical decision model for the multinational manager.

ETHICAL RELATIVISM VERSUS ETHICAL UNIVERSALISM

Throughout our study of multinational management, this text shows the extensive effects of differences in cultural values on all areas of management. However, this is nowhere more apparent than in the difficulties multinational companies face in determining how to deal with ethical differences among the countries in which they do business. Do you impose your own country's ethical system everywhere you do business or do you follow the maxim, "When in Rome, do as the Romans do"?

In Chapter 2, the text introduced the concept of cultural relativism. As you remember, cultural relativism represents the philosophical position of the science of anthropology: All cultures are legitimate and viable as a means for people to guide their lives—that is, what people consider right or wrong, pretty or ugly, good or bad, depends on their cultural norms and values.

Ethical relativism

Theory that each society's view of ethics must be considered legitimate and ethical.

There is a similar concept in business ethics, called **ethical relativism**. Ethical relativism means that a multinational manager considers each society's view of ethics as legitimate and ethical. For example, if the people in one country believe something like assisted suicide to be morally wrong, then for them it is morally wrong. If, on the other hand, people from another country believe that assisted suicide is morally correct, then for them it is not immoral. For multinational companies, ethical relativism means that, when doing business in a country, managers need only follow local ethical conventions. Thus, for example, if bribery is an accepted way of doing business in a country, then it is okay for a multinational to follow local examples, even if it would be illegal at home.

Ethical universalism

Theory that there are basic moral principles that transcend cultural and national boundaries.

The opposite of ethical relativism is **ethical universalism**. Ethical universalism holds that there are basic moral principles that transcend cultural and national boundaries. All cultures, for example, have rules that prohibit murder, at least of their own people.

The difficulty in using ethical universalism as a guide for multinational business practices is that there is little agreement on which moral principles exist in all cultures. Moreover, even when the same principles are used, there is no guarantee that all societies use the principles in the same way. For example, two societies may prohibit murder. However, so that the group has a better chance of surviving, a society with food resources marginal for survival may force the aged to commit suicide or may kill newborn girls to keep the population down. They certainly do not consider this "murder," but an ethical way to ensure the survival of the group. Most societies tolerate some form of killing, such as in executions of criminals or in wars. Even though people die by human action, these acts are not defined as murder but as legitimate acts of society.

Convenient relativism

What occurs when companies use the logic of ethical relativism to behave any way they please, using the excuse of differences in cultures.

For the multinational company, however, there are practical problems for following either ethical relativism or ethical universalism. Some ethicists argue that cultural relativism, while a necessary condition for conducting unbiased anthropological research, cannot be applied to ethics. Thomas Donaldson, for example, argues that multinationals have a higher moral responsibility than ethical relativism (Donaldson 1992b). He notes that, at the extreme, ethical relativism can become "**convenient relativism**." Convenient relativism occurs when companies use the logic of ethical relativism to behave any way that they please, using the excuse of differences in cultures. Donaldson gives the example of child labor in developing countries. In some cases, children as young as seven work for a pittance wage producing products that eventually are used by large multinational companies.

Extreme moral universalism also has its pitfalls. The assumption that one can identify universal ethics that all people should follow can lead to a type of ethnocentrism that Donaldson calls cultural imperialism. That is, managers who assume that they know the correct and ethical ways of behaving can easily view the moral systems of foreign cultures as inferior or immoral. This is particularly dangerous when the multinational is a big and financially powerful company with subsidiaries located in the developing world.

INDIVIDUAL ETHICAL DECISION MAKING FOR THE MULTINATIONAL MANAGER

Although companies develop policies, procedures, organizational cultures, and business practices that have ethical consequences, individual managers ultimately must make decisions.

Economic analysis

Of an ethical problem, focuses on what is the best decision for a company's profits.

The first duty for a manager is to consider whether a decision makes business sense. This is called the **economic analysis**. In the economic analysis, the prime interest is what is the best decision for a company's profits. However, if profits alone guided ethical decision making, managers could worry little about how their decisions affected anyone except the owners of the company. Some argue that this is not ethics at all, since businesses could engage in deceptive and dangerous practices with only the marketplace to control their actions.

After considering the business impact of a decision, a multinational manager must consider the legal and ethical consequences of his or her actions (Hosmer 1987).

Exhibit 4.9 gives a decision flowchart that illustrates the issues multinational managers must consider beyond profits when confronted with ethical decisions.

Legal analysis

Of an ethical problem, focuses on only meeting legal requirements of host and parent countries.

In the **legal analysis** of an ethical problem, the manager focuses first on meeting the laws of the country in which his or her company is operating, or, if required, the home country as well. Should the law not forbid something, it is ethical. In a combination of pure economic and legal analyses, managers should seek to maximize profits within the confines of the letter of the law. The law in this sense provides the "rules of the game" under which companies and people compete. Since different countries have different legal systems, a multinational manager using only a legal analysis of an ethical problem is free to behave within the law in each country, provided that his or her own country does not require following its own laws. Some scholars, such as the Nobel Laureate Milton Friedman, believe that profit maximization—within the rules of the game of open and free competition—is the main ethical responsibility of business (Friedman 1970). Many multinational managers also believe that the legal analysis includes not only a test of whether a behavior or its consequences meet legal standards in the home and host countries, but also a comparison against international standards. These standards come from the international agreements among nations, identified earlier, and the resulting code, summarized in Exhibit 4.8.

Although managers in profit-making businesses must consider the economic and legal implications of any decision with ethical consequences, few managers fail to consider the additional ethical implications of any actions or practices with consequences for people. These additional issues include their individual moral beliefs on how to act, the company's policies regarding the proper way to behave in treating all constituents (e.g., customers, employees, society), and the cultural context of the ethical issue (Victor and Cullen 1988).

Thus, besides the economic and legal analysis, multinational managers must give an **ethical analysis** to problems. In an ethical analysis, one goes beyond simply responding to profit goals and legal regulations. To determine what is "*really* the right thing to do," managers take into account additional issues in their business decisions.

Ethical analysis

One that goes beyond focusing on profit goals and legal regulations.

The ethical analysis has three components: one's organization, the national culture in which the business operates, and personal ethical beliefs.

In the organizational ethical analysis, managers must look to their written codes of ethics and the unwritten norms of the company culture. Many organizations have ethical codes that specify the principles by which managers must guide their decision making and behaviors. When referring to the ethical code as a guide, a manager uses deontological ethical reasoning—you know and follow the written rules. In addition, all organizations have company cultures that have unwritten rules that prescribe or proscribe behaviors. In some companies, for example, all managers would know informal rules, such as, "Profit is more important than the environment as long as you follow the letter of the law." or "Give the bribe if it gets the job done and no one gets hurt or caught." A manager might better understand the ethical bases of the company's culture by understanding the moral language used. For example, is it maximizing the greatest welfare or is it avoiding harm?

Multinational managers are guests in other nations. As such, their ethical decision making must go beyond legal constraints and following company rules and cultural norms. The manager must ask himself or herself whether what they are doing is consistent with and respectful of local cultural norms. For example, should one have employees work on a religious holiday in one country because other units throughout the world are having regular business days?

A manager may begin these analyses at different points. For some issues, one may consider personal moral beliefs first. For other issues, it may make more sense

Exhibit 4.9

Decision Points for
Ethical Decision Making
in Multinational
Management

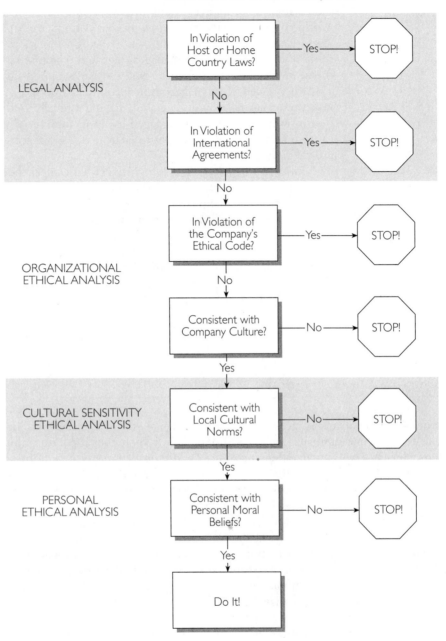

Is the Behavior or Its Consequence:

to consider the law. At some point, however, after considering all components in managerial decision making, the manager must make a personal moral judgment. Is it right for you? You are ultimately responsible. Most courts of law throughout the world will not accept the defense "The organization made me do it."

Thus, for the multinational manager, the purely ethical issues in a decision must be weighed against the economic and legal analyses that also influence the decision. A business must make a profit to survive, people don't want to go to jail or be fined, and most people want to behave ethically as they understand it. Often there will be no easy answer. For example, should a manager move a factory to a country with a cheaper labor force—even if it hurts the people who will lose their jobs? Should a multinational company sell potentially dangerous but useful products to a Third World country because the people in that country can only afford the cheaper but less safe products? Should a multinational company ignore the use of child labor by some of its suppliers, if the managers realize the children's families desperately need the money and their competitors will use these suppliers if they don't?

When faced with such complex conflicts among economics, law, and ethics, how do managers know if they are behaving ethically? Although there is no resolution to every ethical dilemma faced by every individual and in every culture, one aid to ethical decision making is to analyze one's decisions using philosophical ethical theories.

Unfortunately, there is no single accepted ethical theory or system that managers can use for a guide when they face difficult ethical problems. Philosophers have debated for millennia the merits of various systems. However, there are generally accepted ethical theories that managers can use to help understand ethical problems and the nature of their ethical decisions.

Although an ethical analysis such as that suggested in Exhibit 4.8 does not give one the "right" answer to an ethical problem, it does help one understand the reasons behind ethical choices. It also raises the businessperson's awareness regarding the ethical nature of business decisions.

Summary and Conclusions

The multinational manager faces ethical challenges similar to the domestic manager, but magnified by the complexity of working in different countries and cultures. Part of this chapter provided essential background information on business ethics useful for ethics management in all settings. Understanding the relationship between ethics and social responsibility, how ethical philosophies underlay much of our ethical reasoning, and the differences among financial, legal, and ethical analyses provide a starting point for understanding international business ethics.

Unlike the domestic-only manager, the multinational manager must be able to assess how a country's social institutions and culture will affect his or her ability to manage ethical behavior. The examples showed that differences in legal and religious institutions and basic cultural values often lead to different perceptions of what is ethical in business. Although there is some evidence of a convergence in business ethics due to the increase in international trade and investment, a multinational manager can never be too sensitive to issues as important as moral behavior in another culture.

Besides understanding the cultural setting in which they operate, multinational managers can never ignore their home country laws. In this regard, the U.S. manager probably faces the strictest constraints. The FCPA represents an important law that constrains U.S. managers from behaving in ways that, while accepted in other societies, are off limits to U.S. managers. All multinational managers, regardless of national origin, should be aware of the international agreements to which their country is party. Following the summary of these agreements, as shown in Exhibit 4.8, will likely help managers avoid legal and ethical difficulties in their international operations.

The chapter concluded with a decision model for making ethical decisions in a multinational setting. Although the model does not tell you what to do, it does provide a variety of issues that a manager should consider. Managing ethically in the international environment is not always easy but certainly it is a challenge that will continue to grow with increasing interactions among nations.

Discussion Questions

1. Discuss some of the issues that make international business ethics more complex than domestic business ethics.

2. How do legal and ethical analyses differ? Give some examples. Can a manager behave ethically just by following the host country's laws? Explain.

3. Discuss the difference between teleological and deontological theories of ethics. Give examples of how an international manager might appeal to either type of theory when faced with the opportunity to offer a bribe.

4. How do social institutions and culture affect the practice of business ethics in different countries? How do these differences affect managers who take the moral positions of ethical relativism and ethical universalism?

5. Discuss the arguments regarding whether businesses from other nations should follow the U.S. FCPA.

6. Discuss reasons why there is a trend toward a universal code of business ethics.

Chapter Internet Activity

Explore the extent and conditions of child labor around the world by visiting the following sites and others that you find. Consider the state of international agreements regarding child labor and the conditions that may make child labor necessary in some countries. Consider how you would react if your job evaluation was based on low cost production and you had supervisory responsibility for factories using low paid child labor.

http://www.dol.gov/dol/ilab/public/programs/iclp/aboutcl.htm

http://www.ilo.org/public/english/comp/child/index.htm

Internet Sites

Selected Companies in the Chapter
Daewoo Corp.   http://www.daewoo.com/
Levi's   http://www.levistrauss.com/
Nordstrom Inc.   http://www.nordstrom-pta.com/
Opel   http://www.opel.com/
Reebok Inc.   http://www.reebok.com/
Sears Inc.   http://www.sears.com/

Sites on Ethical Issues for Multinationals on the World Wide Web
http://www.cceia.org/   *Carnegie Council on Ethics and International Affairs.*

http://www.transparency.de   *Transparency International monitors business corruption worldwide.*

http://www.iabs.net/   *International Association for Business and Society.*

http://www.dol.gov/dol/ilab/public/Programs/iclp/welcome.html   *The International Child Labor Study Office.*

http://www.ciesin.org/   *Social Indicators of Development, 1995. The World Bank's most recent assessment of the social effects of economic development.*

http://www.heritage.org/heritage/index/   *Most recent Index of Economic Freedom.*

http://www.ilo.org   *International Labour Organization provides data on labor conditions, human rights, labor laws, and even translations of labor terms in several languages.*

Chapter Activity: Rex Lewis's Ethical Dilemma

Step 1: Reread the section on Thomas Donaldson's views on moral languages.

Step 2: Read the following scenario.

Rex Lewis is a 25-year-old manager for ICS Corp., a small U.S. manufacturer of dietary supplements. After graduation, Mr. Lewis worked at company headquarters in Lexington, Nebraska, in a variety of positions. As a former international business major, Mr. Lewis jumped at the chance to take a position as country manager in Matinea. Mr. Lewis studied the Matinean language for four years and visited the country for a summer while an undergraduate. He feels confident that he can handle this position since he has both the managerial and cultural experience.

ICS's major product is SUPALL, a dietary supplement that is inexpensive to produce and can provide children with all of their basic nutritional needs. This product is very attractive to poor countries such as Matinea, where agricultural production is not sufficient to feed the population and recent droughts have made the situation even worse. Although cheaper than a well-rounded basic diet, one child's monthly supply of SUPALL costs about one-quarter of an average worker's salary at current prices, and most families are quite large.

In his first week in Matinea, Mr. Lewis makes a variety of startling discoveries. In spite of the relatively high price of SUPALL, demand in the Matinean market is quite strong. Moreover, ICS is making a 50 percent return on SUPALL! Now Mr. Lewis realizes why the revenues from SUPALL have been able to support his company's crucial R&D research on other products. When he worked back in the States, the CEO told him personally that, if they don't come up with new products soon, the big companies will soon have a SUPALL copy and the price will fall drastically.

Mr. Lewis, who considers himself a good Christian, begins to wonder whether the price is fair for the Matineans. The price of SUPALL is cheaper than food, but it takes virtually all a family's income to buy it. Yet, ICS needs the profits to survive. Mr. Lewis has the authority to set prices in the country, but he must justify his decision to headquarters back in the United States.

Step 3: Divide the class into six teams, one for each moral language. Each team represents a version of the ICS Corp. but with a corporate culture dominated by one of the moral languages.

Step 4: As a team, review Exhibit 4.9 and conduct the relevant analyses. Come to a consensus and give a recommendation to Rex Lewis.

Step 5: Present and discuss your findings with the whole class.

References

Becker, Helmut, and David J. Fritzsche. 1987. "Business ethics: A cross-cultural comparison of managers' attitudes." *Journal of Business Ethics* 6:289–95.

Borrus, Amy, Stewart Toy, and Peggy Salz-Trautman. 1995. "Investigations: A world of greased palms." *Business Week Online*, November 6.

Brull, Steven, and Margaret Dawson. 1995. "Why Korea's cleanup won't catch on." *Business Week Online*, International Edition, December 18.

Buchholz, Rogene A. 1989. *Fundamental Concepts and Problems in Business Ethics*. Englewood Cliffs, N.J.: Prentice Hall.

Business Week. 1983. "The arbitrary act splits executives," September 19, 16.

Business Week Online. 1995. International Editions. Editorial, "Germany, where bribery is tax deductible." August 7.

Cullen, John B., Bart Victor, and Carroll Stephens. 1989. "An ethical weather report: Assessing the organization's ethical climate." *Organizational Dynamics* 18:50–62.

Donaldson, Thomas. 1989. *The Ethics of International Business*. New York: Oxford University Press.

———. 1992a. "The language of international corporate ethics." *Business Ethics Quarterly* 2:271–81.

———. 1992b. "Can multinationals stage a universal morality play?" *Business and Society Review*, 51–55.

Doxey, John. 1995. "Bringing the Koran to the corner office." *Business Week Online*, February 13.

Economist. 1999. "A global war against bribery." *Economist.com*, January 16:Story_ID=182081.

Edmondson, Gail, Silvia Sansoni, Karen Lowry Miller, and Linda Bernier. 1995. "Europe's new morality." *Business Week Online*, International Edition, December 18.

Frederick, William C. 1991. "The moral authority of transnational corporate codes." *Journal of Business Ethics* 10:165–77.

Friedman, Milton. 1970. "The social responsibility of business is to increase its profits." *New York Times Magazine*, September 13, 122–26.

Getz, Kathleen A. 1990. "International codes of conduct: An analysis of ethical reasoning." *Journal of Business Ethics* 9:567–78.

Graham, John. 1983. "Foreign Corrupt Practices Act: A manager's guide." *Columbia Journal of World Business* 18:89–94.

Hosmer, Larue Tone. 1987. *The Ethics of Management.* Homewood, Ill.: Irwin.

Koretz, Gene. 1996. "Bribes can cost the U.S. an edge: In some spots, honesty doesn't pay." *Business Week Online*, April 15.

Marion, Vivian. 1996. "What's fit to buy?" *Lewiston Morning Tribune,* June 30, 1e, 5e.

Mendenhall, Mark E., Betty Jane Punnet, and David Ricks. 1994. *Global Management.* Cambridge, Mass.: Blackwell.

Organization for Economic Cooperation and Development. 2000. http://www.oecd.org/daf/nocorruption/instruments.htm.

Rossant, John. 1995. "Dirty money." *Business Week Online*, International Edition, December 18.

Schlegelmilch, Bobo B., and Diana C. Robertson. 1995. "The influence of country and industry on ethical perceptions of senior executives in the U.S. and Europe." *Journal of International Business Studies*, Fourth Quarter, 859–81.

Templeman, John, and Bill Javetski. 1994. "*Achtung!* Insider trading is a crime." *Business Week Online,* International Edition, December 5.

Transparency International. 2000. "1999 bribe payers index." http://www.transparency.de/documents/cpi/index.html.

U.S. Code, Title 15-Commerce and Trade, Chapter 2B-Securities Exchanges, Section 78dd-1.

Velasquez, Manuel. 1992. "International business, morality, and the common good." *Business Ethics Quarterly* 2:27–40.

Victor, Bart, and John B. Cullen. 1988. "The organizational bases of ethical work climates." *Administrative Science Quarterly* 33:101–25.

Vogel, David. 1992. "The globalization of business ethics: Why America remains distinctive." *California Management Review* 35:30–49.

Zachary, G. Pascal. 1994. "Levi tries to make sure contract plants in Asia treat workers well." *Wall Street Journal,* July 28, A1, A5.

Part 1 Integrating Case 1

Organizational and National Cultures in a Polish/U.S. Joint Venture

This case looks at differences in cultural values and beliefs of Polish and U.S. managers employed in a joint venture in Poland. The case comes from data collected from interviews with Polish and expatriate U.S. managers.

BACKGROUND

THE U.S./POLISH COMPANY

The company was a joint venture with a Polish partner and a wholly owned subsidiary of a U.S. multinational corporation located in Poland. The U.S. company started operations in Poland in 1990. The joint venture started two years later.

The joint venture was a small, nonbureaucratic organization with 140 employees. Everybody knew each other and a family type of relationship existed among the managers. Both local Polish managers and U.S. expatriates reported a friendly work climate even though all top managerial positions were held by the U.S. expatriates.

POLISH ATTITUDES REGARDING U.S. MANAGEMENT

When asked why they chose to work for this company, Polish managers often described U.S. business as "real," "healthy," "tough," "honest," and "fair," although they had never had the opportunity to work with U.S. Americans before. In addition, they felt that features of Polish national culture such as "ability to work in difficult situations" and "experience of struggle with hardship of communism" combined well with American management expertise. In addition, Polish managers reported that working for a U.S. company was a major bonus for their future success and careers. Multinational corporations give employment security because they have a low risk of bankruptcy. In comparison with state companies, the organization was perceived as having a very efficient organizational design dedicated to efficiency and profit making. Reflecting on his experience in state-owned operations, a Polish manager from the Customer Service Operation unit noted:

Source: This case was prepared in 1992 by Krystyna Joanna Zaleska of the Canterbury Business School, University of Kent, Canterbury, England, while a postgraduate student at the Central European University, Prague. Reprinted with permission of the author.

The basic difference between state companies and this company is that the organization of U.S. firms contains many necessary and indispensable elements. Whereas, in Polish companies, many elements were not needed and, even in some cases, disturbed the effective functioning of the company as a whole. Profit was not a major goal, only apparent activities. Many jobs and even whole companies were created when they were not needed. They were unproductive. Here we have only jobs and departments which help the company to function effectively.

The Polish managers expressed a great deal of enthusiasm and excitement for learning U.S. business know-how. Polish managers felt that they learned something new each day, not only from formal training but also from on-the-job training. Often Polish managers compared the company to a university. For the first time since entering a market economy, they felt they had the opportunity to learn business functions such as marketing, distribution, and logistics. These pro-American attitudes created an eagerness among the Polish managers to accept expatriate ideas concerning new work priorities. The attitudes also worked to legitimate the power and leadership of the U.S. Americans in the company.

The Polish managers believed that, unlike under the previous communist system, the new organization encouraged the development of the individual. They believed that the U.S. system of management inspired self-expression and achievement. It respected individuals and their unique personalities. There was a strong belief that hard work would bring success. Talented people who were willing to work could advance and succeed.

These organizational values were quite new for the Polish managers. In their previously state-controlled organizations, competence and good performance were not the main bases for a promotion and compensation. Party membership was the key to a successful managerial career. Rewards and promotions depended on fulfilling a political role rather than on achieving economic goals.

THE CULTURAL CONFLICTS

In spite of the very positive attitudes of the Polish managers toward a U.S. management style, there were still many conflicts between expectations based on Polish cultural traditions and an organizational culture based on the national culture of the United States.

MANAGERIAL SELECTION

Many Polish employees wanted to be hired immediately as managers, without any experience in basic business functions. The magic word "manager" was associated by them with a higher status and success. U.S. managers, however, felt that "you had to earn your spurs first." The U.S. expatriate District Manager recalled:

People applying for positions in the sales department do not want to do basic business first, to be a sales representative, they want to be immediately managers. People that I interview want to be only managers. How you can manage sales representatives if you don't know what they do? They lack a concrete answer for my question.

MERIT, AGE AND SENIORITY

The corporate culture encouraged rewards primarily based on competence in key skills and performance against objective criteria. Both local and expatriate managers believed that individuals were appointed and promoted based on their knowledge and professional expertise. This situation often resulted in much younger managers having older subordinates. As one U.S. manager from the Finance Department stated:

The company gives a lot of authority to young people very quickly. You never know, the guy who is looking younger than you could be a vice president already.

Although Polish managers appreciated promotions based on competence, the issue of age presented some problems of adjustment. Traditional expectations hold that, when one is young, it is impossible to be knowledgeable and have the necessary experience and competence to manage successfully. As a Polish assistant manager from the Marketing Department admitted:

I prefer to have an older boss because it would be very stupid if I have a boss younger than me. He has less life experience and a shorter marriage. He is younger and he is not authority to me. I would prefer someone who has more life experience. I realize that it is a very Polish thing that I find this to be a problem.

THE SALARY SYSTEM

Polish managers expressed difficulty in adjusting to the confidentiality of the new salary system. The Polish and U.S. managers differed in the beliefs regarding what information was personal and what information should be public. Polish managers wanted to know as much about each other's salaries as possible. They had no problems asking another employee about exactly how much they were paid. To the Polish managers, this served as a means of establishing their relative status. As a Polish assistant Brand Manager indicated:

I like this system but I would like to know how I am in comparison with the others. If I knew that the person who works together with me had a higher salary than me, I would be very unhappy.

For the expatriate U.S. Americans, however, it was not part of the company culture to reveal explicit salary information. Salary information was considered personal and confidential. Most felt that revealing salary information disrupted the family climate of the organization. Instead, the Americans expressed faith in the system of assessment and reward allocation. As the expatriate head of the Finance Department noted:

Poles make mistakes when they say: "Americans don't share salaries in this system." I would say it is not that straightforward at all. In the American system, in our company's system, we don't share specifics on what any one person makes. We try very hard to share the system by which you make more salary. We make it very clear that your salary is based on your performance. If you perform well you will make a lot of money.

TEAM GOALS

Working not only for your own interests but also for the success of the team or the whole company was a challenge for many Polish managers. This was especially true for those who had their initial managerial experiences in a state-controlled economy. One Polish manager noted:

Americans want to hire the best, because the organization will gain from them and you as a boss should be not afraid if you hire a person who is more clever than you. You will benefit from it because the company will benefit. In state companies you had to protect yourself by not cooperating—a new, better employee was your potential enemy.

Another Polish assistant Marketing Manager mentioned:

In a state company, if somebody has a problem, he or she solves it with their own interests in mind. Here we are thinking in terms of the benefit of the whole company. I made a mistake and I regarded it as my mistake because I was responsible for it. But the problem was judged [by the Americans] as a problem and loss for all of us. This is a different way of thinking, and this is the attitude of this company. Success belongs to everybody and so does failure. This is better than making one person responsible for it.

THE PSYCHOLOGICAL CONTRACT

From the perception of the Polish managers, the organization required them to accept a new psychological contract between organization and the individual. On the one hand, they felt positive about the degree of personal involvement and responsibility in the daily activities of company affairs. On the other hand, they were confused where to draw the line between professional and private lives. Many of the Polish managers felt that, for them to succeed as employees, the organization demanded too much of their private lives. As the Polish Marketing Manager said:

Americans look differently at the firm. They associate themselves very closely with it. They are part of the firm. In the past I never felt such a relationship with the firm.

Another Polish District Manager mentioned:

This new way of thinking, that you have to have a strong psychological connection with the firm, surprised me. You have to show you are interested. In the past you escaped from your job as quickly as possible.

TRUST

A U.S. cultural trait found surprising by Polish employees was the perception of an underlying good faith in people. Both the company culture and the expatriate managers had positive valuations regarding the intentions of people within the organization. As a Polish accountant stated:

What was new for me was that Americans have the assumption that you are acting for the good of the firm and that you are honest and that people are good. If you go to a restaurant for a business meal, nobody will tell you that you are nasty and that you used the company money and did it for a bad purpose.

A Polish assistant Brand Manager added:

A positive attitude toward people, trust in people—this is a basis for everything. Americans don't wait to catch you in a mistake. We are more suspicious of people. Our immediate assumption is that a person wants to do something bad.

The Polish managers expressed much more negative attitudes regarding the nature of people. These were evidenced in many aspects of the daily business life of the organization: subordinate–superiors ("My boss wants to harm me"), employee–peers ("My colleagues would only criticize me"), customer–product ("Americans are trying to sell us bad products"), employee–product ("I don't believe in the value of this product"). A U.S. expatriate Brand Manager describing the Polish managers indicated:

I have never met a group of people that was more skeptical of the future and more distrusting. Everyone we do business with is convinced that we are dumping a less quality product on the market. The Polish customer is very skeptical. They don't believe that they can get products as good as anybody else in the world.

Distrust, fear, and a disbelief that the boss wishes well for the employees were common attitudes observed by the U.S. expatriates. One U.S. expatriate from Customer Service Operations remarked:

Sometimes they [the Polish managers] don't understand that the company is trying to do the right things for individuals. Sometimes there will be questions which assume that the employer is going to take advantage of them and is going to treat locals badly. It is not a good assumption that the company and manager are not trying to help them if they have a problem.

INFORMALITY

U.S. managers valued blunt and direct speaking. Saying exactly what you mean was considered a virtue, and the U.S. managers had a low tolerance for ambiguity. Therefore, expatriate managers took most explanations at face value. Reacting to this, Polish managers often described Americans as very "open," "direct," "spontaneous," and "natural" during communication. However, this style of communication clashed with the indirect communication habits of Polish employees. As the American head of the Marketing Department stated:

Communication with Polish employees is difficult, especially when an employee has a problem. There is a general unwillingness to talk directly about oneself and one's problems. Poles will gladly talk about somebody else. They will not talk about their own needs. They don't like direct questions about things which are important to them. Perhaps it is considered impolite, too bold, or inappropriate for them.

Polish managers adapted to the U.S. directness by developing an informal network of communication among themselves. This informal network served as a buffer between the U.S. and Polish managers. To deal with their U.S. superiors, Polish managers first talked among themselves. Then one person would become responsible for going to a U.S. manager and telling him or her about someone else's problems. Expatriate managers found it unusual when subordinates who needed to communicate problems resorted to this informal channel. However, this buffer in communication provided a comfort zone for the Polish managers. As the Polish assistant Marketing Manager noted:

Poles more easily criticize things among themselves, but it is difficult for them to criticize things in the presence of Americans. It is as if they don't believe in their strengths, and are afraid that their opinions are either untrue or irrational. They are afraid of being funny.

Americans also introduced an informal style of communication by addressing everyone in the office on a first-name basis. Expatriates expressed the belief that their organizational culture provides an opportunity to "lead by competence, not by formality in relationships between superiors and subordinates." They were proud of their openness and equality in forming business relations. To the expatriates, those Polish managers who resisted the informality appeared to be cold and distrusting. Expatriates interpreted it as the "director syndrome," or an example of an attitude from the communist-controlled past. The expatriate head of the Sales Department described it as follows:

I respect their history. I respect the cultural aspects. Every time they call me "Mister Director" I remind them to call me by my first name. I am constantly telling them that I have a culture, too. This company has a culture, one that I want to build here. I don't like the environment that formality fosters and the environment that it creates. It is a barrier for effective communication. You almost have too much respect, and then you stop talking to me, soon you stop coming and saying, "I have a problem."

The majority of Polish managers adjusted to the norm of a first-name basis very quickly in dealing with the Americans. However, this did not mean that they wished to be on a first-name basis when speaking among Polish managers, especially with their Polish subordinates. Using first names for older people or for superiors is not a Polish norm. Some Polish managers were afraid that they would lose the ability to lead by being so informal. They believed that distance between superiors and subordinates helped them in direct management of lower staff. The Polish head of the Human Resource Department said:

There are some people in the firm with whom I will never be on a first-name basis. I am on a first-name basis with some people and on a Ms./Mr. basis with others. I don't know why, but I will not change that.

Informality also contrasted with Polish views that managers should symbolically show their status and success. Polish managers gave much value to formality, titles, and signs of status, such as having a good make of car. Superiors were expected to have these trappings as a demonstration of their authority over subordinates. In contrast, the U.S. expatriates regarded many of these status symbols as counterproductive and meaningless. A U.S. Brand Manager mentioned:

Poles are passionate about getting ahead in status. People are looking for examples of badges to wear for the rest of the populace to know that you have made it. My boss must be in a big car. "What car are you going to drive?" I was asked by a Pole in the first meeting in Poland.

POSITIVE FEEDBACK ON THE JOB

There were significant differences between Polish managers and expatriate Americans in the type of feedback given on the job. Consistent with U.S. views of management practices, the U.S. managers were quick to recognize achievements publicly and privately. Polish managers were generally positive about this approach and perceived it as motivating. However, in spite of this reaction, positive feedback was not a popular management technique among the Polish managers. They preferred to give criticism and generally negative feedback in front of subordinates and peers. Reacting to the U.S. approach, a Polish District Manager described the situation as follows:

If you are good, Americans can send you a congratulatory letter. Once I had got such a letter from an American colleague of mine even though he had no particular responsibility for my job. He was not my boss. I would never think of doing so. It was so spontaneous.

CONCLUSIONS

Coming from a culture that lacked experience and contact with U.S. businesses before 1989, Polish managers generally had positive but stereotypical views of U.S. business practices. In the short term, such attitudes played a highly motivating role in attracting managers to the joint venture. In the long term, however, despite the initial enthusiasm, basic cultural differences may lead to disillusionment among Polish managers.

CASE QUESTIONS FOR DISCUSSION

1. How can the joint venture managers take advantage of the initial enthusiasm of the Polish managers to build a stronger organization?
2. What cultural adaptations would you suggest to the U.S. expatriate managers regarding their management styles?
3. Using the Hofstede and the value orientations cultural models, how can you explain some of the cultural differences noted in the case?

Part 1 Integrating Case 2

Tee-Shirts and Tears: Third World Suppliers to First World Markets

"The hottest places in hell are reserved for those who, in a period of moral crisis, maintain their neutrality."

—*Dante*

Recent media attention has heightened our awareness of labor conditions in third world countries. While Americans otherwise may have been able to write off substandard labor conditions as another case of cultural variations, these recent cases garnered domestic interest as a result of the parties involved. Their names are about as American as apple pie: The Gap, Kathie Lee Gifford, even Michael Jordan. These are the contractors, the investors, the spokespeople who represent "sweatshops" where, allegedly, young girls are allowed only two restroom visits per day and, allegedly, the days sometimes consist of twenty-one straight hours of work.

LABOR CONDITIONS IN THE UNITED STATES

America's garment industry today grosses $45 billion per year and employs more than one million workers.[1] Uproar began in the Fall of 1995 when Secretary of Labor Robert Reich announced the names of several large retailers who may have been involved in an El Monte, California sweatshop operation. Notwithstanding the fact that the retailers are not liable for the conditions if they have no knowledge of them, the companies involved in this situation agreed to adopt a statement of principles which would require their suppliers to adhere to U.S. federal labor laws.[2]

Reich followed this announcement with an appearance on the *Phil Donahue Show* where he discussed a situation at another plant that employed Thai workers at less than $1.00 per hour and kept its workers behind a barbed-wire fence. Retailers respond that it is difficult, if not impossible to police their suppliers and

Source: This case was prepared by Laura Pincus Hartman, Kellstadt Graduate School of Business, DePaul University, as a basis for classroom discussion rather than to illustrate either effective or ineffective handling of an administrative situation. Copyright © 1997 by Laura Pincus Hartman.

Copyright South-Western and Thomson Learning Custom Publishing (ISBN 0-324-00303-X). For information regarding this and other CaseNet® cases, please visit CaseNet® on the World Wide Web at http://casenet.thomson.com.

subcontractors, who may total more than 20,000 in some cases. And the pressures of the situation are only becoming worse. The apparel industry, which has borne the brunt of Reich's focus, is highly competitive, and extremely labor-intensive. Competition from companies in other countries that do not impose similar labor condition requirements is fierce. Consequently, one is not surprised to learn that a 1994 Labor Department spot check of garment operations in California found that 93% had health and safety violations.[3]

Manufacturers may have a bit more to be concerned about than retailers. Reich has recently invoked a little-used provision in the Fair Labor Standards Act that holds manufacturers liable for the wrongful acts of their suppliers and that allows for the confiscation of goods produced by sweatshop operations.

Reich has now appealed to the retailers and manufacturers alike to conduct their own random spot checks. "We need to enlist retailers as adjunct policemen. At a time when business says to government, 'Get off our back. We can do it ourselves,' we're giving them the opportunity," Reich notes.[4] In June, 1995, Reich established a consortium to police working conditions made up of manufacturers. The group, called "Compliance Alliance," will police contractors conducting regular audits and will identify firms that pay less than minimum wage or otherwise violate the provisions of the Fair Labor Standards Act.[5]

The Clinton Administration's voluntary Model Business Principles, published in May, 1995, are relevant to this discussion. The principles encourage all businesses to adopt and implement voluntary codes of conduct for doing business around the world and suggest appropriate code coverage. In addition, under former secretary Robert Reich's direction, the Department of Labor has established a "No Sweat" campaign to encourage American apparel manufacturers to end sweatshop labor throughout the world.[6] The campaign is based on the belief that consumers will be willing to pay more for garments under a manufacturer guarantee on the label that the product was made without sweatshop labor. On the other hand, critics of the campaign claim that the proposed label is like "the Good Housekeeping seal of approval to a kinder, gentler sweatshop,"[7] and that the agreement to monitor conditions and to use these labels does not go far enough, basically calling for practices already adopted by firms.

AMERICAN ATTENTION DRIFTS TOWARD OTHER COUNTRIES

Neil Kearney, general secretary of the International Textile, Garment and Leather Workers' Federation, describes the garment workplace as follows:

The reality today is that most of the 30 million jobs in the fashion industry around the world are low paid, often based in export processing zones where worker rights are usually suppressed. Wages are frequently below the subsistence level and falling in real terms. . . . Management by terror is the norm in many countries. Workers are routinely shoved, beaten, and kicked, even when pregnant. Attempts to unionize are met with the utmost brutality, sometimes with murder.[8]

Once the American public considered its own conditions, it looked to other countries to see how labor was treated there. Following Reich's slap on the hand to American manufacturers, media attention turned toward the conditions in third world countries and toward American responsibility for or involvement in those conditions. In 1970, there were 7,000 multinational companies in the world. Today, there are more than 35,000.[9] The topic of conditions in those multinationals was destined for afternoon talk shows once it was announced that television personality Kathie Lee Gifford endorsed a line of clothing that had been made for Wal-Mart in Honduran sweatshops. These operations employed underage and pregnant women for more than 20-hour days at $0.31 per hour. The conditions were extremely hot and no worker was allowed to speak during the entire day.

The situation was brought to the attention of the press by Charles Kernaghan, director of the National Labor Committee based in New York City. Kernaghan informed Gifford, and the press, of the conditions in the plant and asked her to respond. Gifford's immediate response was to immediately break off her relationship with the company.[10] Unfortunately, this is not what is always best for the exploited workers. Instead, Kernaghan impressed upon her the need to remain involved and to use her position and reputation to encourage a change in the conditions at the plants.

These arguments may remind the reader of those waged several years ago regarding divestment from South Africa. Proponents of investment argued that the only way to effect change would be to remain actively involved in the operations of the South African business community. Others argued that no ethical company should pour money into a country where apartheid conditions were allowed to exist. The same arguments can and have been made about conducting business in third world countries, and Gifford found herself right in the middle of them.

THE EL SALVADORAN LABOR ENVIRONMENT

El Salvador is a country that has been ravaged by internal conflicts culminating in a civil war that lasted for many years. In 1992, with the advent of peace, the country sought to rebuild what it had lost during wartime and is now considered one of the fastest growing economies in Latin America.[11] The objective of the El Salvadorans involved in the rebuilding process was to help the poor to overcome the conditions of poverty, dependence and oppression that they had experienced during the conflict. While the objectives of private investors may be different, all seem to share a common interest in social stability and development. Economist Louis Emmerij notes that the leading cause of social unrest is "the lack of sufficient and renumerative employment opportunities, bad living conditions, and the lack of perspective and hope."[12]

In developing countries like El Salvador, long-term strategies for improving a poor household's ability to generate disposable income on a sustained basis must consider if households have the skills, education, and know-how to allow them to operate in the market. These strategies include support for training and education, access to markets and access to technology and credit. A large part of the labor problem in the *maquiladores* is the lack of agreement between the workers and management as to the minimum level of productivity expected per day, the level of compensation for a worker who achieves that level, and who should assume the burden of training in order to increase productivity.

Yet, low wages are the prime magnet for multinational firms coming to El Salvador. In 1990, a glossy full-color advertisement appeared in a major American apparel trade magazine showing a woman at a sewing machine and proclaiming, "Rosa Martinez produces apparel for U.S. markets on her sewing machine in El Salvador. *You* can hire her for 57 cents an hour." One year later, the same ad announced that Rosa's salary had gone down—"*You* can hire her for 33 cents an hour."[13] It appears that the publicists felt that Rosa's salary originally looked too high, in the eyes of the market players.

Critical to understanding these conflicts is an understanding of the Salvadoran culture itself. Salvadoran workers are not exempt from the consequences of their history. When they enter the work place, they expect to be exploited and do not trust management. In addition, as a result of the repressive conditions in El Salvador during the war, the society suffers from a general lack of candor and a tendency on the part of individuals to protect themselves by not telling the truth.[14] But this quality is different from the deception that occurs in American business dealings. In this situation, it serves as a means of self-protection in a culture that offers little else. Moreover, the government does not protect individual and business interests, thereby allowing cartels to develop, flourish, and continue.

The author of this case had the opportunity to travel to El Salvador in 1996 in order to observe a class in financial administration at an El Salvadoran university. During the course of a quiz in the class, the professor had reason to leave the classroom for a moment. Upon his return, he found that the students were now collaborating on the answers to the quiz. During the discussion that later ensued regarding the students' actions, the students articulated a need to help each other to succeed. They felt that they should bind together in order to help them all to move forward. If this meant helping a colleague who did not have time to study because he had to work to support his family, in addition to attending school, that seemed acceptable, if not necessary and ethical.[15]

During that same course, the graduate students (most, if not all, of whom worked full time in professional positions) were asked to identify the principal barriers to trust in Salvadoran business relationships, and the means by which those barriers could be broken down. Students responded as follows (translated from Spanish):

One barrier is that the big businesses are formed at the level of families and friends that form a close nucleus, prohibiting others from entering.

The government does not enact laws to guarantee business interests and growth without the intervention of stronger, "bully" businesses.

There is a failure of information—only certain people have access to the most important, business-related information. There is no requirement that business share information, even at a level that would mimic the American SEC requirements.

Create legal mechanisms that sanction companies violating the rules. These sanctions do not exist. Companies use illicit means to take advantage of their competitors and employing the same means is the only way to compete.

The period since the war has seen an increase in vandalism at an individual and corporate level, making it difficult to carry on a business.[16]

Consider the expectation of conflict in this scenario recounted by Fr. David Blanchard, Pastor of the Our Lady of Lourdes Church in Calle Real Epiphany Cooperative Association:

In February of 1994, the cooperative had a serious labor conflict. The women became quite adept at sewing lab coats. But in February, 1994, when the only contract available was for sewing hospital bathrobes, a serious labor conflict arose. Unfortunately, the women who were elected by their peers to negotiate with the contractor made some serious errors in judgment when they calculated the time required to sew this item.

At the time, some women were earning 80 colones daily (twice the minimum wage). Most were making 50 colones. Only a few apprentices were making less than the minimum wage.

With the transition to sewing bathrobes, production and therefore income, was cut in half. Six of the highest wage earners subsequently staged a sit-down strike at their machines, claiming that they were being oppressed.

Father Blanchard asked, "Who negotiated your contract?"

"Our representatives," they said.
"Who elected your representatives?"
"We did."
"Who will suffer if this work is not completed?"
"We will."

These women had entered this project with no prior skills. They had received high-quality and expensive technical, legal and social training. They were all self-employed, but when their wages plunged, they felt oppressed, frustrated and angry, and ended up leaving the cooperative. . . . Some of these women will continue to suffer in poverty. It is certain that they are victims. But they are the victims of hundreds of years of oppression and not of the immediate circumstances sewing hospital bathrobes. They responded to the problems created by the lack of education and their lack of abilities by generating conflict.[17]

Blanchard remarks that Salvadoran industrialists and managers are even more strident in generating conflict in the work place. For instance, consider the case of the Mandarin factory and many other similar plants throughout El Salvador.

THE MANDARIN PLANT AND ITS LABOR CONDITIONS

The San Salvador Mandarin International plant was established in order to assemble goods to be shipped to the U.S. under contract with major U.S. retailers such as The Gap and Eddie Bauer. The plant was built in the San Marcos Free Trade Zone, a zone owned by the former Salvadoran Army Colonel Mario Guerrero and created with money from the Bush Administration's U.S. Agency for International Development (USAID). David Wang, the Taiwanese owner of the plant, subsequently hired Guerrero as its personnel manager. In addition, the company also hired ex-military, plain-clothed armed guards as security for the plant.[18] Factories in El Salvador, as in the U.S., need protection for workers, personal property and for real property.

While personnel managers are not security guards, such appointments have become commonplace with Salvadoran industrialists precisely because they expect conflict in the workplace. However, in many situations, their personnel managers generate the conditions of conflict and attempt to control the conflict through the same methods employed during wartime.[19] For example, Colonel Guerrero himself told the workers at one point, "I have no problem, but perhaps you do; either the union will behave, leave, or people will die."[20]

While The Gap was one of the first companies to have a code of conduct for overseas suppliers (along with Reebok) this strategy might not be effective in the El Salvadoran business environment. Charles Kernaghan, Director of the National Labor Committee in Support of Democracy and Human Rights in El Salvador (NLC), believed that a pre-existing code of conduct was practically useless and stated the following in an interview with *Business Ethics Magazine* in June, 1996:

Consider the history of El Salvador's military, which specialized in the killing of nuns and priests and trade unionists. It is laughable to think that these same people will carry out a company's code of conduct. And there were no legal avenues to challenge any violation because the ministry of labor there is so ill-funded and ill-trained. So you can't depend on the laws. And the women were afraid to speak out.[21]

The following is a summary of events leading to the current situation between the Gap and the Mandarin plant, written by Charles Kernaghan, the Director of the National Labor Committee in Support of Democracy and Human Rights in El Salvador (NLC), a coalition of groups with shared interests in workers' rights.

Women maquiladora workers under attack in El Salvador at a plant producing for J.C. Penney, The Gap, Eddie Bauer, and Dayton-Hudson.[22]

In late January, 1995, the women at Mandarin organized a union—the first union ever established in a free trade zone in El Salvador. At the time, the Salvadoran government and the Maquiladora Association pointed to Mandarin as living proof that workers' rights and unions are respected in El Salvador. Reality proved otherwise.

Mandarin International immediately lashed out at the new union, at first locking out the workers and then illegally firing over 150 union members. The company hired two dozen ex-military plain-clothed, armed "security guards." The women workers were told their union will have to disappear one way or another or "blood will flow."

Groups of five workers at a time are now being brought before their supervisors and told to renounce the union or be fired. Union leaders are followed around the plant by company security guards. At work, the women are forbidden to speak to one another. Colonel Guerrero himself has told workers at the San Marcos zone, "I have no problem, but perhaps you do . . . either the union will behave, leave, or people may die."

These women want their union and they are struggling to keep it alive, but they are afraid. Along with the threats, the company is now systematically firing—a few each week—every union member and sympathizer. They cannot hold out much longer. They are appealing for solidarity.

The Salvadoran Ministry of Labor, which could be fining Mandarin $5,700 a day for violating the Labor Code, has done nothing to reinstate the fired workers or demilitarize the plant.

Mandarin produces clothing for J.C. Penney, The Gap, Eddie Bauer, and Dayton-Hudson. These companies have codes of conduct, which are supposed to govern their offshore operations, but the workers at Mandarin had never heard of or seen any of these codes. No codes of conduct are posted in the San Marcos free trade zone.

CONDITIONS AT MANDARIN/WHY THE WORKERS ARE STRUGGLING FOR A UNION

For eight hours of work at Mandarin, an employee earns $4.51 for the day or 56 cents an hour. This comes to $24.79 for the regular 44-hour work week. However, overtime at Mandarin is obligatory, and if you do not stay for extra shifts whenever they demand it, even if it is at the last minute, you are fired the next day. A typical week includes at least eight hours of obligatory overtime.

Conveniently for itself, Mandarin pays the workers in cash in envelopes which do not list regular hours worked or overtime hours, or at what premium it was paid. This makes it almost impossible for the young workers to keep track of whether they are receiving proper pay.

The Mandarin plant is hot and the workers complain of constant respiratory problems caused by dust and lint. There is no purified drinking water, and what comes out of the tap is contaminated and has caused illnesses. The bathrooms are locked and you have to ask permission to use them—limited to twice a day—or you are "written up" and fired after three such sanctions.

Talking is prohibited during working hours. The women say the piece-rate quota for the day is very high, making the work pace relentless. The supervisors scream at the workers to go faster. The women told us of being hit, pushed, shoved, or having had the garment they were working on thrown in their face by angry supervisors.

The workers say that if you are sick, the company still refuses to grant permission for you to visit the Social Security health clinic during working hours. Nor does Mandarin pay sick days. There is no child care center, which is a critical issue for the women, most of whom are mothers.

Working under these conditions, you earn $107.45 a month, $1,397 for the entire year, if you are paid your Christmas bonus. These wages provide only 18.1% of the cost of living for the average family of four.

The women say that even by scrimping and eating very cheaply just to stay alive, meaning going without meat, fish and often milk, food for a small family of two or three people still costs over 1,000 colones a month, or $114.29, which is more than they earn. Rent for three small basic rooms costs around $57 a month, which they cannot afford. There are other basic expenses as well. Round-trip bus transportation to and from work can cost over $6.00 a week. Tuition for primary school costs $8.00 a month. For a maquiladora worker to eat a simple breakfast and lunch at work costs approximately $2.50 a day. The wages of the maquila workers cannot possibly meet their expenses. Many of the Mandarin workers are forced to live in tin shacks, without water and often lacking electricity in marginal communities on vacant land, along roadsides or polluted river banks. Asked if they had a T.V., a radio, or a refrigerator, the workers laughed. They could not afford those things, we were told. All the Mandarin workers can afford to purchase is used clothes shipped in from the U.S.

It is a myth on the part of the multinationals and their maquiladora contractors that the cost of living in El Salvador is so much less than in the United States, that 56 cents an hour is really not a bad wage. In El Salvador, a "Whirlpool" washer costs $422.26, which is equal to 17 weeks' worth of wages for a maquiladora worker. A refrigerator costs $467.35, or 19 weeks' worth of wages. A queen-sized bed costs $177.85 on sale, or more than seven weeks of wages. A maquiladora worker would have to work three and a quarter hours to afford a quarter-pound cheeseburger, which costs $1.82. A two-pound box of Pillsbury pancake mix costs $2.67, or nearly five hours of wages.

We asked mothers, now that they are working in the maquiladoras, if their children were better off. They told us no, that with their wages they simply could not afford the right food for their children. In Honduras and the Dominican Republic, there is growing evidence that malnutrition is rising among the children of maquiladora workers.

HOW THE MAQUILADORA SYSTEM WORKS

Mandarin sews women's 3/4 sleeve T-shirts for The Gap, which had $3.6 billion in sales last year and made over $300 million in profits. The Gap T-shirts made at Mandarin sell for $20 each in the U.S.

A production line of 40 workers at Mandarin produces 1,500 The Gap T-shirts a day. These T-shirts sell for $30,000 in the U.S. ($20 × 1,500). The 40 Mandarin workers who make these 1,500 T-shirts earn, collectively, $180.23 for the day (40 $\times$ $4.50/day wages). This means that the Mandarin workers earn .6%, or just a little more than one-half of one percent of the sales price of the Gap shirt they make. What happens to the other 99.4%?

Under the U.S. government's Caribbean Basin Initiative trade and aid benefits, maquiladora exports from El Salvador to the U.S. grew by an amazing 3800% between 1985 and 1994, increasing from $10.2 million to $398 million. The number of maquiladora workers producing for the U.S. market increased 14-fold, from 3,500 to 50,000. At the same time, the real wages of the maquiladora workers were slashed 53%—to the current 56 cents an hour or $4.50 a day, which provides only 18% of a family's basic needs.

This is what trade benefits look like from the perspective of the maquiladora worker on the ground. This is what happens when worker rights are divorced from trade and denied in reality. From the perspective of The Gap, however, it means the system is working fine.

MANDARIN AND ITS YOUNG WORKERS

What kind of a company is Mandarin? Child labor came into focus as an issue toward the end of 1994, following the release of a U.S. Labor Department study and a Senate Hearing, where the National Labor Committee showed a short film documenting child labor in Honduran maquiladoras producing for the U.S. In February, 1995, afraid it might get caught, Mandarin summarily fired at least 100 minors between 14 and 17 years old who had been illegally hired. In El Salvador, minors can work only with special authorization from the Labor Ministry, and even then they cannot work more than seven hours a day. Mandarin, of course, worked the minors like everyone else, including forcing them to work overtime. Given that the average work week was 52 hours at Mandarin, this means that the minors were illegally forced to work 17 hours a week more than they should have by law (7 hours $\times$ 5 days = 35; 52 - 35 = 17).

Mandarin, J.C. Penney, The Gap, Eddie Bauer, and Dayton-Hudson have the responsibility to pay these fired minors back wages in the form of overtime payments to compensate them for the 17 hours a week they were forced to work illegally.

It is also interesting to note the absence of the Salvadoran Labor Ministry here as well. Even when it comes to monitoring and protecting child labor, the Ministry is nowhere to be found. It would be worthwhile to ask to see the Ministry's records on Mandarin.

THERE ARE NO LABOR RIGHTS IN EL SALVADOR

Any attempt to organize in the booming maquiladora sector in El Salvador must be clandestine. The mere mention of a union, even the suspicion of interest, will get you fired.

Between 1992 and 1994, maquiladora exports from El Salvador to the U.S. leapt nearly 2.5-fold, growing from $166 million to $398 million. The number of maquiladora plants soared 73% from 120 in April 1992, employing 30,000, to 208 assembly companies by December 1994, employing 50,000. The most recent figures show that the surge is continuing. A comparison of January and February, 1994 with the same two months of this year shows maquiladora exports from El

Salvador to the U.S. increasing 60%—a growth rate faster than any other country in the region.

During this same boom period over the last three years, the International Labor Organization (ILO) estimates that at least 1,000 workers have been illegally fired in El Salvador for trying to organize in the maquilas. In a devastating report on El Salvador released at the end of April, 1995, the ILO concludes: ". . . to speak of union freedoms and the right of unionization in the maquiladora enterprises is impossible, quite simply because such rights do not exist . . . ." This comes on top of an April 6 ILO condemnation of El Salvador for permitting systematic and grave abuses of worker rights, including assassinations, beatings, arrests, and illegal firings for union activity.

The history of worker rights violations at Mandarin fits the above to a "t."

A HISTORY OF REPRESSION AT MANDARIN

In November, 1993, the maquiladora workers at Mandarin formed a local union. The minute the company was notified that the Ministry of Labor had granted legal status to a union at its plant, management illegally fired 100 workers, including the entire leadership of the new union. When the workers fought this, the Ministry of Labor said it could not help and that they would have to turn to the courts (where such a case would drag out for at least two years). Mandarin then told the fired workers point blank to accept the firings, take your severance pay and clear out, or else you will be blacklisted and never again work in the maquila.

This fits in with what we were told in August, 1992, during a National Labor Committee/*60 Minutes* investigation in El Salvador. Posing as potential investors, we met with John Sullivan, who directed USAID's private sector program in El Salvador during the Bush Administration. Sullivan told us we would not have to worry about unions in the free trade zones, since zone management used a computerized blacklist to prevent the unions from penetrating the zones.

Sullivan also told us that we could make a lot of money in El Salvador, where there were world class wages, about 40 cents an hour. If we put our workers on piece-rate and raised the production quota, we could make even more money. Further, Sullivan encouraged us to fire our workers every year—keeping them on a year-to-year contract—rather than allow severance benefits to build up. Lastly, the USAID official suggested we form a Solidarista Association—a phony company union—which would help increase our security from disturbances. As we shall see, Mandarin did all these things.

REPRESSION AT MANDARIN WORSENS

Facing such repression, it was not until January, 1995, that the workers at Mandarin were able to reorganize their union—the Union of Workers of the Mandarin International Company (SETMI). The union was organized by the Democratic Workers Central (CTD), which maintains fraternal relations with the AFL-CIO. When the Ministry of Labor granted SETMI legal status, it became the first union ever recognized in a free trade zone in El Salvador.

The Minister of Labor told union leaders that he would see to it that the union was accepted without delay by the Mandarin company. This was a time of considerable pressure on labor ministries across Central America and the Caribbean to demonstrate concrete advances in the respect for worker rights. In October, 1994, the National Labor Committee was able to delay U.S. Congressional approval of $160 million a year in increased tariff benefits to maquila companies across the region until worker rights conditions improved.

However, despite promises from the Labor Minister, when the company was notified on February 7 that a legal union had been established at Mandarin, it responded by locking out all 850 workers the next day.

Mandarin representatives said that they would rather fire all of the workers than accept a union. The workers refused to leave the industrial park and spent that day and night camped out in front of the factory. On the following morning, February 9, one of the San Marcos Free Trade Zone administrators, Ernesto Aguilar, and several security guards attacked and beat a number of the women. Aguilar punched one woman in the face several times until she was bleeding badly.

An emergency commission was formed to mediate a resolution to the crisis, made up of National Assembly deputies, United Nations delegates, representatives of the Human Rights Ombudsman's Office, several Labor Ministry officials—including Inspector General Doctor Guillermo Palma Duran—as well as union officials and Mandarin management. At 6:00 P.M., February 9, an agreement was reached and signed by all of the participants.

Mandarin committed itself in writing to end the lock-out, to strictly comply with the Salvadoran Labor Code from this point forward, to recognize the union, and to continue negotiations to reach a collective contract. The company also stated that there would be no reprisals against union members.

Between the day Mandarin signed the agreement, along with officials from the Labor Ministry, and today, Mandarin has illegally fired over 150 union members, in a systematic campaign to destroy the union and spread fear among the workers. The agreement Mandarin signed was not worth the paper it was written on.

The Ministry of Labor could be fining Mandarin $5,700 a day for violating the country's labor code but, for lack of power or will, nothing has been done.

Colonel Guerrero has responded to the workers' attempt to organize to defend their basic rights by "militarizing" his San Marcos Free Trade Zone. Colonel Guerrero hired ex-military people both as zone administrators and armed security guards. One of his administrators, Colonel Amaya, told the women at Mandarin that every single union affiliate at the plant will be fired until the union disappears, which is exactly what is happening. As has already been pointed out, over 150 union members have already been illegally fired, including the entire union leadership—something which is clearly prohibited by the Salvadoran Labor Code.

Five at a time, workers are being brought into management's offices and told to renounce the union or be fired.

Mandarin has brought in nearly two dozen ex-military to act either as plain-clothed, armed security guards or to pose as mechanics so that they can spy on the workers. Armed guards are posted at all four Mandarin entrances. Whenever union leaders must move about the plant, armed company security guards follow them. If workers are seen speaking to a union leader, the guards immediately intervene. During working hours, the workers are not allowed to speak to each other.

Colonel Amaya, along with the security guards, has told the women workers that "blood will run" if the union does not leave Mandarin and the San Marcos Zone.

The union leaders fear that even their homes are at times under surveillance. On April 25, Mandarin's Chief of Production, Liou Shean Jyh, along with his bodyguard and two other company staff, went to the home of union leader Alonso Gil Moreno. When he refused to let them enter his home, they pushed the door open. Their message was simple: renounce the union. They also offered him a bribe.

Mandarin was worried that despite the systematic repression and threats, the union continued to grow. Even under these conditions, 300 workers had signed up to affiliate to the union. It was clear, that if it were not for the fear of losing one's job, the overwhelming majority of the 850 workers would side with the union. The union was asking for a secret ballot to determine support for their union.

Mandarin's response has been to step up the pace of the firings and to demand that workers join Mandarin's Solidarista Association or lose their job.

The union was about to be destroyed.

THE WORKERS FIGHT BACK

The U.S. State Department's latest "Country Reports on Human Rights Practices for 1994" (released in February, 1995) observes that in El Salvador's maquiladora sector, there are both documented cases of the illegal firing of union organizers and of physical abuse being used in the maquiladoras. In the face of these abuses, the State Department concludes: "[Salvadoran] Government actions against violations have been ineffective, in part because of an inefficient legal system and in part because of fear of losing the factories to other countries." Nor can the workers turn to the Ministry of Labor for protection. According to the State Department report, "The Ministry [of Labor] has very limited powers to enforce compliance, and has suffered cutbacks in resources to carry out certification and inspection duties, which curb its effectiveness."

The ILO report, mentioned earlier, found the Labor Ministry to be so under-funded and its staff so poorly paid that "this precarious situation in terms of human and financial resources is the best guarantee that not even legally recognized labor rights in the area of union freedom are applied in the companies."

As of Monday, May 15, Mandarin had fired around 100 union members. Every day more unionists were being systematically dismissed. Mandarin was picking up the pace in its campaign to wipe out the shrinking union.

On Monday, May 15, at 9:30 A.M., the union called a work stoppage to protest the mass of illegal firings. As the union leaders stood up to announce the work stoppage, company goons moved in and attacked the union leaders. At one point seven company guards were punching and kicking Dolores Ochoa. They broke her leg. Marta Rivas and Esmeralda Hernandez were also beaten. Elisio Castro Perez, General Secretary of the SETMI union, was beaten and detained for several hours by company security guards.

Once again, Mandarin responded by locking out all 850 employees and firing 50 more union members, including the union's entire leadership. Another commission was formed and another agreement was reached with the company. At 8:00 P.M. Monday evening, Mandarin committed itself to reopen the plant the next morning and to reinstate all of the fired workers.

As in the past, this agreement turned out to be worthless. When the fired workers showed up on Tuesday morning, May 16, the armed guards refused to let them enter the plant. When the union protested, the guards again roughed up the women.

At this moment, the union workers and their supporters—a majority of workers—have stopped working and left the plant to stand in solidarity with their fired sisters and brothers.

The workers are desperate and they are asking for our solidarity.

THE WORKERS' DEMANDS

The fired workers want their jobs back and they want their union and they want their security guaranteed. They specifically seek:

1. The immediate reinstatement, with back pay, of all fired workers;
2. The demilitarization of the Mandarin plant and the San Marcos Free Trade Zone, which means removing the armed security guards;
3. To end completely the firings, the repression, the threats being directed against union affiliates and their supporters;
4. Mandarin's strict compliance with the Labor Code, including the union's right to organize free of company reprisals;
5. That Mandarin negotiate in good faith a collective contract with the SETMI union.

As North Americans became more and more aware of the working conditions in El Salvador, they began to take action against the retailers. On August 16, 1995, more than one hundred workers from UNITE (Union of Needles Trades and Industrial & Textile Employees) demonstrated in front of a Gap outlet store in downtown Toronto in protest of the working conditions at Gap suppliers. At the same time, thousands of miles south of Toronto, Guerrero claimed that "the working conditions here are good for us and good for the Salvadoran workers, but bad for those seeking to keep jobs in the United States . . . [Without the jobs in the maquilas,] young women would have few other work options apart from prostitution or crime."[23] The story becomes further blurred, however, when Guerrero's comments are compared with an earlier statement by Mandarin owner David Wang in connection with the wages paid to Mandarin workers: "If you really ask me, this is not fair."[24]

Workers' wages make up less than 1% of the retail cost of The Gap shirts. Is it any wonder that the company made $310 million in 1994 and paid its CEO Donald Fisher $2 million plus stock options?"[25]

From The Gap Sourcing Principles & Guidelines: "Workers are free to join associations of their own choosing. Factories must not interfere with workers who wish to lawfully and peacefully associate, organize, or bargain collectively. The decision whether or not to do so should be made solely by the workers."[26]

Based on claims of a violation of its sourcing principles and in an effort to ameliorate the situation, The Gap decided to discontinue its relationship with the Mandarin (following in the footsteps of other previous Mandarin contractors such as Eddie Bauer, Liz Claiborne, J. Crew and Casual Corner); however, this action prompted strong cries of concern from labor activists. Contrary to the intentions of The Gap, this resolution was viewed as irresponsible and lacking in accountability.[27] Those concerned with the rights of workers in El Salvador contested The Gap's decision, claiming that this would be the worst possible solution to the problems in a country where 60% of the labor force is unemployed.[28] As a result of other pullouts, the Mandarin has had to cut its work force from 1,300 to 300, and 32 other maquilas have already shut down.[29] "Instead of acting responsibly and seeing that conditions are improved at Mandarin, The Gap is trying to wash its hands and to shift production to other maquilas in other countries with equally bad conditions."[30]

The Gap's original perspective is not without its supporters. Joan Spero, business executive and Secretary of State for Economic Affairs, explains, "A world community that respects democracy and human rights will provide a more hospitable climate for American trade and commerce . . . . Repression fosters instability in the long run and puts investment at greater risk of expropriation and loss."[31] Consider as well the following comments of John Duerden, former President of Reebok:

> As a public company, we have an ethical responsibility to build value for Reebok's shareholders—but not at all possible costs. What we seek is harmony between the profit-maximizing demands of our free-market system and the legitimate needs of our shareholders, and the needs and aspirations of the larger world community in which we are all citizens.[32]

"A VICTORY FOR ALL OF US WHO ARE DETERMINED TO ELIMINATE SWEATSHOPS AT HOME AND ABROAD"[33]

The situation took a drastic turn in December, 1995 when Reverend Paul Smith called a meeting between The Gap Senior Vice President for Sourcing, Stan Raggio, The Gap sourcing guidelines director, Dottie Hatcher, The Gap consultant James Lukaszewski, Reverend David Dyson of the Interfaith Center for Social Responsibility and Charles Kernaghan (NLC). The Gap was feeling pressure from all sides. On the one hand, labor, religious, consumer, solidarity, children's and women's groups were arguing for dramatic changes in working conditions. On the other hand, the National Retailers' Federation contested the complaints and encouraged The Gap to ignore the demonstrations.

The Gap responded to the consumers, issuing a letter stating that it is "committed to ensuring fair and honest treatment of the people who make [its] garments in over 40 countries worldwide,"[34] and, in the words of the NLC, "took a major step forward in accepting direct responsibility for how and under what conditions the products it sells are made."[35] As a result of the meeting, the Gap agreed to implement an independent monitoring system in El Salvador, using the Human Rights Ombudsperson in El Salvador to monitor factories' compliance with its labor guidelines, as long as the Mandarin agreed to rehire the fired union activists.

The NLC and others saw this decision by The Gap as a benchmark against which all other multinational retailers will be measured. Says Kernaghan, "The message is clear: If you make it, you are responsible."[36] Not everyone agrees with Kernaghan's assessment. Larry Martin of the American Apparel Manufacturer's Association believes otherwise: "They've [labor] given us a black eye that most of us don't deserve. Most of us monitor contractors we use here and offshore."[37] One might understand Martin's concerns for the rest of American retailers when one considers the comments of U.S. Labor Secretary Robert Reich, "This raises the question for other big retailers who haven't moved in this direction—why not?"[38]

THE MONITORING PROCESS BEGINS

The Gap's reputation and image since the December 15, 1995, meeting has been rehabilitated in connection with workers' rights.[39] In fact, the response was almost instantaneous. On December 22, 1995, the Department of Labor added The Gap to its list of "good guy" businesses (the "Fair Labor Fashion Trendsetter List") that have pledged an attempt to avoid selling products manufactured in sweatshops.[40] The Gap consulted with Aaron Cramer, Director of the Business and Human Rights Program at California's Business for Social Responsibility (an association of over 800 firms for clearinghouse and consulting purposes). Cramer contacted several individuals in El Salvador to discuss the most effective means by which to establish the independent monitoring system at the Mandarin. One of these individuals was Father David Blanchard, Pastor of Our Lady of Lourdes in the Calle Real Epiphany Cooperative Association and Father Esteban Alliete, Pastor of Santiago in Ciudad Delgado Vicariate for Human Development. Their evaluation of human rights monitoring in El Salvador follows:

The Monitoring of Human Rights in the Marketplace: The Case of El Salvador

Your letter of February 5, 1996 asks to define independent monitoring.

First, the monitoring of human rights must be assumed by Salvadoran organizations. This is important because of the characteristics of organized labor, traditions of work, and work codes that are unique to El Salvador. For example, in the United States, unions choose to support one or another (and sometimes both) political parties in an election. They do this to maximize their interests. In El Salvador, the relationship of political parties to unions is often the reverse. Political parties establish and control unions as a means to expand their power base.

Understanding the union's role in a labor dispute thus demands understanding the political culture that surrounds the conflict. Therefore, those who monitor the labor conflict in El Salvador must be independent of both the union, the political allies of that union and management. But they must be close enough to this situation to interpret accurately the possible sources and manifestations of the conflict.

The best agency to do this in El Salvador is the government Procurator for Human Rights. The Procurator for Human Rights guarantees that government offices function in ways that respect human rights. The Procurator is responsible for the supervision of the ministry of labor, which must assure compliance with work codes. It provides vigilance over the ministry of justice which must prosecute violations. It monitors the role of the security forces.

Should additional verification be required, the Vicariate for Human Development of the Archdiocese of San Salvador and the Human Rights Office of the University of Central America (IDUCA) both enjoy an international reputation for fairness and objectivity. The Vicariate for Human Development of the Archdiocese includes the social secretariat and CARITAS, both of which have promoted productive enterprises, and of course, Tutela Legal. In addition to its legal staff, IDUCA also has access to economists, academics in the faculty of management and business administration and other important intellectual resources.

Not to focus the monitoring process in local agencies such as these seriously undermines reconstruction efforts in El Salvador. These agencies have earned their right to speak out for justice. The vicariate for Human Development and IDUCA have paid for this right with the blood of faithful colleagues. The Procurator's Office for Human Rights was created as a result of the 1992 peace accords. Its integrity is unblemished and it deserves a chance to take its place in the forum for human rights.

You ask how the effectiveness of the monitoring process should be measured. There are two measurable criteria.

First, as Lic. Maria Julia Hernandez has pointed out, each factory should minimally be made to follow the law. This includes the right to organize. Cases of violations should be prosecuted. The number of cases prosecuted and the results of these cases should be published.

Secondly, over the long term, the work force will become more qualified and more productive. When the minimal legal requirements are respected, a stronger work force has greater possibility to negotiate the value of its labor collectively and individually. The result will be seen in greater productivity, profits and an increased standard of living for the work force.

How can an independent monitoring process be established in a cost-effective manner? It would certainly reduce costs greatly if monitoring is concentrated in Salvadoran institutions. Perhaps the interfaith Center on Corporate Responsibility and the National Labor Committee can collaborate asking the private foundations and donors who support your efforts to contribute to the Procurator for Human Rights, Tutela Legal and the IDUCA. Eventually, such monitoring will have to receive its support from local sources—workers, unions and corporations.

You ask how independent monitors should present their findings. Honestly. Individual cases should not be presented as representing a pattern. When patterns exist, they should be clearly presented. Also, all parties should attempt to de-personalize the way cases are presented and strive for objectivity. Where real cases of suffering and abuse exist, these should be treated immediately. Suffering should not be exploited to achieve a public relations victory.

Your question, "how should we gain input from concerned organizations in Central America?", suggests that the independent monitoring is something that should be done from outside, with data obtained from local organizations. Our response is that local organizations should gather the data; they should analyze this data and present their findings to organizations such as yours for dissemination.

Monitoring began and problems ensued. An impasse was reached in March, 1996, followed by a Resolution Declaration regarding the rehiring of union activists at the plant. The Resolution also included a commitment of the signatories to:

1. peace and harmony among workers;
2. the maintenance of the existent peace between workers and management;
3. insofar as possible, a promise to aggressively contact and encourage clothing retailers and manufacturers to direct orders to Mandarin International to help demonstrate that agreement and independent monitoring can and will work.[41]

By April, 1996, the Mandarin plant was in serious trouble. David Wang, owner of the plant, informed the monitoring team at an April 18 meeting that there was an 80% chance that the plant would have to be closed by May, 1996. Wang claimed that only a miracle would keep the plant from closing. Fr. Blanchard responded, "I personally believe in miracles, but they are nothing to base a business on."[42] The problem at the Mandarin plant was not much different that at any other manufacturing plant: contracts. The Mandarin was not going to be able to stay afloat without additional contracts. Its renewed contract with the Gap was simply insufficient alone to satisfy the financial needs of the plant. Because Wang believed the closing was imminent, he refused to provide the monitoring team with the information it required to conduct its responsibilities.

At the same time, The Gap hired two Central American Sourcing Compliance Officers "whose sole responsibility [was] to ensure that Gap contractors operated in full compliance with local laws and [its] Code of Vendor Conduct."

Moreover, the Salvadoran Minister of Labor established a government commission to review conditions in the free trade zone and indicated that foreigners would no longer be permitted to monitor the implementation of work codes in El Salvador.[43] This begs the question of why The Gap doesn't simply allow the El Salvadoran government to monitor the work conditions of the plant? Father Blanchard offers the following response:

We must consider what are the global consequences for disbanding this effort after less than one month in existence.

For example, recently we have learned that the Commerce Department of the United States has informed the international fishing industry that it will not allow the importation of shrimp that are caught with nets that also snare turtles. All fisherman who use nets and who wish to sell their produce in the United States must use turtle-free nets. What is more, the industry must allow independent monitoring by outside agencies.

Salvadoran law permits the use of turtle-snaring nets. The United States has no authority to control the Salvadoran shrimp industry (one of the largest sources of external revenue for the Government of El Salvador). It has complete authority to determine the conditions under which shrimp may be imported into the United States.

The question remains: why not simply rely on the government of El Salvador to supervise compliance, especially given the importance of the shrimping industry in this country.

The answer lies in norms for the modernization of government and general guidelines for development being promulgated by the World Bank, the InterAmerican Development Bank and other loaning agencies. Governments that contribute to international loaning agencies insist on downscaling government and allowing compliance to be monitored by the private sector in alliance with independent monitoring groups. In this scheme, Congress passes the law defining the kinds of nets that are required in the shrimp industry; people concerned about the welfare of turtles contribute to organizations like the International Wildlife Fund to guarantee that these laws are enforced; organizations like the International Wildlife Fund in turn collaborate with the fishing industry to guarantee that the norms are followed. When all is said and done, if nobody cares about the welfare of turtles, the laws are not passed and compliance never takes place.

What is good for turtles is also good for human beings.[44]

THE STORY CONTINUES

Not only do these events continue to occur in El Salvador in connection with the Mandarin plant and others in the Free Trade Zone, but these same issues are also prevalent elsewhere throughout the world. A recent study by the Committee for the Defense of Human Rights in Honduras found that 90% of the women who work in assembly plants there are forbidden to join a union.[45] The same study also found that women between ages 15 and 30 were required to submit to pregnancy tests and to pledge to use contraceptive pills in order to ensure attendance on the job, rather than pregnancy leave.[46] Ralph Lauren's Chaps brand shirts are made under martial law in Myanmar where workers are paid only $.06 per hour for their assembly.[47] Notwithstanding these conditions, the United States apparel industry has increased its imports from Myanmar 330% since 1992.[48]

Further atrocities are evidenced by these comments made by Douglass Cassel, Director of the International Human Rights Law Institute, before the Chicago Council of Foreign Relations.

Shell in Nigeria

A hands-off stance was adopted by Shell Oil last year when Nigeria executed author and environmental activist Ken Saro-wiwa. For years Saro-Wiwa had led an activist group of the Ogoni ethnic minority in the Niger River Delta. The Ogoni claimed that Shell drilling and pipelines had polluted their waters and poisoned their lands, ruining not only their environment but their livelihoods, which depended on fishing and farming.

And, they claimed, they did not benefit from this exploitation of their land. Although Shell says it has supported dozens of community projects and recently boosted its budget for environmental improvements to over $100 million, the Ogoni say that most of the oil money that stayed in Nigeria went into the pockets of corrupt military officers.

In the early 1990's, members of Saro-Wiwals group allegedly sabotaged Shell's equipment, to the point where Shell ceased operations in Ogoniland in 1993. Still, to preserve its investment, Shell called upon—who else?—the local authorities.

Now in normal circumstances, summoning the gendarmes to protect one's property would seem to be the proper thing to do. In Nigeria, however, it is akin to calling in the Mafia. Nigeria is ruled by a corrupt, repressive, military regime, currently headed by General Sani Abacha. Its most recent election resulted in the imprisonment of the civilian winner.

When Shell called, the colonels responded predictably: by allegedly razing thirty Ogoni villages, killing more than 2,000 Ogoni, and displacing some 80,000.

But even this did not suffice to quell the unrest. So the regime had Mr. Saro-Wiwa and several other activists arrested, jailed, and prosecuted on trumped-up murder charges. British Prime Minister John Major later called the trial "fraudulent." At its conclusion last October, Saro-Wiwa and his co-accused were sentenced to death.

As the trial unfolded and its unfairness became apparent, international protests mounted. Yet Shell kept mum. When the death sentence was announced, protests poured in from the United Nations Human Rights Commission, the United States and British governments, South African Nelson Mandela, Amnesty International, and countless others.

But not from Shell, whose joint venture with Nigeria's state oil company supplies more than half the revenue for General Abacha's regime. "It is not for a commercial organization," the company explained, "to interfere with the legal processes of a sovereign state such as Nigeria."

Only after the General's Military Council confirmed the death sentences did Shell's Chairman send a last-minute letter "requesting clemency on humanitarian grounds." But this gesture was too little, too late; a few days later, Ken Saro-Wiwa and his colleagues were hanged.

Before the dirt on Saro-wiwa's grave could settle, Shell announced that it would go ahead with a $4 billion joint venture natural gas plant in Nigeria. Its partner: General Abacha's state oil company.

THE SULLIVAN PRINCIPLES

Still, during the 1970s and 80s, there was one striking experiment in corporate codes of conduct for human rights: The Sullivan Principles for South Africa. Developed by Reverend Leon Sullivan, a General Motors Board member, these principles were initially adopted in 1977 by twelve U.S. firms including GM. By 1986, some 200 of the 260 U.S. corporations doing business in South Africa had adopted the Sullivan Principles.

By adopting the Sullivan Principles, these firms adopted unprecedented, far-reaching commitments to corporate social responsibility toward human rights violations—albeit limited to a single country, and spurred by a desire to deflect a growing call for divestment from that country.

Sullivan firms committed themselves not only to racially nondiscriminatory employment, but also to pay fair wages well above the minimum cost of living; to provide managerial training programs for Blacks and other non-whites; to provide them supportive services for housing, health care, transportation and recreation; and to use their corporate influence to help end apartheid in South Africa. And each firm's performance was subject to outside audit and public reports by A.D. Little.

Might events in Nigeria have turned out differently, had Shell undertaken similar commitments for the Ogoni?

Far-reaching as they were, however, the Sullivan Principles failed both in their ostensible goal—to bring down apartheid—and in their tactical goal—to offer a publicly palatable alternative to divestment from South Africa. By 1977, even Reverend Sullivan pronounced his principles a failure and disassociated himself from their further use. When apartheid ultimately did fall in South Africa, it was not because of the Sullivan Principles.

NORTHERN IRELAND: THE MACBRIDE PRINCIPLES

In the mid-1980s, a similar experiment called the MacBride Principles was initiated for Northern Ireland. Their purpose differs from the Sullivan Principles: they aim not to deflect divestment (for which there has been no serious support) but instead to secure equal treatment for Catholic workers in Protestant-majority Northern Ireland. Their content is more limited, focusing on non-discrimination, without mandating higher wages and social services.

MacBride firms do, however, make one unusual commitment with potential applications elsewhere: to make reasonable, good faith efforts to protect the personal safety of their Catholic workers not only at the work place but while travelling to and from work.

As of February, 1995, 32 of the 80 publicly traded U.S. firms operating in Northern Ireland had signed on to the MacBride Principles. Sixteen states, including Illinois, and more than 40 cities, including Chicago, have passed MacBride Principles laws.[49]

Another highly publicized case of substandard working conditions involves the Nikomas Gemilang factory in Serang, Indonesia (where 1.2 million pairs of Nike shoes—more than a third of its products—are constructed each month), where the resolution has not come so quickly as with The Gap. In Serang, workers faint from exhaustion, humiliation of the workers is commonplace and, in contrast to Nike spokesperson Michael Jordan's multi-multimillion dollar salary, the workers earn $2.23 per day. One labor activist comments, "From the outside it looks like heaven, but for workers on the inside, it's hell."[50] In fact, only one worker interviewed at the Nikomas factory had even heard of Nike's Code of Conduct.[51] *New York Times* columnist Bob Herbert claims that the problem is that Nike overlooks atrocities such as the government-sponsored murder of thousands of innocent civilians "if there is a large enough labor force willing to work for next to nothing."[52]

In response to questions concerning his role as Nike spokesperson, Michael Jordan said, "It is up to Nike to do what they can to make sure that everything is correctly done. I don't know the complete situation. Why should I? I'm trying to do my job. Hopefully, Nike will do the right thing."[53] On the other hand, consumers *are* concerned. Herbert reported in another *New York Times* article that a woman from New York wrote the paper to state that she "simply cannot sit back and watch my two children frolic in their vacation surf knowing that other children suffer to enable my kids to have cute bathing suits."[54]

Other companies are well known for their intolerance of inhumane conditions. Levi Straus and Timberland received accolades for their 1993 decision to discontinue operations in China as a result of that country's stance on human rights. Reebok, as well, refused to operate in China under its martial law conditions following the Tian An Men Square massacre in 1990. In 1992, Sears, Roebuck and Co. refused to import products produced by prison or other involuntary labor in China.[55] Recently, Talbots, K-Mart, and J.C. Penney have introduced compliance programs specifically implementing monitoring procedures for suppliers.[56] Talbots' policy requires that a supplier must *actively* work to prevent sweatshop abuses if that supplier wants to do business with Talbots.[57]

Multimillion dollar globalized firms have the opportunity to make a difference in the countries in which they conduct business. That difference may be for the worse if they are seen to condone the poor labor conditions and treatment of workers in those countries or may be for the better if they use their financial leverage to force a change in the conditions. But what is the responsibility of a foreign firm? If The Gap's costs increase as a result of its activities in El Salvador, are its customers willing to pay the price? If Nike's shoes cost more at the store, will its sales go down? The ultimate question of responsibility appears to be on the shoulders of every person with a dollar to spend.

CASE NOTES

1. Dept. of Labor, "No Sweat Initiative: Fact Sheet." http//www.dol.gov/dol/esa/public/forum/fact.htm

2. Susan Chandler, "Look Who's Sweating Now," Business Week (Oct. 16, 1995):96, 98. [In March, 1996, 72 Thai workers at the El Monte sweatshop were awarded more than $1 million in backwages in connection with the scandal. George White, "Sweatshop Workers to Receive $1 Million," L.A. Times (Mar. 8, 1996):B1.]

3. Ibid. p. 98. The study also found that 73% of the garment makers had improper payroll records, 68% did not pay appropriate overtime wages, and 51% paid less than the minimum wage.

4. Ibid., p. 96. Self-inspection may also be necessitated by the drop in the number of inspectors assigned by the Labor Department to investigate wage and hour law violations. Since 1989, that number has fallen from almost 1000 to less than 800. Ibid., p. 98; Andrea Adelson, "Look Who's Minding the Shop," New York Times (May 4, 1996):17.

5. Stuart Silverstein, "Self-Regulatory Group to Police Clothes Makers' Work Conditions," L.A. Times (June 20, 1995):D1.

6. Pat Widder, "'No Sweat' Proposal Aims to Prevent Abuses of Labor," Chicago Tribune, April 15, 1997, electronic version; Barbara Sullivan, "Label Plan Gets Mixed Reaction," Chicago Tribune, April 15, 1997, electronic version.

7. Sullivan, op. cit., p. 2.

8. http://www.dol/gov/dol/opa/public.forum/kearney.txt

9. Douglass Cassel, "Human Rights Violations: What's a Poor Multinational To Do?" remarks before the Chicago Council on Foreign Relations, Feb. 7, 1996, p. 10.

10. "Gifford Counters Sweatshop Charges," May 2, 1996, p. 40 (Reuters).

11. Michael McGuire, "Lost in the Junkyard of Abandoned U.S. Policy," Chicago Tribune Sec. 2 (April 7, 1996):1, 4.

12. Louis Emmerij, Social Tensions and Social Reform: Toward Balanced Economic, Financial and Social Policies in Latin America (Washington, DC: Social Agenda Policy Group, Inter-American Development Bank, 1995) p. 7, cited in letter from Fr. David Blanchard, Pastor, O.L. Lourdes in Calle Real Epiphany Cooperative Assn. to Aaron Cramer, Director, Business and Human Rights Program, Business for Social Responsibility, February 6, 1996, p. 2.

13. Bob Herbert, "Sweatshop Beneficiaries," New York Times (July 24, 1995):A13.

14. Letter from Fr. David Blanchard, Pastor, O.L. Lourdes in Calle Real Epiphany Cooperative Assn. to Aaron Cramer, Director, Business and Human Rights Program, Business for Social Responsibility, February 6, 1996, p. 8, citing research by Fr. Ignacio Martin-Baro, a social psychologist and one of the six Jesuit priests slain in November 1989 at the University of Central America in El Salvador.

The war has additional effects on the people of El Salvador, even if they were not alive at the time of the recent conflicts. For example, one American student recorded in his journal, "9/3/95: One of the little children handed me an old bullet that he must have found. I imagine there must be many bullets out there in the field. I just wanted the day to be over, for me and for this little boy." (Student manuscripts, in possession of the author.)

15. First-hand experience of the author, February, 1996.

16. Student Manuscripts, in possession of the author (June, 1996).

17. Letter from Fr. David Blanchard, Pastor, O.L. Lourdes in Calle Real Epiphany Cooperative Assn. to Aaron Cramer, Director, Business and Human Rights Program, Business for Social Responsibility, February 6, 1996, p. 5.

18. Terry Kelly, "The GAP: Brutality Behind the Facade," part of World History Archives located at http://neal.ctstateu.edu/history/world.history/archives/canada/canada002.html, p. 1 (1995).

19. Letter from Fr. David Blanchard, Pastor, O.L. Lourdes in Calle Real Epiphany Cooperative Assn. to Aaron Cramer, Director, Business and Human Rights Program, Business for Social Responsibility, February 6, 1996, p. 6.

20. Terry Kelly, "The GAP: Brutality Behind the Facade," part of World History Archives located at http://neal.ctstateu.edu/history/world.history/archives/canada/canada002.html, p. 2 (1995).

21. Mary Scott, "Going After The Gap," Business Ethics Magazine (May/June, 1996):20.

22. Charles Kernaghan, Urgent Action Alert (June 3, 1995), http://www.miyazaki-mic.ac.jp/classes/compoliss/ElSalvadorlabor.html

23. Letta Taylor, "Salvadoran Clothing Factory Accused of Worker Abuse," Roanoke Times and World News (Dec. 31, 1995):D4.

24. Bob Herbert, "Not A Living Wage," New York Times (Oct. 9, 1995):A17.

25. Terry Kelly, "The GAP: Brutality Behind the Facade," part of World History Archives located at http://neal.ctstateu.edu/history/world.history/archives/canada/canada002.html, p. 2 (1995).

26. Gap, Inc., Code of Vendor Conduct, Section VIII, 1996. See also Christian Task Force on Central America, "Urgent Action El Salvador," http://www.grannyg.bc.ca/CTFCA/ act1295a.html (Nov. 29, 1995) p. 1.

27. Letta Taylor, "Salvadoran Clothing Factory Accused of Worker Abuse," Roanoke Times and World News (Dec. 31, 1995):D4; Joanna Ramey, "Worker Rights Groups Slam Gap for Ending El Salvador Contract," Women's Wear Daily, Nov. 30, 1995.

28. Letta Taylor, "Salvadoran Clothing Factory Accused of Worker Abuse," Roanoke Times and World News (Dec. 31, 1995):D4.

29. Ibid.

30. Christian Task Force on Central America, "Urgent Action El Salvador," http://www.grannyg.bc.ca/CTFCA/act1295a.html (Nov. 29, 1995) p. 2.

31. Douglass Cassel, "Human Rights Violations: What's a Poor Multinational To Do?" remarks before the Chicago Council on Foreign Relations, Feb. 7, 1996, pp. 9.

32. Ibid.

33. Words of Jay Mazur, UNITE President, in National Labor Committee, "Gap Victory," http://www.alfea.it/coordns/work/industria/gap-victory.html (Feb. 1996).

34. Christian Task Force on Central America, "Urgent Action El Salvador," http://www.grannyg.bc.ca/CTFCA/act1295a.html (Nov. 29, 1995).

35. National Labor Committee, "Gap Agrees to Independent Monitoring Setting New Standard for the Entire Industry," http://www.alfea.it/coordns/work/industria/gap.agrees. html

36. Industrial Workers of the World, "Unions Win Victory in Gap Battle," *The Industrial Worker*, http://fletcher.iww.org/~iw/feb/stories/gap.html (February, 1995). See also Mary Scott, "Going After The Gap," *Business Ethics Magazine* (May/June 1996):18–20 ["What the Gap has done is historic. It will be a good pilot project to see if third party monitoring works," said Conrad McKerron, social research director of Progressive Asset Management.]

37. Paula Green, "The Gap Signs Accord on Conduct Code with U.S. Labor Group," *The News-Times*, http://www.newstimes.com/archives/dec2295/bzf.htm (12/22/95), p. 2.

38. United Auto Workers, "The Gap Agrees to Improve Conditions in Overseas Plants," *Frontlines*, http://www.uaw.org/solidarity/9601/frontlinesjan96.html (January 1996) p. 1.

39. See, e.g., Paula Green, "The Gap Signs Accord on Conduct Code with U.S. Labor Group," The New-Times, http://www.newstimes.com/archives/dec2295/bzf.htm (12/22/95); Mary Scott, "Going After The Gap," *Business Ethics Magazine* (May/June, 1996): 18–20.

40. Stuart Silverstein, "Labor Department Adds Gap Inc. to 'Good Guy' Retailer List," *L.A. Times*, Dec. 22, 1995, p. D2.

41. Resolution Declaration, March 22, 1996, signed by: David Wang (Mandarin International), Hector Bernabe Recinos (Centra), David Blanchard (Archdiocese of San Salvador), Maria Julia Hernandez (Tutela Legal del Archdiocese), Benjamin Cuellar (Univ. of Central America), Lucia Alvarado Portan (Mandarin International Workers Assn.), and Eliseo Castro Perez (for former SETMI union leaders).

42. Memo from Fr. David Blanchard to Mark Annerm Coordinator, Independent Monitoring Team, April 19, 1996, p. 1.

43. Ibid.

44. Memo from Fr. David Blanchard to Mark Annerm Coordinator, Independent Monitoring Team, April 19, 1996, p. 5-6.

45. Thelma Mejia, "Slaves for Hire," *Chicago Tribune*, 45., sec. 13 (June 22, 1997):10.

46. Ibid.

47. National Labor Committee, "Ralph Lauren and Warnaco Working Hand in Hand With Brutal Dictators in Burma," *Urgent Action Alert* (June 13, 1997):1.

48. Ibid.

49. Douglass Cassel, "Human Rights Violations: What's a Poor Multinational To Do?" remarks before the Chicago Council on Foreign Relations, Feb. 7, 1996.

50. Mark L. Clifford, "Pangs of Conscience: Sweatshops Haunt U.S. Consumers," *Business Week* (July 29, 1996):46.

51. Ibid., p. 47.

52. Bob Herbert, "Nike's Bad Neighborhood," *New York Times* (June 14, 1996):A15.

53. Bob Herbert, "Nike's Pyramid Scheme," *New York Times* (June 10, 1996):A19.

54. Bob Herbert, "Buying Clothes without Exploiting Children," *New York Times* (August 4, 1995):A27.

55. Douglass Cassel, "The Gap: Getting Serious about Sweatshops," broadcast on *World View*, WBEZ, 91.5FM (Jan. 3, 1996) p. 3.

56. Office of Public Affairs, U.S. Dept. of Labor, "Reich Applauds Significant Steps Taken by Retailers to Combat Worker Abuses in the U.S. Garment Industry," press release, June 17, 1996.

57. Ibid.

Strategy Content and Formulation for Multinational Companies

CHAPTER 5
Basic Strategies for the Multinational Company: Content and Formulation

CHAPTER 6
Multinational and Participation Strategies: Content and Formulation

Basic Strategies for the Multinational Company: Content and Formulation

LEARNING OBJECTIVES
After reading this chapter you should be able to:

- Define the generic strategies of differentiation and low cost.

- Understand how low-cost and differentiation strategists make money.

- Recall multinational examples of the use of the generic strategies.

- Understand competitive advantage and the value chain and how it applies to multinational operations.

- Understand how offensive and defensive strategies are used by multinational firms.

- Understand the basics of multinational diversification.

- Understand how the traditional strategy formulation techniques, industry and competitive analysis, and company situation analysis are applied to the multinational company.

Preview Case in Point **International Competition is Tough: Airbus and Boeing Battle Over the Super Jumbo**	The U.S. company Boeing and Airbus Industrie (80 percent owned by European Aeronautic Defense & Space Co. [EADS], a recently created German, French, and Spanish company, and 20 percent by BAE systems from England) are in a heated battle over which firm will control the next generation of super-jumbo jets. After Singapore Airlines committed to buy 16 of the A3XX super jumbos, a yet to be built next generation plane, Airbus is closer to the 40 orders it needs to commit to start the project. Boeing now holds a monopoly in this market with its 747 and promises an expanded version of this plane soon. The risks are high. It will cost almost 11 billion to develop the A3XX but "only" 4 billion to upgrade the 747. Airbus is close to betting the company on the existence of a worldwide market for the super jumbo plane. Airbus predicts a demand of 1400 and Boeing estimates the demand at only 400, too low to legitimate an 11 billion investment. The success of Airbus will rest on accurate assessment of the market and their ability to counter Boeing's revised 747 or perhaps another new model developed by Boeing after Airbus tests the market. Sources: Based on *Economist* 2000d and Rossant 2000.

The Preview Case in Point indicates how two multinational firms, one U.S. American and another built from a consortium of organizations from several countries, compete in the world's commercial aviation industry. In this highly competitive environment, the multinational managers in these organizations craft the basic competitive strategies that they hope will guide their companies to profitability and long-term success. This chapter introduces the basic strategies that all multinational managers must be prepared to face and to master.

To develop an understanding of these strategies, this chapter presents the major components of the strategic management process. The chapter has two main sections. The first provides background on basic strategy content applied to the multinational firm, including the strategic options available to companies. The second main section reviews the basic principles of strategic formulation with applications for the multinational, including the processes by which managers analyze their industries and companies to select a strategy for their company.

After reading this chapter you should understand how the basic elements of the strategic management process apply to multinational operations. You should also understand how the multinational manager is faced with more complex challenges than those faced by a domestic-only manager.

BASIC STRATEGY CONTENT APPLIED TO THE MULTINATIONAL COMPANY

Multinational companies use many of the same strategies practiced by domestic companies. An overview of common organizational strategies is provided next. For students with coursework in strategic management, this will serve as a partial review. However, the discussion illustrates specifically how multinational companies use basic strategies. In particular, the Cases in Point and Multinational Management

Briefs show how real multinationals use basic strategic options in international business. After this introductory chapter, the text focuses on the strategic options that are unique to the multinational company.

COMPETITIVE ADVANTAGE AND MULTINATIONAL APPLICATIONS OF GENERIC STRATEGIES

Generic strategies

Basic ways that both domestic and multinational companies keep and achieve competitive advantage.

Competitive advantage

When a company can outmatch its rivals in attracting and maintaining its targeted customers.

Differentiation strategy

Strategy based on finding ways to provide superior value to customers.

Low-cost strategy

Producing products or services equal to those of competitors at a lower cost than competitors.

Generic strategies represent very basic ways that both domestic and multinational companies achieve and sustain competitive advantage. **Competitive advantage** occurs when a company can outmatch its rivals in attracting and maintaining its targeted customers. Porter (1990) identifies the two primary generic strategies that companies use to gain competitive advantage as differentiation and low cost.

Companies that adopt a **differentiation strategy** find ways to provide superior value to customers. Superior value comes from sources such as exceptional product quality, unique product features, or high-quality service. For example, BMW competes in the world market by providing customers with very high-quality and high-performance sport touring cars. IBM competes worldwide in its mainframe computer business by offering not only high quality and performance but also superior after-sales service.

Companies that adopt a **low-cost strategy** produce or deliver products or services equal to those of their competitors. However, low-cost companies find the means to produce their products or to deliver their services more *efficiently* than the competition. That is, they lower the costs of their products without sacrificing quality. The cost savings that improve efficiency may occur anywhere from the creation of the product to its final sale. Examples include finding sources of cheaper raw materials, employing cheaper labor, using more efficient production methods, and using more efficient delivery methods. Porter (1990) notes, for example, that Korean steel and semiconductor firms often perform well against U.S. and Japanese firms, using low-cost strategies. These Korean firms save money with low-cost and productive labor combined with advanced and efficient production methods.

HOW DO LOW-COST AND DIFFERENTIATION FIRMS MAKE MONEY?

Differentiation leads to higher profits because people will often pay a higher price for the extra value provided by the superior product or service. Levi's jeans have higher prices in the world market because of the special appeal of the Levi's brand. The Swiss firm Tobler/Jacobs can charge more for its specially produced chocolate than can Hershey for its mass-produced product. In comparison to Hershey, Tobler/Jacobs uses higher quality ingredients, a longer processing time, and specialized distribution channels. These factors produce a higher-quality product that commands a higher price (Porter 1990).

High quality, service, or other unique characteristics of a differentiated product usually increase costs; that is, it takes more expensive labor or higher quality materials to make a differentiated product or to provide a differentiated service. In addition, to make customers aware of the special value of their products or services, firms must spend more on marketing. Consequently, to provide a good profit margin, the differentiating company must charge higher prices to offset its additional costs.

Low-cost firms produce products or services similar to their competitors in price and value. Their competitive advantage and their additional profits come from cost savings. Every dollar, mark, or yen they save contributes to the bottom line by increasing their profit margins. Exhibit 5.1 shows how the relationships among

Exhibit 5.1
Costs, Prices,
and Profits for
Differentiation and
Low-Cost Strategies

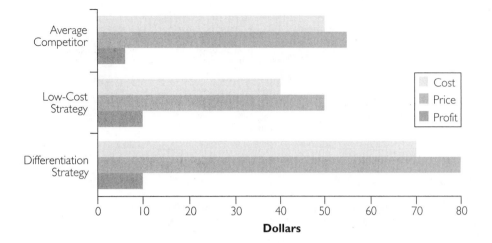

costs, prices, and profits work for the differentiator and the low-cost strategist as compared to the average competitor. As Exhibit 5.1 shows, both the differentiator and the low-cost strategist have higher profits than the average competitor.

Competitive scope

How broadly a firm targets its products or services.

Porter (1990) identifies another competitive issue regarding the two basic generic strategies, called **competitive scope**. Competitive scope represents how broadly a firm targets its products or services. For example, companies with a narrow competitive scope may focus only on limited products, certain types of buyers, or specific geographical areas. Companies with a broad competitive scope may have many products targeted at a large range of buyers. Auto manufacturers such as BMW target a high-income market with a few models, while most U.S. and Japanese auto manufacturers target a broad income market with many models. Exhibit 5.2 shows the four subdivisions of Porter's generic strategies. The following Case in Point illustrates how even a small multinational company can gain competitive advantage in the international marketplace by meeting its customers' quality and reliability needs with a focused differentiation strategy.

COMPETITIVE ADVANTAGE AND THE VALUE CHAIN

A firm can gain a competitive advantage over other firms by finding sources of lower cost or differentiation in any of its activities. These range from getting necessary raw materials, through production, to sales, and to eventual follow-up with after-sales service. For example, a company may find cost savings with cheaper raw materials or cheaper labor in other countries. A multinational may base its differentiation on the excellent R&D produced by its subsidiary located in a country where engineering talent is cheap and of high quality. Many multinational software-design companies, for example, take advantage of the very high number of quality engineers in India and Singapore.

Value chain

All the activities that a firm uses to design, produce, market, deliver, and support its product.

One convenient way of thinking about a firm's activities is called the **value chain**. Michael Porter uses the term "value chain" to represent all the activities that a firm uses "to design, produce, market, deliver, and support its product" (Porter 1985). The value chain identifies areas where a firm can create value for customers. Better designs, more efficient production, and better service all represent value added in the value chain. Ultimately, the value a company produces represents what customers will pay for a product or service. Exhibit 5.3 shows a picture of the value

Exhibit 5.2

Porter's Generic
Strategies

Scope of Competitive Target	Source of Competitive Advantage	
	Lower Cost	Differentiation
Broad Market	General cost leader	General differentiator
Niche Market	Focused cost leader	Focused differentiator

Source: Adapted from Porter 1990.

Exhibit 5.3 The Value Chain

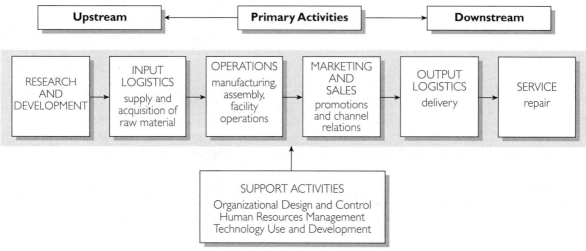

Source: Adapted from Porter 1985.

chain. Later you will see that the value chain provides a useful way of thinking about how multinational companies operate.

Porter divides the value chain into primary and support activities. These activities represent (1) the processes of creating goods or services and (2) the organizational mechanisms necessary to support the creative activities. *Primary activities* involve the physical actions of creating (or serving), selling, and after-sale service of products. Early activities in the value chain, such as R&D and dealing with suppliers, are called *upstream*. Later value-chain activities, such as sales and dealing with distribution channels, represent *downstream* activities. *Support activities* include systems for human resources management (e.g., recruitment and selection procedures), organizational design and control (e.g., structural form and accounting procedures), and a firm's basic technology.

The value chain identifies the areas in the input, throughput, and output processes where multinational companies can find sources of differentiation or lower costs. To achieve higher value or lower costs for its products or services than do rivals, companies must take advantage of the distinctive competencies in their value chain. What are distinctive competencies and where they come from is the topic of the next section.

Case in Point

Focus and Differentiation in a Multinational Subsidiary, or How a "Wee" Outfit in Scotland Decked IBM

A small Scottish subsidiary of NCR, the Dayton, Ohio, maker of office equipment and computers, used a focus-and-differentiation strategy to drive IBM virtually out of the ATM business.

When James Adamson took over NCR's operation in Dundee, Scotland, NCR gave him six months to turn the plant around or face closure. His first decision: focus on one product—the ATM. Early orders proved disastrous. Two major customers, the British banks National Westminster and Barclays, returned low-quality, unreliable machines.

To find out what his customers wanted, Adamson visited customers constantly, all over the world. He also brought customers to Dundee every day the plant was in operation. Engineers, executives, and marketers interviewed the customers daily. Reliability and quality were the key qualities that customers desired. Once he realized what the market wanted, he challenged his engineers to produce a machine twice as reliable as the competitors'. They responded by producing a machine three times as reliable.

Within three years NCR stopped production of ATMs in the United States, switching all production to Scotland. Less than five years after that, NCR passed its two major rivals, Diebold and IBM, in total units installed.

Source: Based on Colvin 1990.

DISTINCTIVE COMPETENCIES

Distinctive competencies

Strengths that allow companies to outperform rivals.

Resources

Inputs into the production or service processes.

Capabilities

The ability to assemble and coordinate resources effectively.

Distinctive competencies are the strengths anywhere in the value chain that allow a company to outperform rivals in areas such as efficiency, quality, innovation, or customer service (Hill and Jones 2001). Distinctive competencies come from two related sources: resources and capabilities. **Resources** are the inputs into a company's production or services processes. Resources can be tangible assets such as borrowing capacity, buildings, land, equipment, and highly trained employees. Resources can be intangible assets such as reputation with customers, patents, trademarks, organizational knowledge, and innovative research abilities. **Capabilities** represent the ability of companies to assemble and coordinate their available resources in ways that lead to lower costs or differentiated output.

Thus, resources provide a company with potential capabilities. They become capabilities only when used effectively. In turn, capabilities are the building blocks of a distinctive competence. However, although capabilities are the prerequisite of building distinctive competencies, this is not enough. To result in long-term profitability and success, capabilities must lead to a sustainable competitive advantage. Next, we consider how companies achieve this state.

SUSTAINING COMPETITIVE ADVANTAGE

Sustainable

Strategies not easily defeated by competitors

For a company to have long-term profitability, a successful low-cost or differentiation strategy must be sustainable. **Sustainable** means that strategies are not easily neutralized or attacked by competitors (Aaker 1989). Sustainability is traced to the nature of a company's capabilities. Capabilities that lead to competitive advantage must have four characteristics (Barney 1991). They must be valuable, rare, difficult to imitate, and nonsubstitutable.

Case in Point

Toyota's
Distinctive
Competencies
Along the
Value Chain:
Strategic
Capabilities
in Cost
Reductions,
Quality, and
Service

Toyota is Japan's No. 1 automaker. Its competitive advantages over other automakers from Japan, Europe, and the United States are the firm's distinctive competencies in cost reduction and high-quality materials and service. Upstream in the value chain, to bring new models to market more quickly and cheaply, Toyota combines manufacturing and production engineering. This eliminates mistakes in production design and reduces cost. Designing a new model takes only 18 months while many competitors take up to 30 months. Toyota designs cars with an objective of fewer parts, fewer production machines, and faster production times. When Toyota redesigned its Corolla model in 1997, the resulting 1998 model had 25 percent fewer parts, was 10 percent lighter, and more fuel efficient. Of the one billion dollars necessary to design a new model and build the plants to produce it, tools and machinery can account for three-quarters of the cost.

The mastery of *kanban,* the just-in-time production system, provides a basis of cost reduction and customer service. Not only do suppliers deliver materials just-in-time, as now happens for many U.S. manufacturers, but the whole value chain also works just-in-time.

Downstream, in the marketing and sales component of the value chain, Japanese dealers use online computers to order models directly from the factory. A built-to-order car arrives in less than two weeks. Special orders can be done in five days. Even with this design flexibility, Toyota uses only fourteen person-hours to assemble a car, as compared with twenty-two for Honda and Ford.

Sources: Based on Taylor 1990 and Peterson 2000.

Valuable capabilities create demand for a company's services or products or give companies cost advantages. Rare capabilities are those that a company possesses but that no competitor or only a few competitors also possess. For example, Boeing and Airbus are two companies with the rare technological capability to design and manufacture large commercial aircraft.

As shown in the preceding discussion of the generic strategies, providing customers superior value or finding a way to deliver products or services at lower cost results in increased profit margins. Competitors seek high profits by imitating or substituting for these capabilities. Thus, sustainable or long-term competitive advantage comes from having capabilities that not only meet the requirements of valuable and rare but also are difficult to imitate or nonsubstitutable.

Difficult-to-imitate capabilities are not easily copied by competitors. One of the most imitated sources of lower costs in the international marketplace is cheap labor. Competitors with access to the same international labor pools quickly duplicate any cost advantage of locating manufacturing facilities in countries with cheap labor. In addition, wage rates in countries with cheap labor often rise faster than productivity; gradually undermining cost advantages based on cheap labor.

Nonsubstitutable capabilities leave no strategic equivalent available to competitors. For example, many early e-commerce companies such as Amazon.com developed capabilities to conduct business over the Internet. Not only have these models been easy to copy, but competitors have also substituted for these capabilities by outsourcing such procedures as Web site building and translation. In contrast, consider the example of Toyota in the preceding Case in Point. It shows how Toyota

Exhibit 5.4 How Distinctive Competencies Lead to Successful Strategies

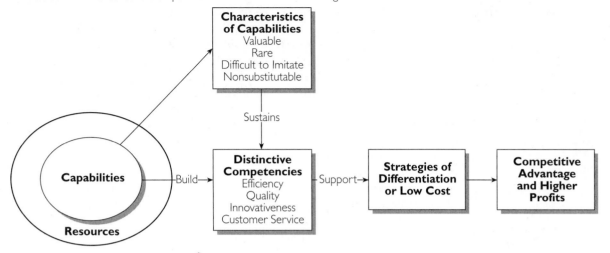

uses strategic capabilities that competitors have found difficult to copy or for which they have been unable to create substitutes.

Exhibit 5.4 summarizes the relationships among resources, capabilities, distinctive competencies, and eventual profitability.

Besides these very basic strategies, companies also develop strategies that directly target rival firms. The following section reviews some of these from the vantage point of the multinational.

OFFENSIVE AND DEFENSIVE COMPETITIVE STRATEGIES IN INTERNATIONAL MARKETS

Competitive strategies

Moves multinationals use to defeat competitors.

Besides using the basic generic strategies in their operations, multinationals use several strategic moves called **competitive strategies**. Competitive strategies can be offensive or defensive. In offensive strategies, companies directly target rivals from whom they wish to capture market share. For example, an attacking company may suddenly drop its prices or add new features to its products that compete with its rival's products. In defensive strategies, companies seek to beat back or discourage the offensive strategies of rivals. For example, a firm might match a rival's lower prices or give distributors volume discounts to discourage customers from shifting to a rival's products.

Offensive competitive strategies

Direct attacks, end-run offensives, pre-emptive strategies, and acquisitions.

Examples of **offensive competitive strategies** include direct attacks, end-run offensives, preemptive strategies, and acquisitions (Thompson and Strickland 1992; Yip 1995). Descriptions of each strategy follow.

- *Direct attacks:* Direct attacks include price cutting, adding new features, comparison advertisements that show lesser quality in a competitor's products, or going after neglected or poorly served market segments.
- *End-run offensives:* With these strategies, companies try to avoid direct competition and seek unoccupied markets. Usually, in international competition, unoccupied markets are countries ignored or underserved by competitors.
- *Preemptive competitive strategies:* These strategies involve being the first to gain a particular advantageous position. Advantages might include getting the best suppliers of raw material, buying the best locations, or getting the best customers. In international markets, being the first with a global strategy can bring

In early 1999, Sega directly attacked Sony's lead in the video-game market. Sega's Dreamcast game console, 128-bit video-game machine was getting rave reviews. In the first three months of 1999, Sega sold 1 million units in Japan and was near to its U.S. release of the game.

Sony felt it needed a response. Video software and hardware account for 42 percent of the Sony group's operating profits. In early March of the same year, Sony announced its PS2, a successor to its highly successful PlayStation. The announcement blunted some of the enthusiasm for Sega's Dreamcast console. But it created a problem for Sony: the machine did not exist yet.

A year later however Sony sold over 1 million of the machines in Japan during the first weekend after its launch and over 500,000 when introduced in the United States. Although still on top, Sony cannot afford to relax. Sega plans a $45 million investment in locking in online portals and carriers of games and video machines. Nintendo has a new machine in the works and Microsoft may enter the market with its "X-box."

Sources: Based on Cohen 2000; Kunii and Rae-Dupree 1999 and Kunii 2000.

great advantages. For example, a multinational company can seek the best raw material in any country. It can also work to become the first company to have its brand recognized worldwide.

- *Acquisitions:* This can be the most effective competitive strategy against rivals, since the acquired competitor no longer exists. An acquisition occurs when one firm buys its competitor. However, if the purchased company does not contribute to the overall company performance, the strategy may not contribute to bottom-line effectiveness. For the multinational firm, acquiring a firm from another country might include other strategic benefits besides profit, such as improving geographical coverage or strengthening the firm's position in important countries.

The preceding Case in Point shows the ongoing battle of Sony and Sega as they attack and counterattack each other in a global battle for the video-game market.

Usually, multinational managers analyze the strengths and weaknesses of their competitors separately in each country. Different countries represent different markets and often require different attack strategies. Consequently, managers develop country-specific plans for dealing with their competitors and deciding whether to attack, take an end-run approach (avoid direct competition), or, possibly, acquire rivals.

In a competitive industry, all managers should expect attacks from rival firms. To counteract these attacks, companies use **defensive competitive strategies**. Defensive strategies attempt to reduce the risks of being attacked, convince attacking firms to seek other targets, or blunt the impact of any attack. Companies may defend at several points on the value chain. For example, a firm may sign exclusive contracts with the best suppliers, thus blocking competitors' access to raw materials. A company can introduce new models that match competitors' lower prices. A firm may get exclusive contracts with distributors or provide better warranties or after-sales service. To scare off potential challengers, firms also make public an-

Defensive competitive strategies

Attempts to reduce the risks of being attacked, convince an attacking firm to seek other targets, or blunt the impacts of any attack.

Case in Point

Unilever Gives and Takes

Unilever is an Anglo–Dutch multinational company with a worldwide presence in consumer products. It has a thousand brands, three hundred thousand employees, and over $42 billion in sales. Unilever is under constant attack from companies of all types—ranging from other multinationals such as its U.S. rival, Procter & Gamble, to powerful local store brands in different countries. Unilever faces strong battles for market share in ice cream, soap, margarine, shampoo, and sauces.

In one attack on Unilever, P&G dropped its prices on competing products in the United States by up to 20 percent. At the same time, P&G increased advertising spending and beat Unilever to the market with a concentrated liquid detergent. The result: Unilever's detergent market share dropped from 35 percent to 27 percent in one year.

In a counterattack by Unilever on P&G in Europe, Unilever introduced a new premier detergent, called Persil Power in Britain and Omo Power elsewhere. Initially, consumers loved the product. It produced extremely clean clothes at very low water temperatures.

However, the defensive move by P&G turned brutally effective. P&G's European research lab discovered that the new soap contained manganese. While that chemical makes the product extremely effective in cleaning, it can weaken clothing fibers in as little as fifteen washes, often resulting in tears and holes. P&G immediately released the lab tests to the public, including pictures of damaged clothes. When independent consumer groups supported P&G's findings, the bottom fell out of the market for Unilever's new product.

Source: Based on Dwyer et al. 1994.

Counter-parry

Fending off a competitor's attack in one country by attacking in another country, usually the competitor's home country.

nouncements of their willingness to fight. Rivals then realize that an attack will be costly and often decide it is not worth the risk. Attacked firms can also **counter-parry**, a popular strategy for multinationals. In international markets, the counter-parry fends off a competitor's attack in one country by attacking it in another country, usually the competitor's home country. This strategy draws resources from the competitor and weakens its attack. It is most successful when the rival firm is forced to protect its established home markets. This is the strategy Kodak used to defend against Fuji. When Fuji attacked Kodak in the U.S. market, Kodak countered by attacking Fuji in Japan. Goodyear used the same strategy against Michelin. When Michelin attacked Goodyear with low prices in the United States, Goodyear countered by attacking Michelin in Europe.

The preceding Case in Point gives examples of Unilever's global offensive and defensive moves in different countries and the responses of its rival Procter & Gamble. After that, we discuss how multinationals use diversification in the international marketplace.

MULTINATIONAL DIVERSIFICATION STRATEGY

Business-level strategies

Those for a single business operation.

Most of the strategic options discussed to this point pertain to the operation of a single business. Consequently, these strategies are called **business-level strategies**. However, many corporations have more than one type of business. Strategies for

Corporate-level strategies

How companies choose their mixture of different businesses.

multi-business companies are called corporate level strategies. **Corporate-level strategies** concern how companies choose their mixture of different businesses. When a company moves from a single type of business into two or more businesses, this is called diversification.

There are two basic types of diversification: related and unrelated. In related diversification, companies start or acquire businesses that are similar in some way to their original or core business. These similarities can exist all along the value chain. There are five typical similarities among companies that can be the basis for a related diversification (Thompson and Strickland 1992). These include:

1. Shared sales forces, advertising, and distribution activities
2. Similar technologies, such as internal combustion engines for motorcycles and lawn mowers
3. Transferable expertise, such as with different types of fast-food chains
4. Related or similar products, as Nike, whose major product is shoes, does with its clothing line
5. Support of another business, as when a professional sports team buys a local TV station

In unrelated diversification, firms acquire businesses in any industry. Their main concern is whether a business represents a good financial investment (Thompson and Strickland 1992). Businesses can be acquired as long-term investments. Usually, in this case, the acquired firm has potential for growth, but it does not have the financial or other resources necessary to grow without help. To reach its potential, the acquired company needs the parent company's financial or managerial resources. Businesses can also be acquired as short-term investments. In this case, the parent hopes to sell off the acquired firm's assets for more than the cost of acquisition. In addition, some firms look for businesses in industries with different economic cycles. In this way, the parent firm can remain profitable even if one industry is in an unprofitable economic cycle.

Like domestic companies, multinationals also pursue diversification strategies. Acquiring a business in another country is a quick way to gain a presence and often a recognized brand name. The multinational with related diversification can also coordinate and use resources such as R&D from different businesses located anywhere in the world to gain competitive advantages. They can also more easily establish global brand names for different but related products. Diversified multinationals can cross-subsidize both across countries and across companies to attack rivals in different countries. Cross-subsidization means that money generated in one country or from one company of a corporation provides resources to sister organizations in other countries or companies to undercut their local competition.

Exhibit 5.5 shows a selection of Global Fortune 500 diversified multinationals with their major lines of businesses. Experts do not agree on which form of diversification is best for multinationals. The related diversifier is better positioned to take advantage of economies of scale and business similarities, and the unrelated diversifier can seek growth industries in attractive countries.

STRATEGY CONTENT: BRIEF CONCLUSIONS

The first section of this chapter provided an overview of the content or makeup of basic strategies: generic, competitive, and diversification. Like solely domestic firms, multinational companies use these strategies to achieve and maintain competitive

Exhibit 5.5 Examples of Diversified Multinationals from *Fortune* 2000 Global 500

Company (Headquarters Location)	Major Lines of Business	Number of Employees	Revenues ($ million)	Profits ($ million)
GE (U.S.A.)	Aircraft engines, aerospace, appliances communications and services, electrical distribution and control, financial services, industrial and power systems, lighting, medical systems, motors, NBC, plastics, transportation	340,000	111,630.00	10,717.00
Siemens (Germany)	Automation and drives, automotive systems, computers, industrial projects and technical services, mobile information and communication, information and communication networks, medical engineering, power distribution and transmission, power generation, production and logistics systems, building technologies, business services, design and exhibition, financial services, real estate management, transportation systems	443,000	75,336.99	1,773.71
Nestlé (Switzerland)	Drinks, dairy products, chocolate and confectionery, culinary products, frozen food and ice cream, food service products, instant food and dietetic products, pet foods, pharmaceutical products and cosmetics, refrigerated products	230,929	49,694.12	3,144.32
Procter & Gamble (U.S.A.)	Health, beauty care, industrial chemicals, beverages and food, laundry and cleaning detergents, food services and lodging, paper	110,000	38,125.00	3,763.00
Mitsui (Japan)	Iron and steel, non-ferrous metals, property, service, construction, machinery, chemicals, energy, foods, textiles, general merchandise	38,454	11,855.00	320.50
Philips (Netherlands)	Lighting, components, consumer electronics, household appliances and personal care, medical systems, industrial and electric acoustic systems, information systems, communication systems, semiconductors, office equipment	229,341	33,556.60	1,919.00

Sources: Based on *Fortune* 2000; Siemens 2000; Mitsui 2000; Procter & Gamble 2000; Philips 2000 and General Electric 2000.

advantage over rivals. The next section reviews traditional strategy-formulation techniques applied to the multinational company.

STRATEGY FORMULATION: TRADITIONAL APPROACHES

Strategy formulation

Process by which managers select the strategies to be used by their company.

There are several common techniques used by managers as aids in formulating their strategies. In general, **strategy formulation** represents the process by which managers select the strategy to be used by their company.

In this section, we review some of the popular types of analyses that provide managers with the information to formulate successful strategies. These analyses help managers understand: (1) the competitive dynamics of the industry in which they operate; (2) their company's competitive position in the industry, (3) the opportunities and threats faced by their company, and (4) their company's strengths and weaknesses. This information allows managers to choose strategies that best fit the unique situations of their companies.

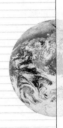

Multinational Management Brief
Cycles of Competition or Mistakes?

In early 1996, the price of dynamic random-access memory chips (DRAMs) dropped by 82 percent. In spite of this dramatic drop in prices, cash-rich companies in Asia built silicon-wafer plants at a breakneck pace. Numerous billion-dollar plants were constructed in Taiwan, Singapore, and Malaysia. At the time, most of the companies investing in these plants were rich, and saw growth as their major strategic goal. Industry experts, however, did not see how the growing number of new plants could survive.

As analysts expected, there was a shakeout between 1996 and 1998. Even by 1999, the world's biggest contract manufacturer of chips, Taiwan Semiconductor Manufacturing Co. (TSMC), was unable to keep its plants running at full capacity. By 2000, the chip manufacturing frenzy heated up again. Chipmakers across East Asia are following the motto: build more and build fast. TSMC and Intel are spending nearly $5 billion each on new factories. Taiwan's No. 2 foundry, United Microelectronics Corp., will spend $2.4 billion and Singapore's Chartered Semiconductor Manufacturing Ltd. has a $2.1 billion plant under construction. Samsung Electronics is making similar investments.

Will this result in a colossal failure replicating the situation faced in the mid-1990s? Maybe. But the chipmakers are no longer dependent on the PC market as their only source of output. They see a rise in chip demand from wireless phones, specialized Internet devices, and video games that are more sophisticated.

Sources: Based on Einhorn et al. 2000 and Engardio, Moore, and Hill 1996.

INDUSTRY AND COMPETITIVE ANALYSES

Industries identify the main competitive arenas of a company's businesses. To formulate good strategies, managers must understand their industries well. This involves understanding the economic characteristics of the industry, and knowing the driving forces of change and competition in the industry.

The dominant economic characteristics of an industry affect how strategies work. Issues that influence strategy selection include market size, ease of entry and exit, and whether there are economies of scale in production (Thompson and Strickland 1992). For example, markets with high growth rates often attract new competitors. Companies in these industries must be prepared to evoke defensive strategies against the new rivals. Michael Porter argues that strategists must also monitor several driving forces of change in an industry (Porter 1980). These include the speed of new-product innovations, technological changes, and changing societal attitudes and lifestyles. For example, rapidly changing technology creates the risk of being quickly overtaken by competitors; firms must respond by emphasizing innovation. Industries are also affected by the extent of their competition. Increased competition comes from such forces as the power of key suppliers and buyers or the threat of potential new entries into the industry (Porter 1979). Knowing your industry can be key to strategic survival. Consider the preceding Multinational Management Brief on the vicissitudes of Asia's semiconductor industry. After reading this brief, consider how you would respond as a multinational manager to this dynamic situation. Would you be willing to increase capacity and take the risk of a future slowdown?

An analysis of an industry helps the manager identify the important characteristics of companies and their products or services that lead to competitive success. For example, in some industries, speed to market with a new product might be key. Intel maintains dominance in the microprocessor industry by continuously beating its rivals to the market with the next generation of computer chips. In other industries, high-quality designs may be most important for competitive success.

Key success factors (KSFs)

Important characteristics of a company or its product that lead to success in an industry.

The factors that lead to success in an industry are called **key success factors (KSFs)**. Each one of these factors can have different degrees of importance in different industries or within the same industry at different points in time. Possible KSFs include (Pearce and Robinson 1994):

- Innovative technology
- Broad product line
- Effective distribution channels
- Price advantages
- Effective promotion
- Superior physical facilities
- Experience of firm in business
- Cost position for raw materials
- Cost position for production
- R&D quality
- Financial assets
- Product quality
- Quality of human resources

A knowledge of industry dynamics and KSFs helps both multinational and domestic managers formulate strategies that best achieve these key goals; that is, with an understanding of what drives competition in the industry and what the successful firms do to achieve and maintain their profitability, managers can formulate strategies that have the best chance of success for their firms. Observe in the following Case in Point how South African Breweries uses a knowledge of KSFs to defend its monopoly in the South African beer market.

Understanding an industry and identifying KSFs represent only some of the knowledge necessary to formulate successful strategies. Formulating the best strategies also demands that you understand and anticipate your competitors' strategies. One technique used to assess rivals is a competitive analysis. A **competitor analysis** profiles your competitors' strategies and objectives. It can help you select an offensive or defensive competitive strategy based on the current or anticipated actions of your rivals.

Competitor analysis

Profiles of your competitor's strategies and objectives.

The competitive analysis has four steps. These include:

1. Identifying the basic strategic intent of competitors. Strategic intent represents the broad strategic objectives of the firm, such as to be the market share leader or to be a company known for its technological innovation.
2. Identifying the generic strategies used and anticipated to be used by competitors (e.g., producing at the lowest cost). This helps managers determine which KSFs are currently most important to competitors and are most likely to be important in the future. For example, cheap labor cost might be an important KSF for a competitor's low-cost strategy.
3. Identifying the offensive and defensive competitive strategies used currently or anticipated to be used by rivals.

Case in Point

Mastery of Local KSFs: SAB (South African Breweries) Defends Its Local Markets

SAB dominates the South African beer market not because its beers have a unique taste or quality but, rather, because they have the distinctive competency to meet the complex demands of the local market.

The key success factor for selling beer in South Africa is mastery of the distribution channel. In South Africa, most beer is sold through *shebeens*, unlicensed pubs left over from apartheid when the sale of alcohol to blacks was illegal. Most are in poor and rural areas with bad roads and unstable electric supply. The government allows these pubs to exist to discourage the use of potentially lethal home brews.

SAB does not sell directly to the illegal pubs but works through local distributors and independent truck drivers. Loyal to SAB, many of the truck drivers are former employees who started their delivery businesses with help from SAB. In remote towns and villages, SAB provides refrigerators and generators to make sure their beer is cold.

Foreign brewers often consider trying to break SAB's monopoly in South Africa. However, they would have to develop the competency to build a competitive channel in this unique region. SAB is also a cost leader with very efficient production allowing them to reduce prices by over 50 percent during the last decade and to serve poor, price-sensitive customers.

Source: Based on *Economist* 2000c.

4. Assessing the current positions of competitors, such as identifying the market leader or companies losing market share.

Understanding current and anticipated competitive moves by rival firms allows managers to plan offensive or defensive strategies for their own firms. For example, if a competitor uses a differentiation strategy based on high-quality products, a company may attack by matching or exceeding that quality at a lower price. The following Case in Point shows how British Airways plans to contrast itself from low cost competitors by switching to a differentiation strategy. If customers are unwilling to pay for BA's superior service, however, the strategy may fail.

To formulate their competitive strategies, multinational companies use a country-by-country competitive analysis. In this way, a company can plan competitive moves, using distinct competitive strategies against different competitors in different countries. Exhibit 5.6 (on page 178) shows hypothetical competitive profiles of four companies in different countries. Using this hypothetical illustration, a multinational manager might decide to avoid attacking Bronson, Inc., in its home market. Bronson is the dominant leader and has threatened retaliation.

COMPANY-SITUATION ANALYSIS

SWOT

The analysis of an organization's internal strengths and weaknesses, and the opportunities or threats from the environment.

Each company faces its own unique situation in the competitive business world. Managers must understand what *their* particular company can and cannot do best, realistically assessing their company's strategic capabilities. In addition, they must identify any opportunities for or threats to their company's unique position in the industry.

The most common tool for a company-situation analysis is called the **SWOT**. SWOT is an acronym for Strengths, Weaknesses, Opportunities, and Threats (Pearce

The two major KSFs in the airline industry are price and service. Most airlines adopt a low-cost strategy and compete based on price, but this often makes profit margins thin. British Airways has decided to compete on service with a differentiation strategy. Though ranked fourth in total revenues in *Fortune Magazine's* Global 500 2000, BA was one of only two of the top nine airlines that lost money that year. BA posted a loss of $33 million.

CEO Bob Ayling's reaction: Stop competing on price with lower cost competitors. Instead, reduce capacity and focus on differentiation for the premium international traveler. BA now has an "economy plus" cabin with eight inches more legroom and wider seats. They put a fully reclining seat in business class on the London to New York route that allows the passenger to sleep on a flat surface.

These changes will cost BA £600 million so BA is betting on passengers paying a premium price for its more luxurious service of better seats, food, and entertainment. BA is also exiting the low-cost competition for other routes in Europe to focus on the more lucrative overseas market. Not all analysts are sure this will work arguing the price is the real KSF.

Hedging a bit on this differentiation strategy, BA is looking at acquiring KLM to outsource low-margin flights primarily to bargain-hunting tourists. This will require drastic cuts at KLM, however, to produce profitable margins.

Sources: Based on *Economist* 2000a; *Economist* 2000b; *Fortune* 2000 and Guyon 1999.

and Robinson 1994). The SWOT has an internal component, which focuses on an organization's *strengths* and *weaknesses*, and an external component, which focuses on *opportunities* or *threats* from the environment.

A strength is a distinctive capability, resource, skill, or other advantage that an organization has vis-à-vis its competitors. Strengths may come from technological superiority, innovative products, greater efficiencies and lower costs, human-resource capabilities, or marketing and promotional strengths, as well as other factors. A weakness is any competitive disadvantage of a company vis-à-vis its competitors. Companies attempt to build their strategies around their strengths. For example, if you can produce at lower costs, you can underprice your rivals. If you can innovate faster, you can be first to market with a new product.

Opportunities represent favorable conditions in a firm's environment. Threats are unfavorable conditions in the environment. Threats come from any changes that challenge a company's position in its industry: new competitors, such as Korean electronics makers in the United States, technological change, political change, and changes in import regulations, for example. Opportunities often come from the same sources. A threat for one company may represent an opportunity for another company. For example, Honda and Toyota view Europe as the next opportunity after the United States for their luxury models Acura and Lexus. BMW and Mercedes, however, view their Japanese rivals' moves into the upscale European car market as a major threat.

The SWOT analysis for the multinational company is more complex than for the domestic company. This is especially true for assessing opportunities and threats. Multinationals face more complex external environments because they operate in two or more countries. Each country provides its own operating environment,

Exhibit 5.6 A Hypothetical Country-by-Country Competitive Analysis of Rivals

Rivals	Strategic Issues	Countries			
		Canada	Mexico	France	Taiwan
Bronson, Inc. (United States)	• Strategic Intent	Dominant leader	Maintain position	Dominant leader	Move into the top five
	• Generic Strategies	Low cost	Low cost	Low cost	Differentiation based on foreign image
	• Competitive Strategies	Defensive based on threat of retaliation	None	Offensive price cutting	Offensive price cutting
	• Current Position	Market leader	Middle of the pack	Increasing share: No. 2	New entry
Leroux (Belgium)	• Strategic Intent	Overtake the leader	Move up a notch	Dominant leader	Survive
	• Generic Strategies	Differentiation based on brand name	Differentiation based on brand name	Differentiation based on brand name	Differentiation based on brand name
	• Competitive Strategies	Price cutting based on counter-parry	Price cutting based on counter-parry	Provide resources for counter-parries	Price cutting based on counter-parry
	• Current Position	Holding at No. 3	Market leader	New entry; too early to tell	Holding at No. 2
Shin, Ltd. (Singapore)	• Strategic Intent	Gain and hold market share	Gain and hold market share	Gain and hold market share	Gain and hold market share
	• Generic Strategies	Differentiation based on high quality	Differentiation based on high quality	Differentiation based on high quality	Differentiation based on high quality
	• Competitive Strategies	Offensive by comparative advertisements	Offensive by comparative advertisements	Defensive, lock in long-term contracts	Defensive, lock in long-term contracts
	• Current Position	Middle of the pack	Middle of the pack, but rising	Market leader	Market leader
Keio, Ltd. (Japan)	• Strategic Intent	To catch and pass the leaders	To catch and pass the leaders	To catch and pass the leaders	To catch and pass the leaders
	• Generic Strategies	Low cost based on cheap labor	Low cost based on cheap labor	Low cost based on cheap labor	Low cost based on cheap labor
	• Competitive Strategies	Heavy discounts based on volume purchases	Heavy discounts based on volume purchases	Heavy discounts based on volume purchases	Heavy discounts based on volume purchases
	• Current Position	New entry, rising fast	New entry, rising fast	Expected to enter this year	New entry, rising fast

which may present opportunities or threats different from those in another country. Consider the following examples. Import or export barriers may also make exporting products or importing supplies prohibitively expensive. Volatile exchange rates may make an otherwise attractive business environment threatening. Local inflation may play havoc with prices for the international market. Changes in government policies may affect the ability to repatriate earnings (get the company's money out).

In conducting a SWOT, multinational managers must conduct extremely thorough analyses of the business environment in each country. A country-by-country SWOT is probably most prudent.

Exhibit 5.7 The BCG Growth-Share Matrix for a Diversified Multinational Company

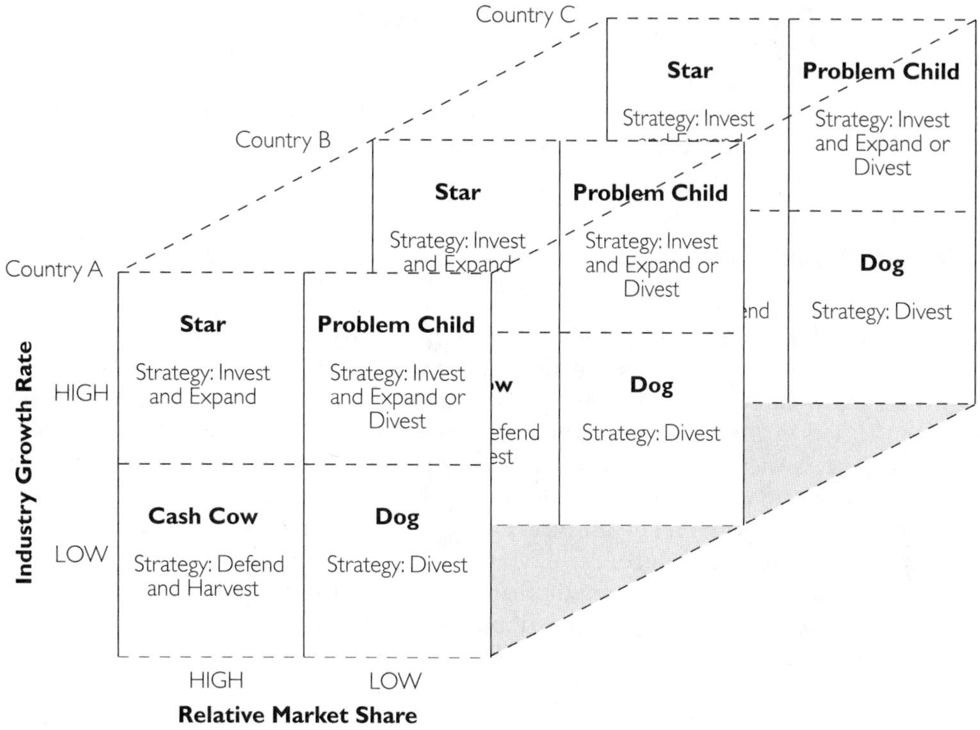

CORPORATE STRATEGY SELECTION

A diversified corporation has a portfolio (a selection) of businesses, with the primary goal of investing in profitable businesses. The major strategic question is deciding which businesses in the portfolio are targets for growth and investment and which are targets for divestment or harvesting. Targets for growth and investment receive additional corporate resources because managers anticipate high returns. Targets for divestment are businesses that managers decide to sell or liquidate. Targets for harvesting are usually mature and profitable businesses that managers see as sources of cash for other investments.

The most popular way of assessing a corporate business portfolio is through a matrix analysis. Several consultants and companies have developed their own business matrix systems to assess business portfolios. The most popular is the growth-share matrix of the Boston Consulting Group (BCG). The BCG growth-share matrix divides businesses into four categories based on the industry growth rate and the relative market share of the business in question. The most attractive businesses are those in fast-growing industries in which the business has a relatively large market share compared to the most successful firm in the industry. Businesses in this category are called "stars." In contrast, "dogs" are businesses with relatively low market shares in low-growth industries. "Cash cows" are businesses in slow-growth industries where the company has a strong market-share position. "Problem children" are businesses in high-growth industries where the company has a poor market share. For each type of business, the growth-share matrix has a suggested strategy. These are shown in Exhibit 5.7.

For the diversified multinational company, the portfolio assessment becomes more complex. The added complexity occurs because market share and industry growth are seldom the same in all the countries in which a multinational competes.

Thus, as illustrated in Exhibit 5.7, portfolio analyses must be conducted for each business in each country or region of operation.

The previous discussion provided a brief review of some analytic techniques used to formulate strategy for the multinational company. The challenge for the multinational manager is to use these and other techniques in the highly complex and evolving world of international competition.

Summary and Conclusions

Few students who read this book will work in industries untouched by global competition. Many will work for multinational companies or their subsidiaries. Others will work for companies that may source their raw materials from international suppliers, sell to international customers, or compete with multinationals (or all three). The business environment becomes increasingly global each day. Consequently, even the managers of domestic firms need a good understanding of multinational business strategy. This chapter provided you with a foundation and basic terminology to understand the strategic issues facing the multinational manager.

The primary ingredients of multinational strategic management are based on general strategic management processes. Like domestic firms, multinational companies employ the generic strategies of low cost and differentiation. To compete with rival firms, multinationals also use offensive and defensive competitive strategies. Diversified multinationals can have both unrelated and related business portfolios. To formulate strategies, multinational managers use many of the same tools available to domestic managers.

Differing from the solely domestic firm, however, the multinational always faces more complex situations. Basic strategies that work in one country may not work in another. Competitive strategies also must be considered on a country-by-country basis. The multinational and its rivals are seldom in the same competitive positions in all the countries in which they compete. Because of these complexities, and the additional complexities of a multi-country economic and political environment, the multinational manager faces continuous challenges in strategy formulation.

Beyond the traditional strategic questions facing all managers, the multinational manager must confront other issues related to strategy. The next chapter deals directly with these issues. Chapter 6 introduces you to the "global vs. local" dilemma faced by multinational companies. For example, multinational companies must decide whether to sell one product worldwide or make unique products for each country. Chapter 6 also introduces you to an array of strategies that multinational companies use to participate in different markets. For example, multinational companies must decide whether to export their products or manufacture their products in other countries.

Discussion Questions

1. Discuss how a multinational firm might use a low-cost strategy in one country while using a differentiation strategy in another country.

2. Identify examples of how multinational companies have used the offensive competitive strategies discussed in the chapter.

3. How can a multinational competitor such as Wal-Mart attack multinational rivals using the counter-parry?

4. Discuss the advantages that multinational companies might have over domestic rivals in sustaining competitive advantage.

5. Identify and discuss the KSFs that are most likely to vary by national context. Discuss why.

Chapter Internet Activity

Explore the Internet sites of three companies noted in the chapter. Go to the investor relations section in the sites and look for information on their multinational strategies. Often, the annual reports contain descriptions of the company's strategy. See if you can tell whether the company is primarily a differentiation or low-cost competitor.

Internet Sites

Selected Companies in the Chapter

AST Research, Inc.   http://www.ast.com/
BMW   http://www.bmw.com/bmwe/
Delta Airlines   http://www.delta.com/
Diebold, Inc.   http://www.diebold.com/
Fujifilm U.S.A.   http://www.fujifilm.com/
Hershey Foods, Inc.   http://www.hersheys.com/
Honda   http://www.honda.com/index.html
IBM   http://www.ibm.com/
Levi's   http://www.levistrauss.com/
National Westminster Bank   http://www.natwest.co.uk/
NCR   http://www.ncr.com/
Nissan   http://www.nissan-usa.com/
Philips   http://www.philips.com/
Procter & Gamble, Inc.   http://www.PG.com/

Samsung   http://www.samsung.com/
Sony   http://www.sony.com/
Toyota   http://www.toyota.com
Unilever   http://www.unilever.com/

Find More Information on Strategy Here

http://cazmedia.com/suntzu/   *Sun Tzu and the Art of Business home page.*
http://www.internationalist.com/business/   *Publicly traded companies throughout the world.*
http://www.yahoo.com/Business_and_Economy/Companies/   *Find a company on the search engine Yahoo!*
http://www.strategy-business.com   *Articles on strategy by Booz, Allen, and Hamilton, an international consulting firm.*

Chapter Case: Bieffebi, S.p.A

The managers of Bieffebi appreciated the continuing favor extended to the machines they manufactured. Their customers in the flexographic printing industry spoke highly of the optical plate mounting and proofing machines that Bieffebi sold around the world, but the managers recognized that there was a limited market for such machines. Technical innovations in the equipment connected with the flexographic printing industry had been extensive in the past, and the managers knew that there would be continued changes in such an advanced printing technique. Thus, the owners of the firm felt somewhat uncertain about the future. They questioned whether they might better remain focused upon the markets with which their small staff was well acquainted, or whether they should launch out on new ventures that more fully capitalized on the core competencies of the organization. Whatever their decision on this matter, they realized that internal changes in their organization might be required to better position their firm in the future.

BACKGROUND AND DEVELOPMENT OF THE FIRM

Shortly after the end of the Second World War, the machine manufacturing firm known as Bieffebi

Source: Alan Bauerschmidt, Professor of Management, College of Business Administration, University of South Carolina. Reprinted with permission.

Figure I Italy and Western Europe

was established in Bologna to provide work for Franco Degli Esposti and Brenno Sambri and to make a living for the Degli Esposti and Sambri families. As in many other portions of Italy, the agricultural region of Emilia-Romagna and the industrial center in Bologna had been devastated during the war. Recovery of the essential infrastructure in the area was delayed by the uncertainty of the political situation and the displacement of the population resulting from change in the organization of the agricultural system in the region. Large agricultural communes and combines had formed to take advantage of the opportunity to farm the rich soil in the broad fields characteristic of this region of Italy, using mechanical equipment. Thus, a large portion of the population sought its fortune in the cities that were beginning to recover or expand their industrial base. Figure 1 offers a map of relevant portions of Europe and the major cities in Italy that are pertinent to understanding the location of Bieffebi.

Members of the Degli Esposti and Sambri families supplied the limited capital necessary to found Bieffebi, and these pooled funds were invested in the machine tools necessary to build presses used in the manufacture of simple rubber stamps. The actions of these two families were not unusual in these times and in this place. Many other family firms were being established in

Bologna, Ferrara, and Modena, as well as in other cities in the immediate region. In each case, the items selected as the focus of the firms were best manufactured in the confines of small, closely knit organizations, drawing on raw materials and components made available or manufactured by firms similarly small and niche oriented.

One explanation for the unusual character of the family firms that emerged in the Emilia-Romagna was the position taken by the powerful Communist party against the intrusion of the large corporations that might have organized industrial development in the area after the war. The capital supplied by the Marshall Plan flowed into Italy through the banking system as directed by the Italian government, but the banks had little interest in the lean enterprises formed by families with little tangible collateral. More of this financial capital flowed into the industrial triangle formed by Milan, Turin, and Genoa, and development in that area was characterized by large, industrial organizations growing still larger. Such better-known Italian firms had an entirely different character than the enterprises to the east, although they still might carry the names of families important in the industrial revolution in Italy before the two world wars.

The modest venture of the Degli Esposti and Sambri families proved successful, and the construction of machines to manufacture rubber stamps was transformed into a firm that provided the equipment needed to produce rubber printing plates used in flexographic printing. Along the way, the partners were able to discover other markets for presses and at one point even considered manufacturing the printing presses using the plates their equipment supplied. The force driving the partners, as Brenno Sambri expressed it, was the desire for personal accomplishment, "to win something through our own effort." Part of that accomplishment was a profit, but Sambri believed the challenge was to win the respect of customers. The close relations that developed between the partners was extended to include the first, few customers, and as the number of the customers grew these relations were extended. Listening to the customer was always a paramount concern: the customers' needs were the basis for the bargain, and, thus, no customer was ever oversold on the value of the equipment manufactured.

Although the firm largely grew in a pattern that paralleled the emergence of flexographic printing and the printing plates used in that field, the application of pressure used in the earliest production of flexographic plates led the firm into other businesses. The original principle of the press has been applied in the manufacture of equipment that uses heat and pressure to compact a variety of light-reactive polymer plastic materials, in addition to natural rubber. An example of such presses was the equipment used to produce the ubiquitous, multilayered circuit boards found in most electronic equipment. However, the firm found itself with strong competition from much larger machine manufacturers in this market. Nevertheless, the fine reputation of Bieffebi as a high-quality machine manufacturer permitted it to hold a small position in this large market. A notable account held by the firm was with the division of Olivetti that supplied circuit boards to the parent firm.

Bieffebi did not face strong competition in all of its markets. It had a virtual monopoly in Europe, as well as in the world market outside the United States, for the machines used to optically mount and proof printing plates used by flexographic printers. There are few substitutes for this precision equipment and Bieffebi manufactured a full line of machines to serve the various trades that used flexographic printing techniques. At one point Japanese manufacturers considered entering this market, but they drew back when they realized the limited nature of the niche and the high quality demanded by customers.

Optical plate mounting equipment is an interesting variation on the plate presses originally manufactured by Bieffebi. An optical mounting and proofing machine is an ancillary piece of equipment used to attach the rubber or photopolymer plates to the impression cylinders used in flexographic printing. Flexographic printing plates are manufactured by applying controlled pressure to rubber or by etching photopolymer materials like the trade-named Cyrel and Nyloflex, using ultraviolet light. If one were to address the natural evolution of the plate manufacturing technology initially pioneered by Bieffebi from an already developed product, one might have expected the firm to manufacture the device used to prepare and etch the photopolymer plates, as one process followed and gradually

displaced the other. Instead, Bieffebi manufactured a piece of equipment that permits the photopolymer plates, stereos, klishees, clichés, or cliche—to use the American, English, German, French, and Italian expressions—to be mounted on the cylinder that makes up part of the impression unit in flexographic printing presses.

Members of the firm reflected on this shift in technique and offered a variety of opinions about the position of the organization in the flexographic printing market. Some considered the firm to have missed an opportunity in the 1970s to manufacture the emerging systems used to produce flexographic printing plates. Such a venture was considered, but the American market for this equipment was dominated by the DuPont Corporation; DuPont shared the market with BASF in Europe and elsewhere in the world. Both of these chemical firms manufactured and sold systems to shape their basic photopolymer products into printing plates for both lithographic and flexographic applications. In fact, the printing plates used in most flexographic printing operations are colloquially called "Cyrels." Such giant organizations as DuPont and BASF would have been powerful competitors for Bieffebi if it had launched itself into a natural extension of its business of providing plate systems to flexographic printers. Meanwhile, the market for mounting equipment was less extensive and remained peripheral to the marketing of photopolymer; optical plate-mounting was also a highly skilled trade in which printers or technicians often specialized because of the precise equipment needed to obtain the register sought in high-quality flexographic printing.

Another explanation for the reluctance of Bieffebi to extend its business of manufacturing presses that made rubber plates used in the early days of flexographic printing was an unwillingness to offer equipment that competed with an existing product. Bieffebi had its beginnings and early success in the manufacture of presses to make rubber plates: to offer a substitute would have helped undermine that market. Rubber plates were serving the printing trades well, and no one was sure that the new technology associated with photopolymer plates would become a successful innovation. The transition from rubber to photopolymer plates in the printing trades was long in development and fraught with difficulties.

The manufacturers of the photopolymer material had to persist to become successful. There are still a few applications where rubber is the preferred medium; however, the perfection of the anilox roller and the reverse doctor blades that portion and spread the ink effectively have firmly established the photopolymer plate as the preferred method in the printing of packaging materials. It became the largest portion of the market for flexographic techniques where the plate mounting equipment like that manufactured by Bieffebi was essential in gaining the register desired in graphic printing. Other markets for large volumes of a single printed matter that have made flexographic printing an economic success continued to grow, however. This included the printing of newspapers, while many other uses were being investigated and pioneered.

COMPETITIVE SITUATION AND STRATEGY

As indicated previously, the evolution of the core technologies in industries served by Bieffebi shaped the position of the firm in the marketplace. The production of rubber presses indirectly drew the firm closer to the packaging industry where flexographic printing techniques were applicable. Unlike firms in the printing trades, most packagers do not manufacture the plates used in printing messages on the containers they produce. The packager normally works with the container manufacturer to decide on the desired graphic design and message. Photographs or digital descriptions of the design are provided to firms that specialize in the preparation of plates. The firms supplying such plates to packagers may use the presses manufactured by Bieffebi or one of its competitors if a rubber plate is to be prepared. While the firms supplying plates used presses or the systems supplied by photopolymer manufacturers, the purchaser of the plates needed some way to mount the plates on the cylinders that would print the message. It was this second requirement that led Bieffebi into direct relations with packagers and, perhaps, drew the attention of the firm away from its original market as the core technology of plate manufacture was undergoing a transition.

The rubber plate-mounting equipment sold to firms in the packaging industry was designed to complement the presses used by suppliers in the manufacture of the plates. When the plate was no longer produced by a press method, but still needed to be mounted on a cylinder precisely, the mounting machine manufactured by Bieffebi and a few others became essential. In fact, Bieffebi quickly adapted its mounting equipment to meet the requirements of the new photopolymer plates supplied by the manufacturers that had been Bieffebi's original customers. In many respects, Bieffebi became a leader among the firms that pioneered the application of the photopolymer plate in package printing.

If Bieffebi missed an opportunity to enter a new line of business that was instrumental in the decline of the original business, it missed few other opportunities. It quickly offered solutions to problems mounting plates during the various stages of plate evolution, and it began to offer a full line of equipment for this crucial task of packagers and other printers using cylinder presses to exploit flexographic technology. Its optical mounting and proofing machines were used in conjunction with presses that print on both plastic and paper. It manufactured small and large plate mounters used with the variety of machines that combine the printing and slotting of the containerboard shaped into boxes. The firm also developed a line of large, sophisticated, optical mounting and proofing machines to serve users who printed on linerboard before it is corrugated to manufacture containerboard. This was a recent innovation in corrugated packaging, and Bieffebi worked with the pioneering firms in both the corrugated packaging and the printing press industries to advance the form of preprinting that was to quickly change the way corrugated boxes were printed.

Bieffebi's optical plate mounting and proofing machines allowed a single operator to fix the prepared plates to the metal impression cylinders used in flexographic printing. A typical color printing job required mounting plates on at least four cylinders that would carry the aniline inks to the paper or plastic impression material. The plates on each cylinder would have to be in register, or match, one another in an exact fashion for a high quality result. The Bieffebi machine used mirrors that allowed the operator to fix the plates to each cylinder in a way that matched. On the more advanced machines manufactured by Bieffebi, a computer attached to the mounting machine used software to assist the operator in obtaining the exact position on each cylinder that would gain the desired register for complicated printing jobs. When the impression cylinders were moved to the different printing stations on the printing press from the plate mounter and fixed in place the printer could easily make the fine adjustments necessary to keep the printing job in register during long, high speed printing runs, as the plates had been properly affixed on the Bieffebi machine to meet the tolerance standards of sophisticated flexographic printing presses.

PRESENT NATURE OF THE FIRM

If Bieffebi were a large, diversified firm it might be easy to explain why it failed to seize the opportunity to produce the systems that replaced the pressing of rubber plates. The original business of manufacturing machines to make rubber stamps had evolved into the manufacture of presses to create flexographic plates, and the firm consistently prided itself on the ability to flexibly serve its customers' technological needs. Bieffebi remained small enough to never lose touch with changes in its markets, and it never had more than 90 employees.

Control of the firm remained in the hands of the two partners, although the firm had become a stock company. Franco Degli Esposti was the president and CEO of the company, and, thus, managed the administration, marketing, and customer relations functions of the firm. Meanwhile, Brenno Sambri focused on the technical operations and production. Later some tasks of Degli Esposti (marketing and customer relations functions) were delegated to the two partners' sons, Daniele Degli Esposti and Stefano Sambri. In spite of the specification of areas of responsibilities and differences in titles, all the major decisions concerning the corporation, including such matters as the nature of the product line, were made jointly by the two original partners and because of the size of the firm directly involved a large portion of the employees. It would be incorrect to presume that when photopolymer plate technology emerged, a manager of the press division failed to consult with the manager of the plate mounting division, as no such division of responsibility existed then or later.

Bieffebi remained a business of families and a family business in its method of management. A high degree of trust was placed in individuals because everyone was a part of the business and the business was small enough to permit each person to understand the nature of the business and its immediate objectives. The core machining technology used by the firm integrated the various lines of products, and the various types of large and small lathes and grinders typical in a machine shop were used in the manufacture of all the items produced. Workers were hired for their skills in the operation of this equipment or they were trained to operate the set of equipment. Thus, a skilled machinist typical of the workers employed in the plant might spend a portion of the day working on the manufacture of a multilayer press and later turn to a task connected with the construction of a plate grinder or mounting machine.

The integrative logic of the core technology is more problematic in respect to marketing because of the two sets of customers served by the firm as it evolved. Later a decision was made to have individuals focus on serving customers in the electronic industry that purchased the multilayer presses, while other persons continued serving the printing needs of the packaging industry directly or through other suppliers of equipment to the packaging industry.

GLOBAL TRANSFORMATION

Maria Teresa Benedetti was hired by the firm in the early 1970s to develop the export market for its equipment, and shipments of packaging equipment to firms outside Italy became the largest part of its business. Exhibit 1 shows the distribution of machine sales in various parts of the world. As already indicated, Brenno Sambri believed the nature of the business required members of the firm to remain as close to customers as possible to understand their emerging needs. Only the printers using the equipment could indicate the problems and limitations of the equipment, while also suggesting solutions that Bieffebi might provide. Marketing representatives like Benedetti, with her command of languages, were a significant part of the needed intelligence network and she worked closely with the technical representatives of the firms to transmit customer requirements. Benedetti was willing to listen to

Exhibit I　Bieffebi S.p.A. Cumulative Worldwide Unit Sales over the Past Twenty Years and Italian Unit Sales for the Past Twelve Years

Type of Equipment/ Area	Other European Community	Other Western Europe	Eastern Europe	Africa	Far East	North America	South America	Central America	Middle East	Oceania	Italy	Total
Rubber Plate Molding Presses	417	156	215	76	41	89	137	47	80	9	811	2,078
Optical Mounting and Proofing Machines for Flexographic Printing	676	190	65	67	39	124	131	35	18	68	241	1,654
Optical Mounting and Proofing Machines for Printer-Slotters	29	10	2	1	2	2	1	2	0	4	39	92
Various Other Equipment for the Packaging Industry	193	71	69	24	26	20	56	20	14	5	296	794
Total Units Sold	1,315	427	351	168	108	235	325	104	112	86	1,387	4,618

Data obtained from an internal corporate analysis performed on March 1, 1991.

the customers and direct their concerns to other members of the organization. Alberto Zanoli, the technical director, was acknowledged as able to solve many of the problems faced by customers with new product designs that could be produced by Bieffebi. Zanoli also had been with Bieffebi for approximately 20 years and was considered by the managers to have a vast knowledge of the technology used by customers while also having all the requisite skills and knowledge to supervise the manufacture of precision machinery with the equipment at hand.

The firm attempted to replicate this approach to successful innovation in the packaging industry in the more difficult printed circuit board market. As mentioned before, the marketing and customer relations tasks in the two areas of business had been divided. Stefano Sambri focused his attention on the electronic markets that trailed the growth in the printing and packaging business to ensure that the difficulties penetrating this more competitive market were overcome. Lorella Scagliarini was hired in 1988 to develop the market for multi-layer presses in the electronic industry—she too spoke a number of languages. The firm sought to develop a team in Bieffebi that could integrate market and production develop-

ment, drawing on the resources of the entire organization. Management hoped such a team approach might avoid missing opportunities to work with the printing and packaging industries. Using a team approach would recognize that Bieffebi was a growing organization entering its second managerial generation. Some believed the traditional, family approach, where everyone knew how everyone else would respond and formal communication and even direct conversation were unnecessary, might no longer serve Bieffebi as well as it had in the past.

Bieffebi served its Italian markets directly. Orders and inquiries were received by mail and telephone, and contracts were negotiated by the administrative staff using existing price lists, frequently drawing on information supplied by the technical design staff. Franco Degli Esposti continued to maintain a wide field of contacts in the country and these generated the largest portion of domestic business. Potential customers in Italy were generally well aware of Bieffebi's reputation and skills, or this was brought to their attention through attempts to solicit new business.

The firm used national distributors elsewhere in the industrialized world. The distributors purchased the machines on customers' orders and some parts manufactured by Bieffebi were stocked. They also serviced and provided any necessary installation and instruction. The products of Bieffebi generally complemented a larger range of equipment and spare parts sold by the distributor, and Bieffebi had no sales offices anywhere in the world. Occasionally machines were sold elsewhere in the world directly from Italy, if no territorial distributor had an active interest.

The price of Bieffebi machines used by the packaging industry ranged up to 130,000,000 Lire.[1] Some of the multilayer presses were valued still higher, and the computer assisted, optical mounting and proofing machine was even more costly. However, Bieffebi equipment was always ancillary to machines that were much more expensive, so these prices were not prohibitive. For example, the cheapest press used in the preprinting of linerboard cost approximately $1.5 million U.S., and the press manufactured in 1990 by Windmöller & Hölscher for Hans Kolb in Ulm, Germany was estimated to have cost approximately DM 10,000,000.[2]

Bieffebi's distributor in the United States was the Wilsolite Corporation: it sent technicians to Bologna for training in the service of the products it purchased from Bieffebi. Bieffebi in turn sent technicians to various parts of the world to deal with customer problems that the distributors could not handle. If the market in the United States grew as expected it would become difficult for a distributor in a single location to handle the demand for products and service; however, Bieffebi was pleased by the attention Wilsolite provided its products. Distributors in the various nations of the European Community and elsewhere in the world did not have the problem faced by Wilsolite providing service over great distances.

INNOVATION AND CHANGE

This global distribution system was one of the results of Maria Teresa Benedetti's activities over a twenty year period. The largest portion of her time was spent outside the country, developing new markets and ensuring that the system of distributors served Bieffebi's reputation for high quality equipment. Another necessary part of her task was gaining information about customer needs in various parts of the world. Some information could be obtained from Bieffebi's dealers,

but this was more often accomplished by establishing reciprocal relations with manufacturers of equipment that Bieffebi's products supported. For example, the plate mounting and proofing machines were considered part of a larger packaging or printing system by ultimate customers. Manufacturers of printer-slotters understood customer needs for a device to mount the plate used on their equipment and were encouraged to recommend the Bieffebi plate mounter to enhance the performance of their own machine.

Innovations in packaging or printing, much as in any area of technology, seldom occurred in isolation. Firms in various segments of the supporting industries cooperated to bring innovations forward and such cooperation often triggered solutions sought by end users of such innovative systems. This was particularly true when an individual supplier lacked the skills and resources to bring entirely new systems forward. Larger firms might attempt to advance entirely new systems by acquiring the skills and resources needed for such innovation, but even such firms would be stymied by the number of complementary innovations required.

Bieffebi often was a part of such cooperating relationships among suppliers, but it was not unique in this respect. And, Bieffebi had been a frequent informal partner with firms in nations outside Italy. Some packaging equipment was manufactured in Italy, but the more significant interrelations were with firms of larger size and contrasting management orientations. The people at Bieffebi learned how to work with others on intricate innovations, while the firm retained its unique properties as a family owned and operated firm.

The innovation in packaging graphics permitted by the printing of linerboard before it is used in the manufacture of containerboard provides a good illustration of the nature of interrelations among several organizations to advance an innovation. Packagers have traditionally been limited in the graphic designs they could print on corrugated boxes by the nature of the containerboard used in the manufacture of boxes. While containerboard has unusual strength and keeping properties, its inner layer of corrugated material can be crushed in the printing process and a ridged pattern can form in the printed design. Printing the linerboard used in the manufacture of containerboard prior to its construction avoids this problem, permitting the best characteristics of paper as a printing medium to be captured in package designs. The problem had been the ability of the printed paper to withstand the heat and moisture associated with corrugating and the ability of box makers to synchronize the printed message with the constructed box.

Solutions to the problems of preprinting linerboard began to emerge during the late 1970s, although a few firms in Europe and the United States had been using existing technologies to provide a limited quantity of the product before that time. The innovations were improved ink distribution for wide paper and electronically controlled knives mounted on corrugating machines that allowed the configuration of the box and the printed message on the linerboard to be synchronized. A crucial part of the task, on which all else depended, was the precise positioning of the plates on the printing cylinders used in the robust, wide-web, flexographic printing presses required by corrugating firms. Pioneering firms handled these printing register problems by trial-and-error methods of manual adjustment, but a better system of plate mounting was needed.

While Bieffebi had competition in providing equipment for the mounting of plates used in the printing of containerboard, none of these competitors were willing or able to provide the precision machine needed for the mounting of the plates used in preprinting of linerboard. In 1981, the first purchaser of a heavy-duty, wide-web cylinder press made especially for the printing of large volumes of linerboard attempted to use a plate mounting machine manufactured by the Harley Corporation in the United States and failed to gain a satisfactory result. Both Harley and Mosstype had the major share of the market for plate mounting and proofing machines used in the printing of containerboard in the United States, where Bieffebi had but a few sales, as suggested by the information supplied in Exhibit 2. Frustrated by its attempts to use a Harley machine, Altonaer Wellpappenfabrik in Hamburg asked Bieffebi for assistance with its problem getting a satisfactory result from the press manufactured by Cobden Chadwick in England, and in short order Bieffebi was able to provide a mounting and proofing machine of a new design that met Altonaer's needs.

The success of this piece of equipment enhanced Bieffebi's reputation. Firms seeking to compete with Cobden Chadwick by manufacturing wide-web printing presses turned to Bieffebi for assistance in advancing their products. Bieffebi became part of the alternative solutions offered by such printing press manufacturers as Windmöller & Hölscher and Fisher & Krecke in Germany. Each of the presses offered by these firms called for advances in optical mounting and proofing machines for the cylinder and belt-presses manufactured. Bieffebi equipment also accompanied the presses manufactured for firms in the United States, opening still newer opportunities for the firm to exploit.

Efforts of the firm in support of the emerging market for preprinted linerboard feed back on the designs of mounting and proofing machines for other markets. Bieffebi began completing manufacture of an optical mounting and proofing machine that used computer assisted design to position graphics plates in printer-slotters used directly in the manufacture of boxes. The firm also had plans to adapt this new computer approach to mount plates in the preprinting of linerboard.

The pace of innovation in optical mounting and proofing machines was hastened by innovations in the packaging industry, particularly by the success of pre-printing in Europe. Some doubted the ability of a small firm such as Bieffebi to commit the resources to meet the challenges of seemingly endless innovation. For example, promising new ways to mount plates on pins drilled into the cylinders used in flexographic printing to improve the printing register were being suggested, and the managers of Bieffebi contemplated responding to this challenge with new equipment that perfected the existing pin-mounting systems.

When Windmöller & Hölscher built the remarkably new printing press for Hans Kolb mentioned previously, it was accompanied by a plate mounting and proofing machine supplied by the manufacturer, based on patents from a firm in Switzerland. This piece of equipment integrated plate mounting and proofing with computer instructions to the main printing press, to speed job changes and productively capture the massive capacity of the machine. Based on the long-standing relations between the two firms, Bieffebi had been approached by Windmöller & Hölscher to supply the unusual type of equipment required by

Exhibit 2 Bieffebi S.p.A. Balance Sheet (All figures are in Italian Lire*)

	12/31/90	12/31/89	12/31/88	12/31/87	12/31/86
Current Assets					
Cash	1,584,951,852	3,683,287,826	4,997,197,794	3,338,788,027	2,729,322,670
Trade receivables	1,680,956,414	2,096,967,267	1,297,290,519	1,696,681,448	1,725,973,718
Trade credits	0	56,633,145	20,077,284	28,143,465	29,714,119
Financial credits	3,801,528,690	0	0	0	0
Other current receivables	3,870,000	0	0	117,683,733	74,375,250
Inventories	1,421,075,807	1,501,959,533	1,214,518,430	1,412,313,909	1,224,222,709
Prepaid taxes	677,317,000	834,624,000	1,083,890,001	1,099,161,246	0
Other prepaid accounts	465,567,750	249,042,478	98,023,794	87,237,829	166,329,825
Fixed Assets					
Buildings	1,921,478,190	1,921,478,190	1,919,628,190	1,873,444,311	1,723,702,286
Equipment	2,909,571,893	2,688,984,521	2,424,167,475	2,145,448,515	1,832,695,348
Stock ownership	281,735,000	281,735,000	281,735,000	280,400,000	120,000,000
Total Assets	14,748,052,596	13,314,711,960	13,336,528,487	12,079,302,483	9,626,335,925
Current Liabilities					
Accounts payable	928,921,109	1,143,013,003	1,035,026,317	1,324,110,579	1,175,623,791
Taxes payable	925,217,484	815,396,000	1,316,155,000	1,074,381,000	315,228,200
Allowances	1,122,643,978	1,161,150,877	1,143,543,651	632,127,945	321,791,602
Funded indebtedness	724,321,395	605,411,304	527,387,869	498,754,735	605,026,054
Longer-term indebtedness	977,788,311	442,667,498	430,031,500	467,707,854	450,657,326
Fixed asset depreciation	3,055,080,961	2,727,479,142	2,529,727,078	2,178,907,531	1,821,409,140
Total Equity					
Paid-in capital	1,933,200,000	1,933,200,000	1,933,200,000	1,933,200,000	1,933,200,000
Past retained earnings	4,070,756,136	3,619,179,071	3,370,112,839	3,003,399,812	2,016,647,795
Current earnings	1,010,123,222	867,215,065	1,051,344,233	966,713,027	986,752,017
Total Liabilities and Net Worth	14,748,052,596	13,314,711,960	13,336,528,487	12,079,302,483	9,626,335,925

Compiled from data published in the annual reports of the corporation.
*During the Summer of 1991 the Italian Lire exchanged at approximately 1300 L. to the U.S. dollar.

the advanced design of the new press, but Bieffebi declined, choosing to continue advancing the design of other equipment with its limited resources. Bieffebi employed a single electronic technician, and it contracted for the writing of software by an outside firm.

OPERATIONS AND FUTURE PERSPECTIVES

Bieffebi added about 60 percent of the value incorporated in its products. Purchases were largely rough forgings and steel slabs and cylinders, along

Exhibit 3 Bieffebi S.p.A. Profit and Loss Statement (All figures are in Italian Lire*)

	12/31/90	12/31/89	12/31/88	12/31/87	12/31/86
Revenue					
Net domestic sales	3,187,873,238	3,390,588,841	3,103,798,539	2,289,088,014	2,558,213,369
Net foreign sales	5,784,544,741	4,665,437,098	6,131,852,465	6,352,566,265	6,401,884,618
Other income	720,727,174	944,287,205	721,788,552	494,679,224	446,858,197
Ending inventory	1,421,075,807	1,501,959,533	1,214,518,430	1,412,313,909	1,224,222,709
Total gains	11,114,220,960	10,502,272,677	11,171,957,986	10,548,647,412	10,631,178,893
Operating Expenses					
Beginning inventory	1,501,959,533	1,214,518,430	1,412,313,909	3,538,604,429	1,142,933,910
Purchases	2,540,331,385	2,799,685,151	2,125,289,399	0	2,555,119,801
Labor	3,016,585,938	2,756,060,644	2,934,791,368	2,847,381,606	2,670,497,748
Other services	1,473,387,338	1,208,479,189	1,149,115,439	1,295,665,276	1,111,394,603
Depreciation	348,733,663	319,441,667	408,285,456	392,567,966	325,662,062
Total operating expenses	8,880,997,857	8,298,185,081	8,029,795,571	8,074,219,277	7,805,608,124
Other charges	1,223,099,881	1,336,872,531	2,090,818,182	1,507,715,108	1,838,818,752
Net gain	1,010,123,222	867,215,065	1,051,344,233	966,713,027	986,752,017

Compiled from data published in the annual reports of the corporation.

*During the Summer of 1991 the Italian Lire exchanged at approximately 1300 L. to the U.S. dollar.

with standard fixtures and electrical and electronic equipment. However, only one or two component parts manufactured by the firm were at the heart of the special features of the equipment produced by the firm. These pieces of machinery would never be contracted for manufacture elsewhere, according to the managers of Bieffebi. The finishing and assembly of the component manufactured and purchased by the firm provided the precision quality of its products.

As the foregoing discussion indicates, Bieffebi had flexibility in its production capability. At the same time the labor market in Bologna could supply most of the skilled machinists needed by the firm. The firm normally had one apprentice in training to learn the basic skills needed by the firm while gaining knowledge about the firm; such persons were considered prime candidates for advancement to supervisory positions in future years. Engineering personnel were more specific to the products manufactured by the firm and it took some time for a newly hired person to advance through the design department and be given both plant and field responsibilities. One

promised Friday delivery was delayed until the following Tuesday because one of the two persons qualified to provide technical approval for a shipment was in Australia working with a customer, while the other was unavailable. The owners of the firm were reluctant to permit a third person to certify the machine as ready for shipment because this person was not ready to be given such responsibility. The firm was committed to meet both promised delivery dates and the specified quality of its products: obviously there was some tension between these two requirements. Benedetti believed that "unlike manufacturers in other countries, an Italian firm cannot afford a single failure in either regard and keep its reputation."

According to Stefano Sambri, Bieffebi wished to be developing at least one or two new products at all times. Any such products would have to fit into one or the other of the existing markets of the firm. He believed the two existing businesses strained the existing marketing capability of the firm. The firm had revenues of 9,150,000,000 Lire in 1990 as shown in Exhibit 3, while the plant had a capacity to produce revenues estimated at

12,000,000,000 Lire without adding to fixed or semi-fixed costs. Sambri was stimulated by some of the new ideas talked about at the Packaging Promotion Fair in Dusseldorf in the Spring of 1991, and he saw a number of innovative products that might fit into the present market niches of the firm.

The president's letter to the stockholders in the most recent annual report indicated that approximately 20 percent of the turnover of the firm in 1990 was obtained from its business constructing presses for the manufacture of multilayered circuit boards. The letter also pointed out that 7 percent of the overall turnover was obtained in the Soviet Union. The president was not optimistic about the business results for 1991, after noting that the results of business in the latter months of 1990 already evidenced a deteriorating economic situation in the United States, coincident with the War in the Persian Gulf. However, Degli Esposti hoped a necessary restructuring of the company would help it weather the economic storm and assist in providing answers to questions about the product line of the firm.

Letters in past years had been equally cautious, reflecting a growing awareness of a heightened competitiveness in the industries in which the firm was engaged. These letters reported steps taken by the firm to control costs and rationalize production, while at the same time spurring new product developments to offset the declining sales of a rapidly aging product line. Each letter indicated a certainty of success, while at the same time reporting the relentless challenge of an innovating competition.

CASE NOTES

1. The Lire exchanged at an approximate rate of 1300 Lire for the U.S. dollar during the Summer of 1991.

2. The German Mark exchanged at an approximate rate of 1.75 to the U.S. dollar during the Summer of 1991.

REFERENCES

Aaker, David A. 1989. "Managing assets and skills: The key to sustainable competitive advantage." *California Management Review* 31:91–106.

Barney, J.B. 1991. "Firm resources and sustained competitive advantage." *Journal of Management*, 17: 99–120.

Cohen, Adam. 2000. "New game." *Time*. October 30, 58–60.

Colvin, Geoffrey. 1990. "The wee outfit that decked IBM." *Fortune*, November 19.

Dwyer, Paula, Zachary Schiller, Laura Zinn, Shekhar Hattangadi, and Lynne Curry. 1994. "Unilever's global fight: Can its new management team win the struggle for growth?" *Business Week*, International Editions, July 4.

Economist. 2000a. "BA's wheel of fortune." February 5. http://www.economist.com.

———. 2000b. "Predators in the air." June 10. http://www.economist.com.

———. 2000c. "South African beer: big lion, small cage." August 12. http://www.economist.com.

———. 2000d. "Thank you, Singapore." September 30. http://www.economist.com.

Einhorn, Bruce, Moon Ihlwan, Michael Shari, and Sebastian Moffett. 2000. "Fat city again for Asian chipmakers." http://www.businessweek.com. March 6. International Edition.

Engardio, Pete, Jonathan Moore, and Christine Hill. 1996. "As the miracle economies slow down, their hidden problems start to appear." *Business Week*, December 2.

General Electric. 2000. http://www.ge.com.

Guyon, Janet. 1999. "British Airways takes a flier." *Fortune*. Vol. 140, September 27. 214–220.

Hill, Charles, W. L. & Gareth R. Jones. 2001. *Strategic Management Theory*. Boston: Houghton Mifflin, 137.

Fortune. 2000. Global 500. http://www.fortune.com.

Kunii, Irene. 2000. "Sony's Samurai." http://www.businessweek.com. March 20.

Kunii, Irene and Janet Rae-Dupree. 1999. "Sony's stealthy shot against Sega in the video-game wars." http://www.businessweek.com. March 3.

Mitsui. 2000. http://www.mitsui.co.jp.

Pearce, John A. II, and Richard B. Robinson, Jr. 1994. *Strategic Management: Formulation, Implementation, and Control*. Burr Ridge, Ill.: Irwin.

Peterson, Thane. 2000. "Toyota's Fujio Cho: Price competition will be brutal." http://www.businessweek.com. April.

Porter, Michael E. 1979. "How competitive forces shape strategy." *Harvard Business Review* 57, March–April, 137–45.

———. 1980. *Competitive Strategy: Techniques for Analyzing Industries and Competitors*. New York: Free Press.

———. 1985. *Competitive Advantage: Creating and Sustaining Superior Performance*. New York: Free Press.

———. 1990. *Competitive Advantage of Nations*. New York: Free Press.

Philips. 2000. http://www.philips.com.

Procter & Gamble. 2000. http://www.pg.com.

Rossant, John. 2000. "Birth of a giant." *Business Week*. July 10, 170–76.

Siemens. 2000. http://www.siemens.com.

Taylor, Alex III. 1990. "Why Toyota keeps getting better and better, and better." *Fortune*, September 19, 66–79.

Thompson, Arthur A, Jr., and A. J. Strickland III. 1992. *Strategy Formulation and Implementation*. Homewood, Ill.: Irwin.

Yip, George S. 1995. *Total Global Strategy*. Englewood Cliffs, N.J.: Prentice Hall.

Chapter 6

Multinational and Participation Strategies: Content and Formulation

LEARNING OBJECTIVES
After reading this chapter you should be able to:

- **Appreciate the complexities of the global–local dilemma faced by the multinational company.**

- **Understand the content of the multinational strategies: transnational, international, multidomestic, and regional.**

- **Formulate a multinational strategy by applying the diagnostic questions that aid multinational companies in solving the global–local dilemma.**

- **Understand the content of the participation strategies: exporting, alliances/IJVs, licensing, and foreign direct investment.**

- **Formulate a participation strategy based on the strengths and weaknesses of each approach and the needs of the multinational company.**

Preview Case in Point	When C.D. Tam became Motorola's first non-U.S.-born head of a major region, the company was in the worst slump of its history. By the late 1990s, for example, in the hot mobile phone Chinese market, consumers considered Motorola's cell phones old fashioned compared with the flashy products of competitors Ericsson and Nokia. The year before Tam's appointment, Motorola lost almost $1 billion and stock prices were plummeting. Tam's responsibilities in Asia were crucial to any turnaround. The Asia–Pacific region accounts for sales over more than $8 billion and represents 27 percent of turnover for Motorola. Within one year of his taking the position, Asia–Pacific sales reached record levels.
Motorola's Turnaround in Asia	In this highly competitive market, Tam used aggressive marketing and discounting to regain market share. However, innovation is the key success factor for sustained competitive advantage. Tam predicts 30 to 50 percent growth in revenues over the next decade based on maintaining the innovation lead.

To keep innovations flowing, Tam uses strategic alliances and global platforms for R&D. Motorola is developing a superior third-generation mobile phone technology called CDMA (Code Division Multiple Access) in an alliance with Japan NTT's DoCoMo. Motorola has R&D labs in India and China, recently adding seven new labs to the existing 18 in China. Motorola has given Chinese labs the lead in developing voice-activated devices such as a planned wristwatch phone.

Sources: Based on Chang and Comparelli 2000 and *Forbes* 2000.

The Preview Case in Point describes a multinational company seeking expertise anywhere in the world to enhance its competitive position. It also shows how a company can use a variety of techniques, from acquisitions to strategic alliances, to go international. In this chapter you will find a review of the essential strategies that multinationals such as Motorola use to bring their companies to international markets and compete successfully. Unlike those in the previous chapter, the strategies discussed here pertain specifically to international operations; that is, besides the basic issues regarding strategy content and formulation, there are additional strategic issues specific to the multinational company. In addition, although the chapter begins with an example of a large multinational company, the strategies of international competition apply also to smaller companies.

This chapter contains two major sections. In the first section, you are introduced to general strategies regarding multinational operations. In the second section, you are introduced to the specific techniques that multinationals use to enter markets. After reading this chapter you should understand how global markets, products, competition, and risk influence the choice of a multinational strategy and the choice of a market-entry strategy. You should also understand that multinational managers face different and more complex challenges than those faced by domestic-only managers.

MULTINATIONAL STRATEGIES: DEALING WITH THE GLOBAL–LOCAL DILEMMA

Local-responsiveness solution

Responding to differences in the markets in all the countries in which a company operates.

Global integration solution

Conducting business similarly throughout the world, and locating company units wherever there is high quality and low cost.

Global–local dilemma

Choice between a local-responsiveness or global approach to a multinational's strategies.

A fundamental strategic dilemma faced by all multinational companies is how to compete internationally. We call this problem the global–local dilemma. On one hand, there are pressures to respond to the unique needs of the markets in each country in which a company does business. When a company chooses this option it adopts the **local-responsiveness solution**. On the other hand, there are efficiency pressures that encourage companies to de-emphasize local differences and conduct business similarly throughout the world. Companies that lean in this direction choose the **global integration solution**.

The solution for the **global–local dilemma**, whether local responsiveness or global integration, forms the basic strategic orientation of a multinational company (Humes 1993). This strategic orientation affects the design of organization and management systems as well as supporting functional strategies in areas such as production, marketing, and finance. Here we consider only strategic implications of the multinationals' global–local dilemma. In later chapters you will see how this fundamental problem of the multinational influences other areas of management, such as human resources management and the choice of an organizational design.

Companies that lean toward the local-responsiveness solution stress customizing their organizations and products to accommodate country or regional differences. The focus is on satisfying local customer needs by tailoring products or services to meet those needs. Forces that favor a local-responsiveness solution come primarily from national or cultural differences in consumer tastes and variations in customer needs. In addition, national differences in how industries work and political pressures can lead companies to favor local responsiveness. For example, government regulations can require a company to share ownership with a local company. Some governments also require companies to produce their products in the countries in which they sell (Ghoshal 1987).

To the largest degree possible, multinational companies that lean toward a global integration solution reduce costs by using standardized products, promotional strategies, and distribution channels in every country. In addition, such globally oriented multinationals seek sources of lower costs or higher quality anywhere in their value chain and anywhere in the world. For example, in such companies, headquarters, R&D, production, or distribution centers may be located anywhere they can provide the best value added with quality or lower cost (Doz 1980; Porter 1986, 1990).

Neither responding to local customer needs nor selling the same product worldwide is a guarantee of success. Multinational firms must choose carefully for each product or business how global or local they orient their strategies. Later in the chapter you will see some of the questions that managers must answer before selecting an appropriate multinational strategy. Before that, however, we will review the broad strategic choices for the multinational manager dealing with the global–local dilemma.

There are four broad multinational strategies that offer solutions to the global–local responsiveness dilemma: multidomestic, transnational, international, and regional. The multidomestic and the transnational strategies represent the bipolar reactions to one side of the global–local dilemma. The international and regional strategies represent compromise positions that attempt to balance these conflicting drives.

MULTIDOMESTIC STRATEGY

Multidomestic strategy

Emphasizing local-responsiveness issues.

The **multidomestic strategy** gives top priority to local responsiveness. The multidomestic strategy is in many respects a form of differentiation strategy. The company attempts to offer products or services that attract customers by closely satisfying their cultural needs and expectations. For example, advertisements, packaging, sales outlets, and pricing are adapted to local standards.

As with most uses of differentiation, it usually costs more for multinational companies to produce and sell unique or special products for different countries throughout the world. There are extra costs to adapt each product to local requirements, such as different package sizes and colors. Thus, to succeed, a multidomestic strategy usually requires charging higher prices to recoup the costs of tailoring a product for local needs. Customers will pay this higher price if they perceive an extra value in having a company's products adapted to their tastes, distribution systems, and industry structures (Ghoshal 1987).

A multidomestic strategy is not limited to large multinationals that can afford to set up overseas subsidiaries. Even a small firm that only exports its products may use a multidomestic strategy by extensively adapting its product line to different countries and cultures. However, for larger organizations, with production and sales units in many countries, using a multidomestic strategy often means treating foreign subsidiaries as independent businesses. Headquarters focuses on the bottom line, viewing each country as a profit center. Each country's subsidiary is free to manage its own operations as necessary, but it must generate a profit to get resources from headquarters. Besides having its own local production facilities, marketing strategy, sales staff, and distribution system, the subsidiary of the multidomestic company often uses local sources of raw materials and employs mostly local people.

TRANSNATIONAL STRATEGY

Transnational strategy

Two goals get top priority: seeking location advantages and gaining economic efficiencies from operating worldwide.

Location advantages

Dispersing value-chain activities anywhere in the world where the company can do them best or cheapest.

Global platform

Country location where a firm can best perform some, but not necessarily all, of its value-chain activities.

The **transnational strategy** gives two goals top priority: seeking location advantages and gaining economic efficiencies from operating worldwide (Bartlett and Ghoshal 1990). **Location advantages** means that the transnational company disperses or locates its value-chain activities (e. g., manufacturing, R&D, and sales) anywhere in the world where the company can "do it best or cheapest" as the situation requires. For example, many U.S. and Japanese multinational companies have production facilities in Southeast Asian countries where labor is currently cheap. Michael Porter (1986) argues that, for global competition, firms must look at countries not only as potential markets but also as "global platforms." A **global platform** is a country location where a firm can best perform some, but not necessarily all, of its value-chain activities.

The resources available in different nations provide the transnational firm with most of its location-based competitive advantages in costs and quality. For the most part, these resources support upstream activities in the value chain such as R&D and production. With upstream location advantages, the transnational can:

- locate subunits near cheap sources of high-quality raw material.
- locate subunits near centers of research and innovation.
- locate subunits near sources of high-quality or low-cost labor.
- seek low-cost financing anywhere in the world.
- share discoveries and innovations made in one part of the world with operations in other parts of the world.

So reads the sign at the gate of the Eastern Seaboard Industrial Estate in Bangkok, Thailand. Site of manufacturing units of Ford and General Motors, the "Detroit" name symbolizes that these two companies account for almost one-third of region-leading Thailand's vehicle exports. Toyota, Honda, Mitsubishi, and Isuzu also manufacture in Thailand.

Manufacturing in Thailand is not just for the local market. Rather, Thailand is a manufacturing platform for both global and regional distribution. Isuzu and Mitsubishi use Thailand as the global manufacturing platform for pickup trucks. GM uses its state-of-the-art $650 million factory for export production to serve Europe, Africa, South America, the Middle East, and other Asian countries. BMW sees three phases of development for its new plant. First, build cars only for Thailand. Second, start exporting to other countries in the ASEAN regional trade association. Third, go transnational and source from or export to anywhere in the world.

One attraction of Thailand is low labor costs. Wages are about $120 a month but still above local averages. Manufacturers also have the pick of the labor pool. GM had 20,000 applicants for its initial 650 jobs. Another attraction is proximity to potentially growing markets in south Asia.

Sources: Based on Tilley 2000 and *Economist* 2000.

Thus, a company adopting a transnational strategy can locate the activities in its upstream value chain based not only on lower costs but also on the potential for creating additional value for its products or services. For example, as shown in the Preview Case in Point, the U. S. multinational Motorola does significant R&D in China because of the abundant supply of excellent and cheap engineers.

Location advantages can also exist for other value-chain activities. These include having locations for cheaper manufacturing, being close to key customers, and locations that serve the most demanding customers. Location in the Japanese market, for example, usually requires that a firm produce products with a quality level acceptable to the whole world. The preceding Case in Point shows how several multinational automobile manufacturers use Thailand as a global platform for production and sales.

Often costs or quality advantages associated with a particular nation are called national **comparative advantage**. This is different from *competitive* advantage, which refers to the advantages of individual firms over other firms. *Comparative* advantage refers to advantages of *nations over other nations*. For example, a country with cheaper and better-educated labor has a comparative advantage over other nations. Comparative advantage is important to organizations because they can use their nation's comparative advantages to gain competitive advantages over rivals from other nations.

Traditionally, scholars viewed comparative advantage as something from which only the indigenous or local organizations could benefit in world competition. Many Japanese and Korean organizations, for example, built their early competitive advantages on the cheap, high-quality, and motivated labor available in their countries. However, the transnational strategy has made this view somewhat out-of-date. The transnational views *any country* as a global platform where it can perform *any value-chain activity*. Thus, the comparative advantage of a nation is no longer just for locals. With increasingly free and open borders, any firm, regardless of its nation of

Comparative advantage

That arising from cost, quality, or resource advantages associated with a particular nation.

ownership, can turn any national advantage into a competitive advantage—if the firm has the flexibility and willingness to locate anywhere.

Location advantages provide the transnational company with cost or quality gains for different value-chain activities. To reduce costs even further, transnationalist firms strive for uniform marketing and promotional activities throughout the world; these companies use the same brand names, advertisements, and promotional brochures wherever they sell their products or services. The soft-drink companies, such as Coca-Cola, have been among the most successful in taking their brands worldwide. When a company can do things similarly throughout the world, it can take advantage of economies of scale. Thus, for example, it is most efficient to have one package of the same color and size produced worldwide in centralized production facilities.

INTERNATIONAL STRATEGY

International strategies

Selling global products and using similar marketing techniques worldwide.

Companies pursuing **international strategies**, such as Toys "R" Us, Boeing, and IBM, take a compromise approach to the global–local dilemma. Like the transnational strategists, firms pursuing international strategies attempt to sell global products and use similar marketing techniques worldwide. Adaptation to local customs and culture, if any, is limited to minor adjustments in product offerings and marketing strategies. However, international-strategist firms differ from transnational companies in that they choose not to locate their value-chain activities anywhere in the world. In particular, upstream and support activities remain concentrated at home-country headquarters. The international strategist hopes that the concentration of its R&D and manufacturing strengths at home brings greater economies of scale and quality than the dispersed activities of the transnational. For example, Boeing in the United States keeps most of its production and development at home while selling planes such as the 757 worldwide with the same sales force. Their marketing approach focuses on price and technology, and even the price and payments are quoted and made in U.S. currency.

When necessary for economic or political reasons, companies with international strategies frequently do set up sales and production units in major countries of operation. However, home-country headquarters retains control of local strategies, marketing, R&D, finances, and production. Local facilities become only "mini-replicas" of production and sales facilities at home (Hill 1994).

REGIONAL STRATEGY

Regional strategy

Managing raw-material sourcing, production, marketing, and support activities within a particular region.

The **regional strategy** is another compromise strategy. It attempts to attain some of the economic efficiency and location advantages of the more global transnational and international strategies combined with some of the local-adaptation advantages of the multidomestic strategy. Rather than having worldwide products and a worldwide value chain, the regional strategist manages raw-material sourcing, production, marketing, and some support activities within a particular region. For example, a regional strategist might have one set of products for North America and another for Mexico and South America. Not only does this allow some cost savings similar to those of the transnational and international strategists, but it also gives the firm flexibility for regional responsiveness. Managers have the opportunity to deal regionally with regional problems, such as competitive position, product mix, promotional strategy, and sources of capital (Morrison, Ricks, and Roth 1991).

Case in Point **Thomson Consumer Electronics' Regional Strategy**	Thomson produces and sells its television sets in two regions, North America and Europe. Although some components for both regions come from low-cost suppliers in the Far East, the two operations run autonomously. Taking advantage of high-quality technical workers in Germany, Thomson produces its large, high-feature, and high-quality sets at its German factory. Taking advantage of lower-cost labor, Thomson's subsidiary, Cedosa of Spain, produces low-cost, small-screen sets. In North America, Thomson uses regional suppliers and low-cost assemblers (largely in Mexico) to serve this market. The North American products appear with RCA and GE nameplates. Source: Based on Morrison, Ricks, and Roth 1991.

Regional trading blocs such as the EU and NAFTA have led to more uniformity of customer needs and expectations within member nations. Trading blocs also reduce differences in government- and industry-required specifications for products. As a result, within the trading bloc, companies can use regional products and regional location advantages for all value-chain activities. The rise of trading blocs has forced some former multidomestic strategists, especially in Europe, to adopt regional strategies. The preceding Case in Point shows how Thomson Consumer Electronics uses a regional strategy in Europe and North America. With this strategy, Thomson gains some of the advantages of local adaptation and some of the advantages of transnational.

A BRIEF SUMMARY AND CAVEAT

Exhibit 6.1 summarizes the content of the four basic multinational strategies. Students of multinational management should realize, however, that these strategies are general descriptions of multinational strategic options. Seldom do companies adopt a pure form of a multinational strategy. Companies with more than one business may adopt different multinational strategies for each business. Even single-business companies may alter strategies to adjust for product differences. In addition, governmental regulations regarding trade, historical evolution of the company, and the cost of switching strategies may prevent a firm from fully implementing a particular strategy. The following Case in Point shows how Ford's attempt at a more transnational strategic orientation (Ford 2000) has yet to pay off.

The array of strategic options for the multinational means that managers must carefully analyze the situation for their company when formulating or choosing a strategy. The following section presents diagnostic questions that multinational managers can use to select a strategy appropriate for their company. These diagnostic questions guide multinational companies in resolving the global–local dilemma.

RESOLVING THE GLOBAL–LOCAL DILEMMA: FORMULATING A MULTINATIONAL STRATEGY

The selection of a transnational, multidomestic, international, or regional strategy depends to a large degree on the globalization of the industry in which a company competes. Multibusiness companies need to consider the degree of globalization within all industries in which they compete.

Exhibit 6.1 Multinational Strategy Content

Strategy Content	Transnational Strategy	International Strategy	Multidomestic Strategy	Regional Strategy
Worldwide markets	Yes, as much as possible, with flexibility to adapt to local conditions.	Yes, with little flexibility for local adaptation.	No, each country treated as a separate market.	No, but major regions treated as similar market (e.g., Europe).
Worldwide location of separate value-chain activities	Yes, anywhere, based on best value to company—lowest cost for highest quality.	No, or limited to sales or local production replicating headquarters.	No, all or most value-chain activities located in country of production and sales.	No, but region can provide some different country location of activities.
Global products	Yes, to the highest degree possible, with some local products if necessary; companies rely on worldwide brand recognition.	Yes, to the highest degree possible, with little local adaptation; companies rely on worldwide brand recognition.	No, products produced in and tailored to the country of location to best serve needs of local customers.	No, but similar products offered throughout a major economic region.
Global marketing	Yes, similar strategy to global product development.	Yes, to the highest degree possible.	No, marketing focuses on local-country customers.	No, but region is often treated similarly.
Global competitive moves	Resources from any country used to attack or defend.	Attacks and defenses in all countries, but resources must come from headquarters.	No, competitive moves planned and financed by country units.	No, but resources from region can be used to attack or defend.

Case in Point

Strategies Are Seldom Pure and Don't Always Work

In June 1996 Ford raised its stake in Mazda to 33.4 percent, enough to take effective control of the company. The objective was to take advantage of Mazda's technical and engineering capabilities, reduce development costs, and extend Ford's reach into Southeast Asia and Japan. Ford hoped to include Mazda as part of its "Ford 2000" strategy. The Ford 2000 strategy, a move toward more of a transnational strategy, aims to use design teams located throughout the world to design and develop cars and trucks for all markets.

However, integrating Mazda into the Ford 2000 strategy proved difficult. Mazda does have the technical capacity to produce excellent designs, like the renowned and successful Miata. However, Mazda and Ford did not resolve Mazda's role in contributing to Ford designs. Ford already had a high-quality engineering design staff in Europe, which is capable of producing small, economical cars for the European market. Ford faced the dilemma of having two design teams and not achieving the global integration of its design, a cornerstone of the Ford 2000 strategy.

Slumping sales in Europe and in some models are causing Ford to reconsider Ford 2000, its more transnational globally integrated approach to manufacturing. For example, the Mondeo, designed in Europe as a world car, failed in its U.S. version.

Sources: Based on Updike and Naughton 1996 and *Economist* 1999.

Globalization drivers

Conditions in an industry that favor transnational or international strategies over multilocal or regional strategies.

What makes an industry global? George Yip calls the trends that globalize an industry the globalization drivers. **Globalization drivers** are conditions in an industry that favor the more globally oriented transnational or international strategies over the more locally oriented multidomestic or regional strategies (Yip 1995).

The globalization drivers fall into four categories: markets, costs, governments, and competition. Each of these areas has key diagnostic questions that the strategist must answer in selecting the degree of globalization of multinational strategies. The more positive the answer to each of these questions, the more likely that companies should select a global transnational or international strategy. (This section draws heavily on Yip 1995.)

GLOBAL MARKETS

- *Are there common customer needs?* Increasingly, in many industries, customer needs are converging. These include industries such as automobiles, pharmaceuticals, and consumer electronics. However, in industries where cultural differences, income, and physical climate are important, common customer needs are less likely.
- *Are there global customers?* Global customers are usually organizations (not individual consumers). They search the world market for suppliers. PC manufacturers usually become global customers for PC components.
- *Can you transfer marketing?* If you can use the same brand name, advertising, and channels of distribution, the industry is more global.

COSTS

- *Are there global economies of scale?* In some industries, such as the disposable-syringe industry, no one country's market is sufficiently large to buy all the products of efficient production runs. To be cost-competitive, firms in this industry must go global and sell worldwide.
- *Are there global sources of low-cost raw materials?* If so, it pays to source your raw materials in those countries with this advantage. If not, it is probably cheaper to produce the product at home and avoid the additional costs of shipping and administration.
- *Are there cheaper sources of highly skilled labor?* If so, as with the case for raw materials, the strategic push is for companies to manufacture in foreign locations. The move of many U.S. manufacturing operations to Mexico and the use of manufacturing plants in Eastern Europe by German companies represent examples of the many companies seeking global sources of lower costs.
- *Are product-development costs high?* When they are, it is often more efficient to produce a few products that a company sells worldwide. Sometimes a single market cannot absorb high development costs. Toyota attempts a global strategy for its higher-end sedan (called Camry in the United States). Keeping as many parts as possible for internal components (the exterior is different in different countries), the company spreads development costs over the world market.

GOVERNMENTS

- *Do the targeted countries have favorable trade policies?* Government trade policies differ by industry and product. Import tariffs, quotas, and subsidized local companies are examples of policies that restrict global strategies. In Japan, for example, import restrictions and heavy subsidies of rice farmers keep foreign competition out and maintain domestic prices that often approach four times the world market price. Trade agreements such as the WTO and trading blocs such as NAFTA and the EU encourage global strategies by lowering governmental trade restrictions, at least among member nations.

- *Do the target countries have regulations that restrict operations?* Restrictions on foreign ownership, on advertising and promotional content, and on the extent of expatriate management present barriers to full implementation of a transnational strategy or an international strategy.

THE COMPETITION

- *What strategies do your competitors use?* If transnational or international companies successfully attack the markets of multidomestic companies, then the multidomestics may have to become more global.
- *What is the volume of imports and exports in the industry?* A high volume of trade suggests that companies see advantages in strategies that are more global.

A CAUTION

The increasingly popular strategy of going global by making uniform products for the world market can sometimes backfire. Cultural and national differences still exist, and even the transnational and international strategist must adjust to key differences in national or regional needs. The following Multinational Management Brief details the struggles in Europe of the U.S. appliance companies Whirlpool and Maytag.

COMPETITIVE ADVANTAGE IN THE VALUE CHAIN

The diagnostic questions just listed help managers decide whether to compete globally or locally in their industry. The globalization drivers represent a balance sheet of forces that move a company either toward transnational or international strategies on the one side, or regional or multidomestic strategies on the other. In addition, the location in the value chain of primary sources of a firm's competitive advantage influences the choice of a generic multinational strategy.

If most of a company's competitive advantages come from upstream in the value chain, as for example from low-cost or high-quality design, engineering, and manufacturing (as with the Toyota example), a company can often generalize these advantages worldwide. A transnational strategy or an international strategy becomes the likely choice. Conversely, if a firm generates most of its value downstream—in marketing, sales, and service—then it is well positioned to engage in a multidomestic strategy, which serves each market individually. Next, we discuss how the globalization drivers push some firms toward the transnational strategy and others toward the international strategy.

Some firms may have competitive strengths in downstream activities, such as customer service, but compete in industries with strong globalization drivers. Other companies may produce high-quality products efficiently but compete in industries with strong pressures for local adaptation. In such circumstances, multinational companies often compromise and select a regional strategy. For the firm with upstream competitive strengths, such as high-quality R&D, the regional strategy

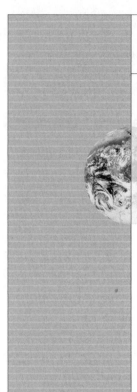

Multinational Management Brief
Local Differences Still Exist

In the late 1980s, the major U.S. rivals in household appliances, Whirlpool Corp. and Maytag Corp., saw western Europe as an untapped market. In western Europe, only 20 percent of the houses have clothes dryers as compared to over 70 percent in the United States. Responding to this perceived opportunity, Whirlpool bought the appliance division of Philips, the Dutch electronics giant. Maytag bought Britain's Hoover. But by 1995, Maytag was out of Europe and Whirlpool was facing flat sales.

Why did these companies fail to achieve their strategic objectives? Consider the case of Whirlpool. Whirlpool took a low-cost strategy and attacked its European rivals with appliance prices well below the competition. For example, Whirlpool's mid-level dishwasher costs over $100 less than a comparable model from its British competitor Hotpoint. They cut costs by using uniform products for the whole European market and centralizing R&D, purchasing, and manufacturing.

Initially, the low-cost strategy seemed a logical approach. Shouldn't price count a lot when, for example, the average European must work twice as many hours as a U.S. American does to buy a refrigerator? Maybe not as much as Whirlpool's managers believed. Quite to Whirlpool's surprise, the strategy failed. The European consumers did not rush to buy the cheaper Whirlpools. Why? Whirlpool misjudged . . .

Source: Based on Berss 1996.

allows some downstream adaptation of products to regional differences. For the firm with downstream competitive strengths, such as after-market service, the regional strategy allows some of the economies of scale produced by activities such as centralized purchasing and uniform products.

Exhibit 6.2 shows how these factors and the pressures for globalization and local responsiveness combine to suggest different multinational strategies.

TRANSNATIONAL OR INTERNATIONAL: WHICH WAY FOR THE GLOBAL COMPANY?

In globalized industries, companies with global strategies tend to perform better than multidomestic or regional strategists. They can usually offer cheaper or higher-quality products or services. How do companies choose between these two approaches to globalization—the transnational and the international?

To select a transnational over an international strategy, the multinational manager must believe that the benefits of dispersing activities worldwide offset the costs of coordinating a more complex organization. For example, a company may do R&D in one country, parts manufacturing in another, final assembly in another, and sales in a fourth. Coordination of these activities across national borders and in different parts of the world is costly and difficult. In a later chapter you will see some of the complexities of organizing a transnational company to accomplish these

Global/Local Responsiveness Pressures	Primary Source of Competitive Advantage in Value Chain	
	Upstream	**Downstream**
High Pressures for Globalization	Transnational strategy or international stategy	Regional strategy compromise
High Pressures for Local Responsiveness	Regional strategy compromise	Multilocal strategy

tasks. The transnational strategist, however, anticipates that the benefits of these dispersed activities in low-cost or high-quality labor and raw materials will offset the difficulties of coordination to produce better or cheaper products.

In contrast to the transnational strategist, the international strategist believes that centralizing key activities such as R&D reduces coordination costs and gives economies of scale. The cost savings from these economies of scale then offset the lower costs or high-quality raw materials or labor that the transnationalist can find by locating worldwide.

The world's largest multinationals seldom adopt a pure international or transnational strategy. Most major multinational corporations, such as IBM, GM, and Siemens, have some mixture of transnational and international strategies. Multibusiness companies may be more international or transnational in different business lines. However, as information systems and communications systems become more sophisticated, many of the traditional international firms are developing transnational characteristics. Boeing, for example, has components of its aircraft produced in Japan and China.

THE GLOBAL–LOCAL DILEMMA: SYNOPSIS

Beyond the traditional strategic questions facing all managers, the multinational manager must confront the global–local dilemma. Markets, costs, governments, and the competition drive the choice of a solution. As the world becomes more globalized (see Chapter 1), we are seeing more companies choosing transnational or international strategies to compete with low cost and high quality. However, cultural and other national differences still exist, and these will continue to provide opportunities to companies with more local or regional orientations.

Once multinational managers choose their basic strategic approach to the internationalization of their business, that is, their multinational strategy, they must also select the operational strategies necessary to enter different countries. The remainder of the chapter discusses these strategic operations in detail.

PARTICIPATION STRATEGIES: THE CONTENT OPTIONS

Regardless of their choice of a general multinational strategy (e.g., multidomestic or transnational), companies must also choose exactly how they will enter each international market in which they wish to do business. For example, multinational

Participation strategies

Options multinational companies have to enter foreign markets and countries.

managers must decide: Will we export only? Or will we build our own manufacturing plant in the country? The strategies that deal with the choices regarding how to enter foreign markets and countries are called **participation strategies**. This section reviews several popular participation strategies, including exporting, licensing, strategic alliances, and foreign direct investment.

EXPORTING

Passive exporter

Company that treats and fills overseas orders like domestic orders.

Exporting is the easiest way to sell a product in the international market. The effort can be as little as treating and filling overseas orders like domestic orders, often called **passive exporting**. Alternatively, at the other extreme, a multinational company can put extensive resources into exporting with a dedicated export department or division and an international sales force. The various export options beyond passive exporting are discussed next.

Although exporting is often the easiest participation strategy, it is an important one. In the United States, most export sales in dollars go to large companies, but most U.S. exporters are small companies. As you will see in the next chapter, exporting is often the only strategy available to small businesses. However, even some very large multinational companies use exporting as their major participation strategy. The aircraft manufacturer Boeing, for example, receives over half of its revenues from exports.

Indirect exporter

Uses intermediaries or go-between firms to provide the knowledge and contacts necessary to sell overseas.

EXPORT STRATEGIES

Once a company moves beyond passive exporting, there are two general export strategies that multinational companies can use: indirect and direct exporting.

Smaller firms and beginning exporters usually find indirect exporting the most viable option. In **indirect exporting**, intermediary or go-between firms provide the knowledge and contacts necessary to sell overseas. Indirect exporting provides a company with an export option without the risks and complexities of doing it alone.

Export Management Company (EMC)

Intermediary specializing in particular types of products or particular countries or regions.

Export Trading Company (ETC)

Intermediary similar to EMC, but it usually takes title to the product before exporting.

The most common intermediaries are the **Export Management Company** (**EMC**) and the **Export Trading Company** (**ETC**). EMCs usually specialize in particular types of products or particular countries or regions. They may have both product and country specializations. Usually for a commission, they provide a company with ready-made access to particular international markets. For example, an EMC might specialize in fruit products for the Asian market, and an apple producer who wished to export to Japan would seek an EMC with that specialization. Good EMCs have established networks of foreign distributors and know their products and countries very well. Export Trading Companies are similar to EMCs and provide many of the same services. The ETC, however, usually takes title to the product before exporting. That is, the ETC first buys the goods from the exporter, and then resells them overseas. The most important advantage of an EMC or an ETC is that a company can quickly get into a foreign market at a low cost in management and financial resources.

Direct exporting

More aggressive exporting strategy, where exporters take on the duties of intermediaries and make direct contact with customers in the foreign market.

The following Case in Point shows how one company found success in indirect exporting. A Japanese trading company helped a U.S. firm overcome problems in exporting its product into a protected market in Japan.

In contrast to indirect exporting, **direct exporting** is a more aggressive exporting strategy. Direct exporters take on the duties of the intermediaries. That is, the exporters make direct contact with companies located in the foreign market. Direct exporters often use foreign sales representatives, foreign distributors, or for-

Case in Point
Export Success for the Small Company

A St. Louis, Missouri, firm, Petrofsky's, devised a way to make frozen bagel dough. The original objective was to freeze bagel dough just to let the firm's bakers have the weekend off. Soon after, Petrofsky's started selling bagel dough to local supermarkets, which in turn sold the bagels as their own. More success followed, and Petrofsky's expanded its business to out-of-state sales.

Jerry Shapiro, the president of Petrofsky's, saw the potential for exports early. He visited Japan in 1985, toasted and buttered eight thousand bagels at a trade show. He adapted the product to local tastes. He made the bagel bigger and softer than the U.S. product. Cinnamon raisin turned out to be the Japanese favorite.

Exporting did not always go smoothly. While penetrating the notoriously difficult Japanese market Petrofsky's hit a snag when Japanese food inspectors barred entry into the country. The reason? "Active bacteria," or yeast, without which no bread product will rise. Shapiro handled this problem by using a powerful Japanese trading company, Itochu. Itochu had the political influence to get the product certified and approved for import.

Source: Based on Norton 1994.

eign retailers to get their products to end users in foreign markets. At the highest level of investment, direct exporters may set up their own branch offices in foreign countries.

Foreign sales representatives use the company's promotional literature and samples to sell the company's products to foreign buyers. Sales representatives do not take title to products, nor are they employed by the direct exporters. Rather, sales representatives have contracts with companies that define their commissions, assigned territories, length of agreements, and other details. Unlike foreign sales representatives, foreign distributors buy products from domestic sellers at a discount and resell the products in a foreign market at a profit. Typically, the foreign distributor is an intermediary selling to foreign retailers rather than to end users.

Some exporters sell directly to foreign retailers. For example, some Korean and Japanese exporters sell electronics products directly to large retail chains in the United States, such as Sears. Usually, for consumer goods, direct exporting requires at least one intermediary before the end user.

However, direct exporters, depending on their resources and local laws, can sell directly to foreign end users. This strategy often works better for selling industrial products to other organizations than for consumer products, such as microwaves for consumers. Some firms reach foreign consumers through traditional catalog sales or Web site catalogues. L. L. Bean (outdoor clothing), Austad (golfing equipment), and Dell Computer (PCs) successfully market through direct mail internationally. REI's e-commerce venture in Japan rivals its more traditional catalog sales.

LICENSING

International **licensing** is a contractual agreement between a domestic licenser and a foreign licensee. A licenser usually has a valuable patent, technological know-how, trademark, or company name that it provides to the foreign licensee. In return, the

Case in Point

Licensing in
the Middle
East

Dave & Buster's (http://www.daveandbusters.com/), a U.S. entertainment restaurant chain with restaurants in several states, is building its global presence with licensing. Working with licensee Al-Mal Entertainment Enterprises from Kuwait, they plan their first store opening in Kuwait City in 2002 with additional stores following not only in Kuwait but also in Bahrain, Egypt, United Arab Emirates, Saudi Arabia, Qatar, Oman, and Lebanon.

With all their international licensees, they collect an initial licensing and development fee followed by royalties based on sales. Their international menus are 95 percent the same as the U.S. menus and 5 percent local. Successful local dishes are tried in other countries. Similarly, the video games, pool tables, and other entertainment offering will remain the same as in the United States. Because of local religious concerns, alcohol will not be served.

Source: Based on Emmons 2000.

Licensing

Contractual agreement between a domestic licenser and a foreign licensee (licenser usually has a valuable patent, technological know-how, trademark, or company name that it provides to the foreign licensee).

foreign licensee provides royalties to the domestic licenser. Licensing provides one of the easiest, lowest-cost, and least risky mechanisms for companies to go international. Licensing, however, is not just for small companies or for companies with limited capital. Even the giant multinationals use licensing when the conditions are right. The preceding Case in Point shows how a growing U.S. entertainment restaurant is expanding its restaurant concept in the Middle East through licensing.

Exhibit 6.3 shows the contents of a typical licensing agreement. The licensing agreement or contract provides the legal specifications of the relationship between the licensee and the licenser. These contracts can be quite complex. They deal with everything from specific descriptions of the licensed product or technology to how the licensing agreement will end. Usually specialized attorneys from both countries work to prepare a document valid in both countries.

SOME SPECIAL LICENSING AGREEMENTS

Many international firms enter foreign markets using agreements similar to the basic licensing agreement. Like the more general forms of licensing, these agreements allow firms to operate in foreign countries without extensive capital investments.

International franchising

Comprehensive licensing agreement where the franchisor grants to the franchisee the use of a whole business operation.

International franchising represents a form of comprehensive licensing agreement. The franchisor grants to the franchisee the use of a whole business operation, usually including trademark, business organization, technologies and know-how, and training. Some worldwide franchisors, such as McDonald's, even provide company-owned stores. To standardize operations, franchisees agree to follow strict rules and procedures. The franchisor in turn receives royalties and other compensation, usually based on sales revenue. U.S. companies, such as Holiday Inn, McDonald's, Seven Eleven, and Kentucky Fried Chicken, dominate the use of franchising as an international participation strategy (Root 1994). The Case in Point on page 208 gives some background on McDonald's franchising strategy.

Contract manufacturers

Produce products for foreign companies following the foreign companies' specifications.

Some international companies contract with local foreign firms to produce the international company's products. Similar to the typical licensing agreement, the foreign company uses the international firm's technology and specifications. They then produce products for their local market or other markets. However, unlike the typical licensing agreement, the international firm still sells the products and controls marketing. This form of agreement is called **contract manufacturing**. It rep-

Exhibit 6.3 Content of a Licensing Agreement

What Is Licensed	Conditions of Use	Compensation	Other Provisions
Know-how: Special knowledge or technology	Who: Which companies can use the licensed property (and whether the use is exclusive)	Currency: In what currency	Termination: How to end the agreement
Patents: The right to use inventions	Time: How long the license lasts	Schedule: When payments must be made	Disputes: What type of dispute resolution mechanism will be used
Trademarks: Brand names, such as Levi's	Where: In what countries the license can or cannot be used	Method: Payments may be lump-sum, installments, royalties as a percentage of profits	Language: What the official language of the contract will be
Designs: The right to copy the design of production or final products	Confidentiality: Provisions to protect trade secrets or designs	Minimum payments: Agreements regarding minimum royalty	Law: What country's contract law will apply
Copyrights: The use of intellectual property, such as book material or CDs	Performance: What exactly the licensee has to do	Other: Fees for technical assistance, product improvements, training, etc.	Penalties: What penalties are in place for lack of performance by either party
	Improvements: Rights of the licensee and licenser regarding improvements in licensed property		Reports: What and when the licensee must report
			Inspections and audits: What the rights of the licenser are

Sources: Adapted from Beamish et al. 1994 and Root 1994.

resents another quick, low-cost entry mode, usually used for small markets not warranting direct investment (Root 1994).

Turnkey operation

Multinational company makes a project fully operational and trains local managers and workers before the foreign owner takes control.

In **turnkey operations**, the international company makes a project fully operational before turning it over to the foreign owner. It is called turnkey because the multinational firm builds the project and trains local workers and managers on how to operate it. After this, the multinational firm gives the owners an operational project, one which they must simply "turn the key" to start.

Turnkey operations occur most often in public construction projects done by multinational companies for host governments. For example, an international construction company, such as Bechtel, might build a hydroelectric power plant for a Middle Eastern government. Besides building the plant, the construction company would provide worker and management training. This would make certain that the plant is fully operational in the hands of local people.

INTERNATIONAL STRATEGIC ALLIANCES

International strategic alliances are cooperative agreements between two or more firms from different countries to participate in business activities. These activities may include any value-chain activity, from R&D to sales and service. There are two basic types of international strategic alliances: the equity international joint venture, known popularly as the IJV, and non-equity-based alliances, usually known as international cooperative alliances.

Case in Point

McDonald's European Franchising

Worldwide, about 70 percent of McDonald's company-owned stores are franchised. In Europe, getting a franchise is a two-year process of screening and selection. Franchisee candidates must work at a store for two years and undergo mandatory training. Those individuals selected pay $45,000 for a twenty-year contract. In return, McDonald's gets a base royalty of 4 percent of sales, another 8.5 percent of sales for rent of the company-owned store, and an additional 4 percent of sales for the franchisee's contribution to advertising. All of these percentages come from gross sales and not profit. However, in spite of McDonald's seemingly heavy take, the average European store has a profit of $200,000 per year. Large, high-volume stores in major cities can triple that sum.

Source: Based on Serwer 1994.

International strategic alliance

Agreement between two or more firms from different countries to cooperate in any value-chain activity from R&D to sales.

International cooperative alliance (ICA)

An agreement for cooperation between two or more companies from different nations that does not set up a legally separate company.

Equity international joint ventures (IJVs) exist when two or more firms from different countries have an equity (or ownership) position in a *separate* company. A multinational company may have a majority, minority, or equal ownership in the new company. A non-equity-based **international cooperative alliance** exists when two or more firms from different countries agree to cooperate in any value-chain activity. This is a contractual agreement for cooperation and does not require setting up a separate company. For example, Ford and Renault have agreed to cooperate in the design, production, and sales of utility vans for the commercial market in Europe. The market for commercial vans is quite profitable, but not big enough for one company to invest in design and production.

Gaining increasing popularity during the last decade, international strategic alliances have become one of the dominant participation strategies for multinational firms. Even firms such as IBM and General Motors, which have resources for and traditions of operating independently, have turned increasingly to international strategic alliances as basic participation strategies (Beamish et al. 1994). As an additional example, the following Case in Point shows the IJVs and non-equity cooperative alliances of Corning Glass Works.

FOREIGN DIRECT INVESTMENT

Foreign direct investment (FDI)

Multinational firm's ownership, in part or in whole, of an operation in another country.

Foreign direct investment (FDI) symbolizes the highest stage of internationalization. You saw already in Chapter 1 how foreign direct investment throughout the world is booming. Although IJVs are a special form of direct investment (i.e., ownership is involved), usually FDI means that a multinational company owns, in part or in whole, an operation in another country. Unlike the IJV, a new firm is not created by parent companies.

Multinational companies can use FDI to set up any kind of subsidiary (R&D, sales, manufacturing, etc.) in another country from scratch. They can use FDI to acquire existing companies in another country.

Greenfield investments

Starting foreign operations from scratch.

According to the World Investment Report (UNCTAD 2000), cross-border mergers and acquisitions (M&A) are now the major driving force in increasing FDI. In 1999, cross-border M&A increased by 35 percent and were worth $720 billion for approximately 6,000 deals. M&A now represent over one third of total FDI. As opposed to **greenfield investments,** starting your own foreign company

Case in Point

Alliance Fever

Seeking economies of scale, unique knowledge, and location advantages, most large multinational companies have numerous international strategic alliances. The U.S. company, Corning Glass Works, is among the leaders, with over half of its profits coming from over twenty joint ventures, two-thirds of which are with foreign firms. Major international joint venture partners with locations in the United States and other countries include (partner percentage ownership and nation in parentheses):

- Corning Ashai Video Product Company, Corning NY (49% Asahi Glass America [Japanese subsidiary])
- American Video Class Company, Pittsburgh PA (25% Asahi Glass America and 25% Sony Corporation [Japan])
- Cometech Inc., Durham, NC (25% Mitsubishi Heavy Industries Ltd.; 25% Mitsubishi Chemical Company [Japan])
- Eurokera, S.N.C., Château Thierry, France and Eurokera North America, Inc. Greenville, SC (both 50% St. Gobain Vitrage S.A. [France])
- Pittsburgh Corning Europe NV, Brussels, Belgium (50% PPG Industries, Inc. [U.S.A.])
- Samara Optical Cable Company, Ltd., Samara Russia (51% Samara Cable Company [Russia])
- Samsung-Corning, Seoul South Korea (3 separate 50% ventures with Samsung Group [Korea])
- Samcor Glass Limited, New Delhi India (45% Samtel Group [India] and Samsung-Corning [Korea/U.S.A]

Source: Based on Corning 1999 Annual Report.

from scratch, the M&A provides speed and access to propriety assets. According to the World Investment Report (UNCTAD 2000), the rapid pace of technological change and the liberalization of foreign investment policies by numerous countries are the major driving factors leading to more M&A as a form of FDI. Exhibit 6.4 illustrates the driving forces behind cross-border M&A activity based on a United Nations report of worldwide levels of FDI.

The most famous and largest of recent mergers is that of U.S. Chrysler and German Daimler Benz to create the company DaimlerChrysler—although some would say that it is a merger of unequals with Daimler truly in charge. Many other multinational firms are using privatizations in former Eastern bloc countries, Europe, and South America to acquire formerly state-owned firms. The decline of the Asian economies has also resulted in acquisition opportunities in Korea and Japan. Part ownership of a foreign company is also common in this area. For example, Ford has a controlling ownership of Mazda (33.4 percent) and Renault owns 36.8 percent of Nissan.

Some multinational companies set up foreign operations only to extract raw materials to support their production at home. This type of backward vertical integration is common in the steel, aluminum, and petroleum industries. Other companies set up foreign operations primarily to find low-cost labor, components, parts, or finished goods. Finished products or components are then shipped home

Exhibit 6.4 The Driving Forces of Cross-border M&As

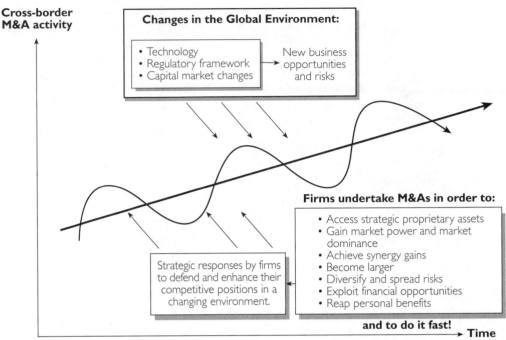

Source: *World Investment Report 2000: Cross-border Mergers and Acquisitions and Development*, Fig. v.i, p. 154, United Nations Conference on Trade and Development, Geneva, Switzerland. Reprinted with permission.

or to other markets. Ford, for example, assembles some automobiles in Mexico and Thailand primarily for export. Market penetration, however, is the major motivation to invest abroad. Companies invest in foreign subsidiaries to have a base for production or sales in their target countries (Root 1994).

The scale of FDI often changes as firms gain greater returns from their investments or perceive less risk in running their foreign operations. For example, a multinational manufacturing firm may begin with only a sales office, later add a warehouse, and still later add a plant or acquire a local company with the capacity only to assemble or package its product. Ultimately, at the highest scale of investment, the firm can build or acquire its own full-scale production facility (Beamish et al. 1994).

Exhibit 6.5 shows the leading FDI companies in the world from the developed and developing countries.

Although multinational companies have many options regarding how to participate internationally, the difficult questions focus on choosing the right participation strategy for a particular company and its products. The next section addresses these questions in detail.

FORMULATING A PARTICIPATION STRATEGY

As in formulating any strategy, formulating a participation strategy must take into account several issues, including the basic functions of each participation strategy; general strategic considerations regarding the company and its strategic intent, products, and markets; and how best to support the company's multinational strategy. We will next deal with each of these issues in turn.

Exhibit 6.5 World's Top Companies Ranked by Foreign Assets

All Companies (Assets in Billions of U. S. Dollars)				
Assets				
Foreign	**Total**	**Company**	**Country**	**Industry**
128.6	355.9	General Electric	United States	Electronics
73.1	246.7	General Motors	United States	Motor vehicles
67.0	110.0	Royal Dutch/Shell	Netherlands/United Kingdom	Petroleum
59.9	237.5	Ford	United States	Motor vehicles
50.1	70.0	Exxon	United States	Petroleum
44.9	131.5	Toyota	Japan	Motor vehicles
43.6	86.1	IBM	United States	Computer
Companies from Developing Economies (Assets in Millions of U.S. Dollars)				
7,926	48,816	Petróleos de Venezuela S.A.	Venezuela	Petroleum exp.
7,024	22,136	Daewoo	Korea	Trade
5,954	9,565	Jardine Matheson Holdings	Hong Kong/Bermuda	Diversified
5,639	10,460	Cemex, S.A.	Mexico	Construction
5,564	26,184	Petronas	Malaysia	Petroleum
4,574	6,475	Sappi Ltd	South Africa	Pulp and Paper
4,100	13,389	Hutchinson Whampoa, Ltd.	Hong Kong	Diversified

Source: Adapted from UNCTAD 2000.

BASIC FUNCTIONS OF PARTICIPATION STRATEGIES

DECIDING ON AN EXPORT STRATEGY

Exporting is the easiest and cheapest participation strategy, although it may not always be the most profitable. However, it is a way to begin to internationalize or to test new markets. Most companies will continue to export even as they adopt more sophisticated participation strategies. However, a company must answer the question: Which form of exporting should it choose?

Each export strategy has some advantages and some drawbacks. As with most business decisions, the greater potential profits of direct exporting are offset by considerations of greater financial risk and commitment of resources (Wolf 1992). In addition, there are considerations regarding the needs and capabilities of the company. The following diagnostic questions can help multinational managers select the best export strategy for their company (Wolf 1992):

- *Does management believe it must control foreign sales, customer credit, and the eventual sale of the product and customer?* If yes, choose a form of direct exporting.
- *Does the company have the financial and human resources for creating an organizational position or department to manage export operations?* If not, choose a form of indirect exporting.

- *Does the company have the financial and human resources to design and execute international promotional activities (for example, international trade shows and foreign-language advertisements)?* If not, rely on the expertise of intermediaries and choose a form of indirect exporting.
- *Does the company have the financial and human resources to support extensive international travel or possibly an expatriate sales force?* If yes, choose a form of direct exporting.
- *Does the company have the time and expertise to develop its own overseas contacts and networks?* If not, rely on the expertise of intermediaries; choose a form of indirect exporting.
- *Will the time and resources required for the export business affect domestic operations?* If not, favor direct exporting.

WHEN SHOULD A COMPANY LICENSE?

The decision to license is based on three factors: the characteristics of the product selected for licensing, the characteristics of the target country in which the product will be licensed, and the nature of the licensing company.

The Product

The best products to license use a company's older, or a soon-to-be-replaced, technology. Companies that license older technologies avoid giving potential competitors their newest innovations, while using the license to still profit from earlier investments.

Often, licensed products no longer have domestic sales potential. The domestic market may be saturated, or domestic buyers may anticipate new technologies. However, older technologies may remain attractive to the international market for several reasons. First, in countries where there are no competitors with recent technology, strong demand may still exist for the licensed product, even if it is based on older technology. Second, the foreign licensees may not have production facilities capable of producing the latest technology. Third, from the licensee firm's point of view, it may still have an opportunity to learn production methods or other information from a licenser's older technology (Beamish et al. 1994; Root 1994).

The Target Country

The situation in the target country may make licensing the only viable participation strategy. Factors that add costs to a product often make licensing more attractive than exporting. Trade barriers such as tariffs or quotas add costs to finished goods that can make exporting them unprofitable. In this situation, rather than transferring a physical product, a company can transfer the intangible know-how through a license. For example, a brewing company that exports kegs of beer may face stiff import tariffs. However, by licensing the brewing process to a local brewer, know-how is transferred, and tariffs or import quotas are avoided.

Similarly, transportation distance between two countries can add significant costs. To continue with the brewing-company example, beers are about 90 percent water—making them quite heavy to transport—and have a limited shelf life. Consequently, overseas shipping is bulky, heavy, and expensive. In such cases, when transportation costs can make a product prohibitively expensive in a target country market, it often makes more sense to license the technology to local producers.

Other issues associated with the target country affect the licensing decision. Sometimes it is the only option. For some military and high-technology products, local governments require that the production be done locally. In other situations, licensing is the low-risk option. Political instability or the threat of a government takeover of companies in the industry can make the lower risks of licensing more attractive. Since a firm neither contributes equity nor transfers products to the host country, they only risk losing the licensing income in an unstable environment. Finally, the market may simply be too small to support any investment larger than licensing (Beamish et al. 1994).

The Company

Some companies lack adequate financial, technical, or managerial resources to export or to invest directly in foreign operations. With licensing, however, the company does not have to manage international operations. There is no need for an export department, a foreign sales force, or an overseas manufacturing site. The company's managers need not know much about operations in the foreign country or how to adapt their product to local needs. The licensee assumes these chores and responsibilities. Thus, licensing is a low-cost option. It does not demand much from the licensing company and is often the most attractive option for small companies (Root 1994).

Having more than one product makes it more advantageous for a company to license. Multi-product companies can license their more peripheral or sideline products but not their key or most important products. This protects their core technologies from potential competitors but still allows additional profits from licensing (Beamish et al. 1994).

Some Disadvantages of Licensing

Although a low-cost and low-risk participation strategy, there are four major drawbacks of licensing as a participation strategy (Root 1994):

First and most important, licensing *gives up control*. Once an agreement is signed and the trademark, technology, or know-how is transferred, there is little the licenser can do to control the behavior of the licensee, short of revoking the licensing agreement. For example, a licensee may not market the product adequately or correctly.

Second, a company may create a *new competitor*. The licensee may use your technology to compete against you not only in the licensee's country but elsewhere in the world market. Even though a contract may prohibit future use of the technology or its use in other countries, local laws may not support this type of clause in the licensing agreement. In addition, even with the protection of local laws, the cost of foreign litigation may make enforcement too costly.

Third, *low income* generally results. Royalty rates seldom exceed five percent. Often licensees are less motivated to sell a licensed product with its shared profits than to sell their own, homegrown products.

Fourth, there are *opportunity costs* to licensing. That is, the licensee removes the opportunity to enter the country through other means, such as exporting or direct investment. Usually the licensing contract grants licensees the exclusive right to use trademarks or technologies in their countries, excluding even the licenser.

WHY DO COMPANIES SEEK STRATEGIC ALLIANCES?

Several motivations lead multinational companies to use strategic alliances. Most of these reasons are based on the logic that two or more companies have different capabilities that, when combined, can lead to competitive advantages. Some of the reasons for forming alliances follow.

Case in Point

BDP
International:
Going Global
with Alliances

BDP International is a privately held logistics and transportation company. Created in 1966 with six employees, it now is a $7 million global logistics company.

Early in the 1990s, CEO Richard Bolte realized that customers were saying that manufacturing was going global so logistics and supply companies must come along or die. To build a global presence in logistics and transportation, BDP formed equity joint ventures and strategic alliances with 104 companies in 96 countries. For example, the BDP and Avi group joint venture, called BDP–Asia Pacific, serves the Chinese, Hong Kong, Indonesian, Malaysian, Singaporean, and Taiwanese markets. Strategic alliances such as BDP/Bernard International with the Bernard Group of the UK are typically used for joint sales or market development activities.

Source: Based on Van Arunum 1999.

The Local Partner's Knowledge of the Market

A major motivation of many foreign companies, especially the smaller ones, is that alliances allow them to take advantage of the local partner's knowledge of the local market. Usually, foreign companies seek partners with similar products who have a good knowledge of local buyers and local channels of distribution. Often such partnerships begin only as sales and marketing agreements. They may progress to joint manufacturing and sourcing of raw material only when the foreign partner is confident that its products or services will succeed in the local market (Beamish et al. 1994). The preceding Case in Point shows how BDP International, a logistics and transportation company, teams with local companies for sales and marketing.

Government Requirements

Especially in developing countries, local governments often require joint ventures as a condition of entry into the country. Local governments want to ensure that local people have an ownership position. It is the only way allowed for a foreign firm to have any direct investment in the country. In countries such as China and in many of the former Eastern bloc countries, the government itself is often a joint-venture partner.

Local government regulations can also be difficult for a foreign firm to understand and manage. Just as local partners can bring knowledge of the local market, they can also bring a good knowledge of how to deal with local government bureaucracies. When equity positions are not required by the government, non-equity-based alliances may also provide necessary contacts and information regarding the local government.

The following Case in Point discusses McDonald's rationale for using joint ventures rather than franchising in parts of the world where management believes that business practices and government requirements require the insights of local people.

Sharing Risks

When two or more companies agree to cooperate on a project, they agree to share not only the potential profits of the relationship but also the risks, should the venture fail. This motivation for entering an alliance becomes particularly popular when either the project is very risky, as for example with an unknown technology,

Case in Point	Even though most of its operations are franchises, McDonald's prefers joint ventures in Asian markets. Following business practices common in collectivist cultures, McDonald's can use the local partners' personal contacts to help overcome cumbersome governmental bureaucracies or supply channels. In Japan, McDonald's' joint ventures are with Den Fujita, an eccentric billionaire with over 1,000 stores.
McDonald's' Joint Ventures in Asia	

Source: Based on Serwer 1994.

or the project requires a heavy investment. Some projects are so expensive relative to the size of the firm that a failure would doom a single firm to bankruptcy. Spreading the risks over more than one company allows each participant in the alliance to take on projects that would otherwise be too risky.

Sharing Technology

Not all companies have the same technological strengths. As a result, many companies seek alliances to find partners with complementary technological strengths. In combination, two or more companies often can bring a sophisticated product to market more quickly and with higher quality. This is the strategy used by the Japanese firm Toshiba and the Korean firm Samsung to improve their technological competitive advantages. They seek alliances with companies throughout the world to gain technical knowledge.

Economies of Scale

By bringing the resources of two or more companies together, strategic alliances often provide the most efficient size to conduct a particular business. Small businesses may team up to compete successfully with larger global firms (Beamish et al. 1994). Even the world's largest firms, such as GE, team up with other companies to make products more efficiently. For example, none of the several European companies that collaborated to form Airbus, the manufacturer of commercial aircraft, could have afforded the level of investment necessary to start an aircraft-manufacturing company with the scale of operations required to compete with Boeing.

Another example of cost savings by economies of scale includes Ford's use of Nissan's design for a front-wheel-drive minivan. Nissan and Ford then share the production costs at Ford's Avon Lake, Ohio, truck-assembly plant. Ford gets the design faster and cheaper and can produce a product that otherwise might not have been cost-effective. Ford also shares design and production roles with Mazda. The Mercury Tracer and the Ford Probe were both designed by Mazda. Ford assembles the Tracer in Mexico, and Mazda builds the Probe in Michigan (Kraar 1989).

Low-Cost Raw Materials or Labor

Alliances between partners from developed and developing countries often have dual motivations. The partner from the lesser-developed country seeks the technology, know-how, or capital investment from the developed country. The partner from the developed country seeks an opportunity to benefit from comparative advantages of the lesser-developed country. These advantages often include cheaper labor and untapped reserves of raw material.

Usually, these alliances take the form of a joint venture. Many U.S. firms use joint ventures with companies from Mexico to take advantage of cheaper labor costs. Both U.S. and Japanese firms often find joint ventures in Southeast Asia attractive for the same reason. The numerous untapped oil and mineral reserves in Russia make joint ventures in that country attractive to many U.S. and European companies.

Key Considerations in the Strategic Alliance Decision

Companies must assess their needs for and abilities to succeed in strategic alliances. Questions to consider include the following:

- *Could other participation strategies better satisfy strategic objectives?*
- *Does the firm have the management and capital resources to contribute to the relationship?*
- *Can a partner really benefit the company's objectives?*
- *What is the expected payoff of the venture?*

In addition to addressing these questions, to maximize their chances of success companies must plan for the design and management of the alliance. Later we will discuss the management and design of strategic alliances in more detail.

Each form of strategic alliance has its benefits. Equity-based IJVs often provide more security than non-equity-based agreements, since firms must invest up front in the creation of the new company. However, since non-equity cooperative alliances do not require the creation of a legal entity, they are often more flexible, easier to create, and easier to dissolve. Cooperative alliances can also be less visible to competitors. Which form of alliance a firm chooses depends on the needs and characteristics of the companies involved as well as on other issues such as local legal requirements.

SOME ADVANTAGES AND DISADVANTAGES OF FDI

All but the most experienced international firms usually try other forms of participation strategies before they select direct investment. Exporting, licensing, or alliances can prepare a firm for FDI and minimize the chances of failure. In any case, however, the advantages and disadvantages of FDI must be weighed. Exhibit 6.6 summarizes the advantages and disadvantages of FDI.

CHOOSING A PARTICIPATION STRATEGY: GENERAL STRATEGIC CONSIDERATIONS

Once a multinational manager considers the general merits of each possible participation strategy, there are several broader strategic issues to consider as part of formulating a participation strategy. In particular, multinational managers must consider: (1) their company's strategic intent regarding profits versus learning; (2) the capabilities of their company; (3) local government regulations; (4) the characteristics of the target product and market; (5) geographic and cultural distance between the home country and target country; and (6) the tradeoff between risk and control (this section relies heavily on Root 1994).

STRATEGIC INTENT

Although ultimately profit is the major goal of all firms, many companies enter international markets with less emphasis on the goal of short-term profit. Other goals—such as being first in a market with potential or learning a new technology—

Exhibit 6.6
Advantages and
Disadvantages of FDI

Advantages	Disadvantages
• Greater control of product marketing and strategy	• Increased capital investment
• Lower costs of supplying host country with the firm's products	• Drain on managerial talent to staff FDI or to train local management
• Avoiding import quotas on raw material supplies or finished products	• Increased costs of coordinating units dispersed worldwide over long distances
• Greater opportunity to adapt products to the local markets	• Greater exposure of the investment to local political risks as expropriation
• Better local image of the product	• Greater exposure to financial risks
• Better after-market service	
• Greater potential profits	

Source: Adapted from Root 1994.

motivate their internationalization efforts. For example, many firms have entered China and the former Eastern bloc countries with the knowledge that profits are possible only in the distant future. In the meantime, their companies are learning the market and making the business contacts necessary to take advantage of future market potential. Joint ventures often serve these purposes well.

If the strategic goal is immediate profit, then entry strategies can be compared using more traditional market-forecasting techniques. Such techniques use the predicted sales to project estimated revenues for each participation strategy (for example, licensing versus exporting). Comparing the forecasted revenues to the costs associated with the investment yields a forecasted profit for each participation strategy. All things being equal, a company will choose the most profitable entry strategy.

However, companies also take into account issues such as financial risk (for example, the cost of the investment relative to the size of the company; the certainty of the profit forecast) and political risk (e. g., the stability of the target country's government). Companies may also consider using participation strategies based on competitive issues, such as using FDI in a counter-parry move.

COMPANY CAPABILITIES

What can a company afford? This fundamental question governs entry choice. For many companies, exporting is the only viable internationalization option. Companies should also consider human resource issues. Do they have the necessary managers to run a wholly owned subsidiary, to transfer to a joint venture, or even to supervise an export department? Production capabilities may be important if the company needs to adapt its products to foreign markets. Finally, even if a firm has the necessary managerial and financial resources to implement a participation strategy, the managers must be committed to using these resources.

LOCAL GOVERNMENT REGULATIONS

Dealing with the complexities of the legal system and government regulations often challenges many firms in their own countries. A company that decides to go international confronts a whole new set of regulations in the target market countries. Many questions must be considered: What kinds of import or export tariffs, duties, or restrictions exist? Excessive import tariffs, for example, may inflate the price of a company's products to a noncompetitive level. What kinds of laws restrict foreign ownership or participation in local firms? In some countries, majority ownership by foreign companies is unlawful. Other legal and regulatory issues also demand careful consideration. Depending on the product, a multinational company might select a participation strategy based on local-content laws (how much of the product or raw material must be produced or supplied locally), patent laws, consumer-protection laws, labor laws, tax laws, and so on.

CHARACTERISTICS OF THE TARGET PRODUCT AND ITS MARKET

Factors related to the product targeted for the international market affect the participation decision in several ways. For example, products that spoil quickly or are difficult to transport might be poor candidates for exporting, whereas products that need little adaptation to local conditions might be good candidates for licensing, joint ventures, or direct investment. Another key issue relates to how and where the product is sold. This means that a company must address the question how to get the product to market. Can it use local channels of distribution? If not, the firm might explore exporting or joint ventures. If it can develop its own channels of distribution, direct investment might provide the best strategy.

GEOGRAPHIC AND CULTURAL DISTANCE

A great distance between two countries, either in geography or culture, affects the participation decision. Physical distance raises several issues. When the producing country is a great distance from the consuming country, exporting may be limited by excessive transportation costs. Even with direct investment for production, it is sometimes necessary to ship components or raw material from another country to the producing country. Distance also makes it more difficult for managers to communicate face to face, and local managers may feel "out of the loop" in corporate decision making.

Cultural distance can often be as important as, if not more important than, physical distance. Cultural distance represents the extent that two national cultures differ on fundamental beliefs, attitudes, and values. Usually, when two countries have distinctly different cultures, the foreign company initially avoids direct investment. Joint ventures, for example, are attractive in these situations because they allow local partners to deal with many local cultural issues. Licensing and exporting further remove the foreign company from direct dealings with the local culture.

POLITICAL AND FINANCIAL RISK OF THE INVESTMENT

Not all potential or otherwise attractive international markets have stable political systems. Governments change, and policies toward foreign firms can change just as quickly. Usually, firms hold off on equity investments (that is, direct investments or joint ventures) until governments show some degree of stability. However, firms that take risks in unstable political environments can sometimes gain first-mover advantage in new international markets. Many companies see the transitioning economies in Eastern Europe as politically and economically risky (see the risk ratings in Chapter 1). However, they also see great potential for growing markets and quality production sites. Thus, many multinational companies are willing to gamble on the current uncertainties in the hope of future payoffs.

Exhibit 6.7
The Risk vs. Control
Tradeoff

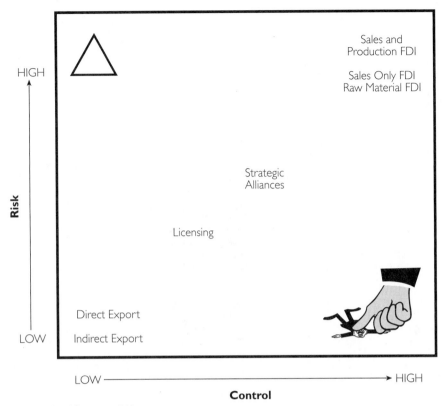

Source: Adapted from Root 1994.

As with political systems, economic systems can be unstable and risky for multi-national companies. Currencies that fluctuate widely in value make international trade difficult. Economic systems that have excessive inflation or recession can affect the profitability of local investments. Unless a joint venture or direct investment has a potential for extremely high profits, most companies stick to licensing or exporting in risky economic environments.

NEED FOR CONTROL

A company going international must determine how important it is to monitor and control operations overseas. Key areas for concern over control include: product quality in the manufacturing process, product price, advertising and other promotional activities, where the product is sold, and after-market service. Companies such as McDonald's that use uniform product quality for competitive advantage often have high needs for control. FDI usually provides the most control.

THE CONTROL VS. RISK TRADEOFF

Usually, participation choices that increase control also have more risks. For example, exporting and licensing are low-risk ventures. However, exporting and licensing also surrender control over the product or service to another party. The various forms of FDI allow firms to maximize control but also expose the firm to the greatest financial and political risks. Exhibit 6.7 shows the tradeoffs between risk and control for common international-participation strategies.

Exhibit 6.8
Decision Matrix for
Formulating
Participation Strategies

Company Situation		Participation Strategies				
		INDIRECT EXPORT	DIRECT EXPORT	LICENSING AND CONTRACTS	IJVs AND OTHER ALLIANCES	FDI
STRATEGIC INTENT	Learn the market			👍	👍👍	👍👍👍
	Immediate profit	👍👍👍	👍👍👍	👍👍	👍	👍
COMPANY RESOURCES	Strong financial position				👍👍	👍👍
	International expertise				👍👍👍	👍👍
LOCAL GOVERNMENT PRODUCT	Favorable regulations		👍	👍	👍👍	👍👍👍
	Difficult to transport			👍	👍👍	👍
	Easy to adapt	👍👍	👍👍	👍	👍	👍
GEOGRAPHY	Long distance between markets			👍	👍👍	👍
CULTURE	Large differences between cultures	👍👍	👍	👍👍	👍👍👍	👍
NEED FOR CONTROL	High				👍	👍👍👍
RISK	Low	👍👍👍	👍👍👍	👍👍	👍	👍

👍 = Favorable conditions for participation strategy

👍👍 = More favorable conditions for participation strategy

👍👍👍 = Most favorable conditions for participation strategy

Source: Adapted in part from Root 1994.

To conclude this section, Exhibit 6.8 summarizes the preferred participation strategies for companies facing different conditions for the issues just discussed. Ultimately, and perhaps most importantly, participation strategies must align with the multinational strategy. Next, the text addresses this final issue in the section on formulating a participation strategy.

PARTICIPATION STRATEGIES AND THE MULTINATIONAL STRATEGIES

Should a transnational strategist use mostly FDI? Should an international strategist use mostly exporting? There are no simple answers to these questions. Even companies with the same multinational strategies may use different participation strategies in the same country. Some of the issues that multinational managers must consider in matching their multinational and participation strategies are discussed next.

Exhibit 6.9 Participation Strategies and the Multinational Strategies

Participation Strategies	Multinational Strategies			
	Multildomestic	**Regional**	**International**	**FDI**
Exporting	Export uniquely tailored products to different countries	Export similar products to each region served	Export home-produced global products world-wide	Export global products produced in most-advantageous locations to any other country or region
Licensing	License local companies to produce products with flexibility to adapt to local conditions	License local companies to produce product with flexibility to adapt to regional conditions	License only when export barriers or other local requirements preclude imports from home country	License only when export barriers or other local requirements preclude imports from optimal production locations or when local risk factors or other barriers preclude FDI
Strategic cooperative alliances	Use when partner's knowledge is required for local adaptation of product or service	Use when partner's knowledge is required for regional adaptation of product or service	Use alliances for upstream value-chain activities when required by own resources (e.g., investment cost); use downstream alliance under same conditions as licensing	Use alliance for upstream value-chain activities when required by own resources (e.g., investment cost or knowledge); use downstream alliance under same conditions as licensing
FDI	Own full value-chain activities in each country—from raw materials to service	Own full value-chain activities in regions—distribute activities within regions for location advantages	Use for downstream sales and after-market services	Invest anywhere in the world for location advantages in sourcing, R&D, production, or sales

Most multinational companies prefer combinations of participation strategies, depending on their reasons for being in a country. Each product and each market may require a different choice. The multinational manager must ask: Why do we want to be in this country? Are we in this market to get raw materials, manufacture products, or sell products? For example, raw-material extraction and manufacturing may favor FDI as a participation choice. A focus on sales only may favor exporting or licensing, especially if the market is small.

The answer to the question why a company is in a specific country follows from the choice of a general multinational strategy. Transnationalists seek location advantages and may be in any country for any value-chain activity. Multidomestics seek local adaptation. They must address the issue of whether this is best done by modifying home-country exports or by locating the entire value chain from R&D to service in each country. Thus, the basic diagnostic question for the multinational manager is what participation strategy best serves the firm's objectives for being in a given country or region. In this sense, participation strategies represent the "nuts and bolts" regarding how a company is actually going to use international markets and country locations to carry out its more general multinational strategies. Exhibit 6.9 describes how companies with various multinational strategies might use the different participation options.

PARTICIPATION STRATEGIES: SYNOPSIS

Companies of all sizes have the option to go international. With the growth of global competition, more and more companies will continue to seek international locations for R&D, raw materials, manufacturing, and sales. This section reviewed participation choices that companies can use to operate in the international marketplace. It also addressed the major issues a multinational manager must consider in formulating a participation strategy.

The selection of a participation strategy depends on a complex array of factors, including, but not limited to, the company's multinational strategy, its strategic intent, and its need for control of its products. Most multinational companies will choose a mixture of participation strategies to fit different products or different businesses.

Summary and Conclusions

The multinational manager faces an array of complex strategic issues. In the previous chapter you saw how basic strategic-management issues apply to the situations faced by multinationals. In this chapter, you built on that knowledge to see how multinational managers confront strategic issues unique to the multinational situation.

All multinational managers, in both large and small companies, must deal with the multinational dilemma of local responsiveness versus the global solution. The choice of a solution to this dilemma was called the multinational strategy—and each multinational strategy has its costs and benefits.

There are benefits to favoring local responsiveness, a form of differentiation. Either through the multidomestic or regional strategy, the multinational can meet the needs of customers by country or region. Tailoring products or services for each country, the pure multidomestic strategy is the most costly, but it allows the company to deal specifically with differences in culture, language, and political and legal systems. The regional strategy, however, goes only part way to local adaptation. Regional adaptation is balanced against the efficiencies of doing things similarly in a whole region.

International and transnational strategists see the world as one market. They try to have global products with global marketing. The goal is to produce high-quality products as efficiently as possible. The transnational strategist differs from the international strategist primarily by using worldwide locations or platforms to maximize efficiency and quality. The transnational will do anything anywhere.

For the multinational company, participation in the international market may occur anywhere in the value chain. At some point, all multinational firms must choose participation strategies that focus on the downstream activities of selling their products or services. All participation strategies, from exporting to FDI can be used for sales. Exporting focuses just on sales, although there may be other strategic benefits such as learning about the market. However, the other participation strategies, including licensing, strategic alliances, and FDI, serve other value-chain activities, including sales. For example, a multinational company might use a strategic alliance for R&D and sales in one country and use FDI for production and sales in another country.

In a globalizing world, the complexities of choosing multinational and participation strategies represent significant challenges to multinational managers. For example, the nature of the product, the government and political systems where the company locates, the risk of the investment, and the needs of the company to control operations (to name only a few issues) come into play in formulating strategic choices for the multinational company. The Cases in Point showed how practicing managers faced and responded to the challenge of formulating multinational and participation strategy.

The next chapter will continue the discussion of strategic issues in multinational management. There you will see some of the problems unique to small entrepreneurial organizations. Many people mistakenly think of international business as the domain of the huge multinational corporations, such as Sony or GM. However, small and medium-sized multinational companies are increasingly significant contributors to the growth of global trade.

Discussion Questions

1. Discuss the conditions when a transnational or international firm is likely to perform better than a multidomestic or regional strategist. Contrast this with the opposite situation, where the multidomestic is more likely to be successful.

2. Contrast the transnational and international strategies in their approach to location advantages.

3. Pick a product and analyze its globalization potential, using Yip's diagnostic questions.

4. How might a small manufacturing company become a global marketer?

5. You work for a small company that has an innovative low-cost production method for laser disks.

A Chinese firm approaches your CEO to license the technology. The CEO asks you to write a report detailing the risks and potential benefits of this deal.

6. You work for a small company that has an innovative low-cost production method for laser disks. A Belgian firm approaches your CEO to form a joint venture with your company. The CEO asks you to write a report detailing the risks and potential benefits of this deal.

7. Discuss some key issues to consider when choosing a participation strategy.

Chapter Internet Activity

Read the chapter case on KNP, N.V. This firm has undergone significant evolution in the last few years. What do you think has happened to this company and why? Do an Internet search and develop a report on the current state of the company. Hint: Look for a company called Buhrmann.

Internet sites

Selected Companies in the Chapter

Bechtel   http://www.bechtel.com/
Boeing Inc.   http://www.boeing.com/
Dell Computers   http://www.dell.com/
Ford Corp.   http://www.ford.com/
General Motors Corp.   http://www.gm.com/
L.L. Bean   http://www.llbean.com/
Mazda   http://www.mazda.com/
McDonald's Corp.   http://www.mcdonalds.com/
Motorola   http://www.mot.com/
Samsung   http://www.samsung.com/
Sears Inc.   http://www.sears.com/
Siemens   http://www.siemens.com/
Toshiba http://www.toshiba.com/
Toys "R" Us   http://www.tru.com/
Whirlpool Corp.   http://www.Whirlpool.com/

Look Inside Multinational Firms and Their Strategies

http://yesonline.com/   *The Transnationalist: The Site Without Borders.*
http://quality.org/html/internat.html   *Information on quality for international business.*
http://www.internationalist.com/business/   *Publicly traded companies throughout the world.*
http://dir.yahoo.com/Business_and_Economy/ Companies   *Find a company on the search engine Yahoo!*
http://www.unicc.org/   *UN Conference on Trade and Development (UNCTAD) reports data on the behavior of transnational corporations.*
http://www.strategy-business.com   *Articles on strategy by Booz, Allen & Hamilton, an international consulting firm.*

Hint: Many company homepages have information on missions and strategies. Often you can read or download the annual report.

Find Out about Risk and Other Issues in the Global Environment

http://www.stat-usa.gov/itabems.html
U.S. Department of Commerce information on political risk and business factors in big emerging markets.

http://www.grai.com/   *Global Risk Assessments, Inc.*

http://www.polrisk.com   *Information on political risk—some of it free.*

http://findlaw.org/01topics/24international/index.html
Information on international law.

http://www.iso.ch   *Home page for the International Organization for Standardization—contains information on the various ISO standards.*

http://www.brint.com/International.htm
BRINT—great site for business environment sources by country.

Locate Trade Shows and Business Investment Opportunities

http://www.info.usaid.gov/welcome/ctis/ctis.html
The United States Agency for International Development provides information on international opportunities for trade and investment.

http://www.tscentral.com/   *Welcome to Trade Show Central.*

http://www.i-trade.com/   *I-TRADE Calendar.*

http://www.tradeport.org/   *Trade Show Calendar.*

http://www.tdb.gov.sg/   *Major Trade Shows in Asia.*

http://asiatrade.com/   *Conventions and Trade Exhibitions.*

http://www.publications-etc.com/russia/business/events.html   *Russian Business & Trade.*

http://www.tdb.gov.sg/   *TRADE FAIRS.* April.

Chapter Case: KNP, N.V.

Koninklijke Nederlandse Paperfabrieken, N.V. (KNP), or Royal Dutch Papermills, produces and sells paper and board products to printing and packaging industries throughout the world. The firm originated in 1850 as a small papermill in Maastricht, the Netherlands. One of the firm's three papermaking mills operates in the city today. Another papermill is located across the Maas River in Belgium. The firm also produces packaging materials at various European locations and has investments in paper merchant operations in a number of countries.

The company's headquarters are in a modern office building in a newer section of the ancient and historic city of Maastricht. It is here that Wilmer Zetteler, the commercial director of KNP België, ponders the emerging international business strategy of KNP and the decisions that will be necessary to meet the challenges faced by the firm.

KNP AND THE WORLD PAPER INDUSTRY

The evolution of the papermaking industry and the emergence of the modern European economic system have shaped KNP. In the year following World War II, the relatively undamaged but depreciated plant at Maastricht produced only 10,000 tons of paper. By 1950 the firm was pioneering the production of coated paper. KNP was the first European producer of such papers to use technology obtained under a license from the Consolidated Paper Company in the United States. A companion plant that produces top-grade coated paper for brochures, art books, and catalogs is located at Nijmegen on the Waal River. Another mill at Meerssen, a town outside Maastricht, produces colored and watermarked paper.

The oil price shock of 1973 led the firm to reconsider its fundamental strategy and further

Source: Alan Bauerschmidt, Professor of Management, College of Business Administration, University of South Carolina, and Daniel Sullivan, Professor of Management, University of Delaware. Reprinted with permission.

specialize in the production of high-grade coated papers to gain prominence in international markets. The firm was already well known for this specialty, but managed to expand its position. A mill was constructed at Lanaken, across the Maas in Belgium, just north of the Albert Canal, to produce more lightweight coated paper. This paper is used for magazines, brochures, catalogs, and promotional material.

A separate packaging division of KNP has nine plants that produce various forms of carton board for the packaging industry and other industrial applications. These products include solid, folding, corrugated, and other board products for making boxes. In addition, the plants at Oude Pekela and Sappemeer produce a greyboard for jigsaw puzzles, books and various types of deluxe packaging.

The plant at Oude Pekela in the Netherlands also produces solid board that is used in making boxes for shipping flowers, vegetables, fruits and various exports. This board product is manufactured on machines similar to those that make paper, but the board machines at KNP use wastepaper rather than virgin pulp as a raw material in the manufacturing process. The firm owns and operates eight wastepaper collection firms that handle 250,000 tons of raw material a year. Some 30,000 tons of capacity were added in 1986 when two more firms were purchased.

A factory in the Dutch town of Eerbeek produces folding box board. The pharmaceutical and food industries use this product, which also is manufactured from wastepaper. Overall, KNP processes 500,000 tons of wastepaper a year.

KNP acquired in 1986 the German firm of Herzberger Papierfabrik Ludwig Osthushenrich GmbH and Co. KG, which manufactures boxes in four locations in western Germany. The Oberstot plant, gained in the Herzberger acquisition, also produces liner and corrugated board used in boxes and other packaging applications. The Herzberg and Oberau plants that were acquired also produce the corrugated materials used in box converting operations. These acquisitions increased the capacity of the packaging division of KNP by 60 percent.

In addition to the four German packaging plants, KNP owns box-making operations in the Netherlands, Italy, and Spain. Each is supplied with board stock manufactured by other divisions of the firm. KNP also has a joint venture with Buhrmann-Tetterode, N.V. in operating a mill that can produce 350,000 tons of paper for the manufacture of corrugated board. With the addition of a fourth machine at the mill in 1986, this joint venture has become one of the principal suppliers of packaging paper of the European market.

KNP began a series of acquisitions of paper merchants beginning in the late 1970s. Each acquisition was a defensive strategy to prevent competitors from capturing existing channels of distribution of KNP products. KNP has paper merchant operations in Belgium, France, and the United Kingdom. The firm also owns a 35 percent interest in Proost en Brandt, one of the two largest paper merchants in the Netherlands, and a 51 percent share in Scaldia Papier B.V. in Nijmegen.

Exhibit 1 displays the group structure of KNP, while Exhibits 2 and 3 summarize the plant capacity of the principal divisions of the company. Figure A shows the location of facilities in the Netherlands.

Internationalizing of the Firm

KNP's activity outside the Netherlands is not surprising. As with most Dutch manufacturers, the firm has always been an exporter and maintained an international perspective. The market for paper in the Netherlands is insufficient to support a plant. Europe is KNP's principal market. In 1986, 75 percent of its paper and 45 percent of its packaging materials were sold outside the Netherlands.

The modern manufacture of paper products depends upon machines that produce large volumes. KNP has state-of-the-art technology that can produce such volumes.

The Netherlands has a population of 15 million, not nearly enough people to support a single modern paper manufacturing plant. On the other hand, the European Community has a population of about 275 million and a modern economy that can easily support a number of competing paper firms.

In most European countries, paper is traditionally marketed through paper merchants who distribute products to converters and printers. These merchants serve national or subnational markets.

Exhibit 1 KNP,
N.V. Group
and Divisional
Organization

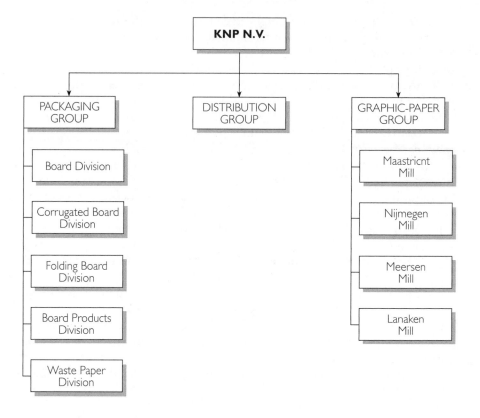

Yet sometimes market development is not straightforward. When the demand for lightweight machine-coated paper emerged in the United States, KNP had a paper merchant on each coast for other products of the firm. But the lightweight coated product required a more direct approach to the printing customer. KNP skirted traditional distributors and developed an exclusive relationship with the Wilcox-Walter-Furlong Paper Company, a paper merchant in Philadelphia that stocked KNP's product in the eastern United States. In the western United States, the firm marketed its product through the offices of MacMillan Bloedel, a firm with a 30 percent stock interest in KNP.

KNP's foreign activities can be divided into two segments and two stages. Part of the first stage has existed since the firm began exporting to adjacent nations in the mid-19th century.

The second stage began with the development of the European Community, which was an important factor in the growth of KNP. The development of the company after World War II was typical of other manufacturers in Europe. Management knowledge and skill was necessary to seize the opportunity provided by the reconstruction of the European economy.

The European Community is designed to break down barriers that prevent economic activity. As the community emerged, paper firms and other businesses used skilled sales agents who were proficient in dealing with the new market. Firms succeeded in extending their markets by meeting the needs of each nation.

Language was not a barrier at KNP, where executives typically speak a number of European languages. Cultural differences also were not a factor.

Outside Europe, KNP initially exported specialized products to Africa and the Middle East. In the early 1980s, the company began exporting to Australia and the Far East and began testing markets in the United States and Canada. No special cultural and language barriers emerged because of the company's previous experience in exporting to European nations.

KNP penetrated the United Kingdom market by working through a sales agent with contacts in

Exhibit 2 KNP, N.V. Plant Capacities of Packaging Group

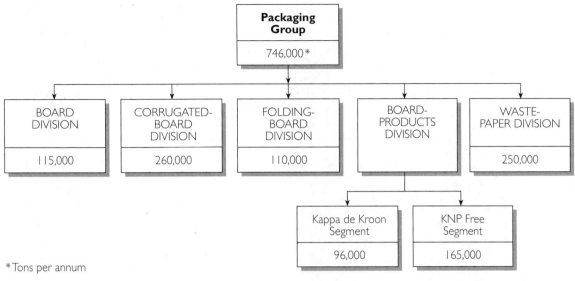

*Tons per annum

Exhibit 3 KNP, N.V. Plant Capacities of Graphic Paper Group

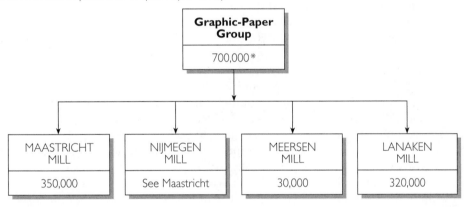

*Tons per annum

the printing trades. Later, the company solidified its position in the United Kingdom by hiring an English paper merchant, Contract Papers Limited, to distribute its products. KNP now owns 45 percent interest in the company.

KNP today is one of Europe's largest exporters of coated paper and a leading producer of board. According to KNP's 1986 annual report, 31 percent of sales were in the Netherlands, 55 percent elsewhere in the European Community, and 14 percent elsewhere in the world.

Globalization of the Firm

KNP cannot be considered a fully globalized company because it does not manufacture products in the markets it serves.

Although the specialized paper products of KNP are global products, their manufacture does not fit the global integrated strategy as described by Yves Doz and other theorists of international business. Therefore, KNP would be best described as following a multifocal international business strategy.

Figure A KNP Plant Locations

The paper industries of Europe and North America have different configurations. American firms tend to be more fully integrated vertically and horizontally in respect to the full range of forest products. European firms, with the exception of the Scandinavians, have little opportunity to buy extensive woodlands in their home countries. Because North American firms have woodlands and a large domestic market, it is difficult for European firms to become established in the market. The Swedes and Finns, on the other hand, have forest resources, but they are handicapped by poor markets for finished paper in their countries.

KNP has acquired foreign paper merchants with connections in various world markets. KNP owns Papetries Libert S.A. in Paris. The firm has a 51 percent holding in Saldiaa Papier, N.V. in Wilrijk, Belgium, and a 45 percent stake in Contract Papers (Holdings) Ltd. in London. In the Netherlands, KNP has a 35 percent interest in Proost en Bandt, N.V. in Amsterdam, and a 51 percent interest in Scaldia Papier B.V. in Nijmegen.

These acquisitions were made in 1978 and 1979 as a defensive move against competitors in the European Community. Competitors had begun acquiring paper merchants that sold KNP products and threatened to use them to promote their own products. Meanwhile, the paper merchants acquired by KNP continue to stock a full range of goods, including those produced by competitors.

No distinct figures are available on KNP's foreign revenues. Overall, distribution provided 2 percent of operating results, while the paper group provided 62.9 percent of operating revenues and 71.7 percent of operating results. The packaging group produced 29.2 percent of operating revenue and 26.3 percent of operating results. These figures ignore the influence of internal transfers, which made up 8.2 percent of the total operating activity of the firm.

Other Aspects of Globalization

In many respects, the creation of KNP België, N.V. in Lanaken is a prime example of the establishment of a greenfield manufacturing operation in a foreign country. The Lanaken paper manufacturing operation was established at the point when the business strategy of the firm shifted toward the production of special grades of coated paper for the printing trades. This decision, just before the energy crisis in the early 1970s, enabled the firm to exploit those grades of specialty paper that had a higher value added in manufacture. The creation of the greenfield operation at Lanaken supported an offensive European niche strategy, while the acquisition of paper merchants in France, Belgium and the United Kingdom was a defensive maneuver to prevent erosion of existing channels of distribution that supported the more extensive range of products produced by KNP.

The plant that was finally constructed at Lanaken had to be located somewhere in the heavy industrial triangle of northwest Europe to minimize transportation costs to key European markets. The Liege-Limburg-Aachen area is close to the heart of this triangle and has the necessary infrastructure for paper production. The nearby Albert Canal provides direct access to the facilities of the port of Antwerp and pulp shipments from worldwide sources.

The situation is somewhat different at the packaging materials operations of KNP in Germany, Italy, and Spain. Raw materials are shipped from KNP operations in the Netherlands and Germany. These locations are strategically situated to minimize transportation costs.

Future Globalization

A more important question is whether KNP would ever consider harvesting forest resources, given the limited opportunity to manufacture pulp in the Netherlands. In contrast, some American and Japanese firms have been enticed by less developed nations to develop and harvest forests so that they have sure sources of pulp. This is one example of globalization. Another example is shipping antiquated paper machines or converting equipment to less developed countries where labor and energy costs are lower.

Future Strategic Developments

The top management team at KNP is aware of these developments in the world paper industry. Zetteler will take these features into account as he helps plan KNP's future, as marketing and production strategies in the industry are already showing signs of change. For example, the firm in early 1987 started a 70,000 ton capacity chemi-thermomechanical pulp line in at the Lanaken mill. This is KNP's first integrated production operation that uses softwood drawn from the Ardennes, instead of the chemical pulp purchased in the international commodity markets. The firm is considering doubling this integrated capacity with a second pulp line in the next few years.

The emergence of KNP and other firms of integrated European producers of special papers would enhance competition in various world markets. The U.S. market has already been penetrated because of the declining value of the dollar and the superior quality of certain European paper products. Any firm that entered the U.S. market, however, would have to consider transportation costs and the advantages of U.S. producers that have forest resources.

CASE QUESTIONS FOR DISCUSSION

1. Should KNP manufacture in other national locations to obtain economies of transportation in raw material and final product?

2. Will competitive pressures require further forward integration by KNP into paper merchant operations?

3. What potential impact (and in what time frame) will new technology have on KNP plant placement production methods and materials producing?

References

Bartlett, C. A., and S. Ghoshal. 1990. *Managing across Borders: The Transnational Solution*. Boston: Harvard Business School Press.

Beamish, Paul, J. Peter Killing, Donald J. Lecraw, and Allen J. Morrison. 1994. *International Management*. Burr Ridge, Ill.: Irwin.

Berss, Marcia. 1996. "Whirlpool's bloody nose." *Forbes*, March 11, 90–92.

Chang, Allen T. and Peter Comparelli. 2000. "Back at the top." http://www.asia-inc.com.

Corning 1999 Annual Report, http://www.corning.com/investor/annual_report.

Doz, Yves L. 1980. "Strategic management in multinational companies." *Sloan Management Review* 21:2, 27–46.

Economist 1999. "The revolution at Ford." August 7. http://www.economist.com.

Economist 2000. "Car making in Asia: politics of scale." June 24. http://www.economist.com.

Emmons, Natasha. 2000. "Dave & Buster's expands to Middle East." *Amusement Business*. 112, September 11, 59–60.

Forbes 2000. "The China factor." November 13. http://www.forbes.com.

Ghoshal, Sumatra. 1987. "Global strategy: an organizing framework." *Strategic Management Journal* 8, 424–40.

Hill, Charles W. L. 1994. *International Business: Competing in the Global Marketplace*. Burr Ridge, Ill.: Irwin.

Humes, Samuel. 1993. *Managing the Multinational: Confronting the Global–Local Dilemma*. New York: Prentice Hall.

Kraar, Louis. 1989. "Your rivals can be your allies." *Fortune*, March 27, 66–70.

Morrison, Allen J., David A. Ricks, and Kendall Roth. 1991. "Globalization versus regionalization: Which way for the multinational?" *Organizational Dynamics*, Winter, 17–29.

Norton, Rob. 1994. "Strategies for the new export boom." *Fortune*, August 22, 125–30.

Porter, Michael E. 1986. "Changing patterns of international competition." *California Management Review* 28:2.

———. 1990. *Competitive Advantage of Nations*. New York: Free Press.

Root, Franklin R. 1994. *Entry Strategies for International Markets*. New York: Lexington Books.

Serwer, Andrew E. 1994. "McDonald's conquers the world." *Fortune*, October 17, 103–116.

Tilley, Robert. 2000. "Detroit moves East." http://www.asia-inc.com. October.

UNCTAD. 2000. *World Investment Report: Cross-border Mergers and Acquisitions and Development*. New York: United Nations.

Updike, Edith Hill, and Keith Naughton. 1996. "Revving up the ailing Japanese carmaker is proving to be a much knottier problem than Ford expected." *Business Week*, International Editions, Asian cover story, October 7.

Van Arunum, Patricia. 1999. "BDP International uses alliances to become a global company." *Chemical Market Reporter*. 255, March 22, 27–30.

Wolf, Jack S. 1992. *Export Profits: A Guide for Small Business*. Dover, N. H.: Upstart Publishing Company.

Yip, George S. 1995. *Total Global Strategy*. Englewood Cliffs, N. J.: Prentice Hall.

Part 2 Integrating Case 1

Airview Mapping, Inc.

In early March 1994, Rick Tanner, the principal of Airview Mapping, Inc., started drafting plans for the upcoming summer season. For him, late winter typically involved making sales calls on the company's established and potential clients for the purpose of determining the expected demand for his services and then drafting his sales forecasts for the upcoming year.

Airview, which had traditionally dominated the aerial surveying markets of Central and Eastern Canada, had recently been faced with increasing competition from other air surveyors from across Canada in its traditional territories. The protracted recession of the early 1990s, combined with the anti-deficit measures introduced by all levels of government, had reduced the overall demand for geomatic services in Canada, producing significant overcapacity in the industry, including the particular markets in which Airview was involved.

This situation had already reduced the company's profits, but the real threat lay in the fact that the new competitors, once established in Airview's region, would stay there, permanently capturing a significant share of the Central Canadian market. These competitors, typically larger than Airview, could expand their market coverage, even if it meant creating a temporary operating base in a distant location. At the same time, their home markets were extremely difficult for small companies from other regions to penetrate due to their fierce price competition.

Rick realized that his company might face difficult times if he could not redirect his attention to some new areas of opportunity. His view was that these opportunities had to be found in international markets. He had already gathered some information on several foreign markets, which looked promising from the company's perspective. It was now time to review the overall situation and decide whether to attempt penetrating any of the identified foreign markets, and, if so, what entry strategy to choose.

Source: Prepared by Kris Opalinski and Walter S. Good of the University of Manitoba as a basis for classroom discussion rather than to illustrate either effective or ineffective handling of an administrative situation. The name of the company and its officers have been disguised. Support for the development of this case was provided by the Centre for International Business Studies, University of Manitoba. Used with permission of the authors.

THE COMPANY

Airview Mapping, Inc. was incorporated in November 1979 by a group of former employees of Aerosurvey Corporation Ltd., with Tom Denning and Rick Tanner as the principal shareholders of the new entity. For the first two years, the company operated without an aircraft, providing mapping services based on externally developed photogrammetric images to clients in Central Canada. Airview's early success provided sufficient capital to acquire an aircraft and a photographic processing laboratory, which, in 1981, was initially placed under the company's subsidiary, Airtech Services Ltd. The two operations were amalgamated in November 1983 under the parent company's name.

When Tom retired in 1990, Rick took over his duties as president and offered key employees 40% of the company's shares, retaining 60% himself.

Airview's sales grew steadily throughout the 1980s, from an annual level of $500,000 in 1981 to $1.2 million in 1989. Sales stabilized during the 1990s at a level of just over $1.1. million.

Airview had traditionally maintained an advanced level of technical capability, investing in the most up-to-date photographic, film processing, data analysis, and plotting equipment. This, combined with the technical expertise of the company's staff, had enabled them to build an excellent reputation for quality, reliability, and professionalism.

PRODUCT LINE

With its extensive technological capabilities, Airview provided a range of services associated with the development of spatial images of terrain; referred to (in Canada) as *geomatics*. The company's primary specialization was related to its ability to acquire airborne images of objects, areas, or phenomena. Its image processing capabilities, however, provided an opportunity to complement its core offering by processing and analyzing externally acquired imagery. The range of services provided by Airview included:

AERIAL PHOTOGRAPHY AND PHOTOGRAMMETRY

Aerial photography occupied a pivotal place in Airview's business. The majority of the complex services provided by Airview were initiated by taking photographs from the air. However, aerial photography was also a separate product, which, depending on the light spectrum applied during the picture taking, could provide information on forest growth and diseases, quality of water resources, wildlife migration, land erosion, and other physical features.

Photogrammetry involved a number of image-processing techniques using aerial photographs as a basis for the development of maps, composite views, or spatially referenced databases. Photogrammetry was distinguished from aerial photography by its capability to identify three-dimensional coordinates for each point on the captured image.

Aerial photography/photogrammetry was very capital intensive, requiring a specially prepared aircraft with specialized cameras and sophisticated photo-laboratory equipment. Airview was considered one of the best equipped aerial photography companies in Canada. Its survey aircraft, with a 25,000-foot photo ceiling was capable of producing photographs at scales of up to 1:10,000. A recently (1992) acquired

Leica camera represented the latest in optical technology, meeting all calibration and accuracy requirements set by North American mapping agencies and accommodating a wide variety of specialized aerial film. Finally, Airview's photo laboratory, which was certified by the National Research Council, processed all types of aerial film used by the company.

AERIAL SURVEYING

Aerial surveying involved taking photographs with the purpose of defining and measuring boundaries and the configuration of particular areas on the earth's surface for a variety of uses, such as establishing ownership rights (*cadastre*); triangulation[1]; locating and appraising mineral resources, forests, and wild habitat; and detecting earth and water movements.

MAPPING

This area included the development of maps from either internally or externally acquired photographic images. Before the 1980s, map making had largely been a manual process of drawing the terrain's contours and elevations and then inserting the accompanying descriptive information. Since the early 1980s, however, the process had been increasingly computer-driven. This resulted in a reduction in the manual labor required and in increased accuracy of the images produced. At the same time, the new technology permitted the storage of maps in a digital format, which created demand for converting maps from the traditional, analog format into a computer-based one.

CADD

This area also dealt with map making, but based on computer-operated scanners supported by CADD/CAM (computer-aided design and drafting/computer-aided mapping) software. With this technology, the digitizing of analog images, such as existing maps or photographs, was fully automated. The scanners interpreted the subject image as a series of dots identified by their coordinates, colors, and illuminance and then produced their digital presentation. The computer-stored images could then be enhanced by adding descriptive information, using a process still performed manually by the CADD operators.

CONSULTING

Over its 15-year history, Airview had developed a multidisciplinary team of specialists, whose expertise had also been employed in providing consulting services associated with the planning and execution of comprehensive mapping projects. This area involved advising clients on the optimal method of gathering spatial information, the interpretation of client-provided data, and supervising data-gathering projects conducted by the client or their subcontractors.

Data capture (aerial photography/photogrammetry) and data-processing (mapping and CADD) projects had traditionally generated (in equal proportions) around 90% of Airview's sales. The remainder had come from consulting projects (9%) and surveying (1%). By 1994, this sales distribution did not reflect the changing structure of the marketplace, where data capture had become a relatively small part of the overall scope of geomatic activities.

CUSTOMER BASE

Airview Mapping, Inc. provided services to a variety of clients locally and nationally. The majority of the company's sales had traditionally come from the public sector. Over the period of 1991 to 1993, government agencies (both federal and provincial), local municipalities, and regional utilities in Ontario, Manitoba, and Saskatchewan had accounted for between 65% and 75% of the company's total dollar sales.

Agencies of the federal and provincial governments as well as provincial utilities were the company's most significant clients. Procurement by public tender, the significant size of individual contracts (from $50,000 to $100,000+), and clear specifications of requirements characterized these projects.

The private sector, accounting for the remaining 35% to 45% of Airview's sales, was represented predominantly by clients from the mining and resource sectors. These contracts were typically in the range of $20,000 to $40,000. Companies representing such diverse areas as construction, recreation, and environmental protection contracted for projects typically valued at up to $20,000 each. Companies from the private sector did not apply a rigorous procurement procedure and frequently needed guidance in defining (or redefining) the requirements of their projects.

GEOGRAPHIC COVERAGE

Airview concentrated its activities within a 1,200-mile radius of its headquarters in the provincial capital of one of the prairie provinces. In this local region, the company was able to deal directly with its clients and had a cost advantage over its competitors from other provinces. It included Northwestern Ontario, Manitoba, Saskatchewan, and Alberta, each contributing equally to the company's revenues.

The company had never attempted to expand beyond the Canadian market, even though the sizeable market south of the U.S.–Canada border was well within its 1,200-mile radius. In the past, this had been justified by the abundance of opportunities available in Canada and restrictions on foreign access to the U.S. market. However, this situation had recently changed on both counts, which caused Rick to consider changing his company's geographic orientation.

ORGANIZATION AND STAFF

The production process associated with the services provided by Airview involved grouping activities into three functional areas; airplane operation and maintenance (two staff members), film development (two), and image processing/output (ten). Regular managerial, marketing, and administrative activities involved four additional staff.

Each production area (aircraft operations, photo lab, data capture, and data conversion) was assigned a coordinator responsible for quality assurance and overall coordination of the workload in the area. These coordinators also provided expert advice to their staff and were responsible for individual projects within their respective production areas.

Airview's production activities were characterized by the relatively small number of concurrent projects (4 to 6) and their modest size. This, combined with the well-trained staff (13 out of 18 had completed postsecondary education in geomatics-related fields), enabled the company to apply a skeleton project management structure.

Coordination of project work among different production areas was the responsibility of the production coordinator, Sean Coleman. Garry Howell was in charge of marketing. Tim Connors, who occupied the position of vice president, also acted as the general manager responsible for all projects. Rick, who was the company's president, oversaw general administration and communication with customers.

PRICING

Each price quotation was based on Garry Howell's assessment of the scope of work required to complete it. This was broken down by category of activity (aircraft operation, film processing, digitization of images, or image analysis). For each of these activity categories, a budget hourly rate was developed, based on historical cost figures (both direct and fixed), the budgeted number of hours for a given planning period, and the company's profit targets. Recently, rates had ranged from $25 for digitization of images to over $900 for aircraft flying time, with an overall average of some $70.

The initial price was determined by multiplying the estimated number of hours required in each category by its budgeted rate and then adding the figures for all activity categories involved in the project. This price was later adjusted by Rick's assessment of the competitive situation (in the case of a tendered bid) or his negotiations with the customer.

Generally, Airview's budgeted rates and—consequently—prices were within the average values prevailing in Canada. This situation reflected their general knowledge of the cost structure of the industry. Any undercutting of price tended to raise suspicions of lower standards. This being the case, the competition between bidders had severely squeezed profit margins, with many firms trying to survive by quoting their services on a break-even basis.

FINANCIAL RESULTS

In the late 1980s and early 1990s, Airview had acquired advanced photographic and mapping equipment and computer hardware and software with a total value of close to $900,000. Financing for these acquisitions had been provided by bank loans and capital leases at interest rates ranging from 12.25% to 17.25%.

During the most recent two years, the cost of servicing this debt load had created a real strain on the company's cash flow, requiring an annual outlay of $200,000, split evenly between interest costs and repayment of the principal. This was extremely difficult for a company traditionally only generating a free annual cash flow in the range of $100,000 to $150,000.

Airview's operating cost structure was characterized by a high proportion of fixed costs. Currently, some 75% of direct costs and 83% of total costs did not vary with changes in their sales level. This cost structure might seem surprising for a business with some 60% of its direct expenses associated with wages and salaries. However, considering the unique nature of the professional qualifications of the company's staff, it was extremely difficult, if not impossible, to vary the number of staff in line with fluctuations in sales levels.

This situation reduced the company's profit at their current sales level, but, at the same time, created significant profit potential with a possible sales increase. It was estimated that the company, barely breaking even at its current sales of $1.1 million, could make over $200,000 in profits by increasing sales to $1.4 million.

Exhibit I
Airview's Corporate
Profile: Current
versus Target
(5-Year Perspective)

	Current	Target
Rank and Size	$1,100,000 sales $0–$25,000 profits 18 employees Medium-sized aerial surveying company No export sales	$2,000,000+ sales $300,000+ profits 30+ employees Medium-sized GIS company $700,000+ export sales
Product Line	Aerial photography—40% Mapping—30% Surveying—1% CAD—20% Commercial—9% 5–10 concurrent projects	Aerial photography—30% GIS—40% Mapping—20% Commercial/consulting—10% 3–5 concurrent projects
Geographic Coverage	Canada—100%	Canada—60% International—40%
Performance Goals	Maintenance of cash flow Profit margin Protecting market share	Sales/profit growth Market penetration Technology adoption New product development Productivity

Strengths	Customer goodwill
	Technological expertise
	Aerial photography
	Digital imaging
		Customer goodwill
		Active marketing
		Geographical diversification
		Flexible offer
		Technological expertise
		   Digital imaging
		   Aerial photography
		   System development

Weaknesses	Marketing Narrow product line Balance sheet	International exposure
Strategy	Passive	Active

OVERALL STRATEGIC PROFILE

Viewed from a strategic perspective, Airview could be characterized as a locally based company with strong technical capabilities but limited expertise in marketing, particularly outside its traditional markets. Rick recognized the importance of having a clear understanding of his company's current position as well as its goals for the next few years. His analysis of Airview's structure and performance led him to develop the company's corporate profile presented in Exhibit 1.

INDUSTRY TRENDS

The term geomatics was widely used in Canada to describe a variety of fields that acquired, managed, and distributed spatially referenced data. The term was generally applied to refer to several disciplines, including the following:

- Aerial photography
- Ground-based (geodetic) and aerial surveying—i.e., assessing and delimiting boundaries of land

- Mapping—i.e., cartography (map making based on ground measurements) and photogrammetry (converting photographic images and measurements into maps)
- Geographic Information Systems (GIS)—i.e., computer-based systems for the storage and processing of spatial information
- Remote sensing—i.e., satellite-borne images and measurements (quite often, airborne images were included in the remote sensing category)

The use of this general term, however, was limited to Canada. In other countries these disciplines were referred to by their individual names. On the other hand, the term remote sensing was frequently used to describe all satellite and airborne observations of the earth's surface, regardless of their purpose and the techniques applied. Although traditionally distinct, these disciplines were becoming increasingly integrated due to the commonality of the computer tools employed to acquire and process the spatial information and generate the final product.

The emergence of satellite-based remote sensing had also affected the geomatics industry worldwide. Its impact on air-based services had been largely positive, despite the fact that both technologies served the same user segments. Advances in satellite technology had received a lot of publicity, which sensitized users of geomatic services to the cost advantages of remote sensing in general and aerial photography/photogrammetry in particular. Consequently, those users who could not use satellite-based services turned to airborne imagery. In many cases, satellite trajectories limited the frequency with which information on a particular earth location could be gathered. This problem was further exacerbated by the prevalence of cloud cover over certain territories. It was expected that, despite recent plans to increase the overall number of remote sensing satellites, aerial photography/photogrammetry would maintain its advantage in applications requiring high resolution capabilities (aerial images could produce resolutions in a 2 to 3 in. range versus a 10 m range available from most satellites) and full-color capabilities.

AIRVIEW'S MARKETS

In the first half of the 1990s, the Canadian geomatics industry was represented by over 1,300 firms from all geomatic disciplines, employing some 12,000 people. The largest number of firms were located in Quebec and Ontario, followed by British Columbia. The distribution of primary activities within the industry was as follows:

Major Line of Business	% of Total Establishments	% of Total Billings
Geodetic (ground) surveying	65%	53%
Mapping	9%	16%
Remote Sensing	5%	11%
Consulting	10%	4.5%
GIS	7%	12%
Other	4%	3.5%

The vast majority (86%) of geomatic firms were small establishments generating sales of less than $1 million. However, the remaining, small number of larger firms generated the majority (68%) of the industry's revenues. Airview belonged to the growing category of medium-sized businesses (10% of all establishments) with sales of between $1 million and $2 million.

The overall market size in Canada was estimated at $630 to $650 million and was dominated by local companies. The industry also generated some $120 million in foreign billings (mainly GIS hardware and software). Interestingly, the export of these services from Canada had traditionally been directed outside of North America and Europe and concentrated in Africa, Asia, and the Middle East.

COMPETITION

Competition in the Canadian geomatics industry was on the increase. The current economic climate, characterized by fiscal restraint in both the private and government sectors, had reduced the growth rate of the demand for the services provided by the industry. As a result, geomatic companies, with their increased production capacities and reduced costs, had become more active in competing for the constant volume of business. This had resulted in a decrease in industry profitability. Overall industry profit levels were the same as in the early 1980s, despite a doubling of overall industry demand.

GLOBAL OPPORTUNITIES OVERVIEW

By March 1994, Rick had spent considerable time reviewing global market opportunities for the company. He had taken a general look at several foreign markets, looking at such major factors as their overall size and growth prospects, political stability and entry barriers, competition, and the availability of funding for geomatic projects.

This step had resulted in rejecting the possibility of entering the markets of Western Europe, which—despite their size—were characterized by ferocious competition and limited growth prospects. Eastern Europe was felt to be too politically unstable (particularly the countries of the former USSR), lacked funding, and were fragmented along national borders.

Rick also felt that the distances associated with dealing with markets in Southeast Asia and Oceania would put a significant strain on the company's financial and human resources, particularly in view of increasing competition from locally based companies. On the other hand, other Asian markets lacked either the size or the financing required to support Airview's long-term involvement.

Finally, he decided that sub-Saharan Africa, although in dire need of the services offered by Airview, was either dominated by companies from their former colonial powers or could not afford any significant level of geomatics-related development, particularly in view of the declining level of support being received from international financial institutions like the World Bank.

On the other hand, Rick found the characteristics of some of the remaining regions quite interesting. Consequently, he decided to concentrate his deliberations on these markets, which included North America (the United States and Mexico), Latin America, and the Arab World (North Africa and the Middle East).

AMERICAN MARKET

The U.S. market was somewhat different from its Canadian counterpart in that it had a larger proportion of geodetic and GIS firms among the 6,300 businesses in its geomatic industry. This larger proportional number of geodetic firms in the

United States was due to its higher population density, which increased the need for cadastral surveying. At the same time, faster adoption of computers in a variety of industrial applications in the United States had stimulated demand for GIS applications and related services.

On the other hand, in comparison to the relative size of the U.S. and Canadian economies, the Canadian geomatic market was disproportionately large. The American market was estimated at $3 billion in 1994; only five times the size of its Canadian counterpart or only half the relative difference in the size of the economies between the two countries. This disparity could be largely attributed to the structural differences between the economies of the two countries. Canada's economy was largely dependent on the mineral and forestry sectors; both industries that supported a relatively large geomatic industry.

The demand for geomatics services in the U.S. market was growing at a 15% annual rate, and was particularly dynamic in the areas of airborne photography and (satellite) remote sensing, digital conversion of existing data, and consulting.

ACCESS TO U.S. MARKETS

In 1994, there were few tariff obstacles to entering the U.S. market. Previous barriers related to licensing and local presence requirements were being removed as a result of the passage of the North American Free Trade Agreement. In some cases, Canadian companies who had succeeded in penetrating the U.S. market indicated that it had been easier for them to cross the international border than to overcome provincial barriers within their home country.

Although there had been some opportunities in the U.S. geomatics market during the 1980s, Canadian firms had traditionally been reluctant to take advantage of them. For aerial surveying companies like Airview, one of the reasons was the fact that American aircraft maintenance and licensing requirements were much more lenient in the United States than in Canada. As a result, a company operating an aircraft out of Canada was not able to compete with American firms on price if there was any significant amount of flying time involved. Although these differences still remained, the recently falling value of the Canadian dollar had all but nullified the cost advantage previously enjoyed by U.S. companies.

In general, the level of competition in the United States was not much different from that in Canada except that the American firms, particularly the larger ones, marketed their services much more aggressively than did their Canadian counterparts.

USER SEGMENTS

It was estimated that local and state governments accounted for some 25% of the total U.S. market for geomatic products and services and that close to half of all local/state budgets allocated to the acquisition of geomatic services was allocated for data capture purposes. The largest potential lay with the 39,000 municipal/ county governments. A trend to modernize the land records and registration systems that document the 118 million land parcels in the United States was the most significant factor in stimulating the demand for data capture, their conversion into a digital format, their subsequent analysis, and graphical presentation.

The average contract performed for local/state governments ranged from $60,000 to $190,000 for aerial photography/photogrammetry services. Although

the Northeast, Southeast, Southwest, and states bordering the Pacific Ocean accounted for the greatest demand, there was also an abundance of opportunities in
the states closer to Airview's base, such as Minnesota (3,529 local government
units), North Dakota (2,795), and South Dakota (1,767).

Federal government agencies represented the second largest user group, accounting for slightly less than 25% of the total U.S. geomatic market. Digital mapping was the major area of demand within this segment. This corresponded closely
to Airview's principal area of expertise.

Contracts with the federal government ranged from $30,000 for surveying pro-
jects to $1.5 million for data-digitizing projects. On average, they tended to be
larger in size than those with state and local governments and were typically
awarded to larger firms. As a result of the U.S. federal government policy of decentralizing the contracting of services, the demand from this user sector was distributed across the country.

The third largest segment in the U.S. geomatic market was the demand from
regulated industries, such as communication firms and gas and electric companies.
They traditionally generated between 20% and 25% of the overall U.S. demand
for geomatic services. Customers from this category were interested in more cost-
efficient management of the large infrastructure under their administration. Consequently, they had been among the early adopters of GIS technology, and their major thrust was in implementing AM/FM (automated mapping and facilities
management) systems, which combined digital maps with information on the operation of their facilities.

The utilities market for geomatic services was spread across the United States,
with the size closely related to the population density of individual regions. These
regional markets were dominated by large companies, such as Baymont Engineering and AT&T, which—due to economies of scale—became very price competitive in catering to the utility sector.

Finally, the rest of the demand for geomatic services came from the private sector, with the most significant segments being the resource industries, viz. mining
and forestry. The rate of adoption of GIS technology in this sector was rather slow,
and remotely sensed data and basic mapping were the primary services contracted
out by these firms.

THE MEXICAN GEOMATICS MARKET

OVERVIEW

By the early 1990s, Mexico had developed significant capabilities in geomatics. Between 40,000 and 50,000 people were employed in all surveying and mapping related disciplines. Yet, in view of the country's problems with rapid urbanization, de-
forestation, and land use change, local demand for geomatics products and services in
the early 1990s exceeded the available supply in some product and service categories.

The primary demand for geomatics services in Mexico was created by cartographic agencies of the federal and state governments. The National Institute of
Statistics, Geography, and Informatics (INEGI) had the primary responsibility for
integrating the country's geographical data, carrying out the national mapping project and developing the national geographic information system.

Each state in Mexico was responsible for undertaking and maintaining a land
survey of its territory and maintaining land cadastre. Therefore, state markets were
the second largest in volume after the federal market.

Several large municipalities were also purchasers of geomatics products and services. In 1993–1994, they were in the process of establishing databases of property boundaries, partly in cooperation with SEDESOL (Directorate of Cartography and Photogrammetry) under the One Hundred Cities Program.

The private sector of the country was also a significant user of spatially referenced information. PEMEX, the state oil monopoly, was by far the largest of those users. It was also in the strongest position to acquire the most technologically advanced products and services in this area.

The total size of the Mexican market for geomatics services in 1993 was estimated at between $160 million and $200 million.

There were two cycles that affected the volume of geomatics work available in Mexico. First, there was the annual rainy season (June to September), which had a negative impact due to limitations on aerial surveying caused by inclement weather. Second, there was the change in Mexico's presidency every six years. As government agencies were the main purchasers of geomatic services, the political environment had a profound effect on business. In general, the first three years of any presidency resulted in minor projects, while the final three years were noted for major works.

The demand for geomatics services in Mexico was increasing. In addition, most Mexican companies competing for this business were interested in foreign participation, particularly if these relationships carried with them better technology and more modern equipment.

Mexico offered a significant operating benefit to Canadian aerial photography firms in that its weather patterns (the rainy season between May and September) counterbalanced those in Canada. This could enable Canadian exporters to utilize their aircraft and photographic equipment during the slow season in Canada (December through March).

COMPETITION

The Mexican geomatics industry was well developed in the traditional areas of ground surveying and cartography. However, its technological and human resource capabilities in the more technical areas, such as digital mapping and GIS were generally limited.

In the area of aerial mapping and surveying, there were about 20 companies, located mostly in Mexico City. Six of these companies, which owned their own aircraft, dominated the national market, whereas the remaining 14 were quite small, did not have their own aircraft, and were fairly new to the industry.

MARKET ACCESS

Public tender was the normal method for obtaining projects in Mexico. Most tenders were open to all companies, but some were by invitation only. The tendency was for contracts to go to those companies that had their own aircraft and the proper equipment. Subcontracting was a popular way for smaller companies to obtain a portion of larger projects.

If a foreign company was awarded a contract, it had to obtain permission from the state geography department and from the Mexican Defense Department. In addition, until 1996, foreign companies were not allowed to operate aircraft over Mexican territory without local participation.

THE LATIN AMERICAN GEOMATICS MARKET

In the early 1990s, the geomatics market in Latin America was at an early stage of transition from traditional to digital technologies for data capture, analysis, and storage. Although general awareness of GIS and remote sensing was widespread, their adoption was largely limited to international resource exploration companies and some public institutions.

The market for geomatics products and services was dominated by the public sector on both the supply and demand sides. However, the private sector was becoming the primary growth area, particularly the resource sector (agriculture, forestry, mining, and energy), where significant investment programs created demand for cadastral surveying, mapping, and GIS. This demand potential, in turn, was providing a growth opportunity for local surveying and mapping companies. This industry had traditionally been dominated by government organizations (mostly military controlled), which, over the previous few years, had gained a significant degree of business autonomy and were actively competing in both local and international markets.

International Financial Institutions (IFIs), such as the World Bank and the Inter-American Development Bank were very active in Latin America. As their major concern was economic development of the entire area, their activities were concentrated in the less developed nations of the region. The IFIs recognized the importance of infrastructure projects and their geomatics components and provided financial support for such basic services as topographic and property mapping and cadastral information systems. As a result of this fundamental focus, geomatics contract activity was not confined to the more economically advanced countries of the region. From the point of view of foreign-based geomatics companies attempting to enter the Latin American market, the IFI-sponsored contracts provided a very attractive opportunity since they were open for public tender.

It was anticipated that the Latin American market for geomatics products and services would grow significantly. It was estimated that from 1993 to 1998, the total demand for geomatics products and services in the region would increase from US $650 million to US $1,500 million.

The provision of spatial information and its conversion to a digital format, as well as the delivery of GIS applications and the provision of training to local staff, constituted the major demand area, expected to constitute three-quarters of the region's market.

GEOGRAPHIC DISTRIBUTION

Brazil was by far the largest market for geomatics products and services, with an estimated 50% of the total demand in the region.

Argentina, with the second largest territory and population in the region, was also the second largest market for geomatics products and services, accounting for 20% of Latin American demand.

Chile, with its significant resource sector, was the third significant geomatics market in the region with a 5% share of total demand.

Interestingly, Bolivia, with its relatively small population and economy, was a disproportionately large market for geomatics products and services (4% of the overall demand).

The other 13 countries of the region shared the remaining 21% of the Latin American market, with Venezuela and Colombia leading the group.

COMPETITION

By the 1990s, Latin American companies had developed substantial capabilities in the areas of surveying and mapping. The mapping sector in the region had originated from the military and, until recent years, had been protected from foreign competition by trade barriers. Consequently, the capabilities of local firms were significant, particularly in the larger countries such as Brazil and Argentina. More significantly, larger surveying and mapping companies had already invested in digital mapping technology and remote sensing. With their developed expertise and low labor and overhead costs, these firms had a significant advantage over their competitors from North America, Europe, and Australia. Their knowledge of the local market was an additional factor placing them ahead of competitors from other continents.

Larger Brazilian and Argentinean firms had used this advantage to penetrate the markets of the smaller countries of the region. Since each national market was characterized by wide fluctuations in the demand for geomatic services, the markets of other countries provided them with an opportunity to stabilize and, possibly, expand their sales. In view of this situation, service firms from outside the region had to compete on the basis of their technological and managerial advantage. Large scale projects, possibly involving digital imaging, provided the best opportunity to compete with local companies.

Despite all these impediments to foreign participation in the Latin American market, European companies had succeeded in capturing a significant share of the region's business. Their success was built on the strong business network established in the region by their home countries. Their penetration strategy was to establish their presence initially (through international assistance programs and the provision of training and education) and then to develop ties with local government agencies and companies from the private sector. European firms were also characterized by their ability to form consortia to pursue larger contracts. These consortia combined European technology and equipment with local labor and market experience.

American firms had achieved significant penetration of these markets for GIS hardware and software. However, their presence in the other sectors was less pronounced, probably due to their uncompetitive cost structure.

Australian geomatics firms involved in Latin America were typically affiliated with Australia's mining and forestry companies active in resource exploration activities in the region.

THE ARAB WORLD (NORTH AFRICA AND THE MIDDLE EAST)

Countries of the Arab world were characterized by the dominance of their oil and gas industries in geomatics-related projects. Their economies and political systems were relatively stable and provided a good foundation for establishing long-term penetration plans by a foreign geomatics company. In addition, in their economic development, countries in this region were less dependent on international aid than was the case of the countries of Latin America. Consequently, their approach to the development of topographic, cadastral, and administrative mapping was based more on long-term planning.

Countries in this region had developed their own companies, typically originating from the national cartographic agencies. In the early 1990s, these agencies still dominated the industry in the region, employing from 30% to 60% of the total number of personnel working in the geomatics field. However, their role had been steadily declining over the past few years.

At the same time, the level of development of locally based firms differed significantly among individual countries. Egypt, Iran, Jordan, Kuwait, Lebanon, Qatar, Syria, and Tunisia each had a substantial number of local specialists in the field (relative to their populations and territory), whereas Algeria, Libya, Iraq, Saudi Arabia, and Yemen had rather limited geomatics capability. Even more significantly, this latter group also had a relatively low proportion of geomatics specialists with university education.

The combined market size for geomatics services in the region was estimated at between $400 million and $600 million in the commercial sector. In view of the political situation in the region, some of the markets were characterized by restrictions on foreign access. Libya and Iraq, for example, were not open to Canadian companies. Also Syria, which had traditionally been very restrictive in granting foreign geomatics companies access to its market, was also of limited attractiveness to Canadian companies.

Iran was the country with the best opportunity for geomatics firms. The climate for Canadian firms in the country was favorable due to Canada's position as a noninvolved country and the technological advancement of the Canadian geomatics industry.

The major opportunities in Iran were associated with several national development programs in the areas of energy production (construction of hydroelectric and nuclear power stations and upgrading the country's power distribution system), expansion of the mining industry (production of iron ore, copper, aluminum, lead/zinc, and coal), the oil and gas sectors, and construction of the country's railway system.

Kuwait and Saudi Arabia had traditionally been the target markets for several Canadian geomatics firms. The expansion of the two countries' oil production and refining capacity had triggered major investment outlays in both countries (for a total of over $20 billion between 1992 and 1994) and would continue (albeit at a slower rate) for a number of years. These two national markets were dominated by American companies and any penetration effort there would require cooperation with Canadian firms from the construction, mining, or oil and gas sectors.

Tunisia represented an example of a country that had developed its own expertise in the area of cartography, which, in turn, had created demand for external assistance in the provision of more sophisticated products and services, such as digital mapping and GIS applications.

Egypt represented yet another type of geomatics market in the region. Its major thrust was now on environmental concerns. The country had developed an environmental action plan that addressed problems with water and land resources management, air pollution, marine and coastal resources, and global heritage preservation, all of which had a significant geomatic component. The cost of implementing Phase 1 of the plan was estimated at some $300 million over the period of 1993–1995.

Egypt also provided opportunities associated with a $3 billion power generation and distribution project and some $2 billion in construction projects associated with the expansion of the country's gas production and oil-processing capacity. Although the majority of work in the geomatics-related field was conducted by local companies, subcontracting opportunities were significant.

Egypt was also a significant market from another perspective. Historically, Egypt had exported its geomatics expertise to other Arab states. Consequently, penetration of this market could be used to leverage access to other markets of the region, particularly in conjunction with Egyptian partners.

MARKET EVALUATION

In order to evaluate each of the four geographic regions from Airview's perspective, Rick developed a summary of the primary characteristics of each of the market areas under consideration. This summary is presented in Exhibit 2.

He also reviewed several possible ways of establishing Airview's presence in any of the regional/national markets. He summarized his considerations as indicated in Exhibit 3, on page 246.

DISCUSSION

In his considerations related to the choice of a potential, new, target market, Rick assumed that once he had arrived at a sensible, coherent marketing plan, Airview could apply for financial support from the government. In fact, he had already discussed this possibility with the Federal Business Development Bank. In addition, he could expect some assistance from the Program for Export Market Development if he chose to establish an office or participate in bidding for projects in a selected market. This assistance could cover 50% of their costs of travel and setting up a permanent foreign office.

His overall concerns included not only the immediate costs of implementing his marketing plan but also the process he should use to select the best market in view of its salient characteristics and the company's goals.

Rick's view of the American market was generally positive. His major concern was with price competition from local firms and possible fluctuations in the exchange rate, which over a short period of time might undermine their cost structure. At the same time, he felt that Airview's technological advantage in the United States was less significant than in other markets. Finally, he assumed that his best opportunity south of the border would be in GIS-related areas, which would require either a substantial investment in obtaining a greater degree of expertise in this area or a joint effort with a GIS company.

The Mexican market was also viewed positively, particularly after the anticipated lifting of flight restrictions in 1996. However, Rick felt that due to the high cost of their staff, Airview would probably be competitive only in complex projects involving both data capture and their conversion into a computer format. At the same time, he was attracted by the operating advantages of having the company's flying season extended beyond the current few summer months.

Latin America seemed to be too competitive to support Airview's solo entry. On the other hand, the region's fragmentation into many small national markets could prove challenging from an operating point of view. Rick felt that seeking an alliance with Canadian mining and resource companies, thereby successfully establishing their operations, might prove to be attractive, particularly if Airview's entry could be supported by the provision of some elements of GIS. As in Mexico's case, the countries of Latin America provided the possibility of operating the company's aircraft during the Canadian off-season.

Exhibit 2 Market Review

Market Characteristics	United States	Mexico	Latin America	North Africa and Middle East
Economic and Political Environment	Stable	Stabilizing	Stabilizing	Fluctuating
Access Restrictions	None	Local agent required No flying in Mexico	All mapping on-site in Brazil	Language Culture
Market Size	Large	Small	Medium	Medium–large
Entry and Operating Costs	Low	Medium	Medium	Medium–high
Growth	Slow, stable	High	High	High
Financing	Cash, immediate	Transfer, delays	Transfer problems IFIs	Ranging from cash to IFIs financing
Contract Procurement	Transparent, fair	Ambiguous, improving	Frequently ambiguous	Ambiguous
Major Products	Digital mapping, GIS	Cadastral mapping, GIS	Topographic and cadastral mapping	Topographic mapping, surveying
Long-Term Advantage (technology, expertise)	Limited advantage	Diminishing, but not disappearing	Slowly diminishing	Sustainable
Primary Customers	State and municipal governments	Federal and state governments	Federal governments Resource sector	Central cartographic agencies Resource sector
Pricing	Competitive, but based on high local costs	Competitive, based on low local costs	Extremely competitive, based on low local costs	Relatively high
Competition	Local, very high	Local, U.S. high	Local, international, extremely high	Local, international, moderate
Entry Strategies	Direct bidding, local partner	Local partner or subsidiary	Network of agents or local partner IFIs projects	Local partner or agent IFIs projects
Strategic Advantages	Close, similar to the Canadian market	Entry to South America Technological advantage Active during Canadian slack	Technological fit Active during Canadian slack	Technological advantage Growing Less competition Long-term prospects
Expansion Opportunities	GIS consulting systems integration	Acquisition of local subsidiary	Training	CIDA project Libya after restrictions

Finally, Rick regarded the markets of the Arab world with particular interest. Airview would definitely have a technical advantage over its local competitors in these markets. At the same time, pricing in this region seemed to be generally less competitive than in the other areas, whereas the similarity of the individual national markets, in most cases based on the demand created by the resource sector, would allow for gradual penetration of the region. At the same time, Rick realized that Airview's lack of experience in international markets in general and in the Arab world in particular would create a very challenging situation for the company's staff.

Exhibit 3 Airview Entry Strategies

Project-Oriented Penetration

This is a strategy suitable for small, niche-oriented firms. The company would have to target a specific area and seek a specific contract. Involvement would be limited to the scope of the specific contract. The main barrier to this approach could be associated with local presence requirements.

Establishing a network of local agents in the countries of interest in the region may provide access to information on upcoming tenders and allow for participation in the bidding process. Bidding for local contracts may serve as a foundation for establishing the company's presence in the region and could be treated as part of an entry strategy.

Subcontracting to Local Firms

This strategy offered the advantage of overcoming local presence restrictions.

Strategic Alliances

An alliance with a Canadian or foreign partner can work quite effectively, provided the firms complement one another in resources and business philosophies.

Establishment of Branch Office

This could be an effective way of overcoming local presence restrictions, provided the firm was sufficiently financed to undertake the costs of setting up such an operation. The choice of location would also be crucial in determining the success of such a venture.

A Corporate Buy-Out

This seemed a somewhat risky proposition, requiring both adequate financing, business acumen to succeed, and lack of restrictions on foreign ownership of local companies. If successful, however, the result would be an immediate presence in the selected market.

Establishment of Head Office Outside of Canada

Although this could enable a company to access the selected market, this possibility could only be considered for large and stable markets, such as the United States.

Foreign Ownership

Like the strategic alliance option, this can offer opportunities, particularly with U.S. firms, provided that this route is in keeping with the long-term goals of that firm and that the two firms are compatible.

Alliances with Local Geomatics Firms

An alliance with a local partner could be beneficial if based on the combination of local experience and inexpensive labor with Airview's equipment and data-processing and mapping capabilities.

Joint Ownership of a Local Company

Acquiring a local company in partnership with another Canadian company may provide some advantages if the partners' product lines complement each other. A provider of GIS software or system integrator may be a good candidate for joint ownership with Airview.

CASE NOTE

1. A specialized technique for defining an accurate three-dimensional coordinate system for determining the location and dimensions of objects on the earth's surface.

Part 2 Integrating Case 2

Whirlpool Europe

OVERVIEW

The only way to gain lasting competitive advantage is to leverage your capabilities around the world so that the company as a whole is greater than the sum of its parts.

Our vision at Whirlpool is to integrate our geographical businesses wherever possible, so that our most advanced expertise in any given area—whether it's refrigeration, technology, financial reporting systems, or distribution strategy—isn't confined to one location or one division. We want to be able to take the best capabilities we have and leverage them in all of our operations worldwide.[1]

This was how David Whitwam, Whirlpool's chief executive officer, articulated the global strategy Whirlpool Corporation launched in 1987. As part of this strategy, Whitwam purchased a large stake in the appliance division of Philips N.V. of the Netherlands. This venture represented the beginning of the emergence of what came to be known as Whirlpool Europe. It was one of four global regions that constituted the Whirlpool Corporation. Besides Europe, other regions included North America, Latin America, and Asia.

In 1994, Whirlpool Europe's revenues were $2.4 billion, about 30% of the total corporate appliance revenues, and net income was $370 million, or about 44% of the total corporate appliance business profit. The company's revenues were growing at about 7% per year for the past two years, while the industry grew at 3%.

Despite this encouraging news, Whirlpool Europe faced some difficult strategic challenges. First, the company was in third place in market share behind two formidable competitors, Electrolux and Bosch-Siemens. These companies had been operating in Europe for years and both had strong financial foundations. Further, the European economy, although improved, continued to suffer from a chronically high unemployment rate of about 12%. The company also faced the challenge of motivating its employees, whose morale was shaken by the company's cost-cutting measures that resulted in the layoff of 2,000 employees.

HISTORY OF WHIRLPOOL CORPORATION

The Benton Harbor, Michigan–based Whirlpool Corporation traced its origins to the early 20th century. The Upton Clothes Washer Company was founded in 1911 by two brothers, Lou and Emory Upton, to manufacture wringer washing machines. Shortly thereafter, the company began to produce electric wringer washers by fitting a motor on the machine.

In 1916, the Uptons forged an agreement with Sears, Roebuck, and Co. to produce two types of wringer washers for the Sears Catalog, Sears's only sales channel at the time. By the 1920s, the Upton Company was Sears's sole supplier of washing machines. Because of this, the company was able to ride the success of Sears when the latter expanded its operations into retail.

To sustain the initial growth, Upton merged with another company, the Nineteen Hundred Washer Company, creating the Nineteen Hundred Corporation in the late 1920s. The merger allowed the two companies to increase production capacity as well as efficiency. In the 1940s, the corporation developed an automatic spinner-type washer which was marketed under Sears's Kenmore brand. In 1948, the company introduced a new spinner washer under the Whirlpool name. The success of the automatic washer and the Whirlpool branding effort led the company to change its name to the Whirlpool Corporation in 1950.

In 1957, the company began its international expansion through the acquisition of several Brazilian appliance manufacturers. This expansion continued in the 1960s. Thus, in 1969, the company penetrated the Canadian market with the purchase of Ignis, a strong Canadian brand name.

Whirlpool continued to grow throughout the 1970s, placing major emphasis on producing, developing, and improving its major home appliance lines. In 1977, for example, the company introduced the first automatic clothes washer with solid-state electronic controls.

In 1982, Jack Sparks became the company's CEO. Under his tenure, a higher priced line of dishwashers, ovens, and other kitchen appliances was added to the family through the acquisition of Hobart Corporation's KitchenAid division.

In 1987 Jack Sparks was succeeded by David Whitwam who fashioned a new aggressive strategy with the goal of transforming Whirlpool into a truly global corporation. The strategy extended Whirlpool's reach into South America, Asia, and Europe.

HISTORY OF WHIRLPOOL EUROPE

As part of David Whitwam's global strategy, Whirlpool purchased a 53% stake in the appliance division of Philips N.V. of the Netherlands in 1988. The division produced major home appliances under the popular brand name of Philips.

Whirlpool Europe was created in 1989, and the Whirlpool brand name was added to the product line. In 1991, Whirlpool took complete control of the Philips/Whirlpool venture by purchasing the remaining outstanding shares of the appliance division.

In addition to the acquisition of the appliance division of Philips, Whirlpool in 1992 entered into a joint venture with Tatramat of Slovakia for the production of appliances in Central Europe. Also in 1992, Whirlpool formed the Hungarian Trading Company as a means of furthering its expansion into Europe. And in 1993, Whirlpool Europe created sales subsidiaries in Poland and the Czech Republic.

Whirlpool Europe had its main operations center in Italy, with manufacturing facilities located in France, Germany, Italy, Sweden, and Slovakia. In addition, the company had 20 sales offices throughout Western and Central Europe.

Whirlpool Europe marketed its products under the brand names of Whirlpool, Bauknecht, Laden, and Ignis. The company grew to be the third largest manufacturer and marketer of major home appliances. European sales of appliances totaled approximately $2.4 billion in 1994, which accounted for 30% of Whirlpool Corporation's total appliance sales of $7.9 billion. Net revenues for the same period were $163 million, accounting for a full 44% of the corporation's total appliance business profit.[2]

INTERNAL ENVIRONMENT

STRATEGIC MANAGERS

The two top senior executives at Whirlpool with the most influence in shaping strategy were David R. Whitwam, Whirlpool Corporation's chief executive officer (CEO), and Jeff M. Fettig, president of Whirlpool Europe.

DAVID R. WHITWAM

David R. Whitwam, 53 years old, joined Whirlpool in 1968 upon graduation from the University of Wisconsin with a bachelor of science degree. Prior to attending college, Whitwam served in the U.S. Army, attaining the rank of captain. Whitwam rose through the ranks of Whirlpool in sales and marketing assignments, including sales manager and division general manager in the Los Angeles area. In 1977, he reached the vice president level.

In 1985, Whitwam was named vice chairman of the board and chief marketing officer of Whirlpool. At that same time, he became a member of the board of directors of the company. Two years later, in 1987, he was promoted to chairman of the board, president, and chief executive officer. Thus, he had been directing the fortunes of the Whirlpool Corporation for 8 years.[3] It was at this time that Whirlpool embarked on a sweeping strategic analysis of its position in the global appliance industry. It was Whitwam who led the corporation through this difficult self-assessment phase and through the subsequent implementation of the corporation's new global direction.

Whitwam believed that Whirlpool needed to make a fundamental change in the way it viewed its industry. Whitwam said, "Before 1987, we didn't see the potential power our existing capabilities could give us in the global market because we had been limiting our definition of the appliance market to the United States."[4]

Whitwam possessed a clear vision of Whirlpool as an integrated global organization. Whitwam's background in sales and marketing led him to believe that external environmental analysis in general and market research in particular could produce positive results. According to him, "Only prolonged, intensive effort to understand and respond to genuine customer needs can lead to the breakthrough products and services that earn long-term customer loyalty."[5]

He was also well aware of the critical importance of leadership to the effective performance of a firm. Whitwam believed that "CEOs have to create the processes and structures to get the organization going and keep people aimed in the right direction, but they cannot achieve anything requiring sustained effort by edict alone . . . a contemporary CEO has to convince employees why transformation [of an organization] is necessary."[6]

JEFF M. FETTIG

The second strategic manager with important influence on Whirlpool Europe was Jeff M. Fettig. Fettig, 37 years old, was president of Whirlpool Europe and executive vice president of Whirlpool Corporation. Fettig joined Whirlpool in 1981 and held a number of management positions in a wide variety of functional areas such as operations, sales, planning, and product development. He served as vice president of marketing for the KitchenAid Appliance Group and then became vice president of marketing for the Philips-Whirlpool Appliance Group of Whirlpool Europe in 1990. Two years later, he was named vice president of marketing and sales for North American Appliance Group. In 1994, he became president of Whirlpool Europe.

SELF-ASSESSMENT: A PRELUDE TO STRATEGY FORMULATION

In the 1970s, U.S. sales of washing machines, refrigerators, and other major appliances were flat. Whirlpool wanted to grow, but taking market share from competitors that survived a major industry shakeout "was seen as an insufficient way to do it."[7] In the mid-1980s, the company's earnings slipped by 61% and the return on shareholders' equity tumbled from 16% to 5%.

In 1987, Whitwam created a task force of senior management to take a critical self-examination and to assess the company's future viable strategic options. During eight months of self-analysis, the participants narrowed down the company's options to three. The first was to continue to operate in the U.S. market and ignore the global market, which, according to Whitwam, would have condemned Whirlpool to a slow death. The second was to wait for globalization to begin and then try to react, which would have put the company in a catch-up mode, technologically and organizationally. And the third option was to aggressively expand the company's operations internationally.[8] The company chose the third option, with the intent of "attaining world leadership in the business of major appliances."[9]

Self-examination, which was used in 1987 to determine the company's scope of operations, eventually became a corporate policy. Each year, the company's top 150 managers would meet to exchange views and engage in internal and external environmental analyses. In addition, all development, marketing, and manufacturing leaders would meet twice a year for global product and technology reviews.

CORPORATE VISION

Whirlpool stated its vision as follows:

Whirlpool, in its chosen lines of business, will grow with new opportunities and be the leader in an ever-changing global market. We will be driven by our commitment to continuous quality improvements and to exceeding all of our customers' expectations. We will gain competitive advantage through this, and by building on our existing strengths and developing new competencies. We will be market-driven, efficient, and profitable. Our success will make Whirlpool a company that worldwide customers, employees and other stakeholders can depend on.[10]

MISSION

In its annual report, Whirlpool articulated the following statement as its mission:

Whirlpool is the leading manufacturer and marketer of home appliances. The company manufactures in 12 countries and markets products in more than 120 countries under major brand names such as Whirlpool, KitchenAid, Roper, Estate, Bauknecht, Ignis, and Laden. Whirlpool is also the principal supplier to Sears, Roebuck and Co. of many major home appliances marketed under the Kenmore brand name.[11]

OBJECTIVES

At the end of the 1987 self-examination meeting, strategists set short-term and long-term objectives for the company. In the short term, the company would seek to achieve strong financial results. In the long term, the company would strive to be a globally integrated concern with the ability to "develop a product anywhere in the world capable of being manufactured anywhere in the world."[12] This meant integrating the company's geographical businesses, so that its most advanced expertise in any given area—be it refrigeration technology, financial reporting systems, or distribution strategy—was not confined to one location or one division. That entailed taking the best capabilities the company had and leveraging them in all of its operations worldwide.

Whitwam sought to create one integrated company worldwide. He thought that the integrative approach would provide the company with a competitive advantage over its competitors who pursued country-by-country strategies without a unifying coordinated plan. In Europe, the integrative approach came to be known as the "pan-European approach," which gave the company a distinct competitive advantage over its competitors.

GRAND STRATEGY

Having determined the company's long- and short-term objectives, Whirlpool's strategists developed a set of criteria that would determine which countries or regions constituted desirable targets for expansion. Possible candidates were judged on three major criteria: ease of entry, growth potential, and government regulations.

Europe received the green light in 1987, when the Netherlands-based conglomerate Philips N.V. made overtures about spinning off its appliance business. In 1989, Whirlpool and Philips entered a joint venture, with Whirlpool buying 53% of Philips's home appliance business (for about $1.4 billion), creating Whirlpool International B.V. In 1991, Whirlpool paid $600 million for the remaining 47%. That move solidified its position in the 12-nation European market of 338 million people.

The acquisition boosted Whirlpool Corp.'s debt to about 50% of capital from 39%, or $1.03 billion. The debt was expected to dilute the company's earnings through 1992. As a result, Whirlpool's stock fell $1 to close at $32.50. Whitwam hoped to trim the debt to one-third, which he considered to be an acceptable level, by relying on the company's strong cash flow.[13]

In addition to the acquisition of the appliance division of Philips, Whirlpool in 1992 entered into a joint venture with Tatramat of Slovakia for the production of appliances in Central Europe. Also in 1992, Whirlpool formed the Hungarian Trading

Company as a means of furthering its expansion into Europe. And in 1993, Whirlpool Europe created sales subsidiaries in Poland and the Czech Republic.

COMPETITIVE STRATEGY

In 1992, Whirlpool analyzed the competitors' products and identified what it called the "value gap" between the U.S. and European markets. Measured by number of hours worked, European consumers paid up to twice as much for major appliances as their U.S. counterparts. With product redesign and cost cutting, Whirlpool was able to give European customers better products and services without a proportional increase in price. Although customer service centers were, for the most part, commonplace among U.S. appliance makers, this was not so in Europe. Whirlpool Europe took steps to change this by creating six fully integrated customer assistance centers in Germany, the United Kingdom, Holland, and Austria. The company planned to expand these centers to other countries.

ORGANIZATION STRUCTURE

To implement its strategy, Whirlpool launched a restructuring campaign that shifted the organization from country-focused sales and marketing to a trade channel focus. A major thrust of the restructuring was a new sales organization that would operate at three levels: a centralized European level with offices in Italy; an "area" level involving four groupings of countries based on similar distribution channel characteristics; and a "local" market level. As a result of this move, sales organizations in 17 countries were replaced by four regional sales offices. The offices were staffed with about 650 sales representatives responsible for servicing about 40,000 trade partners (i.e., dealers).[14] As part of Whirlpool's pan-European strategy, the new sales organizations were primarily structured along product lines rather than countries.

The restructuring also involved an effort to reduce costs. The number of warehouses, for example, was cut from 30 to 16. Eventually, the company hoped to reduce these to five or six. In the human resources area, the company planned to eliminate 2,000 positions, or 15% of its European workforce of 13,000.

MANUFACTURING

The Philips appliance business that Whirlpool acquired was an amalgam of independent national companies that produced different appliances for different markets. Washing machines built in Italy and Germany did not share a single screw, and the division was steadily losing market share.

After acquiring the Philips division, Whirlpool shifted manufacturing to common "platforms" that had European and U.S. appliances sharing the same technology. For example, 85% of Whirlpool's products began to be built around a common interior. Whirlpool also rationalized Philips's scattered assets, slashing $400 million, in annual costs. In addition, it trimmed 36 warehouses to 8 and cut Philips's 1,600 suppliers by half. The move reduced inventories by one-third.

Whirlpool saw Europe as a uniform market, something with which its European competitors disagreed. According to a Bosch-Siemens executive, there were "differences in customer demands and needs from country to country."[15] Whirlpool's CEO, Whitwam, disagreed. According to him, "This business is the same all over the world. There is great opportunity to leverage that sameness."[16] To him, washing technology was washing technology. A product aimed at the German market might have more features and, thus, might be more costly than one with fewer features aimed at the Italian market, but the inside of both machines did not vary a great deal.

One of the products that was developed in the United States and became popular in Europe was a new clothes dryer that had 22% fewer parts and featured an oversized door, a feature that was not commonly found in European products.

PRODUCTS

Whirlpool Europe manufactured dryers, washers, dishwashers, freezers, microwave ovens, ranges, and refrigerators. In the United States Whirlpool built a ladder of brands, with KitchenAid on the top rung, Whirlpool and Kenmore labels in the broad middle, and Roper and Estate in the lower, or "value," ends. Whirlpool pursued the same strategy in Europe. Thus, at the high end was the pricey Bauknecht brand, then Whirlpool in the middle, and at the lower end was the no-frills, utilitarian, lower-priced Ignis and Laden products. The latter two targeted the Eastern and Central European countries.

RESEARCH AND DEVELOPMENT

Research and development was carried out at two regional technology centers that worked closely with similar Whirlpool centers worldwide. In 1994, Whirlpool Europe launched six new products. The company hoped that by 1998, about 85% of sales would come from models that did not exist in 1993. Because the R&D effort focused on improving quality, performance, and energy consumption of products, the company's newest automatic washer design retained fewer than 1% of the parts and components of its predecessor.[17]

One of the innovative products the company made was a washing machine (with horizontal axis) that tumbled clothes like dryers (with vertical axis). The machine used about one-third of the water and energy used by conventional machines that churned clothes with agitators. The new machine proved to be unpopular in the United States partly because it was more expensive and loaded from the front instead of the top.

Although data on Whirlpool Europe's R&D expenditures were not available, Whirlpool Corporation's overall R&D costs increased from $113 million in 1992, to $128 million in 1993, and to $152 million in 1994.

CUSTOMERS

Whirlpool did not consider retailers as its customers. Rather, it was the ultimate consumer that constituted its customers. In the past, Whirlpool treated its retailers as customers. As a result, it developed products for the retailer's specifications. That approach changed to one that focused on serving the end user.

MARKET RESEARCH

Because Whitwam sought to create a consumer-focused organization, market research took on a special importance. He attempted to develop a good understanding of the consumer in a way that would enable the company to translate that understanding into clearly superior product designs, features, and after-sales support. In his words, the company's goal was "for consumers to prefer the Whirlpool brand because it offers greater overall value than competing products. Achieving that goal requires taking a giant step back from our business and rethinking who our customers are and what their needs are."[18] To understand customers' needs, the company studied consumer behavior from the time people took off their dirty clothes at night until the clothes had been cleaned and ironed and hung in the closet. Management felt that whoever came up with a product to make this process easier, simpler, or quicker was going to "create an incredible market."[19]

One of the goals of market research was to help the company build the "perfect" product. Reaching that level meant studying consumers' lifestyles in meticulous details to decipher what they might want even if they could not articulate that desire in terms of a specific product request. One of the initial findings that market research in Europe yielded was that the trends, preferences, and biases of consumers, from one country to another, were becoming smaller rather than larger. According to Hank Bowman, former president of Whirlpool Europe, "Although regional preferences will remain, Whirlpool sees a chance to take advantage of the move toward a less fractured Europe."[20]

DISTRIBUTION

Whirlpool distributed its products under the brand names of Bauknecht, Whirlpool, Ignis, and Laden through independent distributors. Products were also sold through the company-owned subsidiaries in Hungary, Poland, the Czech Republic, Slovakia, and Greece. In addition, Whirlpool Europe sold its products to Whirlpool Corporation's wholly owned companies in Asia, Latin America, and dealers in Africa and the Middle East.

ADVERTISING

In 1990, Whirlpool Europe began an estimated $110 million program to introduce the Whirlpool name to the European marketplace and phase out the Philips brand name. At first, Whirlpool paired its brand name—with which Europeans were unfamiliar and which many had difficulty pronouncing—with the familiar Philips nameplate to introduce customers to its products. The company planned to remove the Philips name on a country-by-country basis as consumers became more acquainted with its brand. Whirlpool Europe's agreement with Philips required it to pay royalties to the latter for using its name beyond 1994.

The dual-branding campaign succeeded in establishing an independent identity for Whirlpool. By the end of 1994, the Philips name had been removed from the product in almost all countries in Europe, including Eastern Europe. In France, Italy, Spain, and Portugal, the complete phase-in of the Whirlpool brand and the removal of the Philips name would not be completed until 1995.

To establish its name as a pan-European company, Whirlpool Europe increased its advertising expenditures from $113 million in 1992, to $128 million in 1993, and to $140 million in 1994.

SALES AND FINANCE

In 1988, before the joint venture with Philips, Whirlpool Corporation's sales in Europe were $244 million with an operating loss of $3 million. In 1991, sales grew to nearly $2.45 billion with operating profits of $83 million,[21] giving the company a 13% market share, just behind No. 2 Bosch-Siemens Hausgeraete.[22] Sales in Central and Eastern Europe accounted for nearly 10% of the total European business.

Exhibit 1
Net Sales by
Business Unit

Business Unit	1994 ($ million)	1993 ($ million)	% Change
North America	5,048	4,559	11
Europe	2,373	2,225	7
Latin America	329	303	9
Asia	205	151	36
Other	(6)	130	—
Total	7,949	7,368	8

Source: Whirlpool Corporation, *1994 Annual Report,* page 27.

Exhibit 2
Operating Profit by
Business Unit

Business Unit	1994 ($ million)	1993 ($ million)	% Change
North America	522	474	10
Europe	163	139	17
Latin America	49	43	16
Asia	(22)	(5)	—

Source: Whirlpool Corporation, *1994 Annual Report,* page 28.

In 1994, Whirlpool Europe's revenues were $2.4 billion, or 30% of Whirlpool Corporation's worldwide sales of $7.95 billion, and its operating earnings were $162 million, or 28% of the parent company's earnings of $576 million. Its operating margin for 1994 was 6.5%, up from 3.6% in 1990. For the net sales and operating profits of Whirlpool Corporation by business unit, see Exhibit 1 and Exhibit 2.

The successful turnaround of Whirlpool's operations in Europe prompted Leif Johansson, CEO of Whirlpool's rival, Electrolux of Sweden, to say, "They took over a company that had lost its way and reinstated direction."[23] Echoing a similar sentiment, Jerry Herman, an analyst at Kemper Securities, Inc. in Cleveland, said, "Whirlpool gets very high marks in its global strategy. They are outpacing the industry dramatically."[24]

Although sales and revenues had been increasing, they fell short of the company's expectations. The company's pretax operating margin of 6.5% was lower than the company's goal of 10% margin, which it already had in North America. Further, earnings were expected to fall in 1995 due to rising raw materials costs and softening demand for appliances in Western Europe. Sales in France and Germany, which accounted for about half of the company's European business, were expected to decline by 20% to 30%.

EXTERNAL ENVIRONMENT

INDUSTRY

With about $19 billion in annual sales, the home appliance industry in Europe was large, accounting for 40% of the global demand. Western Europe represented 24% of this, with Eastern Europe contributing 14%.

The European market was highly fragmented and competitive. Europe had a collection of 200 brand names, many of them popular in just one country. About 35 Western European manufacturers competed in the market. The top four companies had 45% to 50% of the markets. By contrast, five major players, led by Whirlpool, controlled 95% of the U.S. market, once shared by 250 companies.

The revivification of Europe's marketplace favored larger companies at the expense of small appliance makers. For this reason, a shakeout was expected in the industry that would leave five or six powerful companies, much as happened in the U.S. appliance industry in the 1970s and 1980s.[25] In the microwave oven market, Western European companies faced competition not only from other European manufacturers but also from manufacturers in Asia, primarily Japan and South Korea.

Of the big players in the industry, Electrolux was the leader with a 25% market share, followed by Bosch-Siemens with 16%. Whirlpool was third with a 13% share.[26]

In general, appliance sales were expected to increase by 4% annually during the next 10 years, compared with just 2% in the U.S. However, the 1995 sales were expected to drop due to projections of low to moderate economic growth rate. Overall sales were expected to drop by one-third in Germany and 20% in France. Industry saturation varied with the type of product. For example, as shown in Exhibit 3, whereas the market for refrigerators was 100% saturated, the market for clothes dryers represented only 10% of market capacity.[27]

COMPETITORS

The two major companies that competed with Whirlpool Europe were AB Electrolux and Bosch-Siemens Hausgeraete GmbH.

AB ELECTROLUX

With 25% average market share, Electrolux, a Swedish manufacturer, was either No. 1 or No. 2 in almost all the European countries where it operated. The company achieved its leading market share through acquisition. Its last purchase, the 1993 acquisition of AEG Hausgeraete, propelled the company to its commanding presence not only in Europe but also in the world.

Despite its large size, which enabled it to achieve huge gains in sales and brand recognition, Electrolux was not profitable. Its return on equity declined from 8.73% in 1992 to 5.78% in 1993. Although its performance improved to 8.04% in 1994, it was still below the 1992 level.[28] The company's poor performance could be attributed to its inefficient operations and to management's preoccupation with assimilating the new acquisitions.

To improve performance, Electrolux planned to shed many of its 40 products and spend more time creating brand images by moving away from commodity-type products. To do this, the company sought to market four different designs. Two of them would be marketed as pan-European products, and the other two would target the emerging markets of Central and Eastern Europe. The company also set as a goal achieving a leading market-share position in Germany.

BOSCH-SIEMENS HAUSGERAETE GMBH

A German company, Bosch-Siemens was the home-appliance arm of its two owners, Bosch and Siemens. Although its market share in Europe was 16%, it was the leader in Europe's largest economy, Germany. Its financial position was stronger than

Exhibit 3

European Market
Saturation by
Product

Product	% Saturation
Refrigerators	100
Cooking Ranges	95
Washers	82
Freezers	30
Microwave Ovens	30
Dishwashers	20
Dryers	10

Source: Whirlpool Corporation, *1994 Annual Report,*
page 12.

other manufacturers' as evidenced by its return on equity, which grew from 18.64%
in 1991 to 20.22% in 1992. Although the return on equity declined to 19.16% in
1993, it represented an improvement over the 1991 level.[29] Because it was owned by
two companies known for their technological prowess, Bosch-Siemens became the
most technologically advanced appliance manufacturer in Germany.

One of Bosch-Siemens's major weaknesses was that it generally operated as a local company in a market (Germany) that was mature. The German market was also
plagued with high taxes, high labor cost, generous welfare benefits, and excessive
regulations. To overcome these difficulties, the company planned to follow a strategy
similar to that of its competitors by expanding into Central and Eastern Europe.

ECONOMY

After three years of recession, the worst in four decades, the economy of Europe
showed some clear signs of revival.[30] This was brought about by higher exports to
the vibrant U.S. economy, cheaper money from falling interest rates, and corporate
restructuring that boosted earnings. Europe's gross domestic product was expected
to grow by 1.3% after a dismal performance of 0.75% a year earlier. In some countries, such as France, Italy, Germany, and Britain, the gross domestic product was
expected to grow by 2.5%. Consumer price inflation was near a 30-year low and
was expected to stay flat at 2.8%, at least through the coming year.

There were, however, some danger signals. The unemployment rate continued
to hover around 12%, representing 20 million workers, and the economy was burdened by massive public deficits. Further, tight fiscal policies in many European
countries, high individual and corporate taxes, rigid labor rules, and rich social programs were likely to slow down the recovery. In Germany, whose economy exerted
strong influence on other European countries, labor unions demanded wage increases, which could drive prices as well as interest rates higher. As a whole, consumer confidence throughout Europe was low, and consumer spending was not expected to increase substantially.

DEMOGRAPHICS

With a total population of about 730 million, the European continent represented
the world's third largest group of consumers after Asia and the Americas. The total

population in the 15 European Union's nations was about 375 million and was growing at about .5% a year, which was below the world's average of 2.5% annually.

The European population enjoyed above-average standards of living, when judged by world standards; and most people had longer life spans, lower mortality rates, and lower birth rates. Lower birth rates and increased longevity in most European countries caused a rising proportion of retired citizens. Further, the average household size decreased from 2.96 persons to 2.62, and the economically active age group of 21–55 decreased, constituting less than one half of the population in most Western European nations.[31]

POLITICS

There was a threat that Europe might move toward outright protectionism due to the high joblessness rate and the inability of governments and industry to bring about competitive reforms. Pressure on European governments to provide fast answers to the employment crisis was growing. Protectionist measures did not have to take the form of external trade barriers. Governments could furnish subsidies to uncompetitive industries to protect jobs. Thus, the more Europe advanced toward free trade, the more likely that its governments could move to intervene for the domestic economy. Protectionism could cause prices to go up, consumers to buy less, exports to become less competitive, and workers to lose more jobs as companies would relocate in other countries.[32]

CONCLUSION

Whirlpool Europe achieved considerable success in penetrating the European home-appliance market. Within a relatively short period of time, it became the third leading manufacturer in Europe. However, the company's 6.5% operating margin fell short of achieving its objective of 10%. This was due primarily to stiff competition from the two well-established European manufacturers, Electrolux and Bosch-Siemens. And the competition is likely to become more intense in the years ahead as these two companies intensify their efficiency-improvement programs as well as their expansion efforts into the emerging markets of Eastern and Central Europe. With strong labor unions and political resistance to layoffs that make cost cutting more difficult in Europe than in the United States, will Whirlpool Europe measure up to David Whitwam's vision of achieving a leadership position in Europe?

CASE APPENDIX

Exhibit A
Consolidated
Balance Sheet
(as of December 31,
in millions of dollars)

	1994	1993
Assets		
Current Assets		
Cash and equivalents	$ 72	$ 88
Trade receivables, less allowances of $38 in 1994 and $36 in 1993	1,001	866
Financing receivables and leases, less allowances	866	814
Inventories	838	760
Prepaid expenses and other	197	102
Deferred income taxes	104	78
Total Current Assets	3,078	2,708
Other Assets		
Investment in affiliated companies	370	320
Financing receivables and leases, less allowances	717	793
Intangibles, net	730	725
Deferred income taxes	171	127
Other	149	55
Property, Plant, and Equipment		
Land	73	69
Buildings	610	586
Machinery and equipment	2,418	2,181
Accumulated depreciation	(1,661)	(1,517)
Total Property, Plant, and Equipment	1440	1,319
Total Assets	$6,655	$6,047
Liabilities and Stockholders' Equity		
Current Liabilities		
Notes payable	$1,162	$ 992
Accounts payable	843	742
Employee compensation	201	177
Accrued expenses	629	651
Restructuring costs	114	33
Current maturities and long-term debt	39	168
Total Current Liabilities	2,988	2,763
Other Liabilities		
Deferred income taxes	221	167
Post employment benefits	481	472
Other liabilities	262	65
Long-term debt	885	840
Total Other Liabilities	1,849	1,544
Minority Interests	95	92
Stockholders' Equity	1,723	1,648
Common stock, $1 par value; 250 million shares authorized, 80 million and 79 million shares outstanding (including treasury stock in 1994 and 1993)	80	79
Paid-in capital	214	152
Retained earnings	1,754	1,686
Unearned restricted stock	(8)	(9)
Cumulative translation adjustments	(93)	(77)
Treasury stock—6 million and 5 million shares at cost in 1994 and 1993	(224)	(183)
	1,723	1,648
Total Liabilities and Stockholders' Equity	$6,655	$6,047

Source: Whirlpool Corporation, *1994 Annual Report,* pages 30–31.

Exhibit B
Consolidated
Statements of
Cash Flows
(as of December 31,
1994, in millions of
dollars)

	1994	1993
Operating Activities		
Net earnings (loss) before cumulative effect of accounting change	$ 158	$ 231
Depreciation	246	241
Deferred income taxes	(28)	(31)
Equity in net losses (earnings) of affiliated companies, including dividends received	(57)	(14)
(Gain) loss on business dispositions	(60)	8
Provision for doubtful accounts	28	75
Amortization of goodwill	20	28
Restructuring charges, net of cash paid	197	10
Minority interests	12	10
Other	25	43
Changes in assets and liabilities, net of effects of business acquisitions and dispositions		
Trade receivables	(125)	(76)
Inventories	(72)	(145)
Accounts payable	107	101
Other—net	(2)	148
Cash Provided by Operating Activities	$ 449	$ 629
Investing Activities		
Net additions to properties	$ (418)	$ (309)
Financing receivables originated and leasing assets purchased	(3,051)	2,603
Principal payments received on financing receivables and leases	3,068	2,888
Acquisitions of businesses, less cash acquired	(28)	—
Net increase in investment in affiliated companies	—	(19)
Business dispositions	124	4
Other	(34)	(57)
Cash Provided by (Used for) Investing Activities	(339)	(96)
Financing Activities		
Proceeds of short-term borrowings	12,727	12,049
Repayments of short-term borrowings	(12,585)	(12,465)
Proceeds of long-term debt	42	32
Repayments of long-term debt	(206)	(173)
Repayment of non-recourse debt	(11)	(26)
Dividends paid	(90)	(85)
Purchase of treasury stock	(16)	—
Proceeds from the sale of preferred stock	—	75
Swap terminations	—	56
Other	13	26
Cash Used for Financing Activities	(126)	(511)
Increase (Decrease) in Cash and Equivalents	(16)	22
Cash and equivalents at beginning of year	88	66
Cash and Equivalents at End of Year	$ 72	$ 88

Source: Whirlpool Corporation, *1994 Annual Report,* pages 32–33.

CASE NOTES

1.   Regina Fazio Maruca, "The Right Way to Go Global: An Interview with CEO David Whitwam," *Harvard Business Review*, March–April, 1994, pp. 137–48.

2.   Whirlpool Corporation, 1994 *Annual Report*, pp. 12–16.

3.   Standard and Poor, *Register of Corporations, Directors, and Executives* (New York: Standard and Poor, 1995).

4.   Maruca, *op. cit.*

5.   *Ibid.*, p. 135.

6.   *Ibid.*

7.   Alan L. Adler, "Whirlpool Puts Its Brand on Europe," *Chicago Tribune*, March 30, 1992, Section 4, p. 5.

8.   Maruca, *op. cit.*, p. 138.

9.   "Dedication to Majors," *Appliance Manufacturer*, Vol. 42, No. 5, May 1994, p. w4.

10.   Whirlpool Corporation, *op. cit.*

11.   Whirlpool Corporation, *op. cit.*

12.   Patrick Oster and John Rossant, "Call It Worldpool," *Business Week*, November 28, 1994, p. 99.

13.   Christina Duff, "Whirlpool Plans to Acquire Rest of Europe Unit," *Wall Street Journal*, June 7, 1991, p. A9.

14.   Joe Jancsurak, "Group Sales: Channel Focused," *Appliance Manufacturer*, Vol. 43, No. 2, February 1995, p. 14.

15.   Oster and Rossant, *op. cit.*

16.   *Ibid.*

17.   Whirlpool Corporation, *op. cit.*, p. 13.

18.   Maruca, *op. cit.*, p. 143.

19.   *Ibid.*

20.   Robert L. Rose, "Whirlpool Is Expanding in Europe Despite the Slump," *Wall Street Journal*, January 27, 1994, p. B4.

21.   Alan L. Adler, *op. cit.*, p. 5.

22.   Rose, *op. cit.*

23.   Oster and Rossant, *op. cit.*, p. 98.

24.   *Ibid.*

25.   Rose, *op. cit.*, p. B4.

26.   Joe Jancsurak, "Holistic Strategy Pays Off," *Appliance Manufacturer*, February 1995, Vol. 43, No. 2, p. w3.

27.   Whirlpool Corporation, *op. cit.*, p. 12.

28.   "Financial Statement Ending December 31, 1994," *Worldscope* (an on-line database).

29.   *Ibid.*

30.   Bill Javelski, "Europe: Exports and Optimism," *Business Week*, April 4, 1994, p. 49.

31.   Quoted in Sujata Banerjee et al., "Federal Express Europe," unpublished paper, June 11, 1996, pp. 12–13.

32.   Terrence Roth and Bhushan Bahree, "Europe, Despite Growing Joblessness, Isn't Likely to Turn to Protectionism," *Wall Street Journal*, April 1, 1996, p. B7D.

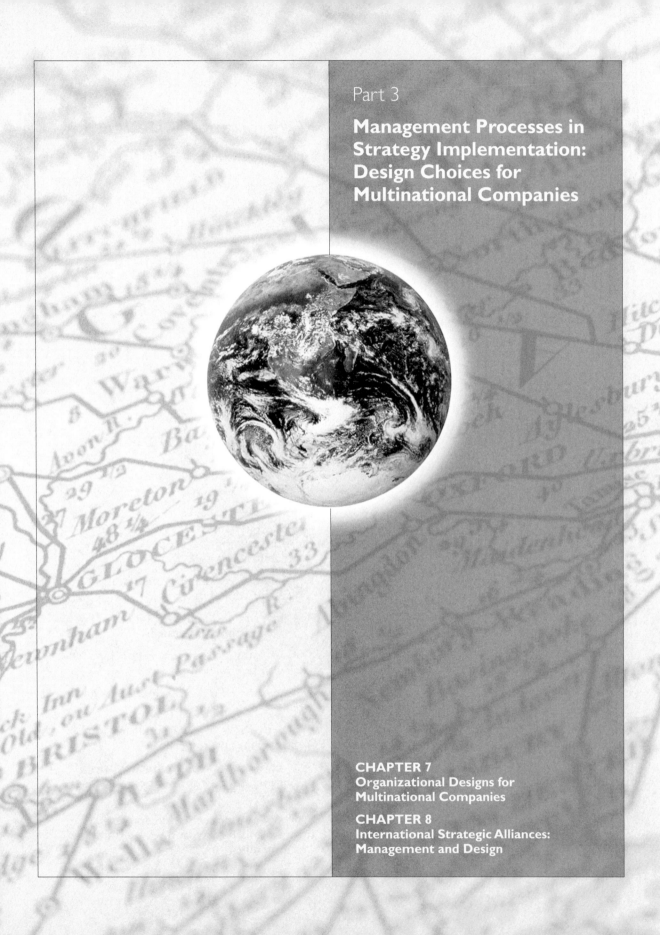

Part 3

**Management Processes in
Strategy Implementation:
Design Choices for
Multinational Companies**

CHAPTER 7
**Organizational Designs for
Multinational Companies**

CHAPTER 8
**International Strategic Alliances:
Management and Design**

Chapter 7

Organizational Designs for Multinational Companies

LEARNING OBJECTIVES
After reading this chapter you should be able to:

- Understand the components of organizational design.

- Know the basic building blocks of organizational structure.

- Understand the structural options for multinational companies.

- Know the choices multinationals have in the use of subsidiaries.

- See the links between multinational strategies and structures.

- Understand the basic mechanisms of organizational coordination and control.

- Know how coordination and control mechanisms are used by multinational companies.

Preview Case in Point	Acer is a Taiwanese PC and consumer electronics firm that is rapidly becoming a world leader in PC sales. Acer started out as a traditional, top-down, Chinese family-controlled business. Now Acer, the third largest PC producer in the world, is not only incredibly profitable (revenues over $6 billion) but it also has a unique organization.
A New Organization Design for Global Competition	Acer is now a loosely configured network of 21 publicly traded companies and 120 affiliated companies in 37 countries around the globe. They all use the Acer name but participation in the group is voluntary. Control from headquarters rests on the willingness of local companies to follow Taiwan's lead.

Acer calls their structure the Internet Organization (iO) because it is modeled after a web with independently viable sites communicating and sharing within the network. To work successfully, members must rely on sharing each other's experience, expertise, and competencies. Acer calls the glue that holds these dispersed units together the "Internet Organzation Protocol" (iOP). The iOP comes from sharing a common brand, participation in the global network, and sharing management experiences. Acer hopes that its competitive advantage lies in the iO's ability to coordinate activities yet remain flexible to respond to changes in the members' local business environments.

Will this organization work? There are doubters, but Acer CEO Stan Shih is committed to this futuristic organizational structure.

Source: Based on http://www.global.acer.com/about/strategies.html 2000.

The best multinational strategies do not ensure success. Implementation of a multinational business strategy requires that managers build the right type of organization—that is, managers try to design their organizations with what they believe are the best mechanisms to carry out domestic and multinational strategies. As shown in the Preview Case in Point, Acer's CEO hopes that its innovative network organization design will provide the right support for their global strategies in the next decade. Below you will see other design choices and consider the complexities of organizing for international competition.

Organizational design

How organizations structure subunits and use coordination and control mechanisms to achieve their strategic goals.

This chapter discusses the organizational-design options available to implement the various multinational strategies. What is organizational design? **Organizational design** represents how organizations structure subunits and coordination and control mechanisms to achieve their strategic goals. This chapter shows how having the right organizational design is crucial for multinational companies to achieve their multinational strategic goals.

The choices regarding how to set up an organization are complex and varied. Each organizational design has costs and benefits regarding the best way to deliver a product or service to the domestic or international customer. Some organizational designs for multinational companies favor flexibility. These designs provide managers with the organizational tools to deliver products adapted to different national or regional markets or to take advantage of resources located in different regions of the world. Other organizational designs favor efficiency. These designs provide managers with organizations best suited to deliver low-cost products worldwide.

Before considering specific designs for multinational organizations, the chapter presents a survey of organizational design and a summary of basic background knowledge on organizational structure. Building on this information, the chapter then discusses the organizational structures used by multinational companies. Finally, the chapter gives a summary of the basic coordination and control mechanisms available to multinational companies.

THE NATURE OF ORGANIZATIONAL DESIGN

The two basic questions in designing an organization are: (1) How shall we divide the work among the organization's subunits? and, after that, (2) How shall we coordinate and control the efforts of the units we create?

In very small organizations, everyone does the same thing and does everything. There is little reason to divide the work. However, as organizations grow, managers divide work first into specialized jobs. Different people perform different tasks. Later, when enough people are doing the same tasks and a supervisor is required, managers divide their organizations into specialized subunits. In smaller organizations, the subunits are usually called departments. In larger organizations, divisions or subsidiaries become the major subunits.

Once an organization has specialized subunits, managers must develop mechanisms that coordinate and control the efforts of each subunit. For example, a manufacturing company must make sure that the production department produces the goods to be available at the time when the marketing department promised the customers. Similarly, a multinational company must ensure that its foreign operations support the parent company's strategic goals. Some companies monitor their subunits very closely. They *centralize* decision making at company headquarters to make certain that the production and delivery of products or services conform to rigid standards. Other companies give subunits greater flexibility by *decentralizing* decision-making control. Later in the chapter we will discuss why multinational companies might choose tight or loose control of their subunits.

An important point to remember is that there is no one best organizational design. The choice of an organizational design depends mostly on the choice of strategy. That is, some design options are more effective for implementing different strategies. In addition, the choice of design options depends on the firm's resources. To modify an organizational design successfully requires that companies have the necessary personnel to staff newly created organizational subunits and the financial resources to support the new organization. For companies operating internationally, as you will see here, the key issue is the degree to which a company has a local responsiveness or global strategic orientation.

A PRIMER ON ORGANIZATIONAL STRUCTURES

Before you can understand the organizational structures necessary for multinational strategy implementation, you need some basic knowledge of organizational structure. To provide this background, the next section gives a brief review of the basic structural options available to managers in designing their organizations. Students who have had course work on organizational design will find this a review.

Organizations usually divide work into departments or divisions based on functions, geography, products, or a combination of these choices. Each way of organizing has its advantages and disadvantages. Companies adopt one or a combination of

Exhibit 7.1
A Basic Functional
Structure

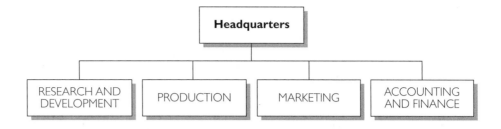

these subunit forms based on management's beliefs concerning the best structure or structures to implement their chosen strategies. In this chapter, some of the advantages and disadvantages of each choice will be explained.

THE BASIC FUNCTIONAL STRUCTURE

**Functional
structure**

*Has departments or
subunits based on
separate business
functions, such as
marketing or
manufacturing.*

In the **functional structure**, departments perform separate business functions such as marketing or manufacturing. The functional structure is the simplest of organizations. As such, most smaller organizations have functional structures. However, even larger organizations often have some functional subunits. Since most organizations use charts to display their organizational structure, the chapter shows each type of organization using exhibits of hypothetical or real organizational charts. Exhibit 7.1 shows an organizational chart for a generic functional structure.

Why do organizations choose a functional structure? The major reason to choose a functional structure for a subunit is efficiency. The functional structure gets its efficiency from economies of scale in each function. Economies of scale result because there are cost savings when a large number of people do the same job in the same place. For example, the organization can locate all marketing or manufacturing people in one subunit, with one staff support group, one telephone system, and one management system. However, because functional subunits are separated from each other and serve functional goals, coordination among the units can be difficult. Responses to changes in the environment can be slow. As such, the functional structure works best when organizations have few products, few locations, or few types of customers. It also works best when the organization faces a stable environment where the need for adaptation is minimal (Duncan 1979).

Organizations face a variety of situations that can undermine the effectiveness of the functional structure. Functional structures can lose effectiveness and efficiency when organizations have many products, serve different customer groups, or locate in widely dispersed geographical areas. The most common reaction by managers to these situations is to organize departments or divisions by product or geography.

THE BASIC PRODUCT AND GEOGRAPHIC STRUCTURES

Product structure

*Has departments or
subunits based on
different product groups.*

**Geographic
structure**

*Has departments or
subunits based on
geographical regions.*

The structural arrangements for building a department or subunit around a product or a geographic area are called the **product structure** and the **geographic structure**, respectively. Exhibits 7.2 and 7.3 show simple product and geographic structures.

Product or geographic organizations must still perform the functional tasks of a business (e.g., marketing, accounting). In contrast to the functional structure, however, product or geographic organizations do not concentrate functions in separate subunits. Instead, functional tasks are duplicated for each product department or geographical-area department. The duplication of these functional tasks

Exhibit 7.2
A Basic Product
Structure

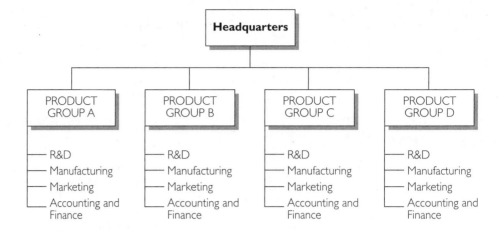

usually requires more managers and more people to run the organization. Duplication of functions also suggests the greatest weakness of the product or geographical structures—the loss of economies of scale in functions. These organizations are usually less efficient than the purely functional organization.

Managers accept the loss of functional efficiencies in product or geographic organizations for two reasons. First, as customer groups and products proliferate, the cost of coordination and control across functions also grows, offsetting basic functional efficiencies. Second, even for small organizations, product and geographic organizations can have competitive advantages over the more efficient functional structure.

The geographic structure allows a company to serve customer needs that vary by region. That is, the geographic structure sets up a mini functional organization in each region. Rather than one large functional organization that serves all customers, the smaller, regional, organization focuses all functional activities on serving the unique needs of the regional customer. Because the organization focuses on specific customer groups, managers can more easily and quickly identify customer needs and adapt products accordingly.

Managers choose product structures when they believe that a product or a group of products is sufficiently unique to require focused functional efforts on one type of product or service. This structure creates strong coordination across the functional areas to support the product group. The pressures that lead to the selection of product structures are products' unique or changing technologies or the association of different customer groups with different products.

Few organizations adopt pure organizational forms. Each organization faces unique tradeoffs based on efficiency, product types, and customers' needs. They design their organizations with mixtures of structures that they believe will best implement their strategies. These mixed-form organizations, which can include functional, geographic, and product units, are called **hybrid structures**.

Hybrid structure

Mixes functional, geographic, and product units.

ORGANIZATIONAL STRUCTURES TO IMPLEMENT MULTINATIONAL STRATEGIES

When a company first goes international, it seldom changes its basic organizational structure. Most companies act first as passive exporters. They simply fill orders using the same structures, procedures, and people used in domestic sales. Even with

Exhibit 7.3
A Basic Geographic
Structure

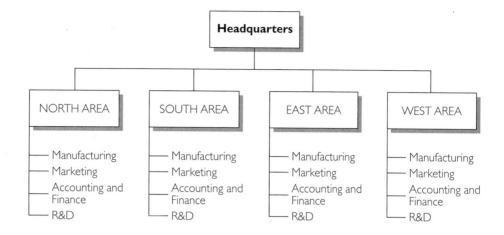

greater involvement in exporting, companies often avoid fundamental organizational changes. Instead, they use other companies to provide them with international expertise and to run their export operations. As shown in Chapter 6, export management companies and export trading companies manage exporting for companies without the resources or skills to run their own export operations.

Similarly, the choice of licensing as a multinational participation strategy also has little impact on domestic organizational structures. The licensor need only negotiate a contract and collect the appropriate royalties. The licensor's corporate attorneys may negotiate the licensing contract, and its managers may monitor the licensing contract. However, the licensee's organization must deal with most of the organizational problems of taking a product or service to the foreign market.

When international sales become more central to a firm's success, more sophisticated multinational and participation strategies usually become a significant part of a company's overall business strategy. As a result, companies must then build appropriate organizational structures to manage their multinational operations and implement their multinational strategies. The following sections focus on the structural options for companies using the multinational and participation strategies discussed previously.

THE EXPORT DEPARTMENT

**Export
department**

*Coordinates and
controls a company's
export operations.*

When exports become a significant percentage of company sales and a company wishes greater control over its export operations, managers often create a separate **export department**. A separate department shows that top management believes that the investment of human and financial resources in exporting is necessary to sustain and build international sales. The export department deals with all international customers for all products. Managers in the export department often control the pricing and promotion of products for the international market. People within the department may have particular country or product expertise. Export-department managers have the responsibility to deal with export management companies, with foreign distributors, and with foreign customers. When the company uses a direct exporting strategy, sales representatives located in other countries may also report to the export-department management. Exhibit 7.4 shows a hypothetical organization with a functional structure and an export department.

Exhibit 7.4
A Functional
Structure with an
Export Department

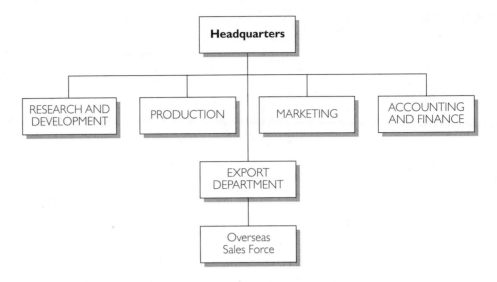

As companies evolve beyond initial participation strategies of exporting and licensing, they need more sophisticated organizational structures to implement more complex multinational strategies. These more complex structures include the international division, the worldwide geographic and products structures, the worldwide-matrix structure, and the transnational-network structure.

Before discussing the more complex multinational structures in detail, some background is necessary on the types of subunits multinational companies set up in foreign countries.

FOREIGN SUBSIDIARIES

Foreign subsidiary

Subunit of the multinational company that is located in another country.

The more complex multinational organizational structures support participation strategies that include direct investments in a foreign country. This means setting up an overseas subunit of the parent firm. These subunits are called **foreign subsidiaries**. Foreign subsidiaries are subunits of the multinational company located in countries other than the country of the parent company's headquarters. Foreign subsidiaries are a growing component of international business. For example, the United Nations estimates that there are over 63,000 multinational corporations with over 7,000,000 foreign subsidiaries worldwide (UNCTAD 2000).

Several types of foreign subsidiaries are used by multinational companies. For companies pursuing a multidomestic strategy, the foreign subsidiary often becomes a "minireplica" of the parent company (Beamish et al. 1994). This type of subsidiary is called the **minireplica subsidiary**. It is a smaller version of the parent company. It uses the same technology and produces the same products as the parent company. However, it runs on a smaller scale. By producing products or services strictly for the local market, the minireplica can adapt to local conditions and support the multidomestic strategy.

Minireplica subsidiary

Smaller version of the parent company, using the same technology and producing the same products as the parent company.

Minireplicas use few expatriate managers. Local managers run the organization, often with little influence from headquarters. Because of its autonomy from headquarters, the minireplica is usually a profit center. In a profit center, corporate headquarters evaluates local managers based on the unit's profitability, using financial-performance information such as return on investment. Seldom do minireplicas

Case in Point

Transferring Local Innovations and Product-Development Skills

In the lucrative European fabric-softener market, Unilever trailed Procter & Gamble's product called Lenor (Downy in the United States). To the rescue came Unilever's German subsidiary. The Germans used a new marketing and product-position strategy focused on Kuschelweich ("Cuddles" in English), the teddy-bear symbol of the clothes softener. Consumers identified with the idea of softness and trust. The idea worked so well in Germany, Unilever used it first throughout Europe and then in the United States. The product became Snuggle in the United States, Huggy in Australia, Cajoline in France, and Coccolino in Italy. Market share tripled in the softener category.

Hewlett-Packard encourages its subsidiaries to become transnationals as the global base for product innovation and development. The plant in Penang, Malaysia holds global responsibility for many microwave component products and for hard-disk drives. At first, its Singapore subsidiary only assembled keyboards. It now is the global production and R&D center for personal calculators, digital assistants, and portable ink-jet printers.

Sources: Based on Bartlett and Ghoshal 1989 and *Business Week Online* 1994c.

Transnational subsidiary

Has no companywide form or function—each subsidiary does what it does best or most efficiently anywhere in the world.

contribute to corporation-wide goals such as providing R&D or manufacturing for other locations around the world.

At the opposite end of the spectrum from the minireplica is the **transnational subsidiary**. This type of subsidiary supports a multinational-firm strategy based on location advantages. The transnational subsidiary has no company-wide form or function. Each subsidiary contributes what it does best for corporate goals.

To respond to local conditions, a transnational subsidiary in one country may produce some products that it adapts to the local tastes. For example, multinational companies often make consumer goods locally. Products such as laundry detergents need adjustments for cultural preferences, washing techniques, and characteristics of the water supply. To contribute to overall corporate efficiency, transnational subsidiaries in other countries may produce products for sale in the worldwide market. To increase organizational learning, transnational subsidiaries anywhere can provide information to the parent company about local markets, help solve problems for any other unit in the world, or develop new technologies. For instance, the Dutch company Philips had its first stereo color TV developed by its Australian subsidiary (Bartlett and Ghoshal 1989).

To implement transnational strategies based on location advantages, multinational companies may place subsidiaries in different countries to take advantage of factor costs (e.g., cheaper labor or raw materials), to take advantage of other resources (for example, an educated workforce or unique skills), or to gain access to the country. For example, DuPont gives worldwide control of its Lycra business to its Swiss subsidiary to take advantage of its concentration of unique production and management skills. Other examples of how multinational companies use their subsidiaries to gain location advantages appear in the preceding Case in Point.

Some foreign subsidiaries begin as only sales offices and then later take on other functions. Before manufacturing a product in another country, companies frequently test the market by opening a foreign sales office. If the market looks promising, companies then invest in the plant and equipment to manufacture locally. In contrast, other subsidiaries begin and remain as suppliers of raw materials for the parent company or other subsidiaries. These units often have no manufacturing or sales capacities. For example, major oil companies such as British Petroleum use many of their subsidiaries only to supply raw material. Finally, some multinationals use their subsidiaries as offshore production or assembly plants for export back to the headquarters' country.

Most subsidiaries are neither pure minireplicas nor pure transnationals. Rather, foreign subsidiaries take many different forms and have many different functions. Multinational companies choose the mix of functions for their foreign subsidiaries based on several issues, including (1) the firm's multinational strategy or strategies, (2) the subsidiaries' capabilities and resources, (3) the economic and political risk of building and managing a subunit in another country, and (4) how the subsidiaries fit into the overall multinational organizational structure.

Foreign subsidiaries provide the structural building blocks for running multinational operations; that is, once companies move beyond simple exporting, foreign subsidiaries become key parts of the organizational designs used by multinational companies to implement their multinational strategies. With the background knowledge of the nature of foreign subsidiaries, we will now consider how multinational companies use the various organizational structures to implement their multinational strategies.

INTERNATIONAL DIVISION

International division

Responsible for managing exports, international sales, and foreign subsidiaries.

As companies increase the size of their international sales force and set up manufacturing operations in other countries, the export department often grows into an **international division**. The international division differs from the export department in several ways; it is usually larger and has greater responsibilities. Besides managing exporting and an international sales force, the international division oversees foreign subsidiaries that perform a variety of functions. Most often, these are sales units. However, units that procure raw material and produce the company's products in other countries are common. The international division also has more extensive staff with international expertise. Top management expects these people to perform functions such as negotiating licensing and joint-venture agreements, translating promotional material, or providing expertise on different national cultures and social institutions.

Exhibit 7.5 gives an example of an international division in a domestic product structure. In this example, the international division handles all products and controls foreign subsidiaries in Europe and Japan and a general sales force in the rest of Asia.

The international-division structure has recently declined in popularity among the large multinationals (Humes 1993). For multiproduct companies operating in many countries, it is not considered an effective multinational structure (Stopford and Wells 1972). However, for companies of moderate size with a limited number of products or country locations, the international division remains a popular and potentially effective organization.

Why do companies often abandon their international divisions as they expand international operations in terms of products and country locations? There are several reasons. First, too many products often overwhelm the capacities of the international division. In sales, for example, it is difficult for people in the international division to know the whole product line and sell it worldwide. Second, when the number of locations in different countries grows, it is difficult for the

Exhibit 7.5
An International
Division in a
Domestic Product
Structure

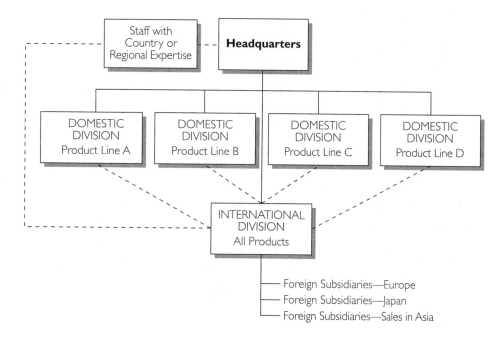

international division to manage multidomestic or regional adaptations. How can a remote headquarters division know local needs and adapt products and strategies accordingly?

Third, the international division makes it more difficult to implement international strategies using worldwide products or location advantages. Because the international division separates international concerns from the headquarters-based product divisions, these divisions are less likely to look at the world as one market. Divisions have a product focus and not a market focus. Home-based product divisions are also less likely to view worldwide production or R&D locations as global platforms. Rather, for most companies with international divisions, the domestic market is king, and international issues are the international division's "problem."

To deal with the shortcomings of the international-division structure, multinational companies have several options. These include the worldwide product structure, the worldwide geographic structure, the matrix structure, and the transnational-network structure. The following section discusses the worldwide geographic and product structures.

WORLDWIDE GEOGRAPHIC STRUCTURE
AND WORLDWIDE PRODUCT STRUCTURE

Worldwide geographic structure

Has geographical units representing regions of the world.

In the **worldwide geographic structure** (as shown in Exhibit 7.6), regions or large-market countries become the geographical divisions of the multinational company. The prime reason to choose a worldwide geographic structure is to implement a multidomestic or regional strategy. Since a company with a multidomestic or regional strategy needs to differentiate its products or services by country or region, it needs an organizational design with maximum geographical flexibility. The semiautonomous regional or country-based subunits of the worldwide geographic structure provide that flexibility to tailor or develop products that meet the particular needs of local or regional markets. Often large differences in an area's

Exhibit 7.6 Apple Computer's Worldwide Geographic Structure

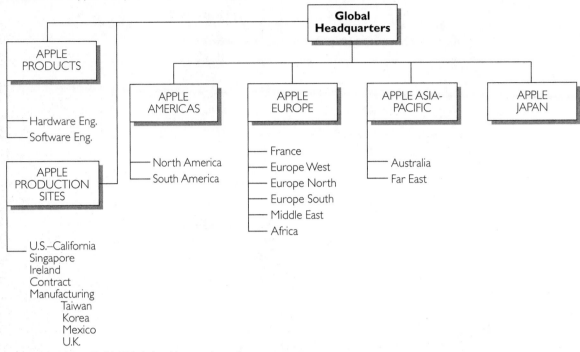

Source: Adapted from Apple's Web site http://www.apple.com/.

product or service needs or in channels of distribution enhance the need for a geographic structure.

For practical purposes, even for the multidomestic strategist, country-level divisions usually exist only when a country's market size is sufficiently large or important to support a separate organization. Separate divisions often make economic sense for large market countries such as the United States, France, Germany, or Japan. Regional divisions combine smaller similar countries such as, for example, a Southern European division for Italy, Spain, and Portugal. For the regional strategist, combinations of countries are as large as possible, based on similarities in customer requirements balanced against the efficiencies of uniform products. Exhibit 7.6 shows the worldwide geographic structure used by Apple Computer. Apple has a separate country-level unit for Japan and regional units for other markets. The Middle East and Africa fall under the control of the European region because Apple judges their market size too small to cover the costs of separate organizations.

Product divisions form the basic units of **worldwide product structures**, as shown in Exhibit 7.7. Each product division assumes responsibility for producing and selling its products or services throughout the world. The product structure supports strategies that emphasize the production and sales of worldwide products. It is usually considered the ideal structure to implement an international strategy. In the international strategy, the company attempts to gain economies of scale by selling worldwide products with most upstream activities based at home.

Worldwide product structures support international strategies because they provide an efficient way to organize and centralize the production and sales of similar products for the world market. The worldwide product structure sacrifices regional- or local-adaptation strengths derived from a geographic structure to gain product-development and manufacturing economies of scale. For example, Ford

Worldwide product structure

Gives product divisions responsibility to produce and sell their products or services throughout the world.

Exhibit 7.7
A Woldwide Product
Structure

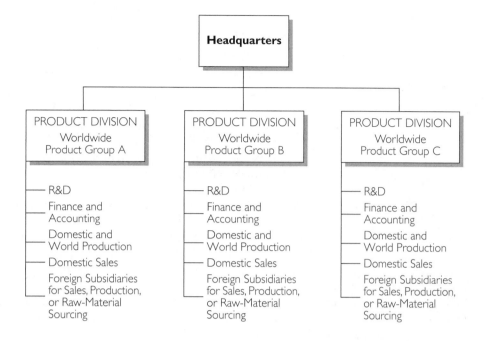

Motor Company implemented its Ford 2000 strategy scrapping Ford of Europe and centralizing product engineering and design in Detroit. They created product groups called "Vehicle Centers" that had worldwide responsibility to develop new trucks and cars. This more product-oriented design has resulted in substantial cost savings from using fewer global suppliers and eliminating duplication in product development (*Business Week Online* 1994a; Treece, Kerwin, and Dawley 1995). However, the current view is that Ford's worldwide product organization lost touch with local customers in Europe (*Economist* 1999b; *Economist* 2000). A danger for Ford—or any other company that emphasizes product over geography—is that the cost savings from more efficiently produced products may not offset revenue losses when products fail to please the local market.

In the ideal worldwide product structure, all the value-chain functions, with the exception of sales, would remain in the company's home country. However, this is seldom possible because strategic, logistical, or political considerations lead a worldwide product structure company to perform some functions (e.g., supply, manufacturing, or after-market service) in foreign locations. In these cases, product-division headquarters still centralizes control of R&D, manufacturing, and international marketing strategy. This means that when foreign subsidiaries are used, they have little autonomy.

Foreign subsidiaries in the worldwide product structure may produce worldwide products/components, supply raw materials, or specialize only in local sales. However, they serve product goals directed from product-division headquarters. Production or supply subsidiaries often have little concern for their local markets. For the sales subsidiaries, there is minimal local adaptation of the headquarters-directed worldwide marketing strategy. Manufacturing subsidiaries in the product structure may produce component products for the global market and export these products back to the division's home country for final assembly. In this case, sister sales subsidiaries may then reimport the finished product for local sales (Beamish et al. 1994). For example, the U.S. aircraft manufacturer Boeing produces many of its aircraft components outside the United States. Its subsidiaries return these

Multinational Management Challenge
Can P&G Change Its Structure?

Procter & Gamble is a $38 billion company with operations in 160 countries. Recently, however, P&G has been losing market share to multinational rivals such as Unilever and Colgate-Palmolive. The problem, according to Durk Jager, the Dutch CEO of this U.S. giant, is that the company is too slow to introduce new products and too inefficient in its organizational structure. The solution: Organization 2005.

In the old P&G model, country or region-level operations were separate fiefdoms, allowing country managers veto power over R&D and sales and marketing decisions.

The new structure abandons the 100 geographic profit centers and replaces them with seven global business units (GBUs) representing product categories: fabric and homecare, food and beverages, feminine hygiene, beauty cream, tissues and towels, baby care, and healthcare. To support these global product divisions in their local marketing, P&G will add eight market development organizations based on regions. It remains to be seen how P&G will coordinate dominant product divisions with their less powerful geographical units.

Sources: Based on Bell 1999; *Economist* 1999a and Murphy 1999.

components to the United States for final assembly. Later, airlines in many of the producing countries buy the completed Boeing planes.

In the competitive world of consumer products, P&G is moving away from a multidomestic sales strategy to a product orientation, as described in the preceding Multinational Management Challenge. To accomplish this shift in strategic orientation, the firm must dismantle its geographic units and build a new product-based organization. What problems would you anticipate in this change?

HYBRIDS AND THE WORLDWIDE MATRIX STRUCTURE

Both the worldwide product structure and the worldwide geographic structure have advantages and disadvantages for multinational strategy implementation. The product structure best supports strategies that emphasize global products and rationalization (worldwide products using worldwide, low-cost sources of raw materials and worldwide marketing strategies). The geographic structure best supports strategies that emphasize local adaptation (managers are often local nationals and are sensitive to local needs). Most multinational companies, however, adopt strategies that include both concerns for local adaptation as well as for the economic and product-development benefits of globalization. Consequently, most large multinationals have structures that are hybrids, or mixtures of product and area units. The nature of the product determines the emphasis given to the product or geographic side of the company (How global are the products?) and the nature of the markets (How complex and different are the major markets?).

Exhibit 7.8 A Worldwide Matrix Structure

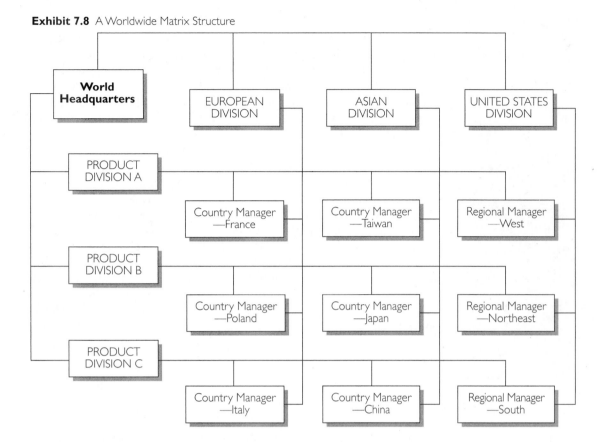

At Sony Corporation headquarters, for example, worldwide product group managers exercise broad oversight over their businesses. However, Sony also focuses on regional needs by dividing global operations into four zones: Japan, North America, Europe, and the rest of the world. The consumer products giant, Unilever PLC, has a regional structure with local managers in three areas: Africa/Middle East, Latin America, and East Asia/Pacific. However, managers in Europe and North America report to worldwide product coordinators (*Business Week Online* 1994a).

To balance the benefits produced by geographic and product structures and to coordinate a mixture of product and geographic subunits, some multinationals create a **worldwide matrix structure**. Unlike most hybrid organizations, the worldwide matrix structure, shown in Exhibit 7.8, is a symmetrical organization: it has equal lines of authority for product groups and for geographic divisions. Ideally, the matrix provides the structure for a firm to pursue both local and more global strategies at the same time. Geographical divisions focus on national responsiveness, and product divisions focus on finding global efficiencies. The matrix structure works well only when there are nearly equal demands from the environment for local adaptation and for product standardization with its associated economies of scale. Without these near-equal demands, the organization tends to evolve into a product or geographic structure, based on which side is more important for competitive advantage.

In theory, the matrix produces quality decisions because two or more managers reach consensus on how to balance local and worldwide needs. Managers who hold

Worldwide matrix structure

Symmetrical organization, usually with equal emphasis on worldwide product groups and regional geographical divisions.

Recently, Cornelius A. J. Herkstruter, Chair of the Royal Dutch/Shell Group, announced a radical restructuring of his company. In a speech delivered simultaneously to corporate headquarters in London and The Hague, he declared that the matrix was out. Instead, global product divisions such as exploration, production, and chemical will report to teams of senior executives. These executives will have centralized decision-making power no longer shared with country or functional managers.

Shell's old matrix was quite complex. Most matrix structures combine two organizational designs, usually geography and product, for the multinational. Shell's matrix was three dimensional, with some managers having functional, product, and area bosses! For example, a finance executive could have a functional boss (for example, chief financial officer), a country-level boss, and a product boss (for example, chemical products).

The current chair believes that, over the years, Shell's complex matrix resulted in too much bureaucracy. The matrix required too many managers. In addition, the meetings and consensus decision making of the matrix slowed decision making. To remain competitive in the oil industry, industry analysts believe Shell must cut many management positions and be quicker to identify business opportunities.

Source: Based on Dwyer and Dawley 1995.

positions at the intersection of product and geographic divisions are called "two-boss managers," as they have a boss from the product side of the organization and a boss from the geographic side of the organization. Product bosses tend to emphasize goals such as efficiency and using worldwide products, while geographic bosses tend to emphasize local or regional adaptation. The conflict in these interests is intended to balance globalization and localization pressures. As such, for managers at all levels, the matrix requires continuously compensating for product needs and geographical needs.

To succeed at balancing the inherent struggles between global and local concerns, the matrix requires extensive resources for communication among the managers. Middle- and upper-level managers must have good human-relations skills to deal with inevitable personal conflicts originating from the competing interests of product and geography. The middle-level managers must also learn to deal with two bosses, who often have competing interests. Upper-level managers, in turn, must be prepared to resolve conflicts between geographic and product managers.

Is the matrix worth the effort? During the 1980s, the matrix structure was a popular organizational solution to the global–local dilemma. More recently, however, the matrix has come under fire because consensus decision making between product and geographic managers has proved slow and cumbersome. In many organizations, the matrixes became too bureaucratic, with too many meetings and too much conflict. Some organizations, such as the Royal Dutch/Shell Group, discussed in the preceding Case in Point, abandoned their matrixes and returned to product structures. Other organizations have redesigned their matrix structures to be more flexible with speedier decision making. In the more flexible matrixes, management centralizes key decisions in the product side or geographic side of the matrix, depending on the need. For example, geographical areas with unique characteristics may require the freedom to have more unique strategies. Facing such a situation, AT&T and Owens-Corning Fiberglas Corp. created highly autonomous units in China. They believed that the local Chinese and Asian markets are so dynamic that local managers (both Chinese and expatriates) need a great deal of freedom to seek opportunities (*Business Week Online* 1994c).

The evolving intensity and complexity of competition in international business has created the evolution of strategies beyond geography and product foci. We saw earlier that this resulted in the transnational strategy. To carry out a transnational strategy effectively, a new organizational form has also arisen. This is the transnational-network structure.

THE TRANSNATIONAL-NETWORK STRUCTURE

Transnational-network structure

Network of functional, product, and geographic subsidiaries dispersed throughout the world, based on the subsidiaries' location advantages.

The **transnational-network structure** represents the newest solution to the complex demands of being locally responsive while taking advantage of global economies of scale and seeking location advantages such as global sources of knowledge. Like the matrix, the transnational network tries to gain all the advantages of the various structural options. It combines functional, product, and geographic subunits. However, unlike the symmetrical matrix structure, the transnational has no basic form. It has no symmetry or balance between the geographic and product sides of the organization. Instead, the transnational is a network that links different types of transnational subsidiaries throughout the world. Nodes, the units at the center of the network, coordinate product, functional, and geographic information. Different product-group units and geographical-area units have different structures, and often no two subunits are alike. Rather, transnational units evolve to take advantage of resources, talent, and market opportunities wherever they exist in the world. Resources, people, and ideas flow in all directions.

The Dutch multinational Philips Electronics N.V. is one example of a transnational network. Working in sixty different countries, the company produces products as diverse as defense systems and light bulbs. There are eight product divisions with over sixty subgroups based on product similarity. The product divisions have subsidiaries throughout the world. Subsidiaries may focus on only one product or on an array of products. Subsidiaries can specialize in R&D, manufacturing, or marketing for world or regional markets. Some subsidiaries focus only on sales. Some units are highly independent of headquarters, while headquarters controls other units tightly.

In terms of geography, Philips divides the world into three groups. "Key countries" such as the Netherlands and the United States produce for local and world markets and control local sales. "Large countries" such as Mexico and Belgium have some local and worldwide production facilities and local sales. "Local business countries" are smaller countries that are primarily sales units and that import products from the product divisions' worldwide production centers in other countries. All these design choices by Philips attempt to optimize efficiency, organizational learning, and local responsiveness (Ghoshal and Bartlett 1990; Humes 1993; Philips Electronics N.V. 1999).

Exhibits 7.9 and 7.10 show two different perspectives on how one can look at Philips' very complex transnational-network structure. One views geographical links among locations, while the other looks at the functions of different locations. Another company often considered to have the prototypical transnational structure is ABB. The Case in Point on page 282 discusses the transnational-network structure of ABB, termed a "loose matrix" by its former CEO.

Exhibit 7.9 Geographic Links in the Philips Transnational Structure

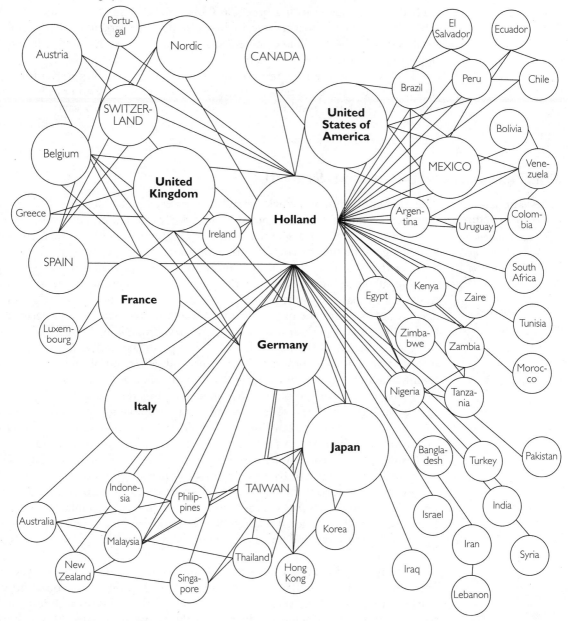

Source: Ghoshal, Sumantra, and Christopher A. Bartlett (1990). "The Multinational Corporation as an Interorganizational Network," *Academy of Management Review*, 15, 603–625. Republished with permission of the Academy of Management; permission conveyed through Copyright Clearance Center, Inc.

Dispersed subunits

Subsidiaries located anywhere in the world where they can most benefit the company.

The basic structural framework of the transnational network consists of three components: dispersed subunits, specialized operations, and interdependent relationships (Bartlett and Ghoshal 1989). The transnational network structure uses the flexible transnational subsidiaries, discussed earlier, as the basic structural unit.

Dispersed subunits mean that management locates subsidiaries anywhere in the world where they can benefit the company. Some subsidiaries take advantage of lower factor costs (e.g., lower labor costs); other units provide information on new

Exhibit 7.10 Product Links in the Philips Transnational Structure

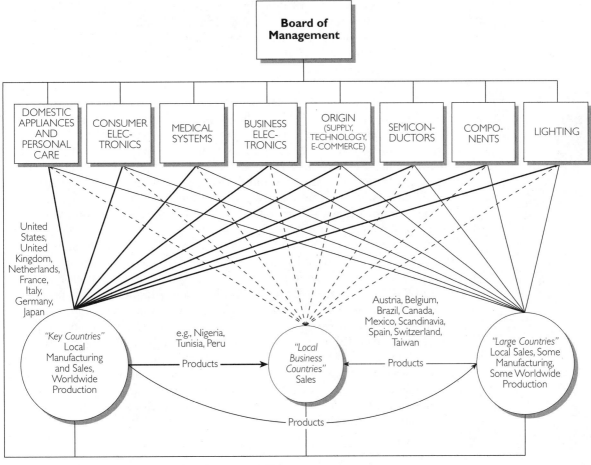

Sources: Adapted from Humes 1993 and Philips Electronics N.V. 1999

technologies, new strategies, and consumer trends. All subunits try to tap worldwide managerial and technical talent. Consider the Case in Point on page 283, showing how two companies use engineers in different countries to produce key products.

Specialized operations mean that subunits can specialize in particular product lines, different research areas, and different marketing areas. Specialization builds on the diffusion of subunits by tapping specialized expertise or other resources anywhere and everywhere in the company's subsidiaries. Philips, for example, has eight research labs located in six countries. Some units have broad mandates, such as Philips' central laboratory in Eindhoven. Other units focus on specific areas, such as the laboratories for solid-state electronics work at Redhill in the United Kingdom (Bartlett and Ghoshal 1989).

Interdependent relationships must exist to manage dispersed and specialized subunits. In interdependent relationships, units share information and resources continuously. To do this, transnationals usually build communication systems based on the latest technology. For example, GE Appliances' CEO J. Richard Stonesifer begins each Friday at 7:00 A.M. in a video conference with colleagues in Asia. For the next five hours he follows the rising sun with more video conferences with

Specialized operations

Subunits specializing in particular product lines, different research areas, or different marketing areas.

Interdependent relationships

Continuous sharing of information and resources by dispersed and specialized subunits.

ABB is a Swiss-based electrical-equipment company that is bigger than West- inghouse and that hopes to take on GE. Although headquarters is in Zurich, Switzerland, the company's thirteen top managers speak only English at their meetings. English is the one common language; but it is a foreign language to all but one manager. The choice of meeting language personifies the global culture of ABB.

ABB's organization is a loose and decentralized matrix, according to Percy Barnevik, ABB's former CEO. ABB has about 100 country managers, most of whom come from the host country. Sixty-five global managers head product divisions from several product segments: transportation; process automation; environmental devices; financial services; electrical equipment; and electric- power generation, transmission, and distribution. The matrix produces two- boss managers at the level of 1,100 local companies. These local company managers must deal with their country-level boss on local responsiveness and their global manager on worldwide efficiency.

The organization is transnational because the matrix is not balanced and the functions of the subunits are not uniform. Depending on the situation, country or global-product bosses may have control. The organizational cul- ture of ABB encourages sharing technology and products within product lines. For example, ABB's U.S. steam-turbine business uses techniques devel- oped in Switzerland to repair the machines built with U.S. technology. There is not a bias against things "not invented here." Management expects even lo- cally run factories to participate in global coordination. For example, thirty- one power-transformer factories located in sixteen countries share all their performance data monthly through global segment headquarters in Mann- heim, Germany. If even one factory has a problem, global headquarters ex- pects solutions from all factories.

Sources: Based on Taylor 1991; Rapoport 1992 and Ferner 2000.

managers from the Americas to Asia (*Business Week Online* 1994c). Ford creates "vir- tual teams" of design engineers from Europe, Japan, and the United States. These engineers communicate electronically sharing both written material and design drawings.

The following Multinational Management Brief gives additional real-world ex- amples of the various transnational activities just discussed.

MULTINATIONAL STRATEGY AND STRUCTURE: AN OVERVIEW

Exhibit 7.11 shows the relationship between the choice of multinational strategy and the choice of an organizational structure. The connections between the boxes for each strategy also show typical ways that multinational structures evolve.

Strategies of national or regional responsiveness (i.e., the multidomestic or re- gional strategies discussed in Chapter 6) suggest the use of geographic structures. An international strategy suggests that managers use a product organization and have worldwide products.

Case in Point

Talent is Everywhere—Finding Low-Cost Talent in a Borderless Company

Fueled by advances in telecommunications and the Information Superhighway, cities such as Taipei, Edinburgh, and Singapore are emerging as centers for technological breakthroughs and worldwide product developments. Multinationals with subsidiaries in such locations can find talented workers in fields ranging from software development to architecture. For example, Motorola, Inc. used 75 local Singapore engineers to design its Scriptor pager. Northern Telecom Ltd. expects to employ 250 Chinese engineers in Beijing to develop and produce software, cellular phones, and multimedia devices.

One big attraction of the overseas intellectual workforce is price. For example, in Taiwan, qualified design engineers for circuit boards earn about $25,000 annually. In China or India, the same top-level talent costs less than $10,000. Equivalent talent in California or Boston costs from $60,000 to $100,000.

Source: Based on *Business Week Online* 1994c.

Multinational Management Brief
Transnational Activities

Since the transnational model has no fixed organizational components and activities, consider how the following companies include transnational activities in the organizational designs.

- *Flattened hierarchies for quick decision making:* Asea Brown Boveri (ABB) operates in over 140 countries but still has only one layer of management between the top ranks and business units.
- *Decentralized R&D for short product life cycles:* Nokia, the Finnish cellular phone maker, puts R&D at the plant level at five factories around the world. Concurrent engineering takes place and the culture supports sharing any valuable engineering information with plants in all country locations.
- *Finding global products:* Texas Instruments created a team with the mandate to search the company worldwide for possible global products.
- *Tapping worldwide talent:* ABB designs locomotives in Switzerland and tilting trains in Sweden. Singapore engineers designed a new pager for Motorola.
- *Integrating the workforce:* To build a collaborative culture between workers in Singapore and workers in their sister plant in the United States, Motorola brought the workers to a Colorado resort for Outward Bound-style team-building games.
- *Using e-mail and information systems:* Unilever PLC has 31,000 employees worldwide communicating by e-mail or Lotus Notes. The Mexican company Cemento Mexicanos can tell with one keystroke the energy use in an oven from its Spanish subsidiary.

Sources: Based on Beamish et al. 1994; *Business Week Online* 1994b; *Business Week Online* 1994d and Forteza and Neilson 1999.

Exhibit 7.11
Multinational Strategy,
Structure, and
Evolution

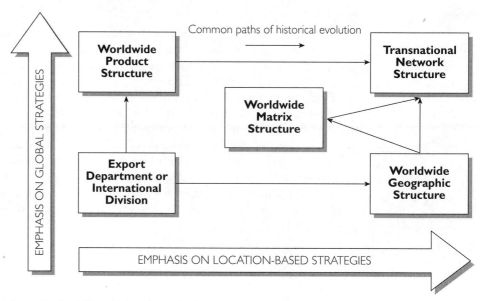

Sources: Based on White and Poynter 1989 and Daft 1995.

Most companies support their early internationalization with export depart-ments or international divisions. Later, as Exhibit 7.12 suggests, and depending on the globalization of their strategy, companies evolve into worldwide product or geo-graphic structures. After this, because of the dual demands of local-adaptation pressures and globalization, many companies move toward a matrix or transnational-network structure. Most companies, however, never quite reach the pure matrix or transnational state. Instead, they adopt hybrid structures with some matrix and transnational qualities. Recently, because of the globalization of more products and the competitive efficiencies gained with global products, there is a growing tendency of large multinationals to give product divisions increased power and to create more transnational subsidiaries.

IMPLICATIONS FOR SMALL MULTINATIONAL COMPANIES

Although smaller multinational companies favor export departments or interna-tional divisions as the organizational structures, they can still implement all the multinational strategies with modifications. For example, within an exporting de-partment or international division, small companies can develop special depart-ments, task forces, or teams to identify, create, and produce global products. Loose structures based on teams and face-to-face interaction may provide a competitive advantage based on speed.

Similarly, small companies can support a multidomestic or regional strategy by adjusting their products sold from their home countries to fit local or regional needs. Although a small company may not have the resources to acquire local subsidiaries close to local markets, there are other sources of local market information. One structural adaptation for the smaller and predominantly exporting company is to hire specialized staff. Such staff should have a good knowledge of the language, cul-ture, business practices, and customer preferences in a country or region. These staff members can travel periodically to the regions or countries of interest and advise product and functional managers on potential product adaptations to serve international customers.

Finally, small companies can have transnational subsidiaries to take advantage of resources throughout the world. For example, one source of cheap transnational networking is to subcontract R&D work to areas of the world with low-cost but high-quality engineers. For the global start-up company, since all units must be built from scratch anyway, building transnational subsidiaries from the beginning may create the most competitively advantaged organization.

Up to this point, we have discussed how to divide the organization into units that best support different strategies. Next, we will see how these units are brought together to accomplish organizational goals.

CONTROL AND COORDINATION SYSTEMS

Selecting different types of subunits to perform specialized tasks and responsibilities represents only one of the major decisions multinational companies make regarding organizational design. In addition, top managers must design organizational systems to control and coordinate the activities of their subunits. This is a difficult task. Foreign subsidiaries differ widely by geographical location, local markets, cultures, and legal systems, as well as by the talents and resources available to the subsidiary (Cray 1984). This section reviews control and coordination systems used by multinational companies to control and coordinate their dispersed activities.

For multinational companies, organizational control represents the procedures used to focus the activities of subsidiaries in directions that support the company's strategies. **Control systems** help link the organization vertically, up and down the organizational hierarchy.

Control system

Vertical organizational links, up and down the organizational hierarchy.

Two basic functions of control systems help focus the activities of the multinationals' subunits to support company-wide strategic goals and objectives. First, control systems measure or monitor the performances of subunits regarding their assigned roles in the firm's strategy. Second, control systems provide feedback to subunit managers regarding the effectiveness of their units. Measurement and feedback help top management communicate strategic goals to subordinates. In addition, measurement and feedback—combined with reward systems (promotion and pay)—help direct subordinates' behavior in appropriate directions.

Coordination system

Horizontal organizational links.

Coordination systems help link the organization horizontally. They provide information flows among subsidiaries so that they can coordinate their respective activities. For example, in implementing its Ford 2000 strategy, Ford plans to use advance information systems so that designers in Europe, the United States, and Japan can coordinate their efforts in designing cars for the world market. Engineers will be able to communicate directly and share complex design information instantaneously. More detail on control and coordination systems follows.

DESIGN OPTIONS FOR CONTROL SYSTEMS

Output control system

Assesses the performance of a unit based on results, not on the processes used to achieve those results.

There are four broad types of control systems: output control, bureaucratic control, decision-making control, and cultural control.

Output control systems assess the performance of a unit based on results, not on the processes used to achieve those results. When used in multinational companies, top management and local management usually negotiate output goals for foreign subsidiaries. These output goals must support the overall corporate strategy.

Control occurs as headquarters evaluates subsidiaries and rewards local managers depending on how well the subsidiaries achieve the output goals.

Responsibility for profit is the most common output control. As noted before, **profit center** is the name given to a unit controlled by its profit or loss performances. Companies compare such units by looking at each profit center's profit or loss. The minireplica subsidiary, discussed earlier, often is a profit center. These profit-center subsidiaries usually set their own strategies, hire local workers, and act independently from the multinational's headquarters. Top managers judge the success of the unit and the unit's managers based on the profits generated for the parent company.

Besides profit, other outcomes such as market share, developing new technologies, and supplying high-quality raw materials provide performance targets used to control multinational subsidiaries. For example, companies with transnational strategies and structures may evaluate each of their subsidiaries differently. One subsidiary may be evaluated based on its development of worldwide products and another evaluated on its market penetration by capturing market share.

Bureaucratic control systems focus on managing behaviors, not outcome, within the organization. Typical bureaucratic-control mechanisms include budgets, statistical reports, standard operating procedures, and centralization of decision making (Daft 1995). These systems work as follows:

- *Budgets set financial targets for expenditures during specific time periods.* Budgets control subsidiary behavior by providing rules that limit how much the subsidiary can spend on any activity. Budgets focus on controlling costs and usually emphasize efficiency goals. That is, efficient subunits produce more output (service or products) on a fixed budget.
- *Statistical reports provide information to top management on nonfinancial outcomes.* For example, a service organization might report on the number of customer complaints each week. A manufacturing organization might report on the number of units produced or the number of units rejected by quality control.
- *Standard operating procedures (SOPs) provide the rules and regulations that identify the approved ways of behaving.* For example, SOPs might prescribe that all subsidiaries should follow a standard practice for personnel evaluations.

Decision-making control represents the level in the organizational hierarchy where managers have the authority to make decisions. Upper management seldom makes all decisions in the organization. However, in decentralized organizations, lower-level managers make a larger number of more important decisions. In centralized organizations, higher-level managers make most of the important decisions. In most worldwide product structures, control over the functional and strategic activities (i.e., production, finance, marketing, and product strategies) is centralized in the product division headquarters. Local country-level subsidiary managers deal only with local administrative, legal, and financial affairs (Beamish et al. 1994). In contrast, decentralized decision making is more common in worldwide area structures. Local country or regional subsidiaries have considerable autonomy from headquarters. Transnational network structures have no general tendency for decision-making control. The transnational has several headquarters, each controlling different types of decisions depending on local expertise and the strategic situation. Depending on the strengths of a subsidiary, decision making may be centralized in the headquarters' nodes or passed down to lower levels.

Profit center

Unit controlled by its profit or loss performance.

Bureaucratic control system

Focuses on managing organizational processes through budgets, statistical reports, standard operations procedures, and centralization of decision making.

Decision-making control

Level in the organizational hierarchy where managers have the authority to make decisions.

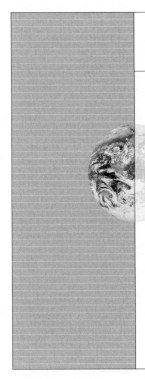

Multinational Management Challenge
Shell's Worldwide Family—How Must It Change?

Until the recent centralization of power in product-division heads, the Royal Dutch/Shell group was a geographical organization with highly independent operating companies in over a hundred countries. To bring cohesion to these units with widely different national interests and conditions and to a headquarters with binational heritage (British and Dutch), Shell developed a strong corporate culture. This culture encourages people to identify with the parent company even while focusing on local interests. The building block of this cultural glue comes from the numerous international assignments of the typical Shell manager. Many managers serve in over four different nations during their Shell careers.

The evolution of the Shell group into a product organization may result in a shift of control mechanisms. When profit and loss responsibilities are transferred to the product-division headquarters, output control will increase in importance. It remains to be seen if Shell can benefit from both its strong culture and output control at product-division level.

Sources: Based on Humes 1993 and Dwyer and Dawley 1995.

Cultural control system

Uses organizational culture to control behaviors and attitudes of employees.

Cultural control systems use the organizational culture (see Chapter 2 for a review) to control behaviors and attitudes of employees. Strong organizational cultures develop shared norms, values, beliefs, and traditions among workers. Such cultures encourage high levels of commitment and support for the organization. Workers and managers understand management goals and direct their efforts in support of these goals. Many experts now argue that a strong organizational culture may be the only way to link a dispersed multinational company with managers from many different national cultures.

Cultural control is the favored control mechanism for transnational-network structures. Although transnational organizations continue to use bureaucratic and output-control mechanisms, the uncertainties and complexities of the international environment make these more formal control mechanisms less effective than culture. For example, budgets or output goals set at Paris headquarters may not be timely for changing situations in Budapest or Singapore. Instead, headquarters relies on the commitment of local managers to corporate goals and trusts that they will adjust appropriately to local conditions.

The Royal Dutch/Shell group has a long tradition of using its strong global culture to bring cohesion to operating companies in more than a hundred countries. In spite of consistently being one of the most profitable companies in the world, Shell is changing its geographic structure to more of a product structure. The challenge for Shell will be to maintain its excellent system of cultural control while gaining the efficiencies of the new product organization. Consider the preceding Multinational Management Challenge. Do you think that Shell will succeed?

Multinational companies use all the control mechanisms to varying degrees, depending on their particular structure. Exhibit 7.12 shows the relationships between the control mechanisms and basic multinational organizational structures.

Exhibit 7.12 Use of Control Mechanisms in Multinational Organizational Structures

| Multinational Structures | Control Systems | | | |
	Output Control	Bureaucratic Control	Decision-Making Control	Cultural Control
International-Division Structure	Most likely profit control	Must follow company policies	Some centralization possible	Treated like other divisions
Worldwide Geographic Structure	Profit center most common	Some policies and procedures necessary	Local units have autonomy	Local subsidiary culture often more important
Worldwide Product Structure	Unit output for supply; sales volume for sales	Tight process controls for product quality and consistency	Centralized at product-division headquarters	Possible for some companies but not always necessary
Matrix Structure	Shared profit responsibility with product and geographic units	Less important	Balanced between geographic product units	Culture must support shared decision making
Transnational-Network Structure	Used for supplier units and some independent profit centers	Less important	Few decisions centralized at headquarters; more decisions centralized in key network nodes	Organizational culture transcends national cultures; supports sharing and learning; the most important control mechanism

DESIGN OPTIONS FOR COORDINATION SYSTEMS

There are six basic horizontal coordination systems: textual communication (memos or reports in electronic or paper form), direct contact, liaison roles, task forces, full-time integrators, and teams (Daft 1995). We discuss first the mechanisms that provide the least amount of coordination and then continue to the mechanisms that provide the greatest amount of coordination.

All organizations use textual communication, such as e-mail, memos, and reports, to coordinate the activities of subunits. Units report on their activities, keeping other units aware of problems, output levels, innovations, or any other important information. With the increased availability of low-cost computer equipment, most memos and reports no longer appear on paper. Companies use e-mail or postings to local Web sites. Such electronic communication is particularly popular for multinational companies since they need rapid interaction over long distances and across many time zones.

Direct contact

Face-to-face interaction of employees.

Liaison role

Part of a person's job in one department to communicate with people in another department.

Direct contact means that managers or workers interact face to face. For multinational companies, direct contact often requires sophisticated video conferencing and a knowledge of a common language. For example, GE Medical Systems uses nearly 1,000 hours of teleconferencing in a year. Ford has computer-aided design and manufacturing links between two continents to allow its engineers in Europe and the United States to communicate design and engineering ideas (*Business Week Online* 1994a).

Liaison roles are specific job responsibilities of a person in one department to communicate with people in another department. A liaison role is only part of a

Full-time integrator

Cross-unit coordination is the main job responsibility.

Task force

Temporary team created to solve a particular organizational problem.

Team

Permanent unit of the organization designed to focus the efforts of different subunits on particular problems.

manager's job responsibilities. For example, in a multinational company, one manager in each country subsidiary might be given the responsibility of coordinating marketing efforts within a region of the world. **Full-time integrators** are similar to liaison roles but have coordination as their sole job responsibility. Often product managers are full-time integrators. Product managers coordinate the development of their product with design teams, the production of their product with the manufacturing departments, and the sales and promotion of their product with marketing. In the multinational company, they often serve as a link between the production units and local-country operations.

Task forces are temporary teams created to solve a particular organizational problem such as entering a new market. They usually link more than one department. For example, to take advantage of new market opportunities in China, Unilever assembled a group of Chinese-speaking troubleshooters selected from its hundred country operations and sent them to China. The troubleshooters built plants, planned strategy and organization, and returned to their home countries when they had completed their task (*Business Week Online* 1994d).

Teams are the strongest coordination mechanisms. Unlike task forces, which have a short-term life span, teams are permanent units of the organization. Teams come from several organizational subunits to specialize in particular problems. For example, a team doing new-product development might include a scientist from R&D and managers from production and marketing. In a multinational example, Texas Instruments uses permanent special-project teams, called Nomads, to set up chip-fabrication plants anywhere in the world—from Italy to Singapore (*Business Week Online* 1994c).

As with the various control options, most multinational companies use several if not all the coordination mechanisms. However, matrix and transnational-network structures have very high needs for coordination. In these types of organizations, one sees a greater use of the more elaborate control mechanisms of task forces, full-time integrators, and teams. For transnational networks, with their extensive geographical dispersion of subunits, teams are increasingly virtual with members seldom meeting face-to-face.

This section completes our consideration of organizational design by showing how managers can control and coordinate the various types of subunits that multinational organizations employ.

Summary and Conclusions

Good strategies will never by themselves guarantee successful multinational operations. Good implementation is equally important. Perhaps the most important part of strategy implementation is having the right organizational design to carry out strategic intents, goals, and objectives. This chapter provided a review of how multinational companies use organizational designs to implement multinational strategies. Organizational design concerns

the choice of subunits (how to divide work) and the choice of coordination and control mechanisms (how to focus the efforts of the subunits).

As supporting background, the chapter reviewed the basics of organizational structure. Functional, product, and geographic structures were described and pictured. They were also compared and contrasted for their strengths and weaknesses. A knowledge of these basic structures is necessary because functional, product, and area structures are the building blocks for the organizational structures used by multinational companies.

As companies internationalize their strategies, they usually progress from using an export department or international division to more complex organizational structures. To use more complex structures, multinational companies need foreign subsidiaries to conduct value-chain activities (e.g., manufacturing) in other countries. Some of these subsidiaries are minireplicas—just reproductions of the home-country organization. Other subsidiaries are transnational—they can do anything or be anywhere depending on the local strengths and the parent company's needs. Companies use different types of subsidiaries depending on the structures that they choose.

If companies adopt a multidomestic or regional multinational strategy, then they usually favor a worldwide geographic structure. This structure emphasizes responding to local markets. In contrast, the worldwide product structure supports the more global international strategy. It is an organizational form that facilitates building and selling global products. Hybrid and matrix structures support compa-

nies with mixtures of strategies for different products and businesses. These structures try to combine some of the benefits of both the geographic and product structures. The transnational-network structure goes beyond the matrix and hybrid. It has no set form, and its subsidiaries respond uniquely to global efficiency pressures, company-learning needs, or local needs, as the strategic situation dictates.

Organizational designs are not complete without integration mechanisms. These mechanisms link subunits and coordinate their activities. Control systems such as bureaucratic and cultural control link the organization vertically. Coordination mechanisms such as task forces and teams link the organization horizontally. Multinational organizations use all these integration mechanisms. However, for the multinational company, cultural control is often considered most important. A strong organizational culture helps the multinational company bridge the national cultures of its employees.

Multinational strategy is not complete without the right structure. In later chapters you will see how the right HRM, leadership, and motivation are necessary to support different strategies in the multinational company.

Discussion Questions

1. You work for a company with three major products. Your CEO has decided to sell these products in the international marketplace. She asks your advice in setting up an organizational structure. What issues would you discuss with her regarding the company's international strategy before making any recommendations?

2. What are the advantages of a worldwide product structure over a worldwide area structure? What type of company would most likely choose each type?

3. What are the costs and benefits of having a matrix structure?

4. What transnational activities might be possible for a small company with only an export department or an international division?

5. Identify some areas in multinational companies where cultural control might work better than bureaucratic control.

Chapter Internet Activity

Read the following brief case. Search online publications such as Economist.com, Fortune.com, or Businessweek.com to build a scorecard on Ford's performance. Has Ford 2000 worked? What adjustments have taken place in the strategy? Answer the questions in the case.

In January 1995, Alex Trotman, Ford's British-born CEO, launched a new strategy for Ford. Called Ford 2000, the strategy was based on cost reduction through greater efficiencies and more rapid product developments to respond to rapidly changing world markets. The strategy relies on building global cars to sell around the world, thus reducing costs in production and development, and highly coordinated efforts by a worldwide production team, thus speeding product development.

One motivation for this design was to increase speed to market by centralizing product decisions. Competitors are faster than Ford. Japanese automakers get new products to market in an average of four years to Ford's five. Chrysler even got its Neon to market in less than three years. Competitors are more efficient. For example, Ford's pretax profit on autos was 5.4 percent, more than doubled by Chrysler's 11.6 percent. Ford produces twenty vehicles per worker, while Toyota gets thirty-seven. Has the product centralization increased or decreased speed to market?

To implement the Ford 2000 strategy it was necessary to completely shake up the worldwide Ford organization. The first problem: merge Ford of Europe and Ford North America into one coordinated organization. The objectives: avoid duplication of designs in Europe and North America, produce similar models for both continents, gain economies of scale in buying from fewer suppliers (fifty thousand in 1995 to five thousand in 1997).

The first step in the merger and redesign was to merge U.S. and European product-development centers. Ford moved fifteen thousand people into five new "Vehicle Centers," each with worldwide responsibility to design specific types of vehicles.

Four are in Dearborn, Michigan. The fifth is split between Dunton, England, and Merkenich, Germany. For example, the Vehicle Center in Europe has worldwide responsibility for small-car development. The center in Michigan has worldwide responsibility for commercial trucks. In addition, vehicles are now designed by permanent teams of engineers, designers, and marketers, a change from the past, where functional specialists were only temporarily assigned to a project. The hope was to produce world cars that have some basic parts (e.g., chassis, steering wheel) in common and need only some minor stylistic changes for local markets. Does Ford have a world car? If so, can they sell it?

The product organization did show some early worldwide efficiencies. Engine-design testing dropped from two years to a hundred days. Approval for a new-car project was reduced from over two months and twenty-two meetings to less than a month. The number of suppliers was reduced.

ACTIVITY REFERENCES

http://www.Economist.com. 1999. "The revolution at Ford." August 7.

http://www.Economist.com. 2000. "For in Europe: in the slow lane." October.

Naughton, Keith. 1995. "Ford's global gladiator: Jacques Nasser starts to overhaul the way it makes cars." *Business Week Online*, December 11.

———. 1996. "Trotman's trails: The Ford chief's reorganization is sputtering, and he needs a successor." *Business Week Online*, April 8.

Treece, James B., Kathleen Kerwin, and Heidi Dawley. 1995. "Ford: Alex Trotman's daring global strategy." *Business Week Online*, April 3.

Internet Sites

Selected Companies in the Chapter

ABB   http://www.abb.com/
Acer Group   http://www.acer.com/
Apple Computers   http://www.apple.com/
AT&T   http://www.att.com
Boeing Inc.   http://www.boeing.com/
DaimlerChrysler   http://www.daimlerchrysler.com/
Ford Motor Company   http://www.ford.com/
GE Medical Systems   http://www.gemedicalsystems.com/
Motorola   http://www.mot.com/
Philips   http://www.philips.com/
Procter & Gamble   http://www.PG.com/
Shell   http://www.shell.com/
Sony   http://www.sony.com/
Unilever   http://www.unilever.com/

Find Multinational Companies and Look at Their Organizations

http://www.ciber.bus.msu.edu/busres/Static/Company-Directories-Yellow-Pages.htm   *Locations of company home pages, many of which describe organizational design.*

http://www.internationalist.com/   *Publicly traded companies throughout the world.*

http://dir.yahoo.com/Business_and_Economy/Companies/   *Find a company on the search engine Yahoo!*

Hint: Company Web pages are often organized around the structure of the company.

Chapter Case: Haute Innovations—International Virtual Teams Case Scenario

SYNOPSIS

As technology communication tools become more advanced and markets more global, cross-border virtual teams are becoming more prevalent. This fictional case study uncovers some of the trials and tribulations of an international virtual team working toward the development and production of an innovative video game product. The manager of the team has to make crucial decisions to keep her team on track and up to speed as they race to the finish line of a successful prototype.

COMPANY BACKGROUND

Haute Innovations was started by Robert "Bob" Grady on December 3, 1984 to produce video gaming software to compete with such early video game development companies as Atari. With little start-up funding, Bob decided to rent a house in Houston, Texas where he set up his offices on the bottom floor and lived upstairs. He hired two of his close college buddies to design and develop video games. They met with immediate success when they sold conceptual gaming software designs to an arcade manufacturer.

Bob developed his initial business attitudes around experimentation, being on the cutting edge of gaming programming and having fun. He hired young, promising programmers who were not "business types" but who had the wild imaginations that were needed to create visually intensive graphics and stimulating games. They set up their computers and design boards in his house and programmed typically until all hours of the night. They considered it challenging fun rather than a "real job." From watching the gaming market, Bob had bigger plans for his business and started to consider his options.

Initially, the company only developed the programming behind the video games and subcontracted to a computer manufacturer to actually produce and package the games for sale. After three years of operation, Bob decided that it would be to his company's advantage to incorporate manufacturing for expansion, quality control, and efficiency purposes. From his profits, he reinvested capital to purchase a small plant in Mont-

gomery, Alabama from Wang Computers with an existing but primitive clean room for technology hardware development. They shifted into manufacturing without many problems and soon needed further expansion to meet their demand.

After a much needed vacation to Scandinavia in 1989, Bob decided that a prime opportunity to stay ahead of the "game" would be to open a European headquarters in Oslo, Norway. This predominately English-speaking country had two big advantages: they liked working with Americans and the companies thrived on the cutting edge technology. Bob purchased a small business office, set up his European headquarters, and hired programmers and support staff to begin his operation.

In 1994, he decided to open a European plant to accelerate his production and lower his costs for the European market. Building a new manufacturing plant in Norway was basically out of the question because of the cost of land and building. He considered many places in Europe but decided that with Stockholm's advances in technology and forward thinking environment purchasing an existing manufacturing plant there would be his best bet. He could retool the plant and then custom train Swedish employees to manufacture the product to his quality specifications. He hired Ingrid Hans, a developer and manager, to oversee quality assurance and proper development of Haute Innovations' products. An R&D site in Copenhagen was added via acquisition just this year.

Haute Innovations experienced much success from the beginning due to Bob's ability to understand both technology and the financial aspect of running a business. He took many risks (that luckily paid off) and considered continued expansion essential. He also placed a tremendous amount of faith in the employees and programmers that he hired—he did not want to "manage" them but rather let them mutually adjust and self-monitor their performance. Often, his programmers set more challenging goals than Bob would have imagined. Setbacks occurred, but Bob didn't mind taking risks as long as everyone learned from them. Bob was so laid back that as long as his programmers produced a quality end product near deadline and near budget, he was happy. He relied on teams to work together and trouble-

Source: Nan Muir Bodensteiner, University of Houston–Clear Lake. Reprinted with permission from the author and the Southwest Case Research Association.

Company Profile

Name: Haute Innovations
Company inception date: December 3, 1984
Company size: approximately 1000 employees worldwide
1998 Net income: $1.6 billion, $500 million dedicated to Research and Development
Main product: handheld video games and video game programming
Headquarters: Houston, Texas
Site locations:

> Houston, Texas—Main headquarters
> Montgomery, Alabama—United States manufacturing plant
> Oslo, Norway—European headquarters
> Copenhagen, Denmark—Research & Development
> Stockholm, Sweden—European manufacturing plant

Team: Bob Grady, Nan King, Georg Lonson, Carl Jensen, Ingrid Hans
Goal: Create a prototype of a voice interactive video game.
Budget: Generous. President's pet project
Deadline for prototype: July 1, 1999
Today's Date: June 10, 1999

---

shoot issues that were out of his specialty. For the most part, these business practices worked well.

PROJECT FORMATION

On October 1, 1998, Bob called for inner-company résumés to form a development team that would create a prototype for a voice interactive video game. The technology had been developed to participate interactively with toys that were due to be released for Christmas sales. Sensing the products would be tremendously popular, he came up with the idea that he could go beyond virtual reality and actually have voice activated instruction applied to handheld video games. This initial product would be very expensive, but it would be Haute Innovations' chance to really make its cutting edge mark. Bob decided this would be his pet project and he developed what he felt was a liberal budget to get the project to a prototype state.

The deadline for résumé submission was November 15, 1998 and he received a total of 15 résumés from which to select. He had never designed a team exactly this way before but was hoping to gain an advantage by picking eager participants who were also the best and brightest. He was very pleased because all of his international divisions submitted a few résumés from which he

could select quality individuals. He contemplated the fact that the experts he wanted all resided in different countries, but decided that he had quality professional people working for him and they would overcome any problems this might present. He assumed their years of experience would mitigate the need for team training. A product such as this would be ideal for global markets and he wanted to be sure the design team understood this and designed it accordingly. This would be his first international virtual team to work on a project of this scale.

The team was announced on December 1, 1998 with their initial phone conference meeting on December 2, 1998. During the initial phone conference, Bob laid out his expectation that the team was to stay in constant open communication and arrive at effective decisions to produce the prototype. Since this product would be on the cutting edge of technology, it was Bob's decision to manufacture the prototype in Sweden—to remove it from the American element. The designs were to be created and tested in the United States, but the actual prototype markup would be completed at the Stockholm plant, by the European developers. The team exchanged e-mail addresses, day and night phone numbers, bio information, and quickly determined their job roles.

Team Profile

Robert "Bob" Grady   Title: President
Role on this project: Moneybags, Idea approver   Location: Houston, Texas
Profile: Robert is a 38-year-old entrepreneur that started this company after he graduated from the University of Alabama with an undergraduate degree in Finance. He is very creative and described as "full of energy." Known for his pet projects and lack of hands-on involvement over these projects—advantages of owning your own company. As long as he is in the black, his company is doing well enough to satisfy him. Even though he does not care to manage, he wants to be kept well informed. Owns a ranch in Palestine, Texas where he holds his annual company meetings.

Nan King, MBA   Title: Research and Development Director
Role on this project: Team Lead, R & D Specialist, Benchmark analyst   Location: Houston, Texas
Profile: Nan is a 35-year-old "go-getter" that joined Haute Innovations after receiving her MBA from Southern Methodist University in Dallas, Texas in 1995. Her background includes working as an R&D consultant with such companies as Texas Instruments and Sega. She is accustomed to being the leader and keeping employees on task.

Georg Lonson   Title: Creativity Director
Role on this project: Idea Generator   Location: Oslo, Norway
Profile: Georg is a 29-year-old programmer with a background in comic book design. Known for his humor and ability to come up with the wild ideas. Bob met Georg at a local Norwegian bar, SMUGET, where their personalities clicked. Georg showed Bob his comic book designs and Bob knew that he had to have him on the team.

Carl Jensen   Title: Design Consultant
Role on this project: Design, Quality Assurance   Location: Copenhagen, Denmark
Profile: Carl is a 35-year-old design engineer. He is quiet and shy—especially when it comes to making decisions about important issues but solves every design problem with exceptional creativity. He works very well with CAD to get his ideas on paper and prefers to meet his teams face to face. He's not very comfortable with advanced software—prefers to have everything in design blueprints as opposed to just looking at a computer screen.

Ingrid Hans   Title: Prototype Specialist
Role on this project: Overseer of prototype development   Location: Stockholm, Sweden
Profile: Ingrid is a 42-year-old prototype specialist for small/handheld video products. She is the local contact in Stockholm for Bob—he places a tremendous amount of faith and expectation in her to control the European production. Her English communication skills tend to waiver on occasion—especially when there are problems with the team. Bob hopes this won't be a problem . . .

Nan, who is located at the main headquarters in Houston, Texas, assumed the role of team leader of the prototype team. With a watchful eye always on the calendar, she is very mindful of ensuring that any of her teams stay on task. Her main role on this team is to make sure the group receives what they need, when they need it, to get the prototype to her on time and reasonably on budget. She often fights the tendency to micromanage, yet insists on regular updates and frequent, often perceived as excessive, communication. She is a stickler for paperwork and integrated design documents.

Georg Lonson, who is located at the European headquarters in Oslo, Norway, is the creativity director over a small group that designs the casings for the toys. It is his responsibility to ensure that his group builds the casing model to Carl Jensen's specifications and then makes it attractive so that consumers will buy it. This is especially important in gaming toys because children and young adults will buy bright eye-catching toys. He must also deal with outside plastics and metal brokers.

Carl Jensen, the design consultant in Copenhagen, Denmark, is the head of a five-person team of design engineers that plans, designs, and builds the inner workings of the video games. He is a highly trained engineer who is more focused on his successes, rather than those of his design team. He is kept on as the head of the team because of his ability to spur everyone to truly innovative designs. His previous successes are the company's most popular products.

Ingrid Hans, the prototype specialist at the European manufacturing plant in Stockholm, Sweden, has the job of bringing it all together and developing it for mass production. She has somewhat limited experience in working with vendors and suppliers but has tremendous knowledge of her manufacturing line and its capabilities. She claims she would much rather work with the automated lines than have to talk with others. Ingrid works very well in a one-on-one situation but not under extreme stress. Nan is well aware of her situation, but agreed with Bob that she would be able to handle the manufacturing inputs into the development of this prototype. Nan raised the issue of an initial team face-to-face meeting and some team training to help them go "virtual" but everyone agreed they were eager to get to work designing their own working groups. Meetings would come later.

Work on the initial designs began. Each member of the virtual team assembled their working groups and solicited confidential input from outside vendors and prior alpha and beta testers as appropriate. Everyone on the team embraced concurrent design principles and acted accordingly. Detailed work schedules were compiled at each site and Nan facilitated the development of an integrated design-to-prototype document that noted all critical interfaces, hand-offs, and milestones for the virtual team. Upstream and downstream concerns at each interface were captured in checklists. Nan discussed the critical interfaces and scheduled handoff dates with each member of the team and made sure everyone agreed to them. Little did she know that while everyone verbally agreed with her, doubts ran rampant. When the team shared the document with their working groups at home, deadlines were considered challenging bordering on impossible. A teleconference was scheduled for the last week of January to discuss initial design issues.

The teleconference made them painfully aware of the fact that everyone had their favorite features and difficult trade-off decisions were inevitable. Thanks to the variety of computer aided design tools on the company intranet, all aspects of the design project were captured and documented. Some decisions were easy once everyone had accessed the full information. Other decisions seemed impossible—everyone stuck with their favorite solution and conflict ruled the day. Some conflicts once resolved improved the design. Other conflicts were starting to get personal . . . They realized it was time to meet face-to-face.

The team had their first and it turned out their only face-to-face meeting at the annual company meeting in the first weekend of March. Bob's ranch provided the means for privacy and relaxation for the team to get to know more about each other. They engaged in the team-building activities that had been scheduled and joked about how late in the life of their team they were finally getting to know one another. They talked about their families, and just had fun together. Between fishing on the lake and picnics, the whole team reviewed the first designs, made some difficult decisions (ones that seemed impossible only a week earlier) and met with Bob. Bob gave his suggestions for modification and then his mark of approval. In the fast and furious three months that the team had been working together, no serious problems had surfaced. However, they knew the most difficult times were at hand. Moving from design to prototype would be the true test. At the annual meeting, questions were raised about their changing roles, how they were going to meet such a demanding schedule, and who was going to take the managerial lead now that Bob had given his approvals. Some on the team expressed their desire for more of Bob's leadership. They felt he could really give their project the push it needed to stay on track. They asked him to visit their respective working groups. Unfortunately Bob's laid back attitude and lack of hands-on style didn't fit. Bob reassured them that Nan would be there for them for project direction and to provide needed resources and coordination. Nan was pleased that he recognized her and started thinking of ways to keep the lines of communication open, the creative juices flowing and conflicts to a minimum. She knew these would be critical to the project's success and she fretted about them for the rest of the weekend. She came up with a list of common pitfalls of virtual teaming and felt her team was vulnerable on all counts. Everyone else enjoyed the rest of the weekend and then returned to their respective locations. The pace intensified.

The work started off at a good pace but then the schedule began to be overbearing. The "I told you we couldn't possibly do this in this time frame" comments surfaced in every working group. The virtual team (v-team) members started to not respond to e-mail, phone calls, and even ignored faxes labeled urgent. They were not very forthcoming with information during conference calls. Nan became more demanding and intensified her forthcoming communication requirements and the team members became defensive and even more closemouthed. They were overwrought with their individual problems and scrambled to find solutions within their groups without keeping other virtual team members informed.

Major conflicts arose when minor changes in one area created big problems for others. Add to that the ill will that developed when it took days and days for the change specifications to be communicated. For example, the materials supplier had excuses as to why motherboards were failing tests when a design flaw was discovered. The redesign changed the specs on the casing materials which then arrived cracked and the vendor was refusing to replace the items. Some of the newest equipment delivered to the Sweden plant to be used in the development of the prototype and manufacturing of the new product was not functioning correctly and the vendor was on holiday. Finally, out of extreme frustration, v-team members began to call Nan at all hours to complain about each other. They all had the perception that their internal problems were minimal—everything was someone else's fault.

Nan, usually calm and collected, began to have sleepless nights and health problems. When she really thought about the problems everyone was calling her about, she realized that she was only hearing the tip of the iceberg. She knew of the schedule and integration problems but knew little of the internal problems in each working group. When she questioned Ingrid about concerns at her site, she responded that she did not want to bother others with her issues and that she thought she had proper control over it. Nan wondered if the other team members were hiding similar issues. Nan decided that she was going to need to be a more involved manager of this virtual team. She wondered what other issues were out there festering. She was in for more problems.

TO COMPLICATE MATTERS. . . .

As Nan started to dig deeper into the health of her team, she found many situations that she was unaware of within her group. She had never dealt with a completely international virtual team, especially when developing a cutting edge prototype. Some of the problems were not too much of a surprise because they are typical of virtual teams but the international distance only accentuated the negative effects of the problems. Some of the problems compounded by the international dimension follow.

Ingrid complained that she was always having difficulty speaking to the manufacturing plant in Alabama because of the time differences. The United States–based plant only worked in two shifts for a total of a 16-hour day. Ingrid would call at 4:00 P.M. her time and could never get in touch with the plant manager. She would leave messages and they would not respond until late in the afternoon. Since Haute Innovations is an open information sharing environment, the American-based plant had her home phone number and would just call her at home in the middle of the night. At first, she was so happy to receive a returned call that she did not complain, but the phone calls became more frequent and for less important reasons.

Not only are Haute Innovations' employees dealing with time zones, they are affected directly by different working schedules and quality of life standards. The Scandinavian standard is to work from 9:00 A.M. to 4:00 P.M. and then to spend the remaining time with their families and friends. They take their holidays and personal time very seriously because of their high standard of quality living and family values. In the United States, the standard working time is 8:00 A.M. to 5:00 P.M., although that is rarely ever followed. The American professionals work much longer hours and drive themselves to achieve a higher quality bank account. They work through their holidays and family time so that they may move up the proverbial promotional ladder. This caused resentment from the American side of the company because they felt that the Europeans were really slacking and not working hard. The Scandinavians perceived they were working smarter and more efficiently to achieve their daily goals, where the Americans were more apt to waste time and company resources.

Carl complained that the American standard operating procedures were too strict and that he felt confined when Nan started inflicting them on his European team. Part of their culture is to have a long working lunch over a few beers while sitting outside a café. This just seemed inappropriate to Nan, so she suggested that the European side cut out the alcohol and socializing in the middle of the working day and often scheduled conferences at the lunch hour. This bothered the whole European group but they did not express it directly to her. They instead built a complaint alliance where they sneered about the "American" rules to make each other feel better. This drove a large wedge between the European and American team, without the Americans even knowing about it.

For the whole virtual development team, there were serious concerns about the stress factor to get the prototype to production level readiness by July 1. As the deadline approached, they felt a general lack of social support. Nan justified this to herself because it happens in all "virtual teams" but she did not quite know how to help. She thought that Bob had built a solid group of very talented people that would work well together. But they were lacking crucial team elements that help defray stress, namely humor and social activities. Because they are all in different countries, it is difficult for them to just "get together" to blow off steam. They sent a few humorous e-mails back and forth, but because of language barriers and wording differences, the interpretations were just not the same. Georg complained that Ingrid would be blunt and less than helpful over the phone and her e-mails were interpreted as being curt. This just added to his stress.

As the stress increased at the Swedish manufacturing plant, Ingrid cut off others by not e-mailing and returning phone calls only when she knew that her other team members would not be in the office. She was so bogged down in her own problems with external issues and plant difficulties that she began to ignore everyone else. Nan knew that this behavior is very typical of stressed team members but Ingrid ignoring everything that was not in her direct line of sight was unacceptable. The final straw was when Ingrid refused to speak English. She claimed she needed to think and it was just too difficult to have to explain her thinking in English. She brought in an interpreter, but Carl was having difficulty being understanding of the communication filter. Carl's native tongue is Danish but he communicates in perfect business English, French, and German. Ingrid was not so lucky—she natively communicated in Swedish only. Her English was not a high priority in her own family, and even though the Swedish schools made her take five years of it, she still struggled. Ingrid was the key team member to pull the whole project together for the deadline and the whole team was growing more concerned that the prototype would not be ready. Despite Nan's anticipation of some of the above issues they seemed to blindside her. She was always a hands-on manager and meant to travel more for the critical face-to-face interaction she knew was important but the timing never seemed right.

The final crises was that what appeared at first to be a minor flaw in the design threatened to necessitate major changes unless the flaw could be worked out in the prototyping phase. Everyone had his or her own idea of how to fix it. Everyone wanted a quick and simple solution that would avoid major changes in the design. Everyone knew the costs of a major change this far into the life of a development effort would be substantial. Yet, they also know that the cost of design changes grows exponentially over the life of the project, fix it now or risk even more later.

CURRENT SITUATION

With three weeks until the prototype is due in Nan's office, the team is still having difficulties. Nan is now faced with trying to get the group to solidify again and push toward the finish line. She walked into Bob's office, plopped down into his leather chair, and exhaled.

Table 1 Team Issues

	Differences between Domestic and International Teams	Combined Needs for Successful Multinational Teams
Managerial Attributes		
Managerial Style		
Communications		
Tools—Technology		
Cross Cultural Issues		
Team Composition and Establishment		
Budget		
Managing Conflict		

Nan: "Bob, I need your help."

Bob: "What do you think went wrong?"

Nan: "I don't know, I thought I had control over the situation but so much happened that they did not tell me about. Could we consider pushing the prototype date back two weeks?"

Bob: "Definitely not! With the Christmas season sales to start in October, we must have the prototype in full production by the end of August. We just do not have the time to delay! They are just going to have to work together to reach their goal."

Nan: "Bob, you do realize that you may be acting a little unreasonable? The team has worked hard but they just need a little help to get back on the right path. Some input from you, some recognition of their hard work could go a long way."

Bob: "Nan, I really want you to handle this. . . ."

Nan walked back to her office and sat down to contemplate her next move. She grabbed a legal pad and quickly sketched out a team issues table (see Table 1) to help her make some sense of the situation. What should she do? Nan thought that with their sound beginning, the face-to-face team bonding, and the lines of communication she tried to maintain, that these issues would not come up. What should she do now?

CASE QUESTIONS FOR DISCUSSION

1. What is your perception of a virtual team? List some key characteristics. Now, give a general description of Haute Innovations' team. How does the Haute Innovations' team fit into your description of a v-team in general?

2. What do v-teams have going for them? What are the strengths of the international virtual team in this scenario and in general?

3. What problems are they having? (Stick to those you recognize in the case scenario.) Suggest solutions.

4. Complete Table 1: Team Issues to assist Nan. How should team members use their time together and time apart to maximize their chances for success?

5. What types of communications tools would a v-team utilize? Which of these tools facilitate the product design task of the team? Revisit the communications issues that this team is experiencing as identified in Table 1. How does the team/task benefit from communicating and working as an international v-team? What could the team manager do to help with the communication problems and facilitate the task?

6. List some barriers to successful virtual teaming. What barriers do you see with this team? How could the team overcome these barriers?

References

Acer, Inc. 2000. http://www.global.acer.com/about/strategies.html.

Apple Computer, Inc. 2000. http://www.apple.com/.

Bartlett, Christopher A., and Sumantra Ghoshal. 1989. *Managing across Borders: The Transnational Solution*. Boston: Harvard University Press.

Beamish, Paul W., J. Peter Killing, Donald J. Lecraw, and Allen J. Morrison. 1994. *International Management*. Burr Ridge, Ill.: Irwin.

Bell, Steve. 1999. "P&G forced by rivals to change old habits." *Marketing*, June 17, 15–19.

Business Week Online. 1994a. "Borderless management: companies strive to become truly stateless," May 23.

———. 1994b. "Grabbing markets from the giants," November 18.

———. 1994c. "High-tech jobs all over the world," November 18.

———. 1994d. "Tearing up today's organization chart," November 18.

Cray, David. 1984. "Control and coordination in multinational corporations." *Journal of International Business Studies*, Fall, 85–98.

Daft, Richard L. 1995. *Organization Theory and Design*. Minneapolis/St. Paul: West.

Duncan, Robert. 1979. "What is the right organization structure? Decision tree analysis provides the answer." *Organizational Dynamics*, Winter.

Dwyer, Paula, and Heidi Dawley. 1995. "The passing of 'the Shell man': An era ends as Royal Dutch/Shell vows to centralize power." *Business Week Online*, International Edition, April 17.

Economist. 1999a. "Procter's gamble." June 12.

———. 1999b. "The revolution at Ford." August 7.

———. 2000. "Ford in Europe: in the slow lane." October 7.

Ferner, Anthony. 2000. "Being local worldwide: ABB and the challenge of global management." *Relations Industrielles*, Summer, 527–29.

Forteza, Jorge H. and Gary L. Neilson. 1999. "Multinationals in the next decade." *Strategy & Business*, 16, Third Quarter 1–11.

Ghoshal, Sumantra, and Christopher A. Bartlett. 1990. "The multinational corporation as an interorganizational network." *Academy of Management Review*, 15, 603–625.

Humes, Samuel. 1993. *Managing the Multinational: Confronting the Global–Local Dilemma*. New York: Prentice Hall.

Murphy, Brian P. 1999. "Bulky P&G looks for speed." *Money*, 28, 11, November, 50–3.

Philips Electronics N.V. 1999. *Annual Report*. February 11, http://www.philips.com.

Rapoport, Garla. 1992. "A tough Swede invades the U.S." *Fortune*, June 29, 76–79.

Stopford, J. M., and L. T. Wells, Jr. 1972. *Managing the Multinational Enterprise*. New York: Basic Books.

Taylor, William. 1991. "The logic of global business: An interview with ABB's Percy Barnevik." *Harvard Business Review*, March-April, 91–105.

Treece, James B., Kathleen Kerwin, and Heidi Dawley. 1995. "Ford: Alex Trotman's daring global strategy." *Business Week Online*, April 3.

UNCTAD (UN Conference on Trade and Development). 2000. *World Investment Report*. New York and Geneva: United Nations.

White, Roderick E., and Toomas A. Poynter. 1989. "Organizing for worldwide advantage." *Business Quarterly* (Summer 1989), 84–89.

Chapter 8

International Strategic Alliances: Management and Design

LEARNING OBJECTIVES
After reading this chapter you should be able to:

- Know the steps for implementation of successful international strategic alliances.

- Understand how multinational companies link value chains in international strategic alliances.

- Understand the importance of choosing the right partners for alliances.

- Know the important characteristics to look for in potential alliance partners.

- Know the differences between equity-based international joint ventures and other types of international cooperative alliances.

- Know the basic components of an international strategic alliance contract.

- Understand the control systems and management structures used in alliance organizations.

- Appreciate the unique problems in human resource management faced by managers in alliance organizations.

- Realize the importance of interfirm commitment and trust for building successful international strategic alliances.

- Understand how multinational companies assess the performance of their international strategic alliances.

- Know when companies should continue or dissolve their international strategic alliances.

Preview Case in Point	U.S.-based Office Depot and the Mexican firm Gigante are one of the success stories in Latin America. They have 35 stores in Mexico. Bruce Nelson, Office Depot's president of its international division, manages two joint ventures. One is in Israel and the other is in Mexico. Nelson notes that the Israeli joint venture is characterized by bickering and never-ending meetings with lawyers. The joint venture with Gigante, however, runs smoothly with little paperwork and conflict. Nelson says, "It all comes down to trust. Both partners put in capital, both partners have had the patience to make it work and each partner brought something to the table."
Retail Joint Ventures in Mexico—The Good and the Bad of Strategic Alliances	Other retailers have not been so fortunate in Latin America. Directed conflict of interest broke the marriage of the French company Carrefour with its Mexican partner Gigante. Joint venture stores competed directly with Gigante operations. Carrefour eventually bought out Gigante's interests. Control was the issue between WalMart and Cifra. Conflicts occurred over store management. WalMart's solution: Buy 51 percent of Cifra, take control, and merge their strengths. Things are now running smoothly.

Source: Based on Poole 1999.

Chapter 6 discussed the importance of the strategic alliance as an international participation strategy. Because strategic alliances are increasingly among the most popular choices for going international, the student of multinational management needs an understanding of strategic-alliance operations and management. Issues discussed in this chapter include: where to link up in the partnering companies' value chain, selecting a partner for a strategic alliance, the options available for designing alliances, HRM issues in managing successful strategic alliances, the importance of building trust and commitment, and how to assess the performance of strategic alliances.

Although strategic alliances are attractive for a variety of reasons (see Chapter 6), they are inherently unstable and provide significant management challenges. Estimates of failure rates range from 30 to 60 percent. As shown in the Preview Case in Point describing retail alliances in Mexico with U.S. and European firms, strategic alliances are risky. Partners may fail to deliver, partners may disagree on how to run the business, and even profitable alliances can be torn by conflict. As such, successful alliances must make strategic sense but also require good implementation. As such, in this chapter you will see the steps necessary to implement a successful strategic alliance. A model of these steps is presented in Exhibit 8.1. We will follow the model in our discussion.

WHERE TO LINK IN THE VALUE CHAIN

Chapter 6 showed you the many benefits of strategic alliances. These include gaining access to a local partner's knowledge of the market, meeting government requirements, sharing risks, sharing technology, gaining economies of scale, and accessing lower-cost raw materials or labor. Which objectives a firm hopes to achieve determine where multinational companies link in the value chain.

Exhibit 8.1

Implementing a
Strategic-Alliance
Strategy

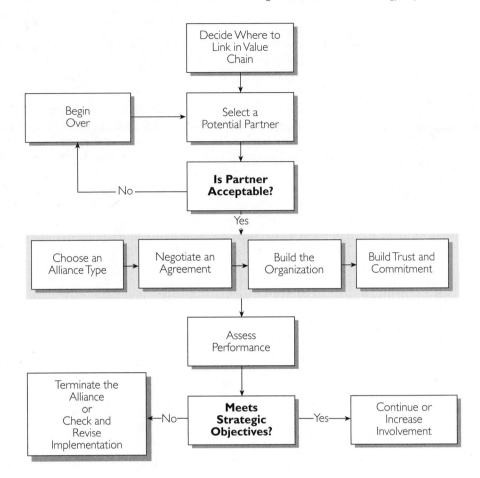

Consider Exhibit 8.2. It shows two value chains and the common areas that companies link to gain strategic benefits from an alliance.

Alliances that combine the same value-chain activities often do so to gain efficient scales of operations, to merge compatible talents, or to share risks. These alliances are attractive when no one company is big enough, has the necessary talent, or is willing to take on an enormously risky venture. In R&D alliances, for example, high-tech multinational companies often use joint research and development to merge different technical skills or to share the risks of developing new or costly technologies. A recent alliance of IBM, Toshiba, and Siemens illustrates these points. These companies bring together engineering talent from three nations with the hope of discovering the next generation of computer chips. Why not do it alone? R&D in computer chips is a highly risky and expensive venture, which no one company wants to attempt by itself. Just designing the chip and fabrication processes is expected to take at least $1 billion (Port et al. 1992).

In operations alliances, multinational companies often combine manufacturing or assembly activities to reach a profitable volume of activity. The Case in Point on page 304 describes an alliance between General Motors Corp. of the United States and Renault SA of France. These companies intend to work together in producing light commercial trucks for the European market.

Exhibit 8.2
Linking Value Chains in
Strategic Alliances:
Some Examples

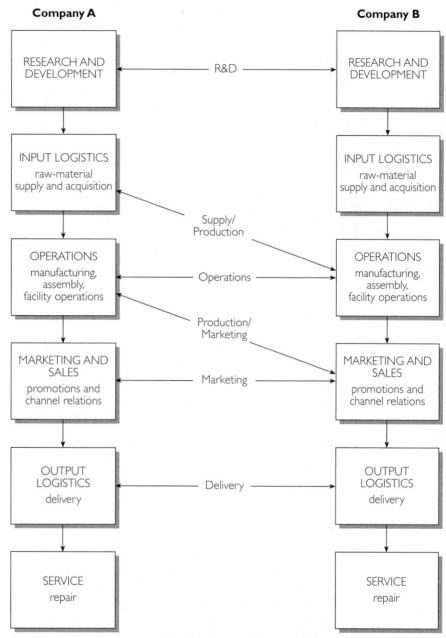

Source: Adapted from Lorange and Roos 1992.

Marketing and sales alliances allow multinational companies to increase the scope and number of products sold. They also allow partners to share distribution systems. Sometimes partners even share logos. In the KLM/Northwest Airlines alliance, the companies share advertising that notes their joint reservation and route systems. In the automobile industry, alliance partners often share each other's dealer systems.

Output alliances to deliver a service are perhaps most popular in the airline industry. International alliances such as those between KLM and Northwest, Swissair

Case in Point

GM and Renault—An Alliance for a Small but Profitable Niche

General Motors Corp. and Renault SA of France have an alliance to develop and market pickups and vans targeted at the light commercial truck market. This market represents approximately 10 percent of the total light truck market, but it is one of the most profitable. The goal of General Motors Europe is to sell between 600,000 and 700,000 vehicles annually. A spokesman for GM noted, "Renault has knowledge and experience in this field so this is a good opportunity—it is better than bringing over a U.S. vehicle that's not adapted to the European market."

Because commercial vehicles are not sold to consumers, automakers are less image sensitive. Consequently, they often don't mind putting their own brand names on a vehicle produced by another maker. In the meantime, GM will sell Renault's existing line of vans in Europe under GM's Opel and Vauxhall brand names.

Source: Based on Tierney 1996.

and Delta Airlines, and British Airways and USAir deliver their services jointly through a process called code sharing (the sharing of reservation codes). In this way, passengers can buy an international ticket in one of the airline's countries, fly to the partner's country, and then get continuing flights with the same ticket on the partner's airline.

Alliances linking upstream and downstream components of the value chain can serve the objectives of low-cost supply or manufacturing. Some supply/operations alliances attempt to find partners where one partner provides low-cost sources of supply or components and the other partner does the manufacturing. Operations/marketing links can also work similarly. One company provides a source of low-cost manufacturing for another company's eventual sales. For example, because of increasing wages in their own countries, many Japanese and Korean companies formed production/marketing alliances with low-wage Southeast Asian companies. Production and assembly occur at the low-cost site, and the Japanese and Korean companies do the downstream marketing and sales.

Operations/marketing alliances can also provide access to markets. This use of the operations/marketing alliance tends to occur when the producing firm needs a local partner with knowledge of local sales and distribution systems. This type of alliance can be necessary when local governments require local participation in foreign businesses. It is often an initial participation strategy for a company with limited knowledge of a foreign market.

For U.S. companies, the majority of international strategic alliances occur in operations. Exhibit 8.3 shows the mixture of value-chain links for the nearly eight hundred publicly announced international strategic alliances created by U.S. multinational companies during a four-year period (Murray 1995).

The links discussed so far and illustrated in Exhibits 8.2 and 8.3 are only some of those possible for international strategic alliances. In building alliances, each company must determine which of its value-chain activities can be enhanced by the relationships. After deciding which value-chain link or links are necessary to achieve their strategic objectives, management faces what is generally considered the most important step in implementing a strategic alliance. This step is selecting the right partner.

Exhibit 8.3

Value-Chain Links in
U.S. International
Strategic Alliances

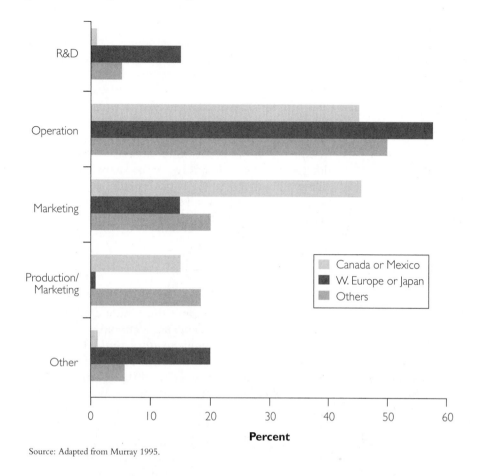

Source: Adapted from Murray 1995.

CHOOSING A PARTNER: THE MOST IMPORTANT CHOICE?

Most experts attribute success or failure of strategic alliances to how well the partners get along. Especially early in the relationship, each party must believe that they have a good partner who can deliver promised contributions and whom they can trust. The following Case in Point shows some of the difficulties that can occur when a company makes mistakes in partner selection.

Experts identify several key criteria for picking an appropriate alliance partner (Geringer 1988):

Strategic complementarity

One that complements the alliance partners.

• *Seek strategic complementarity*. Before forming the strategic alliance, potential partners must have a good understanding of each other's strategic objectives for the venture. Each should know what the other hopes to achieve from the venture both in the short term and in the long term. It is not necessary, however, that partners have the same objectives. While similar strategic objectives, such as rapid growth, are beneficial, objectives can be complementary. For example, a U.S. or Japanese firm may have an advanced computer component-manufacturing technology attractive to a Chinese firm. The Chinese firm may dominate the Chinese market and could provide a potential powerful sales and distribution outlet for the alliance partner. These companies have complementary strategic objectives. The U.S. or the Japanese company desires growth in its

When the U.S. steelmaker, Carpenter Technology from Reading, PA, invested $45 million for a 19 percent stake in a joint venture with Walsin Lihwa Corp. of Taipei, Taiwan they were optimistic for a profitable venture. Unfortunately, the local partner could not deliver. Plans to build a high tech stainless steel and carbon bar plant met resistance from the Taiwanese government. Local farmers protested the location, delayed the installation of electric power, and the plant opened two years late. In the meantime, a competitor added similar products and the profits didn't materialize. In three years, the dropped their interest to 5 percent and two years later they abandoned the venture. Robert Cardy, chairman and CEO of CarTech noted: "That one didn't work out the way it had been planned . . . there was more of a speculative interest by the Taiwanese than we found comfortable sometimes."

Source: Based on Bagsarian 2000.

Chinese market share and the Chinese company desires access to the other side's advanced manufacturing technology.

Complementary skill

One that enhances but does not necessarily duplicate an alliance partner's skills.

- *Pick a partner with **complementary skills**.* Partners must contribute more than money to the venture. Each partner must contribute some skills or resources that complement those of the other partner. J. Michael Geringer asserts that technical complementarity is most important (Geringer 1988). A typical complementary alliance, for example, occurs when one company contributes technical skills (usually the foreign company) and another company contributes marketing skills (usually a local company from the host country). Another recommendation is to find partners with similar but not identical products or markets. This avoids the increased difficulties of working with direct competitors (Main 1990).
- *Seek out companies with compatible management styles.* Lord Weinstock, the managing director for twenty-seven years of Britain's General Electric Company (not related to the U.S. company GE) is a strategic alliance expert. He has seen many alliances succeed and fail. One recent failure, an alliance of GEC with Germany's Siemens, flopped. Consultants noted that Siemens is an engineers' company, consistent with many values in German business culture, and GEC is a financiers' company. The managers simply didn't get along. Weinstock noted that for alliances to succeed, "You have to suppress the ego—it's absolute poison in a joint venture" (Main 1990).
- *Seek a partner that will provide the "right" level of mutual dependency.* As in any marriage, mutual dependency means that companies must rely on each partner to contribute to the relationship. With a good match, partners feel a mutual need to supply their unique resources or capabilities to the strategic alliance. Both partners see their contribution as critical to the success of the relationship and, ultimately, to the success of the strategic alliance. The best level of mutual dependency is balanced. With a balanced dependency, both companies feel equally dependent on the outcome of the venture. Geringer (1988) suggests maintaining this mutual dependency by building safeguards into the strategic-alliance agreement. These might include types of "alimony" payments and restrictions on entering the same business over a specified period. The "alimony" payments would require payments to the partner if the relationship should break up before a specified period.

Exhibit 8.4

International Strategic Alliances for Small Multinational Companies: Incentives and Concerns

Incentives

- Gain Legitimacy
  Acts as a seal of approval

- Develop Links in Distribution Channel
  Use large firm's existing channels

- Access to Resources
  Helps speed access to market

- Diversify Risk
  Share risk with richer partner

Concerns

- Relative level of contribution
  Must commit relatively more assets than larger firm

- Entering a large scale of operations
  Lack of experience with large-scale operations

- Risk of unequal proprietary information disclosure
  Access to smaller firm's information easier

- Mismatch of interacting managers
  Small firm entrepreneur with large firm functional or product specialists

- Loss of control
  Concerns of large firm dominate relationship

Source: Adapted from Peridis 1992.

Anchor partner

A partner that holds back the development of a successful strategic alliance because it cannot or will not provide its share of the funding.

Elephant-and-ant complex

Occurs in strategic alliances when two companies are greatly unequal in size.

- *Avoid the "anchor" partner.* **Anchor partners** hold back the development of a successful strategic alliance because they cannot or will not provide their share of the funding. Potential partners should study carefully each other's financial position and investment plans. A potential partner with a weak division or expansion in other areas may drain financial support from the alliance. If a potential partner is financially weak but still attractive for other reasons, precautions are advised. For example, a contract might specify that the division of the alliance's profits (or other alliance outputs) among the partners will vary in proportion to each partner's financial contribution to the venture.

- *Be cautious of the "elephant-and-ant" complex.* The **elephant-and-ant complex** occurs when two companies are greatly unequal in size. For an international strategic alliance between companies of unequal size, managers must consider serious potential problems. First, the larger firm may dominate the smaller firm, controlling the strategies and management of the alliance. Second, the corporate cultures probably differ to a significant extent. For example, bureaucracy and slower decision making usually characterize larger and older companies. Smaller companies are often more entrepreneurial and informal. Thus, because of cultural differences, a small firm's executives may see the larger firm's managers as ignoring the immediate problems of the venture. The larger partner's executives may see the smaller partner's managers as less professional. In spite of these potential problems, however, elephant-and-ant alliances do succeed. When other factors, such as complementary skills, exist, managers find ways to overcome size differences. Exhibit 8.4 contrasts in more detail some of the incentives and concerns for small businesses in "elephant-and-ant" international strategic alliances.

- *Assess operating-policy differences with potential partners.* Marriage partners need to work out how to squeeze the toothpaste, when to have dinner, who makes the beds, who cleans the house, and all the other operational details of running a

Many multinational companies seek alliances in the transition economies as opportunities to enter new markets, be close to European customers, and find low-cost platforms for manufacturing. Recent data suggest that three-quarters of these alliances meet or exceed expectations of the foreign partner. Below are some examples:

- *Interbrew:* This Belgian company is the fourth-largest brewer in the world. Its joint venture with Hungary's Borsodi brewery led to expanded market share in Europe, increased sales from the large local beer drinking market, avoidance of the high Hungarian import taxes, and a knowledge base of how to move into similar countries in the area.
- *Kalon:* This paint manufacturer from the UK used an alliance with the Polish paint company Polifarb to set up a distribution network to sell its products produced at home.
- *ARCO:* This U.S. oil company used a joint venture with the Russian oil company LukOil to jumpstart its presence in the region and overcome the first mover advantage of several international competitors. Other companies entered Russia when it was part of the former Soviet Union.
- *Wedel Company:* This Polish confectionary firm's joint venture with PepsiCo led to new product lines, capital, increased knowledge of the industry worldwide, and training in management practices.
- *Zetor:* This Czechoslovakian tractor company's alliance with John Deere led to increased product quality, customer service, and improved technological capabilities.

Source: Based on Rondinelli and Black 2000.

household. Similarly, potential partners in a strategic alliance most likely have operational differences in how their companies are run on a day-to-day basis. Accounting policies, human resource management policies, financial policies, reporting policies, and so on, may all differ because of organizational or cultural differences. For example, potential European partners may want to close operations during certain holiday periods. Potential Japanese partners may want the strategic alliance to respect the age hierarchy of management. For the strategic alliance to function smoothly, and before the strategic alliance comes into operation, partners should agree on mutually satisfactory operational policies.

- *Assess the difficulty of cross-cultural communication with a likely partner.* Even if partners speak each other's languages, cross-cultural communication is never as easy as within one's own culture or organization. Managers must expect slower communication and more errors of understanding. For example, in a joint venture between a Japanese company and the U.S. aircraft manufacturer Boeing, the agreement required that fuselage panels be produced with a "mirror finish." The Japanese workers interpreted this literally. They polished the metal to a mirror finish. The result was excessively high labor costs and the need for further discussion to resolve the meaning of "mirror finish" (Geringer 1988).

The preceding Case in Point shows successful partnerships in central and Eastern Europe based on compatible win–win strategic needs and sufficient commitment and trust to overcome cultural differences.

After finding potentially satisfactory partners, multinational mangers from all companies involved in the alliance must decide on the form of the alliance that they wish to build. Next, we consider the popular choices in types of international strategic alliances.

CHOOSING AN ALLIANCE TYPE

Informal international cooperative alliance

An agreement not legally binding between companies to cooperate on any value-chain activity.

There are three main types of strategic alliances (Lorange and Roos 1992). These are **informal international cooperative alliances**, **formal international cooperative alliances**, and **international joint ventures**. International joint ventures are usually called **IJVs** and international cooperative alliances are usually called **ICAs**. Exhibit 8.5 outlines the major differences among the types. We consider each of these next.

INFORMAL AND FORMAL INTERNATIONAL COOPERATIVE ALLIANCES

Formal international cooperative alliance

A nonequity alliance with formal contracts specifying what each company must contribute to the relationship.

International joint venture (IJV)

A separate legal entity in which two or more companies from different nations have ownership positions.

IJV

International joint venture.

ICA

International cooperative alliance.

Informal ICAs are nonlegally binding agreements between companies from two or more countries. They can be agreements of any kind and provide links between companies anywhere on their value chains. For example, a local company might agree informally to market and sell a foreign firm's products in exchange for exclusive distribution rights. Although neither firm would be legally bound to continue this relationship, the companies might use this informal agreement as a test of their ability to work together in agreements that are more formal. If it does not work, the alliance can end at any time.

Since there is no legal protection from a contract, managers usually limit the scope of their involvement with the other company. This means that there is usually a reluctance to dedicate sizable resources to the relationship; for example, product changes for the partner's benefit. In addition, multinational companies in informal alliances resist revealing a company's proprietary information to the partner. Proprietary information refers to information that a company considers its own and wants to keep secret from competitors. An example might be special manufacturing processes.

A higher degree of involvement between or among companies occurs with the formal ICA. This type of alliance usually requires a formal contract specifying exactly what each company must contribute to the relationship. Contributions to the relationship could be managers, technical specialists, factories, information or knowledge, or money. To make some strategic gain that a single company cannot do by itself, companies must usually share some knowledge, skill, or specialized resources through a formalized ICA. This sharing of proprietary information or knowledge raises the level of involvement between the companies. It means that both companies must give away something valuable to the partner to get something in return. In addition, in combination with the obligations specified in a contract, this sharing of proprietary knowledge makes backing out of a formal alliance more difficult than for alliances with informal agreements.

Formal ICAs are very popular in some high-tech industries because of the high costs and risks of R&D. This is particularly true in the semiconductor industry. The Multinational Management Brief on page 311 shows some of the reasons why.

The next level of alliance involvement is the international joint venture.

Exhibit 8.5 Types and Characteristics of International Strategic Alliances

Alliance Type	Degree of Involvement	Ease of Dissolution	Visibility to Competitors	Contract Required	Legal Entity
Informal International Cooperative Alliance	Usually limited in scope and time; a marriage of convenience	Easy, at the convenience of either side	Often unknown to competitors	No	None
Formal International Cooperative Alliance	Deeper involvement requiring exchange of proprietary company knowledge and resources	More difficult to dissolve prior to end of contract due to legal obligations and commitment of resources by companies	Often visible to competitors through announcements in business press but details can be secure	Yes	None
International Joint Venture	Deep involvement requiring exchange of financial, proprietary company knowledge, and managerial resources	Most difficult to dissolve since companies invest significant resources and have ownership in a separate legal entity	High visibility since joint venture company is a separate legal entity	Yes	Yes, separate company

INTERNATIONAL JOINT VENTURES

An international joint venture (IJV) is a separate legal entity owned by parent companies from different countries—companies have an equity or ownership position in an independent company. The simplest IJV occurs when two parent companies have 50/50 ownership of the venture.

Not all joint ventures have only two partners, although two-partner joint ventures are probably the most common. When a large number of companies form a joint venture, the resulting IJV is often called a consortium. Airbus Industries, for example, is a consortium that includes Aérospatiale from France, Messerschmitt Böklow Blöhm from Germany, British Aerospace, and Construcciones Aeronáuticas from Spain.

Companies need not have equal ownership to form a joint venture. Often one partner will have a majority ownership. In some countries, the local law requires that the local partner has the dominant ownership position. In such cases, for example, the foreign company could not own more than 49 percent of the IJV's stock in a two-company venture. Companies may also increase or decrease their ownership share. Prior agreements may require a foreign company to surrender its ownership after a limited time. The first McDonald's in Russia, for example, was a joint venture designed to revert eventually to sole Russian ownership. Some parent companies also increase or decrease ownership depending on the IJV's performance or the parent company's strategic goals. One company may buy out its partner and take over the joint venture as a wholly owned subsidiary.

One difficulty in determining the initial ownership of a joint venture arises from equity contributions other than cash. It is not necessary that companies contribute equal monetary shares to a venture to have equal equity positions. Partners may bring resources to the venture other than financial resources. If the partners

Multinational Management Brief
Semiconductor Alliances

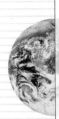

The semiconductor industry produces the "chips" that drive computers and provide memory for storage. It is a fast-moving industry in which companies must innovate continuously. Strategic alliances are very popular because companies can share talent and risk and move products faster from research to the market. Consider these snapshots of some of the international strategic alliances planned or in place:

- *Samsung Electronics Co.:* Looking for partners for $1 billion chip-manufacturing plants in Europe, Asia, and the United States. Signed a chip-purchasing agreement with NEC Corp. of Japan.
- *IBM, Toshiba, and Siemens:* Signed an eight-year, $1 billion agreement to produce the next generation of chips for the 21st century. Two hundred engineers from the three countries report to a Toshiba manager located at IBM's Advanced Semiconductor Technology Center located in New York. An informal side of the agreement allows Toshiba to share with another company (Motorola) technology developed with its IBM and Siemens partners.
- *Texas Instruments:* Teams with Hitachi, Sharp, Canon, and Motorola to develop memory-chip technology.
- *Fujitsu:* Allies with Advanced Micro Devices Inc. for research and production of EPROMs (electronically programmable read-only memories) and flash chips. They split the cost of a $700 million plant and bought 5 percent of each other's stock as insurance for the deal. AMD also has a relationship with Sony for microprocessors.
- *Beijing Stone Group Company:* Created the company Mitsubishi-Stone Semiconductor Co with Mitsubishi Electric Corp. This $2 billion investment will produce state of the art SRAM chips in two new fabs in the special economic development zone of Shezhen.

Sources: Based on Glain 1995; Lei 1993; Port et al. 1992 and Pecht, Liu, and Hodges 2000.

accept that the resources contributed have an economic value, then these resources become part of a firm's equity contribution to the venture. For example, one parent company in a 50/50 joint venture may contribute only its advanced technology, whereas the other partner may provide all of the financial contribution.

The choice of an international alliance type is similar to the choice of a participation strategy discussed in Chapter 6. The alliance types range from those that are flexible and informal and require minimal investment to those that are legally binding, require heavy investment, and are difficult to dissolve. The choice of form thus depends on the strategic intent of the firm, the nature of the firm's products and industry, the resources of the firm, and the requirements of the country of location.

Formal ICAs and IJVs require formal agreements. Next you will see some of the issues considered by multinational managers in negotiating their alliance agreements.

NEGOTIATING THE AGREEMENT

After picking a partner or partners for an IJV or a formal ICA, it is necessary to negotiate and sign contractual agreements. Similar to licensing agreements, alliance contracts are the legal documents that bind partners together. The formal agreements, however, are never as important as the ability of managers to get along. Exhibit 8.6 shows some of the questions that must be addressed as **IJV negotiation issues**.

IJV negotiation issues

Include points such as equity contributions, management structure, and "prenuptial" agreements regarding dissolution of the relationship.

Negotiations for alliance agreements have no consistent timetable or form. Some companies sign agreements almost immediately after they receive a proposal. Other agreements can take years for companies to complete. For example, the joint venture partnerships that eventually resulted in the first McDonald's in Russia took nearly ten years of negotiations. In some situations, even when both parents sign a partnership agreement, the alliance venture never gets off the ground. One or both parents fail to deliver and the venture dissolves.

In general, experts recommend that negotiation teams with technical and negotiation experience negotiate any alliance agreement. The types of preparation for this cross-cultural negotiation would follow the steps discussed previously in Chapter 3 on international negotiations.

Once a firm has a partner and an agreement, it is necessary to build the organization to run the alliance. This includes organizational design and human resource management issues. First, we consider structure and design.

BUILDING THE ORGANIZATION: ORGANIZATIONAL DESIGN IN STRATEGIC ALLIANCES

The design of strategic alliances depends on the type of alliance chosen. Informal ICAs often have no formal design issues. Managers from different companies cooperate without any formal control. Formal ICAs may require a separate organization unit housed in one of the companies, with employees from all the parents. The IBM/Toshiba/Siemens alliance located in New York is an example of an organizational unit setup for an ICA. However, some formal ICAs may share information or products with minimal organizational requirements. For example, two airlines may book each other's routes but need no common organization. IJVs, however, are separate legal entities. This requires that parent companies set up a separate organization for the IJV to carry out the objectives of the alliance.

In this section, we consider two key issues in managing an alliance organization: decision-making control and the management structure. These design issues are applicable mostly to IJVs but also to formal ICAs that require organizational settings. For example, the IBM/Toshiba/Siemens alliance created an organization headquartered at an IBM location but managed by a Toshiba engineer.

DECISION-MAKING CONTROL

Parent companies must consider two major areas of decision making when designing their alliance organizations: operational decision making and strategic decision making. Operational decisions include management decisions associated with the day-to-day running of the organizations. For example, the size of production runs or the hiring of assembly line workers represent operational decisions. Strategic decisions focus on issues that are important to the long-term survival of the alliance

Exhibit 8.6
Selected Questions for
a Strategic-Alliance
Agreement

For Both ICAs and IJVs

- What products or services does the alliance produce?

- Where is the new alliance located?

- Under which country's law does the agreement operate?

- What are the basic responsibilities of each partner? These might include issues such as which company provides the production technology, the plant location, the training of the workforce, the marketing expertise.

- What are the partners' contributions of senior managers?

- What are the partners' contributions of other employees?

- How will royalties or profits be divided?

- How should the company be controlled?

- How is the company organized?

- Who owns new products or technology developed by the new company?

- To whom and where will the strategic alliance sell its products?

- Is a prenuptial agreement needed?

- How can the alliance be dissolved?

Primarily for IJVs

- What is the name of the new JV company?

- What are the equity contributions of each partner?

- What is the makeup of the JV's board of directors?

organization. For example, opening a new plant or introducing a new product are strategic decisions.

Majority ownership of an IJV does not necessarily mean that the parent company controls operational and strategic decision making for the IJV. Similarly, providing the location for a formal ICA does not mean that the parent controls operational and strategic decision making for the alliance. Depending on each partner's skills, parent companies may agree to assign different managerial decision making duties to different partners.

In the IJV, strategic decision making usually takes place at the level of the IJV's board of directors or the top management team. To gain more control over strategic decision making, some IJV parent companies place more of their managers on the IJV company's board of directors or on the IJV's top management team. IJV parent companies that wish to control the operational decision making of the IJV usually have most of their people serving as mid- to lower-level managers.

In nonequity ICAs, strategic decision making usually remains with the parent companies. Alliance managers focus on operational decision making related to delivering the product or knowledge to the parent companies.

MANAGEMENT STRUCTURES

The mix of strategic and operational decision-making control among alliance partners is often complex and unique to each relationship. However, to formalize the nature of decision-making control in a strategic alliance, partners must choose a management structure. Management structures specify formally the division of control responsibilities among partners. There are five typical management control structures used by multinational companies for their ICAs or IJVs. These include (Gray and Yan 1992; Killing 1988):

Dominant partner

The partner that controls or dominates strategic and operational decision making.

Shared management structure

Occurs when both parent companies contribute approximately the same number of managers to the alliance organization.

Split-control management structure

Partners usually share strategic decision making but split functional-level decision making.

Independent management structure

Alliance managers act more like managers from a separate company.

- *Dominant parent:* The **dominant parent** is usually the majority owner of an IJV or, in some cases (especially where majority ownership is not possible), the major contributor of critical resources to an ICA. In this structure, one parent controls or dominates strategic and operational decision making. Its managers hold most of the important positions in any IJV or ICA organization. For IJVs, the dominant parent treats the IJV as if it were just another one of its subsidiaries.
- *Shared management:* In the **shared management structure**, both parents contribute approximately the same number of managers to positions such as the board of directors, the top management team, and the functional areas of management (e.g., production or marketing).
- *Split control:* The **split-control management structure** is similar to the shared management structure in that partners usually share strategic decision making. However, at the functional level (for example, marketing, production, and research and development), partners make decisions independently. Often one partner has a unique skill or technology that it does not want to share completely. This partner insists on independent decision making in these protected areas.
- *Independent management:* In the **independent management structure**, the alliance managers act more like managers from a separate company. This structure is more characteristic of mature IJVs—IJVs must be legally separate organizations—and seldom occurs in ICAs. Especially for operational decisions, IJV managers have nearly complete decision making autonomy. Because of their independence, IJVs with this structure often recruit managers and other employees from outside the parent companies' organizations.
- *Rotating management:* Key positions in the management hierarchy rotate between or among partners in the rotating management structure. For example, the alliance's top manager or management team may change each year. Each partner then appoints its own managers on a rotating basis. The rotating management structure is popular with alliance partners from developing countries. It serves to train local management and technical talent and transfer this expertise to the developing country (Vernon 1977).

CHOOSING A STRATEGIC ALLIANCE MANAGEMENT STRUCTURE

Many characteristics of the alliance relationship influence the choice of a management structure. Usually, if one parent has a dominant equity position or contributes the most important resources to the alliance, this dominant parent will favor a dominant management structure, at least for strategic decision making. Alliance partners with equal ownership shares (for IJVs) or equal resource contributions (for ICAs) tend to avoid the dominant management structure. Instead, they adopt one of the more balanced managerial control systems, such as the shared, split, or rotating structures.

Management structures can change as companies' needs change or their contributions to the alliance change. When an Italian motorcycle helmet manufacturer found that inexperienced Belarussian managers had difficulty running the opera-

Multinational Management Challenge
Finding the Right Management Structure

AGV is a small but highly successful Italian manufacturer of motorcycle helmets. Although AGV has only 190 employees, it is the second leading producer of helmets in the world. AGV exports to over thirty countries and has nearly two thousand sales outlets in different countries.

Seeking a presence in the former Soviet republics, and a cheaper source of raw materials, AGV formed a joint venture with Steklovolokno, a fiberglass producer located in Belarus. AGV took a 40 percent ownership share in the joint venture company called AGV-Polotsk.

Management control problems surfaced quickly. As the minority owner, AGV was forced to use local managers from the Belarus partner. The Italian side discovered that these managers, trained and developed in a formerly state-run organization, had no concept of marketing and no concept of meeting time goals in production. To solve the problem, AGV first attempted retraining. They brought thirty managers to Italy for training in the AGV management methods. However, the Belorussian managers proved reluctant to change their old practices and this program was eventually abandoned.

To gain dominant management control of the venture, AGV bought an additional 20 percent of AGV-Polotsk. They then installed an Italian CEO and Italian managers in sales and production. Because of the cost and difficulty of hiring and maintaining expatriate managers in Belarus, AGV sees this as only an intermediate step. They are now training a cadre of younger Belorussian managers with the hope that they will eventually take over the positions now held by Italian expatriate managers.

Source: Based on United Nations Economic Commission for Europe & ILO 1993.

tion, they faced a serious challenge to the viability of their IJV. The preceding Multinational Management Challenge shows how they solved the problems. How would you react?

Additional considerations in the choice of a management structure relate to the strategic and organizational characteristics of the parent companies and the nature of their industry. That is, parent company and industry characteristics make different management structures more effective or more attractive to the companies involved (Gray and Yan 1992). A recent summary of alliance research summarized several of the factors that multinational managers take into account when designing a management structure for their international strategic alliances. These include (Gray and Yan 1992):

- If partners have *similar* technologies or know-how and they contribute this knowledge *equally* to the alliance, partners prefer a shared management structure.
- If partners have *different* technologies or know-how and they contribute this knowledge *equally* to the alliance, partners prefer split management structures.
- If the alliance has more strategic importance to one partner, a dominant management structure is more likely.

For joint ventures in particular:

- Mature joint ventures move to independent structures as the joint venture's management team gains more expertise.
- Joint ventures in countries with a high degree of government intervention produce IJVs with local partner dominance.
- Independent management structures are more likely when the market is expanding, the venture does not require much capital, or the venture does not require much R&D input from its parents.

All organizations need more than the formal control and coordination systems set up by management. An equally important key for building successful alliances is finding the right people to staff the alliance organization. As such, we now consider the human resource management (HRM) issues in alliance management.

BUILDING THE ORGANIZATION: HUMAN RESOURCE MANAGEMENT IN STRATEGIC ALLIANCES

The HRM functions of international strategic alliances include recruiting and staffing for all alliance positions and evaluating alliance personnel. These issues are made more complex because managers and other employees come from two or more companies and from two or more national cultures.

Experts identify several critical HRM problems and issues that multinational managers must address in the implementation of international strategic alliances (Datta and Rasheed 1993; Lorange 1986; Pucik 1988):

- *HRM planning:* Many companies spend considerable time and effort planning the strategic use of strategic alliances. Perhaps just as important to the eventual success of the alliance is the communication of that strategic intent to the employees who will staff the alliance organization; that is, employees at all levels need to understand why the alliance exists and need to be aware of the parent companies' goals for the alliance.
- *Parent involvement:* The degree of parent company involvement in the alliance's human resource functions depends largely on the age, size, and intended life span of the alliance organization. Newer organizations, especially those with dominant parent or revolving management structures, tend to maintain HRM practices inherited from parent companies. However, for IJVs in particular, due to the need to mesh two or more organizational and national cultures into a legally separate organization, HRM practices soon become different from either parent. In addition, as all alliance organizations get older and larger, they tend to develop their own organizational cultures. This often leads to a need for their own HRM practices.
- *Staffing the alliance management and technical personnel:* Selecting managers or a technical specialist for an assignment in an international strategic alliance is a crucial but risky decision. On one hand, these individuals must have the necessary abilities to contribute the skills required to ensure the success of the alliance. Companies must resist the temptation to unload unwanted personnel on the alliance. On the other hand, parent companies must realize that an IJV or ICA assignment may last a long time. Managers, engineers, or other employees may never return to their parent company. Both these immediate and long term staffing needs of the alliance require that parent companies ensure that they

have enough management and technical talent to give the alliance the necessary people.

- *Staffing the alliance workforce:* Most ICAs involve the exchange of primarily technical and managerial personnel. However, independent IJV organizations often hire lower level workers who are not employees of the parent company owners. In these situations, partners must determine if local workers with the required skills are available at the IJV location. Local labor supply, labor laws, and local cultural values regarding work also determine HRM planning for an IJV. For example, an IJV may require skilled workers that are scarce at the IJV location. In such a case, HRM planning must include the necessary training of the local workforce.

- *Assigning managers strategic or operations tasks:* Depending on the form of managerial control structure and the type of international strategic alliance, parent companies must assign the proper number and types of managers. Crucial to this decision is whether the managers will take primarily strategic or operational roles in the alliance. Managers with strategic-level decision-making responsibility usually have more experience and come from higher levels of management in the parent companies. Operations-level managers, such as a production manager, usually come from lower levels of the parent company's management.

- *Performance assessment:* People who work in alliances need performance assessment for retention, promotion, and salary decisions. However, whenever two or more companies cooperate, it is unlikely that their performance-assessment techniques match exactly. As such, it is usually best to avoid adopting the system of one partner. This may lead to unavoidable cultural biases against employees from partner companies. In the early life of an alliance, performance judgments of employees may follow their parent company guidelines. Managers or other employees from each parent are evaluated on the bases of their parent companies' performance-evaluation systems. Later, it is common for joint performance review committees to take over performance evaluation from the parent companies as the alliance venture matures.

- *Loyalty:* Managers and other employees in ICAs or IJVs may feel a dual loyalty—to their parent organization and to the alliance organization. The intensity of loyalty tends to vary with the term of the alliance assignment. If employees perceive that they are "on loan" from their home organization, as is more often true with ICAs than IJVs, they will usually remain loyal to the parent. If employees believe that their assignments to the alliance organization are long term, they will usually develop a stronger loyalty to the alliance. Multinational managers must realize that loyalty to the alliance organization and the parent company can and should vary depending on the nature of an individual's assignment. Dealing with this fact must be a part of a strategy for human resource management for all alliance organizations.

- *Career development:* To motivate managers or other employees to perform successfully in international strategic alliances, the IJV or ICA assignment must be relevant to a future career and provide some job security. As with many international assignments, there is often a fear that one will be forgotten while away from the home organization. Companies actively pursuing multinational strategies based on international strategic alliances must provide clear information on how alliance assignments fit into an employee's career path and planning. For assignment to long-term joint ventures or cooperative alliances, the career ladder may exist entirely within the alliance.

Exhibit 8.7

HRM Issues in Strategic
Alliances

HRM Planning

- Communicate strategic intent
- Take a long-term dynamic approach

Staffing

- Give time for staffing decisions
- Provide high-quality people to the alliance
- Don't depend on the partner for staffing

Training and Development

- Train for cross-cultural competence
- Make sure training includes all partners
- Build a career structure of IJV participation

Appraisals and Rewards

- Appraise based on long-term goals
- Build incentives for strategic goals—learning or profits
- Tie rewards to global strategy

Source: Adapted from Pucik 1988.

- *Cultural differences:* The cultural differences inherent in all forms of international strategic alliances operate at all levels of culture, especially the national, business, and organizational levels. Different culturally based HRM practices can result in conflict over HRM practices. For example, the Japanese concern for age seniority or the U.S. concern for promotions based on individual achievement regardless of age affect many U.S./Japanese alliances because parents cannot resolve differences in HRM policies.
- *Training:* Managers, engineers, and other employees who work together in international strategic alliances perform better if they have prior training to develop cross-cultural interaction skills. The amount of required investment in training depends on the degree of cultural differences between national cultures, the length of the assignment, and the international experience of the employees of the alliance. Larger cultural differences, long-term assignments, and employees with limited international experience require more training.

Exhibit 8.7 summarizes many of the key issues for successful HRM practices in strategic alliances. A strategic alliance is like a marriage. Without mutual trust and commitment, the relationship will fail. We now examine how these issues are handled in strategic alliances.

COMMITMENT AND TRUST: THE SOFT
SIDE OF ALLIANCE MANAGEMENT

A common theme among managers from both failed and successful strategic alliances is the importance of building mutual trust and commitment among partners. No matter how mutually beneficial and logical the venture may seem at its start, without trust and commitment the alliance will either fail entirely, or it will fail to reach its strategic potential.

THE IMPORTANCE OF COMMITMENT AND TRUST

Commitment

In a strategic alliance, occurs when partners take care of each other and put forth extra effort to make the venture work.

Attitudinal commitment

The willingness to dedicate resources and efforts and face risks to make the alliance work.

Fair exchange

In a strategic alliance, occurs when partners believe that they receive benefits from the relationship equal to their contributions.

Calculative commitment

Alliance partner evaluations, expectations, and concerns regarding potential rewards from the relationship.

Credibility trust

The confidence that the partner has the intent and ability to meet promised obligations and commitments.

Benevolent trust

The confidence that the partner will behave with good will and with fair exchange.

Commitment in a strategic alliance means taking care of each other and putting forth extra effort to make the venture work. Committed partners are willing to dedicate resources and effort and face risks to make the venture work. This is called **attitudinal commitment**. Formally, attitudinal commitment is the psychological identification with the relationship and a pride of association with the partner and with the alliance.

Aspects of attitudinal commitment in international strategic alliances are expressed in many ways. These include the following: a fair financial commitment, a commitment to support the partner's strategic goals, a commitment to the partner's employees, and a commitment to understand the culture, politics, and economics of the partner's country.

If all partners involved in the alliance demonstrate these aspects of commitment, the venture will develop based on the principle of **fair exchange** (Lane and Beamish 1990). Fair exchange means that all partners believe that they receive benefits from the relationship that equal their contributions.

Why is commitment important? The marriage of two or more distinct companies from different cultures creates a strong potential for conflict and mistrust. Without a sense of mutual obligation to each other and to the alliance, partners often fail to work out problems. Instead, they retreat to their own companies or cultures leaving issues unresolved and often feeling the venture is not worth the effort. Lane and Beamish (1990) point out: "A successful relationship requires constant attention and nurturing. As one executive explained, 'Good local partners have to be cherished and taken care of.'"

Commitment also has a practical side, **calculative commitment**. Calculative commitment comes from the evaluations, expectations, and concerns about the future potential for gaining rewards in a relationship. Businesses require tangible outcomes for a relationship to continue. A recent study of commitment in IJVs suggests that commitment increases when both partners achieve their strategic goals. These goals may be financial or other strategic goals such as market entry or learning a new technology. However, it is not necessary that partners have the same strategic goals for the relationship to endure or grow in commitment (Cullen, Johnson, and Sakano 2000; Cullen, Johnson, and Sakano 1995). Perhaps, like any marriage, if partners select each other carefully, it is easier to develop complementary strategic goals and eventual commitment to the relationship.

Trust and commitment usually go hand in hand. As with commitment, there are two forms of trust. **Credibility trust** is the confidence that the partner has the intent and ability to meet their obligations and make their promised contributions to the alliance. Trust is also the confidence that the partner will behave with goodwill and with fair exchange, called **benevolent trust** (Johnson et al. 1996).

The development of trust between partners in an alliance may take time. Alliance partners often begin a relationship suspicious of each other's motives. Typical fears and questions include the following: Do they want to steal my technology? Are they trying to take me over? Am I building a new competitor? Am I giving away too much? Will they or can they provide what we agreed on? Such initial suspicions make trust difficult.

Most experts on trust believe that trust builds in what are called "trust cycles." Just like people in relationships, partners in IJVs and ICAs often feel vulnerable. This early vulnerability makes partners tentative in their involvement in the

Exhibit 8.8
The Trust/Commit-
ment Cycle

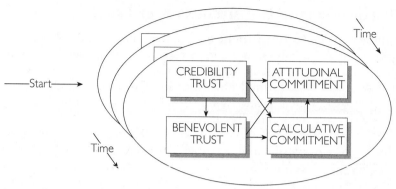

Source: Cullen, Johnson, and Sakano 2000.

relationship and reluctant to reveal true motives, business "know-how," or technology. Gradually, as each side deals repeatedly with its partner, suspicion declines and
reciprocal trust grows (Johnson et al. 1996; Ring and Van De Ven 1992). Exhibit 8.8
shows an example of the trust and commitment cycle in strategic alliances.

Why is trust important? Because successful cooperation requires alliance participants to contribute quality inputs into the alliance organization. When partners do
not trust each other, they hold back information or take unfair advantage of each
other if given the opportunity. When this happens, the alliance seldom produces all
the mutual benefits possible from cooperation.

Trust is also necessary because formal contracts can never identify all the issues
that arise in strategic alliances. It is impossible to write a contract with sufficient
detail to cover every foreseeable situation. Much of what happens between partners
in alliances develops informally as the alliance matures. In addition, the technology
and know-how of organizations contain "tacit knowledge." Tacit knowledge includes rules, procedures, and ways of doing things that are parts of the organization's culture. They are not written down and often people are not aware that they
exist. As a result, for two organizations to share sensitive knowledge and go beyond
the details of a formal contract, trust must exist.

BUILDING AND SUSTAINING TRUST AND COMMITMENT

There are several key factors that multinational managers need to consider to build
and sustain commitment and trust in international strategic alliances (Cullen, Johnson, and Sakano 2000). These include:

- *Pick your partner carefully:* As a major step in alliance implementation, picking a
  partner must include consideration of more than potential strategic complementarity and resource contributions. Alliance partners must believe that they
  can trust each other and they must believe that mutual commitment is possible.
- *Know your strategic goals and those of your partner:* Mutual revelations of strategic
  goals build a crucial step in the trust cycle. It also allows partners to realize early
  in the relationship whether they can commit to each other's strategic goals.
  However, alliance partners must realize that strategic goals for the ICA or IJV
  may change.
- *Seek win–win situations:* To achieve and maintain mutual commitment in an alliance there must be a balance in which each side gains something of importance from the relationship. Although the outcomes from the alliance need not

Exhibit 8.9
The Right Level of Trust
and Commitment

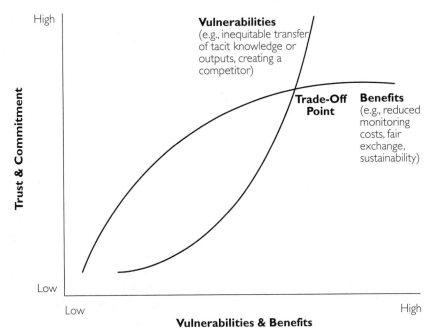

Source Cullen, Johnson, and Sakano 2000.

be the same, both sides must perceive them as a fair exchange if commitment and trust are to evolve.

- *Go slowly:* Participants in international strategic alliances must realize that problems arise and take time to work out. Trust and commitment develop in cycles and not necessarily all at once.
- *Invest in cross-cultural training:* As in all international ventures, managers with cross-cultural sensitivity and language competence will likely have more success in understanding partner needs and interests. Quality cross-cultural interactions between partners' employees will avoid conflict and misunderstandings and lead to greater trust and commitment between partner companies.
- *Invest in direct communication:* To overcome national, business, and organizational cultural differences, alliance partners are more successful at building trust and commitment when they deal with issues face-to-face.
- *Find the right level of trust and commitment:* Exhibit 8.9 shows the trade-off between the vulnerability that comes with trust and commitment and their benefits.

Companies form IJVs or ICAs to benefit their companies either in the short or long term or both. As such, as with all strategic decisions, companies must assess the performance of their strategies. In the next section, we consider the complex problems of assessing the performance of international strategic alliances.

ASSESSING THE PERFORMANCE OF AN INTERNATIONAL STRATEGIC ALLIANCE

As with all business ventures, strategic alliances should contribute eventually to their parents' profitability. When the strategic intent of the alliance is to produce immediate results, assessment of the alliance's performance is not difficult. Standard financial and efficiency measures of performance, such as profit, sales revenue, or number of units produced, are common. Often such alliances, particularly IJVs, become stand-alone profit centers that provide direct financial benefits to the parents. Profit-center alliances produce and sell their own products on the open market. Parents evaluate profit-center strategic alliances similarly to their other corporate divisions, based on traditional financial profitability ratios, such as return of investment.

Other types of strategic alliances provide mostly indirect strategic contributions to parents. Such alliances may never generate profits from the alliance organization. Rather, these strategic alliances produce other valued outputs such as new technologies with potential benefits for their parents. Indirect benefits from strategic alliances may come from penetrating risky markets, learning new markets or technologies, developing new technologies, overcoming local political barriers, developing a presence in a market, or supporting other competitive tactics (Lei 1993).

Boeing's ventures with Japanese companies provide one example of indirect benefits from alliances. Boeing uses alliances with Japanese aircraft-component makers as a defensive strategy. These alliances prevent its competitor, Airbus, from working with the Japanese. Another example is McDonald's joint-venture operations in Russia. McDonald's wanted to be the first fast-food chain in this emerging market—even though managers realized that profits would be hard to repatriate and that the venture would eventually convert to complete Russian ownership.

Eventually, all companies hope to make money from their ICA or IJV investments. The alliance itself may not produce the profit, but the knowledge gained may allow the parents to succeed in the future. In the meantime, however, how can upper management assess the performance of a strategic alliance and the performances of the managers responsible for the ICA or IJV? What is distinctive about **IJV and ICA performance criteria**?

IJV and ICA performance criteria

Often must include criteria other than financial, such as organizational learning.

Financial performance measures alone are seldom good indicators of performance for strategic alliances created for indirect strategic benefits. Depending on the unique objectives of the alliances, parents must develop more subjective performance criteria. These criteria include factors such as creating harmony among the partners, identifying product adaptations for a new market, or capturing market share to gain first-mover advantages over their competitors (Anderson 1990).

Assessing the performance of all types of alliances demands that parents match the strategic objectives of their alliances with the measures used for assessment. If immediate profit is the strategic goal, then profit must be in the assessment. If long-term goals, such as learning a new market or technology, are the main goals of the alliance, then immediate profit must be de-emphasized in favor of other performance measures.

Exhibit 8.10 shows a list of potential performance measures that parent companies use to evaluate their strategic alliances.

Not all alliances achieve their strategic intent; therefore, managers must plan for how to handle a nonperforming alliance. The next section addresses this issue.

IF THE ALLIANCE DOES NOT WORK

If the alliance fails to meet strategic goals, managers have two basic choices (see Exhibit 8.1). Providing that they keep their same strategic intent, they can negotiate an end to the agreement or improve their implementation.

Exhibit 8.10
Selected Performance
Criteria for Strategic
Alliances

Management Processes

- Good partner relationships—no conflict or handled well

- High worker morale

- Meeting goals of social responsibility

- Development of human resources

- Dealing with the local government

Organizational Learning

- Understanding a new market

- Learning a new technology

- Developing new management techniques

- Developing innovative technologies

- Generating other potential opportunities

Competitive

- Gaining market share

- Affecting competitors (e.g., preventing them from gaining a foothold in the country)

Marketing

- Total sales

- Customer satisfaction

- Facilitating the sale of other products

Financial

- Return on investment

- Return on assets

Source: Adapted from Anderson 1990.

The art of managing strategic alliances is knowing when to quit and when to invest more time and resources in building the relationship. There are really no hard-and-fast rules and each case is unique. Often, the personal relationships among alliance managers become the key for turning around a nonperforming alliance.

A particular danger in all questionable alliance relationships is the escalation of commitment (Cullen, Johnson, and Sakano 1995). The **escalation of commitment** means that managers continue in relationships longer than necessary because of past financial and emotional investments. They believe that "just one more day" or "just a little more money" will make the relationship work and make their past investments worthwhile. The truly difficult choice is knowing when to take the loss and dissolve the alliance.

Improving the implementation means going over each step in the implementation process to determine what, if any, changes can be made. Perhaps, for example, partners failed to develop an appropriate design for the alliance organization or chose a weak alliance manager. Of course, if one side decides that it just has the wrong partner, it must dissolve the relationship and, if necessary, seek another alliance partner.

Escalation of commitment

Companies continue in an alliance relationship longer than necessary because of past financial and emotional investments.

A recommended strategy of alliance formation is to plan for the end of the alliance from its beginning. Alliance contracts can contain "prenuptial" agreements, which specify how the alliance can be dissolved. These agreements note the procedures to end the alliance and review periods when both sides must agree to keep the alliance alive. They may also specify penalties for early termination of the contract by either side. The advantage of including such agreements up front, before the alliance begins, is that negotiations occur in a positive and friendly stage of the relationship. They do not occur later, when there is often conflict between the partners and a high level of distrust.

The death of a strategic alliance should not be confused with a failed relationship. Many alliances are intended to be short term. Once partners achieve their strategic goals, they both go their own ways. For example, an alliance may end after a new technology is developed, a new market is penetrated, or a temporary product gap is remedied. In addition, IJVs are often acquired by one of the partners and move to the next level of direct investment.

Summary and Conclusions

The use of international strategic alliances as a major participation strategy continues to grow in international business. Implementing this strategy demands a good knowledge of the problems and prospects associated with alliance management. This chapter provided a basic understating of issues in alliance management, including where to link in the value chain, how to select a partner, designing an alliance organization, HRM practices in an alliance, building trust and commitment in an alliance, assessing performance, and what to do if the alliance fails.

Perhaps the most important decision in managing successful strategic alliances is picking the right partner. Picking a compatible partner with the appropriate skills determines the eventual fate of most strategic alliances.

Strategic alliances have no set structure for ownership, decision-making control, or management control. Partners must negotiate structures that support their mutual strategic goals. The ICA or IJV manager faces HRM problems similar to those in all international operations. However, there is added complexity because parent companies must come to some agreement regarding the HRM practices used in alliance organizations.

Most experts consider trust and commitment as basic foundations for IJV or ICA success, second only to picking the right partner. Commitment and trust take on such importance because not everything can be stated in a contract. For long-term success, partner companies must trust each other to deliver agreed-upon outputs and to not take advantage of partners in the relationship.

Because strategic goals for strategic alliances are varied and subtle, the performance of an IJV or ICA is often difficult to determine. Usually, companies expect a strategic alliance to generate more than short-term financial returns. Objectives such as organizational learning and market penetration often represent major goals of alliances and must figure strongly in their performance assessment.

Strategic alliances are inherently unstable and many will fail. Consequently, when an international strategic alliance fails to meet strategic goals, multinational managers must be prepared to improve their implementation efforts or to abandon the alliance. However, many strategic alliances will die natural deaths when they meet their strategic objectives or are bought out by one of the parent companies.

Discussion Questions

1. What are the characteristics of a good partner in a strategic alliance? How do these partner traits help make a strategic alliance successful?

2. Which of the alliance contract issues shown in the text do you think are most important? Why?

3. Discuss some costs and benefits of the different management structures available for a strategic alliance. Under what conditions should a firm choose any particular structure?

4. What types of personnel are usually assigned to strategic alliances? For each type of personnel, what kind of impact does the IJV assignment have on future careers?

5. What are some of the difficulties of assessing IJV or ICA performance? How do these differ for companies with different strategic goals?

Chapter Internet Activity

Most multinational companies have many joint ventures or strategic alliances. Search the Web sites of the companies discussed in the chapter and see if you can trace their alliances. Draw a network map of the alliances you find.

Internet Sites

Selected Companies in the Chapter

Advanced Micro Devices Inc.   http://www.amd.com/
Airbus Industries   http://www.airbus.com/
British Airways   http://www.british-airways.com/
Canon   http://www.canon.com
Carpenter Technology   http://www.cartech.com
DuPont   http://www.dupont.com/
Fujitsu   http://www.fujitsu.com
GE   http://www.ge.com/
Hitachi   http://www.hitachi.com/
IBM   http://www.ibm.com/
Interbrew   http://www.interbrew.com
LukOil   http://www.lukoil.com
McDonald's Corp.   http://www.mcdonalds.com/
Motorola   http://www.mot.com/
Northwest Airlines http://www.nwa.com/
PepsiCo   http://www.pepsico.com
Renault   http://www.renault.com
Samsung   http://www.samsung.com/
Sharp Electronics   http://www.sharp-usa.com/

Siemens   http://www.siemens.com/
Texas Instruments   http://www.ti.com/
Toshiba   http://www.toshiba.com/
USAirways http://www.usair.com/

Look Here for More Information on Strategic Alliances

http://www.allianceanalyst.com
http://fatty.law.cornell.edu/topics/joint_ventures.html
http://www.ciber.bus.msu.edu/   *Locations of company home pages, many of which describe organizational design.*
http://www.internationalist.com   *Publicly traded companies throughout the world.*
http://www.yahoo.com/   *Find a company on the search engine Yahoo!*

Hint: Many companies show their equity alliances on their home pages. Some alliance organizations have their own home pages.

Chapter Case: PBS (B): The ABB PBS Joint Venture in Operation

The PBS board meeting to make the decision whether or not to accept the ABB proposal for a joint venture lasted 18 hours. In the end, the PBS board voted in favor and the joint venture was agreed. Several legal and contractual issues were quickly resolved, and the deal was signed in late December 1992.

STRUCTURE AND ORGANIZATION

ABB První Brnénská Strojírna Brno, Ltd. (ABB PBS) was a joint venture in which ABB has a 67 percent stake and PBS a.s. has a 33 percent stake. The PBS share was determined nominally by the value of the land, plant and equipment, employees, and goodwill. ABB contributed cash and specified technologies, and assumed some of the debt of PBS. The new company started operations on April 15, 1993.

The ABB PBS company was a joint venture in its formal structure and governance. PBS a.s. had seats on the board, had part ownership, and was a supplier to the joint venture. The core operations of PBS a.s. were its Brno-based power generation business, its experience with turnkey operations, and its engineering and manufacturing capabilities with its customer base of installed equipment. The joint venture included the turnkey power plant business, boilers, and turbines (but not turbochargers). All of the PBS facilities in Brno and the outlying plant in Mikulov that made turbine blades went into the joint venture. In sum, about 4,000 employees from PBS a.s. went to the joint venture; about 3,400 remained in PBS a.s. About 80 percent of the revenue of PBS a.s. became part of the joint venture.

Profit was to be divided in ⅔ − ⅓ shares according to ownership when it was earned and distributed; initial plans called for reinvestment of all profits and no dividends paid out to corporate parents.

ABB PBS was organized by product lines: power plants, turbines, boilers, and external services (the latter was added in 1995). Centralized functions such as marketing, finance, human resources, quality control, and information systems reported vertically to the general director and are matrixed horizontally with the business units or product divisions. The internal service division (maintenance) served the four product divisions. Each product division also had some of the same functions (Exhibit 1).

ABB PBS was assigned geographic regions as its market territories by the ABB power generation segment and used the ABB selling network in these territories. Other ABB companies in the same lines of business had other territories, so head-to-head competition among ABB sister companies for the same customers was minimized.

The ABB regional selling network assisted ABB PBS to identify business opportunities. ABB PBS was the prime contractor for projects that are obtained. For turbines and boilers that were not part of a turnkey project, or in cases in which another ABB company was the primary contractor, ABB PBS participated as a subcontractor. ABB PBS had its own vice-president for export sales and an export sales force for direct selling as well as selling in cooperation with the ABB regional network.

In the domestic market, ABB PBS continued to use its own sales force and customer contacts. There were two domestic competitors, Škoda Turbiny (a company in the Skoda Koncern) and Vitkovice, whose principal business was steel.

BUSINESS RESULTS

Financial Performance

Business for the joint venture in its first two full years was good in most aspects. Orders received in 1994, the first full year of the joint venture's operation, were higher than ever in the history of PBS. Orders received in 1995 increased seven percent over 1994 in nominal terms. Revenues for 1995 were 2½ times those in 1994 (Exhibit 2). The company was profitable in 1995 and ahead of 1994's results with a rate of return on assets of 2.3

Source: By Stanley D. Nollen, Karen L. Newman, and Jacqueline M. Abbey, of the School of Business, Georgetown University, Washington, D.C. 20057. Copyright © by the *Case Research Journal* and Stanley D. Nollen, Karen L. Newman, and Jacqueline M. Abbey.

Exhibit I   ABB PBS Organizational Chart in 1995

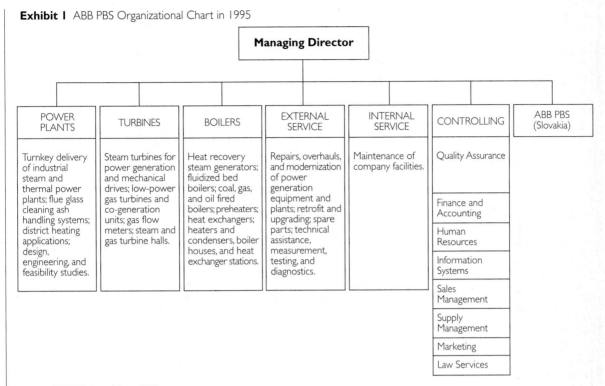

Source: ABB PBS *Annual Report* 1995.

percent and a rate of return on sales of 4.5 percent (Exhibit 3).

The 1995 results showed substantial progress toward meeting the joint venture's strategic goals adopted in 1994 as part of a five-year plan. One of the goals was that exports should account for half of total orders by 1999. (Exports had accounted for more than a quarter of the PBS business before 1989, but most of this business disappeared when the Soviet Union collapsed.) In 1995 exports increased as a share of total orders to 28 percent, up from 16 percent the year before.

The external service business, organized and functioning as a separate business for the first time in 1995, did not meet expectations. It accounted for five percent of all orders and revenues in 1995, below the 10 percent goal set for it. The retrofitting business, which was expected to be a major part of the service business, was disappointing for ABB PBS, partly because many other small companies began to provide this service in 1994, including some started by former PBS employees who took their knowledge of PBS-built power plants with them. However, ABB PBS managers hoped that as the company introduced new tech-

nologies, these former employees would gradually lose their ability to perform these services, and the retrofit and repair service business would return to ABB PBS.

ABB PBS dominated the Czech boiler business with 70 percent of the Czech market in 1995, but managers expected this share to go down in the future as new domestic and foreign competitors appeared. Furthermore, the west European boiler market was actually declining because environmental laws caused a surge of retrofitting to occur in the mid-1980s, leaving less business in the 1990s. Accordingly, ABB PBS boiler orders were flat in 1995.

Top managers at ABB PBS regarded business results to date as respectable, but they were not satisfied with the company's performance. Cash flow was not as good as expected. Cost reduction had to go further. "The more we succeed, the more we see our shortcomings," said one official.

Restructuring

The first round of restructuring was largely completed in 1995, the last year of the three-year restructuring plan. Plant logistics, information

Exhibit 2
Orders and Revenues
for ABB PBS Businesses
in 1994 and 1995

Business	1994		1995	
	Kč million	% of total	Kč million	% of total
Revenue	490	23	3,062	52
Orders	3,230	49	3,687	47
Turbines				
Revenue	707	34	1,118	19
Orders	938	14	1,389	18
Boilers				
Revenue	900	43	1,353	23
Orders	2,439	37	2,452	31
Services	(not reported			
Revenue	separately	314		5
Orders	in 1994)	381		5
Total	2,097	100	5,847	100
	6,607	100	7,909	100

Notes: Kč are in nominal terms. The sum of revenues and orders across businesses in this table exceeds the total revenue and orders figures reported in the income statement data in Exhibit 3; the percent distributions in this table are figured on the sum of revenues and orders in this table.

Source: ABB První Brněnská Strojírna s.r.o., *1995 Business Report* and *1994 Business Report*.

systems, and other physical capital improvements were in place. The restructuring included:

- Renovating and reconstructing workshops and engineering facilities
- Achieving ISO 9001 for all four ABB PBS divisions (awarded in 1995)
- Transfer of technology from ABB (this was an ongoing project)
- Installation of an information system
- Management training, especially in total quality assurance and English language
- Implementing a project management approach

A notable achievement of importance to top management in 1995 was a 50 percent increase in labor productivity, measured as value added per payroll crown. However, in the future ABB PBS expected its wage rates to go up faster than west European wage rates (Czech wages were increasing about 15 percent per year), so it would be difficult to maintain the ABB PBS unit cost advantage over west European unit cost.

The Technology Role for ABB PBS

The joint venture was expected from the beginning to play an important role in technology development for part of ABB's power generation business worldwide. PBS a.s. had engineering capability in coal-fired steam boilers, and that capability was expected to be especially useful to ABB as more countries became concerned about air quality. (When asked if PBS really did have leading technology here, a boiler engineering manager remarked, "Of course we do. We burn so much dirty coal in this country, we have to have better technology.")

However, the envisioned technology leadership role for ABB PBS had not been realized by mid-1996. Richard Kuba, the ABB PBS managing director, realized the slowness with which the technology role was being fulfilled, and he offered his interpretation of events:

ABB did not promise to make the joint venture its steam boiler technology leader. The main point we wanted to achieve in the joint venture agreement was for ABB PBS to be recognized as a full-fledged company, not just a factory. We were slowed down on our technology plans because we had a problem keeping our good, young engineers. The annual employee turnover rate for companies in the Czech Republic is 15 or 20 percent, and the unemployment rate is zero. Our engineers have many other good entrepreneurial opportunities. Now we've begun to stabilize our engineering workforce. The restructuring helped. We have better equipment and a

Exhibit 3

Selected Income
Statement, Balance
Sheet, and Other
Operating Data
for ABB PBS, 1994
and 1995 (Kč million
current)

Variable	1994	1995
Revenue	1,999	5,015
Orders received	6,208	7,088
R&D expenditure	29	64
Investment	435	388
Total assets	5,115	9,524
Fixed assets	1,773	2,186
Trade receivables	451	509
Trade payables	197	817
Bank loans	690	710
Equity	1,130	1,110
Exports (percent of orders)	16%	28%
Employees (number)	3,600	3,235
Labor productivity (value added/salaries)★	Kč 109/Kč	Kč 163/Kč

Note: ★Value added is revenue minus purchased inputs. The labor productivity figures are not meaningful as absolute numbers but rather are used for overtime comparisons.

Sources: ABB První Brněnská Strojírna s.r.o., *1995 Business Report* and *1994 Business Report.*

cleaner and safer work environment. We also had another problem, which is a good problem to have. The domestic power plant business turned out to be better than we expected, so just meeting the needs of our regular customers forced some postponement of new technology initiatives.

ABB PBS had benefited technologically from its relationship with ABB. One example was the development of a new steam turbine line. This project was a cooperative effort among ABB PBS and two other ABB companies, one in Sweden and one in Germany. Nevertheless, technology transfer was not the most important early benefit of the ABB relationship. Rather, one of the most important gains was the opportunity to benchmark the joint venture's performance against other established western ABB companies on variables such as productivity, inventory, and receivables.

MANAGEMENT ISSUES

The toughest problems that ABB PBS faced in the early years of the joint venture were management issues. There were two: How to relate to ABB sister companies in other countries, and how to transform the human capital of the company.

Relationships with Other ABB Companies

Managing a joint venture company was always difficult, and joining a global corporation compounded the start-up challenges. The Czech managers at ABB PBS had to learn fast. One set of problems arose from the relationship of ABB PBS to its ABB sister companies. Richard Kuba and his colleagues were accustomed to working together with other companies on big projects; before the Velvet Revolution, PBS worked with other companies in the škoda group. But ABB was different. Cooperation coexisted with competition, and that was outside Kuba's experience. Sibling rivalry among companies was very much a fact of business life, he discovered. Kuba related an unhappy episode about his company's unfamiliarity with these business relationships. He said:

We underestimated the cultural differences between Czechs and other west European people. We have to learn how to say "no." We have to be better in claim management. We have to fight more in order to succeed in this environment.

This fact of corporate life was confirmed by Erik Fougner, the ABB country manager in the Czech Republic, who also noted that excess capacity in Europe caused the older ABB companies to be particularly anxious about the arrival of the Czech newcomer. Some were concerned that there would not be room for three ABB power generation industry companies in Europe in the future.

Human Capital Transformation

The physical and organizational restructuring of ABB PBS was nearly completed by 1996. The transformation of the thinking and behavior of employees had just begun. The ways that were adaptive, or at least tolerated, under central planning would not succeed in a competitive market economy. Changing employees' "mentality" —the term used by Czech managers—was human capital restructuring. It was proving very difficult to do, and it was going very slowly.

In several respects, ABB PBS was nicely positioned to accomplish human capital restructuring. The top management of the joint venture was stable, it was thoroughly Czech but with a keen awareness of the mentality issues, and the ABB parent company tried to offer assistance in a variety of ways. Czech management was supported by two or three expatriates taking non-executive positions in project management, supply management, and workshop planning.

The ABB PBS managers believed a background of knowledge of local history, culture, and business practices was essential. These Czech managers, as in most Czech companies, knew they had to change the attitudes and behaviors of their employees. Richard Kuba said,

It is easy to change the structure of the company, and it is easy to change the facilities, but it is not easy to change people's minds. Employees don't yet understand the consequences of their actions. They don't take responsibility. There is low unemployment so they can leave and get a less stressful job instead of taking responsibility here.

ABB PBS had never laid off any employees for lack of work. Managers appreciated the good reputation this brought the company, but they also wondered if it dampened employees' motivation to work hard. Without the threat of layoff, would managers' human resource initiatives be listened to?

Fougner, a Norwegian located in Prague since 1992, saw the same "mentality" problem:

This is a bigger challenge than I thought it would be. The first level of change in Czech companies comes easily. To make nice new offices and new factory layouts is quite simple. But the transfer of real human resource learning is slow. Responsibility and initiative are poor because it was not rewarded for two generations in these formerly centrally planned economies. Under central planning, you were given a task, you did it, and nothing bad would happen to you. The tasks themselves were compartmentalized—I did mine and you did yours. I did my duty so I'm okay. Even managers did not see the whole picture and could not take responsibility for it. The functional organization of companies [with the archetypal "functional chimneys"] made it worse.

What could be done? The company took three approaches. At the corporate level, ABB PBS tried to instill a sense of mission. The annual report for 1995 noted the efforts of top management to find agreement on corporate goals and values in order to strengthen employee identification with the company.

ABB, the parent company, tried to assist, but did not want to send too many expatriates to ABB PBS. Rather, local managers had to bring about the mentality changes themselves. ABB loaned some of the people from its internal consulting unit to the joint venture on a part-time basis. Their job was to train the (local) trainers, and to sit beside the production and engineering managers and supervisors and work through attitude change material with them. Line managers were the ones who would implement the human capital restructuring, not personnel managers.

The compensation system was the third line of attack. Before the Velvet Revolution, factory worker pay at PBS was based on a piece rate system that was surprisingly common in the Czech Republic. However, it was badly manipulated so that it did not motivate workers to raise output. Real or imagined equipment problems or shortages of parts—both of which occurred frequently—would excuse workers from meeting desired rates of output, or workers would stockpile output and then slack off. The system fostered the attitude among some workers that "you get a

Exhibit 4
Economic Conditions in Czech Republic, 1993–1995

Variable	1993	1994	1995
Gross domestic product, real %	−0.9	2.6	4.6
Industrial production, real %	−5.3	2.3	9.0
Consumer price inflation, %	20.8	10.0	8.9
Interest rate, %	14.1	13.1	12.8
Exchange rate, Kč/$, annual average	29.3	28.8	26.3
Unemployment rate, %	3.5	3.2	3.0

Sources: Economist Intelligence Unit, *Country Report: Czech Republic and Slovakia*, 1st quarter 1996; 2nd quarter 1994. London, 1996, 1994. International Monetary Fund, *International Financial Statistics*, March 1996, January 1994. Washington, D.C., 1996, 1994.

wage to show up, and anything extra you do gets you extra pay." This attitude reflected working conditions under communism where wages were an entitlement rather than a payment for labor services rendered.

ABB PBS introduced a new incentive pay scheme that was not without its problems. Employees were accustomed to stability and predictability in earnings. Another problem was that the time horizon for the incentive pay was too long—year-long profit sharing schemes were too distant for production workers because they could not see the link between their performance and their reward that far ahead. The scheme was modified in 1996 to reintroduce some smaller discretionary bonuses that were granted when the bonus-worthy work took place.

THE FUTURE

The ABB PBS joint venture was only three years old in the spring of 1996. By that time, the legal privatization of industry in the Czech Republic was essentially completed. The first five years of the transition from central planning to market economy for Czech companies was over. This meant that some of the most extreme external stresses on companies, such as loss of markets and lack of finance, were behind them. The Czech economy appeared to be strong and growing (Exhibit 4).

By 1996, most of the major restructuring of ABB PBS was completed. Most of the easier internal changes had been made. Plant and equipment had been improved, and product quality was in

good shape. Richard Kuba and his colleagues had accomplished a lot, but they were not satisfied. Some of the hard changes were yet to be made, and the outlook for the company was mixed.

Doing business in competitive western markets was much more rugged than Kuba expected. Financial results were sufficient given the difficult business conditions the company faced, but they were not good enough for a mature market economy. Kuba knew there was overcapacity in the industry worldwide. There were tens of relatively small companies like his, and some of them would not survive. Belonging to the ABB network had advantages of course, but it also brought problems. Cooperation with ABB sister companies in marketing and technology was mirrored by competition and sibling rivalry with companies from cultures with which Kuba and his colleagues were unfamiliar. Internally, the transformation of ABB PBS's considerable human capital required renewed focus. Kuba could not rest easily yet.

CASE QUESTIONS FOR DISCUSSION

1. How does the joint venture meet the needs of both companies? Where does it fall short?

2. What are likely to be the greatest challenges for the joint venture? What role might cultural differences between ABB and PBS play?

3. What actions are necessary for ABB PBS top management to undertake to secure the long-term success of the company?

References

Anderson, Erin. 1990. "Two firms, one frontier: On assessing joint venture performance." *Sloan Management Review,* Winter, 19–30.

Bagsarian, Tom. 2000. "The lessons learned from overseas partnerships." *Iron Age New Steel* 16, 34–37.

Cullen, John B., Jean L. Johnson, and Tomoaki Sakano. 2000. "Success through commitment and trust: The soft side of strategic alliance management." *Journal of World Business* 35: 3, 223–40.

———, ———, and ———. 1995. "Japanese and local partner commitment to IJVs: Psychological consequences of outcomes and investments in the IJV relationship." *Journal of International Business Studies* 26:1, 91–116.

Datta, Deepak K., and Abdual M. A. Rasheed. 1993. "Planning international joint ventures: The role of human resource management." In *Multinational Strategic Alliances,* edited by Refik Culpan, 251–71. New York: International Business Press.

Geringer, J. Michael. 1988. *Joint Venture Partner Selection.* Westport, Conn.: Quorum Books.

Glain, Steve. 1995. "Samsung mounts big push to diversify." *Wall Street Journal,* February 10, A6.

Gray, Barbara, and Aimin Yan. 1992. "A negotiations model of joint venture formation, structure, and performance: Implications for global management." *Advances in International Comparative Management* 7:41–75.

Johnson, Jean L., John B. Cullen, Tomoaki Sakano, and Hideyuki Takenouchi. 1996. "Setting the stage for trust and strategic integration in Japanese-U.S. cooperative alliances." *Journal of International Business Studies* 27:981–1004.

Killing, J. P. 1988. "Understanding alliances: The role of task and organizational complexity." In *Cooperative Strategies in International Business,* edited by F.J. Contractor and P. Lorange, 241–45. Lexington, Mass.: Lexington Books.

Lane, Henry W., and Paul W. Beamish. 1990. "Cross-cultural cooperative behavior in joint ventures in lDCs." *Management International Review* 30, Special Issue, 87–102.

Lei, David. 1993. "Offensive and defensive uses of alliances." *Long Range Planning* 26:32–44.

Lorange, Peter. 1986. "Human resource management in multinational cooperative ventures." *Human Resource Management* 25:1, 133–148.

Lorange, Peter, and Johan Roos. 1992. *Strategic Alliances.* Cambridge, Mass.: Blackwell.

Main, Jeremy. 1990. "Making global alliances work." *Fortune,* December 17, 121–26.

Murray, Janet Y. 1995. "Patterns in domestic vs. international strategic alliances: An investigation of U.S. multinational firms." *Multinational Business Review* 13:7–16.

Pecht, Michael, Weifeng Liu, and David Hodges. 2000. "Newer fabs in China." *Semiconductor International* 23, 156–60.

Peridis, Theodoros. 1992. "Strategic alliances for smaller firms." *Research in Global Strategic Management* 3:129–42.

Poole, Claire. 1999. "Love on the rocks." *Latin Trade* August: http://www.findarticles.com.

Port, Otis, Richard Brandt, Neil Gross, and Jonathan B. Levine. 1992. "Talk about your dream team." *Business Week Online,* July 27.

Pucik, Vladimir. 1988. "Strategic alliances, organizational learning, and competitive advantage: The HRM agenda." *Human Resource Management* 27, 77–93.

Ring, Peter Smith, and Andrew H. Van De Ven. 1992. "Structuring cooperative relationships between organizations." *Strategic Management Journal* 13, 483–98.

Rondinelli, Dennis A. and Sloan Black. 2000. "Multinational strategic alliances and acquisitions in Central and Eastern Europe: Partnerships in privatization. *Academy of Management Executive* 14, 85–98.

Tierney, Christine. 1996. Reuters news service, June 24. Downloaded from America Online, June 25.

United Nations Economic Commission for Europe & ILO. 1993. "The management challenge in Belarus: The case of AGV-Polotsk." In *Management Development in East-West Joint Ventures,* 33–36. New York: United Nations.

Vernon, R. 1977. *Storm over Multinationals.* Cambridge, Mass.: Harvard University Press.

Part 3 Integrating Case 1

STS Manufacturing in China:
Mark Hanson Returns from Vacation

It was late February 1998 and a bitterly cold day in Shenyang as Mark Hanson made his way to his office at STS Manufacturing (STS), a joint venture between Shanrong Manufacturing of China (Shanrong) and Tellsan Products of the United States (Tellsan). STS manufactured components for automotive steering assemblies and was a supplier to Volkswagen's joint ventures with Shanghai Automotive Industry Corp. and First Auto Works. Hanson, the young general manager of the joint venture, had just returned from a long overdue week's vacation in Thailand. As he began going through the stack of paperwork and messages on his desk, Hanson realized that just because he had been away for a week, the issues and problems in the joint venture had not disappeared. Moreover, after working at Tellsan for 18 months, he was seriously questioning whether or not Tellsan had made the right decision about even being in China.

CHINA'S FOREIGN INVESTMENT CLIMATE

Understanding the challenging business environment that China poses for foreign investors requires some knowledge of China's history and relations with the outside world. One of the oldest civilizations on earth, stretching back some five thousand years, China's history was both impressive and tragic. It was impressive in the tremendous technological innovations that have come from China, including paper money, gunpowder, printing press, and fertilizer. It was tragic in that famine, poverty, warlordism, civil war, and encroachment and conquest by outside forces have characterized much of China's recent history. In the last two hundred years of China's history, foreign powers have carved up China into spheres of influence, imposed their own legal systems within Chinese territory, imported opium on a massive scale to settle imbalances in trade accounts, and brutally massacred hundreds of thousands of Chinese citizens. This history shaped China's often suspicious and volatile relationship with the outside world and partially accounted for China's leeriness toward foreign investors. Despite all of this, China has at times admired and welcomed foreigners and their technologies. However, at other times China rejected foreigners and everything they had to offer. As early as 1792 the Chinese emperor dismissed Western attempts to engage in trade, stating, "We possess all things and have no need for the strange or ingenious manufactures of foreign barbarians."

From 1948 to 1978, China was in the midst of an inward-looking phase and had limited contact with the outside world. The door was closed to outside investors and capitalism. With Mao Tse Tung's death in 1976 and the realization that China's economic progression required new technologies and skills from the West, China's new leader, Deng Xiao Ping, opened the door to outside investors and began loosening the government's iron grip over economic activity. Gradually, market forces were allowed to play a more significant role in the economy. Referring to the cautious and gradual manner in which China would make this transformation to a more market-based economy, Deng said, "You cross the river by stepping on the stones." This statement captured the incremental and cautious manner by which China was attempting to introduce market forces and, once again, allow foreigners a foothold in the Chinese economy.

Beginning in the countryside under the Household Responsibility System, family and collective farms were allowed to sell some of their produce in an open market, and government quotas for production were gradually reduced. Similar to the farm sector, manufacturing enterprises were encouraged to locate buyers and sell products at market-determined prices once quotas were satisfied. Over time, as quotas were diminished and more products flowed to the expanding market segment of the economy, the percentage of total goods sold at market prices in China far exceeded goods produced for quota. As this occurred, China began to resemble a market economy, although not a privatized one. By 1997, privatization had not occurred in China on a significant scale. Despite the lack of privatization, China was able to develop an incentive-based system harnessing the motivations of individuals and firms. Incentives to produce arose from the government allowing an increasing percentage of household or firm earnings to remain in the hands of the workers and managers. Under Mao, all income was repatriated to the central government ministries in Beijing and then distributed as the leadership saw fit. There was no linkage between firm or farm performance and the welfare of its employees.

This changed under Deng Xiao Ping. Although this system of complete and arbitrary control over the economy changed as market forces were introduced, some decisions remained in the hands of the government planning authorities. Decisions of a more strategic nature such as the decision to expand into new markets or the building of factories remained under the control of often multiple supervisory ministries at the local, provincial, and central government levels.

Another significant milestone in China's effort to interject market forces into their economy involved relaxation of restrictions on products produced. Prior to the policy change, firms were limited to producing products that were clearly associated with the ministry of which they were a part. For example, Shanghai Pharmaceutical Factory No. 1 was restricted to producing pharmaceuticals because of its ownership by the Shanghai Municipality's Ministry of Pharmaceuticals, which was in turn controlled by the central government's Ministry of Pharmaceuticals located in Beijing. Similarly, a firm associated with the Ministry of Posts and Telecommunications could not venture beyond producing telecommunications-related products. Policy reform relaxed these restrictions and allowed firms to invest wherever they discovered a market opportunity, regardless of the industrial sector/ministry to which they belonged. This change undermined the silo nature of the Chinese economy and complicated the task of foreign investors in understanding the Chinese market. Whereas prior to the reform it was relatively simple to identify potential joint venture partners and competitors, the removal of restrictions on investment and the breakdown of the silos meant that both potential partners and/or competitors could come from any sector.

All the reforms, while providing annual double-digit growth rates in the economy and raising the living standards of the Chinese people, had the additional effect of decentralizing decision-making and undermining the control of the central government. By introducing a myriad of policy changes and decentralizing decision-making, foreign investors were constantly confronted with contradictory regulations coming from central, provincial, and local government authorities. While China deserved considerable credit in creating a legal framework of rules and regulations governing foreign investment where none existed prior to 1978, the lack of consistency in enforcement continued to confound investors. Furthermore, limited private ownership of property and the socialization of ownership meant that managers in state-owned enterprises did not necessarily view rate of return as a primary objective. Instead, multiple government agencies, each with their own agenda, competed to influence decision-making in a bureaucratic free-for-all. Managers were often evaluated and promoted to positions not on the basis of merit or rate of return, but on the basis of how politically astute they were in catering to the interests of other higher-level government officials in other ministries.

In 1998, although the door for foreign investors was open and market forces were becoming prominent in China's economy, the Peoples' Republic of China (PRC) government tightly controlled and regulated all the activities of foreign firms operating in China. Issues for foreign investors such as plant location, market access, technology transfer, and foreign exchange management were just a few of the areas exposed to government regulation and constant meddling.

THE CHINESE AUTOMOBILE INDUSTRY

The Chinese automobile industry in early 1997 was suffering from serious overcapacity. Although 1996 sales increased by 19% to 382,000 units, capacity reached more than 700,000 units and was growing quickly with new investments under way by General Motors, Daimler-Benz, Citroën, Honda, and other firms. The Chinese government announced that it would not license any more automobile manufacturing joint ventures and revised its projections for future car demand from 1.2 million units in 2000 to 850,000. Adding to the competition was rampant smuggling of vehicles from Japan and South Korea, which was estimated to have reached 100,000 units.

Most of the foreign automobile firms in China were struggling. For example, in 1993 Peugeot began investing in its joint venture plant in Guangzhou to increase production to 150,000 units. In 1996 the Peugeot plant produced less than 3,000 units, down from 6,600 in 1995. Citroën produced only 13,000 vehicles in 1996, even though its joint venture agreement permitted production of up to 300,000 units. Nevertheless, Citroën was expanding steadily. With the possible exception of Peugeot, none of the automakers appeared willing to withdraw from China, and Japanese firms, latecomers to China, were scrambling to gain a foothold.

Shanghai VW, the joint venture between Volkswagen and Shanghai Automotive Industry Corp., was unique in two respects: it was the only foreign joint venture to be profitable, and the only one to have achieved commercially viable levels of production. Shanghai VW was formed in 1984 as the first foreign automotive venture in China. By 1996, Shanghai VW was producing more than 200,000 vehicles and had built strong supply and distribution channels. Nevertheless, until recently, Shanghai VW had minimal serious competition and, consequently, invested little in product development. The Santana model produced by Shanghai VW was more than a decade old. In addition, Volkswagen's second joint venture with First Auto Works in Changchun, formed in 1988 to produce the Jetta model, was in serious difficulty. Sales in 1996 were 25,000 units, half the target output and far less than the plant's 150,000-unit capacity. The joint venture lost just over $100 million in 1996.

STS MANUFACTURING (STS)

STS was formed in 1994 as an equity joint venture between Shanrong Manufacturing of China and Tellsan Products of the United States. Tellsan had a 60% equity share in the venture and Shanrong had 40%. Tellsan's relationship with Volkswagen in China was linked to the firm's experience as a Volkswagen supplier in Germany through a majority-owned German-based joint venture. Tellsan had been encouraged by Volkswagen to invest in China to support its increased investment and, in particular, the joint venture with First Auto Works. Because the First Auto Works-Volkswagen business was doing poorly, STS had not achieved its performance objectives. In 1997 the venture lost close to $1.5 million, and 1998 did not look like it would be much better.

The joint venture with Shanrong epitomized the problems foreign companies often experienced when venturing with a local Chinese partner. While Tellsan had highly motivated shareholders in the United States with the clear objective of maximizing profits, it was often difficult for the Tellsan team to comprehend what was motivating Shanrong. Part of this was due to the multiple lines of authority that criss-crossed the Shanrong organization. While the Chinese National Automotive Industrial Corporation (CNAIC) assumed lead responsibility for all automobile assembly operations in China, including the First Auto Works, as a parts supplier, Shanrong was under the direction and influence of multiple bureaucracies including, but not limited to, the Liaoning provincial government and the provincial level authorities of the Ministry of Machinery Industry (MMI). The Liaoning provincial government's interest was in maximizing the contribution of the joint venture to the development of Liaoning province as a whole. In turn, MMI's provincial arm, the Chinese Heavy Machinery Bureau had responsibility for maximizing the growth and profitability of a broad range of machinery industries, of which steering assemblies was only one.

Wu Fan was the joint venture's Deputy General Manager. He was appointed at about the same time as Mark Hanson. Mr. Wu's hometown was Fushun, a sizeable town 60 kilometers east of Shenyang. Shenyang is Liaoning's largest city and the location of the provincial government. Mr. Wu was considered to be a promising manager with a strong future within the MMI. At 42, he was one of the oldest Chinese employees at the joint venture. As was typical of individuals his age in China, Wu was a victim of the Cultural Revolution. Because of his education and visibility, he had been forcibly sent to the countryside to be re-educated and work as a peasant for four years in the early 1970s. Trained as an engineer at China's prestigious Qinghua University, his work experience included serving as the Chief Engineer and Party Secretary at other MMI plants. Wu also held advisory positions within the planning department of the CNAIC and the State Science and Technology Commission. The latter organization was responsible for China's acquisition of foreign technologies.

Career paths for Shanrong executives involved advancing up the organizational ladder within MMI, often moving to larger manufacturing facilities within the same industrial sector or moving into management positions within the provincial level of the MMI or another bureaucracy. The factors that determined career advancement for Shanrong executives went well beyond the narrowly-focused merit-based criteria that Tellsan executives operated under. Guanxi, or connections, was an important factor affecting promotions in China's highly relationship-oriented society. Mr. Wu was known for having a particularly broad range of connections.

Mark Hanson was 34 years old and the second general manager in the joint venture. The first general manager was Steve Johnson, an American from Tellsan. Johnson had been quite effective in getting the plant built and production started. However, his relationship with Wu had been strained by various issues. In August, 1996 Johnson returned to Tellsan in the United States and was replaced by Hanson. Hanson had a master's degree from a well known Southwestern business school and had studied Chinese. Although not fluent, he understood enough to hold a basic conversation. After graduation in 1993, Hanson worked with a large automotive supplier before joining Tellsan in 1995.

QUALITY ISSUES AT STS

STS produced a steering wheel assembly for the new VW 2000 sedan widely sold in China. Quality standards had to be high for this precision part but, unfortunately, problems with quality control had plagued the joint venture from the very beginning. Production was falling further and further behind schedule, largely because of the high failure rate in the final inspection. The joint venture was not even close to achieving the same level of productivity as comparable plants in Toledo and Germany. Prior to July 1996, the Shenyang plant had been limited to assembling kits and had not attempted to manufacture component parts from raw materials. Now, STS was struggling to manufacture several precision components for the steering wheel assembly. For each component, the failure rate remained too high.

At a meeting in December 1997, Wu Fan made three recommendations to address the problem: 1) the quality standards could be lowered slightly; 2) additional line workers could be hired; and 3) the highest precision products could be manufactured during overtime work where management could be more discriminating in selecting the workers.

Hanson and Dietrich Werner, Tellsan's Director of Operations and Chief Engineer, did not believe any of the three options were viable long-term solutions because each failed to identify and address the fundamental problem. First, the quality standards at STS were no higher than those achieved at Tellsan's two other plants in Toledo and Germany. Moreover, to ensure quality components in China, VW had recently acquired suppliers of other precision components similar to the steering wheel assembly. If the quality at STS could not be improved, there was a real risk that VW would shift sourcing to one of STS's highly competent competitors, or begin producing the assembly itself.

Second, the ratio of line workers in Shenyang to the number of line workers in Germany and Toledo was 5:1 and 6:1, respectively. All three plants used comparable manufacturing equipment and processes. When forming the joint venture in 1995, Tellsan had agreed to keep on the payroll a much larger number of workers from Shanrong's existing plant than they needed. As far as Hanson and Werner were concerned, many, if not most, of STS's workers were already redundant.

Third, while using select high-quality workers on an overtime basis to produce critical components had been a strategy successfully employed by many Sino foreign joint ventures operating in China, STS management wanted to avoid what would be at best a temporary solution. Instead, Hanson and Werner decided to probe deeper to uncover the fundamental problem and find a solution. Upon close investigation, they found that the causes of the quality problem at STS were multiple and complex and were more deeply entrenched than STS executives had anticipated.

Despite all the work that Hanson, Weinrich, and Hanson's predecessor had done over the past three years, the sobering reality was that below the management level STS had a total absence of a quality control system, no notion of continuous improvement, and no comprehension of quality being more broad-based than testing end products and throwing the defective ones away. In one instance, Werner found that instead of regularly replacing contaminated chemical solutions with clean solution, the workers were simply reusing solution in order to conserve. In other instances, workers could be observed filing precision components manually to meet specifications. Particularly alarming was that there seemed to be no focus on prevention of problems. Quality control involves process control, statistical control, efforts to narrow deviations, and corrective action, all of which seemed to be missing. When a problem appeared, it was perceived to be a random idiosyncratic event and no effort was expended to determine the root cause.

Werner did not believe that technical and engineering skills were the problem: China has the best reverse engineers in the world. Give them the plans, specifications, tool designs and a step-by-step process sheet and they can manufacture virtually anything without the assistance of foreign engineers.

Werner described the cultural problems surrounding quality and lean production efforts: Our partner has a core group of managers assigned to work in the joint venture and these people make all the decisions. Lean manufacturing is an easy subject to discuss but it takes years of experience to implement. There is a physical side that is relatively easy to understand. There is a psychological side that is based on leadership and a willingness to empower teams to manage their own destiny. Lean manufacturing is based on assigning responsibility to lower levels of the organization. To the Chinese, this shatters their view of the world and the Confucian notion of hierarchy and orderliness. Decision-making in China happens at the top of the organization, not the bottom. Below the senior management level hardly anybody makes decisions. The Chinese view of hourly workers is that they make parts. They don't need to be thinking about safety and continuous improvement and quality; somebody else in the organization is responsible for that.

SUPPLIER SELECTION

Local content was a key element of China's automotive policy. Nevertheless, Hanson realized that the Chinese operating environment offered several challenges; and from the perspective of one of his colleagues, "the deck is stacked against us." First, the partner said that Tellsan could not use suppliers based in the United States. Then, Shanrong began exerting pressure on Tellsan to select suppliers from firms in Shanrong's network. The longer Hanson spent in China, the more he realized how important networks were to Chinese organizations and how impenetrable they could appear to non-Chinese. Shanrong was involved in several other joint ventures and made it clear that it expected these joint ventures would become STS suppliers. In one case, Shanrong wanted Shen-Tech, a joint venture between Shanrong and a German firm, to be a key supplier for STS. After six weeks of extensive reviewing, Tellsan concluded that Shen-Tech was not qualified to get the business. Another firm was selected as the supplier. However, Shanrong was determined that Shen-Tech would get the business. Land for Shen-Tech's expansion had been acquired across from the STS plant site. In September 1997, a review was held with the government so that Tellsan could try to disqualify Shen-Tech as a supplier. Tellsan offered Shen-Tech part of the business but the offer was refused. The issue remained undecided.

In another case, Shanrong's choice of a supplier for a critical rotary part did not pass the quality review. The supplier's management then suggested that the specifications could be changed. Not surprisingly, Hanson said no. Next, the firm called a meeting and announced a recovery plan that would allow them to meet the quality standards. To the two Tellsan managers at the meeting, it was clear that the supplier was hoping for a miracle. Hanson said no again. Other Shanrong suppliers were expanding with the hope of getting STS business, even though these firms had not gone through the quality assurance process. Shanrong had analyzed its strategic objectives for STS and came up with a list of components that it funneled to its supplier base, without any input from Tellsan.

Hanson explained some further concerns: We have had, and continue to have, a whole lot of detailed questions from the Liaoning government and the other people reviewing this. The problem is that they don't understand the scope or the business challenges. They have been soured by other joint venture experiences and want this joint venture to be a showcase. They were more interested in the facade on the STS administration building—they had artist renderings that look like Las Vegas hotels. They knew they would be parading politicians through and making this a technology showcase.

Our partner agrees that we have to have quality components. But, if it comes down to the wire and there are two suppliers with equal quality and Shanrong's supplier is 5% higher, we know who will get the business. We have agreed that we will help improve China's supplier base, so we know that we will have to balance what we said we would do with our financing plan.

We have some leverage because we are sticking to the objectives of the deal. We are not going to budge off that. We are trying to make it clear to our partner that you guys need to realize that you are not an export player. You have a huge stigma regarding quality. You can make almost anything but it is going to fall apart in two days. Moreover, now that we have been designated a "trusted company" with the Customs Administration, we can expedite the processing of component parts through Customs and save some inventory costs and shipping time there. Although we have noticed that the duties on a select range of our imported components have been gradually inching upward.

We are also in the middle of what has been a lengthy negotiation with the Ministry of Foreign Trade and Economic Cooperation (MOFTEC) to establish our own import-export corporation. Once in-house, this could save us the 1½% commission that we currently pay the Chinese Heavy Machinery Bureau's foreign trade corporation every time we import or export a part. It's hard to tell the politicians from the people who run the plants. I took a team of six Tellsan executives on some supplier visits. On one of the plane trips we had a representative from China's

Heavy Machinery Bureau with us. We had a reception and sitting at the table, each with their own interpreter, was the Heavy Machinery representative and a project manager from the MMI. Also present were representatives from the provincial divisions of the State Science and Technology Commission, State Planning Commission, and the Liaoning Customs Administration. They talked candidly about the planned economy and how they were trying to change.

TRAINING

The joint venture agreement specified that joint venture employees would receive various types of training and that Tellsan would participate in the process, both in China and in the United States. But the training efforts were getting bogged down in numerous delays involving arguments over the selection of candidates for the training, costs, problems with travel documents, etc.

We are trying to use the best systems Tellsan has and shoot for very high standards. We do not want to compromise just because this is China. But we are having lots of problems with our partner. The joint venture agreement says that Tellsan will assist in training STS employees and the joint venture will be required to pay its fair share of the costs. Recently, we had two engineers scheduled to go to Toledo. Three days before they were supposed to leave, we found out they had no visas. Shanrong was supposed to have applied for visas weeks ago. We had to shorten the training period and the only reason we got the visas was because the embassy did us a favor. So far, the three trips we have planned for STS Chinese employees have run into travel problems with travel documents that we have had to fix. Each time we are assured by Shanrong that it won't happen again and each time it does. We have one guy who has told us he does not to expect to work since he is in the Communist Party.

Also, if STS suppliers have to be trained by Tellsan, Tellsan's view is that STS should pay for the training, not Tellsan. Because of the disagreements about the responsibility for startup costs for the previous two months, we, meaning Tellsan, have instituted a policy of getting a written agreement from our partner before spending any training money. Unfortunately, the policy is solving few disagreements, and only slowing things down because Shanrong managers are reluctant to sign any agreements.

STS AND TELLSAN HEADQUARTERS

Just before he went on vacation, Hanson had a long conversation with Jack Pitfield, his boss in Toledo, Ohio. They discussed a variety of different issues and as the conversation went on, Pitfield expressed frustration with the pace of change in the joint venture.

Pitfield: Mark, you have been telling me about these problems for a year-and-a-half but nothing seems to get resolved. What is the problem?

Hanson: Well, Jack, this is China and things move a bit more slowly than in the States.

Pitfield: I have been hearing that "this is China" ever since we first decided to get involved in the joint venture. Now that the business is up and running, and we have a 60% share in the business, I expect you to make some decisions to get things under control. Maybe our partner will not be too crazy about some of these decisions, but you need to empahsize that we are the majority owner and for some things, we are going to do it the Tellsan way.

Hanson: It is not that easy. My predecessor did that once and it took us over a year to get the relationship back to what it was.

Pitfield: If we can't use our majority ownership position, why do we have it? I just came back from our German joint venture and I can assure you that we certainly take advantage of our majority position. Why, just last week our partner wanted to . . .

With that, the line went dead, "Perhaps fortunately," thought Hanson. "All I need is another lecture about how our German joint venture works like clockwork and STS is a disaster. Pitfield just does not understand what we are up against here. If we use our majority position and outvote our partner, we will kill this relationship."

WHAT NEXT?

Hanson explained some of the issues surrounding the partner relationship:

Every single issue with our partners involves a protracted negotiation. If we say ten, they will say five. It doesn't matter whether the issue is significant or not. If we say let's do "Y" because "Y" makes sense, they will challenge us. It is as if they must leave a meeting with a lower number than we proposed, even if our first number was the right one. When we go to meetings we talk for two hours to see who will turn the lights on. Often we will agree on something on Monday, and then on Tuesday they will deny that we had an agreement. They will even sign off on an issue and then want to renegotiate. Or, they will keep delaying until it is too late to do what we want to do and we have to do it their way. Even minor decisions require senior management approval. There is a tremendous unwillingness for anybody in our partnership to accept risk. When I try to explain to Pitfield and other people in the United States why things are moving slowly, they just say, "What is the problem—make a decision!"

We are not doing business just with Shanrong. Nobody there has the power to make decisions. We get frustrated and then we realize that we are really doing business with China, Inc.

I am used to following a system and being evaluated on performance. Our partner gets assessed on relationship-building. There are certain objective steps that must be followed to achieve an outcome. Our partner finds the objective steps very difficult to understand.

We are dealing with talented people in Shanrong. The top people assigned to the STS project are the best they have. Unfortunately, when you get below these people the talent leaves a lot to be desired. The depth of management is a function of relationships. And the senior people don't know how to delegate. As a result, lots of things fall through the cracks. When things go wrong, we are not sure whether our partner is deliberately trying to mess things up, or they genuinely don't know how to get things done but won't tell us because they would lose face.

HANSON'S DILEMMA

Hanson glanced across the bare concrete floor of the spartan room and saw Dietrich Werner busy at his desk. Despite outside temperatures in the upper 20s, without any prior notice, the heat in the plant and administrative offices had been turned off by the Ministry of Energy in order to conserve electricity. Since typing on the computer was almost impossible wearing gloves, all the managers and staff had cut off the fingertips of their gloves so that they could type and still keep the remainder of their hands warm. Conditions were even colder at the other end of the factory where the Shanrong managers' offices were located, because that part of the factory had virtually no insulation.

As Hanson sorted through the mass of paper that had accumulated in his absence, he decided that the first thing to do was to establish some priorities. The problem was where to start. What were the most critical problems? Pitfield expected action, quickly, but Hanson knew that as far as Shanrong was concerned, the most pressing problem was that workers were beginning to grumble about rumors of layoffs. Without reducing headcount and solving the quality problem and getting quality suppliers, the joint venture had a grim future. To make matters worse, Mr. Wu had just told Hanson that the municipal government was planning a new highway that might require STS to give up some land or even move the factory. In contrast to Hanson's uncertainty and concerns, Mr. Wu not only did not share his opinion, he was proposing a very expensive banquet to celebrate four years of the special relationship between Shanrong and Tellsan. "How," Hanson wondered, "can I convince my partner that the problems at STS are serious and the future of the joint venture is far from certain?"

Part 3 Integrating Case 2

Enersis: Global Strategy in the Electric Power Sector

INTRODUCTION

Enersis, the Chilean multinational electricity company, has grown into a $US 3.7 billion (market capitalization) leader in the South American market by December of 1997. Beginning as the privatized version of the Santiago regional power distribution company, Enersis has become a true multinational, with major operating subsidiaries in Argentina, Peru, Brazil, and Colombia, along with those in Chile.

As the company prepares for the next century, conditions are either opportune for additional growth and profitability, or threatening with the possible arrival of major multinational electric companies from North America and Europe in the region. As the process of privatization of the sector proceeds throughout Latin America, Enersis is encountering increasing challenges from companies such as EDF (France), AES (US) and Iberdrola (Spain). Mr. Pablo Ihnen, CEO of Enersis, has a clear vision of the need for Enersis to expand through the region and to build a portfolio of businesses around the core electric generation and distribution activities.

At the same time that Enersis is exploring expansion opportunities abroad, the company is experiencing limitations on its ability to expand at home. As the largest electric power company in Chile, Enersis is always under public scrutiny for its pricing, service quality, and environmental protection issues. As one of the largest companies in the country, Enersis again is subject to constant public discussion. This reality makes it difficult for the company to pursue expansion activities in Chile, though recently Enersis did bail out a failing water utility (Lo Castillo), and other power generation projects have been started (such as a natural gas-powered plant in Atacama in northern Chile[1]).

Perhaps the greatest limitation on growth in the domestic market is its size; Chile's population of 14 million people is already fairly well supplied with hydro-electric power and some coal/gas thermo-electric power. The limit to domestic growth is very relative, however. In North American terms, the economic growth rate of Chile at more than 6% annually, with power needs at least matching that rate, is fairly attractive. Still, the need for increased electric power supply within Chile is expected to grow less rapidly than the demand elsewhere in Latin America.

Total capital investment in power generation in Latin America has been growing at a value of about $US 10 billion per year during the 1990s. Chile's investment in power generation has grown at about $US 600 million per year during that time, and appears likely to continue at this rate for the next five years. As Enersis expands in the rest of the region, capital investment needs are growing almost exponentially. Exhibit 1 depicts this environment.

If privatizations of state-owned power generation and distribution companies continue on the current path, the need for capital investment is expected to reach $US 100 billion over the course of the next five years. To continue its role as the largest, highly profitable private power company in the region, Enersis needs a huge amount of additional financial resources.

The global (or regional) strategy being developed by Enersis was simply unthinkable only ten years ago. With the Latin American region in the late stages of an enormous external debt crisis and prolonged recession, the economic conditions were singularly unfavorable. The electric power industry at that time was almost entirely government-owned throughout Latin America. Chile was the first country in the region to privatize both the electric power generation industry and also the electricity distribution industry.

In December of 1997, as the leaders of Enersis considered the whirlwind process that had led the company to its current level of activities and internationalization, they realized that the process could not stop now. The competition in electric power generation was heating up in Brazil, in Colombia, and in other target markets for Enersis. The possible entry of foreign power providers was very real, and even in Chile competition was possible from providers in Argentina and Brazil. The distribution business was less subject to market entry, since all countries in the region had non-overlapping power grids, and thus new entrants would have to build an entire infrastructure to compete. Nevertheless, even in distribution Enersis wanted to compete with other firms to buy privatizing companies in South America, and the bidding was often cutthroat. Mr. Ihnen and other Enersis top managers began to wonder if the process that they had begun was really sustainable.

In addition to the competitive pressures, Enersis felt constrained by the government of Chile, which was very concerned about the monopoly power held by the company. With Enersis' 47% share in electric power generation and 45% share of electricity distribution in Chile, this was a very real concern. Thus far, Enersis had avoided any anti-trust violations, but the risk of becoming subject to a complicated investigation was significant.

BACKGROUND ON ENERSIS

Enersis is the Chilean energy company that was formed from the dismantling of the Compañia Chilena de Electricidad in 1981. In that year three new companies were formed, including: the Compañia Chilena de Generacion de Electricidad, Chilgener; the Compañia Chilena Metropolitana de Distribucion Electrica, Chilectra; and the Compañia de Electricidad de la Quinta Region, Chilquinta. These new companies were then privatized in 1987 in separate auctions.

The new owners of Chilectra included Chilean pension funds, company employees, institutional investors, and thousands of small shareholders. In 1988 the company changed its name to Enersis, which was structured to operate as a hold-

Exhibit 1
Installed Capacity
(MW)

	1998	1999	2000	2001	2002	2003	% participation
Argentina	20,799	22,284	23,875	25,579	27,406	29,362	13
Bolivia	877	939	1,007	1,078	1,155	1,238	1
Brazil	61,591	65,988	70,700	75,748	81,156	86,950	37
Chile	6,712	7,191	7,705	8,255	8,845	9,476	4
Colombia	11,287	12,093	12,956	13,881	14,872	15,934	7
Ecuador	2,934	3,143	3,368	3,608	3,866	4,142	2
México	36,997	39,638	42,469	45,501	48,750	52,230	22
Perú	6,795	4,066	4,356	4,667	5,001	5,538	2
Venezuela	20,225	21,669	23,216	24,874	26,650	28,553	12
TOTAL	**165,216**	**177,012**	**189,651**	**203,192**	**217,700**	**233,244**	

ing company. The principal operating subsidiary of Enersis was and is Chilectra, which is the main electricity distribution company in Santiago, the capital of Chile.

Soon after the privatization, Enersis began to move aggressively into a diversification program, mainly in other electricity-related activities. A major shareholding in Endesa, the largest electric power generating company in Chile was taken in 1990. Today Enersis owns 25% of Endesa, and is the largest single shareholder. A computer equipment and services subsidiary, Synapsis, was established to provide these services to the Enersis group. Manso de Velasco, a real estate and construction company, was acquired to be the main vehicle for buying land and building facilities for both Endesa and Chilectra throughout the country. The company's organization chart appears in Exhibit 2. The various operating companies are described in the next section.

Enersis in 1997 has become the largest privately-owned electric power generation and distribution company in Latin America. The company has operations that it manages in Chile, Argentina, Brazil, Colombia, and Peru. While focused principally on the electric power sector, Enersis is also active in real estate ventures through its subsidiary, Manso de Velasco.

To finance its growth, Enersis sold shares in the Chilean stock exchange, borrowed domestically and internationally, and sold ADRs in the US market, bringing its total financial structure in 1996 to 75% equity/25% debt, and a total asset value of $US 9.736 billion—December 1996. The distribution of shareholdings is shown in Exhibit 3.

OPERATING COMPANIES AND AFFILIATES

The initial business of Enersis, and still its single largest activity, is electricity distribution in the Santiago region of Chile through the operating company *Chilectra*. Chilectra Metropolitana was created in 1981 as part of the dismantling of the Compañia Chilena de Electricidad. In 1985 the company was placed into a privatization process, which resulted in Chilectra being 100% privately owned by 1987. The name of the overall company, as previously noted, was changed to Enersis in 1988, and Chilectra became its main distribution subsidiary.

Exhibit 2 Enersis

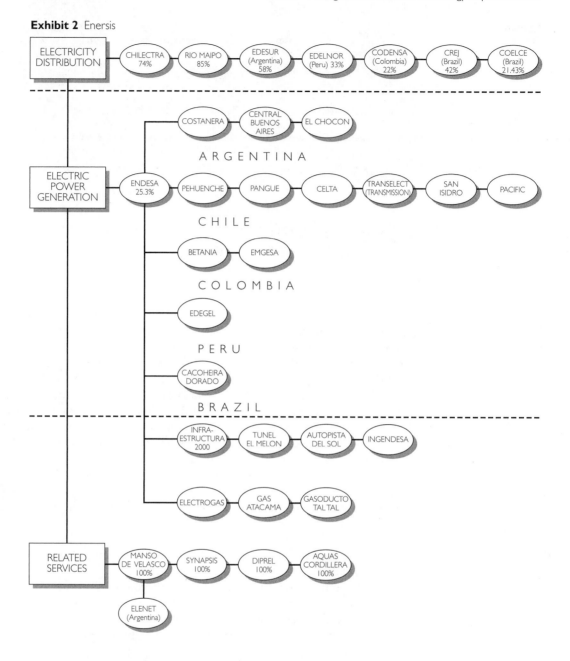

Chilectra today is owned 74% by Enersis and the rest by individual and institutional shareholders through the Chilean stock exchange. Exhibit 4 shows the distribution of ownership of Chilectra, and demonstrates that this affiliate of Enersis has its own international capital structure, with ADRs issued in New York and a broad base of ownership among pension funds, foreign investment funds, and individual shareholders

Chilectra purchases most of its electric power from domestic generating companies, led by Endesa (which also belongs to Enersis). Endesa provided 30.1% of Chilectra's electricity in 1997, followed by Chilgener with 24.1%, Pehuenche with 16.9%, Pangue with 14%, Colbun with 10.6%, and others with 4.3%. This portfolio

Exhibit 3
Ownership of Enersis,
December 1997

Shareholder	Number of Shareholders	Number of Shares	%
Pension Funds	13	2,164,892,601	31.84
Employee Companies	5	1,981,587,840	29.16
ADRs	1	1,132,239,300	16.65
Foreign Equity Funds	19	150,909,038	2.20
Other Shareholders	13,153	1,370,371,221	20.15
TOTAL	**13,191**	**6,800,000,000**	**100.00%**

Source: Enersis Annual Report, 1997.

Exhibit 4
Percent Ownership by
Major Shareholder

Main Shareholders	% Dec. 97
Enersis S.A.	74.12
Morgan G.T.C. (A.D.S.)	11.35
Deposito Central de Valores (Dcv)	3.44
Stockbrokers, Insurance Companies, Mutual Funds	2.66
Foreign Funds	2.41
Others	6.02
Total Shares (11,051 Shareholders)	**100.00**

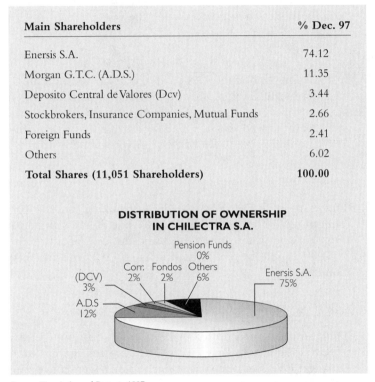

Source: Enersis Annual Report, 1997.

of energy sources is expected to shift with the arrival of imported natural gas from Argentina. The natural gas will replace some of the Chilean system's use of coal for thermoelectric power generation.

RIO MAIPO

Rio Maipo is Enersis' second largest distribution system in Chile. This company was created from a division of Chilectra, with the goal of serving the Maipo Valley region. After sale of shares on the stock exchange, Enersis maintains 85% ownership of Rio Maipo.

Rio Maipo had approximately 255,000 customers at yearend 1997 and sold about 955 GWh of power during the year.

EDESUR (ARGENTINA)

Electricidad del Sur (Edesur) is the power distribution company for the southern half of the city of Buenos Aires, Argentina. Initially, in 1992, Enersis purchased 20% of the shares of Edesur in the privatization process. In 1995 Enersis purchased another 39% of Edesur, such that today Enersis holds 59% of the outstanding shares. As with the other distribution and generation companies, Enersis holds a majority of seats on the board of directors of Edesur, and thus is assured management control of the firm.

In 1997 Edesur had approximately 2,042,000 customers in the Buenos Aires region, producing revenues of about $US 66.9 million for the year. Edesur distributed 11,160 GWh of power during the year.

EDELNOR (PERU)

In 1994 Enersis bought 33% of the Peruvian firm, Empresa de Distribucion Electrica del Norte, Edelnor, in a public auction. This investment gave Enersis control of the firm and the right to place a majority of directors on Edelnor's board.

Edelnor served about 805,000 customers in the northern district of Lima in 1997 and sold 3,256 GWh of electricity during the year.

AGUAS CORDILLERA

This company is the main provider of drinking water and also of wastewater treatment in several districts of Santiago, Chile. Aguas Cordillera produces and distributes drinking water, and collects and disposes of wastewater, for a population of 310,000 people in the communities of Lo Barnechea, Vitacura, and part of Las Condes.

COMPAÑIA ELECTRICA DE RIO DE JANEIRO (CERJ-BRASIL)

This company was acquired in 1996, and it distributes electricity through the state of Rio de Janeiro in Brazil. CERJ had 4.4 million customers at the end of 1997. During 1997, after one year under the management of Enersis, CERJ sold 6,424 GWh of electric power, 12% more than in the previous year. Energy losses were reduced by 4 percentage points, remaining at 25.3% at yearend 1997. CERJ had 1,340,573 clients at the end of the year, growth of 10.1% over the previous year.

DISTRIBUIDORA DE PRODUCTOS ELECTRICOS SA (DIPREL)

The main business of Diprel is distribution and marketing of materials, products, and large-scale equipment to electric power companies. Since its creation in 1989, Diprel has followed a path of diversification of its products. In addition to equipment and materials for electric companies, Diprel now distributes similar products for construction, mining, and other industrial companies.

Dipres has been successful in penetrating the Chilean market through establishment of a major network of sales offices. The company is also developing a network of representatives throughout the rest of Latin America.

Exhibit 5
Installed Electric Power
Capacity in Chile

	Capacity (MW)				Production (GWH)		
	Endesa	Total	% Endesa		Endesa	Total	%
SIC	2,641	4,594	57.5	SIC	12,868	22,421	57.4
SING	97	1,131	8.6	SING	30	5,545	0.5
TOTAL	**2,738**	**5,725**	**47.8**	**TOTAL**	**12,898**	**27,996**	**46.1**

Source: Endesa Annual Report, 1996.

CODENSA (COLOMBIA)

Codensa distributes electricity to 1,536,035 clients in the city of Bogota; this constitutes about 24% of the entire country. The volume of power sold during 1997 was 7,929 GWh, with an energy loss of 23.8%.

CENTRAL HIDROELECTICA DE BETANIA (COLOMBIA)

This was Enersis' first investment in Colombia, in 1996. Betania has an installed capacity of 540 MW, and in 1997 generated 2,070 GWh.

EMGESA (COLOMBIA)

Emgesa is the largest electric power generating company in Colombia. It has eight generating plants with a total of 2,458 MW of capacity. Emgesa produced 11,200 GWh of power during 1997.

ENDESA (CHILE)

The Empresa Nacional de Electricidad, S.A., *Endesa*, is the main electric power generating company in Chile. The government sold partial ownership to the private sector in 1989, when Enersis bought a 5% interest. Subsequently, additional share purchases have given Enersis a 25.3% holding in Endesa by 1995, and the right to place a majority of directors on Endesa's board. Endesa is now reported as a consolidated affiliate of Enersis on the holding company's books.

Endesa's main business is the generation of electric power, which it then transmits mainly through the Central Interconnected System (SIC). In addition, Endesa participates in the generating system in the northern part of the country as a part owner and operator of the Interconnected System of Norte Grande (SING). Exhibit 5 describes the production of electricity in Chile in 1996 and Endesa's role in it.

An interesting twist to Endesa's leadership in the Chilean power generation market is that it utilizes mainly hydroelectric power sources (i.e., rivers coming down from the Andes mountains). In the mid-1990s, Chile experienced a prolonged drought, which reduced the generating capacity of the hydroelectric plants and caused the country to become more dependent on thermoelectric power (from coal, oil, or natural gas). This drought caused Endesa to lose market share, since competitors were more able to deliver thermoelectric power during this time. Paradoxically, Endesa enjoys a major cost advantage when weather conditions are normal, since hydro power costs approximately one-tenth as much as thermo power to generate.

Endesa made its first foreign investment in Argentina in 1992, where it purchased the power plant, Central Costanera. With three plants operating in 1996, Endesa produced 9,513 GWh of electricity, constituting about 16% of total Argentine production.

In 1995 Endesa invested in Peru, buying 60% of the Empresa de Generacion Electrica de Lima, Edegel. Edegel has installed capacity of 689 MW of electricity, representing about 24% of total installed capacity in Peru. In 1995 Edegel produced about 2,650 GWh of electricity.

INGENIERIA E INMOBILIARIA MANSO DE VELASCO

One of the key activities in generating and distributing electric power is the construction of power plants, transmission lines, and connections to users. While plant construction is contracted out to major construction firms, the engineering and construction of electric distribution lines and links was originally carried out within Chilectra. This last activity in 1988 was placed into the wholly-owned subsidiary, Manso de Velasco.

Manso de Velasco continues to be the engineering and construction firm used by Chilectra for constructing electricity distribution facilities. In addition, Manso de Velasco has contracted to offer services to a wide range of outside users, such as constructing lighting and power facilities for the Santiago metro system and also installing lighting for public parks and gardens in the city.

SYNAPSIS

Enersis has extensive activity in information technology to operate its power generation and distribution businesses. This activity has been placed into the subsidiary, Synapsis, which in addition sells information technology services to outside clients.

Financial statements for Enersis and each of the major subsidiaries are presented in the Appendix.

THE CHILEAN CONTEXT

Chile is one of the most industrialized countries in Latin America. With a per capita income of over $US 3000 per year, Chile ranks at the top of the Latin American region. Its population is highly educated, with adult illiteracy at just 5 percent of the population. The country has embraced a free-market capitalist economic model since the overthrow of the Marxist regime of Salvador Allende in 1973. Initially under the military regime of Augusto Pinochet, Chile began to liberalize its economy long before this policy framework became popular in the region. The 'Chicago Boys' trained by University of Chicago free-market economists such as Arnold Harberger and Milton Friedman followed a highly successful set of policies to reduce barriers to competition and to stimulate investment. Tariffs were gradually lowered to a uniform 10% ad valorem by 1976, the least restrictive in Latin America. The door was opened to foreign direct investment in 1976, when Chile withdrew from the protectionist Andean Pact integration group and implemented its own liberal foreign investment regime.

The results of this economic opening in the 1970s were clearly very positive. To a certain extent they were assisted unintentionally by the rise in raw materials prices that accompanied the oil crises. Chile's main export product has long been copper, and copper prices rose dramatically in the late 1970s. This alone produced solid economic growth in the country during those years. When oil and other raw materials prices dropped in the early 1980s, and when the foreign debt crisis hit the region in 1982, Chile unfortunately was dragged down as well, and it took several years until the economy rebounded. In comparison with other Latin American countries, however, Chile did pull out of the crisis more rapidly. By 1986 GDP was growing by a positive 6 ½% per year, and this continued through the rest of the decade. In the early 1990s Chile's economy remained near the top of the Latin American list, with an average growth rate of 7.4% per year.

Chile's government began in the 1970s a process of *privatization*, or sell-off of state-owned companies, that has been followed in various degrees throughout the rest of Latin America in the late 1980s and 1990s. At a time when the economic model of import-substituting industrialization was widely followed in the region, Chile turned its back to that view and aggressively began a process of open markets and export-led growth. Since the government participated in the economy as owner of well over half of industry, a major step to opening markets was the denationalization of companies. This was begun with the sale of Compañía de Cervecerías Unidas (beer), Cemento Melón (cement) and Celulosa Arauco (paper) in the late 1970s, and with subsequent sales of electric power, telephone, airline, and other government-owned businesses in the 1980s.

In the 1990s the Chilean model uses the government as regulator and overseer of the economy, much as in the industrial countries of Europe and North America—with a few key exceptions such as the national copper company, Codelco, which still remains in state hands.

Interestingly, there has been a very considerable consensus in Chile on the free-market economic policies that have been followed. This policy framework was closely associated with the Pinochet military regime, which, as any such government, was criticized for being authoritarian. Without debating that issue, it can be concluded that the Pinochet regime did indeed strongly support the open-market policy framework, and consistently maintained it through economic booms and recessions. When Pinochet stepped down as President in 1988, the elected government of Patricio Alwyn continued the economic policy framework, as have subsequent Chilean governments. The result was an economic performance (e.g., growth, inflation, balance of payments) superior to all other countries in Latin America from 1975–1995.

RECENT HISTORY OF CHILE'S ELECTRICITY SECTOR

The electric power sector in Chile is divided into three stages: generation, transmission, and distribution. The generation sector consists of companies that generate electricity from hydroelectric and thermal electric sources and sell their production to distribution companies, other regulated and unregulated customers, and to other generation companies. The transmission sector consists of companies that transmit high-voltage electricity from the generating companies. These companies are all subsidiaries of the main generation and distribution companies. Distribution companies purchase electricity from generating companies at the nodes of the country-wide system, typically at low voltage (23 kV or less), and then distribute it for sale to the public. Each of these segments is privately owned, with government regulation on pricing and oversight on service quality. Exhibit 6 describes the system.

The national electricity industry is divided into two large geographic grids, the Central Interconnected System (SIC) and the Interconnected System of Norte Grande (SING). In addition there are several other systems, including systems

Exhibit 6 Stages in the Electric Power System

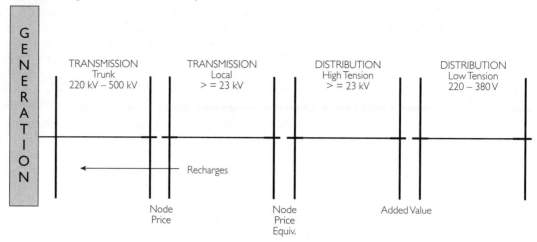

owned and operated by individual industrial companies (e.g., copper companies) for their own use, typically in remote areas.

As discussed above, Endesa dominates power generation in Chile, with approximately a 50% market share. Endesa owns and operates 16 power plants connected to the SIC and another three power plants connected to the SING.

At the level of distribution, there are eight major companies and several smaller ones. Their characteristics are described in Exhibit 7.

Chilectra and Rio Maipo are both part of the SIC network, which provides power to Santiago and to about 90% of Chile's total population.

LEGAL FRAMEWORK

Chile's electricity law essentially allows private ownership of all stages of electric power production and distribution, with public-sector regulation and price controls. The National Electricity Commission (CNE) sets prices and plans expansion of the system. The SEF sets and enforces technical standards for the system. And finally, the Ministry of Economy has final authority over electricity prices, and it regulates the granting of concessions to electric generation, transmission, and distribution companies.

Probably one of the key continuing problems faced by Enersis was the complex system of price controls placed on the electricity sector. Negotiation of prices of power generation for sales to distributors and of power distribution for sale to final customers takes place on a four-year cycle, and in general prices fall behind costs by the end of each cycle. Endesa and Chilectra regularly seek to keep their output prices in a profitable range, but the negotiation process often is drawn out and leads to periods of very low profit.

The electricity law seeks to provide objective criteria for electricity pricing and resource allocation. The regulatory system is designed to provide a competitive rate of return on investments in order to stimulate private investment, while ensuring electricity to all who request it. Under the law, companies engaged in electric power generation must coordinate their activities through the association of power suppliers, CDEC (Centro de Despacho Economico de Carga), for either the SIC

Exhibit 7
Distribution of
Electricity in Chile
by Company

Company	Number of Customers	%	Sales GWH	%
Chilectra (ENERSIS)	1,099	36	6,676	50
CGE	498	16	1,918	15
Chilquinta	335	11	1,122	9
Rio Maipo (ENERSIS)	230	7	763	6
Saesa (COPEC)	319	10	939	7
Emec	151	5	426	3
Frontel (COPEC)	149	5	336	3
Emel	130	4	169	1
others	170	6	759	6
TOTAL	**3,081**	**100**	**13,108**	**100**

Source: Comision Nacional de Energia, 1995.

or the SING, to minimize the operating costs of the electric system. Generation companies meet their contractual sales requirements with power that they either generate themselves or buy on the open market. Because Endesa's production in the SIC is primarily hydroelectric, its marginal cost of production is generally the lowest in the system, and therefore Endesa generates most of the power it sells there. Generation companies have to balance their contractual obligations with their delivery of power by buying any needed electricity at the spot market price, which is set hourly by the CDEC based on the marginal cost of production of the last generation facility utilized.

The main purpose of the two CDECs in operating the power assignment system is to ensure that only the most efficiently-produced electricity reaches customers. The CDECs also seek to ensure that every generation company has enough installed capacity to produce the electricity needed by its customers. Sales of electric power may be made through short-term or long-term contracts, or between generation companies, in the spot market. Generation companies may also contract to deliver power among themselves at negotiated prices. Generation companies are free to determine whether and with whom to contract, the duration of contracts, and the amount of electricity to be sold.

Sales of electricity to distribution companies for resale to regulated customers (customers with demand for capacity less than or equal to 2 megawatts) must be made at the node prices then in effect at the relevant locations or 'nodes' on the interconnected system. Two node prices are paid by distribution companies: node prices for capacity and node prices for energy consumption. Node prices for capacity are calculated based on the annual cost of installing a new diesel fuel gas turbine generation facility. Node prices for energy are calculated based on the projected short-term marginal cost of satisfying the demand for energy at a given point in the interconnected system, quarterly during the succeeding 48 months in the SIC and monthly during the succeeding 24 months in the SING. To calculate the marginal costs a formula is used that takes into account 10-year projections of the principal variables in the cost of energy such as water reservoir levels, fuel costs for thermoelectric power, maintenance, demand levels, etc.

A generation company may need to purchase or sell energy or capacity in the spot market at any time depending on its contractual requirements in relation to the amount of electricity that it is able to produce. These purchases and sales are transacted at the 'spot marginal cost' of the interconnected system, which is the marginal cost of the last generation facility to be dispatched.

Energy supply prices are unregulated for final customers with a connected capacity greater than 2 MW (referred to as 'large customers'), for temporary customers, and for customers that have special quality requirements. Customers not subject to regulated prices may negotiate prices freely with distribution and/or generation companies. All other customers are subject to the maximum prices established by the tariffs.

As far as electric power *distribution* is concerned, tariffs are established to allow distribution companies to recover their costs of operation, including allowed losses, and a return on investment. The operational costs include: selling, general and administrative costs of distribution; maintenance and operating costs of distribution assets; cost of energy and capacity losses; and and expected return on investment of 10% per year in real terms including the cost of renewing all the facilities and physical assets used to provide the distribution services, including interest costs, intangible assets and working capital. The various costs are based on an average of those incurred by electricity distribution companies. operating in Chile. Thus, more efficient companies may earn more than 10% returns, and less efficient ones less.

KEY COMPETITORS IN CHILE

The main competitor in Chile is most importantly Chilgener. Chilgener is a major competitor in power generation, with thermoelectric plants in Santiago, Valparaiso, and in Copaipo. In addition, Chilgener owns several electricity distribution companies operating in both the central and the northern power grids. Chilgener consistently bids for electric power projects in Chile and elsewhere in Latin America (especially Argentina) against Chilectra and Endesa. In a highly-publicized recent duel for construction of a natural gas pipeline between Argentina and Chile, a consortium led by Chilgener beat Enersis and gained a major new power source. Other smaller electric companies such as Chilquinta also compete domestically and abroad with Enersis.

Separate from the two major electric distribution grids, the electric companies serve 'non-regulated clients', which are large-volume electricity users that are permitted to buy electricity directly from generating companies. The non-regulated clients are customers that use more than ^{2} megawatts hours of power—typically large industrial companies such as copper mines.

GLOBAL STRATEGY AT ENERSIS

According to company documents, "The Company's business strategy is to use its accumulated utility experience and expertise to improve the profitability of its existing electric distribution and generation businesses in Chile, Argentina, Peru, Brasil, and Colombia, and to enhance the value of other businesses it may acquire in Latin America. The Company believes it has proven expertise in managing privatized utilities, including experience in reducing energy losses of distribution businesses, constructing and operating generation facilities, implementing proprietary billing and accounts receivable management systems, improving labor relations, increasing work force productivity, streamlining information systems, and operating under tariff and regulatory frameworks that reward efficient operations."

Following this broad statement in 1995, Enersis has continued to expand its activities in Latin America with the purchase of controlling interest in the Rio de Janeiro power distribution company, CERJ, and the Colombian power generation company, Betania. In addition, the company has diversified more widely in Chile, with the purchase of the water utility Lo Castillo in Santiago in 1996 and various real estate activities through the Endesa subsidiary, Infraestructura 2000.

STRATEGIC ALLIANCES OF ENERSIS

Enersis has used strategic alliances frequently in its short history. When building the information systems part of its business, Enersis formed Synapsis as a joint venture with Unisys Corporation of the United States. After three years of operation, Enersis bought the partner's interest and now runs Synapsis as a wholly owned subsidiary.

In overseas ventures Enersis has worked exclusively with local partners in each country, as well as with other foreign investors on some occasions. For its initial foray into Argentina, a joint venture (Distrilec) was formed with Perez Companq (a large Argentine conglomerate) and PSI (from the U.S.) to own the power distribution company, Edesur. Likewise, when entering Peru to buy the power generation company, Edelnor, the company formed a joint venture with Endesa of Spain, Compañia Peruana de Electricidad, and Banco del Credito del Peru. Subsequently, when bidding for and winning the ownership of CERJ in Brazil, Enersis formed a joint venture with Endesa (Spain) and Electricidad de Portugal. No Brazilian partner participated in the consortium with Enersis on this occasion, but the consortium itself has Electrobras as a local partner in the total shareholding of CERJ. For capital and technology resources, Enersis has found the Spanish electric company, Endesa, to be a valuable partner in these and other projects.

As a policy, Enersis management asserts that strategic alliance partners will continue to be sought in each foreign venture undertaken, to assure knowledge of the local market and treatment as a local (at least partly local) company. The bias against foreign companies is particularly strong in Enersis' situation, for example, because Argentine companies and government agencies often view Chilean firms as smaller, less capable competitors, and because Peruvian companies and government agencies often view Chilean firms as antagonists, given the history of conflicts between the two countries. To defuse some of this opposition, in addition to gaining local market knowledge, Enersis will continue to work with local partners in future Latin American ventures.

Even as Enersis continues to actively use strategic alliances in its international ventures, the company maintains a clear policy of seeking to exert the highest possible degree of managerial influence in the businesses undertaken. It always follows an intention of long-term ownership, and generally obtains majority control of the board of directors (i.e., operational control) of affiliates.

DIVERSIFICATION STRATEGY

Enersis management has defined the strategy of the firm to be focused on the electric power industry and on related activities. These related activities began with the establishment of a subsidiary for information technology and one for real estate and construction activities. Since that time, additional activities have largely fallen into the categories of electric power generation and distribution outside of Chile and diversification into other sectors inside Chile. In 1996 the water company, Lo Castillo, was purchased. This move was justified as a step into additional infrastructure that accompanies electric power. In fact much of the distribution and physical facilities' construction are quite similar between the two businesses, so the diversification may be reasonably related to the core business after all.

Enersis, through Manso de Velasco, has spread its activities far from electric power, investing in construction of apartment buildings in Viña del Mar, a highway tunnel connecting Santiago with the coast (El Melon), and other ventures that have much to do with real estate and construction but virtually nothing to do with electricity other than relating to infrastructure development. While the real estate/infrastructure ventures do move the company away from power generation, these activities constitute well less than 10% of the total business, and the intention is to keep this type of diversification limited to a small percentage of total Enersis activity.

THE CHALLENGE OF OPERATING MULTINATIONALLY

Enersis has now been involved in business outside of Chile since 1992. This experience has not been without some missteps. For example, when expanding into Argentina, Enersis faced the inability to reduce staffing at the Edesur electricity distribution company, due to local labor rules. As well, there was a relatively low level of motivation of the labor force there, due to a history of state ownership of the electricity sector and the lack of performance-related incentives for the workers. It took Enersis managers more than two years to carry out the needed staffing reductions and to install modern performance measures and incentives.

As the Latin American region became more attractive for foreign investment during the 1990s, electric power utilities became important targets for foreign companies in the region. Once the threat of the external debt crisis had been extinguished by about 1991, interest began to pick up. At the beginning of the decade, Enersis had very few competitors when it bid for power companies that were being privatized in Argentina, Peru, and Brazil. By the middle of the decade, American companies such as Houston Energy, AES, Duke Power, and others had entered the bidding in Brazil, Mexico, and elsewhere. At the same time European power companies such as Iberdrola (Spain), Electricite de France, ENE (Italy) and Electricidad de Portugal also entered the fray.

Enersis found that the most useful strategy for dealing with the foreign competition, and being a foreign company itself outside of Chile, was to ally with a local power company in the target market and with one or more industrial-country companies. This package of Enersis management skills, local knowledge held by the local partner, and capital plus technology contributed by the U.S. or European partner, turned out to be a winning combination in bids for Edelnor in Peru, CERJ in Brazil, and Betania in Colombia.

A continuing problem for Enersis in overseas business is the fact that most electric power business remains in government hands throughout Latin America. This problem extends as well to the generation of electricity, where, for example, Argentine government-owned companies operate nuclear power plants that compete with Endesa to supply power to the distribution networks.

Appendix A

Enersis S.A. and Subsidiaries
Consolidated Statements of Income Years Ended December 31, 1997 and 1996 (Expressed in Thousands of Chilean Pesos—M$)

	1997	1996
Operating Results:		
Revenue from Operations	1,334,976,829	1,233,788,841
Cost of Operations	(857,443,897)	(763,248,909)
Gross Profit	477,532,932	470,539,932
Administrative and Selling Expenses	(115,128,805)	(124,625,967)
Net Operating Income	362,404,127	345,913,965
Other Income (Deductions):		
Interest Income	37,867,295	31,892,890
Equity in Income of Related Companies	31,999,177	17,610,537
Other Income	59,736,909	72,550,465
Equity in Loss Of Related Companies	(987)	(9)
Amortization-Goodwill	(35,006,194)	(24,132,148)
Financial Expenses	(158,395,649)	(108,835,106)
Other Expenses	(43,947,488)	(29,052,406)
Monetary Correction	41,053,618	24,285,123
Non-Operating Income	(66,693,319)	(15,780,654)
Income Before Income Taxes and Minority Interest	295,710,808	330,133,311
Income Taxes	(57,002,970)	(40,701,164)
Income Before Minority Interest	238,707,838	289,432,147
Minority Interest	(157,945,493)	(179,094,920)
	80,762,345	110,337,227
Amortization-Negative Goodwill	22,753,925	2,307,295
Net Income	103,516,270	112,644,522

Source: Enersis Annual Report, 1997.

Appendix A
(continued)
Consolidated Balance
Sheet Years Ended
December 31, 1997
and 1996
(Expressed in
Thousands of
Chilean Pesos—M$)

	1997	1996
Liabilities and Stockholders' Equity **Current Liabilities**		
Due to Banks and Financial Institutions— Short-Term	56,328,049	79,321,790
Due to Banks and Financial Institutions— Current Installments	56,185,075	81,251,887
Bond Issues	39,622,264	52,059,672
Long-Term Obligation—Current Installment	6,097,099	9,682,682
Dividends Payable	18,714,200	48,621,825
Accounts Payable	80,828,450	62,828,616
Notes Payable	359,140	794,334
Miscellaneous Payables	43,054,841	44,174,656
Notes and Accounts Payable to Related Companies	7,519,838	5,337,297
Provisions	39,198,551	33,500,327
Wlthholdings	58,220,021	32,738,280
Deferred Income	6,253,329	19,733,523
Deferred Taxes	167,726	182,949
Other Current Liabilities	19,571,116	19,602,614
Total Current Liabilities	432,119,719	489,930,452
Long-Term Liabilities		
Due to Banks and Financial Institutions	1,707,736,423	969,611,840
Bond Issues	963,287,650	611,034,148
Notes Payable	28,725,949	24,893,286
Miscellaneous Payables	7,712,680	3,784,433
Provisions	19,301,360	8,558,077
Other Long-Term Liabilities	43,157,727	43,455,860
Total Long-Term Liabilities	2,769,921,789	1,661,327,644
Minority Interest	2,272,352,449	1,558,254,355
Stockholders' Equity		
Paid-In Capital	372,505,262	372,505,262
Premium On Sale Of Own Shares	22,600,111	22,600,111
Other Reserves	21,594,889	22,163,444
Retained Earnings:		
Prior Years	232,469,742	196,759,783
Net Income For The Year	103,516,270	112,644,522
Interim Dividends	(46,665,681)	(43,883,980)
Total Retained Earnings	289,320,331	265,520,325
Total Stockholders' Equity	706,020,593	682,789,142
Total Liabilities and Stockholders' Equity	6,180,414,550	4,392,201,593

Source: Enersis Annual Report, 1997

Appendix B
Ownership of Enersis
as of 12/31/97

Shareholder	Number of Shareholders	Number of Shares	%
ENDESA Spain	5	1,981,587,840	29.16
Pension Funds	13	2,164,892,601	31.84
ADRs (Citibank as Depositary Bank)	1	1,132,239,300	16.65
Foreign Equity Funds	19	150,909,038	2.20
Stockbrokers, Mutual Funds, and Insurance Companies	97	364,098,443	5.35
Other Shareholders	12,665	1,006,272,778	14.80
TOTAL	**12,800**	**6,800,000,000**	**100.00**

As of December 31, 1997, Enersis S.A. was owned by 12,800 shareholders of record. The twelve largest shareholders of the company were:

Name of Shareholder	Number of Shares	%
Citibank N.A. (Depositary Bank)	1,132,239,300	16.65
A.F.P. Provida S.A.	424,999,771	6.25
Compania de Inversiones Luz y Fuerza S.A.	445,061,585	6.55
Compania de Inversiones Chispa dos S.A.	445,061,585	6.55
A.F.P. Habitat S.A.	439,578,489	6.46
Compania de Inversiones Los Almendros S.A.	445,061,585	6.55
Compania de Inversiones Chispa Uno S.A.	445,061,585	6.55
A.F.P. Santa Maria S.A.	297,490,170	4.37
A.F.P. Proteccion S.A.	224,955,672	3.31
A.F.P. Cuprum S.A.	264,364,775	3.89
Endesa Desarollo S.A.	201,341,500	2.96
Compania de Inversiones Luz S.A.	194,412,126	2.86
Subtotal (12)	4,959,628,143	72.95
Other Shareholders (12,788)	1,840,371,857	27.05
TOTAL SHAREHOLDERS (12,800)	**6,800,000,000**	**100.00**

Source: Enersis Annual Report, 1997.

Enersis's Subsidiaries

Compared Balance Sheets for the Years Ended 1996 & 1997 Consolidated Financial Statements (in th Ch$)

Company	Chilectra S. A.		Compania Electrica Del Rio Maipo S. A.		Ingenieria E Inmobiliaria Manso De Velasco S. A.	
	1996	1997	1996	1997	1996	1997
Assets						
Current Assets	95,932,965	113,655,826	6,905,251	5,103,062	80,165,281	57,556,408
Fixed Assets	164,847,753	178,162,696	23,685,481	26,250,384	59,234,937	61,332,698
Other Assets	379,964,688	437,704,746	744,612	633,057	68,835,658	71,321,779
Total Assets	640,745,406	729,523,268	31,335,344	3,198,650	208,235,876	190,220,885
Liabilities						
Short-Term Liabilities	58,650,663	82,328,872	7,339,729	6,480,372	100,203,749	83,691,072
Long-Term Liabilities	306,420,814	349,552,396	7,780,720	8,172,423	13,411,853	8,332,892
Minority Interest	123,453,124	12,323,641	0	0	16,522,817	18,695,577
Equity and Reserves	223,769,192	231,755,351	14,156,363	15,223,794	10,287,095	10,094,723
Subsidiary's Organization Cost	0	0	0	0	(104,700)	(155,125)
Accumulated Profits/Losses	11,628,679	23,463,597	906,555	908,673	57,375,144	60,480,194
Net Income	75,613,700	81,219,326	7,679,842	8,008,277	19,208,102	19,386
Less Interim Dividends	(47,682,766)	(51,119,915)	(6,527,865)	(6,807,036)	(8,671,184)	638
Total Liabilities and Equity	640,745,406	729,523,268	31,335,344	31,986,503	208,235,876	(10,304,986)

Compared Income Statements for Years Ended 1996 & 1997

Company	Chilectra S. A.		Compania Electrica Del Rio Maipo S. A.		Ingenieria E Inmobiliaria Manso De Velasco S. A.	
	1996	1997	1996	1997	1996	1997
Operating Income						
Operating Revenues	292,409,961	278,601,779	36,909,063	35,611,809	55,715,923	61,322,185
Operating Costs	(204,231,674)	(189,633,558)	(26,344,032)	(25,452,716)	(33,144,910)	(38,505,737)
Operating Margin	88,178,287	88,968,221	10,565,031	10,159,093	22,751,013	22,816,448
Administrative and Selling Expenses	(27,950,367)	(22,535,093)	(3,635,883)	(2,653,949)	(5,834,837)	(4,168,383)
Operating Income	60,227,920	66,433,128	6,929,148	7,505,144	16,736,176	18,648,065
Non-Operating Income						
Non-Operating Revenues	64,013,747	74,206,722	3,781,890	3,456,969	9,132,738	7,365,254
Non-Operating Costs	(35,929,075)	(49,392,093)	(1,935,881)	(1,933,976)	(8,493,689)	(8,404,216)
Monetary Adjustment	458,642	3,231,872	146,227	642,586	2,744,554	3,394,882
Non-Operating Income	28,543,314	28,046,501	2,092,236	1,865,579	3,383,603	2,355,920
Income Tax	(11,296,447)	(11,569,453)	(1,341,542)	(1,362,446)	(1,499,578)	(2,192,476)
Minority Interest	(1,861,087)	(1,690,850)	0	0	(1,320)	(22,037)
Negative Goodwill Amortization	0	0	0	0	58,922	597,166
Net Income	75,613,700	81,219,326	7,679,842	8,008,277	19,208,102	129,386,638

Source: Enersis Annual Report, 1997.

Enersis's Subsidiaries *(continued)*

Compared Balance Sheets for The Years Ended 1996 & 1997 Consolidated Financial Statements (in th Ch$)

Company	Chilectra S. A.		Compania Electrica Del Rio Maipo S. A.		Ingenieria E Inmobiliaria Manso De Velasco S. A.	
	1996	1997	1996	1997	1996	1997
Assets						
Current Assets	5,298,555	7,315,617	5,300,799	6,182,065	1,419	76,797
Fixed Assets	1,303,521	971,981	401,102	412,784	1,466	1,172
Other Assets	36,818	5,798	62,053	47,484	327	288
Total Assets	6,638,894	8,293,396	5,763,954	6,642,333	3,212	78,257
Liabilities						
Short-Term Liabilities	3,120,286	4,426,779	3,946,667	4,842,934	2,563	998
Long-Term Liabilities	97,082	60,452	129,139	106,039	0	0
Minority Interest	326	196	0	0	0	0
Equity and Reserves	3,519,754	3,519,754	1,374,800	1,374,800	65,987	69,561
Subsidiary's Organization Cost	0	0	0	0	0	0
Acumulated Profits/ Losses	(1,236,720)	(98,554)	2,982	5,011	(62,432)	(65,338)
Net Income	1,138,166	2,060,079	2,043,231	2,088,050	(2,906)	5,082,808
Less Interim Dividends	0	(1,675,310)	(1,732,865)	(1,774,501)	0	(5,009,772)
Total Liabilities and Equity	6,638,894	8,293,396	5,763,954	6,642,333	3,212	78,257

Compared Income Statements for Years Ended 1996 & 1997

Company	Chilectra S. A.		Compania Electrica Del Rio Maipo S. A.		Ingenieria E Inmobiliaria Manso De Velasco S. A.	
	1996	1997	1996	1997	1996	1997
Operating Income						
Operating Revenues	9,960,829	11,163,764	21,133,538	20,201,295	0	0
Operating Costs	(6,795,779)	(7,132,759)	(15,706,397)	(15,115,664)	0	0
Operating Margin	3,165,050	4,031,005	5,427,141	5,085,631	0	0
Administrative and Selling Expenses	(1,914,044)	(2,009,342)	(3,005,473)	(2,583,994)	(2,848)	(3,286)
Operating Income	1,251,006	2,021,663	2,421,668	2,501,637	(2,848)	(3,286)
Non-Operating Income						
Non-Operating Revenues	526,984	770,727	273,882	146,180	60	5,088,892
Non-Operating Costs	(316,216)	(169,111)	(192,207)	(226,786)	0	(4)
Monetary Adjustment	(95,182)	(199,020)	(48,717)	(14,779)	(118)	(2,794)
Non-Operating Income	105,586	402,596	32,958	(95,385)	(58)	5,086,094
Income Tax	(218,389)	(364,196)	(411,395)	(318,202)	0	0
Minority Interest	(37)	16	0	0	0	0
Negative Goodwill Amortization	0	0	0	0	0	0
Net Income	1,138,166	2,060,079	2,043,231	2,088,050	(2,906)	5,082,808

Source: Enersis Annual Report, 1997.

CASE NOTES

1. This project is actually fairly complex, including the construction of a natural gas pipeline across the Andes from Salta in Argentina to Mejillones in northern Chile, building a power plant in Mejillones, and connecting it to the national power grid (SING) at Atacama. Enersis is co-owner of both the pipeline and the power plant, along with partner CMS. CMS operates the gas pipeline, and Enersis operates the power plant—which is connected to both the SIC and SING distribution networks.
2. See, for example, "El Precio de una Derrota," *Que Pasa*, July 22, 1995, pp. 52–56.

Chapter 9

Multinational E-Commerce: Strategies and Structures

LEARNING OBJECTIVES
After reading this chapter you should be able to:

- Define the forms of e-commerce.

- Appreciate the growing presence of e-commerce in the global economy.

- Understand the structure of the Internet economy.

- Identify the basic components of a successful e-commerce strategy.

- Understand the attractions of and deterrents to building a multinational e-commerce business.

- Know the basic multinational e-commerce business models.

- Identify the practicalities of running a multinational e-commerce business.

- Understand the function of enablers in multinational e-commerce operations.

<table>
<tr><td>

**Preview
Case in Point**

**Global
Internet
Economy
Indicators:
Selected Facts**

</td><td>

- World Wide Web–user population was *171 million in 1999.*
- The global e-commerce market will surpass *$1.2 trillion by 2001.*
- By mid-2000, over *50 percent* of the online population came from *outside the United States.*
- By 2005, the number of users *outside the United States* is expected to rise *70 percent* to *one billion users.*
- By mid-2000, *35 percent of Internet users could not understand English-only sites.*
- *Business Web users* are *three times* more likely to make a *purchase* when using an e-commerce site in their *own language.*
- Internet access will be in *47 million European homes* by *2003.*
- *Latin America* will have over *24.3 million* Internet users by *2003.*

Source: Adapted from The Internet Economy Indicators 2000.

</td></tr>
</table>

Although still small by comparison to the traditional economy, the Internet economy is booming and growing faster than any other business trend in history. As shown in the Preview Case in Point, the Internet economy is not only growing exponentially but it is also a worldwide phenomenon. Consequently, multinational managers must be well versed in all aspects of e-commerce and be prepared to use the Internet as a new global platform for multinational business transactions.

Earlier chapters discussed many of the intricacies involved in developing multinational strategies and building the organizations to implement these strategies effectively. In this chapter, you will see that new opportunities exist for companies to expand their multinational operations via the World Wide Web and the Internet.

Many of the issues involved in doing multinational business over the World Wide Web are similar to those faced by traditional multinational companies. However, the next generation of multinational managers must address many unique issues in formulating and implementing multinational strategies for the Internet economy.

This chapter will provide you with essential background on the nature of e-commerce and the Internet economy. First, the chapter considers basic e-commerce strategy, structure, and operations. Second, the chapter considers issues unique for the multinational company including the costs and benefits of globalizing via the Internet, basic multinational e-commerce models, and practical issues associated with multinational e-commerce such as Web-site design. After reading this chapter and considering the array of multinational management issues considered earlier, you should gain a good understanding and appreciation of the e-commerce challenges multinational companies must face now and in the immediate future.

THE INTERNET ECONOMY

WHAT IS E-COMMERCE?

E-commerce

The selling of goods or services over the Internet.

E-commerce refers to the selling of goods or services over the Internet. These goods or services include those delivered offline, such as UPS shipping a book purchased through Amazon.com to a customer anywhere in the world. They also include goods and services delivered online, such as downloaded computer software.

B2C

Business-to-consumer transactions.

B2B

Business-to-business transactions.

When most people talk about e-commerce, they focus on two types of transactions. The first is the business-to-consumer transactions such as buying toys from eToys. The acronym **B2C** is commonly used to refer to these transactions. The second type represents selling among businesses, or business-to-business transactions. This is the **B2B** component of e-commerce. B2B transactions make up 70 to 85 percent of current e-commerce business.

One of the most important reasons for the significance of B2B e-commerce comes from the revolution in supply chain management made possible by electronic links between businesses and suppliers. Information sharing between business customers and suppliers allows suppliers to know what their customers want and allows businesses to know price, availability, and product characteristics immediately.

For example, Ericsson, the Swedish mobile phone giant, has gone to paperless procurement. They use the company's local network or intranet to find approved suppliers. The intranet provides links to the supplier's Web sites and a purchase is made within predefined levels. Prior to this system, Ericsson spent an average of $100 on every order processed. The reduction in paperwork has reduced the average transaction cost to $15 (http://www.ebusinessforum.com 2000).

C2C

Consumer-to-consumer transactions.

C2B

Consumer-to-business transactions.

In addition to these e-commerce models, there exist other forms of business transactions spawned by the Internet. These also have global possibilities although they are often not thought of as e-commerce. For example, ebay is a global player in the **C2C** (consumer-to-consumer) business of auctions. Anyone can sell something online and place bids. Other forms of business transactions to consider might be **C2B** (consumer-to-business). Examples of these firms include price comparison Web sites such as http://www.addall.com, which searches online bookstores throughout the world to provide price comparisons and shipping and delivery information.

Secure server

An Internet host that allows users to send and receive encrypted data.

Internet hosts

Computers connected to the Internet with its own IP address.

What is the current global presence of e-commerce? Recent reports from OECD (Organization for Economic Cooperation and Development) use two indicators (Coppel 2000). One is the number of secure servers. A **secure server** is an Internet host that allows users to send encrypted data so that those outside the connection cannot see the information. Such servers are necessary for e-commerce to thrive because they encourage users to send credit card information over the Net. A second indicator of the presence of e-commerce is the number of **Internet hosts**. Any computer connected to the Internet with its own Internet Protocol address is considered a server in OECD statistics. An Internet Protocol address is a unique address that a computer has on the World Wide Web so that other Internet users can access the public information on the computer.

According to a recent report (Coppel 2000), OECD countries dominate the Internet with over 90 percent of the world's Internet hosts. OECD countries represent most of the developed economies in the world (although China is not a member). By March 2000, OECD countries had 66801 secure servers, a 97 percent increase in just one year. Exhibit 9.1 shows the secure server and Internet host rankings for selected countries in the OECD. Projections are that the U.S. dominance in Internet use will decline gradually over the next decade.

The basis of e-commerce, Internet use, expanded geometrically from 1991 to 1999. In 1991, three million people used the Internet, but almost none used it for e-commerce. In contrast, approximately one-quarter of the 250 million users in 1999 made purchases from electronic commerce sites. Projections are that, in less than five years, at least 5 percent of business-to-business transactions (B2B) and business-to-consumer transactions (B2C) will be based on e-commerce.

The growth in the use of the Internet or the World Wide Web for e-commerce is so dramatic that its impact is difficult to estimate. Some say that the Internet will

Exhibit 9.1

Secure Servers (per million inhabitants) and Internet Hosts (per thousand inhabitants) in Selected OECD Countries

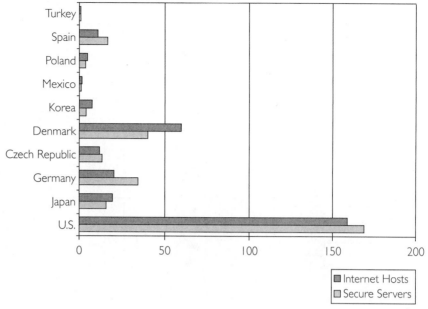

Source: Adapted from Coppel 2000.

have more impact on the world than the industrial revolution. Consider the estimates shown in Exhibit 9.2 by several multinational consulting firms of the expected worldwide e-commerce growth between 1999 and 2003. Such growth suggests tremendous opportunities for multinational companies to use the Internet as a tool for conducting business worldwide at any point in the value chain from procurement of raw materials to eventual sales. Before considering the strategy and structure of using e-commerce in multinational business, the chapter next provides background material on the nature of the Internet economy.

THE INTERNET ECONOMY

According to a team of experts at the University of Texas at Austin, the Internet economy has four levels (Barua and Whinston 2000). These layers are (1) the Internet infrastructure, (2) the applications infrastructure, (3) the Internet intermediaries, and (4) the Internet commerce layer.

Layer 1 includes the backbone of the Internet including Internet service providers (ISPs) such as America Online, telecommunication companies, and the manufacturers of networking systems. Companies on this level include:

- Communications (Qwest, MCI, Worldcom)
- Internet Service Providers (Mindspring, AOL, Earthlink)
- Networking (Cisco, Lucent, 3Com)
- Hardware (Dell, Compaq, HP)

Layer 2 includes the companies and consultants that build Web systems and supporting software. Companies on this level include:

- Consultants (Scient)
- Commerce applications (Netscape, Sun, IBM)
- Web development software (Adobe, Netobjects)

Exhibit 9.2 Estimates by E-Commerce Consultants of Worldwide E-Commerce (Billions $)

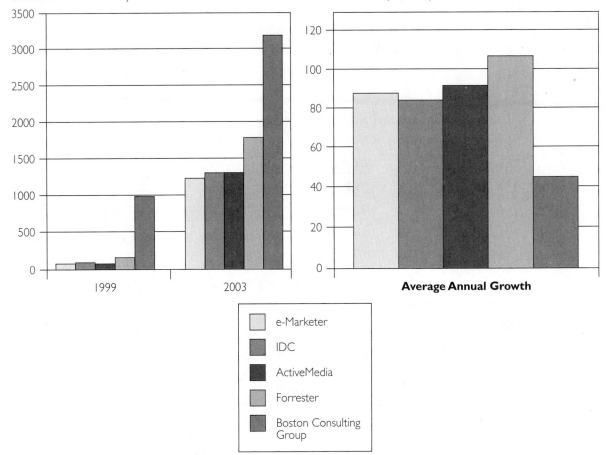

Source: Adapted from Coppel 2000.

- Search engine software (Verity)
- Web-enabled databases (Oracle)

Layer 3 includes a new type of company that provides linking services on the Internet and derives its revenues from commissions, advertising, and membership fees. Examples of these companies include:

- Online travel agencies (TravelWeb, Travelocity.com)
- Online brokerages (Etrade)
- Content aggregators (Cnet, Zdnet)
- Online advertising (Yahoo!)

Level 4 includes companies that conduct commercial transactions over the Web. Amazon.com and drugstore.com provide examples of companies from this layer. Other examples include:

- E-retailers (wine.com, diamond.com)
- Manufacturers selling directly (hpshopping.com, Dell)
- Subscription-based companies (vrbo.com)
- Transportation services (most airlines)
- Shipping services (FedEx, UPS)

Exhibit 9.3
E-Commerce Business
Models: Openings
and Barriers for
Going Global

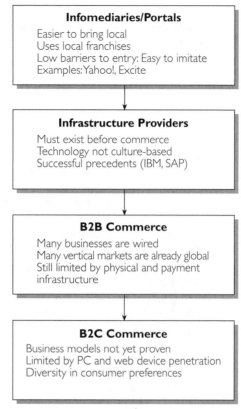

Infomediaries/Portals
Easier to bring local
Uses local franchises
Low barriers to entry: Easy to imitate
Examples: Yahoo!, Excite

Infrastructure Providers
Must exist before commerce
Technology not culture-based
Successful precedents (IBM, SAP)

B2B Commerce
Many businesses are wired
Many vertical markets are already global
Still limited by physical and payment
infrastructure

B2C Commerce
Business models not yet proven
Limited by PC and web device penetration
Diversity in consumer preferences

Source: Adapted from Sawhney and Mandal 2000.

E-commerce is evolving quickly. However, the failures of many e-commerce start-ups in the year 2000 demonstrated that the Internet economy is not without risks. Each layer of the Internet economy has its threats and opportunities. Exhibit 9.3 provides a summary of these threats and opportunities.

FUNDAMENTALS OF E-COMMERCE STRATEGY AND STRUCTURE

The previous sections provided background information on the current state of the Internet economy. In this section you will learn current strategies used by successful e-commerce companies.

FIVE STEPS FOR SUCCESSFUL E-COMMERCE STRATEGY

E-commerce strategizing is a new and evolving management challenge. The multinational manager must build on sound, basic strategizing as a prelude to multinational operations. One expert (Venkatraman 2000) suggests five basic steps for building a successful e-commerce strategy. These include:

- *Build on current business models and experiment with new e-commerce models.* Search for ways to use the e-commerce business to reduce costs or enhance services offered by the traditional business. E-commerce transactions can be cheap, yet they can add value to customers. Customers can get timely updates such as American Airlines Alert, an e-mail service to notify customers of changes in schedules.

- *Meet the challenge of developing an e-commerce organization.* The basic choice involves a distinction between either a separate autonomous entity for e-commerce business or a seamless integration into the current model. The integrated model works best when it is difficult to separate e-commerce from the existing organization without confusing the customer. This also requires senior management commitment to using the Net aggressively as part of the company's strategy. Not only senior management but the entire firm must be prepared to embrace the e-commerce model, as did Egghead Software when it moved entirely to a Web-based business.
- *Allocate resources to the e-commerce business.* A successful e-commerce strategy must commit financial, human, and technological resources to developing e-commerce capabilities. If these capabilities do not exist internal to the organization, then selected e-commerce operations are outsourced to third parties or to strategic alliance partners. For example, companies like Viant help build e-commerce operations for partners like Radio Shack and Kinko's.
- *Build a superior e-commerce infrastructure as a basis of a differentiation strategy.* Possible sources of differentiation include the following. Build Web sites with superior online experiences; Venkatraman uses the example of Gulfstream selling multi-million-dollar jets on its interactive site (http://www.gulfstreampreowned.com). Personalize the interaction to each customer. Streamline and simplify transactions.
- *Make sure the entire management team aligns with the e-commerce agenda.*

The Internet economy has spawned numerous new companies; at the same time, it has provided opportunities for traditional companies to use this evolving business tool. Next, you will see one of the major issues faced by traditional companies when they add e-commerce to their current businesses.

E-COMMERCE STRUCTURE: INTEGRATED OR AUTONOMOUS

Each company needs to decide how e-commerce fits into its existing organizational design and management systems. Writing in the *Harvard Business Review*, Ranjay Gulati of Northwestern University and Jason Garino of the Boston Consulting Group (2000) call this the "right mixture of bricks and clicks." They mean that companies must decide how much to integrate their evolving Internet operations into their traditional business operations. In the evolving e-commerce jargon, traditional business operations are often called the **"brick-and-mortar"** part of the company.

Brick-and-mortar

Traditional or non-virtual business operation.

The degree of integration between brick-and-mortar operations and the Internet business can occur anywhere in the value chain from procurement of raw material to after-sales service. Additionally, the degree of integration can range from the near seamless operation of an Office Depot to the mostly independent operations of Barnes & Noble and Barnesandnoble.com.

Each choice has benefits. The independent operation can move faster and be more entrepreneurial when freed from corporate bureaucracy. It can seek funding from the deep pockets of venture capitalists willing to invest in e-commerce companies. The integrated operation, on the other hand, can benefit from cross-promotion of shared products, shared customer information, increased large-quantity purchasing leverage, and economies of scale by using the same distribution channels (Gulati and Garino 2000).

The choice between seamless integration and a fully autonomous unit is not simple and seldom is clear cut. The best option for most companies is something in between. As with most strategy implementation issues, managers must evaluate their company's particular situation to make an informed decision. Exhibit 9.4 shows a

Exhibit 9.4

Key Decisions in the
Web Business
Integration Versus
Separation Decision

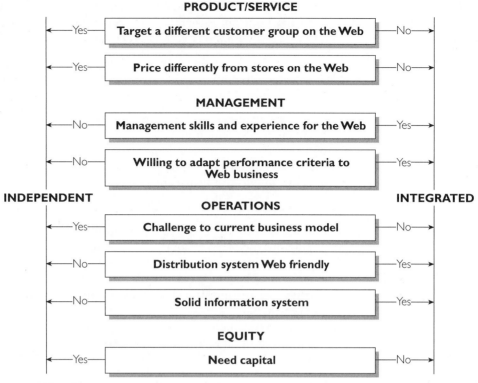

Source: Adapted from Gulati and Garino 2000.

decision model with the questions that managers must consider in choosing the best level of integration for the e-commerce unit.

Although the level of e-commerce integration is a crucial decision in implementing an e-commerce strategy, there are also numerous other operational challenges to consider. These are discussed next.

ADDITIONAL OPERATIONAL CHALLENGES FOR AN E-COMMERCE BUSINESS

What challenges can a company anticipate in developing an e-commerce business? Towers Perrin, the New York consulting firm, surveyed over 300 major companies from the United States and Europe. The survey, called the Towers Perrin Internetworked Organization Survey, found that although many companies see the advantages of e-commerce, they also recognize there will be many problems and challenges. The following section reports the important findings of the 1999/2000 Towers Perrin survey on the management issues companies face when running an e-business.

• Finding partnerships and alliances with customers or third parties is critical for success.
• Because of the shortage of people with e-commerce skills, it is difficult to attract, retain, and, develop employees in the e-commerce unit.
• Training and development in e-commerce are not yet adequate.
• Finding ways to provide individuals with growth opportunities and job fulfillment drives employee retention in e-commerce.

- Deciding what e-commerce functions to outsource is difficult. Most survey companies outsource many e-commerce functions, but are reluctant to do so for functions with direct customer contact.

How can companies meet these challenges? Towers Perrin suggests different strategies depending on whether the company is a pure e-business or a unit of a traditional business. Pure e-business companies must:

- Develop information and management systems to respond to rapid growth.
- Maintain rapid decision making, creativity, innovation, and flexibility.
- Build external relationships with e-commerce support companies and customers.
- Attract and retain e-commerce-capable talent.
- Develop an effective management team.

Traditional companies with e-commerce units must:

- Build a common vision and commitment to the e-commerce operation throughout the organization.
- Change the organizational structure to emphasize quick reconfiguration of assets and capabilities.
- Change the organizational culture to create a supporting environment for e-commerce.
- Attract and retain e-commerce-skilled employees.
- Alter HR programs to suit the different skill requirements of e-commerce employees.

Exhibit 9.5 gives a comparison of the past and expected organizational changes multinational companies are making to implement their e-commerce strategies.

The preceding sections reviewed the basic strategies, structures, and challenges managers face when developing an e-commerce business. In the following sections, you will see some of the additional challenges faced when companies choose to move their e-commerce operations into the multinational domain.

GLOBALIZING THROUGH THE INTERNET

Although a Web site immediately gives the entire world access to a company's products or services, many of the challenges of globalization faced by traditional brick-and-mortar companies remain. A company must still solve the global–local dilemma discussed in detail in Chapter 6. Managers must decide whether the company's products or services are global in content and delivery or require localization to national or regional levels. In addition, the traditional problems of multinational business relating to currencies/payments, local laws, infrastructure for delivery or procurement, and national and business cultures must be addressed by e-commerce companies. Other chapters consider these issues in more detail. This section adds to the understanding of multinational strategy formulation and implementation by considering some issues unique to the e-commerce operation.

MULTINATIONAL E-COMMERCE STRATEGY FORMULATION

THE NATURE OF THE BUSINESS

What kind of e-business is easiest to take global? To a large degree, it depends on the types of products or services offered through e-commerce. The next section reviews these differences.

Exhibit 9.5

Recent and Expected Organizational Changes in Major Multinational Companies Building E-Commerce Businesses

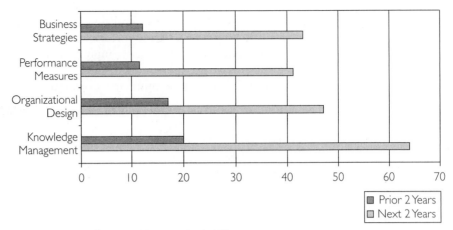

Source: Adapted from research by Towers Perrin 2000.

According to e-commerce experts, Mohanbir Sawhney and Sumant Mandal (2000), e-commerce companies work in three areas. Some move bits or computerized information; others move money in payment flows; still others move physical products. Each type of operation requires an infrastructure to support the transaction. Telecommunications infrastructures support moving bits. A payment infrastructure allows the movement of money. To move physical goods requires physical infrastructure. The ease of taking e-commerce international depends mostly on the mix of infrastructures required.

Sawhney and Mandal argue that there is a hierarchy of difficulty in e-commerce depending on infrastructure requirements. Portals and infomediaries provide gateways to the Internet. Portals are primarily search engines to locate Web sites, while infomediaries go a step further by providing not only links but also information such as current news. They were also the first e-business forms to have a global presence.

At the next level are businesses such as Travelocity, digital music, and software vendors. Although they do not move physical objects, they still must rely on local infrastructure to take payments for their products. The technical and managerial challenge comes from dealing with issues such as credit card payments (fraud and lack of use in some areas), currency conversion, and a bewildering array of tax jurisdictions. Most difficult to globalize are e-commerce businesses that rely on a physical infrastructure. Like their brick-and-mortar counterparts, these businesses must ship goods that fulfill customer orders and manage their supply chains located throughout the world. In addition, they must deal with the challenges of receiving payments through a variety of payment infrastructures.

For e-businesses that also require a physical infrastructure in the countries where they operate, large multinational firms that enter e-commerce with an existing global presence often have an advantage. The have in place brick-and-mortar units or they have the resources to establish a physical base in each country of operation to maintain localized Web sites. Smaller firms and firms new to the complexities of multinational commerce face more challenges in establishing an international presence.

BASIC OPPORTUNITIES AND THREATS OF MULTINATIONAL E-COMMERCE

In deciding whether to globalize their e-commerce operations—either as an existing brick-and-mortar company or a pure e-commerce company—managers need to weigh the attractions and deterrents of international e-commerce (Rosen and Howard 2000). Again, this is a traditional strategy formulation problem: they must consider the opportunities and threats before deciding on a strategy. However, the e-commerce environment has some unique characteristics. Consider the attractions and deterrents noted below.

The major attractions of e-commerce globalization are:

- *Cost reduction*. It can be less expensive to reach international customers via the Web.
- *Technology*. The technology to reach anyone with an Internet-linked computer is readily available.
- *Efficiencies*. Electronic communication and processes can be more efficient.
- *Convenience*. The Web is in operation seven days a week and twenty-four hours a day regardless of location.
- *Speed of access*. Once a Web site is running, a company's products or services can be accessed immediately from anywhere in the world.

Some deterrents include:

- *Return/receipt burden and cost of delivery*. If the pattern follows catalogue sales, businesses should expect a 30 to 40 percent return rate for online purchases (Rosen and Howard 2000).
- *Costs of site construction, maintenance, upgrades*. Web site construction and maintenance in multiple languages, currencies, and tax locations can cost companies millions of dollars per year.
- *Channel conflicts*. Distributors and retailers that sell a company's products may be undermined by competition from a company's Web site that sells directly to end users. This is a major fear of many automobile dealers if the manufacturers were to sell directly from the factory. Consider what is happening to travel agents as more people buy tickets online directly from the airline companies.
- *Easily copied models*. Local competitors can easily see and copy a multinational's product or service or business model if it is displayed on the Web.
- *Cultural differences*. Web sites must not only be multilingual but, also, must present a format that is appropriate culturally.
- *Traditional cross-border transaction complexities*. These include issues such as pricing for exchange rates, different taxes, and government regulations.

The following Case in Point gives an example of how QXL.com overcame one deterrent, cultural differences, to succeed in the United Kingdom It also shows how the eBay-auctioning model was copied and modified to fit the U.K. business environment.

PICKING A MARKET

One expert, Clay Shirky (2000), suggests that Web entrepreneurs should target countries based on two factors. First, attractive markets for e-commerce are those with market inefficiencies. Shirky claims that many formerly state-controlled markets have suboptimal economic performance. In these markets, e-commerce shopping allows buyers to get better quality and cheaper prices because they are free from state control. Second, target markets with attractive demographic characteristics. These include locations with an Internet population of at least 5 percent, a high literacy rate (to predict future growth of the Internet population), a country that participates in at least one free trade agreement, and a government with a viable legal system.

Case in Point

Electronic Auctioneering in the United Kingdom

According to Jim Rose, the U.S.-born CEO of QXL.com (a U.K. auction platform similar to eBay in the United States), Web-based business models are easy to imitate. Pricing, Web page design, and distribution strategies are visible to anyone with a Web browser. Rose argues that sensitivity to cultural distinctions separates winners from losers. In the United States, eBay was able to immediately exist as an auctioning platform for consumers to sell anything they wanted to list, a C2C company. Observers in the United Kingdom noted that this worked in the United States because of the "yard sale" mentality of U.S. culture. In contrast, Rose began QXL as a B2C company. QXL bought an inventory of goods and auctioned the carefully picked merchandise to British consumers. Only after consumers became comfortable with this model did QXL add consumer-to-consumer sales.

Source: Adapted from Nickell 2000.

In Shirky's opinion, e-commerce potential is great in South America because of the Mercosur trade group and in those southeast Asian countries with membership in the Asean trade group. He also suggests the European Union is the next boom area for e-commerce because many countries such as France, Italy, and Germany retain market inefficiencies from pre-Union days. The open borders and common currency in the EU should be a fertile ground for e-commerce growth.

The enormous growth in e-commerce shows that the benefits of global e-commerce clearly outweigh the risks. Firms increasingly use the Internet as a tool to globalize operations. However, in the rapidly growing Internet environment, the competition is heating up. In particular, achieving sustainable competitive advantage is difficult when competitors can easily copy business models. The following Multinational Management Challenge shows some of the threats to the dominance of e-commerce by U.S. companies.

MULTINATIONAL E-COMMERCE STRATEGY IMPLEMENTATION

Successful implementation of a multinational e-commerce strategy requires building an appropriate organization and developing the necessary technical capabilities to conduct electronic transactions. The following sections provide an overview of various options available to multinational managers.

THE MULTINATIONAL E-COMMERCE ORGANIZATION

What is the organization of a multinational e-business? Professors Sawhney and Mandal (2000) see Amazon.com and Yahoo! providing the most likely models. These organizations are three-tiered, mixing global and local functions. Corporate headquarters represents the global core that provides the vision, strategy, and leadership that drive the electronic marketing of worldwide products or services. Headquarters also provides shared services such as the network infrastructure. Managers at headquarters, and in the shared functional areas, have worldwide responsibility for their operations.

Local subsidiaries, which actually deliver the goods, take charge of functions better done locally such as managing the supply chain and dealing with local regulations. These organizations try to solve the global–local dilemma with the

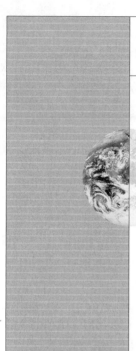

Multinational Management Challenge
Can U.S. Companies Stay on Top?

The United States hosts 90 percent of all commercial Web sites and three quarters of all e-commerce takes place here. The magazine, *Economist,* asks: will the United States continue to dominate e-commerce? Maybe not. Although the existence of Web sites that people can access from anywhere in the world makes crossing borders easier, the *Economist* cautions that going global may not be so easy.

Three barriers seem to exist. First, especially for retail trade, is the difficulty of delivery. As a result, some U.S. companies refuse orders from abroad. Second, at least for Europe, tax and regulatory barriers deter many U.S. e-commerce vendors. There is a perception among many Silicon Valley companies that Europe is prone to regulate everything and e-commerce is not yet developed sufficiently to face such a challenge. Third, many U.S. retailers left their domestic-only operations too late. Local companies in Europe and Asia are taking first-mover advantage to capture the estimated $9 billion of e-commerce retail sales in Europe and the estimated $6 billion in Asia.

Source: Based on *Economist* 2000.

global integration of similar technical functions such as Web-server design, while still making necessary local adaptations such as Web-site translations (Sawhney and Mandal 2000). Exhibit 9.6 pictures the levels and functions of this type of organization.

Yahoo! provides a Case in Point of a successful mover of information within a multinational e-commerce model. Yahoo! shows an effective balance among the global and local requirements of an e-commerce site.

TECHNICAL CAPABILITIES AND IMPLEMENTATION OPTIONS FOR MULTINATIONAL E-COMMERCE

Components of a successful multinational online presence require electronic capabilities throughout the value chain (Hudgins 1999). Such capabilities include:

- Software to process pricing in multiple currencies. The most sophisticated software not only supports payment-processing systems that show prices in multiple currencies but also accepts payment in the customer's preferred currency.
- Systems that calculate and show purchase information on international shipping, duties, and local taxes such as the VAT (value-added tax common in Europe).
- Systems that check regulatory compliance with local and international laws.
- Ability to give support in multilingual service centers.
- Fraud protection.
- Electronic payment models in addition to credit cards (not used as commonly as in the United States). Only 14 percent of U.S. e-commerce companies support debit/invoice payments as compared to 88 percent of European companies.

Exhibit 9.6
Organizational
Structures of the
Multinational
E-Corporation

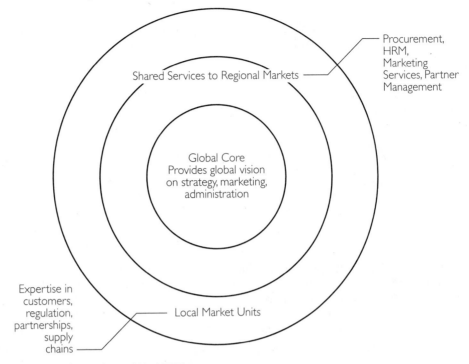

Source: Adapted from Sawhney and Mandal 2000.

Case in Point	Yahoo!, a leading Internet search engine, operates in 22 countries using 13 different languages. Evan Neufeld, director of international research for Jupiter Communications calls Yahoo! the poster child of globalization.
Yahoo!: Go Global; Act Local	What is the Yahoo! formula? Yahoo! takes its basic model of site construction, making the look and feel similar everywhere, but modifies content and advertising as a country-level localization strategy. Yahoo! partners with local companies such as Spain's *Conzaón* and the BBC in England.
	Conzaón provides Spanish audiences the society gossip they desire while the BBC provides U.K. users with news. In Europe, Yahoo! claims 20 of the 38 million Internet users. In Europe alone Yahoo! has 350 content partnerships. For e-commerce partners overseas, they favor local companies over U.S. companies.
	Source: Adapted from Pickering 2000.

Many areas of the world do not use credit and debit cards, which poses a significant problem for e-commerce. The following Case in Point shows how 7-Eleven manages its electronic payment model without the use of credit cards.

TO BUILD OR OUTSOURCE TECHNICAL CAPABILITIES?

Similar to companies choosing an export strategy (direct exporting or indirect exporting with the aid of export management companies), e-commerce companies that wish to globalize their operations have two basic options. They can run

Case in Point

7-Eleven Shifts Thinking for Payments

E-commerce in many parts of the world is restricted because the use of credit cards is not common. How do you pay electronically without credit or debit cards? Even in an advanced industrial nation such as Japan, credit card use is much less common than in the United States. For example, in Japan, less than 10 percent of the transactions involve credit card payments.

In Japan, people often pay utility bills at convenience stores. Thinking creatively, 7-Eleven Japan took advantage of this existing payment structure for Web purchase payments. Japanese users of 7dream.com can select "Payment at 7-Eleven Store" as an option allowing them to pick up and pay for their online purchase at any of the 8,000 7-Elevens in Japan.

Source: Adapted from Sawhney and Mandal 2000.

E-commerce enablers

Fulfillment specialists that provide other companies with services such as Web site translation.

all e-commerce functions themselves or they can outsource these functions to e-fulfillment specialists called **e-commerce enablers**. The enablers provide services and software that translate Web sites, calculate shipping, value-added tax, duties, and other charges unique to each country. For example, NetSales (http://www.netsales.com/) offers a complete line of e-commerce services targeted at medium-sized businesses. Services range from supply procurement to setting up Web-based stores.

The enablers of multinational e-commerce exist because many companies—even some that are very large—do not have the internal resources or capabilities to conduct all e-commerce functions. In addition, in such a rapidly changing competitive environment, few companies have the time to develop such strategic capabilities. For example, Forrester Research estimates that 85 percent of U.S. e-retailers cannot fill international orders—they do not have the capability to deal with the complexities of shipping across borders. As such, even some very large companies such as Nike and Blockbuster outsource to enablers. Enablers take on functions such as receiving the customers' purchased goods, storage, packing, and eventual shipment to the customer. As with good export management firms, successful order-fulfillment enablers understand local business culture and know how to comply with taxation and regulatory issues (Wilkerson 2000).

Many enablers now exist that specialize in helping companies to globalize their e-commerce. Companies such as Global Site and Idion help create multilingual versions of Web sites for their customers. These companies have automated the translation process so that updates to Web sites can occur faster. This type of service has become so popular that Forrester Research expects a 50 percent a year increase in this service.

For some companies, localization of Web sites is minimal. Dell Computer has Web sites in 50 countries using 21 different languages; however, they use the same layout for the sites in all countries. In contrast, Chipshot.com, which sells golf equipment online, tailors its sites to local cultural needs. In Japan, to take advantage of the Japanese golfer's sensitivity to brand names, the Chipshot site shows brand names conspicuously and emphasizes the availability of custom-made clubs. By comparison, the U.S. site appeals to the more cost conscious U.S. customers by emphasizing the 50 percent discount (Engler 1999).

The following Multinational Management Brief gives an overview of the services offered by NextLinx, one of the first global e-commerce enablers (Ghosh 2000).

Multinational Management Brief
Looking at a Global E-Commerce Enabler's Services

NextLinx identified long-term obstacles to international business that can be simplified by its services. These obstacles include:

- Export and import regulations and duties.
- Complex border crossings.
- Multi-region/country expertise needed.
- Extensive documentation required.
- Coordination of multiple transportation legs.
- Total landed cost often unknown until after the shipment is delivered.

The NextLinx software reduces the global e-commerce transaction to three phases on a Web site. In the "pre-click" phase, the buyer reviews transportation options and costs; gets import duties, VAT, excise, and other governmental charges, and determines total landed cost. In the "click" phase, the buyer orders and determines door-to-door shipping. This phase also screens for customers with denied access to purchase and checks to determine if a license is required. In the "post-click" phase, documentation is printed and tracking of the shipment begins until it reaches the destination.

The NextLinx system covers 100 exporting and importing countries. It covers all 99 chapters of the Harmonized Tariff Schedule with all the HTS headings and subheadings in the schedule. There are 19,000+ HTS codes for both export and import. The software calculates customs duty rates including all trade preferential programs. It also calculates governmental charges such as VAT, excise taxes, merchandise-processing fees (MPF), and port charges. NextLinx can host the technology on its Web site for a company or it can provide software and technical support to clients who use their own servers.

Source: Adapted from http://www.nextlinx.com.

In addition to e-commerce enablers that provide transaction services, numerous companies also do Web translations. Some of these companies have automated the translation process. One challenge of the translation process is to keep up with the frequent, often costly changes in global Web sites. In addition, culturally sensitive enablers go beyond simple translations. Like any advertisement or promotion in different countries, the Web site must be sensitive to cultural and religious differences. Colors, symbols, pictures, and variance in local use of the same language may cause different reactions in different countries.

Some suggestions for modifying a site to go global follow.

E.F. Sheridan (2000), president of the Web of Culture, suggests 10 "mission-critical" factors that a corporate Web site must use to communicate to a global audience. These include:

1. Linking all international sites to the corporate Web site.
2. If your site includes feedback or comment sections, it should also contain all non-electronic local contact information. See <u>http://www.novell.com</u> for an example.

Multinational Management Challenge
Can eBay Recover?

Failure to heed the issue of local adaptation left eBay, the U.S. electronic auction company, with only 3 percent of its sales from outside the United States. eBay launched its European site in dollars-only currency and was quickly left behind by QXL.com. QXL.com has sites throughout Europe that cope with different languages and currencies. eBay responded by buying the large German auctioneering company, Alando.de, with the hope of localizing operations. Will this strategy succeed?

Source: Adapted from *Economist* 2000.

3. Provide a prominent list of languages used by the company's Web site. This makes international use easier and shows a commitment to globalization. See http://www.lexmark.com for an example.
4. If your site includes downloads, use a page for Global Downloads for different languages.
5. Localize by language the parts of the parent company Web site that receive the most access.
6. Provide a site map for the parent company Web site that includes links to all local content.
7. Provide the firm's privacy statement in all local languages.
8. Guard against local piracy by putting your policies in local languages. Many pirates of U.S. Web material claim they did not know it was illegal to copy since they did not understand English.
9. Localize your graphics as well as your written material.
10. Localize content management. Web sites need continuous monitoring for updating material. This is a particular challenge for the multinational company, as this must be done in different languages.

As the preceding Multinational Management Challenge notes, a failure to attend to local cultural differences can seriously hurt an otherwise excellent e-commerce business model.

The following Case in Point gives a situation where Dow Chemical used only a moderate adaptation of its Web sites to different countries. This seemed to work well in some countries, but not in Japan.

Developing a global Web site adds additional challenges to organizations beyond cultural sensitivity and language differences. Many organizations discovered that they needed to adapt their organizations to the information flow and customer demands created by Web locations accessed from anywhere in the world. This often resulted in changes in organizational structure and changes in internal information systems to make the company more integrated globally.

The results of the Forrester Research survey reported in Exhibit 9.7 suggest that organizational challenges are among the most important issues to Web-site globalization.

Case in Point	Dow entered its e-commerce program in the middle of 1999 with 200 customers worldwide. Their site for registered users, MyAccount@Dow, provides customers with such e-commerce functions as purchasing, order status, account history, and payment information. By the end of the year, they hope to have 50 percent of customers online. In the year 2000, they invested $100 million in e-commerce. In January of 2000, they began e-commerce in Asia. Because their products are global, they plan similar e-commerce strategies for North America, Europe, and Asia. They now have customers in Australia, Singapore, Malaysia, and China. However, challenging their assumption that a similar e-commerce strategy would be effective worldwide, they had few Japanese customers because their sites were English-only. By the end of the year, they now plan to have sites in several Asian languages.
Dow Chemical's B2B E-Commerce Strategy	

Source: Adapted from Van Savage 2000.

Exhibit 9.7 Major Problems Identified in Web-Site Globalization

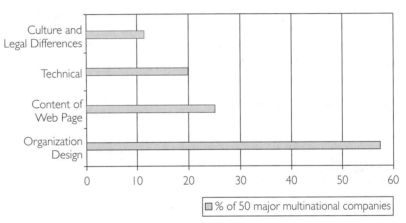

Source: Adapted from research by Forrester Research reported in Engler 1999.

Summary and Conclusions

This chapter introduced the basic concepts of e-commerce in general and multinational e-commerce in particular. The chapter discussed the basic forms of e-commerce including B2C, B2B, C2C, and C2B. Presently B2B dominates the Internet economy. However, expectations are that B2C will eventually gain a major share of e-commerce transactions. Overall, e-commerce is expanding geometrically. Although the United States currently dominates e-commerce, statistics show that other areas of the world are quickly catching up.

The fundamentals of e-commerce strategy emphasize building on traditional business models and experimenting with cost reductions and areas of differentiation that Internet use might provide. This means that there is no easy formula for building a successful e-commerce business. Innovative and creative managers will find ways to use e-commerce tools to enhance cost leadership or differentiation strategies. Because the World Wide Web makes e-commerce models transparent and easy to copy, only the most innovative and rapidly moving companies are likely to survive.

Companies conducting multinational operations via the Internet face most of the same challenges faced by brick-and-mortar multinational companies. The global versus local dilemma and the problems of conducting business in different cultural and institutional environments remain. The World Wide Web, however, provides instant access to the world for all companies willing to navigate the e-commerce world and will probably become one of the most important drivers of globalization in the future.

Discussion Questions

1. Define e-commerce and discuss the types of e-commerce transactions.

2. Identify and discuss the levels of the Internet economy. How has the Internet created new types of businesses?

3. Compare and contrast the costs and benefits of a fully integrated-brick-and-mortar and e-commerce company.

4. What are the advantages and disadvantages of e-commerce businesses over traditional brick-and-mortar businesses when taking their operations global?

5. Discuss the advantages and disadvantages of outsourcing global e-commerce activities to enablers.

6. Discuss the characteristics of a successful multinational Web page.

Chapter Internet Activity

As noted in the chapter, successful multinational e-commerce requires Web sites in different languages. There are free services that allow you to translate a Web page into several languages. One way to test a translation is called "back translation." This means that you translate from one language to another, then you translate back to see if the original is still correct.

Go to the translation service provided by Altavista (http://world.altavista.com/). Find a favorite Web page. Translate it from its original language to two other languages. Test the translation by back translating into the original language.

Internet Sites

Selected Companies in the Chapter
3com   http://www.3com.com/
Cisco Systems   http://www.cisco.com
Dell Computer   http://www.dell.com/
eBay   http://www.ebay.com
eTrade   http://www.etrade.com
Netscape   http://www.netscape.com
Quest   http://www.quest.com/index_nn.asp
QXL   http://www.qxl.com/uk/
UPS   http://www.ups.com

Vacation Rentals by Owner   http://www.vrbo.com/
Worldcom   http://www.worldcom.com/

Look Here for More Information on E-Commerce Practices and Statistics
http://www.oecd.org/subject/e_commerce/   *OECD information on e-commerce.*
http://www.oecd.org/dsti/sti/it/cm/stats/   *OECD indicators of Internet use.*

http://www.towers.com/towers/   *A consulting firm with e-commerce expertise.*

http://www.ebusinessforum.com/   *Information from the Economist on e-commerce. A very useful site. It includes information on best practices and how to do e-commerce business in different countries.*

http://www.business2.com/   *A contemporary e-commerce magazine.*

http://www.forrester.com/Home/   *A consulting firm with e-commerce expertise.*

Chapter Activity: Build a Web Store

Step 1: Your instructor will divide the class into groups.

Step 2: Select an agricultural or industrial product produced in the region of the country where you are located. If possible, interview a small-business person concerning his or her perspectives on the international opportunities for their product. In the United States, one way of finding a potential business owner is through the small-business development centers attached to many U.S. universities. Your instructor may assign you a business or product.

Step 3: Using the steps shown in Exhibit 10.5, the chapter on small business management, and information from World Wide Web sources (such as those in Exhibit 10.7) and your library, identify a foreign market or markets for the product or products.

Step 4: Build a simulated or actual Web site in your own language that shows the company's products or services. If you have the technical capabili-ties and are working with a real business, you can build a Web store. Simple, no-cost versions of Web storefronts can be done from sources such as http://www.authstores.com/. Periodically search the Web for additonal free e-commerce sources, as new sites frequently become available.

Step 5: Translate your Web site into the language of the country or countries that represent your target market. Use the free translation software available on the Web (See the Internet locations for translations at the end of Chapter 3). Apply the ten steps noted in this chapter to make sure your site is culturally appropriate.

Step 6: Test your translation and site layout with native speakers. If a real site, wait for orders.

Step 7: Present your site and its performance to your class and to the small-business person, if possible.

References

Barua, Anitesh and Andrew B. Whinston. 2000. "Measuring the Internet economy" University of Texas, www.Internetindicators.com, June 6.

Coppel, Jonathan. 2000. "E-commerce: Impacts and policy challenges." *OECD, Economics Department Working Papers*, No. 252, Paris, June 23.

ebusinessforum.com. 2000. "Ericsson: "The promise of purchasing cards." http://www.ebusinessforum.com, December 18.

Economist. 2000. "Survey e-commerce: first America, then the world," February 4, 2000. http://www.economist.com/editorial/freeforall/10000226/su0724.html.

Engler, Natalie. 1999. "Global e-commerce," *InformationWeek*, 755, October 4.

Ghosh, Chandrani. 2000. E-trade routes," *Forbes*, August 7, 108.

Gulati, Ranjay and Jason Garino. 2000. "Get the right mix of bricks & clicks," *Harvard Business Review*, May-June, 107–114.

http://www.nextlinx.com.

Hudgins, Christy. 1999. "International e-commerce." *Network Computing*, 10, 23, November 15, 75–50.

The Internet Economy Indicators. 2000. "The global Internet," July 21, http://www.Internetindicators.com/global.html.

Nickell, Joe Ashbrook. 2000 "Auction THIS, eBay." *Business 2.0*. May, 183, 185, 187.

Pickering, Carol. 2000. "The world's local yokel," *Business 2.0*, May, 188, 193.

Rosen, Kenneth T. and Amanda L. Howard. 2000. "E-retail: gold rush or fool's gold?" *California Management Review*, 42, 3, Spring, 72–100.

Sawhney, Mohanbir and Sumant Mandal. 2000. "Go global." *Business 2.0*, May, 178–213.

Sheridan, E.F. 2000. http://www.Webofculture.com/corp/commandments. html.

Shirky, Clay. 2000. "Go Global or Bust." *Business 2.0*, March 1, 145–6.

Towers Perrin, 2000. http://www.towers.com/towers/services_products/frame_tp_hi.asp?target=TowersPerrin/ebusiness.htm.

Towers Perrin, Reported in Kathleen Melymuka. 2000. "Survey finds companies lack e-commerce blueprint." *Computerworld*, Vol. 34, No. 16, April 17, 38–39.

Van Savage, Eleanor. 2000. "In its infancy: e-commerce in Asia," *Chemical Market Reporter*, Vol. 257, No. 16, April 17, F12–F16.

Venkatraman, N. 2000. "Five steps to a dot-com strategy: how to find your footing on the Web." *Sloan Management Review*, Spring, 15–28.

Wilkerson, Phil. 2000. "Enabling global e-commerce." *Discount Store News*, 39, 8, April 17, 15–16.

Chapter 10

Small Businesses as Multinational Companies: Overcoming Barriers and Finding Opportunities

LEARNING OBJECTIVES
After reading this chapter you should be able to:

- **Understand the basic definitions of small business and entrepreneurship.**

- **Explain how small businesses can begin as global start-ups or follow the stages of internationalization.**

- **Understand how small businesses can overcome barriers to internationalization.**

- **Identify when a small business or entrepreneur should consider going international.**

- **Understand how small businesses or entrepreneurs can find customers, partners, or distributors abroad.**

- **Understand how new venture wedge strategies can be used in foreign markets.**

Colite International Ltd. is a U.S. company that makes signs for businesses. In 1992 the Brown brothers bought a South Carolina local operation (they were the only employees) with little international experience. By 2000, they were a $10 million a year business with 55 employees and doing business in 50 countries. Twenty-eight percent of revenue comes from international sources.

How do they outcompete larger international rivals? The Brown brothers say they use speed, technology, and the Web to better the competition. They take digital pictures of a customer's signs. They change the design and then post the design on their Web site (http://www.colite.com) for the customer's approval. This takes just 24 hours and they deliver the signs within four weeks, beating the industry average of 10 weeks.

Colite is typical of the boom in exporting by small U.S. companies. One survey estimated that companies with fewer than 500 employees account for over 30 percent of U.S. export dollars and represent 90 percent of the number of exporters.

Sources: Based on Barry 2000 and McClenahen 2000.

Small businesses contribute significantly to most national economies. The Preview Case in Point shows the growing influence of smaller U.S. companies in the international market. Even in the developed nations of Europe, North America, and Japan, over 98 percent of all businesses are small. In these countries, small businesses employ more than 50 percent of the workforce and produce nearly 50 percent of the countries' GNPs (OECD 1996; UNCTAD 1993). During the recent periods of downsizing by large firms in the United States, small companies created more than two-thirds of the new jobs (Scarborough and Zimmer 1996).

Given the importance of small businesses to the growth of national economies and to the increasing globalization of business, it is not surprising that small businesses seek opportunities outside their national boundaries—just as their larger brothers and sisters do. When going international, small businesses can use the same participation strategies and multinational strategies available to larger businesses. They can export, form a joint venture, license, and engage in FDI. Small businesses can also act like multidomestic strategists in product adaptation or develop transnational networks for supply, manufacturing, and distribution. However, because they are small and often controlled by the entrepreneur or founder, small businesses face some circumstances different from those of larger multinational corporations. This chapter presents examples and reviews the barriers small businesses face and must overcome in internationalization. It also shows how some basic entrepreneurial strategies can serve small business in taking their products or services to the global marketplace. Topics covered in the chapter include defining the nature of a small business and an entrepreneur, identifying how small businesses go international—from global start-ups to the following stages of internationalization, identifying how small businesses break the barriers to internationalization, and the strategies companies can use to find international markets and to succeed in new international ventures.

"Small" business

UN definition: less than 500 employees. Popular press definition: less than 100 employees. U.S. Small Business Administration's definition: varies by industry and uses both sales revenue and the number of employees.

WHAT IS A SMALL BUSINESS?

There are many definitions of what makes a **"small" business**. A recent study by the United Nations defined small and medium-sized businesses as those having less

Already successful at home, Medical Resources, a medical equipment company, first sensed international opportunities when its Web site generated inquiries from Saudi Arabia. Getting advice from the U.S. Commerce Department's Commercial Service (service for small businesses going international) on how to set up systems for shipping and payment, Medical Resources generated $1 million in sales in its first year of international business.

Medical Resources now has a Saudi partner and a distribution center in Saudi Arabia to serve the Middle East. CEO and owner Randy Reichenbach hopes to sell $100 million of equipment throughout the Middle East in the next few years.

Due to Medical Resources' success, Reichenbach was named Ohio's "Exporter of the Year" in 2000.

Sources: Based on Barry 2000 and http://www.medicalresources.com.

than 500 employees (UNCTAD 1993). The popular press usually considers small businesses as those with less than a hundred employees. The U.S. Small Business Administration has a more complex definition. The definition of small varies by industry and uses both sales revenue and the number of people as indicators of size. For example, to be classified as small by the U.S. Small Business Administration, annual receipts cannot exceed $17 million in the general construction industry, but may range up to $22 million in wholesale trade industries. In manufacturing industries, the maximum number of employees for small businesses ranges between 500 and 1,500, depending on specific industry (Scarborough and Zimmer 1996).

WHAT IS AN ENTREPRENEUR?

Entrepreneur

Person who creates new ventures that seek profit and growth.

New ventures

Entering a new market; offering a new product or service; or introducing a new method, technology, or innovative use of raw materials.

An **entrepreneur** creates new ventures that seek profit and growth. An entrepreneur deals with the risk and uncertainty of new and untested business. **New ventures** exist when a company enters a new market, offers a new product or service, or introduces a new method, technology, or innovative use of raw materials. Risk results from new ventures because their outcomes, such as survival and profitability, are variable. Some companies survive; some die; others make a profit and grow; others remain small. Uncertainty results because a new venture founder can never fully predict which of the variable outcomes will befall his or her company (Dollinger 1995).

Some consider entrepreneurship the driving force of all small businesses (Scarborough and Zimmer 1996). Without an entrepreneurial spirit, few small businesses would exist. That is, at some point, it was necessary for an entrepreneur to face the risk and uncertainty of starting the business.

Moving into the international market is one increasingly important entrepreneurial activity of small businesses. To go international, companies such as Medical Resources, in the preceding Case in Point, must accept the additional risk and uncertainty of receiving payments from foreign customers, partnering with foreign distributors, and entering a new and often strange, foreign market.

INTERNATIONALIZATION AND THE SMALL BUSINESS

How do small businesses go international? This section examines two ways by which small businesses enter the international arena. First, some organizations go

**Small-business
stage model**

*Process of internation-
alization followed by
many small businesses.*

international by following stages of international involvement. Each stage leads to a greater involvement in international business. Second, organizations can begin as global companies. They start international operations at the same time they start domestic operations. The incremental view of internationalization for the small business is called the **small-business stage model**. Going global from day one of the company's life is called a **global start-up**. The next sections discuss these two processes of small-business internationalization in more detail.

THE SMALL-BUSINESS STAGE MODEL OF INTERNATIONALIZATION

Global start-up

*Company that begins
as a multinational
company.*

The traditional view of small-business internationalization follows the stage model. That is, small companies take an incremental approach to internationalization. Such companies begin as passive exporters, filling international orders but not actively seeking international sales. Later, the company may add an export department or an international division, with a more proactive approach to international sales. Joint ventures and other forms of direct investment follow. The stage model probably applies to the majority of small-business efforts at internationalization. Most, but not all small businesses, do not have the managerial and financial resources for immediate globalization.

The typical stages of internationalization for a small entrepreneurial business include (Dollinger 1995):

- *Stage 1—Passive exporting:* The company fills international orders but does not seek export business. At this stage, many small-business owners do not realize that they have an international market.
- *Stage 2—Export management:* The CEO or a designated manager specifically seeks export sales. Because of resource limitations, most small businesses at this stage rely on the indirect channel of exporting (see Chapter 6). However, this stage is often a major change in orientation for the entrepreneur or small-business manager. Exporting is seen as an opportunity for new business.
- *Stage 3—Export department:* The company uses significant resources to seek increased sales from exporting. Managers no longer see exporting as a prohibitive risk. The key for most small businesses is finding a good local partner for distribution.
- *Stage 4—Sales branches:* When demand for the company's product is high in a country or region, it justifies setting up local sales offices. Small businesses must have the resources to transfer home managers to expatriate assignments or to hire and train local managers and workers to run these operations.
- *Stage 5—Production abroad:* Production moves a company beyond downstream value-chain activities. It allows companies to gain local advantages such as easy local product adaptation or production efficiencies. Companies may use licensing, joint ventures, or direct investment. This is often a very difficult stage for a small business because the cost of a failed direct investment can put the whole company at risk for survival.
- *Stage 6—The transnational:* Small size does not preclude a business from developing a globally integrated network that characterizes the transnational corporation. As we will see, some entrepreneurs begin their small businesses as transnationals.

Many small and some large companies find the deliberate process of internationalization by stages adequate for their strategic situation. Following the stage model allows companies to minimize their exposure to risk and develop their international expertise gradually. In contrast, other entrepreneurial companies have

Multinational Management Challenge
Can You Go Global from Day One?

Since its founding in 1998, going global was the heart of Eagle Building Technologies Ltd's strategic plan. The reason? CEO Anthony D'Amato said it is because of the size of the foreign market.

Eagle's main product is a stacked, mortarless wall system originally designed at Brigham Young University. Eagle licenses the technology from Integrated Masonry Systems International.

Eagle's first major contract was in China. They have a joint venture with Double Dragon Cement Works, a Chinese state-owned enterprise, and contract for 5 million square feet of residential construction. In addition to China, Eagle does business in India and Mexico. Operations in Turkey, Croatia, and Yugoslavia are planned.

In 2000, the first year of revenues, this 47-person company generated 90 percent of its income from foreign sources.

Source: Based on McClenahen 2000.

products that often require them to go international immediately or to move rapidly through the internationalization stages. In the next section, we discuss the growing phenomenon of global start-ups to show how rapidly some beginning businesses become global operations.

SMALL-BUSINESS GLOBAL START-UP

Global start-ups occur when companies begin as multinational companies. Impossible?—not in today's international marketplace. The preceding Multinational Management Challenge shows how Eagle Building Technologies used going global as the heart of its strategic plan to generate 90 percent of its first year's revenue from foreign sources.

Global start-ups require unique conditions and organizations. One viewpoint argues that six key elements favor global start-ups (Oviatt and McDougall 1995). Not surprisingly, these elements are similar to the globalization forces that favor transnational companies of all sizes. They include:

- *Dispersed human resources*: Conditions favor global start-ups when key skills exist in different locations throughout the world. To tap these human resources, companies must locate wherever the best and cheapest skills are found.
- *International sources of venture capital:* Conditions favor global start-ups when entrepreneurs have sources of capital from within their native country and from sources in other countries. When a company has a global presence, it can move quickly to the most available and cheapest sources of funds.
- *The existence of a global demand:* Conditions favor global start-ups when demand for the product or service exists in many countries. The existence of global demand was a key driving factor for Eagle Building Tecnologies, discussed in the foregoing Multinational Management Challenge, to go global immediately on founding.

- *The lack of a geographically protected market:* Conditions favor global start-ups if the flow of information and communication break down barriers of geography and allow competitors from other nations to imitate a new venture. Companies must go global immediately to gain a foothold in competitors' domestic markets.
- *The necessity of worldwide sales to support the venture:* Conditions favor global start-ups when no one market can produce sufficient sales to support the business. A company may capture near total market share in its domestic market but still not have sufficient sales revenue to survive. High-tech businesses with large R&D expenses often require the large sales of global markets to offset the cost of the R&D investment.
- *The potential to avoid later resistance to internationalization:* Conditions support global start-ups when it is easier to begin globally than to change to global later. All organizations develop a history and culture that, if initially successful, inhibit later change. Domestic success may squelch an entrepreneurial spirit and lead to missed international opportunities later in the organization's life.

Although a global start-up is not always possible for a new venture, when the conditions are right, the global start-up represents an increasingly popular choice for many new companies.

Liability of newness

A large percentage of new businesses fail within a year.

Liability of size

Being small often makes business failure more probable, because small size usually means limited resources.

All new small-business ventures face a **liability of newness** and a **liability of size**. That is, being new and small often make business failure more probable than success. Small size usually means limited resources, and young age often means new and untried ideas. Although all entrepreneurial ventures are risky, global start-ups are more risky than domestic ventures. However, even with the increased risk and complexity of immediately going international, global start-ups may offer the only avenue of success for new ventures in rapidly globalizing industries (Oviatt and McDougall 1995).

The next section reviews some of the obstacles that often prevent small businesses from going international, either by stages or by global start-ups.

OVERCOMING SMALL-BUSINESS BARRIERS TO INTERNATIONALIZATION

Conventional wisdom argues that small businesses face many barriers that retard their becoming multinational companies. Small size often means limited financial and personnel resources to dedicate to international activities. Small size can also mean a lack of sufficient scale to produce goods or services as efficiently as larger companies. Small companies often have top managers with limited international experience. These managers may have negative attitudes toward becoming multinational. Such managers view international ventures as too risky and not potentially profitable. Negative managerial attitudes and past success at home lead to organizational cultures with a strong domestic orientation.

Global culture

Managerial and worker values that view strategic opportunities as global and not just domestic.

In spite of these difficulties with internationalization, many small businesses aggressively enter international markets and succeed. Next, we consider some of the barriers to internationalization and examples of how small businesses and entrepreneurs have overcome these barriers to achieve successful multinational operations.

DEVELOPING A SMALL-BUSINESS GLOBAL CULTURE

A **global culture** occurs when an organization has managerial and worker values that view strategic opportunities as global and not just domestic. At all levels of the organization, members share a common language to describe international operations. This common language gives organizational members a framework to interpret and understand their company's actions in the international arena (Caprioni, Lenway, and Murtha 1994).

Generally, increased international competition and exposure to international markets have forced larger companies, such as those in the automobile industry, to develop more of a global culture. Survival made it necessary for top executives of all nationalities to respond to global competition.

Smaller businesses, however, often ignore international opportunities because key decision makers and the culture of their organizations view competition only as domestic. In a true global culture, entrepreneurial owners develop a global mindset for themselves and their companies. Thinking globally permeates everything that happens in the company. People believe that national boundaries are less relevant. They also believe that the company can do business and conduct value-chain operations (e.g., R&D, manufacturing, raising capital) anywhere in the world.

Several characteristics of the key decision makers in an organization affect the development of a global culture (Dichtl, Koeglmayr, and Mueller 1990). These include:

- *Perceived psychic distance to foreign markets:* This represents the extent to which managers believe that foreign markets are "just too different" for involvement. When key managers overcome this belief, a global culture is more likely to exist.
- *International experience:* Managers with little training in foreign languages and little international travel often resist internationalization. However, managers with previous international experiences, even just personal travel and sightseeing, have a greater propensity to recognize global opportunities. Often even a chance meeting during a foreign vacation can trigger an international small-business venture.
- *Risk aversion:* Managers who are unwilling to take risks have difficulty supporting internationalization of the firm. Going international requires an entrepreneurial spirit and thus the willingness to face risks.
- *Overall attitudes toward international strategies:* Some managers just find the idea of international strategies too dangerous to the status quo. Others see international opportunities as beneficial to the company and to their careers. A global culture will develop when the owner/entrepreneur promotes company values that support and reward looking for international opportunities.

Those companies with a global culture and key decision makers that view the world as an opportunity will more likely become multinational companies. The following Case in Point shows how the international experience of the CEO helped one organization overcome the lack of a global culture.

CHANGING ATTITUDES OF KEY DECISION MAKERS

Both the stage model and the global start-up model focus on the attitudes of the primary decision makers as key to the development of an international culture in small or medium-sized business. For companies that internationalize their business through stages, each stage demonstrates the key executives' increasing commitment to internationalization.

Early in internationalization, managers perceive foreign markets as risky, with high costs to enter and with low potential benefits. Because of these somewhat negative attitudes toward internationalization, most international sales for small and

Case in Point

Growing a Transnational in Five Years

In 1986 Dennis Gillings was chief executive of a four-year-old pharmaceutical research company with one U.S. location and only thirty-five employees. Gillings, however, had an international mind-set. Raised in England but managing a U.S. business, he saw the opening of the unified EC market as a great opportunity for his company. Gillings reasoned that if he started European operations early in the unified EC, he would have a tremendous competitive advantage.

When Gillings proposed a European office for his four-year-old company, he now recalls, "Everyone within the company thought I was verging on crazy." He had an international mind-set but his company did not. To develop an international culture, he started cautiously. Gillings visited thirty prospective European customers before lining up sufficient work to open the London office. Within five years, Gillings' company, Quintiles Corp., had offices in five countries.

To develop a more international culture, Quintiles Corp. starts an operation with expatriate managers. However, the firm hires local managers as soon as possible to take advantage of their local contacts. Quintiles uses a sophisticated electronic communication system to keep everyone in touch. Beginning as a small U.S. professional service business, Quintiles is now a fast-growth multinational company. Through the years of its international expansion, Quintiles' sales grew from $1.9 million to over $60 million.

Source: Based on Mangelsdorf 1993.

medium-sized businesses come from countries that are close in culture and in geography. For example, most Canadian companies begin exporting first to their geographically and culturally similar neighbor to the south. These cautious moves to increase internationalization help top managers overcome initial skepticism regarding international markets. In later stages of internationalization, these attitudes change, with the international market often perceived as more profitable than the domestic market (Calof and Viviers 1995; Miesenbock 1988). Exhibit 10.1 shows that exporters and nonexporters in the U.S. industrial-equipment industry have quite different attitudes regarding internationalization.

Positive attitudes toward international markets are perhaps more necessary for global start-ups than for companies that move slowly into the global marketplace. Experts (Oviatt and McDougall 1995) argue that successful global start-ups require the founders to communicate a global vision to everyone in the organization. Managers like Anthony D'Amato, discussed in the previous Eagle Technologies Case in Point, use their global vision to help their companies become multinational from birth.

GAINING EXPERIENCE: DUTIES AND THE PERSONAL LIFE OF THE SMALL-BUSINESS CEO

The effects of internationalization on the personal life and duties of the CEO may play a more important role in the international activities of small and medium-sized companies than for larger firms. The owner of a small business is often the CEO and the driving entrepreneurial force in the business. When internationalization

Exhibit 10.1

Attitudinal Differences
Concerning Inter-
nationalization for
Small-Business
Exporters and
Nonexporters

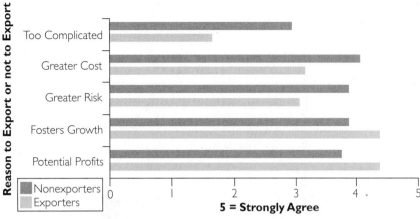

Source: Adapted from Kedia and Chhokar 1985.

affects this individual, it threatens the whole underlying fabric of the organization (Wright 1993).

For a small firm, opening new markets is often the CEO's personal responsibility. Although small-company CEOs spend only 20 percent of their time managing export and other international functions, the CEO must be willing to incur more than economic costs for the venture (Beamish and Munro 1987). There are social and business costs to the CEO who engages in internationalization. The CEO's responsibilities for the new international venture often result in increased travel and stress from undertaking a new venture. Many CEOs feel that these activities adversely affect family life. They also dislike being away from the daily management of their businesses (Wright 1993).

In addition, the job of the small-business CEO may change when the company becomes multinational. A study of Canadian manufacturers who had recently begun exporting found that over 50 percent of the CEOs felt that their duties changed since going international. The impact seemed to affect CEOs more than their workers. Only a little over 20 percent of the employees in the same companies had their jobs restructured and needed retraining due to the firms' international business (Wright 1993).

As new multinational managers, the Canadian CEOs also believed that they needed skill upgrading for international business. Exhibit 10.2 shows key skills that the CEOs felt they needed.

IS SIZE A BARRIER FOR SMALL-BUSINESS INTERNATIONALIZATION?

Larger firms have a greater tendency to enter export markets. They have more resources to absorb the risk of exporting and often have a greater incentive to export when domestic markets become saturated (Bonacorsi 1992).

Many academic researchers and small-business managers argue that only larger companies have the resources to become multinationals (Bonacorsi 1992). In fact, most studies find that the larger the business, the more likely the firm exports its products (Christensen, da Rocha, and Gertner 1987). Even among those firms that do export, larger firms tend toward committed exporting, while smaller firms tend toward passive exporting. Larger firms also serve more national markets. For example, one study of Canadian firms found that companies with total sales of over

Exhibit 10.2
Training and Knowledge Needs of Small-Firm CEOs Entering Internationalization

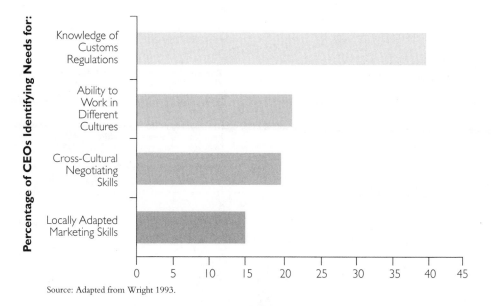

Source: Adapted from Wright 1993.

Size barrier to internationalization

It is often more difficult for small businesses to take the first step in internationalizing their organization.

International sales intensity

Amount of international sales divided by total sales of the company.

$50 million exported on average to twenty-seven different countries, while smaller firms averaged only slightly more than twelve countries (Calof 1993).

However, the **size barrier to internationalization** may exist only in the initial internationalization decision. That is, larger size makes it easier for a company to begin exporting or direct investment. But once firms do choose to take on an international venture, experts suggest that the international sales intensity of small firms equals, if it does not exceed, that of larger firms (Calof 1993). **International sales intensity** represents the amount of international sales divided by the total sales of the company. Thus, once involved in international ventures, small multinational companies often gain sales revenues proportionally equal to or greater than those of larger multinational companies (Bonacorsi 1992).

The same study of Canadian firms also shows how small multinational firms can outperform larger companies on international sales intensity. The researchers found that smaller companies using foreign direct investment produced over 68 percent of their revenues from foreign sales as compared to 48 percent for larger firms with similar investments. Similarly, smaller exporting firms were as likely as larger exporting firms to generate about one-third of their revenues from exporting (Calof 1993).

In addition, even with their lower total volume of international sales, the smallest multinational companies (those with fewer than twenty employees) can achieve significant export success. Estimates suggest that these micro companies account for 12 percent of U.S. exports (*Inc. Online* 1994a).

USING THE SMALL-BUSINESS ADVANTAGE

In spite of some barriers to internationalization, the small business has some advantages over larger and often more entrenched organizations. In fact, the trend-spotting author of *The Global Paradox*, John Naisbitt, predicts that small multinational businesses will have even greater advantages in the increasingly global economy. He argues that small companies can change products and internal operations faster to take advantage of evolving technologies. In contrast, larger organi-

Small-business advantage

Fast-moving entre-preneurs can use their competitive advantage of speed. Being first to market, they can cap-ture significant sales before larger com-petitors react.

zations often must overcome extensive bureaucratic procedures when adopting new products or new management operations. The bureaucratic procedures of larger organizations slow down decision making often leading to missed opportu-nities in the global marketplace.

For the small business, speed becomes the **small-business advantage**. When larger companies are slow to react to rapidly changing conditions, fast-moving en-trepreneurs can use their competitive advantage of speed. Being first to market, they can capture significant sales before the larger competitors can react (Scarborough and Zimmer 1996). The small-business advantage is particularly important for the multinational company because, increasingly, the global economy requires fast change to take advantage of new markets.

THE FUTURE: FALLING BARRIERS TO MULTINATIONAL SMALL BUSINESSES AND MORE GLOBAL START-UPS

Many of the barriers to small-business internationalization are becoming easier to overcome. Government programs that support small-business exporting and sales are expanding. High-impact trade agreements such as NAFTA and the WTO make trade less complex and reduce the resource requirements that previously held back many smaller firms. The rapid growth of international business information pro-duced by governments and other sources such as the World Wide Web provide a wealth of readily available information to entrepreneurs regarding international op-portunities. In turn, this knowledge of international business opportunities encour-ages more entrepreneurs to consider global start-ups and makes it easier for estab-lished small businesses to become multinationals.

The increase in the number of small businesses engaged in international activi-ties also makes it easier for other businesses to develop a global culture. Now, po-tential international entrepreneurs not only have a better knowledge of business opportunities abroad, but they can also copy the cultures of other successful small multinational companies. In addition, as more managers gain experience in inter-national business, negative attitudes among small-business owners and entrepre-neurs toward international sales will decrease.

Although the barriers to small-business internationalization may be falling, managers still need to assess whether their firm is ready to go international. The next section provides a series of diagnostic questions that can help small-business owners and managers make the internationalization decision. The following sec-tion describes how small businesses can make the contacts with customers and po-tential partners necessary to succeed in foreign sales.

WHEN SHOULD A SMALL BUSINESS GO INTERNATIONAL?

The small business must respond to many of the same questions as the larger busi-ness when considering multinational options. However, the limited number of products or services—and the limited resources—of most small businesses make certain drivers of internationalization more important for them.

Several questions, when answered affirmatively, suggest that a small business is ready to become a multinational company. These include:

- *Do we have a global product or service?* A global product or service can be sold worldwide with minimal changes for each country. Since small businesses seldom have the resources to adapt each product to local needs, producing a

Exhibit 10.3 Questions to Consider in the Small-Business Decision to Go International

Management Objectives

• What is the reason for going international?

• How committed is top management to the internationalization decision?

• How quickly does management expect the internationalization effort to pay off?

Management Experience and Resources

• What in-house international expertise does the firm have (international sales experience, language capabilities, etc.)?

• Who will be responsible for the international organizational component of the company (e.g., export department)?

• How much senior management time should be allocated?

• What organizational structure is required?

Production Capacity

• How is the present capacity being used?

• Will international sales hurt domestic sales?

• What will be the cost of additional production at home or in a foreign location?

• What modifications of the product or service are required?

Financial Capacity

• What amount of capital can be committed to international production and marketing?

• What level of operating costs for international operations can be supported?

• What other financial requirements may compete with the internationalization efforts?

• By what date must the internationalization effort have positive returns?

Source: Adapted from U.S. Department of Commerce 1998.

standard worldwide product makes globalization easier. As discussed in Chapter 6, if customers have similar needs, or customers seek a product or service from anywhere in the world, then there exists a greater opportunity for globalization (Yip 1995).

• *Do we have the managerial, organizational, and financial resources to internationalize?* Internationalization, even with the more simple participation strategies, requires significant availability of financial and personnel resources. Exhibit 10.3 gives some of the questions concerning resource requirements that a small business facing the prospect of going international needs to address.

• *Even if we do have the resources, are we willing to commit those resources and face the risks of internationalization?* Small-business managers must view internationalization as similar to other start-up ventures. For the right company, with the right products, the eventual returns from a new international venture may exceed the investment and make the exposure to risk worthwhile. To seek these potential returns, managers must overcome the psychological and cultural boundaries already noted.

• *Is there a country in which we feel comfortable doing business?* Without the resources to understand the cultural and business practices in many countries, small-business managers often first seek international opportunities in national cultures similar to their own.

• *Is there a profitable market for our product or service?* Even with good products or services, a key question focuses on which countries to enter. For example, research

Exhibit 10.4 Steps in Picking a Foreign Market

1. **Screen Potential Markets**

   - Get statistics that show the extent of the relevant products exported to or produced in potential countries.

   - Identify five to ten countries with large and fast-growing markets for the products. Examine the trends in the market in past years and different economic circumstances.

   - Identify additional countries with smaller, newly emerging markets. These may provide first mover advantages.

   - Target three to five of the most promising markets. Mix established markets with emerging markets, depending on management's tolerance for risk.

2. **Assess Targeted Markets**

   - Examine market trends for company products or services and related products or services that could affect demand.

   - Identify demographic trends (income, age, education, population, and so on) that identify the users of the company's products or services.

   - Estimate the overall consumption of the product or service and the amounts provided by foreign and domestic producers.

   - Identify sources of competition from domestic producers and other foreign competitors, including price, quality, features, and service.

   - Identify local channels of distribution.

   - Assess what modifications of the product or service are required.

   - Identify cultural differences that may influence participation strategies available.

   - Identify any foreign barriers to exporting or other participation options (tariffs, limitations on percentage of ownership, home-country export controls, etc.).

   - Identify any foreign or home-country incentives to enter the market.

3. **Draw Conclusions and Make the Choice**

Source: Adapted from U.S. Department of Commerce 1998.

by managers at Ekkwill Tropical Fish Farm indicated that collecting fish was a popular hobby in many countries. One-third of its production now goes to markets in Asia, Latin America, Canada, and the West Indies (Knowlton 1988).

- *Which country should we enter?* A thorough strategic analysis is required. Firms need to identify potential threats and opportunities by country. For example, current and future demand for a product may vary by country. Each country also has different competitors as well as different barriers to entry (tariffs, complex distribution systems, and so forth). Exhibit 10.4 gives a summary of the steps that small businesses can follow to find customers abroad.

- *Do we have a unique product or service that is not easily copied by larger multinational companies or local entrepreneurs?* Although small firms may have the advantage of speed to market, large multinationals may use their advantage of economies of scale to imitate an innovation, using a lower-priced product. To maintain their competitive advantage over larger firms, small multinational companies must have rare resources (i.e., not easy to copy) and valuable resources (factors that allow the company to produce a product or service valued by customers). These rare and valued resources may include technical superiority, innovation, or high quality. They give the company the muscle to produce continuously superior products or services (Barney 1991).

- *Do location advantages exist upstream in the value chain?* Internationalization of a small firm need not be just a downstream activity in the value chain, such as marketing. When there are advantages of lower cost or higher quality in supply or manufacturing, small multinational companies can seek the same location advantages available to larger companies by sourcing raw materials or manufacturing in other countries. For example, Northwest River Supply Corp., a small firm producing high-quality whitewater rafts in Moscow, Idaho, found significant cost advantages by manufacturing in Mexico. It could produce better-quality products with cheaper prices than its large-company competitors.

- *Can we afford not to be a multinational?* There are several factors, even for the small business, that may make becoming a multinational company necessary for survival. A shrinking home market may require a firm to internationalize to maintain sales revenue. Finding international sources of lower costs of raw material or production facilities may be necessary to match competitors' prices and maintain profit margins. Small multinational companies may find the positive image of being a multinational firm necessary for attracting new customers and attracting investors.

The next section reviews the use of different participation strategies for the small multinational company.

GETTING CONNECTED TO THE INTERNATIONAL MARKET

PARTICIPATION STRATEGIES

Small and medium-sized multinational companies have the same participation options, as do larger firms, including exporting, licensing, joint ventures, and foreign direct investment. Most often, however, the small business emphasizes exporting as its major international-participation strategy. For the small firm without knowledge of potential foreign customers or sufficient resources to set up an overseas sales office, indirect exporting makes the most sense. These firms use the services of ETCs or EMCs to get their products to the international market.

However, even an internationally inexperienced small business can jump to direct exporting or more advanced stages of internationalization when they can find the right foreign distribution channel. The following Multinational Management Challenge contrasts the advantages of going alone to develop your own distribution system to building a close relationship with a foreign distributor. This Multinational Management Challenge gives an example of how one entrepreneur confronted the choice of using direct foreign sales or sales through foreign distributors.

FINDING CUSTOMERS AND PARTNERS

Customer contact techniques

Trade shows, catalog expositions, international advertising agencies and consulting firms, government-sponsored trade missions, and direct contact.

To go international, small businesses must find ways to reach their foreign customers, either by direct contact or by teaming up with foreign partners (distributors, joint venture partners, or licensees) who deal with the ultimate customers. As with larger multinational companies, there is no set formula for finding partners or customers. Much depends on the nature of the product, countries involved, and the nature and resources of the company involved. However, there are some standard techniques readily available to small multinational companies. In this section, we show some of these common **customer contact techniques**.

- *Trade shows:* National and international trade shows give small businesses inexpensive mechanisms to contact potential customers or business partners. Trade

Multinational Management Challenge
Going Alone or Working with a Foreign Distributor

Just three years after its founding, Evolutionary Technologies International, a software company, was asked by a European company: "Who represents you in Europe? We're ready to buy." EFI founder, Robin Curle was in shock; they had no one in Europe or anywhere else outside the United States for that matter.

Curle took direct responsibility for the European operation. She hired a European manager from France. She then faced the decision of whether to sell directly or through local distributors.

Their product requires extensive support so they chose to sell directly in Europe. She did not believe a local distributor would provide the required service.

Next stop was Japan. In Japan, EFI found that they did not have local knowledge to sell directly. They hired a consultant who linked them with local distributors.

Curle notes that both strategies work and the entrepreneur must study local situations carefully. EFI now generates 55 percent of its revenue from international sales.

Source: Based on Curle 1998.

shows give businesses the opportunity to set up displays of their products and to provide brochures and other documents that describe their product or service. Businesses may rent space at the shows individually or as part of a larger group. The U.S. Commerce Department now runs a virtual trade show called E-ExpoUSA (http://www.e-expousa.doc.gov/). This Web site offers constant access to U.S. suppliers and international buyers. The site shows product descriptions, photos, and videos (Barry 2000).

- *Catalog expositions:* Catalog expositions are similar to trade shows except that a business does not have its product or people at the show. Rather, product catalogs, sales brochures, and other graphic presentations show a firm's goods or services at some site. Some U.S. embassies and consulates provide catalog expositions for U.S. goods. Because a company need only send printed matter, catalog expositions provide a low-cost way of testing international markets.

- *International advertising agencies and consulting firms:* International advertising agencies and consulting firms have offices throughout the world; often with specialists in different products or services. International advertising agencies can provide advertising and promotional services geared to a local national environment. Consulting firms often have a good knowledge of local regulations, local competitors, and local distribution channels. A business that uses these services can expect to pay significant compensation. However, local-market expertise and contacts may make the expenditure worthwhile.

- *Government-sponsored trade missions:* To foster growth in international trade, governments often sponsor trade missions. These missions represent companies or

Exhibit 10.5

Selected U.S. Government Programs for Making International Contacts

Department of Commerce Contact Programs

- *Export contact list service:* provides mailing lists of foreign distributors, manufacturers, retailers, service firms, and government agencies.

- *Trade opportunities program (TOP):* provides sales leads from foreign firms that seek to buy or represent U.S. services or products.

- *Agent/distributor service (ADS):* a custom search service for U.S. exporters seeking foreign import agencies and distributors.

- *Commercial news USA(CNUSA):* provides an illustrated catalog and electronic bulletin boards available through U.S. embassies and consulates.

Department of Commerce Trade-Event Programs

- *Certified trade-fair program:* provides U.S. Department of Commerce assistance and support to trade-fair organizers who agree to give special assistance to small businesses and new-to-export businesses.

- *Foreign buyer program:* provides overseas promotional support for selected trade shows where U.S. businesses can meet potential foreign buyers, distributors, licensees, or joint-venture partners.

- *Matchmaker trade delegations:* organized and led by Department of Commerce personnel, these delegations introduce new-to-export and new-to-market firms to prescreened international prospects.

- *Trade missions:* similar to matchmaker delegations, these missions introduce U.S. makers and service providers to foreign contacts.

U.S. Department of Agriculture

- *Commodity and marketing programs:* provide businesses with data on consumption, trade, stocks, and marketing information on specific agricultural products.

- *High-value product services division:* provides trade shows, trade leads from overseas buyers with an interest in U.S. agricultural products, and free advertising of U.S. products overseas.

- *Trade assistance and planning (TAPO):* provides an information source for U.S. agricultural exporters.

Source: Adapted from U.S. Department of Commerce 1998.

industries looking to open new markets in the countries visited. Host governments usually provide introductions to potential local sales representatives, distributors, and end users.

- *Direct contact:* Although it is often more difficult and costly, small-business entrepreneurs and managers can seek channel partners, joint-venture partners, and end users directly. As noted earlier in a Multinational Management Challenge, Robin Curle of Evolutionary Technologies International went directly to customers in Europe, but used local distributors in Japan. If the managers/entrepreneurs can find key intermediaries—that is, potential alliance partners or distributors—or can get direct access to potential customers, then direct contact may work best.

Exhibit 10.5 shows some of the programs the U.S. government provides to businesses seeking international contacts or potential customers. Other countries provide similar services. Exhibit 10.6 shows some sources on the World Wide Web that any multinational company can access to find trade leads. And the Case in Point on page 403, on Water Systems International, shows how one small company

Exhbit 10.6 A Sample of International Trade Leads on the Web

B2B for Tomorrow

This site is designed to support all companies by providing an electronic B2B marketplace where buyers and sellers can advertise their products or services on the Internet. This is still a fairly new site, so there isn't a great number of companies, but the site is continually being updated. Registration is free and allows the user to post and view leads. This site lists companies from all over the world in a number of different sectors.

International Business Forum

The International Business Forum provides information about business opportunities in the international marketplace. The Forum is divided into numerous sections: a company directory, business opportunities listings, business event listings, business education sources, resources, and associations.

Mpost

In addition to various trade discussion boards including Traders board and World Exhibition Board, Mpost also features a Trade Resources area where users can search for chambers of commerce, world exhibitions, worldwide hotel, and other useful information for the International Business professional.

Online Trade Leads

Onlineleads.com provides a global depository of trade leads for importers, exporters, and related services. Functions such as posting, buying, selling, and searching currently are free of charge and the provider-company is attempting to keep them this way.

The Import-Export Bulletin Board (The IEBB)

The Import-Export Bulletin Board is a global trade leads portal. In conjunction with Trade Compass, this Web site provides a searchable trade leads database, a listing of most recent leads, and articles on how to utilize trade leads. The site claims that the trade leads posted by IEBB members are published regularly in the Journal of Commerce.

The Trading Floor

A very interactive and complete trading site. Offering online trading, confidential negotiations, private group conferences, a Blackboard of multimedia-enhanced trade leads and inquiries, an information-rich Trader Directory, and unique multimedia brochures and catalogs, The Trading Floor is a comprehensive interactive trading facilitator available on the Internet for firms involved in international trade. There is a lot of informative information as well, such as product and industry reports, and a list of required documentation for every country. There is a subscription fee for the use of this site.

TradeExpress International

TradeExpress International is a bulletin board service for importers and exporters. It consists of products offered and a products wanted bulletins. There is a subscription fee to post offers, while viewing posted offers is free.

TradeZone

The Tradezone International Business Opportunities page provides access to a trade leads database which is for manufacturers, exporters, importers, trade services, and opportunity seekers. Access to the database is free.

Venture-Web

This bilingual site (English and Japanese) offers a meeting place for international traders worldwide. Any individual or company looking to sell or buy a product, looking for specialized personnel, trying to raise capital, or searching business partners can post messages and browse the listings.

World Trade Markets

World Trade Markets in cooperation with the United Nations Conference on Trade and Development (UNCTAD) have adapted the WTM renowned Trade/SEARCH system to cater for the capturing, dissemination, and searching of Trade Point Trade Leads (ETO's-Electronic Trade Opportunities) throughout the world. The WTM database is updated daily by the United Nations, Trade Points, WTM Agents, and Research Staff as well the Internet Public.

World Trade Zone

Another site dedicated to fostering international trade. The site offers a categorized company directory as well as a searchable listing of trade leads. The site also hosts a mailing list for trade leads. For more information about the list, check the mailing list section of this index.

WorldBid.com

Worldbid.com is an international network that brings together buyers and sellers from around the world for interactive trade. Site receives over 1,000 new posts daily from over 18,000 companies in 100 countries. Registration is required, but free.

(continued)

Exhbit 10.6 A Sample of International Trade Leads on the Web *(continued)*

AFRICA: MBendi—The African Trading Space

Hosted by the premier African business information site, trade enquiries posted can be searched by product and offer type. Companies wishing to buy or sell items can post and update trade enquiries. There is no charge to use this service.

ASIA: Asia's Marketplace

Another bulletin board separated into three sections: For sale, To buy, and Business opportunities.

EUROPE: ECeurope.com

A business to business trading bulletin board that serves small-to-medium sized companies in accessing trade leads. Membership is required and it's free. Multi-lingual site.

Angola: Business Opportunities Bulletin Board

The Embassy of the Republic of Angola in Washington, D.C. has established a Business Opportunities Bulletin Board due to the many requests for information on business contacts in Angola's economic sectors. Individuals can post relevant trade and investment opportunities to others with similar interests in the business community.

Brazil: Franchising Net

Franchising Net is a Web site with business opportunities, news, and information related do the franchising business in Brazil. The Brazilian Franchising Index has more than 1200 different franchising opportunities divided by categories into 35 sections. Site is currently (Aug. 2000) under heavy construction.

China: China Business Bulletin Board

A bulletin board that allows traders all over the world to use. It is free.

Czech Republic: Export-Import Express

A bulletin board for business persons with interest in the Czech market. Offers to sell, buy, business opportunities, and partner searches can all be posted.

Egypt: Egyptian Ex-Im Bulletin Board

A simple bulletin board dedicated to Egyptian Export and Import activities. Posting is free.

India: India Trade Board

India Trade Board is an exclusive forum for posting business to business messages. This board does not cross-post to any other board, list, or newsgroups nor does it allow auto posting. Search, Buy, and Sell are available.

Ireland: ITW—Business to Business

The Irish Trade Web is offering a free new service to Irish and Foreign businesses. A very helpful site for those interested in entering the European market through an agency in Ireland, or are looking for Irish products to import.

Mexico: Desde-mexico

Catalog of Mexican companies focused on exports, ordered by industry in English and Spanish. However, most contact information is in Spanish.

Poland: BMB Promotions Business Information Services Poland 2000

This site is created to foster international trade with Poland. One section offers a listing of cooperation proposals from a large number of domestic businesses through a searchable interface. The Special Economic Zone section provides information about tax, investment, and more.

Russia: Russian Business, Trade, and Investment

A site dedicated to providing information for business persons and investors interested in the former Soviet Union (FSU): Russia, the CIS and NIS. Lots of information including trade newsletters, company directories, trade show listings, industry specific information, and trade opportunity listings. Currently (Oct. 2000) under major renovations. The old version is still accessible at http://www.publications-etc.com/russia/index2.html

Taiwan: Taiwan Products Online

Search for trade leads with China and Taiwan using the product or supplier search. Includes trade information as well as links to other useful information for the international trader.

Turkey: BusinessTurk

This site hosts bulletin boards for offers to buy, sell, and various business opportunities for the international business persons interested in Turkish markets.

Source: Michigan State University, CIBER Web site, http://ciber.bus.msu.edu/busres/Static/Trade-Leads.htm, March 5, 2001. Used with permission.

Case in Point	To help U.S. small businesses contact business partners and customers throughout the world, the U.S. Commerce Department has a program called Matchmakers. Matchmakers has overseas offices in numerous countries and access to local government trade officials. The service is available in 35 countries and links to over 100 Export Assistance Centers in the United States.
Water Systems International Finds Partners Through Matchmaker	Local businesspeople visit the Matchmaker offices and link up with trade specialists in the United States who have U.S. supplier product information and capabilities.
	Water Systems International produces equipment to remove impurities from water such as excess fluoride or other harmful chemicals. WSI used the Matchmaker program to make major equipment sales to the governments of India and West Bengal.
	Source: Based on Barry 2000.

used the U.S. government's "matchmaker" program to build a growing international enterprise.

READY TO GO AND CONNECTED: A SYNOPSIS

The forgoing sections provide the diagnostic questions a small-business person can use to decide when to take his or her business international. These questions focus first on whether a firm has the right products and adequate resources to go international. The questions then prompt the entrepreneur to consider the competition and the country environments where he or she hopes to do business.

If the company is ready to go international and the foreign opportunities are attractive, then there exists a variety of mechanisms popular among small multinational businesses to make international contacts for customer and partners. The previous section reviewed many of the readily available sources. However, an enterprising small-business person will find that many more sources exist and that detailed research will increase the likelihood of the international venture's success. Finding the right overseas partner may be the most crucial decision of all.

Even with the right company, the right product, and a potential customer, a small business needs a good wedge to break into a new market. The next section shows how small businesses can use some traditional entrepreneurial wedge strategies in starting and building an international venture.

NEW-VENTURE STRATEGIES FOR SMALL MULTINATIONAL COMPANIES

Entry wedge

Company's competitive advantage for breaking into the established pattern of commercial activity.

New ventures, whether initial start-up operations such as global start-ups or new international operations for an ongoing business, need some type of entry wedge to gain an initial position in a business opportunity. Karl Vesper, the renowned expert on new ventures, defines the **entry wedge** as "a strategic competitive advantage for breaking into the established pattern of commercial activity" (Vesper 1980). In this section, the chapter examines how some of the common entrepreneurship entry wedges work for the small multinational business. The section also includes numerous examples of small businesses using entry wedges for their multinational activities.

New Product or Service and First-Mover Advantage

First-mover advantage

That of the entrepreneur who moves quickly into a new venture and establishes the business before other companies can react to the opportunity.

Technological leadership

Being first to use or introduce a new technology.

One basic entrepreneurial wedge strategy focuses on being the first to introduce a new product or service (Dollinger 1995). This strategy tries to capture **first-mover advantage**. First-mover advantage occurs when the entrepreneur moves quickly into a new venture and establishes the business before other firms can react to the opportunity. To succeed, the new product or service must be not only innovative but also comprehensive. Comprehensive means that the product must meet customer expectations in areas such as warranty, customer service, and expected components. Without a comprehensive introduction, the new product or service is easy for competitors to imitate.

Technological leadership provides the most common source of first-mover advantage. The first company to use or introduce a new technology often has the best understanding of how to produce a product. It did the initial research and development and has the greatest familiarity with the product's characteristics. Such firms can build on this knowledge to keep ahead of competition by using their head start to introduce new product developments and innovations.

Several other situations give first movers an advantage. They may have first access to natural and social resources, such as mining rights and close relationships with research universities. The first movers can choose the best locations not only for raw materials but also for proximity to customers. Finally, and perhaps more important in international business, first movers can have the best access to social relationships. Social relationships lead to the personal contacts necessary to build effective channels of distribution. They also lead to trust and commitment from business partners and customers.

Switching costs

Expenses involved when a customer switches to a competitor's products.

The final advantage of being first comes from switching costs. **Switching costs** occur when customers face some loss in turning to a competitor's products. Customers become familiar with products and they often invest time and effort learning to use the products. For example, many people do not switch between Apple- and Windows-based computers because they already know one operating system well. In addition, because of brand loyalty, many customers may not want to face the discomfort of switching to another brand of a product or service.

Copycat Businesses

Copycat businesses

Those following the "Me too" strategy, whereby they adopt existing strategies for providing products or services.

Copycat businesses follow the "me too" strategy. A company adopts existing products or services. Competitive advantage comes from varying the nature of product or service characteristics or how the company provides the product or service (Vesper 1980). Successful copycats do not copy existing businesses identically. They find a niche or slight innovation to attract customers away from existing businesses. Sometimes the innovation can be as simple as a new location more convenient for customers. Some suggestions for successful copycats include the following (Dollinger 1995):

- *Be the first to change to a new standard:* New standards of quality or internationally recognized specification standards offer powerful entry wedges for new competitors.

Itron, Inc., a small manufacturing corporation in Spokane, Wash., produces handheld computers used by utility companies to read and record data from electric, gas, and water meters. A few years ago, Itron faced a bleak future. The U.S. market was saturated. Most of the big utilities had already purchased their meter-reading computers. Itron faced downsizing and near bankruptcy.

Fortunately for Itron, growth opportunities still exist in the international market. When Itron landed its biggest, and toughest, customer, they were back in the black. Tokyo Electric Power Co.'s $9 million order for 5,300 handheld meter-reading devices was one of their largest sales. It took six years to achieve, with two years dedicated just to field trials. The field trials demonstrated the high quality and high reliability that allowed Itron to beat out such major competitors as NEC, Hitachi, and Mitsubishi.

Itron is now in Europe with a wholly owned subsidiary and a strategic alliance with the German high-tech giant Schlumberger. Keeping ahead of the competition is important and Itron is pushing its automatic meter-reading system (it reads meters remotely from a vehicle or stationary location) for the demanding European market.

Sources: Based on Caldwell 1995; Caldwell 2000 and Lisa 1998.

- *Go after the toughest customers:* Often established firms shy away from some customer groups. Highly price-sensitive or quality-sensitive customers may offer an opportunity for a niche market for the new competitor. Itron, discussed in the preceding Case in Point, went after a notoriously tough Japanese customer and succeeded in turning around the company.
- *Play to minor differences in customer needs:* Established firms often ignore minor differences in customer needs and leave open an opportunity for doing new business with these customers.
- *Transfer the location:* A business that works in one part of the country may work equally well in another part of a country or in another country. The success of U.S. franchises like McDonald's throughout the world shows that this is a viable strategy for creating a new business.
- *Become a dedicated supplier or distributor:* A dedicated supplier finds another firm that needs its goods or services and focuses all efforts on that major customer. For example, a small firm in Washington state provides cargo containers for Boeing airplanes. This small company serves Boeing directly and sells indirectly to users of Boeing jets throughout the world.
- *Seek abandoned or ignored markets:* The major players in any industry do not always serve every market fully and well.
- *Acquire existing business:* Acquiring an existing business is a common start-up strategy for small businesses in domestic markets. However, opportunities also exist in foreign countries to acquire businesses. In particular, formerly state-controlled businesses in eastern Europe provide potentially good acquisition targets for entrepreneurs from around the world.

Summary and Conclusions

Small businesses are a key factor in the economies of all nations. Often they provide the most jobs, the most economic growth, and the most innovation. Increasingly, small businesses must face the challenges of becoming multinational companies and entering the international marketplace. The small business does, however, face some unique problems and prospects when entering global competition. In this chapter, therefore, we have extended the study of multinational and participation strategies to focus on situations with particular application to small multinational companies.

After defining the basic characteristics of a small business and entrepreneurship, we reviewed the processes by which small businesses go international—through stages or through global start-ups. Increasingly, global start-ups are replacing stages of internationalization, especially for high-tech entrepreneurial companies in fast-changing industries.

A small business must overcome certain traditional barriers that may inhibit its internationalization. The chapter discussed how a small business can develop a global culture, change the attitudes of key decision makers, gain crucial international experience, and overcome the size barrier of internationalization. The chapter also presented the diagnostic questions that a small-business person can ask in deciding when the company is ready to enter the international marketplace.

Crucial to a small business is finding ways to access foreign customers and business partners. Small businesses have the same participation-strategy options as larger firms. However, small businesses often do not have the in-house resources to identify or go directly to foreign customers. Fortunately, there are many public and private resources available to the businesses wishing to become multinational. This chapter provided an overview of some resources pertinent to small businesses, available from government and private sources. Increasingly, electronic media, such as the World Wide Web, provide easy and quick access to information on markets throughout the world. Exhibit 10.6 provided just a small sample of this growing source of multinational-business information.

For the small business, entering the international market is an entrepreneurial venture. Entrepreneurial ventures require successful entry-wedge strategies if the company hopes to have any chance of success. Traditionally, books on entrepreneurship consider entry-wedge strategies only in terms of the domestic market. This chapter, however, showed how entrepreneurial entry-wedge strategies could work in the global marketplace. Several Cases in Point showed how actual entrepreneurs used entry-wedge strategies to compete successfully with larger international rivals.

Small business will continue to be an important and growing component of international trade and investment. As a result, small-business managers will need many of the same multinational management skills used by managers from larger companies. This chapter provided you some background on key multinational strategy issues faced by the small-business person.

Discussion Questions

1. Why are small businesses important for most economies?

2. What are the advantages of a small business going international through incremental stages rather than as a global start-up?

3. The Multinational Management Challenge on Eagle Building Technologies showed a successful global start-up. Discuss the conditions that made this strategy the correct choice.

4. Identify two or three small-business barriers to internationalization. If you were a recently hired manager of a small business facing great opportunities in a foreign market, how would you go about overcoming these barriers?

5. As a recent business-college graduate, a small-business manager asks you to help her decide whether she should enter the export market. What questions would you ask her and why?

6. Discuss ways that a small-business manager can make the contacts necessary to implement an exporting strategy.

7. Consider three of the suggested strategic moves for copycat businesses. What additional difficulties will a company face in using these strategies in the international market as opposed to the domestic market?

Chapter Internet Activity

Identify a local small business. Go to the CIBER site at Michigan State University (http://ciber.bus. msu.edu/busres/Static/Trade-Leads.htm). Explore the numerous trading Internet sites and find potential joint venture partners located in several different countries.

Internet Sites

Selected Companies in the Chapter
Colite International Ltd.   http://www.colite.com
Future Tech International
   http://www.holosuites.com/
Itron, Inc.   http://www.itron.com/
Medical Resources   http://www.medzone.com/
Northwest River Supply Inc.   http://www.nrsweb.
   com/
U.S. Department of Commerce   http://www.doc.gov

General Information for the Multinational Small Business
http://www.sba.gov   *U.S. Small Business Administration.*
http://www.usatrade.gov   *Small business assistance centers.*
http://www.iso.ch   *Home page for the International Organization for Standardization—contains information on the various ISO standards.*
http://www.lowe.org   *The Edward Lowe Foundation home page contains links to the SmallbizNet, a source of over 4,000 full text documents on small-business issues, and Edge Online, an online magazine of information on running a small business.*
http://www.entreworld.org   *The Ewing Marion Kauffman Foundation provides a Web search engine specifically for articles on entrepreneurship.*

http://www.arabbiz.com/   *Information on and hints about doing business in Arab countries.*

Where to Find Trade Shows and Trade Events
http://www.tscentral.com/   *Welcome to Trade Show Central.*
http://www.tradeport.org/cgi-bin/tradenet2/ tradebase-form   *Trade Show Calendar.*
http://www.tdb.gov.sg/   *Trade Develoment in Singapore.*
http://asiatrade.com/Convention/index.html   *Conventions and trade exhibitions.*
http://www.publications-etc.com/russia/business/ events.html   *Russian business and trade.*

Chapter Activity: Take a Product International

Step 1: Your instructor will divide the class into groups.

Step 2: Select an agricultural or industrial product produced in the region of the country where you are located. If possible, interview a small-business person concerning his or her perspectives on the international opportunities for their product. In the United States, one way of finding a potential business owner is through the small-business development centers attached to many U.S. universities. Your instructor may assign you a business or product.

Step 3: Using the steps shown in Exhibit 10.4 and information from World Wide Web sources (such as those in Exhibit 10.6) and your library, identify a foreign market or markets for the product or products.

Step 4: Using Web sources (such as those in Exhibit 10.6) identify potential trade shows, trading partners, or other intermediaries (e.g., ETCs) that would help you get the product to the international marketplace.

Step 5: Present your findings to your class, and to the small-business person, if possible.

References

Barry, Doug. 2000. "From Appalachia to India: U.S. small businesses are going global." *Business Credit* 102, 6: 49–50.

Barney, J. B. 1991. "Firm resources and sustained competitive advantage." *Journal of Management* 17:99–120.

Beamish P. W., and H. J. Munro. 1987. "Exporting for success as a small Canadian manufacturer." *Journal of Small Business and Entrepreneurship* 4:38–43.

Bonacorsi, Andrea. 1992. "On the relationships between firm size and export intensity." *Journal of International Business Studies*, Fourth Quarter, 605–33.

Caldwell, Bert. 1995. "Japanese customer thanks Itron." *Spokesman-Review*, March 7, A6, A9.

———. 2000. "Itron shake-up proves to be a profitable move." Spokesman-Review, June 29, A8.

Calof, Jonathan L. 1993. "The impact of size on internationalization." *Journal of Small Business Management*, October, 60–69.

———, and Wilma Viviers. 1995. "Internationalization behavior of small- and medium-sized South African enterprises." *Journal of Small Business Management*, October, 71–79.

Caprioni, Paula J., Stefanie Ann Lenway, and Thomas P. Murtha. 1994. "Understanding internationalization: Sense-making process in multinational corporations." In *Small Firms in Global Competition*, edited by Tamir Agmon and Richard Drobnick, 27–36. New York: Oxford.

Christensen, C., Angela da Rocha, and Rosane Gertner. 1987. "An empirical investigation of the factors influencing export success of Brazilian firms." *Journal of International Business Studies*, Fall, 61–78.

Curle, Robin Lea. 1998. "Expanding internationally: Grow as you go." *Entre-World.org*, May 1, http://www.entreworld.org.

Dichtl, Drwin, Hans-Georg Koeglmayr, and Stefan Mueller. 1990. "International orientation as a precondition for export success." *Journal of International Business Studies*, First Quarter, 23–40.

Dollinger, Marc J. 1995. *Entrepreneurship*. Burr Ridge, Ill.: Irwin.

Fenn, Donna. 1995. "The globalists." *Inc. Online*, Archive Doc. No. 14950161. Inc. 500 Special Issue.

Inc. Online. 1994a. "Who's going global?" Archive/Doc. No. 03941341. March.

Kedia, Ben, and Jagdeep Chhokar. 1985. "The impact of managerial attitudes on export behavior." *American Journal of Small Business*, Fall, 7–17.

Knowlton, Christopher. 1988. "The new export entrepreneurs." *Fortune*, June 6, 98.

Lisa, Harrell. 1998. "Itron eyes German subsidiary." *Journal of Business*, 13, A1.

Mangelsdorf, Martha E. 1993. "Building a transnational company." *Inc. Online*, Archive/Doc. No. 03930921. March.

McClenahen, John S. 2000. "Global gold." *Industry Week* 249, 12: 71–76.

Miesenbock, Kurt J. 1988. "Small business and internationalization: a literature review." *International Small Business Journal* 6:42–61.

Organization for Economic Cooperation and Development [OECD]. 1996. *Small Firms as Foreign Investors*.

Oviatt, Benjamin M., and Patricia Phillips McDougall. 1995. "Global start-ups: Entrepreneurs on a worldwide stage." *Academy of Management Executive* 9:30–44.

Scarborough, Norman M., and Thomas W. Zimmer. 1996. *Effective Small Business Management*. Upper Saddle River, N.J.: Prentice Hall.

UNCTAD. 1993. *Small and Medium-sized Transnational Corporations*. New York: United Nations.

U.S. Department of Commerce. 1998. *Basic Guide to Exporting*. Washington, D.C.: Government Printing Office.

Vesper. Karl M. 1980. *New Venture Strategies*. Englewood Cliffs, N.J.: Prentice Hall.

Wright, Phillip C. 1993. "The personal and the personnel adjustments and costs to small businesses entering the international market place." *Journal of Small Business Management*, January, 83–93.

Yip, George S. 1995. *Total Global Strategy*. Englewood Cliffs, N.J.: Prentice Hall.

Part 4 Integrating Case 1

Xeltron

We are a small high technology firm in Costa Rica with an innovative technology. However, our current applications are for only a limited market. We are concerned about how we can expand our market by applying our technology to analogous problems. In addition, we worry about how we can expand geographically to other parts of the world.

Fernando Castañeda
President, Xeltron

In the early 1970s, a group of technical experts, representing different disciplines, decided to improve on the existing coffee sorting technology. In countries where coffee production was one of the most important sources of export earnings, such as Costa Rica, there was a clear need to improve this method. In 1974, the group, headed by Fernando Castañeda, had developed an optical analyzer and a mathematical model for absolute color analysis that would revolutionize the local coffee industry. They applied for and were granted patents for these inventions. These patents and the group's technical knowledge formed the basis for the corporation known as Xeltron.

Fernando Castañeda, now the President of Xeltron, is struggling with the question of how to stay ahead of its competitors with its technology and how to continue to offer innovative products. The company has been highly successful in the past few years. However, the applications are now changing from their original product, which is automated coffee bean sorting, to the separation of other products such as beans, rice, and nuts, using optical analyzers. Furthermore, competitors in the United States now offer machines that can perform the function of high-speed optical separation of granules. Having just about filled the Costa Rican coffee bean separation market and knowing the limitations of concentrating on a single product, the President worries about how best to develop new machines for the separation of other products, how to stay in the Costa Rican culture and still enter new markets, and how to service these markets.

Source: This case was prepared by Professor Arthur Gerstenfeld, Worcester Polytechnic Institute. This information was gathered as part of a grant from the Department of Education, Business and International Education Program as a basis for classroom discussion rather than to illustrate either effective or ineffective handling of an administrative situation. Copyright © 1998 by Arthur Gerstenfeld.

Copyright South-Western and Thomson Learning Custom Publishing (ISBN 0-324-00970-4). For information regarding this and other CaseNet® cases, please visit CaseNet® on the World Wide Web at http://casenet.thomson.com.

THE SEPARATION MACHINES

The foundation of the business is based on the fact that most coffee bean selection today is still based on workers using their eyes and hands, and as the workers' eyes get tired, quality of work decreases. The selection of good beans from bad beans is done by color and the machine patented by Xeltron makes the selections using photocells and fiber optics. If the machine "sees" a bad bean, a solenoid puts a short blast of air against that bean and pushes the bad bean into a separate bin or on to a separate conveyor belt. This all happens very quickly, perhaps 300–600 times per second.

In the machine and the optical analyzer, the beans pass through an analyzer and a set of thirty-four optical fibers. The analyzer does not use artificial references; rather, it utilizes a halogen light installed in a separate receptacle.

Each sorting channel is fed by a vibrator controlled by a small built-in computer. Thus, the number of beans per second that reach the color analyzer can be adjusted. The beans are supported on an air cushion generated by a pair of stainless steel cylinders to minimize friction while the beans are accelerated using gravity.

Color analyzers used by the competition require a reference background. This limitation results in a partial view of the beans and is one of the main sources of inaccuracy, since they are not able to detect all the bean defects. In the Xeltron system, the light is transmitted by means of optical fibers to a set of lenses and focused with great precision on the beans.

Every time 500 beans pass through the optical analyzer, the built-in computer adjusts the signal levels for optimum sorting efficiency. A digital screen continuously displays both the sorting parameters and the results of the sorting process. The results are shown as percentages of overall grain rejection and percentages of rejection for each of the selection criteria. Each time a grain is rejected, an LED turns on, indicating the selection criteria.

The company is now working hard to modify the analyzer for sorting other products. For example, there is interest in sorting good from bad macadamia nuts. However, as might be expected, the problems are different. The shapes are different, the colors are different, and each parameter raises new technical challenges.

CULTURAL DIFFERENCES

There are very large cultural differences among firms in Latin America and firms in the United States even with all the close communication that takes place today. For example, in the United States we would think of the word "mañana" as "tomorrow." However, in most of Latin America, "mañana" means some time in the future. Similarly, the concept of time is clearly different. In the United States, if a meeting (or a class) were to start ten minutes late, that would be frowned upon. In Latin America, it is an accepted norm to start at least one-half hour or more later than scheduled.

Are there really differences among firms in developing countries such as Costa Rica and firms in developed countries such as the United States? As might be suspected, there are similarities and there are differences. Two problems that Xeltron faces are that they are a mainly Spanish-speaking firm (an advantage for work within the country but a disadvantage for work outside of the country) and are somewhat isolated from their competitors and customers. However, there are benefits to staying in Costa Rica that keeps Xeltron from relocating.

Like most firms in Latin America, at the upper levels almost everyone speaks English. However, the day-to-day interactions within the firm are only in Spanish.

In the past that has not presented a problem, but it could well present problems for the future. For example, as sales increase to English-speaking countries, as it becomes necessary for one of the technicians to work directly with a customer, and the technician speaks only Spanish, problems arise. Conversely, as Xeltron attracts more English-speaking professionals from the U.S., they need these employees to learn Spanish so they can interact effectively with Spanish-speaking workers and suppliers. Most of these employees learn Spanish quickly when they are immersed in the language and culture; however, Castañeda wonders if Xeltron needs to offer language (English and Spanish) courses to its employees.

A problem faced by some of the engineers is the difficulty of benchmarking. Benchmarking is often done by studying competitors' catalogs and by evaluating machines from the competition exhibited at trade shows. Another method of benchmarking compares actual performance with competitive models while operating at the customer's plant. It is difficult to try to see a competitor's machine that is manufactured thousands of miles away. Similarly, it is difficult to examine new equipment for manufacturing or for research that is so many miles away. Obviously, trade shows help on both of these items, but Xeltron's location in Costa Rica makes it more difficult to compete.

However, an advantage that they do have in Costa Rica is that the labor rate is approximately a quarter that of the United States. For example, in Costa Rica, a lathe operator might make $3 per hour, while in the U.S. he or she might make $12 to $15 per hour. A starting engineer in Costa Rica makes $10,000 a year, while a counterpart in the United States makes $35,000 per year.

For many Costa Rican natives, staying in their own country offers them simply a better "way of life." "One reason why I moved to Costa Rica was that I would rather have my children brought up in a society where they don't have to go through a metal detector in order to go to school," explained Massoud Gougani, in charge of production. While this statement might be an exaggeration-in actuality, most U.S. schools don't use metal detectors-the point remains that many employees at Xeltron feel as if the Costa Rican lifestyle is more to their liking.

For some, they are willing to give up the higher income for the preferred lifestyle. In many cases, the lifestyle choice is weighed against the lower salaries and a cost of living similar to that in the U.S. This issue seems to present a constant tug and is a particular problem for Costa Rican engineers or managers educated in the United States, who upon graduation receive offers of salaries three times the salaries offered in Costa Rica.

SERVING INTERNATIONAL CUSTOMERS

This section first considers what services are required by Xeltron. In general, the world today expects more service than ever. When a product is purchased, we expect it to work; if training is needed, we expect to be able to receive that training quickly and easily; if manuals are appropriate, we expect clear and understandable manuals; if machines break, we expect to receive instant service with little aggravation and fuss; and if technical support is needed over the telephone, we expect to receive it quickly and intelligibly.

Having recognized the above, is Xeltron able to service the English-speaking markets? Will expansion into some of these markets become prohibitive because of cost? Xeltron has been selling color-sorting machines for the past fifteen years to South America, and for the past five years they have kept a plant in Brazil.

One idea they are considering is to have a technical liaison in the United States who could serve as both a monitor of new technologies and as a service person. But is one person sufficient? Perhaps it needs to be a team and, if so, where would they be stationed and what will the costs be?

The firm seems to have two distinct advantages in the South American market. It clearly has a technology that is unique, viable, and patented, and offers labor rates that are far less than those in the United States. Finally, they are close to their initial market in Costa Rica.

"I worry much about management and organization," said Massoud. "We need a company with strong management. For example, for our new products one cannot wait six months for delivery. It is a problem if marketing brings in more than production is able to turn out. It is necessary to level these functions."

Once or twice a year Xeltron services the machines. They do not consider this a high service cost. The most frequent problems encountered are as follows:

1. The client does not have good electrical or compressed air installation.
2. Often the person who is operating the machines has a limited level of education. Thus, when a problem arises, they are unable to follow the technical manual or technical advice over the telephone.
3. Human error. Sometimes Xeltron encounters difficulties with running the machine and expects it to be some major difficulty where a Xeltron technician is required, when in fact the problem may be a very simple one. The customer may have replaced a burnt 3 amp fuse with a 5 amp fuse even though it is clearly marked on the fuse box that a 3 amp fuse should be used.

While the major savings are in labor for the Xeltron products, this device was developed in a country where the labor rate is relatively low. The motivation for users is obviously quality rather than labor costs savings. However, it is often harder to sell quality than it is to sell cost savings; this can be more easily quantified by the users and prospective users.

SUMMARY AND FUTURE DIRECTIONS

This product made its start in Costa Rica, because that is where the coffee is produced. There has been a reputation in Costa Rica that the quality of the coffee is very important. As Xeltron moves into new products, the company will be at a disadvantage. The challenge is to adapt the technology to other products. It is not only getting the samples and working out the engineering for sorting but also determining when the selling season is, how the market is structured, and what the standards of quality should be.

The mindset of the Xeltron staff is to supply machines to sort different products using the same general technology. They can change the software and the feeding system but sometimes a major change is needed.

New product development is still driven by the president and by his personal instincts for the market. This might have been appropriate during the early years, but now the company is facing new products and new markets. Is this still the best way to proceed? There is no systematic way at present to supply market information to the product development team. Can and should Xeltron go to a system of concurrent engineering? How can they better link marketing to R&D?

Part 4 Integrating Case 2

Softbank Corp.: Internet and Technology-Related Acquisitions and Global Strategy

Softbank, a Tokyo-based company, was started by Masayoshi Son in 1981. Softbank ranks as one of the largest distributors of software and technology-related products as well as a provider of internet-based information in the world. Softbank, the largest investor in the Internet, e-commerce, and technology-related areas in the world, has grown since 1992 into one of the most influential and dynamic players in the Internet and e-commerce industry. Because of Son's unique entrepreneurial style and flamboyant personality, the Western media often called him *The Bill Gates of Japan, Cyber-Mogul, Master of the Internet, Japan's Mr. Internet*, etc. Some observers (Webber 1992) even rated his entrepreneurial style as totally different from the Japanese-style entrepreneurship. Son founded Softbank after receiving his degree in economics from the University of California at Berkeley in 1980. Since 1994, Softbank's shares are traded on the Tokyo over-the-counter market. In 1998, Softbank's consolidated revenues reached $4.38 billion with a pre-tax profit of $339 million. In 1999, Softbank's market capitalization surpassed $11.5 billion and the company employed 7,000 workers worldwide (see Exhibit 1: *Business Week* 1999a&b; *Financial Times* 1997a-c; *The Wall Street Journal* 1996,1999a-c).

In the last six years, Softbank has sought aggressive global diversification by acquiring high-profile internet companies and invested millions of dollars in long-term Internet technologies. In September 1999, Softbank's selected acquisitions and majority share holdings include: Yahoo, Yahoo Japan, E-Trade-Japan, E-Trade Group, Buy.com, Concentric, E-Loan, USWeb, ZDNet, Ziff Davis, ZD Comdex, Kingston Technology, SB Networks, and Japan Digital Broadcasting Services (see Exhibit 2). Softbank's venture capital subsidiary (Softbank Technology Ventures) has actively pursued and sought equity-related investments in companies from the areas of digital information technology, internet communications, network services, and e-commerce.

Softbank's shift in its core-competence and long-term strategies result from a massive growth in the Internet and technology-related markets in the United States, Japan, and Western Europe. According to industry analysts, Softbank plans to become one of the largest Internet and technology communication companies in

Source: Syed Tariq Anwar, T. Boone Pickens College of Business, West Texas A&M University. Reprinted with permission.

Exhibit I

Softbank Corp.:
Selected Financial and
Corporate Date (as of
March 31, 1999)*

	U.S.$	Yen
A: Financial Data		
Consolidated Revenues:	$4.3 billion	528 billion yen
Consolidated Pre-Tax Profit:	$339 million	40.9 billion yen
Consolidated Net Profit:	$311 million	37.5 billion yen
Market Capitalization:	$11.3 billion	1,392 billion yen
Common Stock Outstanding:	$104.8 million shares	
B: Corporate Data		
Head Office:	24-1, Nihonbashi-Hakozakicho, Chuco-ku, Tokyo, Japan	
Shareholders Worldwide:	50,000	
Employees Worldwide:	7,000	
Incorporated:	September 3, 1981	
Stock Information:	Stock traded on Tokyo Stock Exchange (first section)	
	Symbol: 9984	
Independent Divisions:	–Software & Network Products Division	
	–Publishing Division	
	–Human Resources Division	
	–Administrative Division	
	–Internet Business Development Department	
	–Electronic Commerce	
	–Business-to-Business and Consumer Services	
	–Media and Content	
	–Network Services	
Board of Directors:	President and CEO: Masayoshi Son	
	Executive Vice President: Ken Miyauchi	
	Executive Vice President and CFO: Yoshitaka Kitao	
	Directors:	
	Ronald Fisher	
	Den Fujita	
	Yoshihiko Miyauchi	
	Kenichi Ohmae	
	Jun Murai	
	Yasumitsu Shigeta	

Source: (1). Softbank Corp., Tokyo, Japan: September 1999, www.softbank.com/corporate_data.htm. (2). *Forbes.* "Master of the Internet," July 5, 1999, pp. 146–151.

*Exchange Rate: US $1 = 120.55 Japanese Yen (March 31, 1999).

the world. Softbank is truly the first-mover company in its product markets. Analysts believe that in the next five years, Softbank will become a major force in the Internet and technology-related and software distribution areas because of increasing demand and growth. On the other hand, Softbank will be impacted by height-

Exhibit 2

Softbank Corp.:
Major Entities and
Product Lines

A: Media and Marketing:

Ziff-Davis, Inc. (HYSE: *ZD*):

Integrated media and marketing company

PC Magazine

PC Week

Computer Shopper

50 licensed publications (combined circulation: 8 million readers)

COMDEX (the largest U.S. show)

ZDNet (NYSE: *ZDZ*)

Web site (news, information, entertainment)

ZDTV

Cable TV Channel—Digital Information Topics

Ziff-Davis—Market Research Division

Computer intelligence unit: market research firm

B: Internet and Technology-Related Companies:

Softbank Technology Ventures

Asymetrix Learning Systems (NASDAQ: *ASYM*): Online trading programs

BackWeb: Markets Software; delivers personalized information

Buy.com: Operates retail Web site

Concentric (NASDAW: *CNCX*): Provides virtual private networks and extranets; operates the *Quicken Financial Network* for Intuit

E-Loan: Online mortgage

E★Trade (NASDAQ: *EGRP*): Online investment brokerage and stock trading services

InterTrust: Develops and sells a software system in the areas of medical records, movies, audio, stock transactions, etc.

MessageMedia (NASDAQ: *MESG*): Develops, markets, and installs messaging systems on the Internet; two-way communications

Reciprocal: Provides service in the areas of selling software, music, magazines and other types of digital property

USWeb/CKS (NASDAQ: *USWB*): Helps design Web sites for Fortune 1000 companies; deals with strategic consulting

Yahoo (NASDAQ: *YHOO*): Premier global Internet media company; Softbank is the largest shareholder of Yahoo which recently acquired *GeoCities*

Source: Softbank Corp., Tokyo, Japan: September 1999, www.softbank.com/corporate_data.htm.

ened global competition and will be challenged by newcomers in the industry. The case is intended to have students look at Softbank's future market growth and its global strategies within the concept of internationalization and competitive advantage issues.

WHO IS MASAYOSHI SON?

Son, born in 1957 on Kyushu Island and grew up in a small town, Tosu City, Saga Prefecture. Son belongs to an ethnic Korean family. His grandparents had migrated to Japan from Korea. In 1973, at the age of 16, Son attended a high school in California and later moved to Holy Names College in Oakland, California. In 1980, Son graduated from the University of California at Berkeley with a B.A. degree in Economics. While an undergraduate student, Son invented a multilingual pocket translator and later sold his patent to Sharp Corp. Son also founded Unison Computer Company which is now owned by Kyocera Corp. (Webber 1992; www.softbank.com/).

In 1981, Son returned to Japan and founded Softbank Corp. The company initially started with two part-time workers and later grew to 570 employees in 1991. Softbank supplied computer software, books and magazines, and other technology-related products to 200 dealer outlets. In 1991, the company expanded at a very fast pace and grew to 15,000 dealer outlets because of the changing market conditions and strong consumer demand for software and computer-related products. In 1991, Son netted $350 million in sales. After 1991, Son started to expand into the Internet-related area and made numerous acquisitions. In 1994, Softbank's stock started trading on the Tokyo over-the-counter market. After four years, Softbank's shares were listed on the Tokyo Stock Exchange. Since 1994, the stock has split four times. Son's recent initiatives, acquisitions, and major alliances include: Nihon Cisco Systems, Ziff-Davis trade show, Comdex, Windows World, Yahoo Japan, and Softbank Technology Ventures (see Exhibits 1–3). In 1994, when the Internet market in North America started to take off, Softbank was the only Japanese company making high-profile acquisitions. This shows Son's visionary personality and aggressive entrepreneurial style (*Business Week* 1996; *Business Week E-Biz* 1999; *U.S. News & World Report* 1999; *Weinberg* 1999). Abrahams & Nakamoto (1999) commented:

Softbank is a unique Japanese company. Led by Masayoshi Son, its flamboyant president, it has been touted as Japan's answer to Microsoft. Son's multimedia empire has expanded at breathtaking speed to become a global enterprise, but in the past year the group's shares have tumbled, raising concerns about Softbank's future.

Forbes (1999) commented on Softbank's massive acquisitions:

Masayoshi Son's golden touch in Web investing has made him fabulously rich. His 42% stake in Softbank gives him a personal worth of $6.4 billion. The $6.4 billion question: Is he really that much smarter than everyone else—or is he just lucky?

Far Eastern Economic Review (1999) commented on Son's bold moves and his entrepreneurial style:

Son's vision is to build Softbank into a global Internet consortium or zaibatsu[1], with the same landscape-shifting impact as the zaibatsu of the Meiji era who created Japan's first modern industries. He is doing this by identifying businesses where substantial efficiencies can be gained by going on-line. In particular, Son has zoomed in on Japan's stuffy world of brokerage, insurance, and banking.—Should Son succeed, he will be known not just as the man who dominates the Internet, but as a major financial-services player.

ACQUISITIONS, DIVERSIFICATION AND GLOBAL STRATEGY

According to *Forbes* (1999), Softbank has invested $2.4 billion in 100 Internet, technology, communications, and computer publishing companies. As of July 1999, the total market value of these companies surpassed $14 billion. In many companies, Softbank became one of the major investors (see Exhibit 4). Softbank's venture capital subsidiary (Softbank Technology Ventures) has provided $906 million to many

Exhibit 3

Softbank's Internet and Technology-Related Revenues (as of June 1999)

A: Software & Network Products

Sales (1998): $1.58 billion (9.7% up)

Operating Profit: $30.1 million (38.4% down)

Major Companies: SB Networks, UTStarcom, Trend Micro

B: Media & Broadcasting

Sales (1998): $0.96 billion (17.3% up)

Operating Profit: $114.2 million (10.8% up)

Major Companies: Ziff-Davis, Japan Digital Broadcasting Corp. (TV, radio and data transmission)

C: Technology Events and Trade Shows:

Sales (1998): $0.3 billion (30.4% up)

Operating Profit: $78.8 million (8.0% up)

Selected Companies: ZD Comdex and Forums, Inc.

D: Technology Services

Sales (1998): $1.35 billion (185.4% up)

Operating Profit: $48.5 million (22.7% up)

Selected Companies: Kingston Technology (memory modules), Pasona Softbank (computer temp. agency)

E: Internet Sector

Sales (1998): N/A

Operating Profit: N/A

Selected Companies: Yahoo Japan (ownership: 51%), E★Trade Japan (58%), GeoCities Japan (60%), ZDNet (online news & magazines)

Source: *The Wall Street Journal.* "Japan's Softbank unveils new Internet deals," 1999. June 25, p. A17.

Exhibit 4 Softbank's Selected Internet and Technology-Related Acquisitions and Market Value (as of July 1999)

Acquisition	Date Acquired	Price Paid ($ million)	Current Holding (%)	Market Value ($ million)
E-Trade Group (*Online Investing*)	July 98	$409	27%	$2,364
Message Media (*Message Technology*)	May–Sept. 98	8	24	124
Pasona Softbank (*Temp. Agency*)	Feb. 95	N/A	20	62
Trend Micro (*Anti-Virus Software*)	Dec. 96	64	27	768
USWeb (*Web Consulting*)	Feb. 96	14	7	131
Yahoo (*Internet Portal*)	Nov. 95–Aug. 98	410	27	8,424
Yahoo Japan (*Internet Portal*)	April 96	10	51	2,287
Ziff-Davis (*Media & Marketing*)	Oct. 94–Feb. 96	1,500	70	833
Total		$2,415		$14,993

Source: (1). *Financial Times.* "Softbank widens its net," 1999. July 9, p. 12. (2). *Forbes.* "Master of the Internet," 1999. July 5, pp. 146–151.

internet firms in the United States and Japan. Analysts believe that Softbank has plans to invest $1.2 billion in the coming months to seek additional acquisitions and new internet start-ups. As of September 1999, Softbank holds 7 to 8 percent ownership in the Internet and e-commerce industry worldwide. Softbank's Internet and technology acquisitions fall into two categories. First, in the area of media and marketing, Softbank owns 70 percent of Ziff-Davis, Inc. which is the largest computer trade show company in the world. Ziff-Davis published computer magazines such as *PC Magazine*, *PC Week*, and *Computer Shopper*. Second, in the Internet, communications, and technology sectors, Softbank has invested in some of the top Internet brands, i.e., Yahoo, Yahoo Japan, E-Trade Group, E-Loan, Concentric, USWeb, Message Media, and Asymetrix Learning Systems. These acquisitions have placed Softbank among the top Internet and technology players in the world.

A quick look at Softbank's global strategy reveals two areas. First, Softbank has ambitions to become the main Internet and communications company in the world. This w3as achieved by acquiring some of the strategic Internet brands in the world markets. Second, Softbank plans to get out of the computer publishing business and will start refocusing on the Internet and e-commerce areas. This could be attributed to high growth in the Internet and e-commerce areas. This could be attributed to high growth in the Internet and e-commerce industry. Although risky in nature this long-term strategic move by Softbank carries an excellent market share and will place it among the top Internet companies in Japan and other markets. Very few Japanese companies have pursued this kind of risky growth strategy in the Internet and e-commerce areas.

GLOBAL OPPORTUNITIES AND PROBLEM AREAS

FUTURE PLANS AND GLOBAL OPPORTUNITIES

Unlike Microsoft, Dell, AOL, Amazon.com, Intel, and other high-tech and e-commerce companies, Softbank has not been able to become a household name in the Western world. Most of its markets and customers are located in Japan and Asian countries. On the other hand, Softbank ranks as a global player in the Internet and e-commerce. In 1999, Softbank's initial investment of $358 million in the Internet and technology-related industry has grown to a value of $10 billion (*Far Eastern Economic Review* 1999). Most of Softbank's visibility lies in Japan where it has changed the traditional Japanese corporate culture. Unlike the American business environment, the Japanese market is limited in venture capital firms. Analysts believe that Japan lags about four to six years behind in the Internet and e-commerce areas. For this reason, Softbank represents on of the few Japanese companies having significant potential and future growth prospects. Very few Japanese companies are well positioned to capitalize on the changing Internet and e-commerce industry.

Unlike other Japanese Internet and service companies, Softbank has acquired companies which are complementary in nature and may carry good growth potential in the future. Since its inception in 1981, Softbank has become a small conglomerate having its influence in many high-tech and Internet sectors. Although Internet and its related industries are still in their infancy in Japan and other developed markets of Asia, Softbank has fully exploited these markets. This is the main reason why Softbank captured significant market share and changed the mainstream Japanese corporate culture. Son's entrepreneurial style made many inroads in the

Japanese corporate environment as well. Son, the main pacesetter in the Internet industry, has forced other competitors to follow him as well. The change process pursued and managed by Softbank represents a classic textbook case study which will result in benefits for Softbank as well as consumers worldwide. As Brown & Eisenhardt (1998) stated on managing the change process:

At one level, managing change means reacting to it. . . . But managing change also means anticipating it. . . . Finally, at the highest level, managing change is about leading change. By this we mean creating the change to which others must react. It means launching a new market, raising the industry standard of service, redefining customer expectations, or increasing the pace of industry product cycles. It means being ahead of change or even changing the rules of the game. At the extreme, the best performing firms consistently lead change in their industries.

Softbank perfectly fits in the change process stated by Brown & Eisenhardt (1998) by not only becoming the industry leader but also forcing others to make changes.[2]

Many analysts believe that in the coming years, Softbank's markets will grow significantly. In the areas of product development and worldwide brand visibility, Softbank holds a good position to capitalize on its learning curve and knowledge-related areas. Some of Softbank's investments in the Internet companies doubled in the last three years and have brought massive fortune to Son. Selected companies include: Yahoo, Yahoo Japan, E-Trade, Ziff-Davis, ZDNet, and Geo Cities. In June 1999, Softbank announced a joint venture with NASDAQ to initiate the process of setting up the NASDAQ-type stock market in Japan (*The Wall Street Journal* 1999b) In September 1999, Softbank announced another strategic alliance with Microsoft and Global Crossing to provide telecommunications services in the Asian markets. Global crossing will take 93 percent equity in the venture whereas Softbank and Microsoft each will invest 3.5 percent in the venture. Softbank and Microsoft may increase their stakes to 19 percent (http://www.quicken.com). These recent alliances and ventures show that Softbank plans to go beyond its traditional Japanese market.

PROBLEM AREAS AND WEAKNESSES

In the coming years, Softbank may face problems because of the changing Internet and e-commerce industry (see Exhibit 5). Some of the problems include:

1. Unlike Microsoft, Dell, AOL, Amazon.com, and other high-tech companies, Softbank is not a household name in the United States and the Western world. The company is very well known in Japan but carries limited influence in other markets.
2. Softbank mostly stayed in Japan and sought its growth through acquisitions. These acquisitions have accumulated debt which may limit future growth if some of its entities go sour.
3. Ziff-Davis, Inc. which published *PC Magazine* and *Computer Shopper* faces problems because of its declining ad revenues, heightened competition, and debt problems. Analysts believe that Ziff-Davis may take some time to recover since the world PC industry now faces lower profits and an invasion of cheaper machines (*Advertising Age* 1998; *Business Week* 1999a; http://cbs.marketwatch.com/news/).
4. Softbank is not listed on the New York Stock Exchange or NASDAQ. This weakens Softbank's ability to attract mutual fund managers and institutional investors from the United States. In addition, this may hamper Softbank's future growth in Japan, the United States and Western Europe.

Exhibit 5 Softbank Corp.: Strengths and Weaknesses

Strengths	Weaknesses
• Softbank is one of the largest and most innovative Internet and communications companies in the world	• Softbank is not a household name in the United States and Western Europe
• Has built/acquired 100 plus Internet companies; aims to be the leader in the Internet and e-commerce industry	• Some acquisitions have gone sour; some of the future startups may also go sour if Softbank expands into unrelated areas
• Excellent potential in the areas of software distribution, web publishing, and computer trade shows	• Softbank may encounter more competition in the Internet market
• Excellent growth through acquisitions	• Softbank's shifting focus on its core strategy may create problems in the coming years
• Recent joint venture with NASDAQ looks very promising	• Softbank may not be able to manage its hundreds of alliances and joint ventures because of changing technologies and competition in the e-commerce areas
• First-mover in the Internet and technology-related industry	
• Excellent learning curve; knows the Japanese market	• The stock is not listed in the United States (NYSE or NASDAQ)
• Knows how to expedite the product development process and target new markets	• East Asian markets are somewhat stagnant; may take some years to recover
• Plans to bring significant changes in Japan's Internet market	• Softbank is a small player in the e-commerce and retailing industry
• Masayoshi Son (President/CEO) is U.S. educated; knows the Western corporate system and culture; also has a good vision	• Ineffective handling of debt and cash flows have created problems
• Good market share in the niche-oriented Internet and communications industry	

5. The East Asian crisis has affected Softbank's expansion in the Asian markets. Although economic conditions are improving, Softbank may be affected because of currency depreciations in the weaker economies, i.e., Indonesia, Thailand, Malaysia, and others.

6. Historically, Softbank has targeted the distribution of software, computer publications, and selected Internet areas. It is still a small player in the e-commerce industry because of entry barriers and heightened competition.

7. Softbank plans to enter into Japan's online financial and insurance industry which is somewhat untapped. Some analysts believe that Softbank may face tough competition because of its unfamiliarity with these sectors. Softbank's strong know-how in the Internet area may not be replicated in the finance and insurance sectors.

8. The Internet and e-commerce industry at the global level is a complex market because of regulations and country-specific standards. Softbank may face these hurdles beyond the Japanese market.

9. Since 1996, Softbank's stock has plunged many times because of its massive acquisitions and debt problems. Some analysts feel concerned about Softbank's handling of its debt and negative cash flows since Sons owns 43 percent of the company (*Fortune* 1997).

10. In the U.S. market, Softbank has devised a new strategy to cope with its new competitors. Some of the smaller companies in the e-commerce industry are perceived to be more successful and profitable.

WHAT LIES AHEAD?

SHORT-TERM VS. LONG-TERM ISSUES

Many analysts see Softbank as a unique Japanese company. Under the leadership of Son, the company stands to reap huge rewards if markets do not tumble. In the short-term, Softbank reaps all the benefits by being the market leader. More acquisitions are expected in the Internet and communications-related areas. Some analysts believe that Softbank plans on consolidating its position in the Internet market in the next two years. It is also expected that Softbank will gradually reduce its holdings in the area of computer publishing and will start concentrating on the Internet and e-commerce areas. There is a huge growth potential expected in these markets. Of course, it may also carry risks because of competition and changing business markets.

THE INTERNET, E-COMMERCE, AND OTHER TECHNOLOGY ISSUES

In the last three years, the Internet and technology-related markets are moving in many different directions in the United States and overseas (*The Economist* 1999; U.S. Department of Commerce 1999). Companies have to be vigilant to capitalize on the changing technologies, growth, and customers. Softbank is well positioned to be part of the growing market. As *Forbes* (1999, p. 151) commented on Son's future plans:

Son wants to be number one in 'eyeball traffic, finance, e-commerce and content' . . . not by controlling a single behemoth like Amazon.com, but by taking sizable stakes in top players in myriad niches.

Softbank's venture capital subsidiary, Softbank Technology Ventures, has established a 40,000-square-foot site in Mountain View, California in September 1999 (*Fortune* 1999). This facility will serve as a "startup incubator" for promising Internet firms. Softbank plans to become a major player in every aspect of the Internet and e-commerce market. This includes telecommunications, finance and banking, insurance, publishing, distribution, retailing, and other web-based service products.

In Japan, Softbank has formed a joint venture with NASDAQ. There is a huge potential in the NASDAQ-style market in Japan. According to one estimate, consumer savings and assets are used inefficiently because of the unavailability of the U.S.-style individual investors. Softbank's initiative in this segment with NASDAQ is expected to bring big structural changes in the stock markets in Japan (*Financial Times* 1999a-c; *The Wall Street Journal* 1999b). In addition, Softbank plans to consolidate its position in Japan's online industry in virtually every sector, i.e., education, e-commerce (business and retailing), banking, finance, insurance and bond markets, distribution, and broadcasting industry. In the Asian markets, Softbank has made an alliance with Global Crossing and Microsoft to provide Internet-related products (http://www.quicken.com). Market analysts believe that Softbank has many new initiatives and joint ventures/alliances in the pipeline. Within the present circumstances, Softbank is rated to be the main Internet company in the world. It will be interesting to see if Softbank can hold its position as the world Internet company or just be run over by another Softbank-type company.

A: Future NASDAQ Market in Japan and Breakdown of Consumer Assets (as of Dec. 1997)

Time Deposits	40.5%
Insurance	24.4%
Demand Deposits	8.6%
Securities	7.3%
Trusts	5.9%
Stocks	4.8%
Cash Currency	3.7%
Bonds	2.5%
Investment Trusts	2.3%
Total Assets	*$10.3 trillion (1,230 Yen)*

B: Global Internet Access by Regions (as of May 1999)

Canada and United States	97.0 million consumers (56.6%)
Europe	40.1 (23.4)
Asia/Pacific	27.0 (15.8)
Latin America	5.3 (3.1)
Africa	1.1 (0.6)
Middle East	0.9 (0.5)
Total	*171 million*

C: Selected Countries with Internet Access: Home and Work (as of 1998)

United States	37%
Canada	36
Nordics	33
Australia	31
United Kingdom	15
Germany	10
Japan	10
France	8

Sources: *Financial Times.* "Electronic trading to open up the world to Japan's investors," 1999. June 16, p. 20. U.S. Department of Commerce. *The Emerging Digital Economy-II*, Washington, DC.: U.S. Dept. of Commerce, 1999. June p. 3.

CASE QUESTIONS FOR DISCUSSION

1. What are your views of Softbank's recent Internet-related diversification and its technology-based acquisitions?
2. Analyze and evaluate Softbank's market niche in the Internet and e-commerce industry.
3. What kind of specific global strategies does Softbank need to undertake to be the key player in the Internet and technology-related markets in Japan, North America and other global markets?
4. What did you learn from Softbank's global diversification initiatives and expansion strategy?

5. Compare and contrast Softbank with other multinationals from Japan and the Western world regarding internationalization, diversification, and global competition issues.

CASE NOTES

1. *Zaibatsu* group of companies' structure was based on the concept of holding companies. These companies were very strong before World War II. After the war, the U.S. dissolved these groups which later took the form of *Keiretsu* companies based on the Main-Bank structure and network connections.
2. For further discussion, see: Kim & Mauborgne (1999a-c).

CASE REFERENCES

Abrahams, Paul & Michiyo Nakamoto. 1999. "Heat turns up on the rising star," *Financial Times*, November 13, 16.

Advertising Age. 1998. "Softbank woes rattle clients of web ad firms," March 23, 1, 48.

Brown, Shona L. & Kathleen Eisenhardt. 1998. *Competing on the Edge: Strategy as a Structured Chaos*, Boston, Massachusetts: Harvard Business School Press.

Business Week. 1996. "Cyber-Mogul: To conquer the net, Masayoshi Son takes to the high wire," August 12, 56–62.

Business Week. 1999a "Ziff-Davis is printing in red ink," January 25, 107.

Business Week. 1999b. "Time for this behemoth to evolve?" September 20, 48.

Business Week-E.Biz. 1000. "The E-Biz 25; Masters of the web universe," September 27, 20–56.

Butler, Steve. 1999. "Empire of the Son," *U.S. News & World Report*, July 5, 48–50.

Far Eastern Economic Review. 1998. "Prodigal Son," January 22, 42–44.

Far Eastern Economic Review. 1999. "Japan's Mr. Internet," July 29, 1112.

Financial Times. 1997a. "Softbank spree has investors in a jitter," April 23, 21.

Financial Times. 1997b. "Softbank shares take further dive," October 4/5, 23.

Financial Times. 1997c. "Softbank falls into the perception gap," December 3, 19.

Financial Times. 1999a. "Softbank set for online investors," April 21, 24.

Financial Times. 1999b. "Electronic trading to open up the world to Japan's investors," June 16, 20.

Financial Times. 1999c. "Softbank widens its net," July 9, 12.

Forbes. 1999. "The world's working rich," July 5, 222.

Fortune. 1997. "Japan's top technology investor takes a hit," September 8, 150–151.

Fortune. 1999. "How Son captured Japan's Internet economy," August 16, 156–160.

Global Crossing, Microsoft, Softbank Announces Asian Network Venture, 1999 September 8, http://www.quicken.com.

Kim, W. Chan and Renee Mauborgne. 1999a. "How to discover the unknown market," *Financial Times*, May 6, 12.

Kim, W. Chan and Renee Mauborgne. 1999b. "How Southwest Airlines found a route to success," *Financial Times*, May 13, 20.

Kim, W. Chan and Renee Mauborgne. 1999c. "From trend to quantum leap," *Financial Times*, June 10, 24.

Softbank, Tokyo, Japan, 1999 September. http://www.softbank.com.

U.S. Department of Commerce. 1999. *The Emerging Digital Economy-II*, (June): Washington, DC.: U.S. Dept. of Commerce.

The Economist. 1999. "The real Internet revolution," August 21, 53–54.

The Wall Street Journal. 1996. "Softbank's buying spree may be hard act to follow," August 19, B4.

The Wall Street Journal 1999a. "Softbank cleans up on the Internet," February 3, B4.

The Wall Street Journal. 1999b. "NASDAQ plans to set up a new stock market in Japan, June 16, A19, 21.

The Wall Street Journal. 1999c. "Japan's Softbank unveils new Internet deals," June 25, A15, 17.

Webber, Alan M. 1992. "Japanese style entrepreneurship: An interview with Softbank's CEO, Masayoshi Son," *Harvard Business Review*, 70(1): 91–103.

Weinberg, Neil. 1999. "Master of the Internet," *Forbes*, July 5, 146–151.

Yip, George S. 1992. *Total Global Strategy: Managing for Worldwide Competitive Advantage*, Englewood Cliffs, New Jersey: Prentice Hall.

Ziff-Davis Rebuts News Corp. Story, 1999, Sept. 13. http://cbs.marketwatch.com/news/

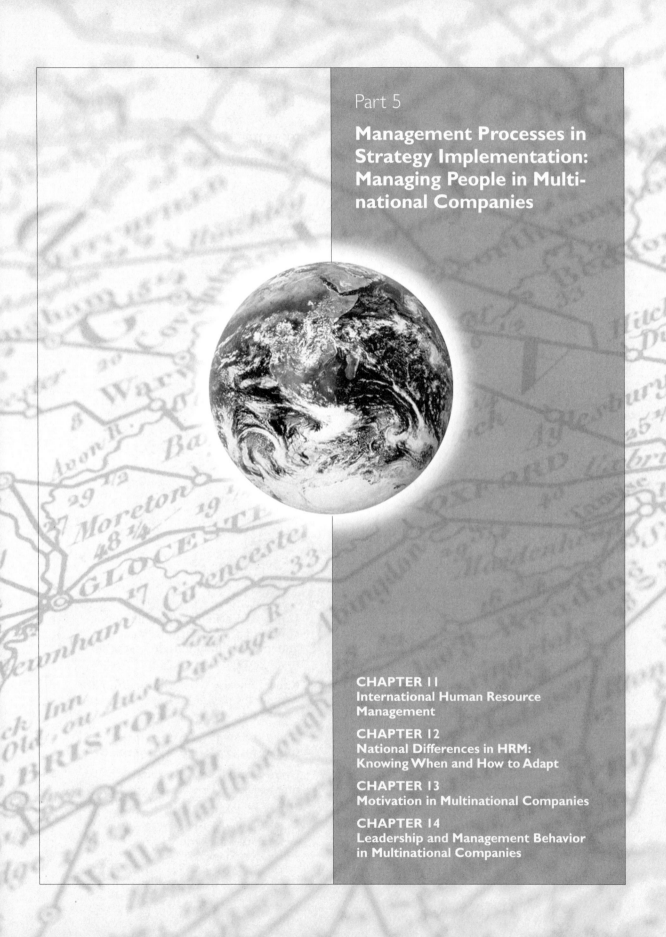

Part 5

**Management Processes in
Strategy Implementation:
Managing People in Multi-
national Companies**

CHAPTER 11

International Human Resource Management

LEARNING OBJECTIVES
After reading this chapter you should
be able to:

- **Know the basic functions of human resource management.**

- **Define international human resource management.**

- **Understand how international human resource management differs from domestic human resource management.**

- **Know the types of workers used by multinational companies.**

- **Understand the four basic orientations to international human resource management.**

- **Understand the relationship between choice of a multinational strategy and international human resource management.**

- **Know how and when multinational companies decide to use expatriate managers.**

- **Know the skills necessary for a successful expatriate assignment.**

- **Understand how expatriate managers are compensated and evaluated.**

- **Appreciate the issues regarding expatriate assignments for women managers.**

<table>
<tr><td>

**Preview
Case in Point**

**Fast-Track
Global
Managers**

</td><td>

In some U.S. companies, especially those with minimal global strategies, mid-level managers avoid international assignments out of fear of negative career implications. The common feeling in these companies is "out of sight, out of mind." Thus, the fear is that by taking an international assignment the individual will not be considered for important projects and promotions at home. A recent study found that only 28 percent of U.S. companies valued global experience, putting the United States third from the bottom of the 16 countries ranked.

However, in many U.S. multinationals, this negative attitude toward international assignments is changing. As U.S. companies search for new customers and markets abroad, they have a growing need for managers with the necessary skills for global assignments. Overseas staffing is growing 10 to 20 percent a year in companies such as Dell Computer Corp., General Motors, Ford, and Gerber Products Co. For such companies, international experience is an important part of the executive experience.

As the global ambitions of U.S. companies grow, so do the global ambitions of managers. Now, many fast-track managers feel they must seek out global assignments as necessary steps in their careers. In many companies, such as Citicorp, Gillette, Texaco, 3M, General Motors, AT&T, General Electric, Procter & Gamble, and Ford, top managers are now being replaced by a new breed of executive. These new top managers have years of global experience and may not even be U.S. nationals. At 3M, for example, 75 percent of the top 100 executives have worked outside the United States. More than half of the top management group at Ford has worked outside of the United States, perhaps not surprising for a company with 60 percent of its workforce in other countries. This new breed of top managers is changing U.S. corporate culture, espousing and insisting on managers' having international experience. As one expert on international staffing noted, when an international opportunity arises, "Either you take up the offer or suffer the consequences later in your career."

Sources: Based on Oster et al. 1993 and Loeb 1995 and Hube 2000.

</td></tr>
</table>

The Preview Case in Point shows that more U.S. companies are seeking internationally experienced managerial talent to run U.S. operations in the global market. This emphasis on building internationally experienced management talent comes from the increasing popularity of global multinational strategies in response to a globalizing world economy.

A key ingredient of implementing any successful multinational strategy includes using compatible human resource management policies. As such, this chapter discusses various options available for human resource management in multinational companies using any of the four multinational strategies discussed in Chapter 6. In combination with the next chapter on comparative views of human resource management, you will see how multinational managers select and implement appropriate human resource management policies to support their multinational strategies.

The chapter first presents a basic definition of international human resource management and shows how international human resource management differs from strictly domestic human resource management. The chapter then discusses how multinational companies must choose a mixture of employees and managers with different nationalities to set up operations in different countries. Following this, there is a discussion of four basic orientations to international human resource management. You will see how each of these orientations best supports different multinational strategies. The last half of the chapter gives particular attention to the role, selection, training, and evaluation of multinational managers who are given international assignments. The chapter concludes with a discussion of issues regarding women with international postings.

INTERNATIONAL HUMAN RESOURCE MANAGEMENT DEFINED

Human resource management (HRM)

Functions are recruitment, selection, training and development, performance appraisal, compensation, and labor relations.

Recruitment

Process of identifying and attracting qualified people to apply for vacant positions in an organization.

Selection

Process by which companies fill vacant positions in the organization.

Business organizations necessarily combine physical (e.g., buildings and machines) and financial assets as well as technological and managerial processes to do some type of work. However, without people, the organization would not exist. Managing and developing human assets are the major goals of human resource management. Thus, **human resource management (HRM)** deals with the entire relationship of the employee with the organization. The basic HRM functions consist of recruitment, selection, training and development, performance appraisal, compensation, and labor relations. They are defined as (Milkovich and Newman 1993; Bohlander, Snell, and Sherman 2001):

- **Recruitment**: Identifying and attracting qualified people to apply for vacant positions in an organization.
- **Selection**: The process by which companies choose people to fill vacant positions in the organization.
- **Training and development**: The processes by which employees acquire the knowledge, skills, and abilities to perform successfully both in current jobs and in the future jobs they will have in their organizational careers.
- **Performance appraisal**: The system used by an organization to measure and assess employees' work performance.
- **Compensation**: The organization's entire reward package, including not only financial rewards and benefits, but also nontangible rewards such as job security.
- **Labor relations**: The continuing relationship between an employer and employees who are represented by labor organizations.

INTERNATIONAL HUMAN RESOURCE MANAGEMENT AND INTERNATIONAL EMPLOYEES

Training and development

Giving employees the knowledge, skills, and abilities to perform successfully both in current jobs and in future jobs.

Performance appraisal

System to measure and assess employees' work performance.

When applied to the international setting, the HRM functions become **international human resource management (IHRM)**. When a company enters the international arena, all the basic human resource management activities remain. However, they take on added complexity. Two issues lead to this complexity for the multinational manager. First, the employees of multinational organizations include a mixture of workers of different nationalities. Second, multinational managers must decide how necessary it is to adapt the company's HRM policies to the national cultures, business cultures, and social institutions where the company is doing business.

TYPES OF EMPLOYEES IN MULTINATIONAL ORGANIZATIONS

IHRM must take into account several types of employees in the multinational organization. **Expatriate** employees come from a different country than where they are working. The expatriate employees who come from the parent firm's home

Compensation

Organization's entire reward package, including not only financial rewards and benefits but nontangible rewards, such as job security.

Labor relations

Ongoing relationship between an employer and those employees represented by labor organizations.

International human resource management (IHRM)

All HRM functions, adapted to the international setting.

Expatriate

Employee who comes from a different country from where he or she is working.

Home country nationals

Expatriate employees who come from the parent firm's home country.

Third country nationals

Expatriate workers who come from neither the host nor home country.

Host country nationals

Local workers who come from the host country where the unit (plant, sales unit, etc.) is located.

Inpatriate

Employees from foreign countries who work in the country where the parent company is located.

country are called **home country nationals**. The expatriate workers who come from neither the host nor home countries are called **third country nationals**. Local workers come from the host country, where the unit (plant, sales unit, etc.) is located. We call these workers **host country nationals**. Usually, home country and third country expatriates belong to the managerial and professional staff rather than to the lower-level workforce. The globalization of the workforce is also breeding a special type of expatriate called the **inpatriate**. Inpatriates are employees from foreign countries who work in the country where the parent company is located.

Adaptation of HRM Practices

An effective IHRM system has both company-wide HRM policies and procedures and HRM policies and procedures adapted to different country locations. Even for transnational companies, there often must be some adaptation of the firm's HRM practices to the traditions, national cultures, and social institutions of host countries. Adaptations of HRM practices are particularly necessary when dealing with non-managerial employees. These employees are usually host country nationals and generally expect a multinational company's HRM practices to fit their local traditions. The unqualified imposition of a multinational's HRM practices on host country nationals risks offending local cultural norms and values, or perhaps may even result in illegal practices.

To avoid costly mistakes in HRM, multinational companies need to consider several key questions regarding local employees such as (Black, Gregersen, and Mendenhall 1992; Reynolds 1997):

- *How can we identify talented local employees?* Nations differ in terms of educational qualifications and formal certifications for job skills. Multinational companies must acquire the necessary knowledge to identify local talent.
- *How can we attract these prospective employees to apply for jobs?* In the United States, newspaper advertising is a popular technique for recruitment. However, in other nations, personal contacts are more important. A multinational must often use local traditions to get the best candidates for jobs.
- *Can we use our home country's training methods with local employees?* Training methods are not always culturally transferable. To make training transcultural, both trainers and written material must be available in all languages.
- *What types of appraisal methods are customary?* Appraisal methods common in one country may not transfer to another country. For example, the Japanese use of age-graded promotions and raises may not be accepted by U.S. workers.
- *What types of rewards do local people value (e.g., security, pay, benefits)?* Cultural and institutional factors often lead people to value different combinations of rewards. In contrast to most European countries, for example, the United States is a society with high wages but low benefits.
- *How can we retain and develop employees with a high potential as future managers?* Countries differ in the training and development applied to lower-level managers with high potential. U.S. companies may identify these managers early in their careers and develop them through rapid promotion coupled with high rewards. In contrast, Japanese companies know they have these managers for their whole career and may take a slower approach, emphasizing experience in many different functional jobs within the company.
- *Do any local laws affect staffing, compensation, and training decisions?* Multinational companies must learn about and work within the web of laws and government policies that govern work in their host countries.

The answers to these questions differ widely, depending on a host country's national and business cultures and its social institutions. As such, effective management of host country workers requires an in-depth knowledge of that country's HRM practices. Chapter 12 explores HRM practices in different countries in considerable detail and provides background necessary to understand local HRM practices and to know when and how to adapt to local conditions.

This chapter next considers other issues that are pertinent to IHRM, including the choice between expatriate and local country managers, the role of women as expatriates, and the relationship of IHRM to a company's multinational strategy. Most of the issues discussed in the remainder of this chapter focus on IHRM practices for managers. The issues discussed in the next chapter are, in general, more relevant to IHRM practices for lower-level Host Country National workers.

One of the most important IHRM issues relating to the implementation of multinational strategies is developing the correct HRM policies and procedures regarding the use of expatriate managers. These managers will often have ultimate responsibility for the firm's international operations and will implement much of a firm's multinational strategy. Consequently, the following section of this chapter focuses on IHRM issues with particular relevance to the use of expatriates.

MULTINATIONAL MANAGERS: THE EXPATRIATE OR THE HOST COUNTRY MANAGER

U.S. companies employ over 7 million people outside the United States. Although most of these employees are lower-level workers, they require a significant number of managers. When are the management positions filled by expatriates? When are they filled by host country nationals? Deciding how many expatriates or local managers to use depends mostly on a company's multinational strategy. Transnational strategists see their managerial recruits as employable anywhere in the world. Multidomestic strategists tend to favor local managers or use expatriates only for short-term assignments. However, regardless of multinational strategy, management teams usually contain a mixture of expatriate and host country nationals. For a particular position, a firm might approach its staffing decisions by answering questions such as (Black, Gregersen, and Mendenhall 1992; Quelch and Bloom 1999; Tung 1981):

- *Given our strategy, what is our preference for this position (host country, home country, or third country national)?* For example, a company with a regional strategy may favor the use of third country nationals as country-level managers.

For expatriate managers (parent country or third country nationals):

- *Is there an available pool of managers with the appropriate skills for the position?* To use expatriate managers, a company must have qualified and available managers within its own ranks. Or it must be able to recruit qualified parent company or third country managers to fill open positions.
- *Are these managers willing to take expatriate assignments?* Not all managers will take assignments abroad. Some managers believe that international assignments can hurt their advancement at home. Increasing numbers of managers have employed spouses, making it impossible to take an international assignment.
- *Do any laws affect our assignments of expatriate managers?* Some countries have strict restrictions on foreigners taking employment. Temporary work visas may be difficult or impossible for employees to obtain.

For host country managers:

- *Do our host country managers have the expertise for the position?* To use host country managers, the local labor pool must have available managers with the training and expertise to fill open positions. Host country managers often lack the expertise of managers from multinational companies.
- *Can we recruit managers with the desired skills from outside our firm?* Even if qualified managerial talent exists in a country, a foreign multinational might not have the reputation or the local connections to attract host country managerial talent. For example, in Japan, many college graduates are reluctant to work for foreign multinationals because they do not provide the security of Japanese companies.

IS THE EXPATRIATE WORTH IT?

IHRM decisions regarding the use of expatriate managers must take into account the costs of such assignments. Total compensation of expatriate managers often exceeds three to four times that of home-based salaries and benefits. Extremely costly locations such as China can be even higher. In China, for example, a bilingual senior U.S. executive can expect a base salary approaching $400,000, hardship allowances as high as 35 percent of salary, two free houses (one in Hong Kong for the weekends and one in China), and chauffeur-driven cars (Melvin 1997).

Exhibit 11.1 shows additional data on the total compensation packages of U.S. expatriate managers posted in some of the more expensive countries.

Even with such high costs, the success of an expatriate assignment is not guaranteed. U.S. companies in particular have poor records of expatriate success when compared with European and Japanese multinational companies. Surveys show that U.S. multinationals often have failure rates for managers in overseas assignments ranging from 10 to 40 percent (Ashamalla 1998). Failure rates include only those managers who were reassigned to the home country for poor performance or who chose to return home because of their own or their family's difficulties adjusting to the local culture. In addition, lower than expected performance levels for expatriate managers are also common.

Typical reasons for U.S. expatriate failure include, in order of the importance of their effects (Ashamalla 1998; Tung 1987):

- Spouse or family members fail to adapt to local culture or environment
- Manager fails to adapt to local culture or environment
- Personality of the manager
- Excess of difficult responsibilities of international assignment
- Lack of technical proficiency
- No motivation for international assignment

Because of the problems associated with using expatriates, some U.S. multinational companies have questioned their use of expatriates. The high costs of locating expatriates in overseas assignments, the high costs associated with failed assignments, and the difficulties of finding U.S. managers with skills like language fluency combine to discourage some companies.

In contrast, however, many multinational companies, especially those with transnational or regional strategies, view international assignments in a broader, longer-term perspective. To compete successfully in the 21st century, such companies see international assignments as having a key strategic role. Consider the following benefits:

Exhibit 11.1
Paying for the
Expatriate Manager

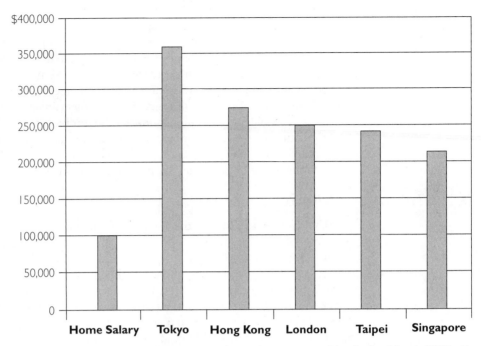

Note: Estimated annual costs for an expatriate manager with a family of four in 2000 with a base salary of $100,000—excludes transfer costs and training costs.

Sources: Adapted and estimated from data reported in the *Economist* 2000 and Runzheimer International 2000.

- *International assignments help managers acquire skills necessary to develop successful strategies in a global context.* Strategic management in the next decades will require managers who understand global competition, customers, suppliers, and markets. Seldom can managers make effective strategic decisions without considering global implications. Without international-management experience, future top managers may not develop talents such as understanding foreign customers or foreign governments. Recognizing such challenges, companies such as Colgate-Palmolive provide a variety of international assignments both for high-potential managers and managers who have recently graduated from college (Gregersen 1999; Lublin 1992).
- *Expatriate assignments help a company coordinate and control operations dispersed geographically and culturally.* Expatriates with a shared vision and objectives for the corporation serve as links to communicate corporate needs and values to culturally and geographically diverse local subsidiaries. In addition, expatriates have first-hand knowledge of local situations and communicate local needs and strategic information to headquarters. In contrast, an overuse of host-country managers may create employees who identify primarily with the host-country subunit rather than with the global organization (Korbin 1988).
- *Global assignments provide important strategic information.* Because of the length of typical expatriate assignments (two to five years) as compared with short visits from headquarters, expatriate managers have sufficient time to gather complex information (Gregersen 1999). For example, in politically risky countries, an experienced expatriate manager can provide the top management of the parent company with critical and timely information. This might include information about key trends in the host country's political, economic, and financial environments (Boyacigiller 1991).

The tradeoff between the strategic benefits of international assignments and the high costs of using expatriates has led some companies to consider a new type of multinational manager. The following section considers this option.

INTERNATIONAL CADRE: ANOTHER CHOICE

The high costs of expatriate managers and the need for managers who think and act globally create conflicting pressures for multinational companies. One reaction by some multinational companies is to use very short assignments for most expatriates while downsizing long-term expatriate staff in favor of more host country managers. Another reaction by multinational companies is to create a separate group of managers who specialize in international assignments. These international specialists are called the **international cadre** or *globals*.

International cadre

Separate group of expatriate managers who specialize in a career of international assignments.

The international cadre has permanent international assignments. They are recruited from any country and are sent to worldwide locations to develop cross-cultural skills and to give the company a worldwide perspective (Quelch and Bloom 2000). Their main job is to promote sharing and learning by all organizational locations and by multinational employees of all nationalities.

Similar to the diplomatic corps of countries, the international cadre spends their career moving from one international assignment to another. They often develop their own international organizational culture, differing somewhat from their companies' main organizational culture (Torrington and Holden 1992). For example, Colgate-Palmolive Co. calls its international cadre the "globalites." Rather than gaining ten years of experience before their first international assignment, as is common in most U.S. multinational companies, the Colgate-Palmolive managers are recent college graduates. These managers expect to have long globe-hopping careers (Lublin 1992). IBM uses a global database to search for talent for any project. Although preference is given to geographically closer managers or engineers, employees who indicate a willingness to move become eligible for global positions (Quelch and Bloom 1999).

The use of a permanent international cadre is more common for European firms than for U.S. multinationals. Perhaps because international issues are so pertinent in post-1992 Europe, many European companies believe it is necessary to develop an organizational culture that promotes international consciousness, tolerance, and cooperation at all levels of the organization (Torrington and Holden 1992). Along with using an international cadre, many European companies also attempt to give international experience to all managers at all levels and at a much earlier age. High-potential managers in particular are singled out for these international experiences (Scullion 1994). For example, Unilever considers 75 percent of its managerial positions "international," and if you take a job with Unilever, international assignments are part of the deal (Quelch and Bloom 1999).

Next, the chapter considers how to use the expatriate manager to maximize strategic advantage.

THE EXPATRIATE MANAGER

Once a company makes the decision to use expatriate managers or to develop a full-time international cadre, successful multinational organizations develop IHRM policies that maximize the potential effectiveness of their expatriate managers. This section shows what we know about the effective selection, training and development, performance appraisal, compensation, and repatriation of the expatriate multinational manager.

SELECTING EXPATRIATE MANAGERS

Traditionally, U.S. multinational companies assume that domestic performance predicts expatriate performance. This assumption leads companies to search for job candidates with the best technical skills and professional competence. When these factors become the major, if not the only, selection criteria for international assignments, companies often overlook other important selection criteria (Tung 1981). What other criteria are important for selecting the best people for expatriate assignments?

Key success factors for expatriate assignments

Motivation, relational abilities, family situation, and language skills.

Several experts on international IHRM have identified **key success factors for expatriate assignments** (Gregerson 1999; Halcrow 1999; Mendenhall and Oddou 1985; Tung 1981). Besides professional and technical competence, the key success factors include relational abilities, family situation, motivation, and language skills. While professional and technical competencies remain prerequisites for the international assignment, these other factors are equally important for success. Consider the following:

- *Technical and managerial skills:* Often an expatriate assignment gives managers more tasks and greater responsibilities than similar-level assignments at home. Additionally, the geographical distance from headquarters can result in the manager having more decision-making autonomy. Only managers with excellent technical, administrative, and leadership skills have a strong likelihood of success in such positions.
- *Relational abilities:* Relational abilities help employees avoid a major pitfall of international assignments, the failure to adapt to different cultures. People with good relational skills have the capacity to adapt to strange or ambiguous situations. They are culturally flexible and sensitive to different cultural norms, values, and beliefs. In addition, they have the ability to modify their own behaviors and attitudes to fit in with a new culture. They favor collaborative negotiation styles and avoid direct confrontation.
- *Family situation:* Selection for an international assignment must also consider the potential expatriate's family situation. An overseas assignment affects the spouse and children as much as the employee. A family situation favorable to the assignment is crucial for expatriate success. Key factors to consider include the spouse's willingness to live abroad, the impact of the potential posting on the spouse's career and the children's education, and the spouse's relational skills. With an increasing number of dual careers, multinational companies may need to provide two positions or compensation for the spouse's lost income to ensure a successful assignment (Latta 1999). The following Multinational Management Brief shows some of the programs companies now use to aid dual-career couples.
- *International Motivation:* To overcome the challenges of more complex jobs, cultural differences, and strains on families, managers must be motivated to accept the expatriate position. Such motivation can come from a commitment to the company's international mission, an interest in the culture of the assignment country, and a good fit with the recruit's career stage. However, few good managers will accept an assignment that they perceive is detrimental to their career.
- *Language ability:* The ability to speak, read, and write the host country language enhances many of the other key success factors. Managers with good language

---

Multinational Management Brief
Managing Dual Careers for the Expatriate

Ten years ago, the typical expatriate was a man with a spouse willing to forsake career and work and relocate to another country. Multinational companies now face many managers refusing international assignments for reasons relating to their spouse's career. One survey found that sacrifice by their spouse is now the number one cause of declining assignments. Companies like Motorola, HP, Royal Dutch Shell, and GE are responding. These firms give allowances for the spouse's career-building activities such as getting work permits or furthering education. Recent data show that 25 percent of the companies give spousal job search assistance, up from near zero in the early 1990s.

Consider some of these adaptations:

- Royal Dutch Shell makes career counselors available for spouses and unmarried partners.
- Shell Oil Company created an information network with 44 centers for finding spouses jobs.
- Sara Lee reimburses spouses for job-seeking expenses.
- Deloitte & Touche provides spouses a job-searching database on the company's intranet.
- 3M provides a one-time dislocation allowance for spouses and allows spouses who are employees to take personal leave.

Sources: Based on Latta 1999 and Thaler-Carter 1999.

---

skills come better prepared to apply their technical and managerial skills. They have more success in dealing with local colleagues, subordinates, and customers. Knowledge of the local language also increases the understanding of the local culture and reduces the stress of adapting to a new cultural environment.

Selecting an expatriate manager with the appropriate array of skills demands more effort than selecting domestic managers. There are more key success factors to consider in international assignments than in domestic assignments. Most successful multinationals use a combination of selection techniques to identify people with the appropriate talent for an expatriate posting. Some popular techniques include interviews, standardized tests of intelligence or technical knowledge, assessment centers (testing centers where candidates solve simulated managerial problems), biographical data, work samples, and references.

Exhibit 11.2 shows some of the characteristics of the key success factors and selection techniques used in the expatriate selection process.

The importance of the expatriate success factors is not equal for all expatriate job assignments. Each success factor has a different priority depending on four assignment conditions. These are (Tung 1981): assignment length, cultural similarity, required communication with host country nationals, and job complexity and responsibility. Each of these conditions affects the selection criteria as follows:

- *Assignment length:* The amount of time an expatriate expects to remain in the host country may range from short postings of a month or less to several years.

Exhibit 11.2 Expatriate Success Factors and Selection Methods

Key Success Factors	Selection Methods					
	Interviews	Standardized Tests	Assessment Centers	Biographical Data	Work Samples	References
Professional/technical skills						
• Technical skills	✔	✔		✔	✔	✔
• Administrative skills	✔		✔	✔	✔	✔
• Leadership skills						
Relational abilities						
• Ability to communicate	✔		✔			✔
• Cultural tolerance and empathy	✔	✔	✔			
• Tolerance for ambiguity	✔		✔			
• Flexibility to adapt to new behaviors and attitudes	✔		✔			✔
• Stress adaptation skills	✔		✔			
International motivation						
• Willingness to accept expatriate position	✔			✔		
• Interest in culture of assignment location	✔					
• Commitment to international mission	✔					
• Fit with career development stage	✔			✔		✔
Family situation						
• Spouse's willingness to live abroad	✔					
• Spouse's relational abilities	✔	✔	✔			
• Spouse's career goals	✔					
• Children's educational requirements	✔					
Language skills						
• Ability to communicate in local language	✔	✔	✔	✔		✔

Sources: Adapted from Black, Gregersen, and Mendenhall 1992 and Ronen 1986.

Selection for short-term assignments usually focuses primarily on technical and professional qualifications.

- *Cultural similarity:* Cultures vary widely, but certain cultures are more similar to each other. The cultural similarity between Japan and Korea, for example, is higher than between the United States and Taiwan or France and Saudi Arabia. Thus, finding the right French or U.S. expatriate for an assignment in the Middle East or Asia requires more emphasis on family factors, relational skills, and language skills. Managers from similar cultures usually find adaptation much easier.

- *Required interaction and communication:* Some jobs require more interaction and communication with host country nationals such as subordinates, suppliers, customers, and joint venture partners. Increased relational skills and knowledge of the host country language and culture become more important in such situations.

- *Job complexity and responsibility:* People in jobs with more complex tasks and greater responsibilities often have significant effects on the success of projects.

Exhibit 11.3
Selecting Expatriates:
Priorities for Success
Factors by Assignment
Characteristics

Expatriate Success Factors	Assignment Characteristics			
	Longer Duration	More Cultural Dissimilarity	Greater Interaction and Communication Requirements with Locals	More Complex or Responsible Job
Professional/Technical Skills	High	Neutral	Moderate	High
Relational Abilities	Moderate	High	High	Moderate
International Motivation	High	High	High	High
Family Situation	High	High	Neutral	Moderate
Language Skills	Moderate	High	High	Neutral

Sources: Adapted from Black, Gregersen, and Mendenhall 1992 and Tung 1981.

For this reason, professional and technical skills are always important. However, the more important the job to the organization, the more the candidate's skills and previous success in related work will count in the selection decision.

Exhibit 11.3 summarizes issues to consider in setting priorities during the expatriate selection process. Different success factors have more importance depending on the expatriate's job assignment conditions.

The efforts to ensure the best chance of the expatriate manager's success do not end with the selection process. Even good raw material needs training and development. Next, we consider training and development for the expatriate.

TRAINING AND DEVELOPMENT

Cross-cultural training

Increases the relational abilities of future expatriates and, in some cases, their spouses and families.

Strong evidence shows that predeparture **cross-cultural training** reduces expatriate failure rates and increases expatriate job performance (Black and Mendenhall 1990; Forster 2000). The main objective of cross-cultural training is to increase the relational abilities of the future expatriate and, when possible, the spouse and family of the future expatriate. The techniques used and the rigor of the training depend on the anticipated situations an expatriate might face in his or her assignment.

In spite of the evidence that training leads to successful expatriate assignments, many multinational companies still do not invest heavily in cross-cultural training (Forster 2000). This situation may be changing. U.S. multinational firms such as American Express, Colgate-Palmolive, and General Electric continuously upgrade their international training concerns. A recent survey by the consulting firm Windham International (2000) of 264 multinational companies with a total worldwide expatriate population of 74,709 found that approximately 63 percent now have cross-cultural training prior to expatriate assignments.

Training rigor

Extent of effort by both trainees and trainers required to prepare the trainees for expatriate positions.

Training rigor involves the extent of effort by both trainees and trainers required to prepare the trainees for expatriate positions (Black et al. 1992). Low rigor means that training lasts for a short period and includes techniques such as lectures and videos on the local culture and briefings concerning company operations. High-rigor training may last over a month. It contains more experiential learning and extensive language training and often interactions with host country nationals. Exhibit 11.4 shows various training techniques and their objectives as the rigor of the cross-cultural training grows.

Exhibit 11.4

Building Blocks of
Cross-Cultural Training
Rigor: Techniques
and Objectives

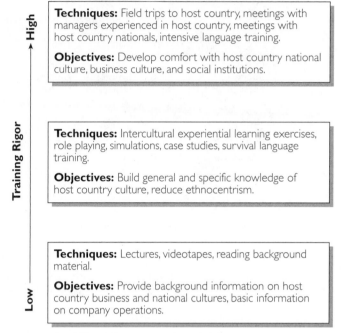

Techniques: Field trips to host country, meetings with managers experienced in host country, meetings with host country nationals, intensive language training.

Objectives: Develop comfort with host country national culture, business culture, and social institutions.

Techniques: Intercultural experiential learning exercises, role playing, simulations, case studies, survival language training.

Objectives: Build general and specific knowledge of host country culture, reduce ethnocentrism.

Techniques: Lectures, videotapes, reading background material.

Objectives: Provide background information on host country business and national cultures, basic information on company operations.

Sources: Adapted from Black, Gregersen, and Mendenhall 1992 and Ronen 1989.

The same conditions that influence the priorities given to expatriate success factors in selection decisions also affect the requirements for an expatriate's training rigor. Increases in the length of the assignment, cultural dissimilarity between home and host country, amount of required interaction and communication with local people, and job complexity/responsibility all suggest a need for increased training rigor as preparation for the overseas assignment (Mendenhall and Oddou 1988; Tung, 1981). Exhibit 11.5 shows how the rigor of training relates to the basic expatriate assignment conditions already discussed. In addition, given that failure of the spouse to adapt is the major cause of expatriate downfalls, assignment conditions help determine the training needs of the spouse and possibly other family members. Training for a long assignment in a dissimilar culture may include training for all family members, not just the prospective expatriate.

In addition to predeparture training, many multinational companies build international experience into management development. The Multinational Management Brief on page 440 gives some examples of these companies.

Once expatriates are on assignment, IHRM does not stop. Multinational managers must have appropriate performance-appraisal techniques for employees in international assignments. Next, the chapter considers performance appraisal for the expatriate.

PERFORMANCE APPRAISAL FOR THE EXPATRIATE

Conducting a reliable and valid performance appraisal of expatriate managers provides one of the greatest IHRM challenges for the international company. Seldom can a company transfer the same performance criteria and measures to a host country operation.

Some of the issues that make expatriate performance appraisals difficult include (Dowling and Schuler 1990):

Exhibit 11.5
Training Needs and
Expatriate Assignment
Characteristics

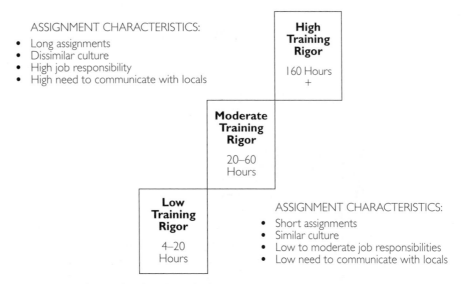

ASSIGNMENT CHARACTERISTICS:

- Long assignments
- Dissimilar culture
- High job responsibility
- High need to communicate with locals

High Training Rigor

160 Hours +

Moderate Training Rigor

20–60 Hours

Low Training Rigor

4–20 Hours

ASSIGNMENT CHARACTERISTICS:

- Short assignments
- Similar culture
- Low to moderate job responsibilities
- Low need to communicate with locals

Source: Adapted from Mendenhall, Dunbar, and Oddou 1987.

- *Fit of international operation in multinational strategy:* As discussed in Chapter 6, companies often enter international markets for strategic reasons other than the immediate profit of that particular international operation. Learning about a new market or challenging an international competitor may be strategic goals that put a subsidiary in the red but still serve a useful purpose for the organization. In these cases, local managers might look quite ineffective for a company that uses economic-performance measures such as return on investment, a standard profitability ratio (roi).
- *Unreliable data:* Data used to measure local subunit performance may not be comparable with the home units' data or data from other international operations. For example, local accounting rules can alter the meaning of financial data. In other cases, production efficiency can look bad because local laws require full employment rather than the occasional use of overtime.
- *Complex and volatile environments:* The international environment is complex and unstable. Economic and other environmental conditions can change rapidly and in ways often unanticipated by managers back in the home country headquarters. Consequently, reasonable and achievable performance objectives developed earlier can quickly become impossible for expatriate managers to achieve.
- *Time differences and distance separation:* Although decreasing in importance with more rapid communication and travel options, the separation of local organizations from the home office by geography and differences in time remains a problem for evaluating local managers. Often "out of sight, out of mind," expatriate and local managers lack the frequency and intensity of communication to keep home-office staff informed on all aspects of local management problems. Without intensive and direct contact, performance appraisals can fail to demonstrate a comprehensive understanding of an expatriate manager's situation.
- *Local cultural situations:* As we have seen throughout this text, countries differ widely on accepted work practices. Factors such as the number of holidays and vacations, the expected hours of work, the training and types of local workers available, and the types of local managers available can affect directly the performances of expatriate managers. Although successful expatriate managers

Multinational Management Brief
Developing Global Management Skills

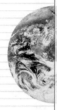

To develop truly global managers, some U.S. companies now offer global training and assignments early in management careers.

- General Electric provides language and cross-cultural training to prepare marketing managers to conduct business in the global environment. GE considers the global outlook important even though some of these managers may never have overseas assignments.
- Training at Procter & Gamble's "P&G College" includes a heavy emphasis on international issues for new and mid-level managers.
- Colgate-Palmolive has global marketing management training for U.S. and other nationals. They become product managers in the United States or abroad and must be able to move from country to country in 6 to 18 months, if they hope to reach higher-levels of management. Some managers have up to three international assignments in their first five years.
- American Express sends its junior managers both from the United States and from other countries for two-year assignments. The aim is to have managers with a global perspective early in their careers and not just when they become vice presidents.

Sources: Based on *Expatriate Management Update* 2000 and Gregerson 1999 and Lublin 1992.

adapt quickly to the local cultural expectations, parent country management and staff seldom have the same appreciation of the local situation. Good international performance appraisals must adjust for local cultural expectations regarding work.

To overcome the difficulty of conducting performance appraisals of international managers and other employees, experts suggest several steps to improve the process (Black, Gregersen, and Mendenhall 1992).

- *Fit the evaluation criteria to strategy:* For example, if the objective is to enter a market for long-term position, it does not make sense to use short-term financial-performance measures.
- *Fine-tune the evaluation criteria:* Senior managers need to consider carefully all their objectives for the international operation. They need to visit local sites to understand more clearly the problems and situations faced by expatriate and local managers. Recently repatriated managers can also provide excellent knowledge about local circumstances.
- *Use multiple sources of evaluation with varying periods of evaluation:* The complexity of the international situation demands more information than similar appraisals done at home. As such, higher-levels of management should rely on several sources of information. Exhibit 11.6 shows several common components of expatriate performance appraisals. These components include sources of evaluation information, evaluation criteria, and evaluation periods.

The next question considered is: How do multinational companies determine the fair and adequate compensation of expatriate managers?

Exhibit 11.6

Evaluation Sources, Criteria, and Time Periods for Expatriate Performance Appraisals

Evaluation Sources	Criteria	Periods
Self-Evaluation	Meeting objectives Management skills Project successes	Six months and at the completion of a major project
Subordinates	Leadership skills Communication skills Subordinates' development	After completion of major project
Peer Expatriate and Host Country Managers	Team building Interpersonal skills Cross-cultural interaction skills	Six months
On-Site Supervisor	Management skills Leadership skills Meeting objectives	At the completion of significant projects
Customers and Clients	Service quality and timeliness Negotiation skills Cross-cultural interaction skills	Yearly

Source: Adapted from Black, Gregersen, and Mendenhall 1992.

EXPATRIATE COMPENSATION

THE BALANCE-SHEET APPROACH

Balance-sheet method

Attempts to equate purchasing power in the host country with the expatriate's purchasing power in his or her home country.

More than 85 percent of U.S. multinational companies commonly apply the **balance-sheet method** for determining expatriate compensation (Overman 2000). The balance-sheet method provides a compensation package that attempts to equate or balance an expatriate's purchasing power in the host country with purchasing power in his or her home country. To balance the compensation received for the international assignment with compensation received in the home country, multinational companies usually provide additional salary. This increased salary includes adjustments for differences in taxes, housing costs, and the costs of basic goods and services. Goods and services include items such as food, recreation, personal care, clothing, education, home furnishing, transportation, and medical care (Dowling and Schuler 1990; Frazee 1998). Exhibit 11.7 pictures a simple view of how the balance sheet approach works.

Besides matching the expatriate's purchasing power, companies often provide other allowances and extra benefits called perquisites to the expatriate manager. These cover the initial logistics of the international move (such as hotel costs while settling in), compensation for lifestyle differences between the home and host country, and incentives to take the assignment. Some of these additional allowances and perquisites include (Black, Gregersen, and Mendenhall 1992):

- *Foreign service premiums:* Multinational companies often provide 10 to 20 percent of base pay for accepting the individual and family difficulties associated with an overseas assignment. Approximately 78 percent of major U.S. multinational companies pay this premium.
- *Hardship allowance:* This is extra money paid for a particularly difficult posting due to issues such as high risk or poor living conditions.
- *Relocation allowances:* Along with the basic costs of moving a family to an international assignment, many companies pay a flat sum equal to one month's salary

Exhibit 11.7
A Balance Sheet
Approach to Expatriate
Compensation

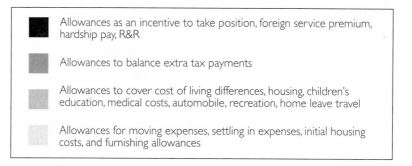

Domestic Assignment: Expenses and Spendable Income:		Expatriate Assignment: Expenses and Balanced Spendable Income + Allowances:
Base Salary	+	Base Salary
	=	
Taxes	=	Taxes
	+	
Goods and Services	=	Goods and Services
	+	
Housing	=	Housing
	+	
Spendable Income	=	Spendable Income

Allowances as an incentive to take position, foreign service premium, hardship pay, R&R

Allowances to balance extra tax payments

Allowances to cover cost of living differences, housing, children's education, medical costs, automobile, recreation, home leave travel

Allowances for moving expenses, settling in expenses, initial housing costs, and furnishing allowances

at the beginning and end of the assignment to cover miscellaneous costs of re-locating.

- *Home-leave allowances:* These provide transportation costs for expatriates and their families to return to their parent country once or twice a year.

OTHER APPROACHES

The high cost of expatriate compensation and the trend for multinational companies to have workers anywhere in the world doing similar work has resulted in companies developing modifications of the traditional balance sheet approach. Some companies simply pay home country wages regardless of location, called the **headquarters-based compensation system**. This works well when parent country wages are high compared with the local assignment's cost of living (Black, Gregersen, and Mendenhall 1992). It can be a problem in high-cost locations such as Paris or Tokyo.

Many experts now recommend that companies wean expatriates gradually from dependence on perks and allowances that allow home country managers to main-

Headquarters-based compensation system

Paying home country wages regardless of location.

tain the lifestyles they have at home, or sometimes live better overseas (Frazee 1998; Overman 2000). These companies assume that there is nothing special about being an expatriate, especially for longer assignments. After an initial period on assignment, allowances are reduced. Firms use local or regional markets to determine compensation. Such companies expect the expatriate to become an efficient consumer by adjusting to local lifestyles and costs of living. This is called the **host-based compensation system**.

Host-based compensation system

Adjusting wages to local lifestyles and costs of living.

Some companies speed this adjustment by offering selections of allowances somewhat similar to a cafeteria benefit plan. Expatriates can, within certain financial boundaries, select the allowances they feel are most appropriate to their needs.

The international cadre, those managers who work for global companies in a series of international assignments, present different problems for compensation. For example, Lawrence Watson, the managing director of the European headquarters of the Hay Group (an international consulting firm for HRM), asks: "So, how do you reward a French citizen who works in the U.K. for a U.S. company? And how do you ensure continuity and equity when that person relocates to Singapore next year?" (Hay Group 1993).

Global pay system

Worldwide job evaluations, performance appraisal methods, and salary scales are used.

To address the problem of compensation for multiple and continuous global assignments, companies develop **global pay systems**. Global pay systems have worldwide job-evaluation and performance-appraisal methods designed to assess the worth of jobs to the company and equitably reward subordinates. To some extent, global pay systems resemble the balance system. Allowances still exist for differences in expenses such as cost of living, taxes, settling in, and housing. However, the system does not balance compensation to produce parity with lifestyles in the home country. Rather, companies use a worldwide standard of compensation and make only necessary adjustments to that standard. The objective is to reduce waste from expatriate perquisites, eliminate the factor of steep differences in compensation from the decision to accept a given job, and promote compensation equity for all long-term international cadre (Overman 2000).

Transnational companies such as Seagram, discussed in the following Case in Point, are moving toward global pay systems that consider worldwide equity in rewards and allow managers to move between countries with minimal effects on lifestyle.

Although international cadre are not expected to "come home," most other types of expatriate managers return to their home company in their home country. This is not always as easy as many managers expect. Hence, multinational companies face the "repatriation problem."

THE REPATRIATION PROBLEM

Repatriation problem

Difficulties that managers face in coming back to their home countries and reconnecting with their home organizations.

Bringing expatriate employees home and back into full participation in the company remains a difficult problem for many organizations. For example, one study in the United Kingdom found that over 70 percent of the companies surveyed reported significant problems regarding reentry of expatriates into the company (Scullion 1994). Studies of North American companies found that 25 percent of managers completing foreign assignments wanted to leave the firm (Gregersen 1999). Turnover might be as high as 50 percent within two years after return (Poe 2000). The difficulties that managers face in coming back to their home countries and reconnecting with the old job is called the **repatriation problem**. However, these difficulties can be solved with proper preparation and planning by the expatriate and the company.

The Seagram Spirits and Wine Group, incorporated in Canada, with HR in London, and its CEO in New York is certainly international. Seagram generates 65 percent of revenue from outside of North America and employs ten thousand people in 60 different countries. They need experienced and dedicated multinational managers—Europeans, Asians, and Americans—who can move easily and effectively between countries as corporate needs change. To facilitate their multinational strategies, they recently developed an international compensation plan called the "international cadre policy" to function as a "global glue."

This compensation policy applies to over 1,000 global managers in the international cadre. Members of the international cadre are not typical expatriates who wish to return to the United States or their parent country after their assignments. These managers expect international positions for their whole career.

The international cadre compensation package begins with a worldwide job-evaluation system so that similar jobs get similar pay. To equalize the compensation system in different locations, Seagram provides a pay system that puts managers in the top quartile of local compensation. However, managers must meet profit performance goals to keep this level of compensation. All bonuses are computed as a percentage of base pay.

Source: Based on Gross and Wingerup 1999.

Expatriates face at least three basic cultural problems when coming home (Black, Gregersen, and Mendenhall 1992). Many of these relate to the phenomenon called "reverse culture shock," where people must relearn the subtleties of their own cultural norms, values, and beliefs. First, the expatriate must adapt to what is often a new work environment and organizational culture of the home office. This may lead to low work performance or turnover after the assignment. Second, expatriates and their families must relearn to communicate with friends and coworkers in the home and organizational culture. Often, as part of adapting to their former host cultures, expatriates are unaware that they now use different communication patterns. Third, although surprising for people who have lived most of their life in their home country, many expatriates need time to adapt to the basic living environment such as school, food, weather, and so on.

There are also organizational problems for the expatriate and the company if repatriation is not handled properly. One survey reported that 61 percent of expatriates felt that they were not given the chance to use their international experience. After years in challenging international postings, three-quarters reported that their present jobs were demotions. Three months after their return home, one-third of the former expatriates were still in temporary jobs (Gregersen 1999).

A variety of strategies exist that allow companies to have successful repatriations of their expatriates (Gregersen 1999; Black, Gregersen, and Mendenhall 1992). These include:

- *Provide a strategic purpose for the repatriation:* Use the expatriate's experiences to further organizational goals. Expatriates often provide excellent sources of information and experiences that companies should plan to use.

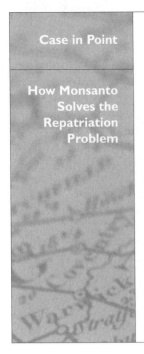

Case in Point

How Monsanto Solves the Repatriation Problem

One recent survey found that 61 percent of returning expatriates felt that their company did not use their foreign experience successfully. Not surprisingly such experiences lead to a turnover rate approaching 25 percent, with some companies even losing all of their returnees.

Effective companies take repatriation seriously.

Monsanto has the usual expatriate preparation of relational training and language training. However, it also has a comprehensive program to maintain a manager's career development and to make reintegration into the home company easier. First, at least three to six months prior to a manager's return, a senior line manager in the home and an HR manager (both with international experience) assess the skills the expatriate has achieved in his or her international assignment. Second, the returning expatriate does a self-assessment and identifies career goals. Third, the senior manager and HR manager identify potential job openings within the Monsanto organization. Fourth, and finally, the three managers meet and decide which available position best matches the expatriate's strengths and the needs of the organization.

The program has existed for six years and has reduced turnover dramatically.

Source: Based on Gregerson 1999.

- *Establish a team to aid the expatriate:* The HRM department and the expatriate's supervisor can help plan for the expatriate's return.
- *Provide parent country information sources:* Many companies assign mentors or sponsors who keep the expatriate informed of current changes in the company including job opportunities.
- *Provide training and preparation for the return:* This preparation can begin as early as six months before the return. Visits home and specific training for the next assignment help ease transition difficulties.
- *Provide support for the expatriate and family on reentry:* To ease the initial adjustments of coming home, companies can aid in finding housing, provide time off for adjustments, and adjust compensation packages if necessary.

The preceding Case in Point shows how Monsanto prepares its expatriate managers for eventual repatriation to the United States.

Traditionally, in most multinational companies, international assignments have been male dominated. Why is this true? Is the practice continuing? Next, we consider these and other issues raised when women take on international assignments.

INTERNATIONAL ASSIGNMENTS FOR WOMEN

The most striking fact about women with international assignments is their paucity in numbers. Estimates are that only 12 percent of expatriate managers are women (Lancaster 1999). The data show that North American multinational companies are reluctant to post women overseas and that personnel managers believe foreigners would be prejudiced against women managers (Jelinek and Adler 1988; Stroh, Varma, and Valy-Durbin 2000). In addition, of the women who do get international assignments, very few have top-management positions (Izraeli and Zeira 1993).

These findings are even more striking when one considers that North American companies probably use more women in international positions than do Asian or European companies.

Why are the barriers so strong to women gaining international positions even in countries such as the United States, where nearly half of the business-school graduates are women?

Culturally based gender-role expectations for women and men enter into many selection decisions. Some managers question whether family problems, a known predictor of expatriate failure, will be greater for women. They doubt whether women are willing to take the time away from their family that is necessary to handle an expatriate position. They ask, How will the spouse fit in? What will happen if there is a dual career? Some even voice the concern that women are not tough enough to face the physical hazards, isolation, and loneliness of some international postings (Adler 1993).

However, the data tend to prove these prejudices wrong. Nancy Adler, a leading expert on women in international management, notes two important "myths" that lead HR executives and top-line managers to overlook qualified and motivated women for international postings. These are (Adler 1993):

- *Myth 1:* Women do not wish to take international assignments. In a survey of women graduating with MBAs, over three-quarters said they would choose an international position at some time during their career.
- *Myth 2:* Women will fail in international assignments because of the foreign culture's prejudices against local women. To address this myth, Adler surveyed over one hundred women managers with international postings for North American companies. Over 95 percent of these women reported successful expatriate assignments, well above the average success rate for men.

More recent data by the New York-based research firm Catalyst (Mallory 2000; Schafer 2000) suggest that these myths still exist and block many women managers from career-building international assignments. Similar to Adler's findings almost a decade earlier, this firm also found that women managers are just as willing as men to take on an international assignment.

SUCCESSFUL WOMEN EXPATRIATES

In spite of their low numbers, women succeed in expatriate assignments (Stroh, Varma, and Valy-Durbin 2000). Contrary to some expectations, expatriate women managers succeed in cultures where few local women reach managerial levels in organizations. In addition, for some assignments, being a woman can be advantageous and lead to performances better than those of male colleagues.

FOREIGN, NOT FEMALE

In a classic article, subtitled "A *Gaijin*, Not a Woman," Nancy Adler debunked one of the key myths regarding women as expatriates (Adler 1987). *Gaijin* is the Japanese word for foreigner. From her research, Adler concluded that it is a mistake to assume that people from foreign cultures, even traditionally patriarchal Asian cultures, apply the same gender-role expectations to foreign women that they apply to local women. Rather, it seems that people from even very traditional cultures can view foreign businesswomen as so different from local women that gender becomes irrel-

Case in Point

The Gender-Free *Meishi*

The Japanese and many other Asian cultures exchange business cards (*meishi* in Japanese) during introductions. *Meishi* serve to define status with one's company and determine how one should interact with business associates, even to the use of polite forms of language.

Two U.S. professors, a husband-and-wife team working on a research project in Japan, observed how the *meishi* determined the pattern of interaction with the woman. If the man was introduced first or the two were introduced as a married couple, Japanese businessmen and professors would focus attention on the man and treat the wife, politely but obviously, as *oksuma* (wife). However, if the woman also produced her *meishi* at the same time as the husband, the role of wife was ignored. Instead, the Japanese responded to the woman in terms of her professional rank. She was *sensei* (a polite form of address for professors) and gender or marital status became irrelevant. However, it seemed particularly important to establish professional rank initially. The Japanese seemed to have more difficulty moving a woman to professional status after they perceived her initially as a wife.

evant for business purposes. For example, one businesswoman working in the Sudan was surprised by the behavior of her Sudanese host. She asked him how it was possible that he could serve her food, give her a cushion to sit on, and wash her arms after the meal? Men never do these things for women according to traditional Sudanese gender-role expectations. The Sudanese host reasoned, "Oh, it's no problem. Women do not do business; therefore, you are not a woman" (Solomon 1989). After establishing a business relationship, according to Adler, the real issues that arise in cross-cultural interactions depend more on how people in the host country culture react to people of the expatriate's nationality rather than to the expatriate's gender.

The preceding Case in Point describes a situation where a woman's business status determined how Japanese men responded to her.

THE WOMAN'S ADVANTAGE

Some studies (Adler 1987) suggest that women may have some advantages in expatriate positions, especially in Asia. Being unique has some benefits. Because so few women have expatriate assignments, those women who do take expatriate positions report being more visible. Local businesspeople were more likely to remember them and often sought out these women more than the women's male colleagues. North American expatriate women also report that local businessmen from traditional cultures assume that the women are "best," "Or why else would you send a woman?"

Women also may be more likely to excel in relational skills, a major factor in expatriate success. Women report that local male managers can be more open in communication with a woman than with a man. Local men, even from traditional cultures, can talk at ease with a woman about an array of subjects that includes issues outside the domain of traditional "male only" conversations. Consequently, being both a businessperson and a woman gives the expatriate women a wider range of interaction options than those available to expatriate men or to local women (Adler 1993).

MORE WOMEN IN THE FUTURE?

Opportunities for women expatriate managers are expected to grow, particularly with global companies. Scholars see several factors leading to more women with international assignments.

Many global and multinational companies face an acute shortage of high-quality multinational managers (Thaler-Carter 1999). At the same time, perhaps because of the rise in dual-career couples, fewer men are willing to take international assignments (Izraeli and Zeira 1993). One way to solve this problem is to tap the available population of women managers. Freed from local cultural barriers that restrict the use of women managers, multinational companies can select the best people for the job regardless of gender. Because of potentially stronger relational skills, women managers may often better qualify for international positions than their male colleagues.

The increasing numbers of women managers, particularly in North America and to a lesser degree in Europe, provide role models for women in management. As a result, during business travel in the West, managers from cultures with traditional role expectations for women more often encounter women in managerial positions. This greater familiarity with women managers by business executives from traditional cultures may encourage global companies to employ more women in expatriate positions, regardless of local female role expectations (Izraeli and Zeira 1993).

In North America, legal and social pressures for equal opportunity have resulted in more women in managerial positions over the last twenty years. Particularly for large U.S. corporations, these pressures should result in greater access to expatriate assignments for U.S. women and women of other nationalities who work for U.S. companies (Izraeli and Zeira 1993). In addition, since equal-opportunity laws exist in many countries that now have few women managers (e.g., Japan), the U.S. experience may signal the future for other countries.

MULTINATIONAL STRATEGY AND IHRM

Multinational companies have several options to develop the appropriate IHRM policies for the implementation of multinational strategies. One way to ascertain a company's approach to IHRM is to examine its IHRM orientation or philosophy. Experts identify four IHRM orientations. These are discussed next, followed by a consideration of how these orientations support the implementation of the four multinational strategies.

IHRM ORIENTATIONS

IHRM orientation

Company's basic tactics and philosophy for coordinating IHRM activities for managerial and technical workers.

The four **IHRM orientations** are ethnocentric, polycentric, regiocentric, and global. These orientations reflect a company's basic tactics and philosophy for coordinating their IHRM activities for managerial and technical workers. Exhibit 11.8 shows how the IHRM orientations relate to some of the basic HRM functions. Each orientation is discussed in more detail next.

ETHNOCENTRIC IHRM ORIENTATION

An **ethnocentric IHRM** orientation means that all aspects of HRM for managers and technical workers tend to follow the parent organization's home country

Exhibit 11.8 IHRM Orientation and IHRM Practices for Managers and Technical Workers

IHRM Practice	IHRM Orientation			
	Ethnocentric	Polycentric	Regiocentric	Global
Recruitment and Selection	Home country nationals for key positions selected by technical expertise or past home country performance; host country nationals for lowest levels of management only.	Home country nationals for top management and technical positions; host country nationals for mid-level management positions; selection of home country nationals similar to ethnocentric; selection of host country nationals based on fit with home country culture, e.g., home country language ability.	Home country nationals for top management and technical positions; regional country nationals for mid-level management and below.	Worldwide throughout the company; based on best qualified for position.
Training for Cross-Cultural Adaptation	Very limited or none; no language requirements.	Limited for home country nationals. Some language training.	Limited to moderate training levels for home country nationals; home and host country nationals use language of business, often English.	Continuous for cultural adaptation and multi-lingualism.
Management Development: The Effects of International Assignments	May hurt career.	May hurt career of home country nationals; host country nationals' advancement often limited to own country.	Neutral to slightly positive career implications; international assignments of longer duration.	International assignments required for career advancement.
Evaluation	Home standards based on contribution to corporate bottom line.	Host standards based on contribution to unit bottom line.	Regional standards based on contribution to corporate bottom line.	Global standards based on contribution to corporate bottom line.
Compensation	Additional pay and benefits for expatriate assignments.	Additional pay and benefits for expatriate assignments; host country compensation rates for host country nationals.	Due to longer assignments, less additional compensation for expatriate assignments.	Similar pay and benefit packages globally with some local adjustments.

Sources: Adapted from Adler and Ghadar 1990 and Heenan and Perlmutter 1979.

Ethnocentric IHRM

All aspects of HRM for managers and technical workers tend to follow the parent organization's home-country HRM practices.

HRM practices. In recruitment, key managerial and technical personnel come from the home country. Local employees fill only lower-level and supporting jobs. Past performance at home and technical expertise govern selection criteria for overseas assignments in the ethnocentric IHRM company (Mendenhall, Dunbar, and Oddou 1987).

Consistent with the use of home country nationals for management and technical positions, evaluations and promotions use parent country standards. The company assesses managers' performances using the same criteria and measures used for home country units. Because of national context variations, companies may be forced to use different approaches for the evaluation and promotion of host country managers. Such local adaptations, however, often have little effect on the ethnocentric company's procedures for promotions beyond the lowest levels of management. As such, limited by facilities and opportunities located in their country, host country nationals usually face a ceiling or barrier limiting how far they may progress in the company.

When an ethnocentric IHRM company uses expatriates, training for the international assignment is often limited or nonexistent. Except for top country-level or region-level positions, most international assignments last only a short time, often only for marketing and sales contacts. The use of home company evaluation and promotion standards, the lack of training, and the often short periods of expatriate assignments limit and discourage cultural adjustments for expatriates. Seldom, for example, do expatriate managers from the parent country know the host country's language.

In the ethnocentric company, when international postings are available, they often have negative effects on the careers of managers or technical specialists. Since ethnocentric organizations usually concentrate key decision making at home, expatriate managers often feel that they have little success in communicating local needs to headquarters. Expatriates also tend to feel isolated and "out of the loop," with little opportunity to network with higher-level management.

An ethnocentric approach to IHRM is not necessarily good or bad. As you will see next, some multinational strategies work perfectly well when a company uses ethnocentric IHRM policies. In choosing this or any other IHRM orientation, managers must consider the costs and benefits of the orientation in the context of their choice of a multinational strategy. Some benefits and costs of ethnocentric IHRM policies include (Dowling and Welch 1988; Reynolds 1997):

Benefits:

- *Little need to recruit qualified host country nationals for higher management:* Local employees will hold only lower-level jobs or mid-level management jobs. Often a "glass ceiling" limits the advancement of host country nationals.
- *Greater control and loyalty of home country nationals:* these employees know that the home culture drives their careers. They seldom identify with the local country subsidiaries.
- *Little need to train home country nationals:* Managers look to headquarters for staffing and evaluation and follow headquarters' policies and procedures.
- *Key decisions centralized:* Personnel decisions are made at headquarters.

Costs:

- *May limit career development for host country nationals:* High potential host country nationals may never get beyond the glass ceiling, and talent is wasted.
- *Host country nationals may never identify with the home company:* host country nationals are governed by local HRM practices and they often realize that the glass ceiling exists. Therefore, they often have more allegiance to the local company than to the home company.
- *Expatriate managers are often poorly trained for international assignments and make mistakes:* Training is not valued and assignments are often short.
- *Expatriates may have limited career development:* International assignments are often viewed as hurting one's career and do not always attract the best people.

Regiocentric IHRM

Regionwide HRM policies are adopted.

Polycentric IHRM

Firm treats each country-level organization separately for HRM purposes.

REGIOCENTRIC AND POLYCENTRIC IHRM ORIENTATIONS

Firms with **regiocentric** or **polycentric IHRM** orientations have greater responsiveness to the host country differences in HRM practices. These orientations are similar in that they emphasize adaptation to cultural and institutional differences among countries. They differ only in that the polycentric company adapts IHRM practices to countries and the regiocentric to regions. Given their similarity in IHRM philosophy, they are discussed together in this section.

Companies with polycentric IHRM orientations treat each country-level organization separately for HRM purposes. The home company headquarters ordinarily lets each country-level subsidiary follow local HRM practices. The regiocentric organization tends to adopt region-wide HRM policies. Consistent with these orientations, companies recruit and select their managers mostly from host countries or regions. Regiocentric companies may also look for key people from the home company who have mastered the cultures and languages of the countries in their regional locations. Qualifications for managers from the host country follow local or regional practices. However, to communicate with the multinational's headquarters, host country managers often need the ability to speak and write in the home company's national language.

Polycentric and regiocentric multinationals usually place home country nationals in top-level management or technical positions. These home country managers are used to control overseas operations or to transfer technology to host country production sites (Adler and Ghadar 1990; Bohlander et al. 2001). As with the ethnocentric IHRM companies, HRM policies applied to home country expatriates remain fixed at headquarters. In addition, unless headquarters values country- or region-specific international experiences, there remains a tendency for international assignments to have negative effects on the managerial careers of home country nationals (Adler and Ghadar 1990).

Unlike the ethnocentric IHRM company, the polycentric IHRM company favors local procedures and standards for evaluations and promotions of most host country managers. Decentralization from headquarters allows country or regional managers to assess their own human resource needs and develop local evaluation and promotion criteria. Local organizational cultures that differ from the home company's also influence the procedures used by organizations to evaluate and promote employees. Regiocentric IHRM companies act similarly to the polycentric companies but develop regional standards for evaluation and promotion.

Some benefits and costs of polycentric and regiocentric IHRM policies (Dowling and Welch 1988; Reynolds 1997) include:

Benefits:

- *Using mostly host country nationals or third country nationals from the region reduces costs for training of expatriate managers from headquarters:* Successful expatriate assignments, especially in a widely different culture, require heavy investments in training.
- *The use of more host country nationals and third country nationals limits the number of home country expatriate employees who face language barriers and adjustment problems:* Local managers speak their area's language. Third country nationals from the region usually come from a similar culture and more likely have local language skills. Consequently, no investment in language training is necessary. The multinational company also faces fewer problems in managing expatriate adjustments to local cultures and in bringing home company expatriates back into the headquarters organization.
- *Host country employees and third country nationals from the region are often less expensive than home country expatriates:* The costs of expatriates are usually quite high.

Costs:

- *Coordination problems with headquarters based on cultural, language, and loyalty differences:* Even when host country or regional managers speak the language of the multinational's headquarters, communication can still be difficult, and misunderstandings can result. Host country managers may have more loyalty to their local organization than to the multinational parent.
- *Limited career-path opportunities for host country and regional managers:* Similar to the case for companies with ethnocentric HRM practices, host country and regional managers may face a glass ceiling for promotions. They may be limited to advancement within a country or region.
- *Limited international experience for home country managers:* Because international experience is often not valued or rewarded, it does not always attract the best managers. Companies with limited managerial talent in international operations often face difficulties if their industry becomes more global with more international operations.

The frustrations and career barriers faced by host country managers can hurt the development of local talent.

GLOBAL IHRM ORIENTATIONS

Global IHRM

Recruiting and selecting worldwide, and assigning the best managers to international assignments regardless of nationality.

Organizations with truly **global IHRM** orientations assign their best managers to international assignments (Quelch and Bloom 1999). Recruitment and selection take place worldwide, in any country where the best-quality employees can be found. The fit of the manager to the requirements of the job far outweighs any consideration of the individual's country of origin or country of job assignment. Thus, capable managers adapt easily and well to different cultures and are usually bilingual or multilingual. In addition, the international assignment becomes a prerequisite for a successful managerial career in companies with global orientations.

In companies with global orientations, managers are selected and trained to manage cultural diversity inside and outside the company. Employees inside their organization have culturally diverse backgrounds, and the company's multiple country locations provide culturally diverse customers, suppliers, and so on (Quelch and Bloom 1999). Besides confronting issues of cultural diversity, global managers must meet the coordination and control needs of corporate headquarters (Bartlett and Ghoshal 1998). To meet these challenges successfully, managers need continual training for cultural adaptation and development of the skills to balance local needs with overall company goals (Quelch and Bloom 1999).

As with other IHRM orientations, however, a global IHRM has its costs and benefits. Some benefits and costs of global IHRM policies (Dowling and Welch 1988; Quelch and Bloom 1999) include:

Benefits:

- *Bigger talent pool:* The available talent pool of managers and technical specialists is not limited by nationality or geography.
- *Develops international expertise:* Multinational companies develop a large group of experienced international managers.
- *Helps build transnational organizational cultures:* Managers identify with the organizational culture more than with any national culture.

Costs:

- *Importing managerial and technical employees not always possible:* Host countries often have immigration laws that limit the use of foreign nationals or make their use very costly.
- *Added expense:* Training and relocation costs are expensive. Expatriate compensation is higher than for host country employees.

Each IHRM orientation has strengths and weaknesses. A multinational's choice of an IHRM orientation depends for the most part on its multinational strategy. Next, we consider how the IHRM orientations support the four multinational strategies discussed in Chapter 6.

FINDING A FIT: IHRM ORIENTATION AND MULTINATIONAL STRATEGY

Exhibit 11.9 shows possible IHRM orientations that support the different multinational and participation strategies discussed in Chapter 6. Matching IHRM to the selected multinational strategy is a major component for successful strategy implementation. Like all strategic decisions for multinational companies, IHRM decisions are based on how the firm faces the global–local dilemma. Some IHRM decisions show a concern for local responsiveness when companies need people with a superior understanding of host country issues. Other IHRM decisions reflect globalization pressures when companies need managers with world-class competence regardless of their passport nationality (Adler and Bartholomew 1992).

Companies with multidomestic strategies concentrate on being responsive to local conditions. As a result, the country-by-country focus of polycentric IHRM provides the appropriate IHRM to maximize nation-level flexibility. In particular, the large use of host country managers and employees provides a company with a built-in knowledge base of local conditions. That is, polycentric IHRM helps support the multidomestic strategy because local managers often better understand local customer tastes, distribution channels, government regulations, worker expectations, and other features unique to the local business environment.

As shown in Exhibit 11.9, regiocentric IHRM practices also may work for multidomestic companies. However, managers in such companies must assess their IHRM needs quite carefully. Three questions are key. Can they find third country nationals who have the necessary knowledge of the business environment in the host country? What kind of training and development are necessary to keep these managers performing at levels that equal or exceed host country managers? What rewards keep these managers committed to their international assignments? In addition, top management must consider whether their investments in the selection, training, development, and retention of third country expatriate managers provide sufficiently greater performance to offset the usually much lower costs of hiring local managerial talent.

The firm with a regional strategy has increased demands for coordinating activities of subunits located in different countries. However, since these subunits are in one region of the world, the regiocentric IHRM strategy most closely supports the strategic intent of the company. Seldom would an ethnocentric IHRM orientation work for the firm with a regional strategy. However, some elements of a polycentric or global IHRM orientation may also support the regional strategy. For example, companies that emphasize regionally coordinated manufacturing may find the

Exhibit 11.9

IHRM Orientations and Mulitnational Strategies

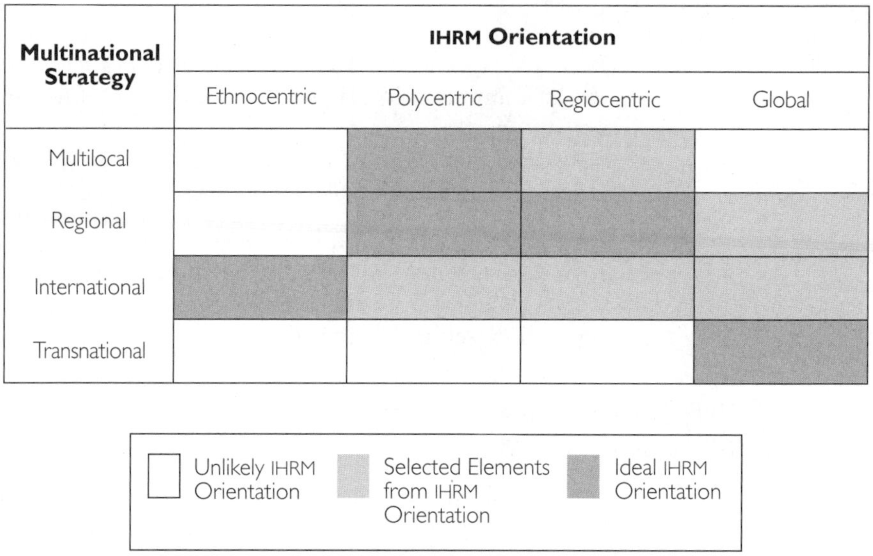

Multinational Strategy	IHRM Orientation			
	Ethnocentric	Polycentric	Regiocentric	Global
Multilocal				
Regional				
International				
Transnational				

	Unlikely IHRM Orientation		Selected Elements from IHRM Orientation		Ideal IHRM Orientation

polycentric approach to IHRM quite satisfactory. Production facilities located in separate host countries can develop locally tailored HRM practices even though their products have regional sales or contribute components to regional products. In such cases, only the top managers in the region need a region-wide perspective and should be managed with regiocentric or global HRM policies. In contrast, companies that share R&D or product knowledge regionally may find that only regiocentric or more global IHRM practices can recruit, select, and develop the people with the right capabilities. In such cases, managers at all levels need knowledge of regional markets, governments, national cultures, languages, and social institutions to perform adequately.

The international strategy emphasizes globalization on the upstream end of the value chain—produce and sell global products with minimal local adaptation and with subsidiary control centralized in the home country. Given the product standardization and centralized control, ethnocentric IHRM probably provides the most efficient and ideal human resource practices. Such IHRM practices work for the more pure international strategists, such as the aircraft manufacturer Boeing. However, for most companies, a pure international strategy is seldom possible. Most international-strategy companies have some products that require adaptation to regional or local needs. Most international-strategy companies have foreign production locations because of low cost, customer proximity, or politics. As such, depending on the unique situation faced by a company, there is usually a need to have some mixture of polycentric, regiocentric, or global IHRM practices. For example, while IHRM for top managers might follow an ethnocentric orientation, local production managers may be treated with a polycentric approach.

Organizations adopting transnational strategies, almost without exception, adopt a global orientation to IHRM. As we have seen in previous chapters, the transnational firm requires a highly flexible organization that can maximize location advantages in its value chain (Bartlett and Ghoshal 1998). As such, transnational companies must select and train managers from diverse national backgrounds who can take assignments anywhere in the world. Multinational managers in transnationals must be prepared to enter global corporate cultures that require managers to deal flexibly with diverse cultures and national social institutions (Black, Gregersen, and Mendenhall 1992).

For any multinational strategy to succeed requires careful assessment of a firm's IHRM practices. Successful companies select IHRM orientations with a major focus on finding the one that best supports their multinational strategy. However, usually no one IHRM orientation exactly fits a company's multinational strategy, and few companies follow any IHRM orientation completely. Rather, each multinational company selects a general approach combined with specific IHRM practices and procedures from other orientations that fit their strategic needs. Since IHRM supports all levels of the value chain, a crucial mistake is to misalign an IHRM orientation with the company's multinational strategy.

Summary and Conclusions

This chapter introduced the basic HRM practices of recruitment, selection, training and development, performance appraisal, compensation, and labor relations. When these practices are applied to a company's international operations, they become IHRM or international human resource management. Besides basic HRM functions, two key issues in IHRM are the choice of the mixture of expatriate and host country managers, and knowing how to adapt home company HRM practices to the host country's situation. This chapter focused on HRM practices for expatriate employees. The next chapter reviews the differences in national HRM practices. A knowledge of these national differences helps multinational managers adapt IHRM practices to local conditions.

Multinational companies tend to adopt basic orientations to IHRM. These are the ethnocentric, regiocentric, polycentric, and global orientations. These orientations reflect HRM philosophies that range from the ethnocentric company's using its headquarters HRM policies worldwide to the global company's transcultural IHRM. Each one of these orientations best supports one of the multinational strategies. For example, transnational companies favor global IHRM orientations, while multidomestic companies favor polycentric IHRM orientations.

Expatriate managers present challenges and opportunities to multinational companies. They are costly, often costing two to three times as much as host country managers. They need special training to succeed. They are not always successful. However, expatriate managers are loyal to the home organization and often have skills that are impossible to find with host country managers. Each multinational company chooses the mix of managers (from home country, third country, or host country) depending on its IHRM orientation and finding the right mix of global or local managerial talent to implement its chosen multinational strategy.

Successful IHRM presents one of the most important challenges to multinational companies in the 21st century. Many globalization trends—the development of large-scale trading blocs, the opening of national boundaries for trade, and the increasing prevalence of international strategic alliances—offer multinational organizations the opportunity to use human resources unrestrained by political, linguistic, and cultural boundaries. Those companies, large and small, that exploit international human resources most effectively will have strong competitive advantages in an increasingly global economy.

Discussion Questions

1. Identify the components of HRM and describe how they differ for IHRM.

2. Describe the types of nationals employed by multinational firms. Note likely situations when each type would be used.

3. Discuss and contrast the four IHRM orientations. Describe how each can support a multinational strategy.

4. Using the basic components of HRM as a guide, describe the likely practices used by a transnational firm.

5. Contrast the positive and negative issues for using short-term and international-cadre expatriate managers. Consider both the organization's perspective and the career implications for the individual manager.

6. Discuss the options available for expatriate compensation. Consider how these options might be used for a transnational and a multidomestic company.

7. Discuss how multinational companies can deal with the repatriation problem.

Chapter Internet Activity

Most companies have only a few expatriates. As such, it is not cost effective to develop expatriate HRM services in-house and the expatriate HRM functions are often out-sourced. To meet this demand, there are many consulting firms. Explore the following Web sites and write a report of the services a multinational company can find to effectively manage its expatriate workforce. See if you can find other providers of expatriate HRM services.

Hay Group   http://www.haygroup.com/about.asp
Runzheimer International   http://www.runzheimer.com
Towers Perrin   http://www.towers.com
Windham International   http://www.windhamint.com/

Internet Sites

Selected Companies in the Chapter

3M   http://www.3m.com
American Express Company   http://www.americanexpress.com/
AT&T   http://www.att.com
Colgate-Palmolive   http://www.colgate.com/
Deloitte & Touche   http://www.us.deloitte.com
GE   http://www.ge.com/
Procter & Gamble, Inc.   http://www.PG.com/
Sara Lee   http://www.saralee.com

Look Here for International HRM Information

http://www.sHRM.org/HRMagazine/index.html
   HRMagazine contains hundreds of articles dealing with international HRM, many are online.

https://www.ubs.com/   *Union Bank of Switzerland economics research location—includes prices and earnings for cities and occupations from around the globe.*

http://www.worldbiz.com   *Worldwide Business Executive Resources—services for expatriates and cross-cultural information—some free and some at moderate prices.*

http://www.embassy.org   *Electronic Embassy provides information on visas and other information for some countries.*

http://www.ilo.org   *International Labour Organization.*

http://www.worldbank.org/lsms/   *World Bank Living Standards Measurement Study.*

http://www.worldbank.org/wdr   *World Development Report.*

http://stats.bls.gov   *U.S. Bureau of Labor Statistics.*

http://www.rici.com   *International Career Info, Inc. (Japan and United States; bilingual).*

http://www.craighead.com/   *Cultural background relevant to business for numerous countries—hard copy is in most university libraries—Internet site has limited country information, free.*

http://www.webcom.com   *Basic information useful for business expatriates and travelers.*

http://www.yahoo.com/business   *Use this Yahoo! search engine basic category to search for more detail on cost of living, taxes, etc.*

http://www.imd.ch/   *The Institute for Management Development publishes a home page with extensive summaries of cross-national economic and trade data as well as survey data on cross-national management and HRM issues.*

http://www.sHRM.org/   *The Society for Human Resource Management's source for HR topics of all varieties.*

Chapter Case: The Road to Hell

John Baker, Chief Engineer of the Caribbean Bauxite Company of Barracania in the West Indies, was making his final preparations to leave the island. His promotion to production manager of Keso Mining Corporation near Winnipeg—one of Continental Ore's fast-expanding Canadian enterprises—had been announced a month before and now everything had been tidied up except the last vital interview with his successor, the able young Barracanian, Matthew Rennalls. It was vital that this interview be a success and that Baker should leave his office uplifted and encouraged to face the challenge of his new job. A touch on the bell would have brought Rennalls walking into the room but Baker delayed the moment and gazed thoughtfully through the window considering just exactly what he was going to say and, more particularly, how he was going to say it.

John Baker, an English expatriate, was forty-five years old and had served his twenty-three years with Continental Ore in many different places: in the Far East; several countries of Africa; Europe; and, for the last two years, in the West Indies. He hadn't cared much for his previous assignment in Hamburg and was delighted when the West Indian appointment came through. Climate was not the only attraction. Baker had always preferred working overseas (in what were termed the developing countries) because he felt he had an innate knack—better than most other expatriates working for Continental Ore—of knowing just how to get on with regional staff. Twenty-four hours in Barracania, however, soon made him realize that he would need all of this

"innate knack" if he was to deal effectively with the problems in this field that now awaited him.

At his first interview with Hutchins, the production manager, the whole problem of Rennalls and his future was discussed. There and then it was made quite clear to Baker that one of his most important tasks would be the "grooming" of Rennalls as his successor. Hutchins had pointed out that, not only was Rennalls one of the brightest Barracanian prospects on the staff of Caribbean Bauxite—at London University he had taken first-class honors in the B.Sc. Engineering Degree—but, being the son of the Minister of Finance and Economic Planning, he also had no small political pull.

The company had been particularly pleased when Rennalls decided to work for them rather than for the government in which his father had such a prominent post. They ascribed his action to the effect of their vigorous and liberal regionalization program, which, since the Second World War, had produced eighteen Barracanians at midmanagement level and given Caribbean Bauxite a good lead in this respect over all other international concerns operating in Barracania. The success of this timely regionalization policy has led to excellent relations with the government—a relationship that had been given an added importance when Barracania, three years later, became independent, an occasion which encouraged a critical and challenging attitude toward the role foreign interests would have to play in the new Barracania. Hutchins had therefore little difficulty in convincing Baker that the successful

Source: Prepared by Gareth Evans for Shell-BP Devleopment Co. of Nigeria Ltd., Intercollegiate Case Clearing House, Soldiers Field, Boston, MA 02163.

career development of Rennalls was of the first importance.

The interview with Hutchins was now two years old and Baker, leaning back in his office chair, reviewed just how successful he had been in the "grooming" of Rennalls. What aspects of the latter's character had helped and what had hindered? What about his own personality? How had that helped or hindered? The first item to go on the credit side would, without question, be the ability of Rennalls to master the technical aspects of his job. From the start he had shown keenness and enthusiasm and had often impressed Baker with his ability in tackling new assignments and the constructive comments he invariably made in departmental discussions. He was popular with all ranks of Barracanian staff and had an ease of manner which stood him in good stead when dealing with his expatriate seniors. These were all assets, but what about the debit side?

First and foremost, there was his racial consciousness. His four years at London University had accentuated this feeling and made him sensitive to any sign of condescension on the part of expatriates. It may have been to give expression to this sentiment that, as soon as he returned home from London, he threw himself into politics on behalf of the United Action Party who were later to win the preindependence elections and provide the country with its first Prime Minister.

The ambitions of Rennalls—and he certainly was ambitious—did not, however, lie in politics for, staunch nationalist as he was, he saw that he could serve himself and his country best (for was not bauxite responsible for nearly half the value of Barracania's export trade?) by putting his engineering talent to the best use possible. On this account, Hutchins found that he had an unexpectedly easy task in persuading Rennalls to give up his political work before entering the production department as an assistant engineer.

It was, Baker knew, Rennalls's well-repressed sense of race consciousness which had prevented their relationship from being as close as it should have been. On the surface, nothing could have seemed more agreeable. Formality between the two men was at a minimum: Baker was delighted to find that his assistant shared his own peculiar "shaggy dog" sense of humor so that jokes were continually being exchanged; they entertained each other at their houses and often played tennis

together—and yet the barrier remained invisible, indefinable, but ever present. The existence of this "screen" between them was a constant source of frustration to Baker since it indicated a weakness which he was loath to accept. If successful with all other nationalities, why not with Rennalls?

But at least he had managed to "break through" to Rennalls more successfully than any other expatriate. In fact, it was the young Barracanian's attitude—sometimes overbearing, sometimes cynical—toward other company expatriates that had been one of the subjects Baker had raised last year when he discussed Rennalls's staff report with him. He knew, too, that he would have to raise the same subject again in the forthcoming interview because Jackson, the senior draftsman, had complained only yesterday about the rudeness of Rennalls. With this thought in mind, Baker leaned forward and spoke into the intercom. "Would you come in Matt, please? I'd like a word with you," and later, "Do sit down," proffering the box, "have a cigarette." He paused while he held out his lighter and then went on.

"As you know, Matt, I'll be off to Canada in a few days' time, and before I go, I thought it would be useful if we could have a final chat together. It is indeed with some deference that I suggest I can be of help. You will shortly be sitting in this chair doing the job I am now doing, but I, on the other hand, am ten years older, so perhaps you can accept the idea that I may be able to give you the benefit of my longer experience."

Baker saw Rennalls stiffen slightly in his chair as he made this point so added in explanation, "You and I have attended enough company courses to remember those repeated requests by the personnel manager to tell people how they are getting on as often as the convenient moment arises and not just the automatic 'once a year' when, by regulation, staff reports have to be discussed."

Rennalls nodded his agreement, so Baker went on. "I shall always remember the last job performance discussion I had with my previous boss back in Germany. He used what he called the 'plus and minus' technique. His firm belief was that when a senior, by discussion, seeks to improve the work performance of his staff, his prime objective should be to make sure that the latter leaves the interview encouraged and inspired to improve. Any criticism must, therefore, be constructive and helpful. He said that one very good way to encourage a person—and I fully agree with him—is to tell him about his good points—the plus factors—as well as his weak ones—the minus factors—so I thought, Matt, it would be a good idea to run our discussion along these lines."

Rennalls offered no comment, so Baker continued: "Let me say, therefore, right away, that, as far as your own work performance is concerned, the plus far outweighs the minus. I have, for instance, been most impressed with the way you have adapted your considerable theoretical knowledge to master the practical techniques of your job—that ingenious method you used to get air down to the fifth-shaft level is a sufficient case in point—and at departmental meetings I have invariably found your comments well taken and helpful. In fact, you will be interested to know that only last week I reported to Mr. Hutchins that, from the technical point of view, he could not wish for a more able man to succeed to the position of chief engineer."

"That's very good indeed of you, John," cut in Rennalls with a smile of thanks. "My only worry now is how to live up to such a high recommendation."

"Of that I am quite sure," returned Baker, "especially if you can overcome the minus factor which I would like now to discuss with you. It is one which I have talked about before so I'll come straight to the point. I noticed that you are more friendly and get on better with your fellow Barracanians than you do with Europeans. In point of fact, I had a complaint only yesterday from Mr. Jackson, who said you had been rude to him—and not for the first time either.

"There is, Matt, I am sure, no need for me to tell you how necessary it will be for you to get on well with expatriates because until the company has trained up sufficient people of your caliber, Europeans are bound to occupy senior positions here in Barracania. All this is vital to your future interests, so can I help you in any way?"

While Baker was speaking on this theme, Rennalls had sat tensed in his chair and it was some seconds before he replied. "It is quite extraordinary, isn't it, how one can convey an impression to others so at variance with what one intends? I can only assure you once again that my disputes with Jackson—and you may remember also Godson—have had nothing at all to do with

the color of their skins. I promise you that if a Barracanian had behaved in an equally peremptory manner I would have reacted in precisely the same way. And again, if I may say it within these four walls, I am sure I am not the only one who has found Jackson and Godson difficult. I could mention the names of several expatriates who have felt the same. However, I am really sorry to have created this impression of not being able to get on with Europeans—it is an entirely false one—and I quite realize that I must do all I can to correct it as quickly as possible. On your last point, regarding Europeans holding senior positions in the Company for some time to come, I quite accept the situation. I know that Caribbean Bauxite—as they have been doing for many years now—will promote Barracanians as soon as their experience warrants it. And, finally, I would like to assure you, John—and my father thinks the same too—that I am very happy in my work here and hope to stay with the company for many years to come."

Rennalls had spoken earnestly and, although not convinced by what he had heard, Baker did not think he could pursue the matter further except to say, "All right, Matt, my impression may be wrong, but I would like to remind you about the truth of that old saying, 'What is important is not what is true but what is believed.' Let it rest at that."

But suddenly Baker knew that he didn't want to "let it rest at that." He was disappointed once again at not being able to "break through" to Rennalls and having yet again to listen to his bland denial that there was any racial prejudice in his makeup. Baker, who had intended ending the interview at this point, decided to try another tack.

"To return for a moment to the 'plus and minus technique' I was telling you about just now, there is another plus factor I forgot to mention. I would like to congratulate you not only on the caliber of your work but also on the ability you have shown in overcoming a challenge which I, as a European, have never had to meet.

"Continental Ore is, as you know, a typical commercial enterprise—admittedly a big one—which is a product of the economic and social environment of the United States and Western Europe. My ancestors have all been brought up in this environment for the past two or three hundred years and I have, therefore, been able to live in a world in which commerce (as we know it to-day) has been part and parcel of my being. It has not been something revolutionary and new which has suddenly entered my life. In your case," went on Baker, "the situation is different because you and your forebears have only had some fifty or sixty years' experience of this commercial environment. You have had to face the challenge of bridging the gap between fifty and two or three hundred years. Again, Matt, let me congratulate you—and people like you—once again on having so successfully overcome this particular hurdle. It is for this very reason that I think the outlook for Barracania—and particularly Caribbean Bauxite—is so bright."

Rennalls had listened intently and when Baker finished, replied, "Well, once again, John, I have to thank you for what you have said, and, for my part, I can only say that it is gratifying to know that my own personal effort has been so much appreciated. I hope that more people will soon come to think as you do."

There was a pause and, for a moment, Baker thought hopefully that he was about to achieve his long-awaited "breakthrough," but Rennalls merely smiled back. The barrier remained unbreached. There remained some five minutes' cheerful conversation about the contrast between the Caribbean and Canadian climate and whether the West Indies had any hope of beating England in the Fifth Test before Baker drew the interview to a close. Although he was as far as ever from knowing the real Rennalls, he was nevertheless glad that the interview had run along in this friendly manner and, particularly, that it had ended on such a cheerful note.

This feeling, however, lasted only until the following morning. Baker had some farewells to make, so he arrived at the office considerably later than usual. He had no sooner sat down at his desk than his secretary walked into the room with a worried frown on her face. Her words came fast. "When I arrived this morning I found Mr. Rennalls already waiting at my door. He seemed very angry and told me in quite a peremptory manner that he had a vital letter to dictate which must be sent off without any delay. He was so worked up that he couldn't keep still and kept pacing about the room, which is most unlike him. He wouldn't even wait to read what he had dictated. Just signed the page where he thought the letter would end. It has been distributed and your copy is in your 'in tray.'"

Puzzled and feeling vaguely uneasy, Baker opened the "Confidential" envelope and read the following letter:

From: *Assistant Engineer*
To: *The Chief Engineer, Caribbean Bauxite Limited*
*14th August, 196_*

ASSESSMENT OF INTERVIEW BETWEEN MESSRS. BAKER AND RENNALLS

It has always been my practice to respect the advice given me by seniors, so after our interview, I decided to give careful thought once again to its main points and so make sure that I had understood all that had been said. As I promised you at the time, I had every intention of putting your advice to the best effect.

It was not, therefore, until I had sat down quietly in my home yesterday evening to consider the interview objectively that its main purport became clear. Only then did the full enormity of what you said dawn on me. The more I thought about it, the more convinced I was that I had hit upon the real truth—and the more furious I became. With a facility in the English language which I—a poor Barracanian—cannot hope to match, you had the audacity to insult me (and through me every Barracanian worth his salt) by claiming that our knowledge of modern living is only a paltry fifty years old whilst yours goes back 200–300 years. As if your materialistic commercial environment could possibly be compared with the spiritual values of our culture. I'll have you know that if much of what I saw in London is representative of your most boasted culture, I hope fervently that it will never come to Barracania. By what right do you have the effrontery to condescend to us? At heart, all you Europeans think us barbarians, or, as you say amongst yourselves, we are "just down from the trees."

Far into the night I discussed this matter with my father, and he is as disgusted as I. He agrees with me that any company whose senior staff think as you do is no place for any Barracanian proud of his culture and race—so much for all the company "clap-trap" and specious propaganda about regionalization and Barracania for the Barracanians.

I feel ashamed and betrayed. Please accept this letter as my resignation which I wish to become effective immediately.

c.c. Production Manager
Managing Director

CASE QUESTIONS FOR DISCUSSION

1. What are the strengths and weaknesses of the performance-review technique used by Baker?

2. Should Baker have anticipated Rennalls' reaction to his performance review? Why?

3. What issues of cultural sensitivity are germane for understanding the case? Was it the performance review or Baker's interaction style that prompted Rennalls' resignation?

4. If you were Baker, what would you do now?

References

Adler, Nancy J. 1987. "Pacific basin managers: A *gaijin*, not a woman." *Human Resource Management* 26:2, 169–91.

———. 1993. "Women managers in a global economy." *HRMagazine*, September, 52–55.

———, and Susan Bartholomew. 1992. "Globalization and human resource management." *Research in Global Strategic Management* 3, 179–201.

———, and Fariborz Ghadar. 1990. "International strategy from the perspective of people and culture: The North American context." *Research in Global Business Management* 1, 179–205.

Ashamalla, Maali H. 1998. "International human resource management practices: The challenge of expatriation." *Competitiveness Review*, 8, 2, 54–65.

Bartlett, Christopher A., and Sumantra Ghoshal. 1998. *Managing Across Borders (2ed).* Boston: Harvard Business School Press.

Black, J. Stewart, and Mark E. Mendenhall. 1990. "Cross-culture training effectiveness: A review and theoretical framework for future research." *Academy of Management Review* 15, 113–36.

Black, J. Stewart, Hal B. Gregersen, and Mark E. Mendenhall. 1992. *Global Assignments.* San Francisco: Jossey-Bass.

Bohlander, George W., Scott Snell, and Arthur W. Sherman, Jr. 2001. *Managing Human Resources*, 12th ed. Cincinnati, OH: South-Western.

Boyacigiller, Nakiye A. 1991. "The international assignment reconsidered." In *Readings and Cases in International Human Resource Management*, edited by Mark Mendenhall and Gary Oddou 148–55. Boston: PWS-Kent.

Dowling, Peter J., and Randall S. Schuler. 1990. *International Dimensions of Human Resource Management.* Boston: PWS-Kent.

Dowling, Peter J., and Denice E. Welch. 1988. "International human resource management: An Australian perspective." *Asia Pacific Journal of Management* 6:1, 39–65.

Economist. 2000. "Living expenses." http://www.Ecomonist.com, July 22.

Economist. 1996. Chart, "Cost of Living." December 14, 118.

Evans, P., E. Lank, and A. Farquhuar. 1989. "Managing human resources in the international firm: Lessons from practice." In *Human Resource Management in International Firms,* edited by P. Evans, Y. Doz, and A. Laurent, 113–43. London: Macmillan Press.

Expatriate Management Update. 2000. "International assignments at Colgate: Focus of succession planning." http://members.aol.com/expatmgmt, May.

Forster, Nick. 2000. "Expatriates and the impact of cross-cultural training." *Human Resource Management Journal*, 10, 63–78.

Frazee, Valerie. 1998. "Is the balance sheet right for your expats?" *Workforce*, 3, 19–23.

Gregerson, Hal. B. 1999. "The right way to manage expats." *Harvard Business Review* March/April, 52–61.

Gross, Steven E. and Per L. Wingerup. 1999. "Global pay? Maybe not yet!" *Compensation and Benefits Review*, 31, 25–34.

Halcrow. Allan. 1999. "Expats: The squandered resource." *Workforce*, 3, July, 28–30.

Hay Group. 1993. "Global pay for global players." In *The Human Resources Yearbook*, edited by Mary F. Cook, 3.14–3.16. Englewood Cliffs: Prentice-Hall.

Heenan, D. A., and H. V. Perlmutter. 1979. *Multinational Organization Development.* Reading, Mass.: Addison Wesley.

Howard, Cecil G. 1992. "Profile of the 21st-century expatriate manager." *HRMagazine* 37:6, 43–102.

Hube, Karen. 2000. "An assignment abroad shouldn't mean career exile." *Business Week Online,* July 18 http://www.businessweek.com.

Izraeli, Dafna, and Yoram Zeira. 1993. "Women managers in international business: A research review and appraisal." *Business and the Contemporary World*, Summer, 35–46.

Jelinek, Mariann, and Nancy J. Adler. 1988. "Women: World-class managers for global competition." *Academy of Management Executive* 11:1, 11–19.

Korbin, Stephen J. 1988. "Expatriate reduction and strategic control in American multinational corporations." *Human Resource Management* 27:1, 63–75.

———. 1991. "Are multinationals better after the Yankees go home?" In *Readings and Cases in International Human Resource Management*, edited by Mark Mendenhall and Gary Oddou, 97–99. Boston: PWS-Kent.

Lancaster, Hal. 1999. "To get shipped abroad, women must overcome prejudice at home." *Wall Street Journal*, June 29, B1.

Latta, Geoffrey W. 1999. "Expatriate policy and practice: A ten-year comparison of trends." *Compensation and Benefits Review*, 31, 35–39.

Loeb, Marshall. 1995. "The real fast track is overseas." *Fortune*, August 21, 129.

Lublin, Joann S. 1989. "Grappling with the expatriate issue." *Wall Street Journal*, December 11, B1.

———. 1992. "Younger managers learn global skills." *Wall Street Journal*, March 3, B1.

Lublin, Joann S., and Craig S. Smith. 1994. "U.S. companies struggle with scarcity of executives to run outposts in China." *Wall Street Journal*, August 23, B1, B3.

Mallory, Maria. 2000. "Women of the world? Hardly. Overseas posts elude female managers." *The Atlanta Journal the Atlanta Constitution*, November 19, R 1.

Melvin, Sheila. 1997. "Shipping out." *The China Business Review*, 24, 30–5.

Mendenhall, Mark, and Gary Oddou. 1985. "The dimensions of expatriate acculturation: A review." *Academy of Management Review* 10, 39–47.

———. 1988. "Acculturation profiles of expatriate managers: Implications for cross-cultural training programs." *Columbia Journal of World Business* 21, 73–79.

Mendenhall, Mark E., E. Dunbar, and Gary R. Oddou. 1987. "Expatriate selection, training and career-pathing: A review and critique." *Human Resource Management* 26:3, 331–45.

Mesa, Costa. 1998. "Is the balance sheet right for your expats?" *Workforce*, 3, 19–26.

Milkovich, George T., and Jerry Newman. 1993. *Compensation.* 4th ed. Homewood, Ill.: Irwin.

Oster, Patrick, David Woodruff, Neil Gross, Sunita Wadekar Bhargava, and Elizabeth Lesly. 1993. "The fast track leads overseas." *Fortune*, November 11.

Overman, Stephenie. 2000. "In sync." *HRMagazine*, 45:3, 86–92.

———. 1992. "The right package." *HRMagazine* 37:7, 71–75.

Poe, Andrea C. 2000. "Welcome back." *HR Magazine* 45:3, 94–101.

Quelch, John A. and Helen Bloom. 1999. "Ten steps to a global human resources strategy." *Strategy & Business*, First Quarter, 2–13.

Reynolds, Calvin. 2000. "Global compensation and benefits in transition." *Compensation and Benefits Review*, 32, 28–38.

Reynolds, Calvin. 1997. "Strategic employment of third country nationals." *Human Resource Planning* 20,1, 33–39.

Ronen, Simcha. 1986. *Comparative and Multinational Management*. New York: Wiley.

Runzheimer International. 2000. "Runzheimer international compensation worksheet." http://www.runzheimer.com.

Schafer, Sarah. 2000. "Women hit another glass ceiling; homebody image costs female middle managers valuable overseas assignments." *The Washington Post*, October 19, E. 11.

Scullion, Hugh. 1994. "Staffing policies and strategic control in British multinationals." *International Studies of Management and Organization* 24:3, 86–104.

Solomon, Julie. 1989. "Women, minorities and foreign postings." *Wall Street Journal*, June 2, B1.

Stroh, Linda K., Arup Varma, and Stacy J. Valy-Durbin. 2000. "Why are women left at home: Are they unwilling to go on international assignments?" *Journal of World Business*, 35, 241–55.

Thaler-Carter, Ruth E. 1999. "Vowing to go abroad." *HRMagazine*, 44:12, 90–6.

Torrington, Derek, and Nigel Holden. 1992. "Human resource management and the international challenge of change." *Personnel Review* 21:2, 19–30.

Tung, Rosalie L. 1981. "Selection and training of personnel for overseas assignments." *Columbia Journal of World Business* 16:1, 68–78.

———. 1987. "Expatriate assignments: Enhancing success and minimizing failure." *Academy of Management Executive* 1:2, 117–26.

Winham International. 2000. "Survey highlights." http://www.windhamint.com.

Chapter 12

National Differences in HRM: Knowing When and How to Adapt

LEARNING OBJECTIVES
After reading this chapter you should be able to:

- Have a basic understanding of how the national context affects HRM practices.

- Identify how recruitment and selection practices differ in various national contexts.

- Identify possible host adaptations in recruitment and selection practices for a multinational company.

- Identify how training and development techniques are used in different countries.

- Identify sources of high-quality workers in different nations.

- Understand how training must be adapted to host country workers.

- Identify how performance evaluation and compensation practices differ in various national contexts.

- Identify possible host country adaptations in performance evaluation and compensation practices for a multinational company.

- Understand how labor costs vary in different nations.

- Have an appreciation of how the national context and historical conditions affect the relationship of management and labor in different countries.

Preview Case in Point	The United States is the only industralized country without government-mandated vacation time. Eighty-one percent of U.S. firms give new employees only two weeks vacation. In contrast, the EU requires that all employees have four weeks of vacation regardless of seniority. Many U.S. managers see the European vacation as excessive and European managers counter that U.S. organizations have misplaced goals.
Following Local Traditions	When Captura Software, an electronic finance service provider from Washington State, opened offices in London and Paris, HR manager Corkye Christensen knew that they had to do more than follow the letter of the law. Average vacation time in most Euorpean countries is more than the twenty days mandated. Her first thought of trading extra vacation time for money wouldn't work—it's illegal in the EU. Their strategy is to blend with local traditions and nearly shut down in August. Even U.S. expatriates are allowed the extra vacation time of their local colleagues.

Source: Based on Poe 1999.

The Preview Case in Point shows just one issue that can affect how multinational companies conduct business in a country. Other issues might include: How do you hire a worker in Mexico? What educational background can you expect from German workers? Can you lay off workers in Denmark? What would happen in Japan if you promoted a 30-year-old to supervise 40-year-old employees? What kind of relationships should you expect with unions in South Africa?

All these questions deal with issues of human resource management (HRM) in different national settings. When multinational companies set up operations abroad or engage in strategic alliances with companies from other countries, managers often need to understand and adapt to local human resource management customs and practices.

To show the impact of the national context (national and business cultures and social institutions) on human resource management, this chapter gives illustrations of varied practices from the United States and other countries. The chapter builds on your understanding of international human resource management, discussed in Chapter 11. Reading both chapters will help you, the multinational manager, select and implement appropriate human resource management policies and, when necessary, adapt these policies to the local national environment.

WHY DO NATIONS DIFFER IN HRM?

National context

National culture and social institutions that influence how managers make decisions regarding the strategies of their organizations.

Cross-national differences in HRM and the pressures to adapt to local conditions arise from the array of factors that make each nation unique. These factors are called the **national context**. The national context includes such things as the national culture, the country's available labor and other natural resources, the characteristics of political and legal institutions, and the types of managers available to firms. The national context includes social institutions, national and business culture, factor conditions, and their combined effects on the business environment. Thus, the national context provides the unique setting for each nation in which managers make decisions regarding HRM practices. Exhibit 12.1 shows a model of

Exhibit 12.1
How the National
Context Leads to
National Differences
in Local HRM Practices

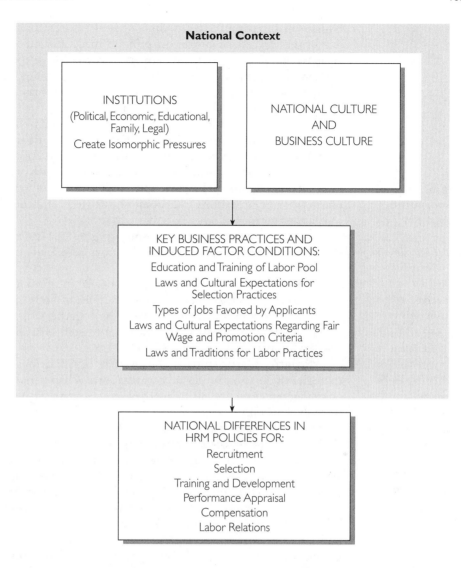

National Context

INSTITUTIONS
(Political, Economic, Educational,
Family, Legal)
Create Isomorphic Pressures

NATIONAL CULTURE
AND
BUSINESS CULTURE

KEY BUSINESS PRACTICES AND
INDUCED FACTOR CONDITIONS:
Education and Training of Labor Pool
Laws and Cultural Expectations for
Selection Practices
Types of Jobs Favored by Applicants
Laws and Cultural Expectations Regarding Fair
Wage and Promotion Criteria
Laws and Traditions for Labor Practices

NATIONAL DIFFERENCES IN
HRM POLICIES FOR:
Recruitment
Selection
Training and Development
Performance Appraisal
Compensation
Labor Relations

how the national context leads to national differences in HRM policies and practices. Each component of the model is discussed as follows.

Social institution

*Enduring system of
relationships among
people, such as an
educational or political
system.*

What are social institutions? A **social institution** is an enduring system of relationships among people. Social institutions include the family system, educational
system, economic system, and the political and legal systems. For example, the family defines the relationships among men, women, children, grandparents, and other
relatives. The legal system defines the formal duties and relationships of people in a
society. All societies have social institutions, and we rely on them—just as we do on
national culture—to provide structure to our lives. Countries differ widely in the
historical developments of their social institutions.

Social institutions are closely linked with national and business culture. Social
institutions, such as the family and the educational system, pass on cultural traditions. Political and legal systems reflect the norms and values of the society.

Organizations must select and implement HRM practices that meet the demands of a society's social institutions. That is, just as social institutions help structure the relationships among people, they help define the correct ways of doing

business in any country. In the United States, for example, anti-discrimination laws, part of the legal social institution, prohibit many recruitment practices common to Japanese and Korean companies. In Japan, for example, the family system relies on women raising children so that men can work long hours at night or be away from home for long periods. As such, there are unwritten biases against women holding managerial positions after they have children.

Because social institutions, especially the legal and political systems, help define what are legitimate and correct management practices in a particular society, organizations in that society tend to adopt similar management practices. This pressure from social institutions to follow similar paths in management practices is called **organizational isomorphism** (Zucker 1987). Within a nation, isomorphism leads organizations to become similar to each other, but different from organizations located in other nations.

Experts identify three types of isomorphism (or pressures for similarity) that are important for organizations: coercive isomorphism, mimetic isomorphism, and normative isomorphism.

Coercive isomorphism means that social institutions coerce or force organizations to adopt certain practices. For example, in both Taiwan and Italy, extended family expectations of living and working together combine with national economic and legal policies to encourage the existence of small firms and discourage the development of large firms (Orru 1991).

Mimetic isomorphism means that organizations purposefully copy the strategies of the most successful organizations. When people start new organizations or change ongoing organizations, they often imitate what seems to work most successfully. This imitation in turn leads to organizations becoming similar to one another within a particular nation.

Normative isomorphism means that organizations indirectly copy the designs, cultures, and strategies of other organizations by conforming to professional and technical norms. Normative isomorphism differs from mimetic isomorphism because copying occurs largely without conscious effort. Movements of employees among companies, availability of the same trade publications, and informal discussions among managers from different organizations can gradually introduce similarity among a group of organizations. Since these processes take place largely within national or cultural boundaries, organizations within a country tend to become similar to one another but different from those of other societies.

Chapter 2 showed that the values and norms associated with national and business cultures result in preferred ways of doing business. These preferences influence all aspects of the organization: strategies, organizational design, and human resource practices. Basic norms and values regarding gender, age, and family and friends influence HRM practices from recruitment to performance appraisal. For example, in more particularistic cultures, managers are more likely to hire people based on personal qualities (e.g., someone from a particular family or village) rather than on more universalistic criteria such as education level.

The national context also includes the pool of resources available for firms. The **resource pool** represents all the human and physical resources available in a country. Examples include the quality of labor, the availability of scientific laboratories, and sources of fuel. If all countries had access to the same resources, there would be fewer differences across nations in management practices. Regardless of nationality, if firms could access the same resources, they would copy the strategies and organizations of the most successful competitors in the world. However, the national endowments of physical resources (e.g., supply of raw materials) and other resources

---

Organizational isomorphism

Pressure from social institutions to follow similar paths in strategy and other management practices.

Coercive isomorphism

The force or power of social institutions to make organizations adopt certain practices.

Mimetic isomorphism

Voluntary imitation by managers of strategies of the most successful organizations.

Normative isomorphism

Imitation by organizations of designs, cultures, and strategies of other organizations, without the conscious effort of mimetic isomorphism.

Resource pool

All the human and physical resources available in a country.

(e.g., culturally based motivations to work, educational systems) are unique to each country.

Where does the resource pool come from? The resource pool represents the factor conditions associated with a country. There are five key factors that influence the resource pool available to firms and in turn the management practices favored by firms in different nations (Porter 1990). These include:

- *The quality, quantity, and accessibility of raw material:* For example, the extensive tracts of fertile land in the United States enable U.S. agricultural firms to compete with low price and high quality on the world market.

- *The quantity, quality, and cost of personnel available:* Germany, for example, has large pools of technically trained workers that support the development of industries and firms where high-quality differentiation strategies abound. In contrast, however, German workers are among the most highly paid in the world, thus making low-cost strategies difficult.

- *The scientific, technical, and market-related knowledge available to firms:* Both Japan and the United States, for example, have abundant stores of scientific and technical knowledge from universities and industry-based R&D. Korean electronics companies do not have the same level of knowledge resources and often rely on Japanese and U.S. technologies. To counter this limitation, companies like Samsung take aggressive cost-leadership strategies by lowering production costs for imported technologies (Steers, Shin, and Ungson 1989).

- *The cost and amount of capital available to firms for operations and expansion:* This factor addresses the question of how firms get financing to run their operations. For example, during the double-digit expansion of the Korean economy, Korean *chaebol* (conglomerates) relied mostly on heavy debt financing from government-controlled banks. More recently, in a post-1998 Korean economy reeling from the shock of failing *chaebol* and a weaker currency, Korean banks are less likely to loan money to debt-ridden companies.

- *The type, quality, and costs of supporting institutions such as the systems of communication, education, and transportation:* Nations differ widely in the supporting resources necessary to run a business. Trained workers are a critical resource. However, factors such as reliable phones and the ability to transport goods cheaply and predictably are also important.

Natural-factor conditions

National resources that occur naturally, such as abundant water supply.

Some resources occur naturally. These are called **natural-factor conditions**. For example, countries with extensive coal and gas reserves favor the development of industries and firms that require high energy consumption. For example, Canada has abundant sources of the water necessary for the efficient production of aluminum.

Induced-factor conditions

National resources created by a nation, such as a superior educational system.

Other resources arise from cultural and institutional pressures. These are called **induced-factor conditions**. For example, the high cultural value placed on education in many Asian societies helps create a well-trained workforce for countries like Singapore and Korea. Social institutions such as the government can also affect induced factor conditions. For example, the knowledge base available to the Japanese robotics industry is facilitated by the more than 180 Japanese universities that created robotics laboratories and the $20 million a year contributed to program development by the Japanese Ministry of International Trade and Industry (Porter 1990).

In general, as noted earlier, companies find competitive advantages by tapping into pools of national resources that are valuable and difficult to copy or rare (Barney 1991). "Valuable" means that the resource contributes quality or cost-competitive advantages to a company's product or service. "Difficult to copy or rare" resources are not easily imitated by competitors. When valuable, difficult to copy, or rare resources are unique to a nation, companies in that nation tend to take advantage of these resource pools and in turn develop similar strategies. Consequently, different resource pools also lead to basic national differences in strategies.

For example, Germany's technically trained workforce is a valuable resource for German industry. As you will see in more detail later, it is a national system supported by a long cultural tradition of craftwork, existing educational institutions, and substantial government contribution to vocational training. As such, it is also difficult for firms in other countries to copy. Thus, many German companies often rely on this pool of technical workers to compete with differentiation strategies for products such as automobiles and cameras.

As the model shows, the national and business cultures combine with isomorphic pressures created by social institutions to affect the business environment and certain factor conditions. In turn, this national context determines the management practices and policies followed by most companies in a nation and the types of HRM adaptations necessary for multinational companies.

Of course, not all components of the national context, such as energy resources, are relevant for HRM. Later, in Chapter 15, you will see how the national context affects strategy and organizational design. This chapter outlines the major characteristics of the national context that affect HRM. Throughout the chapter, you will see how the following issues affect national differences in HRM:

- *Education and training of the labor pool:* The type and quality of labor available to companies is a key issue in HRM. A country's educational system provides the raw human resource material for companies. How much training a person will need to be a qualified worker and the meaning of educational credentials for selection are examples of issues determined by a nation's educational system. A well-educated labor force is a factor condition induced by governmental and cultural support for education. Later, for example, you will see how the German system of specialized training dominates key aspects of German HRM.

- *Laws and cultural expectations for selection practices:* The laws of a country and the people's expectations that arise from the national and business cultures tell managers the "right" way to find new employees. In some nations, for example, you are expected to hire your relatives. In other nations, it might be against a company's policies to do so. In some nations, it is considered common and necessary to ask women job applicants if they plan to get married soon. However, asking a job applicant such a question in the United States would be illegal and discriminatory.

- *Types of jobs favored by applicants:* Japanese college graduates prefer to be hired by big companies. They are attracted to the security of working for a large company. Most Chinese businesses are family dominated, and family members expect to work for and with other family members. These examples illustrate cultural values and norms regarding the "best" and the "right" places to work.

- *Laws and cultural expectations regarding fair wages and promotion criteria:* Should older workers make more money than younger workers? Should men be promoted faster than women? Should people who enter the company together make the same salary and be promoted together? Should a worker's family situation influence his or her salary? Due to cultural expectations and institutional pressures, questions such as these are often answered differently in different national contexts. As such, values, norms, and institutional expectations influence

Exhibit 12.2
Steps in the Recruiting
Process

- Jobs Open
- Applicant Characteristics Identified
- Recruitment Strategies Applied
  - Walk-ins
  - Newspaper and other Advertising (e.g., Internet)
  - Job Positions Posted in Organization
  - State and Private Employment Services
  - Educational Institutions
  - Emplyee Referrals
- Applications Received

Sources: Adapted from Werther and Davis 1993 and Bohlander, Snell, and Sherman 2001.

compensation decisions and the relationship between performance appraisals and compensation. For example, U.S. multinational managers often find that the link between compensation and performance, considered legal and fair in U.S. companies, is often considered less important in other nations.

- *Laws and traditions regarding labor practices:* The legal position and power of unions and the historical relationships between management and labor have profound influences on HRM practices regarding labor relations. For example, in some nations there exists long-term historical precedents for labor–management conflict. Labor conflict, however, differs widely by national context. Additionally, the popularity of unions among workers differs by national context.

The remainder of this chapter illustrates the impact of national context on HRM practices in several nations. These illustrations only hint at the extent of differences among national HRM practices. To understand any particular host country's HRM practices, multinational managers must pay careful attention to the values, norms, and laws that bear directly on HRM.

For comparison purposes, each basic task of HRM is treated by contrasting dominant practices in the United States with examples of practices from other nations. The HRM tasks considered, in order of presentation, are: recruitment, selection, training and development, performance appraisal, compensation, and labor relations.

RECRUITMENT

Exhibit 12.2 summarizes the major steps in recruitment. First, managers determine that jobs are available. These vacancies may occur in anticipation of expansion or as replacements for workers leaving the organization. Second, employers determine the types of people and skills that are necessary for the job. Third, employers generate a pool of applicants for the job.

Recruitment strategies generate the applicant pool and include:

- Walk-ins or unsolicited applications.
- Advertisements placed in newspapers or on the Internet.
- Company Web site job posting—listings of vacant positions on the firm's Web site.

- Internal job postings—company listings of vacant jobs targeted at current employees.
- Public and private personnel agencies.
- Placement services of educational institutions.
- Current employee recommendations.

Managers hope that one or more of these recruitment strategies will generate a pool of applicants who are qualified for the vacant job.

Most national differences in recruitment occur in the preferences for using different recruitment strategies. National and business cultures have the dominant effects on the "right way" to find employees, but organizational and occupational cultures also have different norms regarding recruitment. For example, firms such as Procter & Gamble in the United States have strong norms favoring recruitment from within the firm. Social institutions such as educational systems also affect recruitment. In Japan, for example, personal contacts between university professors and managers are often a prerequisite for university students to get good jobs in big companies.

RECRUITMENT IN THE UNITED STATES

U.S. companies use all types of recruiting strategies. However, U.S. managers do not judge all recruitment strategies as equally effective. Exhibit 12.3 shows recruitment strategies believed most effective for companies in the United States.

For all types of positions, U.S. managers see newspaper advertising as one of the most effective recruitment channels. College or university recruitment was judged among the most effective only for professional and technical jobs. Managers believed that employee referrals produced only marginal success. There is some concern in the United States that employee referrals result in the recruitment of only those employees with similar backgrounds to current employees. There is also a fear that recruitment by personal contacts (common in many other nations) may result in potential biases against certain groups, such as women and minorities (Bohlander, Snell, and Sherman 2001).

The belief in the United States that open and public advertisements are the most effective recruiting strategy reflects U.S. individualistic cultural values. Managers in the United States and other individualistic societies view potential workers as unique combinations of skills. These skills are purchased by the company on the labor market. Public advertisements of jobs maximize the pool of available talent and, from the workers' point of view, support egalitarian norms that all can compete for open jobs. In contrast, recruitment in collectivist societies tends to focus on the in-group such as the family and friends of those already in the organization (Hofstede 1991). Next, for comparison, the chapter considers recruitment in Korea.

RECRUITMENT IN KOREA

Backdoor recruitment

Prospective employees are friends or relatives of those already employed.

Korea ranks moderately low on Hofstede's individualism scale (21st percentile) and has HRM practices more representative of collectivist cultures. Recruitment in Korea originated from a mixture of Confucian values and Western pragmatism (Steers, Shin, and Ungson 1989). Hard work, dedication, loyalty, and a respect for seniority combine with Western influences to produce a mixed recruitment system.

Most Korean companies recruit blue-collar workers by **backdoor recruitment**, a form of employee referral. That is, prospective employees are friends or relatives of

Exhibit 12.3
Most Effective Recruiting Sources for U.S. Companies (by job category)

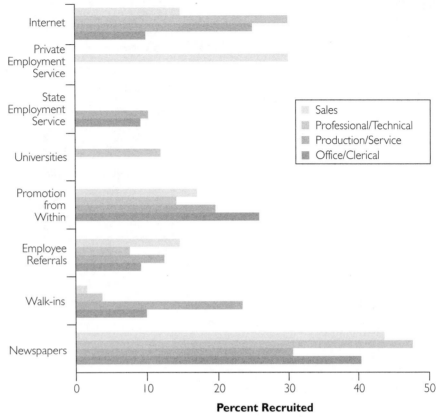

Sources: Estimated percentages adapted from the Bureau of National Affairs 1988 and Cook 1997 and Terpstra 1996.

those already employed. From the company's perspective, friends and relatives represent a good pool of candidates. If prospective employees are relatives or friends, then one can vouch for their trustworthiness and industriousness. Smaller companies and those in rural areas tend to rely more on backdoor rather than open recruitment.

Like the Japanese system, the Korean recruitment of managers emphasizes looking for candidates at prestigious universities. Also, like the Japanese, Korean companies prefer recent graduates to managers with experience. Companies assume that younger people will mold more easily to fit the particular company's culture. However, a form of backdoor recruitment occurs at this level, primarily through old school ties. Companies tend to favor graduates of particular universities. Often a disproportionate number of a company's managers come from a particular university.

After attracting a pool of applicants, the next stage in the HRM process is selection.

SELECTION

SELECTION IN THE UNITED STATES

U.S. experts on human resource management identify a series of steps in the selection process (Bohlander, Snell, and Sherman 2001; Werther and Davis 1993). Exhibit 12.4 shows these steps, from the initial application to the final hiring.

The aim of typical U.S. selection practices is to gather quality information on a candidate's job qualifications. The ideal selection then results in a match between

Exhibit 12.4
Typical Steps in U.S.
Personnel Selection

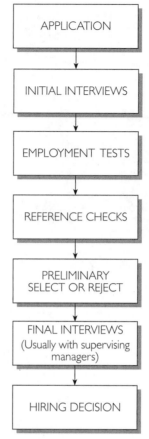

Sources: Adapted from Bohlander, Snell, and Sherman 2001 and Werther and Davis 1993.

the specific skills of the job applicant with the specific job requirements. As with the recruitment process, an individual is seen as a bundle of skills that the organization can purchase. The United States's individualistic culture promotes a focus on individual achievements (e.g., education, natural ability, experience) and not on group affiliations such as the family. As a result, many U.S. companies have prohibitions against nepotism, the hiring of relatives. In addition, many U.S. companies have policies forbidding managers to supervise family members.

Previous work experience, performance on tests, and perceptions of qualifications from interviews help inform personnel or hiring managers about the applicant's qualifications. To avoid discrimination or favoritism, laws and cultural norms in the United States prescribe that information gathered during the selection process must be valid; that is, the information gathered from prospective employees must relate to performance on the vacant job. Job-qualification tests must predict job performance. For example, lifting a hundred pounds would not be a valid selection test for most clerical jobs. Personal information gathered during the selection process, such as height and weight, must also be relevant to the job.

Next, we consider contrasting selection practices in collectivist national cultures.

SELECTION IN COLLECTIVIST CULTURES

Hofstede (1991) captures the essence of hiring in collectivist cultures. He notes: "The hiring process in a collectivist society always takes the in-group into account.

Usually preference is given to hiring relatives, first of the employer, but also of other persons already employed by the company. Hiring persons from a family one already knows reduces risks. Also relatives will be concerned about the reputation of the family and help correct misbehavior of a family member."

In many Asian and Latin American collectivist cultures, businesses are often small and family owned. The hiring of family members is a natural extension of family activities. However, modernization and urbanization challenge some of these traditions. In Mexico, for example, newspaper advertisements and executive-placement agencies are increasingly used in larger urban companies. In these larger companies, there are simply not enough relatives to fill all positions (Kras 1995).

In selecting employees, collectivist cultural norms value potential trustworthiness, reliability, and loyalty over performance-related background characteristics. Personal traits such as loyalty to the company, loyalty to the boss, and trustworthiness are the traits that family members can provide. However, larger and technically oriented companies may need professional managers and technicians with skills not available inside the family. In these cases, the selection process still prioritizes personal characteristics over technical characteristics. If one cannot have a family member, then the priority is to find employees who have the personality characteristics and background necessary to fit into the corporate culture. Younger male recruits are preferred because they have not been corrupted by another company's values, and cultural role expectations expect them to be more dedicated to work than women with children.

For example, in managerial selection in the collectivist Korean culture and the moderately collectivist Japanese culture, high school and university ties substitute for family membership. At Daewoo Corporation in Korea, the chairman and six of the eight top executives attended Kyunggi High School. Seoul National University graduates make up 62 percent of the highest executives in seven of Korea's most important *chaebol* (industrial conglomerates) (Steers, Shin, and Ungson 1989). Graduates from two public (Tokyo and Kyoto) and two private (Keio and Waseda) universities dominate both business and public leadership in Japan. Executives who graduated from elite universities use their personal contacts with university professors to provide information on a recruit's worthiness to the company. Often, the recruit's area of study at the university is of much less concern than the more subjective assessments of fit with the company.

IMPLICATIONS FOR THE MULTINATIONAL: RECRUITMENT AND SELECTION

Recruitment of host country workers and managers requires that the managers of a multinational company understand and adapt to local practices. Thus, for example, foreign multinationals in the United States probably have most success using the typical U.S. recruitment practices—advertising in newspapers and going to college campuses. In other countries, the multinational manager will also need to discover and use local recruitment and selection practices.

Adaptation to local recruitment and selection practices may not always be easy. In societies where backdoor or personal contacts are acceptable recruitment strategies, foreign multinationals may not have access to the appropriate recruitment channels. In Japan, for example, most foreign multinational companies do not have the personal contacts with Japanese professors necessary to attract the best potential managerial talent. For U.S. companies, such recruitment methods may violate ethical codes that require competitive access to all open jobs.

Multinational Management Challenge
Avoiding Discrimination in the United States

Companies from high masculinity countries often face a clash of cultures concerning personnel practices in the United States. When U.S. consultants tell their clients not to ask job applicants personal questions, the managers react with surprise. They respond, "Without information on employees' religion, upbringing or home life, how are we going to know them and trust them?"

To go beyond the formal qualifications listed on the résumé or application, some managers probe with questions many people in the United States would consider illegal—or at best inappropriate and an invasion of privacy (e.g., How many children do you expect to have?). Questions such as these arise when expatriate managers fail to accept U.S. law and cultural norms.

For any company operating in other cultures, such mistakes can be costly. For example, Hyundai Semiconductor America Inc., a division of Korea's Hyundai Group, was ordered to pay $9.5 million to a U.S. corporate headhunter. Technical Resources Inc. filed the suit because they were fired by the Hyundai human resource manager for refusing to consider gender in hiring engineers. Many foreign companies face lawsuits related to HRM practices, most often for gender, race, and age discrimination. If they lose a case, a company may pay as much as $20 million in damages, plus litigation fees.

Source: Based on *Wall Street Journal* 1999.

What happens when a company does not follow local norms in recruitment and selection? First, it may not get the best potential employees. Second, it may offend local cultural norms or break host country laws. Thus, multinational managers must always assess the trade-off between following home practices that get what they believe are the "right" people for the job against the costs and benefits of following local traditions. Consider the problems that companies from more masculine cultures face in the United States, as described in the preceding Multinational Management Challenge.

After identifying a pool of applicants and selecting those to be hired, the next step in the HRM process is training and development of the employees.

TRAINING AND DEVELOPMENT

In any country, training and development needs vary widely. Different industries, technologies, strategies, organizational structures, and local labor market conditions affect an organization's training and development needs and programs. However, broad national differences in training and development do exist among countries.

The cross-national differences in training and development are most associated with institutional differences in national educational systems. Educational systems lead to large differences in recruits' qualifications in basic skills and in attitudes toward work. For example, over 90 percent of the 25 to 34-year-olds in Norway, Japan, and Korea finished secondary school. Turkey and Portugal had only 24 per-

Exhibit 12.5 Training Systems around the World

Type	Example Countries	Features and Sources of Institutional Pressures
Cooperative	Austria, Germany, Switzerland, and some Latin American Countries	Legal and historical precedents for cooperation among companies, unions, and the government.
Company-Based Voluntarism/high labor mobility	USA and the UK	Lack of institutional pressures to provide training. Companies provide training based on own cost-benefits.
Voluntarism/low labor mobility	Japan	Low labor turnover encourages investment in training without institutional pressure.
State-Driven Incentive Provider	Hong Kong, Korea, Singapore, Taiwan, China	Government identifies needs for skills and uses incentives to encourage companies to train in chosen areas.
Supplier	Developing countries in Asia and Africa, transition economies	No institutional pressures for companies to train. Government provides formal training organizations.

Source: Adapted from ILO 1999.

cent (OECD 2000). For another example, consider Germany. It has a strong technical education program and an apprenticeship system originating with the guild system of the Middle Ages.

Cultural values regarding types of educational credentials and other personnel practices such as lifetime employment, also influence training and development needs. For example, though threatened by economic practicalities and often maligned as inefficient, the Japanese retain the ideal of long-term employment. For companies like Ricoh, which continues to avoid layoffs at all costs, it allows management training and development to take place slowly, through extensive job rotations. Managers learn by doing. They have many different job assignments early in their careers.

Exhibit 12.5 gives an overview of work-related training systems in use throughout the world. Next, for a more detailed example, we will discuss training and development differences between the voluntary system of the United States and the cooperative system of Germany.

TRAINING AND DEVELOPMENT IN THE UNITED STATES

U.S. companies with over one hundred employees invest more than $60 billion in training costs (Van Buren and King 2000). Exhibit 12.6 shows the types of skills taught to employees by these U.S. organizations. The most popular training topics are management development and computer skills. However, other types of training, such as those needed for new methods and procedures, reach more people on all levels of the organization. In spite of the billions of dollars invested in training, training in the United States does not reach all workers. Estimates are that U.S. employers provide training only to one out of every fourteen workers (Cook 1993).

Exhibit 12.6
Skills Taught by U.S.
Organizations

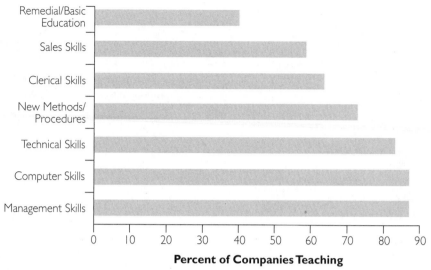

Percent of Companies Teaching

Source: Adapted from Filipezak 1992.

Because of weaknesses in U.S. secondary education, the pressure on U.S. businesses to supplement basic educational training will also increase. Thirty percent of U.S. students do not finish high school. Many of those who do graduate do not have sufficient reading and mathematical skills for current and future jobs (Cook 1993). For example, 40 percent of the companies in Exhibit 12.6 already see the need to provide remedial and basic education.

Predictions of high needs for training have resulted in some calls from business and government for German-style apprentice programs. In such programs, the government requires industry to provide vocational training to workers in exchange for tax benefits. However, in the United States, training not specifically tailored for a company is often viewed as something that the employee may eventually take to a competitor. This makes some companies reluctant to invest in training without a more immediate and positive cost–benefit analysis regarding their own bottom line (Bondreau 1991).

Next we describe what is perhaps the most acclaimed model of vocational training.

TRAINING AND VOCATIONAL EDUCATION IN GERMANY

Dual system

Form of vocational education in Germany that combines in-house apprenticeship training with part-time vocational-school training, and leads to a skilled certificate.

Meister

In Germany, a master technician.

German companies are renowned worldwide for their high-quality technical products. A sophisticated and standardized national system of vocational education and training provides a major human resource for German industry.

There are two major forms of vocational education in Germany. One form consists of general and specialized vocational schools and professional and technical colleges. The other form is called the **dual system**. The dual system combines in-house apprenticeship training with part-time vocational-school training leading to a skilled-worker certificate. This training can be followed by the *Fachschule,* a college giving advanced vocational training. Ultimately, one can achieve the status of a **Meister**, or master technician. The system of vocational education in Germany is summarized in Exhibit 12.7.

The dual system is probably the most important component of German vocational training. The training and certificate qualifications are standardized through-

Exhibit 12.7
Skilled Worker Training
in Germany

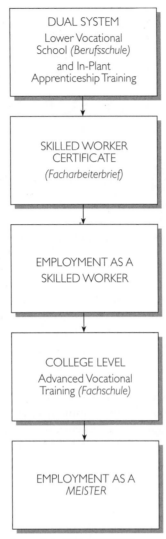

Sources: Lane 1989 and ILO 1999.

out the country. This produces a well-trained national labor force with skills that are not company specific. Apprenticeships exist not only for manual occupations but also for many technical, commercial, and managerial occupations. Apprenticeships are not limited to the young. Older workers often seek apprenticeships and resulting certificates to enhance their development. There are nearly four hundred nationally recognized vocational certificates (Arkin 1992b; ILO 1999). Unions, organizations, and the government are now identifying new groups of certificates to represent qualifications for high tech jobs in the new economy.

The dual system results from a collaboration of employers, unions, and the state. The costs are shared between companies and the state, with the companies paying approximately two-thirds of the costs. Employers have a legal obligation to release young people for vocational training. However, recently, cutbacks in German companies and high German unemployment have resulted in fewer apprenticeships being offered than there are workers applying. Many firms have cut the number of apprentices to cut costs or called for more company-specific skills (see Exhibit 12.8). Emerging information technology industries are also challenging the system

Exhibit 12.8
Germany's
Apprenticeship
Program under
Pressure

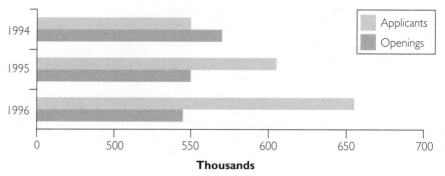

Source: Adapted from *Business Week Online* 1996b.

as their job requirements are not served by the traditional German educational structure (*Business Week Online* 1996b; ILO 1999).

Besides their national system of vocational education, German companies invest heavily in training, with four out of five workers receiving some in-house training. For example, at Mercedes Benz, the company's internal training center offers 180 vocational courses. Besides the six hundred young people in vocational training and a modular management-development program, four thousand employees per year take formal training at the company's training center (Arkin 1992b).

Not only do training and development practices differ for entry-level workers, but also the national context affects the situation for managers. Next, we examine management development in the United States as compared with that in Europe and Japan. Management development focuses on the programs that companies use to identify and groom managers for careers in an organization.

MANAGEMENT DEVELOPMENT IN THE UNITED STATES

Many U.S. companies have programs to identify and develop managerial talent. The objective is to develop quality managers who will spend their entire careers within the company. The prime steps include identifying managers with the talent for promotion and matching them with organizational needs for managerial talent.

Several techniques help identify and develop managerial talent (Bohlander, Snell, and Sherman 2001; Werther and Davis 1993). Many U.S. companies charge senior-level managers with the responsibility of identifying managerial potential. Managerial performance appraisals often contain estimates of managerial readiness. Some companies use more direct approaches, such as assessment centers to identify managers. The assessment center is a testing procedure presenting individuals with a series of situations or problems. Observers judge how well potential managers respond to the situations or problems presented at each station in the assessment center. Managers may be promoted or identified as having high potential based on their performances in the assessment center. Mentoring occurs when a senior-level executive becomes the coach, guide, and advisor for a junior manager. This may be either a formal or an informal relationship. Some U.S. companies develop "fast-track" careers for junior managers destined for higher-level management. Usually, a company assigns fast-track managers to a variety of challenging positions early in their careers, and such managers, if successful, receive rapid promotions.

However, in an individualistic culture such as the United States, career management remains the responsibility of the individual. These individual goals may not correspond to filling the current organizational assignment or to participation in management development. Therefore, U.S. companies cannot assume the long-term loyalty of their better managers. Retrenchments, limited company growth, short career ladders, and even the relatively young age of superiors may prevent career advancement. Individual career opportunities may simply be better somewhere else, and good managers may resign.

Next, we examine management-development approaches used by the Japanese.

MANAGEMENT DEVELOPMENT IN JAPAN

Permanent employment

In Japan, continuous employment, often to the age of 55.

An understanding of management development in Japan must be set in the context of a system undergoing increasing pressure to change, strong cultural traditions relating to age seniority, and the philosophy of **permanent employment**. The association of age with wisdom is a Confucian value that leads Japanese companies to believe that managers cannot be fully capable until they have reached a certain age. The philosophy of a permanent-employment system also arises from Confucian values of familial duties. The company, serving in the parent role, must protect and take care of the worker, and the worker in turn owes loyalty to the paternalistic company. The permanent-employment system also has institutional roots in law. Article 27 of the Japanese Constitution states, "All people shall have the right and obligation to work" (Schlender 1994). This is a point that many larger companies, within economic constraints, take literally. The following Multinational Management Brief gives a more specific description of the traditional Japanese permanent-employment system.

Japanese managerial recruits come directly from universities and join the company as a group. Most are approximately the same age. Because many Japanese companies still hope to make a long-term if not lifetime commitment to managers, they select recruits largely based on personal qualities and potential fit with the corporate culture. For all but the most technical jobs there is little consideration given to college major. The managerial recruit (most likely a man) also must choose his company carefully. He will likely work for the company until age 55. He ties his fate to the fate of the company.

The low emphasis given to technical qualification for managers versus personal qualifications means that companies must have a long-term view to management development. The first years of managerial careers focus on initiation into and learning the company's culture. After an initial basic training, new managers move often between departments, learn the nature of the company's business, and develop job skills. Managers may have over ten different jobs before they have any real responsibility (Abegglen and Stalk 1985). Learning the company's culture is also enhanced by extensive after-hours socializing and drinking with other managers. The typical Japanese manager may arrive at the office at 9 AM, leave work around 7 PM, and join his colleagues for drinks until 10 or 11 PM.

Lack of flexibility due to lifetime employment commitment leaves many organizations with little choice but to hire fewer recruits from college. The result is that many Japanese organizations now struggle with the prospects of an aging and more expensive managerial workforce. During the boom of the Japanese economy the average age of managers was 25. It is now 35. (*Economist* 1999)

Traditionally, there has been little public or formal emphasis in Japanese companies on identifying high-potential managers early in their careers. For the most part, during the first eight to ten years, managers following a traditional Japanese system are promoted and paid the same as others in their age cohort. Most positions have a minimum age, and no one will be promoted before this age. However,

Multinational Management Brief
Permanent Employment in Japan: A System Under Fire

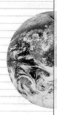

Lifetime or permanent employment often received credit for producing the loyal and motivated workforce that supported the dramatic growth in the Japanese economy. It was touted as something to be imitated by companies from other nations. However, more recently, it has been criticized for leading to Japanese organizations bloated with too many middle managers. Japanese companies are modifying the system but still feel committed to senior workers who came on board in a time of greater Japanese prosperity.

Basic characteristics of lifetime employment and current modifications include the following:

- Lifetime employment remains an ideal goal tempered by economic reality. Some estimate that only 15 to 18 percent of the workforce actually has lifetime security.
- It is mostly for men. Few Japanese women get the opportunity to enter career-track occupations.
- Lifetime employment is mostly a characteristic of large companies and, currently, only some of those large companies can afford it.
- Managers, more than workers, receive the protection of lifetime employment.
- The "lifetime" only lasts to approximately age 55. Companies offer incentives for older employees (especially managers) to become part time or to take jobs with satellite companies.

How does it work?

- Many companies use a three-track system. Full-time (mostly male) workers commit for lifetime employment. Part-time (mostly female) workers can be let go or reduced in hours as necessary. Temporary workers (also mostly women but some specialist jobs for men) join the company not expecting lifetime employment. A look at the age structure of most Japanese companies shows that very few women continue work beyond their mid-20s, the expected age of marriage and first child. These recruitment policies allow companies to protect a core of male full-time workers.
- Temporary and sometimes permanent transfers to satellite or subsidiary companies keep people employed but reduce the workforce of the main company.
- The financial flexibility of the bonus system allows companies to make drastic cuts in wages and salaries during times of poor company performance.
- Large Japanese companies use subsidiaries and small companies dependent on the large company to provide flexibility when demand for their products increases or decreases. In tough times, the smaller companies take most of the blows if production or work must be cut back. Again, this protects the core workers in the main firm.
- The use of temporary workers and transfer to satellite companies is increasing even including professional and managerial employees. NTT, for example, created independent subsidiaries and staffed them with 5,000 former employees.
- Much to the dismay of Japanese college students, the hiring of new graduates has slowed to a trickle.

Sources: Based on Thorton 1999; *Economist* 1999; Mroczkowski and Hanaoka 1989 and Takahashi 1993.

some Japanese companies have kept secret files on their most promising juniors. They believe that identifying publicly a high-potential junior would be too disruptive to the social harmony of the group.

Although Japanese culture sanctions standing out from the group, economic reality is changing many organizations. Consider the following (http://www.managementfirst.com):

- Asahi Breweries now ties evaluations to promotions for all managerial levels—a change accepted by younger managers but criticized by older managers.
- Matsushita now has a merit pay system for its 4,500 managers.
- Honda ties the bonus system to profitability and is gradually phasing out seniority as the criteria for pay and promotions.

Most management training and development focus on company-related skills. Unlike in the individualistic United States, the development of human resources is not considered an individual's personal investment; managers do not view their training and development as an accumulation of skills and competencies that can be marketed to other companies. With the mutual commitment of permanent employment, both the organization and employees accept that investment in management development is an investment for the well-being of the company.

In addition to technical issues such as marketing skills, Japanese managerial training contains what the anthropologist Thomas Rohlen calls a "spiritual" education (Terpstra and David 1991). Spiritual education emphasizes character development, such as the ability to persevere in difficult times, the acceptance of social responsibility, and the habit of cooperation. Toward this end, some Japanese companies have recently popularized military-style boot-camp training centers, where managers undergo rigorous physical and psychological stress. As with military basic training, spiritual training sometimes includes hazing and self-deprecation, which are used to build stronger characters.

Because managers join the company directly after completing an undergraduate degree, technical management training inside the company focuses on company-specific skills. General management education, such as the MBA degree, has little personal value for Japanese managers. That is, having an MBA degree provides a manager no competitive advantage over other managers of the same age. Consequently, until recently, only a few universities, such as Keio and Waseda in Tokyo, had U.S.-style MBA programs.

Major Japanese companies often do, however, send selected managers to prestigious universities in the United States or Europe for the MBA and other management degrees. In such cases, the company's objective is not to develop the individual's managerial skills. Rather, most companies hope that the returning manager will serve the firm by learning the language and culture of a foreign market and providing an understanding of competitors' business practices. Returning managers expect only to rejoin their age cohort in managerial rank and pay.

Exposure of Japanese managers to Western managerial training is not without cost for Japanese companies. Not all returning managers are willing to go back to the slower-paced Japanese system of management development. Because they are somewhat disillusioned with traditional Japanese HRM practices, these MBAs are often good candidates for positions in foreign multinational companies. Many also join high tech firms too new to be dominated by traditional Japanese business culture.

Having seen examples of training and development in different national contexts, we can now consider how these differences affect the multinational companies operating in different countries.

Exhibit 12.9
Workers of the Future: Student Math and Science Scores from Selected Countries

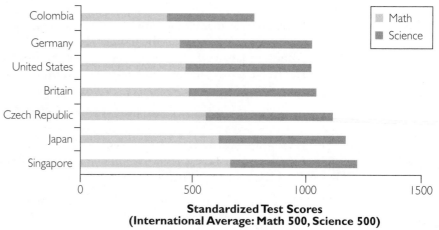

Standardized Test Scores
(International Average: Math 500, Science 500)

Source: Adapted from *Economist* 1997.

IMPLICATIONS FOR THE MULTINATIONAL: TRAINING AND DEVELOPMENT

Before setting up operations in a host foreign country, multinational managers must consider the quality of the workers and sometimes the managers available in the host country. They must also examine the feasibility of exporting their company's training techniques to the host country. For example, a transnational company might need workers with basic skills in math and science to staff plants of the future. Rather than invest in basic education to train a low-cost workforce, the company can locate in countries with the best educational systems. Thus, for example, a multinational company with a requirement for technical workers might examine which educational systems produce the best students in mathematics and science. Consider the implications of the data (shown in Exhibit 12.9) on the math and science performance for 13-year-olds. What does this suggest about the next generation of workers in different countries? Match this information with the data on differences in compensation (Exhibit 12.13 on page 491). Where would you seek location advantages?

No matter what the basic talent of host country workers, exporting and adapting training are requirements for using host country nationals. The following Case in Point describes efforts by Mercedes to train Tuscaloosa, Alabama, workers in Germany and by Motorola to train workers from sites throughout the world.

Adaptation of management-development practices to different national contexts depends significantly on the intended use of host country managers. If host country nationals are limited to lower management levels, then multinational companies may follow local management-development practices. This would be a likely approach for a multilocal company with a polycentric IHRM orientation. Such companies develop local managerial talent for careers in one country. Host country managers often never expect to work at the multinational's headquarters or in another country location.

In situations where multinational companies allow and expect host country nationals to rise to higher levels of management, however, the parent company's corporate culture dominates management-development policies, and such multinationals expect managers of all nationalities to be, for example, Motorola or Ford managers—not British or Mexican or Malaysian.

Most multinational companies realize that training pays. Consider these examples from Brazil to the United States.

- When the major automobile manufacturers go to developing countries to set up production sites, they often must take responsibility for the training of local workers. Evidence from Brazil suggests that leading companies provide basic education in reading and math and now average 50–80 hours a year in off-the-job training. Production workers need capabilities in measurement, statistical procedures, and the ability to read sophisticated manuals. To encourage participation in the training, companies link promotion to multi-skilling, education, and training.

- All Motorola employees must have forty hours of training a year. Motorola spends more than 4 percent of its payroll expenses on training. Motorola U. is headquartered in Schaumburg, Illinois, and has fourteen branches throughout the world.

    Motorola training is a mixture of technical and corporate cultural education. The technical education focuses on making sure that all production is of the same quality throughout the world. The cultural training is to export a transnational culture that, for example, emphasizes equal opportunity no matter where the location. Translators ensure that the messages are transcultural. Sports metaphors, for example, common in the U.S. courses, are replaced by stories about families in Asian countries. Where there are no exact translations for ideas such as "empowerment," everyone uses the English words.

- When Mercedes set up a brand-new plant in Alabama, the firm had forty thousand applicants for 650 jobs—a large pool of candidates from which to select higher-quality workers. However, the U.S. workers did not have the German apprenticeship training, and very few had ever worked in an automobile-assembly plant. The Mercedes solution: They shipped the U.S. workers to Germany for up to six months to work side by side with German employees. After that, seventy German trainers returned to the United States to continue the training. To appeal to U.S. cultural expectations, they abandoned the hierarchical business culture of the home plant, gave workers more autonomy on the assembly line, and emphasized teamwork.

Sources: Based on Kelly and Burrows 1994; Humphrey 1998 and Vlasic 1997.

Next, the chapter considers differences between performance appraisal in the United States and performance appraisal in collectivist cultures.

PERFORMANCE APPRAISAL

Regardless of the national setting, all companies at some point must deal with the human resource problems of identifying people to reward, promote, demote, develop and improve, retain, or fire. Not everyone can move up the ladder of the organizational pyramid. Not everyone can be a leader. Not everyone will perform at acceptable levels. Even in countries like Japan, with its high value for lifetime employment, the survival of the company now often requires layoffs.

The fundamental assumption in the West, and in particular, in the more individualistic cultures, is that performance-appraisal systems provide rational and fair solutions to these human resource problems. That is, ideally, appraisal systems provide management with objective, honest, and fair data on employee performance. Consequently, human resource decisions, such as pay or promotion, can be based on these performance-appraisal data. Although issues regarding seniority, experience, and security are not ignored, the cultural ideal is a meritocracy, where good performers get more rewards.

PERFORMANCE APPRAISAL IN THE UNITED STATES

The U.S. performance-appraisal system represents cultural values that espouse links among individual rights, duties, and rewards, as well as a legal system that promotes equal opportunity. Thus, the ideal U.S. performance-appraisal system is highly rational, logical, and legal.

The textbook view of the U.S. performance-appraisal system contains four elements: performance standards, performance measures, performance feedback, and human resource decisions related to remuneration, promotion, or termination (Werther and Davis 1993).

Performance standards reflect management's goals regarding acceptable quality and/or quantity of work output. These standards include work-related knowledge, quality, volume, and initiative. For example, a secretary may be expected to type a certain number of words per minute. Performance measures are techniques intended for objective and often comparative assessment of employees on the performance standards. The most popular measures use some form of rating scale (Locher and Teel 1988). The employee is rated on a variety of traits (e.g., work quality), usually by managers, but occasionally by peers or subordinates. Teacher evaluations by class members and peer evaluations of contributions to a student group project are examples of performance ratings.

Performance feedback usually occurs in a formal interview between superior and subordinate. Three methods are common in the United States (Bohlander, Snell, and Sherman 2001). First, in the tell-and-sell method, the supervisor gives feedback and explains the evaluation. Second, in the tell-and-listen method, the supervisor gives feedback and listens to the subordinate's reactions. Third, in the problem-solving method, the supervisor and subordinate work to identify problems and propose solutions for improvement.

What are the typical human resource consequences of the U.S. performance-appraisal system? Most U.S. organizations use performance appraisals for compensation decisions. Other major but less common uses include performance improvement, feedback, documentation, and promotion (Bohlander, Snell, and Sherman 2001).

Because of the concern in the United States that human resource decisions be fair and equitable to all individuals, performance-appraisal systems have institutionalized legal pressures to follow similar procedures. The following Multinational Management Brief summarizes the **U.S. legal requirements for appraisals**.

U.S. legal requirements for appraisals

Regulating performance-evaluation practices to ensure their fairness.

The U.S. performance-appraisal system is rooted in an individualistic culture and an institutional system that aspires to protect equal rights and equal opportunities. Cultural stories such as "the American dream of rags to riches" support the idea that all can achieve wealth and success through their own efforts. Next, we will see how the institutional systems and cultural values of other nations result in quite different aspects of work performance being valued and evaluated.

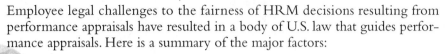

Multinational Management Brief
The U.S. Legal Requirements for Performance Appraisals

Employee legal challenges to the fairness of HRM decisions resulting from performance appraisals have resulted in a body of U.S. law that guides performance appraisals. Here is a summary of the major factors:

- *Performance evaluations must relate clearly to the job*: Evaluation systems must evaluate only performances on tasks or outcomes that the job is designed to achieve.
- *Performance standards must be provided in writing*: Access to specific written standards must be available to all concerned while working and before any appraisal.
- *Supervisors must be able to measure the behaviors they rate*: Systems that rate or evaluate a worker must be valid. This means that the company must be able to demonstrate that an evaluation system does measure what it is supposed to.
- *Supervisors must be trained to use evaluation measures*: Companies must be able to demonstrate that supervisors have the necessary skills and training to use evaluation tools such as interviews or observations.
- *Supervisors and subordinates must discuss appraisals openly*: Unlike in some Japanese firms, appraisals cannot be secret. There must be procedures in place to discuss appraisals.
- *Appeals procedures must be in place*: The employee must have some formal access to higher management or other appeal mechanism to challenge his or her superior's evaluation.

Source: Based on Bohlander, Snell, and Sherman 2001.

PERFORMANCE APPRAISALS IN COLLECTIVIST CULTURES

In collectivist cultures, age and in-group memberships (usually family or social status) provide a large component of the psychological contract with the organization; that is, the employer and employee accept as correct and fair that human resource decisions should take into account personal background characteristics more than achievement. Since who you are and how old you are may count more than how you perform, the usefulness of a Western-style performance-appraisal system is less clear. For example, if only family members are eligible for promotion, it makes little sense to evaluate all employees for management potential.

None of this implies, however, that information regarding performance is not communicated to people in collectivist cultures. Members of work groups often know the best and the worst performers. Because it is important to work for the benefit of the group, members may subtly praise or punish other workers based on work performance. Managers also may work indirectly to sanction poor performance. Behaviors such as withdrawing normal favors or working through intermediaries (who are often relatives) are common. For the Japanese, the supervisor can communicate negative feedback for poor work performance simply by ignoring his subordinate. Thus, even without formal appraisal systems, feedback occurs indirectly.

According to Hofstede (1991), managers in collectivist societies often avoid direct performance-appraisal feedback. An open discussion of performance may clash with the society's norm of harmony, which takes precedence over other values. For example, during the first eight to ten years of their careers, Japanese managers may never encounter the appraisal system. Even if one exists, it is often secret and lacks direct feedback to the employee. Instead, all beginning managers get the same salary and promotions, based on age and seniority. Reducing competition among managers and maintaining harmony among the group are higher-priority values than identifying or developing high-performers.

Steers, Shin, and Ungson (1989) point out that the preference for seniority-based promotions, rather than appraisal-based promotions, is even greater among Koreans. They note that while job performance is important and most companies do have appraisal systems, seniority is most important for advancement. This follows "from the Confucian tradition that strives to preserve harmony (since it is unseemly for younger employees to supervise older ones). It is also easier to use seniority to make promotion decisions than to rely on imprecise personnel evaluation methods to discriminate between a group of high achievers" (101).

Perhaps because of the long-term orientation of Korean culture, Korean performance-appraisal systems focus on evaluating and developing the "whole man" for the long-term benefit of the company. They evaluate sincerity, loyalty, and attitude on an equal footing with job performance. Only for senior management, where the logic of an organizational pyramid dictates a smaller number of top positions, does the performance evaluation focus on actual performance and contribution to the company (Steers, Shin, and Ungson 1989).

At least from the U.S. perspective, performance appraisals provide the information necessary for promotion and compensation decisions. Next, we will see how compensation practices in other national contexts differ from the U.S. model.

COMPENSATION

Compensation includes wages and salaries, incentives such as bonuses, and benefits such as retirement contributions. There are wide variations both among countries and among organizations within countries concerning how to compensate workers. A country's economic development, cultural traditions, legal institutions, and the role of labor unions all affect compensation. Consider these examples:

- Japanese workers earn over three times the wages of the workers in other East Asian countries such as Taiwan, Singapore, and Korea (U.S. Department of Labor 1995).
- Although not required by law, Korean and Japanese workers expect bonuses at least twice a year.
- In Denmark, over 80 percent of employees belong to unions, and agreements between unions and employers' associations determine minimal and normal pay (ILO 1997a).
- In the EU, there is a statutory minimum of four weeks of vacation.

COMPENSATION PRACTICES IN THE UNITED STATES

Conditions external and internal to the company affect the wages and salaries of workers and managers (Bohlander, Snell, and Sherman 2001). External factors include local and national wage rates, government legislation, and collective bargaining. Internal factors include the importance of the job to the organization, the affluence of the organization or its ability to pay, and the employee's relative worth to the business (merit).

Taking into account these external and internal factors, most U.S. companies develop formal and systematic policies to determine wages and salaries. The Personnel Policies Forum, a group of personnel managers representing companies of all sizes and from all industries, found that 75 percent of their member companies had formal written policies for wage and salary administration (Bureau of National Affairs 1990). What are these policies? Consider the following additional results from the Personnel Policies Forum study.

To establish that their companies' wages and salaries are competitive in the labor market, the Personnel Policies Forum study showed that 94 percent of U.S. companies used data from comparative wage and salary surveys to determine compensation. Comparative wage and salary surveys tell companies how their compensation packages match up with those of competitors. Two-thirds of the companies check on comparative wage and salary data at least once a year. Nearly 40 percent assess their competitive wage and salary position more than seven times a year.

Perhaps more than any other society, the highly mobile U.S. labor market requires this hefty concern with external equity (i.e., Do we pay at or above market level?). The individualistic U.S. culture views careers as private and personal, and mobility, advancement, and higher wages often require leaving a company. Thus, unlike in countries such as Japan and Korea, where company loyalty often prevails over opportunities for higher remuneration, U.S. companies must rely on competitive wages to maintain a quality workforce.

Most U.S. companies also develop procedures to establish that people receive equitable pay for the types of jobs they perform. Seventy-five percent of the companies surveyed by the Personnel Policies Forum (Bureau of National Affairs 1990) have formal systems to evaluate how much particular jobs (independent of the people doing them) contribute to the company. A variety of methods helps establish a hierarchy of jobs based on worth to the company. Issues such as responsibility, skill requirements, and the importance of the job's tasks to the organization contribute to the worth of a particular job. Those who occupy the higher-ranked jobs are paid higher.

Although the worth of a job to the company largely determines the base pay assigned to a certain position, raises in pay are determined mostly by merit (Hansen 1998). As previously noted and discussed in more detail in the following section, this is particularly unlike the seniority-based systems of Korea and Japan.

As part of the total compensation package, benefits have grown substantially in the United States during the last few decades. Major employee benefits in the United States include pension plans, health-care benefits, insurance coverage, vacation pay, sick leave, and paid holidays. Social Security insurance, unemployment insurance, family leave, and workers' compensation insurance for work-related accidents are required by law. However, as the following Multinational Management Brief shows, U.S. benefits still lag behind those that a multinational company should expect to pay in Europe.

Next we will see an example of the changing compensation system in Japan. In response to competitive pressures, ten years of recession, and globalization of Japanese organization, Japanese firms are moving toward a Western style of compensation management. However, it still differs from the U.S. approach in its emphasis on age and group harmony as factors to account for in pay packages.

COMPENSATION IN JAPAN

As with U.S. firms, Japanese companies determine base salaries to a large degree by the classification of positions. Positions have skill and educational requirements.

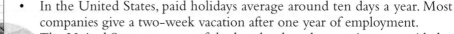

Multinational Management Brief
A Comparison of Some Benefits in the
United States and the European Community

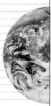

- In the United States, paid holidays average around ten days a year. Most companies give a two-week vacation after one year of employment.
- The United States was one of the last developed countries to provide legal protection for maternity. The Family Leave Bill, passed in 1993, requires employers of more than fifty people to provide up to twelve weeks of unpaid leave for the care of newborns.
- In Denmark, paid holidays accrue at 2.5 days a month. Maternity leave is four weeks before the birth and twenty-four weeks after the birth, with either parent taking the last ten weeks.
- In Italy, there are ten national public holidays a year along with paid vacations. Women are entitled to maternity leave of two months before and three months after the birth of a child.
- In the EU, law requires a minimum of 20 paid holidays, but most German workers have many more, averaging around thirty. In the state of Bavaria, for example, German workers get the national average of six weeks' vacation along with Bavaria's fourteen state holidays. Maternity leave is fourteen weeks at normal salary.

Sources: Based on Arkin 1992a; Arkin 1992b; Caplan 1992; Benjamin 1993; Langer 1993 and Poe 1999.

Those who occupy the more demanding positions receive higher wages and bonuses depending on their classification.

There are two effects of seniority on the Japanese compensation system. First, besides educational qualifications, each position has minimum age requirements. As the Japanese worker gains in seniority he, and less often she, becomes eligible to move up to more valued and more highly paid positions. Second, seniority factors into pay decisions, but at a declining rate. That is, seniority counts more for pay raises earlier in one's career and diminishes after age 45. The logic of this system is that more money is required early, when family responsibilities such as buying a home or paying for children's education are highest. These responsibilities decrease after middle age. In fact, early in a career it is not uncommon for marital status and family size to affect wages or salary.

In more recent times, merit (as the Japanese interpret it) affects pay raises to a greater degree than under the traditional position/seniority system. As has been noted, the Japanese view of merit does not match exactly the Western view, stressing attitudes as much as job performance. However, experts on Japanese personnel policies predict that merit and achievement—at least Japanese style—will continue to have a greater impact on Japanese compensation and promotions (Macharzina 2000). Exhibit 12.10 shows the traditional compensation formula as it is being modified for pay raises in use in many Japanese companies today. The major shift that is occurring is the weight given to merit over seniority.

Economic pressures on the Japanese compensation system are growing. This is in part due to the increasing costs of compensating a large management staff re-

Exhibit 12.10

The Japanese Pay Raise Formula: Changing the Balance

Sources: Adapted from *Economist* 1999 and Mroczkowski and Hanaoka 1989.

Nenpo System

New Japanese compensation system based on yearly performance evaluations that emphasize goals—although goals are not always the same as in Western companies.

Bonus system

In Japan, employees often receive up to 30 percent of their base salary, usually given twice a year during traditional gift-giving seasons.

cruited from the baby-boom generation. As a result, some Japanese companies are taking the "radical" approach of basing management compensation only on merit. Honda was among the first to introduce this type of system, called the ***nenpo* system**, in 1992. At Honda, there are no cost-of-living raises, housing allowances, family allowances, or automatic pay raises. Instead, superiors determine a manager's pay by yearly performance evaluations that emphasize goals (Takahashi 1993; Schmidt 1997). Although seniority remains important for holding certain positions, trends in Japanese human resource practices show a convergence with practices used in the United States and other Western nations. A recent survey shows that 90 percent of Japanese companies have or plan to introduce performance into their pay and promotion systems (*Economist* 1999).

Along with raises based on age, promotions, and merit, a significant component of Japanese compensation is the **bonus system**. Many Korean companies use similar systems. Bonuses come twice a year, usually during traditional gift-giving seasons. During the high of the Japanese boom economy, employees often received up to 30 percent of their base salary in the form of bonuses. Successful large companies paid up to 100 percent of base salaries in bonuses in particularly good years. However, with the current economic situation in Japan, such levels are now infrequent.

Ostensibly, the bonuses depend on the performance of the company. They serve to motivate all employees to work for company success. However, the biannual bonuses have become such an expected part of the Japanese compensation system that most companies and employees see the bonuses as mandatory. People plan major purchases and savings based on expected bonuses.

For the *kaisha* (Japanese company), bonuses add flexibility into the compensation system. Bonuses reduce payments for required benefits based on a percentage of the base pay, such as health-care insurance. Rather than pay weekly or monthly salaries, Japanese companies retain the use of the money for a longer period for alternative investments. The bonus system also makes a significant percentage of an organization's total compensation a variable cost. Wages and salaries paid to employees can be varied by the firm's financial performance without layoffs.

Benefits packages in Japan are fairly uniform (Kodama 1992). The government regulates a health-insurance program that provides Japanese employees free choice of physicians and hospitals. Pension plans are also similar in most companies.

Because Japanese companies typically have a greater involvement in the personal lives of workers, Japanese workers receive benefits that might be considered unusual in the United States or other Western nations. Such benefits might include subsidized housing based on family size, free or low-cost access to company-owned vacation resorts, golf club memberships, and transportation subsidies or company cars and drivers. Some of these benefits, such as golf club memberships can cost over half a million dollars.

In the mid-1990s, Japanese HRM managers received nearly $30,000 in perquisites. By 2000, as you can see from Exhibit 12.11, Japanese bonuses and overall compensation were lower than many of their counterparts from other countries.

Exhibit 12.11 Who Gets What and From Where: Compensation for a Vice President of Human Resources

	Japan	Germany	U.S.	Argentina	China	South Africa	Venezuela
Base Compensation	$167,853	$124,381	$168,540	$202,608	$46,622	$92,349	$148,234
Bonus	$16,244	$32,447	$25,281	$51,327	$5,828	$21,729	$53,903
Long-Term Incentives	$0	$0	$73,034	$18,910	$0	$21,729	$0
TOTAL CASH COMPENSATION	$184,097	$156,828	$266,855	$272,845	$52,450	$135,808	$202,138
Compulsory Benefit Contributions	$10,829	$10,816	$11,236	$51,327	$5,828	$13,507	$29,647
Voluntary Benefit Contributions	$29,780	$13,520	$28,090	$13,507	$0	$19,013	$24,257
Perquisites	$10,829	$8,112	$0	$16,209	$0	$24,313	$16,171
TOTAL NON-CASH COMPENSATION	$51,439	$32,447	$39,326	$54,029	$5,828	$43,458	$70,074
TOTAL INCOME	$235,536	$189,275	$306,181	$326,874	$58,278	$179,266	$272,212

Source: Adapted from data reported in Towers Perrin 2000.

Such change reflects the movement of Japanese HRM practices to more Western models and the financial state of many of their organizations.

IMPLICATIONS FOR THE MULTINATIONAL: PERFORMANCE EVALUATION AND COMPENSATION

As with recruitment and selection, multinational companies must match their performance-evaluation system to their IHRM orientation and multinational strategies. For example, transnational companies with global IHRM orientations will likely favor one system of performance evaluation for all managers, with some possible modifications for lower-level host country managers and other employees. Companies with multidomestic multinational strategies and polycentric IHRM policies will often follow local HRM practices. More ethnocentric IHRM companies often impose home country HRM practices regardless of the reactions of host country nationals. For example, even top managers for Japanese companies in the United States often report that they must adjust to the ethnocentric HRM practices of their Japanese parents. The U.S. managers are uncomfortable with ill-identified career paths and the lack of specialization. Moreover, many U.S. managers working for Japanese companies believe that headquarters management posts are blocked by the glass ceiling. As Bill Bsand, executive vice president for Hitachi America, notes: "There are very few Americans who work for Hitachi in Japan and usually at a very low level" (Lancaster 1996).

A multinational company with locations in several nations may need several different compensation systems, especially for host country nationals. For each host country, worker compensation levels must match wage levels in the local labor market. Compensation must also meet local minimum-wage rates. Examining information, such as that reported in Exhibits 12.12 and 12.13 on pay rates for labor, can give multinational managers the general data necessary to estimate the costs of host country workers and competitive wage and salary levels. Country-level comparative compensation data are available from many government, private, and international sources. Information on compensation laws is usually available from host country governments. However, multinational managers must also consider re-

Exhibit 12.12

Labor Costs and Hours
Worked per Week in
Selected Countries

Country	Average Cost of Labor per Hour in U.S. $	Average Hours Worked per Week
United States	19.2	38
Korea	6.71	47
Sri Lanka	0.47	43
Denmark	22.96	32
Germany	26.18	33
Greece	8.91	36
Japan	20.89	36

Sources: Adapted from ILO 2000b; U.S. Department of Labor 2000.

Exhibit 12.13

The Compensation
Score Card: Annual
Gross Wages in Cities
Around the World

City	Employee Groups				
	Automobile Mechanics	Laborers	Skilled Industrial Workers	Department Manager	Engineers
Bangkok	4,500	1,700	7,100	15,700	11,100
Bombay	1,500	1,100	2,400	10,200	4,700
Berlin	21,700	20,600	26,300	56,400	43,900
Cairo	2,500	1,800	3,000	4,200	4,900
Houston	37,700	29,000	42,500	59,500	52,900
Istanbul	4,000	3,100	13,500	34,100	23,900
Manila	2,300	1,800	3,200	8,700	6,300
Mexico City	4,200	1,700	4,400	9,000	12,100
Nairobi	1,500	300	1,500	3,500	2,900
Shanghai	3,500	1,900	3,200	12,300	7,000
Warsaw	4,300	3,700	5,100	9,900	8,400

Source: Adapted from UBS 2000.

gional differences within countries. Both labor costs and regional government laws may be different. Consider the situation for Mexico in the following Brief.

A look at the relatively low cost of labor, managers, and engineers in Eastern European countries and India shows why many multinationals seek location advantages in these countries. Children from these countries also score well in cross-national comparisons of math and science ability. This suggests that these locations will provide excellent future workers in technical occupations.

However, some experts argue that competitive advantages based on wage rates are only short term. They look at the situation for many Japanese, Korean, and Taiwanese companies that based their early competitive advantages on quality, low-cost labor. Most manufacturing companies in these countries have moved plants to cheaper locations in China or Southeast Asia. The implication for multinational companies is that, when local wage rates rise, the company will be forced either to keep pace or to seek another low-cost location.

Multinational Management Brief
Some Legal Requirements of Compensation in Mexico

- A bonus of 15 days' pay at Christmas.
- Ten percent of the company's taxable income paid to employees as profit sharing.
- Twelve days' paid vacation after four years of working.
- Full pay to employees on strike.

Source: Based on Sunoo 2000.

Failure to meet local wage standards can result in poor workers and bad relationships with host governments. In addition, inadequate pay in other countries might bring negative reactions at home. For example, the Indonesian suppliers of Nike manage to pay workers only $2.23 per day, less than the Indonesian minimum wage of $2.59 per day (*Business Week Online* 1996a). This and other potentially abusive labor practices has caused Nike and other U.S. offshore manufacturers to face criticism at home over labor abuses in low-wage countries.

In the next section, the chapter concludes by looking at labor relationships from a comparative perspective.

A COMPARATIVE VIEW OF LABOR RELATIONS

The patterns of labor relations in different nations arise not only from cultural differences but also from the unique histories of unionization in each country (ILO 1999; Poole 1986). Historical factors, such as the state of technological development during early unionization and the time when governments recognized the legality of unions, influence current union structure and activities. Some unions were developed for ideological reasons such as overthrowing the capitalist system or representing religious values. Others developed simply to improve wages and working conditions. Management views of unions also differ from country to country. The astute multinational manager will be well versed in the history, structure, and ideology of unions in the countries in which her or his company operates. Consider some of the difficulties of labor relations in India as shown in the following Case in Point.

Before entering a country, one major HRM issue to consider is the popularity of unions. An indicator of union popularity is called union-membership density.

UNION-MEMBERSHIP DENSITY

Union membership density

Proportion of workers in a country who belong to unions.

A strong indicator that multinational managers can use to tell how much unions influence companies in any country is the **union-membership density**. Union-membership density refers to the proportion of workers who belong to unions in a country. Estimates of union density are always approximate because some reports do not consider white-collar workers or professional unions.

Union membership in the United States has declined considerably over the last thirty years. However, European and other industrialized countries still have quite

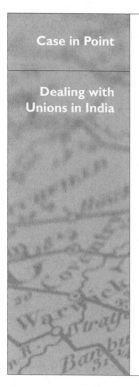

India's free-market reforms have attracted multinational firms General Electric, Otis Elevator Co., and Unilever, to name only a few. However, these firms face a national context in which strong institutional pressures give power to unions and encourage union militancy.

India has more than forty-five overlapping, sometimes conflicting and most often confusing major labor laws. These laws allow unions to be formed by as few as seven people. Some companies must deal with as many as fifty different labor groups. The laws also make it difficult to fire employees or close money-losing operations. A company with more than 10 workers needs government permission to fire employees—something almost never given.

How are multinationals adapting? Siemens AG, Whirlpool Corp., and Philips Electronics NV are using golden handshakes to buy out workers. Rather than confronting unions directly, these companies offer workers voluntary retirement and payoffs. For example, with little fanfare, Siemens shed 1,300 of 7,500 employees from its bloated Indian operation for a maximum payout of $16,160—low by European standards but high for India. Many multinational managers sense unions are ingnoring such practices because of a growing realization by unions that Indian businesses must be more efficient to compete internationally.

Source: Based on Karp and Williams 1997.

high proportions of workers who are union members. In major industrialized countries, union membership is declining but still averages greater than 50 percent. Some decline is due to the end of compulsory union membership in the transition economies of Eastern Europe. However, in countries such as South Africa, with the opening of unions to the formerly barred black population, unions have more than doubled in size (ILO 1997a; 1997b). Exhibit 12.14 gives a summary of unionization density in various parts of the world.

SOME HISTORICAL AND INSTITUTIONAL DIFFERENCES

Historical conditions during the early days of unionization in a country and the unions' relationships with social institutions such as the government tend to influence the activities of contemporary unions. Consider the following differences among German, French, British, and U.S. unions observed by Professor Lane (1989).

British unions began early in the 19th century, corresponding to the rise of major factory-based industries. Ignored early on by government, British unions developed without government interference. Not until the 1980s was there much legal control of management–labor conflict. If workers went on strike, neither the company nor the workers had any legal obligation to solve the conflict, such as honoring the workers' right to return to work. According to Lane (1989), the lack of government intervention led management and workers to develop strong adversarial relationships that remain in existence in contemporary Britain. Lane characterizes the British situation as fragmented and highly conflictual.

Perhaps because German culture ranks high on uncertainty avoidance, labor relationships have a more orderly tradition. The government recognized the union

Exhibit 12.14
Union Density and
Change in Selected
Countries

Country	Union Density	Change 1985–95
Egypt	38.8%	−9.1%
South Africa	40.9	130.8
Cuba	70.2	−29.8
United States	14.2	−21.1
Japan	24.0	−16.7
Denmark	80.1	2.3
Hungary	60.0	−25.3
Sweden	91.1	8.7

Sources: Adapted from ILO 1997a; ILO 1997b.

movement in the mid-1880s. The strong role of the state served to develop more harmonious relationships between labor and management. The result in current-day Germany is a formalized, legalistic, low-conflict situation with centralized bargaining between large unions and large corporations. Lane argues that the government serves as an intermediary between unions and management.

French unions began much later and developed more slowly than did British or German unions. According to Lane (1989), there were many small companies and this fragmentation of businesses retarded union growth. In some industries, legal recognition of the right to bargain collectively occurred as late as 1969.

The lack of legal protection of French workers and the difficulties of unionization led to highly militant unions. French unions often have strong ideological orientations. They adopt anticapitalistic stances based on a belief in the unavoidability of class conflicts between owners and workers. The French ideological unions tend to compete for union members within the same organizations, the consequence of which sometimes has favored management. In many cases, management simply ignores the unions.

In the United States before 1926, there was little legal support for union activity. The Wagner Act, passed in 1935, provided the most important legal protection for unions. It granted federal protection of the right to organize and bargain collectively. U.S. unions tended early on to focus on bread-and-butter issues of wages, benefits, and working conditions. They never developed the ideological orientations of the French unions or the formal union–management cooperation of the Germans. Union membership peaked soon after the Wagner Act, during the 1940s. However, with the decline of many traditionally unionized industries and the movement of United States manufacturing offshore, union strength in the United States has continuously weakened.

In Asia, unionization has taken several different paths. As described in more detail later, formerly militant Japanese unions were absorbed in the corporate structure and now largely support management. However, Korean unions have evolved a more conflictual relationship with industry and government. For example, recent Korean labor legislation introduced more freedom for companies to fire workers. This led to student unrest and strikes costing over $2 billion in lost output in just one month (*Economist* 1997). However, in tightly controlled economies such as Singapore, where unionization has gained little, there were no days lost to industrial disputes between 1992 and 1994 (IMD 1996).

Reflecting their different ideologies and orientations, unions from different countries tend to adopt different structures. Next, you will see a summary of basic union structures in use in different countries today.

UNION STRUCTURES

Enterprise union

Represents all people in one organization, regardless of occupation or location.

Craft union

Represents people from one occupational group, such as plumbers.

Industrial union

Represents all people in a particular industry, regardless of occupational type.

Local union

Represents one occupational group in one company.

Ideological union

Represents all types of workers based on some particular ideology (e.g., communism) or religious orientation.

White-collar or professional union

Represents particular occupational group, similar to craft union.

Works council

In Germany, employee group that shares plant-level responsibility with managers over issues such as working conditions.

The type and structure of unions also reflect institutional pressures and historical traditions regarding unionization. Several major types exist. **Enterprise unions** represent all people in one organization, regardless of occupation or location. **Craft unions** represent people from one occupational group, such as plumbers. **Industrial unions** represent all people in a particular industry regardless of occupational type. **Local unions** usually represent one occupational group, in one company. However, they are often affiliated with larger craft or industrial unions. **Ideological unions** represent all workers based on some particular ideology (e.g., communism) or religious orientation. **White-collar or professional unions** also represent particular occupational groups. The nature of union structures also influences the collective-bargaining process and the general relationship between management and workers.

Enterprise unions are most often associated with Japanese labor relations, although they are not the only unions that exist now or have existed in Japan. However, most radical Japanese ideological and industrial unions were effectively crushed during the first half of the twentieth century and were replaced by enterprise unions. Sometimes called (critically) "company" unions, these unions have close associations with management. In fact, one-sixth of the executives in major Japanese companies were previously union executives (Abegglen and Stalk 1985). Not surprisingly, there is often close cooperation between union and management, with unions viewing management goals as their own.

German unions favor the industrial form of organization. There are seventeen major industrial unions, and collective bargaining generally takes place between the unions and employer associations (groups of employers). At the plant level, an elected **works council** negotiates directly with the employer over working conditions, although industry unions negotiate wages at the national or regional level. The following Multinational Management Brief shows how the works council is integrated into management decision making in Germany and is globalizing its influence following the globalization of German companies.

As noted previously, the most common objective of French unions is to organize all workers based on ideological positions. As such, union structure does not necessarily follow industry, occupation, or enterprise lines. Instead, one union will represent a variety of workers who adhere to the same ideological beliefs. Any one company may have several of these groups organizing workers.

The local union remains the major structural feature of U.S. unions. Most locals associate with some craft, industry, or mixed national union. There are approximately 170 national unions in the United States. Local craft unions tend to represent workers in a local region, while local industrial unions tend to represent workers at the level of the plant. Although most collective bargaining takes place at the local level, in some instances, such as in the automobile industry, unions attempt to make company-wide or industry-wide agreements.

IMPLICATIONS FOR THE MULTINATIONAL:
THE SEARCH FOR HARMONY

When they use local workers, multinational companies have no choice but to deal with local labor practices and traditions. As a result, the impact of dealing with

Multinational Management Brief
Globalization of the Works Council

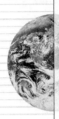

Co-determination, or, in German, *Mitbestimmung*, means that management surrenders to workers a share of the control of the organization reserved traditionally for management and owners. In Germany, co-determination exists at two levels. At the plant level, workers elect the works council. This group has certain prerogatives supported by law. Some decisions are shared with management, such as selection criteria. Some management decisions can be vetoed, such as reassignment. Finally, management must consult and inform the works council on other decisions, such as accident protection. These rights are detailed in Exhibit 12.15.

At the level of the enterprise, industrial democracy in Germany gives many workers equal representation on the board of directors with those elected by the shareholders. In practice, however, most of these arrangements include policies that favor owners and managers in tight votes. For example, one of the worker-selected representatives must be a manager.

For the Volkswagen Group, the works council has followed its globalization with the formation of the World Works Council in 1999. Although the World Works Council does not have the participatory rights granted German groups by Germany's Industrial Constitution Law, it is funded out of corporate operations and has some powers to influence the Volkswagen Group's worldwide strategic decisions.

Exhibit 12.15 Examples of Decisions and Levels of Participation by German Works Councils

Co-Determined with Management	Veto Power over Management	Consulted; or Information Provided by Management
Compensation System	Selection Criteria	Major Business Plans
Piecework Rates	Training	Introducing New Technology
Job Design	Recruitment	Introducing New Equipment
Holiday Planning	Dismissal	Financial Information
Accident Prevention	Reassignment	

Sources: Based on Lane 1989 and ILO 2000a.

Co-determination

Surrender by management to workers of a share of control of the organization, traditionally reserved for management and owners.

unions and related labor laws must be considered in any strategic decision regarding locating in another country. Consider these examples. In the United States, Japanese companies have avoided locations in the more union-friendly northern states, favoring instead southern locations with less union activism. The militant unions in western Europe have led some multinational companies to look for locations in countries like the Czech Republic, where not only are wages lower but labor conflict also seems low.

The state of a country's labor relations is just one of many factors that must be considered in designing a multinational company's IHRM policies and procedures.

Exhibit 12.16
Who Gets Along?

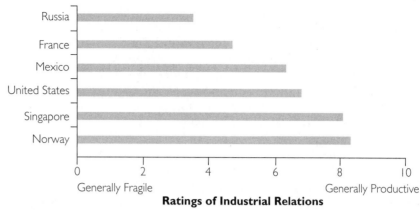

Ratings of Industrial Relations

Source: Adapted from *The World Competitiveness Yearbook 1996*, 6.25, IMD, Switzerland. Used with permission.

However, like local wage rates and worker quality, a country's labor-relations patterns also influence location decisions. Where are the favorable locations? An international survey of managers rating their own countries' relationships between managers and employees gives some hints in Exhibit 12.16.

Summary and Conclusions

This chapter highlighted fundamental national differences in the HRM processes of recruitment, selection, training and development, performance appraisal, compensation, and labor relations. The chapter also showed how multinational operations are affected by the HRM practices prevalent in host countries.

To understand why HRM practices differ, the chapter presented a model of how the national context affects HRM practices. We saw that national culture, business culture, and key social institutions—education and the legal system—affect a nation's dominant HRM practices.

To show how the model works in different national contexts, the chapter provided numerous illustrations that contrasted U.S. HRM practices with those of other nations. Countries with collectivist cultures were often chosen for comparisons because of their cultural distances from the highly individualistic U.S. national culture. The contrasts purposefully showed large differences in HRM practices to give some sense of the variety of HRM practices in the world. However, no one chapter, or book for that matter, could explain adequately all the worldwide differences in human resource management. Thus, the examples given serve only to sensitize multinational managers to the complexity of their task in the HRM area.

The chapter compared U.S. recruitment and selection practices with those in more collectivist societies. In contrast to managers used to working with the more public and legalistic U.S. practices, managers from collectivist societies believe that personal contact is the best method to recruit and identify the best employees.

The chapter noted that training of entry-level workers depends largely on the institutional structure of the educational system. U.S. managers are increasingly concerned that workers do not have the basic educational skills necessary to succeed in jobs that are more complex. In contrast, Germany has perhaps the best system of technical training, based on a collaboration of companies, unions, and the government. Many other countries, however, including some of the transitioning economies and developing countries, have educational systems that produce potential workers with good mathematics and science skills.

Later in the chapter we saw that management-development practices are embedded in cultural expectations regarding the relationship of managers with their organizations. U.S. companies face the dilemma of investing to develop top management talent and then risk that these managers will go to another company. In more collectivist national cultures, such as Japan and Korea, managers have more commitment to remain with the organization (they often have little choice). As such, companies can take a long-term view of investing in extensive management development and training.

To avoid legal ramifications of race, gender, and age biases, the discussion showed that U.S. performance-evaluation systems tend to be formal and public. In collectivist societies, in contrast, performance appraisal tends to be informal and more secret. In the United States, rewards—in particular, compensation—are linked to the results of performance appraisals. In collectivist societies, factors such as age, family situation, loyalty to the company, and relationship to the owners often influence rewards more than performance does.

Most multinational companies are attracted to production sites in countries where the wages are low but the talent pool is strong. As such, they tend to adopt host country wage and salary levels. However, the extent of adaptation of other HRM practices depends largely on the IHRM orientation of the multinational company. Usually, polycentric companies let local managers follow local HRM practices. Ethnocentric companies try to follow headquarters' practices as much as they can. They adapt only if they must. Firms with transnational strategies and global IHRM practices tend to develop worldwide HRM systems that are flexible enough to fit most host country locations.

Transnational strategists also use similar management-development practices throughout the world: a global IHRM system for managers that recruits, selects, and develops the best talent regardless of nationality. In contrast, companies with polycentric, regiocentric, or ethnocentric IHRM orientations often have a glass ceiling for host country managers. This ceiling retards extensive management development for host country nationals.

Confronting and dealing with differences in traditions and volatility of labor relationships are unavoidable activities in running operations in different countries. Multinational companies can seldom change a country's traditions of labor relations. Consequently, the volatility of host country labor often becomes a key factor in choosing host locations.

Whether a company establishes a joint venture in another country or sets up wholly owned operations in another country, a detailed study of the HRM practices of the local environment is required. History, tradition, culture, and social institutions (education and legal and government systems) create unique HRM practices in each country. Moreover, even countries that are similar culturally often have different historical and traditional patterns of labor relations. Thus, a successful multinational manager comes prepared not only with a knowledge of local culture but also with an understanding of how HRM practices evolved to become part of a host country's business environment.

Discussion Questions

1. Describe and discuss the major factors in the national context that affect a nation's HRM practices.

2. Compare and contrast recruitment and selection strategies in the United States and in nations with more collectivist cultures. Discuss legal and cultural problems that multinational managers might face using a collectivist approach to recruitment and selection in the United States and using a U.S. approach in more collectivist cultures.

3. Some U.S. politicians have called for the development of a German-type apprenticeship-training system in the United States. If you were a manager of a U.S. Fortune 500 multinational company, how would you respond to this proposal and why?

4. Discuss the advantages and disadvantages of a permanent-employment system for managers. Discuss how this system might work for non-Asian countries besides the United States.

5. You have been given the assignment of setting up a training program for first-level managers in a formerly government-owned Eastern European company. How would you go about developing a curriculum? Why?

6. Compare and contrast the appraisal and compensation systems in the United States and more collectivist-culture nations. Discuss legal and cultural problems that multinational managers might face using a collectivist approach to these systems in the United States and using a U.S. approach in more collectivist cultures.

7. Contrast the different types of unions and discuss the challenges each type might pose to a multinational manager.

Chapter Internet Activity

Check the latest data on wages and salaries around the world. The United Nations (http://www.un.org), the U.S. Department of Labor (http://www.dol.gov), the International Labour Organization (http://www.ilo.org), and Union Bank in Switzerland (http://www.ubs.com) provide the data you need.

Internet Sites

Selected Companies in the Chapter

Asahi Breweries   http://www.asahibeer.co.jp
Captura Software   http://www.captura.com
Ford Corp.   http://www.ford.com/
GE   http://www.ge.com/
Hyundai Group   http://www.hmc.co.kr
Keio University   http://www.keio.ac.jp/
Kyoto University   http://www.kyoto-u.ac.jp/English
Mercedes-Benz   http://www.mercedes.com
Motorola, Inc.   http://www.mot.com/
Otis Elevator Co.   http://www.otis.com/
Technical Resources, Inc.   http://www.techrecruiting.com
Unilever   http://www.unilever.com/
Waseda University   http://www.waseda.ac.jp/

Look Here for HRM Practices for Countries throughout the World

http://www.ilo.org   *International Labour Organization provides data on labor conditions, human rights, labor laws, and even translations of labor terms in several languages.*

http://www.ubs.com/   *Union Bank of Switzerland economics research location—includes prices and earnings for cities and occupations from around the globe.*

http://www.sHRM.org/   *The Society for Human Resource Management's source for HR topics of all varieties.*

http://www.worldbank.org/   *World Bank Living Standards Measurement Survey, World Development Report.*

http://stats.bls.gov   *U.S. Bureau of Labor Statistics.*

http://www.rici.com   *International Career Info, Inc. (Japan and United States; bilingual).*

http://www.imd.ch/   *The Institute for Management Development publishes a home page with extensive summaries of cross-national economic and trade data, as well as survey data on cross-national management and HRM issues.*

Chapter Activity: The HRM Component in a Multinational Company's Location Decision

Step 1: Read the following multinational problem.

You are now a vice president for human resources for the XYZ company located in the United States. Your company manufactures components for industrial robots. Employees need U.S. high-school-level ability in reading and mathematics to maintain job skills.

You have just come from a meeting where the CEO has asked all functional-area vice presidents to prepare a report concerning the location advantages or disadvantages of country _____. Marketing and production VPs will look at issues such as potential market size and the availability of raw materials and supply and sales distribution channels. Your job is to consider the nature of the labor force should your company decide to set up operations in _____. You will need to plan for a host country national workforce of two hundred production workers, ten first-line managers, and two mid-level managers.

Step 2: Picking teams and countries.

Your instructor will divide you into teams of three to five people. Each team will choose a different country for a prospective location. Your team will act in the role of the vice president for human resources and will prepare the report called for in Step 1. Your instructor may also require that you work within a specific industry.

This is a library research project. Your instructor may provide you with general data sources. You may also use information from the text.

Step 3: Prepare reports.

Reports may be written, oral, or both. A typical report analyzes the implications of economic, cultural, and institutional factors as they might affect all of the HRM functions discussed in this chapter. Below are some key topics that must be addressed. Your instructor may assign additional topics to consider.

A. Economic considerations:
Comparative wage and salary levels of this country with other countries.
Employment levels including workforce participation of women and youth.
Employer-provided benefits.
Characteristics of labor relations (e.g., likelihood of work stoppages).

B. Institutional conditions:
Availability of educated workers.
Extent of government intervention in employment—wage levels, benefit requirements, policies for layoffs, mandated holidays, other labor legislation.
Legal power of unions.

C. National and business cultures:
Effects of dominant religion and language on labor relations.
Cultural effects of the relationship of the employee with the organization—long term, family dominated, preference for larger or smaller organizations, etc.
Traditions regarding union types and labor.

D. Analysis:
Costs and benefits of locating in this country.
Solutions for potential problems.
Recommendation to the president.

Step 4: Present your findings.

Oral reports for this exercise will take between one-half to one and one-half hours, depending on your instructor's requirements.

Source: Adapted from Balfour 1988–1989.

References

Abegglen, James C., and George Stalk, Jr. 1985. *Kaisha: The Japanese Corporation.* New York: Basic.

Arkin, Anat. 1992a. "Personnel management in Germany: At work in the powerhouse of Europe." *Personnel Management,* February, 32–35.

———. 1992b. "Personnel management in Denmark: The land of social welfare." *Personnel Management,* March, 32–35.

Balfour, Alan. 1988–1989. "A beginning focus for teaching international human resources administration." *Organizational Behavior Teaching Review* 13:2, 79–89.

Barney, J.B. 1991. "Firm resources and sustained competitive advantage." *Journal of Management,* 17: 99–120.

Benjamin, Daniel. 1993. "Losing its edge: Germany is troubled by how little work its workers are doing." *Wall Street Journal,* May 6, A1, A4.

Bennet, Amanda. 1992. "Executive pay: An international survey." *Wall Street Journal,* October 12, B6.

Bohlander, George W., Scott Snell, and Arthur W. Sherman, Jr. 2001. *Managing Human Resources.* Cincinnati: South-Western.

Bondreau, John W. 1991. "Utility analysis in human resource management decision." In *Handbook of Industrial and Organizational Psychology,* edited by M. D. Dunnette and Latta M. Hough, 1111–43. 2d ed. Palo Alto: Consulting Psychology Press.

Bureau of National Affairs. 1988. *Recruiting and Selection Procedures, Personnel Policies Forum.* Washington, D.C.: Bureau of National Affairs, Inc. No. 46, May, 9–11.

Business Week Online. 1996a. "How Nike's pay stacks up." July 9, chart.

———. 1996b. August 23, chart.

Caplan, Janice. 1992. "Personnel management in Italy: It's the climate that counts." *Personnel Management,* April, 32–35.

Cook, Mary F. 1993. *The Human Resources Yearbook 1993/1994 Edition.* Englewood Cliffs, N.J.: Prentice Hall.

———. 1997. "Choosing the right recruitment tool." *HR Focus,* 74, s7–s8.

DeMente, Boye. 1988. *Korean Etiquette and Business Ethics in Business.* Lincolnwood, Ill.: NTC Business Books.

Economist. 1997. "The trouble with South Korea." January 18, 59–60.

———. 1997. "Who's top?" March 29, 21–22.

———. 1999. "Putting the bounce back into Matsushita." May 20, http://www.Ecomomist.com.

Filipezak, Bob. 1992. "What employees teach." *Training,* October, 44.

Guttmann, M. (ed.). 1994. *Prices and Earning around the Globe.* 1994 ed. Zurich, Switzerland: Union Bank of Switzerland.

Hansen, Fay. 1998. "Incentive plans are now commonplace in large firms." *Compensation and Benefits Review,* 30, 8.

Hofstede, Geert. 1991. *Cultures and Organizations.* London: McGraw-Hill.

Humphrey, J. 1998. "Globalisation and supply chain networks in the auto industry: Brazil and India." In *International Workshop, Global Production and Local Jobs.* Geneva: Interntional Institute for Labour Studies.

IMD. 1996. *The World Competitiveness Yearbook 1996.* Lausanne, Switzerland: IMD.

International Labor Organization (ILO). 1997a. *World Employment Report 1996–97.* Geneva: International Labor Office.

———. 1997b. *World Labour Report 1997–98.* Geneva: International Labor Office.

———. 1999. *World Employment Report 1998–99.* Geneva: International Labor Office.

———. 2000a. "Globalization of works council activities." *World of Work,* 36, http://www.ilo.org/public/english/bureau/inf/magazine/36/.

———. 2000b. *Key Indicators of the Labor Market 2000.* Geneva: International Labor Office.

Kelly, Kevin, and Peter Burrows. 1994. "Motorola: Training for the millennium." *Business Week Online,* March 28.

Karp, Jonathan and Michael Williams. 1997. "Firms in India use buyouts to skirt layoff rules." *Wall Street Journal,* October 13, A 16.

Kodama, Tomomi. 1992. "Observations on the differences and similarities in the Japanese and U.S. benefits system." *Employee Benefit Notes,* August, 1–2.

Koretz, Gene. 1990. "Why unions thrive abroad." *Business Week,* September 10, 26.

Kras, Eva S. 1995. *Management in Two Cultures.* Yarmouth, Maine: Intercultural Press.

Lancaster, Hal. 1996. "How you can learn to feel at home in a foreign-based firm." *Wall Street Journal,* June 4, B1.

Lane, Christel. 1989. *Management and Labour in Europe.* Aldershot, England: Edward Elgar.

Langer, Steven. 1993. "The Abbott, Langer & Associates Compensation & Benefits Reports." In *The Human Resource Yearbook 1993/1994 Ed.,* edited by Mary F. Cook, 5.12–5.38. Englewood Cliffs, N.J.: Prentice Hall.

Lee, Chris. 1992. "The budget blahs." *Training* 29:10, 31–58.

Locher, Alan H., and Kenneth S. Teel. 1988. "Appraisal trends." *Personnel Journal* 67:9, 139–45.

Macharzina, Klaus. 2000. "Editorial: The Japanese model—out of date?" *Management International Review,* 40, 103–6.

Management First.com. 2001. "Job cutting, Japanese style." http://www.managementfirst.com.

Milkovich, George J., and John W. Bondreau. 1994. *Human Resource Management.* Homewood, Ill.: Irwin.

Mroczkowski, Tomasz, and Masao Hanaoka. 1989. "Continuity and change in Japanese management." *California Management Review,* Winter, 39–52.

OECD. 2000. *Education at a Glance: OECD Indicators.* Organisation for Economic Co-operation and Development.

Orru, Marco. 1991. "The institutional logic of small-firm economics in Italy and Taiwan." *Studies in Comparative International Development* 26:3–28.

Poe, Andrea C. 1999. "When in Rome . . . European law and tradition back generous vacation policies." *HR Magazine,* 44, HR Magazine Online Archive, http://www.my.sHRM.org.

Poole, M. 1986. *Industrial Relations: Heritage and Adjustment.* Oxford: Oxford University Press.

Porter, Michael E. 1990. *The Competitive Advantage on Nations.* New York: Free Press.

Rohlen, Thomas P. 1983. *Japan's High Schools.* Berkeley: University of California Press.

Schlender, Brenton R. 1994. "Japan's white collar blues." *Business Week,* March 21, 97–104.

Schmidt, Richard. 1997. "Japanese management, recession style." *Business Horizons,* 39, 70–75.

Steers, Richard M., Yoo Keun Shin, and Gerardo R. Ungson. 1989. *The Chaebol: Korea's New Industrial Might.* New York: HarperBusiness.

Sunoo, Brenda Paik. 2000. "Employment laws in Mexico." http://www.workforce.com.

Takahashi, Shunsuke. 1993. "New trends on human resource management in Japan." In *The Human Resource Yearbook 1993/1994 Ed.,* edited by Mary F. Cook, 1.37–1.38. Englewood Cliffs, N.J.: Prentice Hall.

Terpstra, David. 1996. "The search for effective methods." *HR Focus,* May, 5 16–19.

———, Vern, and Kenneth David. 1991. *The Cultural Environment of International Business.* Cincinnati: South-Western.

Thornton, Emily. 1999. "Corporate Japan: No room at the top." *Businessweek Online,* August 9.

Towers Perrin. 2000. *Worldwide Total Remuneration: The Evolution of Global Compensation Strategies.* http://www.towers.com/wtr/.

Union Bank Switzerland. 2000. *Prices and Earnings.* http://www.ubs.com.

U.S. Census Bureau. 1999. *Statistical Abstracts of the United States, Comparative International Statistics.* Washington, D.C.: U.S. Government Printing Office.

U.S. Department of Labor. 1993. *Employment and Earnings, January 1993.* Washington, D.C.: U.S. Government Printing Office.

———. 1995. *Hourly Compensation Costs for Production Workers, June 1995.* Washington, D.C.: U.S. Government Printing Office.

———. 2000. "International comparisons of manufacturing costs and labor productivity trends." http://stats.bls.gov/special.requests/ForeignLabor/flsprod4.pdf:.

Van Buren, Mark E. and Stephen B. King. 2000. "ASTD's annual accounting of worldwide patterns in employer-provided training." *Training & Development.* Supplement, The 2000 ASTD International Comparisons Report, 1–24.

Vlasic, Bill. 1997. "In Alabama, the soul of a new Mercedes?" *Business Week Online,* April 1.

Wall Street Journal. 1999. "Hyundai unit to pay recruiter $9.5 million in discrimination case." April 26, B 8.

Werther, William B., and Keith Davis. 1993. *Human Resources and Personnel Management.* New York: McGraw-Hill.

Zucker, L.G. 1987. "Institutional theories of organization." *Annual Review of Sociology.* 13:443–64.

Chapter 13

Motivation in Multinational Companies

LEARNING OBJECTIVES
After reading this chapter you should be able to:

- **Know how people from different nations perceive the basic functions of working.**

- **Know how people from different nations view the importance of working.**

- **Understand how the national context affects the basic processes of work motivation.**

- **Be able to apply common theories of work motivation in different national contexts.**

- **Be able to design jobs for high motivational potential in different national cultures.**

Preview Case in Point	A challenge for multinational managers is to find the right mix of rewards that local workers find motivating. The move of multinational companies into China has created an intense competition for good workers. In a country where the average wage is $250 a year, money talks, especially in recruitment and retention. Skilled secretaries get monthly salaries that match or even double the yearly national average. When companies don't match the local market wages, job performance drops and turnover increases.
Rewards in China	Rapidly increasing salaries for new recruits can be demotivating for current employees, says Debbie Lieu, a consultant in Shanghai. Internal pay equity is a concern when current employees make less than new hires. Surprisingly, however, this equity imbalance is not a problem if the highly paid are expatriates and not local Chinese nationals.

Good pay, however, is not sufficient to keep a motivated Chinese workforce. Opportunities for training such as Johnson & Johnson's executive MBA program with the University of Singapore and opportunities for promotion are high motivators for Chinese managers. One Hong Kong based consultant notes that a corporate culture that signals respect for employees and clear pathways for advancement produces the most motivated Chinese workers.

Source: Based on Johnson 1998. |

To implement multinational strategies successfully, earlier chapters showed how managers select the best organizational designs and the best international HRM policies. However, the best strategy, the best organizational design, and the best international HRM practices will not guarantee success. The multinational manager must also understand how to motivate and lead international employees with diverse cultural backgrounds and different expectations about work. Thus, this chapter focuses on motivation in the multinational enterprise. The next chapter will build on your understanding of motivation to identify leadership options in the multinational setting.

All managers must motivate their subordinates to accomplish organizational goals. However, as the Preview Case in Point shows, motivational techniques vary by cultural setting. Multinational companies in China face an array of challenges to attract, retain, and motivate a workforce in a rapidly changing labor market. All multinational companies face the difficult task of motivating culturally diverse workers in an array of national settings. To provide the background necessary to understand how to motivate workers in multinational organizations, this chapter reviews international differences in work values and the meaning of work, discusses major theories of motivation and their multinational applications, and reviews U.S. and European views of designing jobs to produce high levels of motivation.

WORK VALUES AND THE MEANING OF WORK

Before we can understand how to motivate or lead people from different national cultures, we must have some knowledge of what work means to people from different societies. There are two basic questions to answer. Why do people work? What do people value in work?

Exhibit 13.1 Ratings of Major Functions at Work

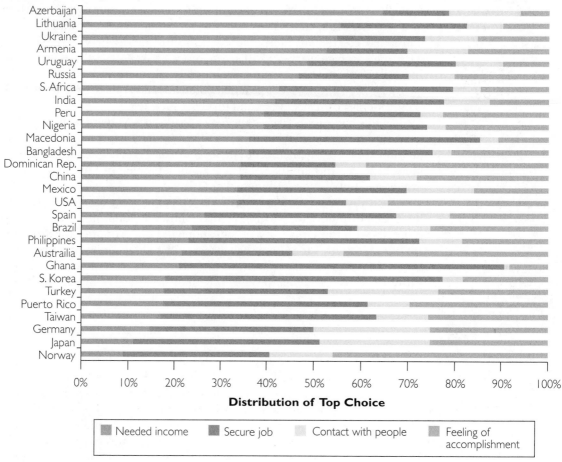

Distribution of Top Choice

- Needed income
- Secure job
- Contact with people
- Feeling of accomplishment

Source: Computed from original data in Inglehart et al. 2000.

WHY DO PEOPLE WORK?

To answer this question, several major international research projects studied thousands of workers from several countries. These studies included workers in all types of occupations: professional, managerial, clerical, service, and production workers (Meaning of Work International Research Team 1987).

The most recent study, the World Values Surveys and European Values Surveys (WVS/EVS) (Inglehart et al. 2000), contains information on people's attitudes toward work and life from 50 countries that include the majority of the world's population.

One question addressed in the surveys that is important to multinational managers is whether people from different countries have different reasons for working. To answer this question, each person was asked what he or she most expected from a job. We call these the **functions of work**. As Exhibit 13.1 shows, four major functions of work were most popular: providing needed income, security, contact with other people, and a feeling of accomplishment.

The most important finding is that people from different nations did not assign the same magnitude of importance to these work functions. Most of the transition economies (e.g., Azerbaijan and Lithuania) and many of the developing nations (e.g., India) rate getting needed income a higher priority than the other functions.

Functions of work

Outcomes such as providing necessary income and providing satisfactory experiences.

Exhibit 13.2
Differences in Work
Centrality in Seven
Countries

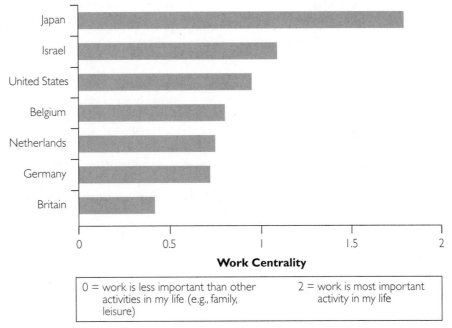

Source: Adapted from Meaning of Work International Research Team 1987.

This probably reflects the situation in many of these countries where the income from work is instrumental to survival. In contrast, many of the collectivist cultures and the social democracies rate contact with and getting a feeling of accomplishment as more important. Consequently, when crafting their motivational strategies for a local workforce, multinational managers must not assume that people from different nations have the same reasons for working.

WHAT DO PEOPLE VALUE IN WORK?

Work centrality

Overall value of work in a person's life.

In addition to the basic functions of work, a second key value related to work is called work centrality. **Work centrality** is "the degree of general importance that working has in the life of an individual at any given point in time" (MOW 1987). Work centrality represents the importance of work in a person's life when compared with other activities, including leisure, family, community, and religion. Exhibit 13.2 shows the differences in work centrality for seven countries. Clearly, work has a dominant role in the lives of the Japanese.

Higher levels of work centrality also closely correlated with the average number of hours worked per week in the country (see Chapter 12 on national differences in human resource management for comparative data): People from countries with greater work centrality usually work more hours. The average Japanese worker, for example, puts in more hours than his or her counterpart in most other industrialized nations.

High levels of work centrality may lead to dedicated workers and effective organizations. However, as the following Multinational Management Brief shows, high levels of work centrality can also have adverse effects on workers. Evidence suggests that the number of hours worked by the Japanese is declining and many workers are complaining of burnout, perhaps indicating a change in work centrality for this country (Grant 1997).

Multinational Management Brief

Karoushi and *Karojisatus*—Sudden Death or Suicide from Overwork

The Japanese word *"karoushi"* translates in English as "sudden death from overwork." *Karojisatus* is suicide from overwork. As we saw in Chapter 12, the Japanese work more hours than people from most other countries do. They also have the highest work-centrality score.

This psychological and time commitment to working probably accounts for some of the Japanese economic growth. However, there is some indication that the benefits may have physical and psychological costs. As most of the managers who led Japan through its period of growth reach later middle age, the costs to them of long working hours and other Japanese business practices (long hours of drinking and smoking with colleagues after work) may be taking its toll. Early evidence suggests that death from work-related stress is on the rise. Police estimate the number of work-related suicides at 1,300 annually, but they have no official classification for this type of death. Some lawyers representing surviving family members put the estimate higher.

Sources: Based on Kageyama 1998 and Tubbs 1993.

Importance of work

Goals that people hope to achieve from working.

Besides examining the functions of work, the WVS/EVS study also looked at the importance of different work characteristics. The idea of the importance of work is closely related to the idea of the functions of work just discussed. However, the values attached to work functions reflect societal norms regarding *why people have to work or what they hope to get from a job.* The **importance of work** characteristics, on the other hand, reflects societal norms regarding *what people value in their current job.*

The WVS/EVS research team asked workers to note what characteristics of a job they believe are important. The rankings of the work characteristics (for 50 countries) are: Generous holidays (73%), An opportunity to use initiative (53%), Good hours (53%), A job respected by people (50%), A responsible job (56%), A job in which you feel you can achieve something (42%), A job that is interesting (39%), A job that meets one's abilities (36%), Good job security (30%), and Good pay (19%).

Note that for an existing job pay ranks as less important than it did in Exhibit 13.1 for the functions of work. Also, the reward of a generous holiday is almost a cultural universal: it is ranked first by nearly all countries. However, as one can see from Exhibit 13.3, the priorities given to different job characteristics do vary by country. Note, for example, that Japan and Russia differ from the world trend of giving a high priority to holidays. In spite of pay being a dominant function of work for many of the transitions and developing nations, no country rated pay as the most important work characteristic.

The earlier Meaning of Work study and the more current WVS/EVS study give us a good beginning picture of how work values differ in national contexts. They suggest the following conclusions:

- In some societies, work is very central and absorbs much of a person's life. People in such societies willingly work long hours and have a strong commitment to succeeding at work.
- All people hope to receive certain benefits from work. Regardless of national context, money is a necessity, but it is not enough. Other emotional and practi-

Exhibit 13.3 Importance Rankings of Work Characteristics in Nine Countries

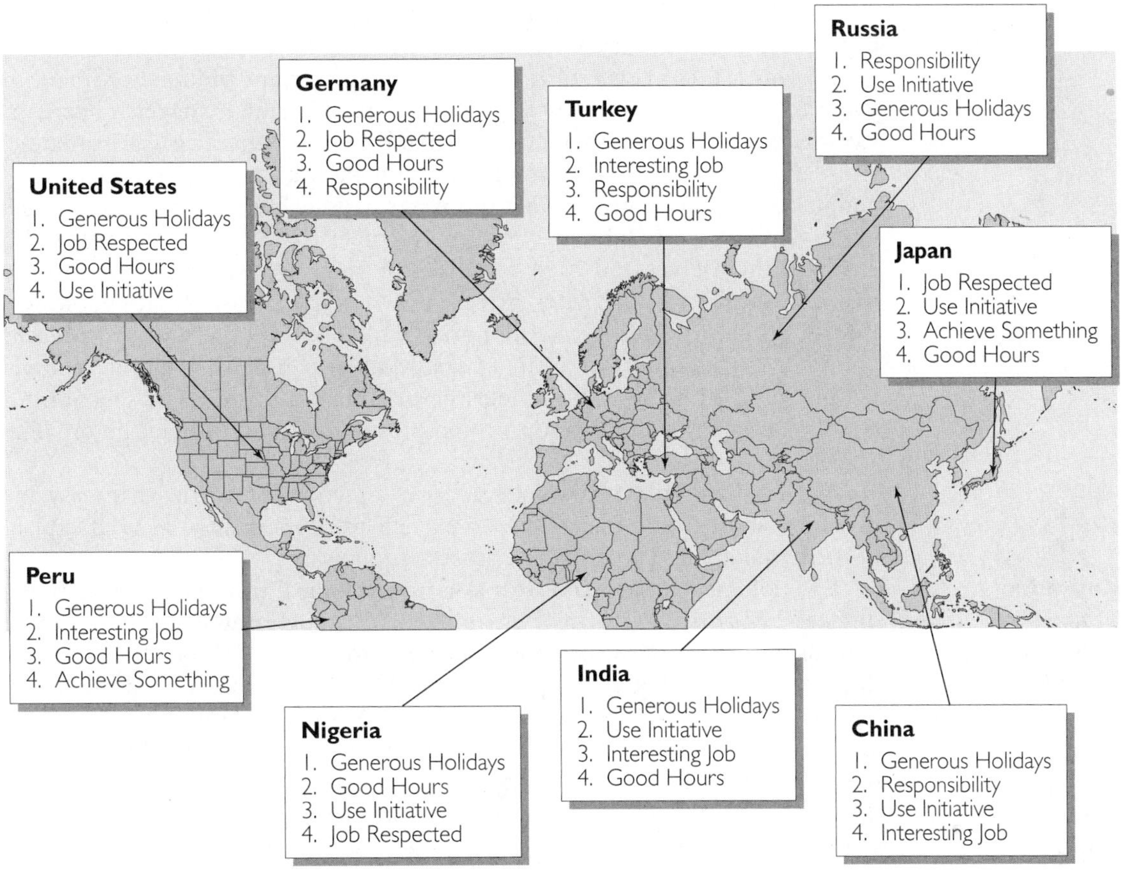

Russia
1. Responsibility
2. Use Initiative
3. Generous Holidays
4. Good Hours

Germany
1. Generous Holidays
2. Job Respected
3. Good Hours
4. Responsibility

Turkey
1. Generous Holidays
2. Interesting Job
3. Responsibility
4. Good Hours

United States
1. Generous Holidays
2. Job Respected
3. Good Hours
4. Use Initiative

Japan
1. Job Respected
2. Use Initiative
3. Achieve Something
4. Good Hours

Peru
1. Generous Holidays
2. Interesting Job
3. Good Hours
4. Achieve Something

Nigeria
1. Generous Holidays
2. Good Hours
3. Use Initiative
4. Job Respected

India
1. Generous Holidays
2. Use Initiative
3. Interesting Job
4. Good Hours

China
1. Generous Holidays
2. Responsibility
3. Use Initiative
4. Interesting Job

Source: Based on data made available by Inglehart et al. 2000.

cal benefits derived from work may have higher priorities. The benefits people hope to get from their jobs vary by national context.

- The first key to successful motivation strategies in multinational companies is understanding the differences among countries in the functions of work, work centrality, and the priorities given to different job characteristics.

Multinational managers must understand that people from different countries often have different reasons for working and priorities regarding the important attributes of their jobs. However, although this knowledge is important, is it sufficient to motivate and manage a multinational workforce successfully? Probably not. To use the knowledge of national differences in work attitudes for motivational purposes, a multinational manager also needs to understand how basic motivational principles work in the multinational environment. To give you this background, the next sections provide reviews of the basic work-motivation process, popular theories of work motivation, and applications of work-motivation theories to multinational settings.

WORK MOTIVATION AND THE NATIONAL CONTEXT

THE BASIC WORK-MOTIVATION PROCESS

Why do some people set goals that are more difficult and put forth more effort to achieve their goals than others? Why do some students seek "A's" while other students feel satisfied with "C's"? Why do some workers seek jobs that are more difficult and work harder at them, even if the pay is not higher? These questions address the issue of motivation.

Motivation concerns all managers. Managers want their subordinates motivated to achieve organizational goals. Toward this end, managers choose incentives (e.g., pay, promotion, recognition) and punishments (e.g., salary reduction), and design work (e.g., with simple or complex tasks) based on their assumptions and knowledge concerning what motivates people. For example, if a manager believes that her subordinates work only to meet basic needs such as feeding and clothing themselves and their families, she may use wages and bonuses as her major motivational tool. Alternatively, if a manager believes that people work to find fulfillment in doing a challenging job well, she might assign subordinates complex, varied, and interesting tasks. Managers usually respond positively to people (e.g., with raises) who help the organization achieve its goals and negatively (e.g., with bad evaluations) to employees who fail to help the organization achieve its goals.

The left hand side of Exhibit 13.4 gives a picture summarizing the psychological processes that most experts use to explain work motivation. A brief explanation of these underlying psychological processes follows.

Motivation

A psychological process resulting in goal-directed behavior that satisfies human needs.

Need

Feeling of deficit or lacking that all people experience at some time.

Goal-directed behavior

One that people use with the intention of satisfying a need.

Psychologists see **motivation** as a psychological process that results in goal-directed behaviors that satisfy human needs. Although **needs** differ for individuals and for cultural groups, all people seek to satisfy needs. A need is a feeling of a deficit or lacking that all people experience at some time. A need might be very basic, such as being hungry for the next meal. A need might be more complex, such as the need to be the best at whatever one attempts. To satisfy the hunger need, you may go to work to earn money to buy food. To satisfy an achievement need, you might practice ice skating daily with the ultimate goal of becoming an Olympic champion. In each case, a person uses **goal-directed behaviors** (work or practice) to satisfy unfulfilled or unsatisfied needs (i.e., hunger or the need for achievement). Goal-directed behaviors are behaviors that people use with the intention of satisfying a need.

Although satisfying needs is a general condition for human motivation, people use the work setting to satisfy many needs. For example, for most people, work is necessary to provide food and shelter. In addition, as you saw from the WVS/EVS study, working provides people with an opportunity to satisfy needs such as affording leisure, having interesting things to do, having responsibility, a chance to use initiative, and developing relationships with other people. Many theories of work motivation have a basic assumption that people will work harder if they can satisfy more of their needs on the job.

Because most goal-directed behaviors take place in a social context, motivation includes more than satisfying needs; that is, when we do things that affect others, people reactive positively or negatively to what we do. In reinforcement theory, we call these reactions reinforcement and punishment. **Reinforcement** means that the consequences that follow a person's behavior encourage the person to continue the behavior. **Punishment** means that the consequences that follow a person's behavior encourage the person to stop the behavior. In the work setting, for example, managers use reinforcement (such as bonus pay) to encourage certain behaviors, such as higher daily output. Managers also use punishment (such as docking pay) to discourage behaviors such as missing days of work. Based on whether they meet their needs at work and how managers react to their behaviors at work, employees may put more or less effort into work, feel satisfied or dissatisfied, or stay with or leave the organization.

Reinforcement

Reactions to a person's behavior that encourage the person to continue the behavior.

Punishment

Consequences of a person's behavior that discourage the behavior.

Exhibit 13.4 The Basic Work Motivation Process and the National Context

Individual Work Motivation	National Context (Culture and Social Institutions)
UNSATISFIED NEEDS	**DEFINES THE IMPORTANCE OF DIFFERENT NEEDS** (being accepted by group more important than individual achievement; low socioeconomic development gives priority to survival needs)
GOAL-DIRECTED BEHAVIOR TO SATISFY NEEDS	**DEFINES LEGITIMATE WORK BEHAVIORS** (long work hours considered normal; labor relations law requires less than a 35-hour work week)
REINFORCEMENT OR PUNISHMENT	**DEFINES WHAT IS REWARDED OR PUNISHED AND HOW** (highest punishment is being ignored by group; laws make firing a worker nearly impossible)
CONTINUE OR STOP BEHAVIOR; STAY OR LEAVE THE ORGANIZATION	**DEFINES RELATIONSHIP WITH ORGANIZATION** (people have moral obligation to remain with organization; labor market allows workers to move easily between organizations)

Sources: Adapted from Hellriegel, Slocum, and Woodman 2001 and Kanugo and Wright 1983.

NATIONAL CONTEXT AND WORK MOTIVATION: A BRIEF INTRODUCTION

Although certain basic needs are common to all humans (e.g., the need for food and shelter), the national context (culture and the social institutions) influences all steps of the motivational process. The right-hand side of Exhibit 13.4 shows the effects of the national context on the work-motivation process. Each box contains two examples. One example shows an effect of national culture on the motivation process. The other example shows an effect of social institutions on the motivational process. More explanation and examples follow.

Cultural values, norms, and supporting social institutions influence the priority that people attach to work in general and the types of needs that people hope to satisfy at work. For example, early education and childhood games encourage people in collectivist societies to develop a need to belong to groups. The national context also helps define what behaviors at work provide legitimate ways to satisfy needs. For example, in countries such as Japan, where work is central to a person's status and self-image, seeking a job in the largest and most prestigious company satisfies a need for achievement.

The national context influences reactions to goal-directed behaviors at work. For example, if a Japanese worker brags about her performance, she is likely to be sanctioned by her work group. The Japanese have a saying: "The nail that stands out gets hammered down." Finally, national culture and social institutions also influence the levels of satisfaction workers expect to receive in an organization and how committed workers are to their organization and its goals. For example, in countries where labor is well organized and militant, resistance to increases in work productivity is considered legitimate.

This brief overview of work motivation and the effects of the national context provides only an introduction to the complexities a multinational manager faces in the motivation of international workers. Next, to explore in more depth the challenges of motivating a culturally diverse workforce, the chapter expands on the basic model of work motivation. In the following sections you will see reviews of several motivation theories and a discussion of how the national context influences the application of each motivation theory and how the theory can be used by the multinational manager.

THEORIES OF WORK MOTIVATION IN THE MULTINATIONAL CONTEXT

Need theory

Of motivation, assumes that people can satisfy basic human needs in the work setting.

Why do we need work-motivation theories? Work-motivation theories attempt to show how the basic motivational processes apply to a work setting. Managers can use motivation theories to develop systematic approaches to motivating employees on the job. There are two basic types of motivational theories, **need theories** and **process theories**. The following section summarizes the major need theories of motivation. More than other motivational theories, need theories have the most international applications. A later section considers process theories.

NEED THEORIES OF MOTIVATION

Process theories

Of motivation, arising from needs and values combined with an individual's beliefs regarding the work environment.

Need theories of motivation rest on the assumption that people can satisfy basic human needs in the work setting. That is, people are motivated to work because their jobs satisfy both basic needs, such as money for food and shelter, and higher-level needs, such as personal growth.

There are four popular need theories of motivation. These are Maslow's Hierarchy of Needs, ERG Theory, Motivator-Hygiene Theory, and Achievement Motivation Theory. Before considering the multinational applications of need theories of motivation, this section provides a brief review of each theory. You can find more detailed reviews of these and other theories of motivation in courses and texts in organizational behavior.

Exhibit 13.5 gives a summary and comparison of the four popular need theories. It also shows the characteristics of jobs that can satisfy the types of needs identified by these theories.

MASLOW'S HIERARCHY OF NEEDS

Hierarchy of needs theory

States that people have five basic types of needs: physiological, security, affiliation, esteem, and self-actualization.

The psychologist Abraham Maslow (1970) offered perhaps the most famous need theory of motivation. The **hierarchy of needs theory** states that people have five basic types of needs: physiological, security, affiliation, esteem, and self-actualization. Physiological needs include basic survival such as food, water, air, and shelter. Security needs include safety and the avoidance of pain and life-threatening situations. Affiliation needs include being loved, friendship, and belonging to a human group. Esteem needs focus on respect, recognition by others, and feeling of self-worth. Self-

Exhibit 13.5 Need Theories of Motivation

Source of Need Satisfaction on the Job	Maslow's Needs Hierarchy	ERG Theory	Motivator-Hygiene Theory	Achievement Motivation
• *Advancement* • *Use of Ability* • *Meaningful Work* • *Achievement* • *Interesting Job*	Self-Actualization	Growth	Motivators • Advancement • Growth • Achievement	Need for Achievement
• *Recognition* • *Influence* • *Esteem*	Esteem			Need for Power
• *Coworker Support* • *Supervisor Support* • *Social Interaction*	Affiliation	Relatedness	Hygiene Factors • Working conditions • Job security • Salary	Need for Affiliation
• *Work Conditions* • *Benefits* • *Security*	Security	Existence		
• *Base Pay*	Physiological			

Sources: Adapted from Daft 1991; Gordon 1987 and Hellriegel, Slocum, Woodman 2001.

actualization needs, the highest level in Maslow's theory, reflect needs of maximizing personal achievement.

Maslow believed that the five basic needs follow a hierarchy from lower-level or basic needs to higher-level needs. First people seek to satisfy lower-level needs, such as the physiological need for food and shelter. After they fulfill these lower-level needs, people seek to satisfy higher-level needs, such as the need for esteem. According to Maslow, once a need is satisfied, it no longer motivates. Thus, for example, if your base pay is adequate for survival, it has no motivational value. Then other charactersitics of the work situation, such as working in teams to meet affiliation needs, become motivational. Current opinion on Maslow's approach suggests that, while there are two groups of needs representing higher- and lower-level needs, the need hierarchy does not work in sequence. Moreover, not all available jobs in a country provide the activities required to meet all levels of needs (Pinder 1984).

ALDERFER'S ERG THEORY

ERG theory

Simplified hierarchy of needs, including growth needs, relatedness needs, and existence needs.

Clay Alderfer (1972) developed **ERG theory** as a simplified hierarchy of needs having only three levels (see Exhibit 13.5 for a comparison with Maslow). These needs include growth needs, relatedness needs, and existence needs. Growth needs are similar to Maslow's self-actualization and esteem needs. Work is motivating when it gives the opportunity for personal growth, such as by using one's creativity. Relational needs are similar to Maslow's affiliation needs. Getting support from one's work group satisfies relational needs. Existence needs are lower-level needs and represent basic survival needs.

In ERG theory, frustration of a need motivates behavior to satisfy the need. In addition, if a person cannot satisfy a higher-level need, she or he will seek to satisfy lower-level needs. For example, if the satisfaction of growth needs is impossible on the job, satisfaction of relational needs becomes the prime motivator.

MOTIVATOR-HYGIENE THEORY

Motivator-hygiene theory

Assumption that a job has two basic characteristics, motivators and hygiene factors.

Proposed by Frederick Herzberg (Herzberg, Mausner, and Snyderman 1959), **motivator-hygiene theory** assumes that a job has two basic characteristics, motivators and hygiene factors. Motivating factors include the characteristics of jobs that allow people to fulfill higher-level needs. For example, a challenging job might allow someone to meet his or her need for high levels of achievement. Hygiene factors include those characteristics of jobs that allow people to fulfill lower-level needs; for example, when good benefits and working conditions satisfy security needs.

Motivating factors arise from the content or the actual tasks that people perform on the job. Hygiene factors focus on the context or the setting in which the job takes place. Thus, for example, tasks that allow you to use your abilities are motivators. However, the size of your desk and color of your office are context or hygiene factors. Unlike other need theories, which assume that the desire to satisfy any type of need can motivate, Herzberg argued that satisfying lower-level needs at work (i.e., the hygiene factors) brings people only to a neutral state of motivation. To go beyond just a neutral reaction to the job, managers must build motivators into the context of a job (e.g., providing interesting tasks). Thus, only the opportunity to satisfy higher-level needs leads to increased motivation.

ACHIEVEMENT-MOTIVATION THEORY

Achievement-motivation theory

Suggestion that only some people have the need to win in competitive situations or to exceed a standard of excellence.

The psychologist David McClelland (1961) identified three key needs as the basis of motivation. These include needs for achievement, affiliation, and power (see Exhibit 13.5). However, most of McClelland's influential work focused on achievement motivation. **Achievement-motivation theory** suggests that some people (approximately 10 percent in the United States) have the need to win in competitive situations or to exceed a standard of excellence. High achievement-motivated people like to set their own goals. They seek challenging situations but avoid goals that they feel are too difficult. Because they like to achieve success in their goals, high achievers desire immediate feedback. They like to know how they are performing at every step leading to a goal.

McClelland believed that achievement motivation is fixed in early childhood. He also believed that different cultures have different levels of achievement motivation. Some evidence supports McClelland's contention of different levels of achievement motivation in different cultures. However, there is no clear evidence regarding whether nations with more achievement-motivated people have better economic performance (Ronen 1986).

NEEDS AND THE NATIONAL CONTEXT

There are both similarities and divergence in the needs that people from different nations seek to satisfy from working. Similarities of needs across cultures occur because people tend to group needs into similar clusters or categories (Ronen 1994); that is, regardless of national background, people see their work-related needs *grouped* in ways that match the broad groups proposed by need theories of motivation (see Exhibit 13.5).

However, national groups vary in two ways on how people see needs being satisfied at work. First, people from different nations do not give the same *priorities* to the needs that might be satisfied at work. For example, as shown in Exhibit 13.6, Hungarians give a high priority to satisfying physiological needs through higher base pay. This is not true for people from some other countries, such as China or Holland. Second, even if workers from different countries have similar needs, they

Exhibit 13.6 Rankings of the Importance of Job-Related Sources of Need Satisfaction for Seven Countries
(H = upper third; M = middle third; L = bottom third; #1 = highest rank)

Job-Related Sources of Satisfaction for:	China	Germany	Holland	Hungary	Israel	Korea	United States
Self-Actualization Needs							
• Advancement	M	M	H	L	H	H	H
• Use of Ability	H	H	H	H	M	H	H
• Meaningful Work	M	H	M	M	M	M	M
• Achievement	#1	M	H	H	#1	#1	H
• Interesting Job	H	#1	#1	H	H	H	#1
Esteem Needs							
• Recognition	M	L	M	H	M	M	M
• Influence	M	L	M	L	L	L	L
• Esteem	H	M	M	M	H	L	H
Affiliation Needs							
• Co-Worker Support	M	H	H	M	M	H	L
• Supervisor Support	M	H	M	#1	H	H	M
• Interaction	L	L	M	M	L	L	L
Security Needs							
• Work Conditions	L	L	L	M	L	M	L
• Benefits	L	H	L	M	M	M	M
• Security	L	H	M	M	L	H	M
Physiological Needs							
• Base Pay	L	M	L	H	M	M	L

Source: Adapted from Elizur et al. 1991.

may not give the same level of importance to satisfying these needs. For example, one cross-national comparison found that interesting work (something that satisfies growth needs) ranked as the most important work goal for Japanese, British, and Belgian workers. However, interesting work was still relatively more important for Belgian workers than it was for Japanese and British workers (Harpaz 1990).

Can multinational managers use need satisfaction as a motivational tool? Yes, it can serve as a motivational tool, if multinational managers take into account the particular needs that people in a nation seek to satisfy in the work setting. Consider the following Case in Point, which gives examples of companies that increased motivation by linking organizational goals to the local employees' needs.

What differences in need satisfaction might multinational managers expect to find in different countries? Exhibit 13.6 illustrates some of the differences in the priorities given to job-related sources of need satisfaction by people from several nations (Elizur et al. 1991). The exhibit divides the rankings of job-related sources of need satisfaction into three groups: High (H) for the top third, Middle (M) for the middle third, and Low (L) for the bottom third. Exhibit 13.6 also shows the job-related sources of need satisfaction in terms of Maslow's need hierarchy. For cross-referencing to other need theories, see Exhibit 13.5, which showed how Maslow's need hierarchy relates to other need theories.

As Exhibit 13.6 shows, people from different nations do not necessarily give the priorities suggested by need theories to the sources of need satisfaction at work. For example, although most need theories suggest that higher-level needs (e.g., self-actualization) should be most important, regardless of national background, many of the job-related sources of satisfying self-actualization needs had only moderate importance. Only the need for interesting work fell into the top

Case in Point

**Finding the
Right Needs in
Eastern
Europe—Job
Security or
Higher Pay?**

Taking over a formerly state-owned firm in Poland turned out to be a motivational challenge for the Finnish paper and power-equipment firm Ahlstrom Fakop. Morale and sales were low, and the new management searched for ways to improve the situation. The first try, offering incentive pay, produced no results.

As workers recently jettisoned into a market economy, the east European employees of Ahlstrom Fakop had other needs than money. Their prime concern was keeping their jobs. When told that their jobs were secure, if sales and productivity targets were met, the workers responded positively with increases in both. It seems that the anxiety produced by the transition to a market economy made keeping a job more important than bonuses for productivity.

When Dow Chemical took over a crumbling chemical plant in the former East Germany, they inherited a bloated workforce and the knowledge that they would need to lay off 400 workers. To ease the culture shock of the transition to a market-based company and increase productivity, Dow built a motivational system based on trust and individual initiative. Many workers adapted well to the system, using the newfound independence to achieve higher levels of performance and promotions. However, some floundered, confused by managers who did not watch their every move and a distrust of those with power.

Sources: Based on Jacob 1995 and Warren 2000.

third classification for all seven countries. High levels of potential need satisfiers on the job were found at all levels of the need hierarchy. In Germany, for example, perhaps because of the social institutional support for labor, job characteristics that could satisfy security and affiliation needs were as important as those related to self-actualization needs.

How can a multinational manager anticipate need differences in countries on which there is little information? Many multinational managers now work in emerging or formerly state-controlled economies where there is little available information on the often evolving employee attitudes toward work. In these cases, skillful multinational managers must anticipate worker needs based on cultural norms and values and institutional conditions. Hofstede's work (1991) gives some hints on how a multinational manager might do this.

Exhibit 13.7 shows some of the motivators at work identified by Hofstede for different types of national cultures (see Chapter 2). Hofstede's work suggests that emphasizing satisfying high-level needs at work may apply better to highly individualistic cultures. In addition, he cautions that need satisfaction may not be a motivator at all in some high power distance countries dominated by norms of service to the elite.

APPLYING NEED THEORIES IN MULTINATIONAL SETTINGS

Some points to consider in adapting need theories of motivation to the international context include the following:

- *Identify the basic functions of work in the national or local culture:* Where work is not central, people may satisfy their needs outside the work setting, limiting the use of need satisfaction as a motivational tool.

Exhibit 13.7
Hofstede's Dimensions
of National Culture
and Motivators at
Work

Cultural Context:
High power distance
Dominant Work Motivators:
Conform to norms and rules
Meet moral obligations to
   leaders
Example Country:
Mexico

Cultural Context:
High individualism
Dominant Work Motivators:
Autonomy
Challenging work
Advancement
Example Country:
United States

Cultural Context:
High uncertainty avoidance
Dominant Work Motivators:
Security
Clear organizational hierarchy
Example Country:
Belgium

Cultural Context:
High masculinity
Dominant Work Motivators:
Pay
Training opportunities
Achievement
Example Country:
Japan

Source: Adapted from Hofstede 1991.

- *Identify the needs considered most important by workers in the national or local culture:* The evidence presented in this chapter shows that need priorities differ by national context. Managers should identify cultural differences in potential need satisfiers at work and focus on providing jobs that satisfy these needs.
- *Sources of need fulfillment may differ for the same needs:* Even if people from different cultures have the same needs, they may find different sources of fulfillment on the job. For example, people from different cultures may find interesting work most important, but they may have quite different ideas regarding what is interesting work. Hofstede's work suggests that individualism and power distance represent important dimensions of national culture that affect how people find need satisfaction at work.
- *Understand the limitations of available jobs to satisfy needs:* Although satisfying higher-level needs is possible in most industrialized countries, the same may not be true in many developing nations. Existing jobs may provide only the satisfaction of basic needs for survival.

To increase the motivation of host-country workers or to solve other motivational problems, multinational managers can also consider other approaches to motivation beyond need theories. Next, the chapter provides reviews of additional theories of motivation and their applications to multinational settings.

PROCESS AND REINFORCEMENT THEORIES OF MOTIVATION

In this section, we briefly review the process theories of motivation known as *expectancy theory*, *equity theory*, and *goal-setting theory*. Process theories are more complex than need theories. They see motivation arising from needs and values *combined* with an individual's beliefs regarding the work environment. Besides the popular process theories, this section also reviews reinforcement theory and its application to multinational settings. These approaches to motivation receive fewer applications in the international setting than do need theories. However, we can draw some tentative conclusions regarding how these perspectives work in various national settings. For a complete review of these theories, students should consult any current organizational-behavior textbook.

EXPECTANCY THEORY

Overview

Expectancy theory

Assumption that motivation includes an individual's desire to satisfy his or her needs and their beliefs regarding how much their efforts at work will eventually satisfy their needs.

Victor Vroom (1964) proposed a view of motivation that is more complex than simple need satisfaction. This theory and its later variants are known as **expectancy theory**. In this theory, Vroom proposed that work motivation is a function not only of an individual's needs or values but also of an individual's beliefs regarding what happens if you work hard. Expectancy theory assumes that part of motivation is an individual's desire to satisfy his or her needs. However, the level of motivation also depends on people's beliefs regarding how much, or if, their efforts at work will eventually satisfy their needs.

The three factors that make up expectancy theory include expectancy, valence, and instrumentality. The theory often is presented in the form of the following equation:

Motivation = Expectancy × Valence × Instrumentality

Expectancy is an individual's belief that his or her effort will lead to some result. For example, if you believe that intensive study over a weekend will lead to a high grade, you have a high expectancy in that situation. *Valence* is the value you attach to the outcome of your efforts. For example, a student may value a high grade in a class, in comparison to the pleasure of going skiing over a weekend. *Instrumentality* refers to the links between early and later results of the work effort. For example, continuing the grade analogy, instrumentality means the link between one outcome of studying, a grade on a test, with a later outcome, a final grade for a course. If the test was worth only 1 percent of the final grade, instrumentality would be low. That is, how one performs on a minor test has little effect on a final grade.

Thus, in the expectancy-theory perspective, motivation is much more than the value people attach to work outcomes. Beliefs regarding whether an effort will lead to success and whether the results of effort will lead eventually to valued outcomes also come into play.

Some suggest that expectancy theory serves best as a diagnostic tool to determine why workers are motivated or not motivated (Gordon 1996). The manager must ask three questions. First, do workers believe that their efforts will lead to successful performance of a task? Second, do workers believe that present success at some task (e.g., no defects for a week) will lead to success at some future valued outcome (e.g., getting a raise)? Third, do employees value the outcomes that follow from their efforts at work?

Applying Expectancy Theory in Multinational Settings

There are two key issues in applying expectancy theory in the multinational company. The first is to identify which outcomes people value in a particular national or local cultural setting; that is, the multinational manager must find and use rewards that have positive valence for employees. The second is to find culturally appropriate ways of convincing employees that their efforts will lead to desirable ends.

In the Case in Point earlier in this chapter, we saw that the workers from one former Eastern Bloc country had a higher valence for secure jobs than they did for bonus pay. When managers from the Finnish parent company recognized this, they promised job security (the workers' ultimate goal) in return for the workers' putting more effort into productivity. As expectancy theory would predict, when workers became convinced that their efforts would lead to their valued goal of security, their motivation increased.

EQUITY THEORY

Overview

Equity theory focuses on the fairness that people perceive in the rewards that they receive for their efforts at work. The rewards people receive from work can include, for example, pay, benefits, recognition, job perquisites, and prestige. Under this theory, the "efforts" people put into the job include not only the quality and quantity of their work, but also such factors as their age, educational qualifications, seniority, and social status (Adams 1963).

Equity theory proposes that people have no absolute standards for fairness in the input/output (effort/reward) equation. Rather, people perceive the fairness of their rewards vis-à-vis their inputs, based on how they compare themselves to others. For example, if two people have the same experience, do the same job, but do not have the same pay, then one is in overpayment inequity and the other is in underpayment inequity. Equity theory predicts that workers who believe that they are underrewarded reduce their contribution to the company (e.g., take longer breaks). Workers in an inequitable situation produced by overrewards increase their work input, at least in the short run.

Applying Equity Theory in Multinational Settings

The first issue to consider in multinational applications of equity theory concerns the importance of equity norms in a society. Developing reward systems based on equity norms may not be motivating when other norms for rewarding people have more importance than equity.

Psychologists identify three principles of allocating rewards that vary in their use in different cultural settings: the principle of equity (based on contributions), the principle of equality (based on equal division of rewards), and the principle of need (based on individual needs) (Erez 1994). A recent review of cross-national reports on the three principles of reward allocation suggests the following:

Equity norms prevail in individualistic cultures: In particular, managerial practices in the United States such as bonus pay, Management by Objectives, and most U.S. performance-appraisal systems use the equity norm. Rewards are based on performance. Good work deserves good pay (Gluskinos 1988). In contrast, in societies where status comes from group membership rather than achievement, rewards based on performance may not make sense. High-status groups are expected to get higher rewards regardless of their performance levels.

Equality norms prevail over equity norms in collectivist cultures: In societies with strong equality norms, at least for the members of one's group or team, group members prefer equal rewards for all. For example, one study of an Israeli company found that 40 percent of the workers perceived a bonus system as unfair even though it increased their income. They suggested that fair rewards should go to the team instead of to individuals (Gluskinos 1988).

The principle of need may prevail over equity in certain conditions: One study found, for example, that Indian managers preferred rewards based on need over rewards based on either equality or equity (Berman and Singh 1985). Collectivist cultures in particular may place more value on other people's needs than on one's own contributions.

Equity theory

Proposal that people perceive the fairness of their rewards vis-à-vis their inputs based on how they compare themselves to others.

Exhibit 13.8
Rewards from Peers
for Contributions to a
Student Group Project

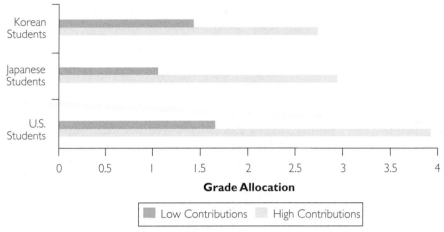

Source: Adapted from data in Kim, Park, and Suzuki 1990.

Exhibit 13.8 shows an example of how the "fairness" of equity or equality rewards can even affect students' responses to grades relative to contributions. The information comes from a study in which Korean, Japanese, and U.S. students assigned peer-evaluation grades for contributions to group projects. Although some equity norms seemingly worked for all students, U.S. students clearly linked rewards to performance much more than did the students from the two Asian societies (Kim, Park, and Suzuki 1990).

The following Multinational Management Brief gives an additional example of how CEO pay levels reflect differences between European and U.S. views regarding fair levels of rewards. The Brief shows that different cultural and institutional traditions come into conflict when considering the fairness and legality of executive pay.

The second and final issue to consider in applying equity theory concerns cultural differences in beliefs regarding the sources of a person's contributions to work. In some cultures, age, social status, and family membership may be more important inputs to work than the actual effort and performance on the job. In many Asian countries, for example, most people would consider it very unfair if a younger worker received more pay than an older worker—particularly if she or he did the same job. Research suggests that, in addition to performance criteria, collectivist cultures judge pay fairness based on factors such as seniority, education, and family size (Hundley and Kim 1997).

GOAL-SETTING THEORY

Overview

Goal-setting theory

Assumption that the mere existence of a goal is motivating.

Goal-setting theory assumes that people want to achieve goals. When they meet or exceed a goal, people feel competent and satisfied. When they fail to meet a goal, people feel dissatisfied. Thus, the mere existence of a goal is motivating (Locke and Latham 1990).

Goal-setting theory has several principles (Hellriegel, Slocum, and Woodman 2001). Goal-setting proponents argue that managers who follow these principles can motivate employees to meet organizational objectives. The principles of goal setting include:

- *Set clear and specific goals:* Employees will know and understand what management expects them to accomplish.

Multinational Management Brief
What Is "Fair" in CEO Salaries—Europeans Battle
over the Globalization of the Comparison Group

Companies in the United States have the largest gap between average worker pay and the pay of the CEO. Although this generates some protest when workers are laid off or have no pay raises, in the highly individualistic U.S. culture most people accept CEO pay and perks as justified if a company performs well.

In Europe, the average annual compensation for a CEO is $389,711. Their colleagues in the United States average $819,428. This discrepancy generates fears in some European companies that U.S. multinationals will lure away the best executives from Europe. Some argue that European executives who compete on the multinational front should receive pay similar to their competitors. Several European multinationals are now using CEO pay packages similar to those in the United States. Defenders of the pay raises call for increasing the compensation of European CEOs to match U.S. levels and for linking CEO compensation packages more to corporate performance.

However, critics condemn the new pay as unjustified and contrary to European traditions regarding fair pay. Stock exchanges in Britain and Sweden changed their rules to require disclosure of executive pay packages. When Lars Ramqvist, the CEO of the telecom-equipment firm Ericsson, received a 100 percent raise, the Swedes were outraged. The head of research of the Stockholm Stock Exchange found the raise "offensive." The deputy prime minister of Sweden accused the CEOs of major Swedish multinationals of acting like "spoiled children" in their quest for pay hikes. The head of Sweden's largest trade union finds such raises by "greedy managers" an affront to workers.

Political and labor leaders in Britain and France took similar critical views. Britain may even go so far as to eliminate stock options—a major compensation incentive for U.S. executives—as components of executive compensation.

Since equity theory predicts that people perceive the fairness or rewards in comparison to others, this case suggests that issues of fair compensation may eventually transcend not only local organizational boundaries but also national boundaries. Not surprisingly, there has been a dramatic increase in the rise of inpatriate CEOs (i.e., those who have nationalities different from their company's).

Sources: Based on *Economist* 2000; Flynn and Nayeri 1995 and Lyons and Stuart 2000.

- *Assign difficult but achievable goals:* If goals are too difficult, there is little incentive to try to achieve them. If goals are too easy, employees may not take them seriously.
- *Increase employee acceptance of goals:* At least in the United States, studies tell us that employees who participate in goal setting have a greater acceptance of managerial goals (Erez, Earley, and Hulin 1987).
- *Provide incentives to achieve goals:* Tying rewards (e.g., salary, bonuses) to goal achievement increases the acceptance of the goals (Locke, Latham, and Erez 1988).

- *Give feedback on goal attainment:* To be motivated, people must understand how well they are doing to achieve their goals.

Applying Goal-Setting Theory in Multinational Settings

Some experts believe that goal setting works to some degree regardless of location (e.g., Erez and Earley 1987). Setting goals does affect behavior in a positive direction. However, cultural expectations vary regarding whether subordinates should participate with managers in setting the goals and whether it is better to set goals for groups or for individuals.

In more individualistic cultures, such as in the United States, setting individual goals may prove more effective than setting goals for a work group. People from individualistic cultures do not easily share responsibility for group outcomes. Thus, they do not find goals assigned to groups as motivating as goals assigned to themselves. In contrast, workers in collectivist cultures may respond better to higher levels of participation in goal setting than people from more individualistic cultures such as in the United States. In societies with cultural values supporting the necessity of belonging to a group, participation may have a greater chance of enhancing the worker's ownership and commitment to goals. Finally, in cultures high on power distance, worker participation in setting goals may not produce any positive effects. Workers expect the leader to set the goals and tell them what to do (Erez 1994).

Exhibit 13.9 demonstrates some of the differences in outcomes that can occur when people from different cultures have different degrees of participation in the goal-setting process. This exhibit is based on a study of U.S. and Israeli university students (Erez and Earley 1987). Three groups of students performed simulated job tasks. For the first group, goals were assigned. For the second group, a representative from the group expressed the students' opinions on goals to the leader. For the third group, the whole group participated in setting goals. Because Israeli culture is more collectivist and lower on power distance than U.S. culture, the experimenters expected that goal assignment would not work very well for the Israeli students.

Participation in goal setting improved the performance of all groups. However, perhaps because U.S. students come from a highly individualistic and moderate power distance national culture, they performed almost as well with assigned goals as they did when given the opportunity to participate in goal setting. This was not true for the Israeli students, who come from a more collectivist and lower power culture. The Israeli students did much better with participation. The implication is that subordinate participation in goal setting is an effective motivational tool in more collectivist nations, but less important in individualistic or high power distance national cultures.

REINFORCEMENT THEORY

Operant conditioning

Model proposes that, if a pleasurable consequence follows a behavior, the behavior will continue, whereas if an unpleasant consequence follows a behavior, the behavior will stop.

Overview

Most managerial applications of reinforcement theory focus on operant conditioning. **Operant conditioning** represents a basic way people learn. The famous psychologist B. F. Skinner identified most of the principles underlying operant conditioning (Skinner 1938).

The operant-conditioning model proposes that behavior is a function of its consequences. That is, in its simplest application, if a pleasurable consequence follows a behavior, the behavior will continue. If an unpleasant consequence follows a behavior, the behavior will stop (Luthans and Kreitner 1985). Unlike most other theories

Exhibit 13.9

Cultural Effects on
Performance by the
Degree of Participation
in Goal Setting

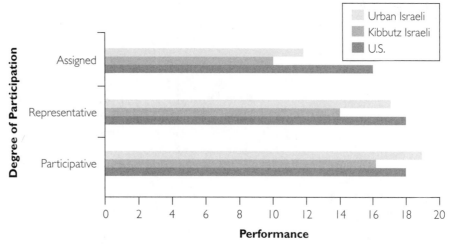

Source: Adapted from data reported in Erez and Earley 1987.

of motivation, operant conditioning focuses on observable behavior and not on the psychological processes (e.g., meeting needs) that affect people's motivation.

The operant-conditioning model has three steps. These are shown in Exhibit 13.10 with a managerial example. The antecedent comes first and stimulates behavior. The behavior follows the antecedent, and the pleasant or unpleasant consequences follow the behavior. The exhibit shows a simple example based on work attendance. In the antecedent, management sets an attendance goal. The employee behaves by either coming to work or missing work. Management then provides pleasant or unpleasant consequences for the behavior.

Positive reinforcement occurs when management responds with a rewarding consequence. The consequence is deemed rewarding only if it increases the desired behavior. Not all people will respond to the same positively intended consequences in the same way. Although often confused with punishment, negative reinforcement increases desired behavior by eliminating some negative consequence. That is, people behave in a certain way to avoid something unpleasant. For example, you may put on a heavy coat to avoid the pain of extreme cold. Punishment occurs when something unpleasant occurs after a behavior. The exhibit shows that docking of pay is an unpleasant consequence that follows the behavior of not coming to work. Extinction occurs when a manager ignores a behavior. However, managers must be careful to avoid extinction when other rewards (e.g., a paid day off) may be operating.

Most management applications of reinforcement theory use positive reinforcement to encourage behaviors desired by management. To reinforce behavior, managers have an array of organizational rewards. These include material rewards (e.g., pay), benefit rewards (e.g., company car), status rewards (e.g., prestigious office), and social rewards (e.g., praise) (Hellriegel, Slocum, and Woodman 2001).

Applying Reinforcement Theory in Multinational Settings

For behaviors that are easily observable and measurable, such as attendance, the evidence from most U.S. studies suggests that positive reinforcement works (Luthans and Kreitner 1985). However, finding appropriate organizational reinforcers remains a major difficulty in the application of reinforcement theory to diverse national groups. We saw earlier in the chapter that people from different nations

Exhibit 13.10 Management Example of Operant-Conditioning Process and Types of Consequences

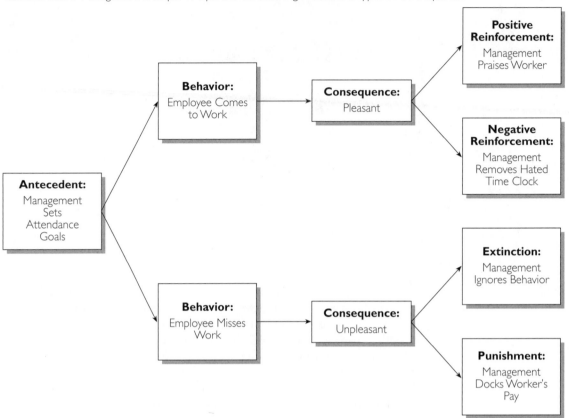

expect different rewards from work. Thus, different groups may respond to different reinforcers.

The challenge for the multinational manager is to understand not only how work values influence potential rewards but also to identify the organizational rewards available in a national setting that she or he can use as reinforcers. National cultures and social institutions define acceptable and legitimate rewards. Consider these two examples. In highly unionized countries such as Germany, pay and benefits are fixed nationally and are not available as organizational rewards targeted to specific behaviors. In Japan, employees often consider public praise embarrassing. It implies that one is somehow better than his or her colleagues. This embarrassment and the potential ostracism by the work group would result not in a reward but instead in punishment, unintended by the culturally ignorant manager.

Evidence exists, however, that when multinational managers can find culturally and institutionally appropriate reinforcers, reinforcement theory does work. For example, companies in Mexico City often use punishment to control tardiness—a one-day suspension without pay for every three days tardy during a thirty-day period. When one company replaced the punishment system for tardiness with a positive-reinforcement program giving bonuses for punctuality, tardiness fell from 9.8 percent to 1.2 percent (Herman 1973).

Exhibit 13.11 shows an example of how proper use of reinforcers can work in different national contexts. In this example, two groups of Russian workers at the Kalinin Cotton Mill responded positively to both extrinsic rewards and social re-

Exhibit 13.11
Effects of Positive
Reinforcement and
Types of Rewards in a
Russian Cotton Mill

Sources: Adapted from Welsh, Luthans, and Sommer 1993 and Luthans et al. 1998.

wards (Welsh, Luthans, and Sommer 1993). One group received extrinsic rewards. These rewards were U.S.-made products such as soap, jeans, T-shirts, and music tapes. The other group received the social rewards of recognition and praise. Both outcomes were similar to those found in U.S. studies. However, the Russian workers responded most positively to the U.S. products as rewards. This positive reinforcement increased the behaviors management desired.

KEY POINTS IN THE MULTINATIONAL APPLICATION OF PROCESS AND REINFORCEMENT THEORIES

The multinational manager should consider several key points when using process and reinforcement theories of motivation in different cultural settings. These include:

- *Expectancy theory:* The major key is identifying the appropriate work rewards that have positive valence for employees in a national setting.
- *Equity theory:* The multinational manager must assess the importance and meaning of the principle of equity in a national context. A multinational manager may find equality norms or norms that base rewards on need to have equal or more importance than equity.
- *Goal-setting theory:* Depending on cultural norms, goal setting may be more effective when assigned to groups rather than individuals. Participation in goal setting may have more positive effects in collectivist cultures than in individualistic or high power distance cultures.
- *Reinforcement theory:* The rewards people value at work may influence the types of reinforcers useful to managers in different cultural contexts. In addition, the institutional environment, such as degree of economic development and the labor-relations system, affects the types of rewards available for managers in any society.

MOTIVATION AND JOB DESIGN: U.S. AND EUROPEAN PERSPECTIVES

Job design attempts to make jobs more motivating by changing the nature of their functions and tasks. Early theories of job design focused primarily on making jobs more efficient through procedures such as time and motion studies. The objective was to make a job as fast and efficient as possible. There was little concern for the psychological state of the worker. Contemporary views of job design take into account the psychological effects on the worker produced by the types of tasks associated with a job. Theories that suggest ways to design jobs for high motivation focus on how job characteristics allow a worker to meet or satisfy motivating needs.

A U.S. APPROACH: THE JOB-CHARACTERISTICS MODEL

Job-characteristics model

Suggests that work is more motivating when managers enrich core job characteristics, such as by increasing number of skills a job requires.

Although there are several approaches to redesigning work for increased motivational potential, one of the most popular in the United States is the **job-characteristics model** (Hackman and Oldham 1980). This model suggests that work is more motivating when managers enrich core job characteristics such as the different number of skills a job requires. In turn, these core job characteristics affect the psychological states of a worker that are critical to motivation. For example, one psychological state considered critical for motivation comes from whether the worker believes his or her job is meaningful. Proponents of the job-characteristics model argue that, if the core job characteristics lead to appropriate psychological reactions, then jobs have a high potential to motivate workers.

The job-characteristics model sees three critical psychological states as motivating. First, a person must believe that his or her job is meaningful. A meaningful job is perceived as important or valuable. Second, a person must believe that he or she is responsible or accountable for the outcome of his or her work. Third, a person must understand how well he or she has performed.

Core characteristics of a job that lead to the motivating psychological states include:

- *Skill variety:* A job with skill variety requires the use of different abilities and activities.
- *Task identity:* Task identity increases when a person can complete a whole piece of work from beginning to end.
- *Task significance:* Task significance increases when a job has important effects on other people.
- *Autonomy:* When people have autonomy they control their own schedules and job procedures.
- *Feedback:* Feedback occurs when the job allows timely information on a person's performance.

Not all people respond positively to jobs with enriched job characteristics. Rather, the model suggests that jobs with high motivational potential work best for people who have a strong need for personal growth and have the appropriate knowledge and skills to perform the job well. Exhibit 13.12 gives a picture of how the job-characteristics model works when a job has a high potential for motivating workers.

Sociotechnical systems approach

Focuses on designing motivating jobs by blending the social system (i.e., organizational structure, culture) with different technologies.

Next, we compare this U.S. perspective on making work motivating with a similar approach developed in Europe.

A EUROPEAN APPROACH: SOCIOTECHNICAL SYSTEMS

The **sociotechnical systems (STS) approach** to building a job's motivational potential was developed originally in England and Scandinavia (Trist and Murry 1993; Thorsrud 1984). The STS approach attempts to mesh both modern technol-

Exhibit 13.12
A Motivating Job in the
Job-Characteristics
Model

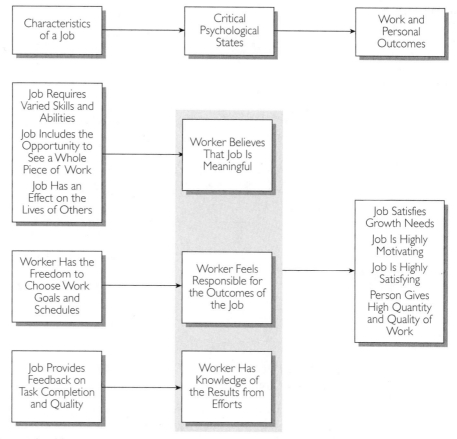

Source: Adapted from Hackman and Oldham 1980.

ogy and the social needs of workers. However, the STS approach does not consider workers just as individuals. Rather, individual workers are part of a social system (i.e., organizational structure, culture) that must blend with different technologies (Cummings 1978).

Autonomous work group

Team or unit that has nearly complete responsibility for a particular task.

The STS approach focuses on the **autonomous work group**. The autonomous work group is a team or unit that has nearly complete responsibility for a particular task. The most famous example is Volvo's Kalmar plant, where autonomous work groups have responsibility for particular components of the automobile (e.g., doors). In autonomous work groups, worker teams control many aspects of their jobs traditionally governed by management; for example, the tasks assigned to individuals and the pace of work (Gordon 1996).

The STS approach builds into a job many of the same motivational job characteristics proposed by the U.S. job-characteristic model just discussed. However, in a crucial difference with the U.S. approach, the team's tasks rather than the individual worker's tasks become the focus of job enrichment (Erez and Earley 1993). The team decides individual task assignments and thus increases skill variety. The team makes autonomous decisions on a variety of matters related to its job, such as which task to complete first. The team has task identity by producing a whole product. The team gets feedback from its work often, by conducting its own quality inspections.

Exhibit 13.13

Comparing the Performance of Chinese, U.S., and Israeli Managers Working Alone and in Groups

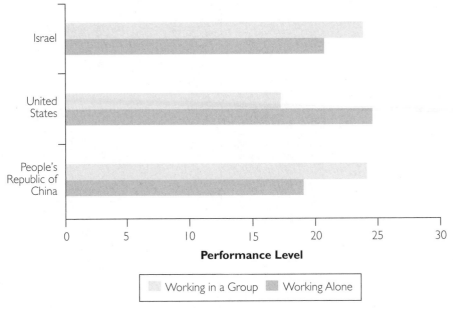

Source: Adapted from Earley 1993.

CHOOSING JOB-ENRICHMENT TECHNIQUES IN MULTINATIONAL SETTINGS

How can a multinational manager choose the best techniques to design motivating work? Some experts suggest that the distinction between individualistic and collectivist cultures should determine the choice of job-enrichment techniques (Erez and Earley 1993). Approaches created in the United States tend to focus on how the *individual* reacts to core job characteristics. They have a cultural bias in favor of individualistic cultures. Approaches designed in more collectivist cultures, including the sociotechnical systems approach and the Quality Circles popular in Japan, focus on the job characteristics of the *team*. They have a cultural bias in favor of more collectivist cultures. Although proponents of both forms of enrichment can point to success stories in several nations, experts recommend a team focus for job enrichment in collectivist cultures and an individual focus in more individualistic cultures.

One explanation of why team-based job enrichment may not work well in individualistic cultures is that people from the more individualistic cultures just do not work as well in groups. Exhibit 13.13 gives an example of this phenomenon. It shows a comparison of three culturally diverse groups of managers working in groups or alone. As you can see, unlike the managers from the more collectivist cultures, U.S. managers performed much worse in groups than they did alone.

Why does performance drop off with the use of teamwork in more individualistic cultures? Some experts explain this by noting that people from individualistic cultures often engage in social loafing. **Social loafing** occurs when people put out less effort when they work in groups. They do this for three reasons. First, working in groups, people do not feel responsible for group outcomes and feel less pressure to perform. Second, workers in groups often believe that the group will make up any slack in their personal efforts. Third, especially in highly individualistic cultures such as the United States, people give their own work and interests priority over

Social loafing

Term used when people put out less effort when they work in groups.

Multinational Management Challenge
Team-Based Job-Enrichment Success Stories in Japan—
Will They Work in the United States and Mexico?

At Sony's plant in Kohda, Japan, teams of four workers do all the assembly and the final testing of camcorders. Output increased over 10 percent from the former conveyer belt assembly line. At an NEC telephone factory, eight-person teams work in a spider-like circle facing each other across a turntable. They pace their own work. Some group members build entire subcomponents and place them on a turntable in front of them. Other group members spin the turntable to get the components and produce the finished phones. Training costs increased because people had to learn new skills. However, thirty-five people now produce as many phones as seventy people did under the previous system.

Will this approach work in the United States? Companies like Compaq Computer Corp. believe so. They used assembly "cells" to assemble whole computer units and saw a 51 percent gain in labor productivity. In spite of this successful incident, however, surveys of businesses show only moderate success by U.S. companies using these group-based approaches. One possibility is that, in the United States, the motivational benefits of group-based job enrichment work best for simple assembly jobs. In this type of work, when the assembly team is small, a manager can more easily identify, provide feedback to, and hold responsible the individual who is a slow performer. Other evidence suggests that, even in more collectivist cultures, groups will perform best when they receive both individual and group feedback.

Will this approach work in Mexico? Mexico is a more collectivist society than the United States leading many multinational managers to expect that the self-managed teams would work well. However, a study of the experience of 243 Mexican executives found that nearly all had problems with the use of enriched jobs based on self-managed teams. Why? Although the idea of working in groups appeals to the Mexican worker, other cultural values offset the effectiveness of the teams. A low tolerance of ambiguity (high uncertainty avoidance) and expectations regarding hierarchical authority make workers uncomfortable without direct supervision.

Sources: Based on Earley, Gibson, and Chen 1999; Nicholls, Lane, and Brechu 1999 and Williams 1994.

the group's. However, in individualistic cultures, some of the detrimental effects of social loafing on a group's performance decline when individuals rather than the groups are held accountable for performance (Earley 1989).

The preceding Multinational Management Challenge confirms the success of team-based job enrichment programs in some Japanese organizations. However, it also suggests that the success of these programs in individualistic cultures, such as in the United States, remains a challenge. Using team-based job designs in the United States and in other individualistic cultures may require that managers retain individual performance assessments even in the team-based company.

Summary and Conclusions

Motivating workers in diverse cultural settings is a constant challenge for multinational managers. As companies both large and small become more global and transnational in their strategic and human resource orientations, the challenge of increasing worker motivation in multinational settings will become even greater. For a multinational company to remain competitive in the global environment, each company and its managers must find ways to motivate an increasingly diverse workforce.

As a guide to developing motivational techniques in multinational settings, this chapter addressed several key issues. First, the chapter showed some of the available information on international differences in work centrality and the importance of work in several different nations. Second, the chapter reviewed the basic processes of work motivation and how these processes are influenced by the national context. Third, the chapter reviewed classic theories of motivation (including need, processes, and reinforcement theories) and the multinational applications of each approach. In these sections you also received specific and practical suggestions on how to apply these theories in different national contexts. Fourth, and finally, the chapter considered both U.S. and European approaches to designing jobs with high motivational potential.

Most of the views of motivation discussed in this chapter were "made in the U.S.A." U.S. academics created the theories and performed much of the research supporting the theories. The approaches to motivation discussed here are also standard fare in U.S. university courses in organizational behavior. However, the dominance of U.S. perspectives as the "country of origin" for many

motivational theories does not invalidate their multinational applications—*if* a manager makes appropriate adjustments for national contexts and various subcultures. Many of the psychological theories that underlie common U.S. approaches to motivation have "culture-free" assumptions and research support; that is, they attempt to explain human behavior independent of cultural setting.

Importantly, however, even if psychological processes that underlie motivational theories are culture free, the applications of motivation theories are not. Even when people respond to work using the same underlying psychological processes, the national context continues to influence other factors, such as what people find rewarding at work and what people feel is fair and moral. For example, a U.S. American and a Brazilian may both respond to the psychological process of positive reinforcement similarly. Their behaviors increase when consequences are pleasant. But this does not mean that they will view the same reinforcers offered by management as rewarding. As we saw throughout the chapter, nations vary widely in their predominant views regarding the functions and meaning of work and in the rewards that people hope to get from work.

A brief discussion of motivation can only sensitize the multinational manager to subtleties of applying any motivation technique in diverse national settings. Although a manager may begin his or her approach to motivating workers with an awareness of the broad stereotypes concerning national cultures, each job situation requires an understanding of the unique organizational, regional, and occupational cultures as well as the individual differences of each employee.

Discussion Questions

1. Compare the Job Diagnostics approach to job design and the Sociotechnical Systems approach. Pick a national culture with which you are familiar (besides your own) and discuss which approach would be most likely to succeed and why.

2. How might a country's educational and political systems affect the effectiveness of redesigning work as a motivational tool?

3. Discuss differences in the attributes of work considered most important in different nations.

How might these differences influence the application to the work setting of expectancy theory and reinforcement theory?

4. Discuss the differences between need and processes theories of motivation. Which type do you think is more applicable to multinational management and why?

5. Discuss the three principles of fairness of rewards. Do you think that equity theory could work

in societies where other principles besides equity operate? If so, how would you apply equity theory as a manager in these countries?

6. Under what conditions would you recommend involving groups in setting goals? Discuss the cultural influences on goal setting, using Hofstede's original four dimensions of national culture.

Chapter Internet Activity

See what's new in motivation. Go to online business periodicals such as http://www.economist.com, http://www.fortune.com, and http://www.businessweek.com. Use their search engines to find information on motivation. Search motivation

concepts such as job design, worker satisfaction, worker commitment, worker performance, work values, and so on. Write a brief report on your findings.

Internet Sites

Selected Companies in the Chapter

Ahlstrom Corp.   http://www.ahlstrom.com/
Compaq   http://www.compaq.com/
Dow   http://www.dow.com
NEC Corp.   http://www.nec.com/
Sony   http://www.sony.com/
Volvo   http://www.volvo.com/

Check Country Background Information for Hints at Motivation Strategies

http://www.odci.gov/cia/publications/factbook/index
  The CIA's World Factbook Master Home Page—includes background information on country geography, people, government, economy, communications, and defense forces.

http://www.webofculture.com/   *The Web Of Culture—articles on cultural differences.*

http://lcweb2.loc.gov/frd/cs/cshome.html   *Country Studies: Area Handbooks—country background on political, economic, and social institutions.*

http://www.craighead.com/   *Cultural background relevant to business for numerous countries—hard copy is in most university libraries—Internet site has limited country information, free.*

http://www.imd.ch/   *The Institute for Management Development publishes a home page with extensive summaries of cross-national economic and trade data, as well as survey data on cross-national management and HRM issues.*

Chapter Activity: Planning Motivational Strategies for Different Countries

Step 1: Read the following multinational problem.

You have just completed your first year as a management trainee for the XYZ company. Your company manufactures components for industrial robots. You have just come from a meeting with

the vice president for personnel. She has told you that XYZ has decided to open a manufacturing plant in the country of _____. Because of your background in international business, top management has chosen you to be the new plant manager. The VP tells you that this is a significant opportunity and challenge, since you would have to wait at least five more years to get this level of responsibility at home. Personnel experts are already in country _____ working on recruitment, selection, and training. Your major job will be to motivate the local workers to reach the plant's full capacity as soon as possible. Given your knowledge of the local culture and social institutions, the VP asks you to prepare a report specifying the motivational strategies that you might use on your new assignment.

Step 2: Picking teams and countries.

Your instructor will divide you into teams of three to five people. Each team will choose or be assigned a different country for a plant location. Your team will act in the role of the new expatriate plant manager. If your instructor chooses, this may also be an individual assignment.

This project may be a library research project or an in-class assignment based on information from the text.

Step 3: Prepare reports.

Reports may be written, oral, or both. A report analyzes the likely effectiveness of motivational approaches given different economic, cultural, and institutional factors in the country in question.

Each report must discuss the strengths and weaknesses of applying the following motivational theories in the selected country:

- Need theory
- Expectancy theory
- Goal-setting theory
- Equity theory
- Reinforcement theory
- Job design

Step 4: Present your findings to the class.

Step 5: Class discussion.

Alternative approach: The whole class works with one country, and each team deals with one approach to motivation.

References

Adams, J. S. 1963. "Toward an understanding of inequity." *Journal of Abnormal and Social Psychology* 67, 422–436.

Alderfer, C. P. 1972. *Existence, Relatedness and Growth: Human Needs in Organizational Settings.* New York: Free Press.

Berman, J. J., and P. Singh. 1985. "Cross-cultural similarities and differences in perceptions of fairness." *Journal of Cross-Cultural Psychology* 16, 55–67.

Cummings, T. G. 1978. "Self-regulating work groups: A sociotechnical synthesis." *Academy of Management Review* 3, 625–34.

Daft, Richard L. 1991. *Management.* 2d ed. Chicago: Dryden.

Earley, P. Christopher. 1989. "Social loafing and collectivism: A comparison of the United States and the People's Republic of China." *Administrative Science Quarterly* 34, 565–81.

———. 1993. "East meets west meets Mideast: Further explorations of collectivistic and individualistic work groups." *Academy of Management Journal* 36, 319–48.

———, Cristina B. Gibson, and Chao C. Chen. 1999. "'How did I do?' versus 'how did we do?' Cultural contrasts of performance feedback use and self-efficacy." *Journal of Cross-Cultural Psychology* 30, 594–619.

Economist. 2000. "Those egalitarian Swedes." http://www.economist.com, June 3.

Elizur, Dov, Ingwer Borg, Raymond Hunt, and Istvan Magyari Beck. 1991. "The structure of work values: A cross cultural comparison." *Journal of Organizational Behavior* 12, 21–38.

Erez, Miriam. 1994. "Toward a model of cross-cultural industrial and organizational psychology." *Handbook of Industrial and Organizational Psychology* 4, 559–607.

Erez, M., and P. C. Earley. 1987. "Comparative analysis of goal-setting strategies across cultures." *Journal of Applied Psychology* 72, 658–65.

———. 1993. *Culture, Self-Identity, and Work.* New York: Oxford University Press.

Erez, M., P. C. Earley, and C. L. Hulin. 1987. "The impact of participation on goal acceptance and performance: A two-step model." *Academy of Management Journal* 12, 265–77.

Flynn, Julie, and Farah Nayeri. 1995. "Continental divide over executive pay: American-style largess is raising howls in Europe." *Business Week,* July 3.

Gluskinos, U. M. 1988. "Cultural and political consideration in the introduction of western technologies: The Mekorot Project." *Journal of Management Development* 6, 34–36.

Grant, Linda. 1997. "Unhappy in Japan." *Fortune* January 13, 142.

Gordon, Judith R. 1987. *A Diagnostic Approach to Organizational Behavior.* Boston: Allyn and Bacon.

———. 1996. *Organizational Behavior.* Upper Saddle River, N.J.: Prentice Hall.

Greenberg, Jerald. 1995. *Behavior in Organizations.* Englewood Cliffs, N.J.: Prentice-Hall.

Hackman, J. R., and G. R. Oldham. 1980. *Work Redesign.* Reading, Mass.: Addison-Wesley.

Harpaz, Itzhak. 1990. "The importance of work goals: An international perspective." *Journal of International Business Studies,* First Quarter, 75–93.

Hellriegel, Don, John W. Slocum, Jr., and Richard W. Woodman. 2001. *Organizational Behavior,* ninth edition. Cincinnati, OH: South-Western.

Herman, J. 1973. "Effects of bonuses for punctuality on the tardiness of industrial workers." *Journal of Applied Behavioral Analysis* 6, 563–70.

Herzberg, F., B. Mausner, and B. B. Snyderman. 1959. *The Motivation to Work.* New York: Wiley.

Hofstede, Geert. 1980. "Motivation, leadership, and organization: Do American theories apply abroad?" *Organizational Dynamics*, Summer, 42–63.

————. 1991. *Cultures and Organizations.* London: McGraw-Hill.

Hundley, Greg and Jooyup Kim. 1997. "National culture and the factors affecting perceptions of pay fairness in Korea and the United States." *International Journal of Organizational Analysis*, 5:4, 325–341.

Inglehart, Ronald, et al. WORLD VALUES SURVEYS AND EUROPEAN VALUES SURVEYS, 1981–1984, 1990–1993, and 1993–1997 [Computer file]. ICPSR version. Ann Arbor, MI: Institute for Social Research [producer], 2000. Ann Arbor, MI: Inter-university Consortium for Political and Social Research [distributor], 2000.

Jacob, Rahul. 1995. "Secure jobs trump higher pay." *Fortune*, March 20, 24.

Johnson, Mike. 1998. "Beyond pay: What rewards work best when doing business in China." *Compensation and Benefits Review* 30: 51–56.

Kageyama, Yuri. 1998. "More Overworked Japanese Killing Selves; Labor: As reflected in court cases, the deaths typically follow months of overtime with few or no days off and little sleep." *The Los Angeles Times*, July 20: 7.

Kanungo, Rabindra N., and Richard W. Wright. 1983. "A cross-cultural comparative study of managerial job attitudes." *Journal of International Business Studies*, Fall, 115–29.

Kim, Ken I., Hun-Joon Park, and Nori Suzuki. 1990. "Reward allocations in the United States, Japan, and Korea: A comparison of individualistic and collectivistic cultures." *Academy of Management Journal* 33, 188–98.

Locke, E. A., and G. P. Latham. 1990. *A Theory of Goal Setting and Task Performance.* Englewood Cliffs, N.J.: Prentice Hall.

————, G. P. Latham, and M. Erez. 1988. "The determinants of goal commitment." *Academy of Management Review* 13, 23–39.

Luthans, Fred, and Robert Kreitner. 1985. *Organizational Behavior Modification.* Glenview, Ill.: Scott, Foresman.

————, A. D. Stajkovic, B. C. Luthans, and K. W. Luthans. 1998. "Applying behavioral management in Eastern Europe." *European Management Journal* 16, 466–75.

Lyons, Denis B. K. and Spencer Stuart. 2000. "International CEOs on the rise." *Chief Executive*, Feburary, 51–3.

Maslow, A. 1970. *Motivation and Personality.* New York: Harper and Row.

McClelland, David C. 1961. *The Achieving Society.* Princeton: Van Nostrand Reinhold.

Meaning of Work International Research Team. 1987. *The Meaning of Working: An International Perspective.* New York: Academic Press.

Nicholls, Chantell E., Henry W Lane, and Mauricio Brehm Brechu. 1999. "Taking self-managed teams to Mexico." *Academy of Management Executive* 13: 15–25.

Pinder, C. C. 1984. *Work Motivation.* Glenview, Ill.: Scott, Foresman.

Ronen, Simcha. 1986. *Comparative and Multinational Management.* New York: Wiley.

————. 1994. "An underlying structure of motivation need taxonomies: A cross-cultural confirmation." *Handbook of Industrial and Organizational Psychology* 4, 241–69.

Skinner, B. F. 1938. *The Behavior of Organisms: An Experimental Analysis.* New York: D. Appleton-Century Company.

Thorsrud, E. 1984. "The Scandinavian model: Strategies of organizational democracy." In *International Perspectives on Organizational Democracy,* edited by B. Wilpert and A. Sorge, 337–70. New York: Wiley.

Trist, E., and H. Murry. 1993. *The Social Engagement of Social Science: An Anthology, Vol. II: The Socio-Technical Perspective.* Philadelphia: University of Pennsylvania Press.

Tubbs, W. 1993. "*Karoushi*: Stress-death and the meaning of work." *Journal of Business Ethics* 12, 869–77.

Vroom, Victor H. 1964. *Work and Motivation.* New York: Wiley.

Warren, Susan. 2000. "Five-year mission: For Dow, a dirty job in Germany presented a chance to clean up—to court eastern Europe, it wrestled a dinosaur from the Communist era—razing 'the glittering hall'." *Wall Street Journal*, May 19, A1.

Welsh, Dianne H. B., Fred Luthans, and Steven M. Sommer. 1993. "Managing Russian factory workers: The impact of U.S.–based behavior and participative techniques." *Academy of Management Journal* 36, 58–79.

Williams, Michael. 1994. "Back to the past: Some plants tear out long assembly lines, switch to craft work." *Wall Street Journal,* October 24, A1, A4.

Chapter 14

Leadership and Management Behavior in Multinational Companies

LEARNING OBJECTIVES
After reading this chapter you should be able to:

- Know the characteristics of global business leadership.

- Understand traditional North American models of leadership, including trait theory, behavioral approaches, and contingency theory.

- Understand the Japanese performance-maintenance model of leadership.

- Be able to apply the cultural-contingency model of leadership.

- Develop sensitivity to national cultural differences in preferred leadership traits and effective leadership behaviors.

- Understand how national culture affects the choice of leader influence tactics.

- Understand how national culture influences subordinates' expectations regarding appropriate behaviors and traits of leaders.

- Understand the role of transformational leadership in multinational settings.

- Understand how the national culture affects a leader's attributions regarding subordinates' behaviors.

- Develop the ability to diagnose cultural situations and suggest appropriate leadership styles to fit the situation.

This is a fictional example of the leadership styles of two CEOs, one from a U.S. pharmaceutical company and other from a Japanese pharmaceutical company. They must lead their subordinates in dealing with a crisis regarding a potentially deadly batch of headache medicine produced by one of their overseas subsidiaries. Although the characters and companies are fictional, the styles are based on real leaders.

Ms. Moore, a U.S. American CEO	Sakano-*san*, a Japanese CEO
7:00 Ms. Moore, CEO of Thorndike Pharmaceuticals, leaves for work with her daughter.	Sakano-*san*, CEO of Kobe Pharmaceuticals, eats a breakfast of a raw egg and rice. Sakano-*san*'s wife wakes their two children in enough time for their 45-minute subway ride to school.
7:30 Ms. Moore leaves her daughter at a private junior high school for girls.	
7:45 Ms. Moore receives a cell-phone call from the Thorndike Pharmaceuticals European area manager to tell her of a death and the poisoning of several people in France as a result of taking tainted headache medication produced by their company. The European area manager asks her what he should do. Moore says she will get back to him.	
8:00 Ms. Moore calls her executive secretary and tells him to plan for an 8:30 videoconference with relevant U.S. and European managers and legal staff.	Sakano-*san* exchanges a polite bow with his driver and begins his limousine ride to Kobe Pharmaceuticals.
8:30 Ms. Moore has a videoconference with the management team and briefs its members on the crisis.	
8:45 Corporate attorneys brief Ms. Moore and the top management team on legal options and liabilities.	
9:00 The director of public relations calls Moore, asking how she can deal with the press.	
9:05 The plant manager of the French facility that produced the tainted drug calls and asks what he should do about the protesters outside the gate.	
9:45 Fearing further deaths and injury, the VP of European operations temporarily shuts down all production of the tainted drug and recalls all drugs produced after a certain date.	Sakano-*san* meets with executives from Bayer to discuss an international joint venture.
10:00 Ms. Moore asks the finance and accounting department to figure out how much this is going to cost.	Around this time, a trusted mid-level manager, a student of Sakano-*san*'s old Tokyo University professor, informs Sakano-*san* discreetly that a problem exists and staff are developing a solution. Sakano-*san* nods his understanding. Staff engage in consensus building (*nemawashi*) to develop a plan of action to deal with the crisis.
10:05 Top management and legal staff meet with Ms. Moore to give her an update.	
10:30 Ms. Moore gives an interview to the press.	
11:30 Ms. Moore has a hurried lunch at her desk. She takes calls from the legal department and from the VP for European operations during lunch.	Subordinates formally inform Sakano-*san* of the problem and their plan to deal with the crisis. He acknowledges the information and thanks them for their quick work.
For the remainder of the day, and to well after 8:00 P.M., Ms. Moore continues at this hectic pace of meetings and phone calls. She calls her husband at 4:00, reminding him to pick up their daughter at school.	With the knowledge that his staff is working on dealing with the crisis, Sakano-*san* continues his regular business day: a two-hour luncheon meeting with government officials to discuss long-term R&D goals for the industry. He ends his day talking with a chemical supply company CEO at 1:00 A.M. in a private bar in Tokyo's entertainment district, *Ropongi*.

Source: Based on the format in a fictional story in Doktor 1990.

Leadership

Process of influencing group members to achieve organizational goals.

What is **leadership**? Leadership is influencing group members to achieve organizational goals. Leadership is more than simply holding a management position. Excellent leaders motivate their employees to achieve more than minimal organizational requirements. Without good leaders, no company can achieve success. Consequently, most managers seek ways to improve their leadership skills, and the popular and academic press is filled with ideas on leadership. However, as we will see, there is no simple answer to the question, What makes a great leader? Many formal theories of leadership exist, and most people have their own beliefs concerning what makes a great leader.

Improving one's leadership skills in a domestic company is a difficult challenge. Becoming an excellent leader in a multinational company is an even greater challenge. This chapter shows that successful multinational leaders choose effective leadership styles based on an understanding of how national culture and a country's social institutions affect leadership. To achieve understanding, this chapter covers two important areas. First, it provides a summary of theories of leadership offered by experts from different countries. Second, the chapter offers key examples of how leaders of different national backgrounds behave in their home cultures. As the Preview Case in Point shows, and the chapter will point out, managers working in different cultures may achieve similar goals using widely different leadership styles.

GLOBAL LEADERSHIP: THE NEW BREED

The rise of transnational companies and the dependence of even the smallest companies on international trade creates a need for a new type of leader. Many of today's companies and more of tomorrow's companies will have units located all over the world and will draw workers and managers from all over the world. In such companies, people like Rajat Gupta, the first non-Western leader of the international consulting firm McKinsey and Co., rise to the top. Born in India, with a Harvard MBA, and with work experience in the United States and Europe, Gupta is a global citizen. At just 45 years old, he was heading the global McKinsey (Byrne 1994).

Global leader

One who has the skills and abilities to interact with and manage people from diverse cultural backgrounds.

A **global leader** must have the skills and abilities to interact with and manage people from the diverse cultural backgrounds that populate his or her multinational company. Next, we consider some of the characteristics of this new breed of leader. Experts on managing cultural differences identify the critical characteristics of a global leader (Harris and Moran 2000; Rosen et al. 2000). According to these experts, the successful global leader is:

- *Cosmopolitan:* sufficiently flexible to operate comfortably in pluralistic cultural environments.
- *Skilled at intercultural communication:* knows at least one foreign language and understands the complexities of interaction with people from other cultures.
- *Culturally sensitive:* uses experience in different national, regional, and organizational cultures to build relationships with culturally different people while understanding his or her own culture and cultural biases.
- *Capable of rapid acculturation:* rapidly acculturates or adjusts to strange or different cultural settings.
- *Knowledgeable about cultural and institutional influences on management:* understands how national culture and a country's social institutions affect the entire management process.

Case in Point

The Toughest Job in Europe

Ron Sommer has the toughest job in Europe. As the CEO of Deutsche Telekom, he has a lot to do in a European Union opened to unlimited competition. Key goals for the survival and growth of Deutsche Telekom include developing its international strategy after selling its share of the Global One joint venture with France Telecom and U.S. Sprint; convincing the entrenched German works council to let him cut nearly 60,000 jobs to improve productivity; convincing U.S. and Japanese investors to invest in a nearly $10 billion planned stock offering; and catching rivals such as AT&T and British Telecommunications, which have a head start competing in a deregulated environment. By the end of 2000, Sommer was on track. Deutsche Telekom had international revenues up 15 percent and, at the same time, employees by 7 percent.

How did Sommer get this job? When the former CEO of Deutsche Telekom resigned, this German company needed a *Wunderkind* with international credentials. Sommer, then president of Sony Europe, and a fluent speaker of German, French, and English, fit the bill. Sommer is a truly global leader and a truly international man.

Sommer was born in Israel to a Russian-Austrian mother and a German father. He moved to Vienna at age 7. By age 21, he had completed his doctorate in math at the University of Vienna. Enamored with the United States during a visit as a teenager, he moved to New York in 1972 and joined a tiny company trying to make a computer. Seeking financing for his company, he met the German entrepreneur Heinz Nixdorf. Nixdorf was so impressed with Sommer, he hired him. After a brief stop in Paderborn, Sommer was running Nixdorf's Paris operations by age 27. From Nixdorf, Sommer went to Sony Corp. in 1980. He was president of Sony Deutschland by 1986. Four years later he was president of Sony of America. In 1993 he became President and Chief Operating Officer of Sony Europa.

Sources: Based on Deutsche Telekom AG 2000; 2001 and Miller et al. 1995.

- *A facilitator of subordinates' intercultural performance:* uses a deep understanding of cultural differences in work and living to prepare subordinates for successful overseas experiences.
- *A user of cultural synergy:* takes advantage of cultural differences by finding a synergy that combines the strengths of each cultural group and by using performance standards understandable across cultural groups. This results in higher levels of organizational performance than that produced by culturally homogeneous companies.
- *A promoter and user of the growing world culture:* understands, uses, and takes advantage of the international advances in media, transportation, and travel that support the globalization of international business.
- *A commitment to continuous improvement in self–awareness and renewal:* understanding and questioning one's self.

The preceding Case in Point presents an example of the new breed of global leader and the challenges he faces in leading Germany's Deutsche Telekom, Europe's largest Telekom company.

The remainder of this chapter provides a background on leadership that multinational managers can use to improve their global leadership skills. Few managers will reach the levels and experience of a Ron Sommer, as just described. But all managers can benefit by gaining a better understanding of leadership and by using this knowledge to develop more of the strengths of a global leader.

THREE CLASSIC MODELS: A VOCABULARY OF LEADERSHIP

The following sections survey three basic models of leadership. These models include leadership traits, leader behavior, and contingency leadership models. Knowledge of these basic views of leadership will help you understand the basic terms used to describe leadership options in a multinational setting.

Similar to the motivation theories discussed in the previous chapter, most, but not all, of these leadership models originate from North America. However, this chapter focuses on the multinational applicability of leadership models, not just on their North American applications.

LEADERSHIP TRAITS

Trait models of leadership evolved from the debate regarding whether leaders are born or made. Early leadership theorists looked at successful leaders in business, politics, religion, and the military, such as Alexander the Great and Muhammad. They concluded that such leaders were born with unique characteristics that made them quite different from ordinary people. This view of leadership is known as the **great-person theory**.

Great-person theory

Idea that leaders are born with unique characteristics that make them quite different from ordinary people.

Although leadership theorists never identified an exact list of leadership traits, decades of research did discover some differences between leaders and their subordinates (Yukl 1998). At least in the United States, successful leaders exhibit the following traits: higher intelligence and self-confidence; more initiative; more assertiveness and persistence; greater desire for responsibility and the opportunity to influence others; and a greater awareness of the needs of others. However, unlike the great-person theory of leadership, contemporary views of leadership traits do not assume that leaders are born. Although leaders are different, aspiring leaders can achieve this difference through training and experience.

LEADERSHIP BEHAVIORS

U.S. PERSPECTIVES ON LEADERSHIP BEHAVIORS

Although leaders have different traits than their subordinates, North American studies of leadership traits have concluded that traits alone do not make a leader. The *behaviors* leaders use to manage their employees may be more important. Classic studies of leadership behaviors in the United States came from two U.S. universities, Ohio State and the University of Michigan. Based on hundreds of studies of North American managers, these teams of researchers identified two major types of leadership behaviors (Likert 1961; Stogdill and Coons 1957). One type of leadership includes behaviors that focus on completing tasks by initiating structure. Leaders who have a principal concern for initiating structure are called task-centered leaders. A **task-centered leader** gives specific directions to subordinates so that the subordinates can complete tasks. These leaders establish standards, schedule

Task-centered leader

One who gives subordinates specific standards, schedules, and tasks.

Exhibit 14.1 Likert's Four Styles of Management

Management Behaviors	Exploitative Authoritative (System 1)	Benevolent Authoritative (System 2)	Consultative (System 3)	Participative (System 4)
General Leadership Style	Autocratic, top-down	Paternalistic but still autocratic	Less autocratic, more attention to employees	Employee-centered
Motivation Techniques	Punishments, some rewards	More rewards, but still punishment dominated	Reward dominated	Employees set own goals and appraise results
Communication Style	Downward, little use of teamwork	Downward, with some limited teamwork	Employees give opinions	Extensive multiway communication both laterally and vertically
Decision-Making Style	Decisions made at top of organization	Management sets boundaries	Management consults but makes final decision	Group or team makes most decisions
Control Mechanisms	Process and output managed from the top	Management sets boundaries	More output control than process	Team appraises results

Source: Adapted from Likert and Likert 1976.

Person-centered leader

One who focuses on meeting employees' social and emotional needs.

Autocratic leadership

Leaders make all major decisions themselves.

Democratic leadership

Leader includes subordinates in decision making.

Consultative or participative leadership

Leader's style falls midway between autocratic and democratic styles.

work, and assign employees tasks. A second type of leadership behaviors focuses on meeting the social and emotional needs of employees. These behaviors represent the style of a consideration or **person-centered leader**. Consideration behaviors include actions such as showing a concern for subordinates' feelings and taking subordinates' ideas into account.

The distinction between person-centered and task-centered leader behaviors also applies to how leaders make decisions. Leaders who adopt an **autocratic leadership** style make all major decisions themselves. Those who employ a **democratic leadership** style include subordinates in the decision making. Most experts accept that a range of leader behaviors exists between the authoritarian leader, who makes all decisions, and the purely democratic leader, who abdicates all decision making to the group (Tannenbaum and Schmidt 1958). A **consultative or participative leadership** style often falls midway between the autocratic and democratic leadership styles.

Taking a somewhat broader perspective than just leadership behavior, Rensis Likert, a famous management and leadership theorist, identified four styles of management that also reflect a similar distinction between the task and the person (Likert 1967). These patterns are exploitative/authoritative, benevolent/authoritative, consultative, and participative. Exhibit 14.1 shows how each management style relates to a manager's general leadership orientation, preferred motivational techniques, communication style, decision-making style, and controlling style.

Based on the early studies of U.S. workers, we can conclude that leaders choose behaviors that focus on initiating structure for task completion or on meeting the social and emotional needs of workers. Which style of leader behavior is best? Perhaps it all depends on the situation. In later sections, you will see that contemporary U.S. leadership theories challenge the assumption that one style of leadership behavior fits all situations. Before considering that issue, however, we will look at leadership through the eyes of the Japanese.

JAPANESE PERSPECTIVES ON LEADER BEHAVIORS

Performance–maintenance (PM) theory

Japanese perspective on balancing task- and person-centered leader behaviors.

The **performance–maintenance (PM) theory** of leadership represents a Japanese perspective on leader behavior. Created in Japan, but similar to many U.S. leadership theories, PM theory has two dimensions (Peterson, Brannen, and Smith 1994). The performance function (P) is similar to task-centered leadership. It represents a style of leadership where the manager guides and pressures subordinates to achieve higher levels of group performance. The performance (P) side of PM leadership has two components. First, the leader works for or with subordinates to develop work procedures, called the planning component. Second, the leader then pressures employees to put forth more effort and to do good work, called the pressure component. The maintenance function (M) is similar to person-centered leadership. It represents behaviors that promote group stability and social interaction.

One key difference exists between the Japanese PM approach to leader behavior and the U.S. perspective on task and person-centered leadership. The Japanese PM leader focuses on influencing groups. The U.S. approach to task or person-centered leadership focuses on how the leader influences individuals.

PM theory suggests that groups perform best when both P and M are present. That is, a leader can pressure a group to achieve higher levels of performance as long as the leader also supports the social interaction needs of the group, the M function. The theory suggests that the positive effects of combining the P and M leadership components should work in all cultural settings. However, in adapting to national differences, many Japanese companies use modified versions of PM theory to manage their overseas operations (Misumi and Peterson 1985).

The next section presents an overview of a more complex view of leadership, called contingency theory. It shows the historical progression of leadership theory beyond the simple trait and behavior models.

CONTINGENCY THEORIES

Contingency theory

Assumption that different styles and different leaders are more appropriate for different situations.

Fiedler's theory of leadership

Proposal that success of task- or person-centered leader depends on relationships between the leader and his or her subordinates; the degree that subordinates' tasks are easily and clearly defined; and the officially granted organizational power of the leader.

The early models of leadership tended to look for leadership universals: Managers and researchers wanted to know which leadership traits or behaviors defined excellent leadership in all situations. After years of study, experts concluded, "it all depends"; no one leadership style works best for all situations. This conclusion led to an approach to leadership known as **contingency theory**. Contingency theories assume that different styles and different leaders are more appropriate for different situations. Thus, to lead successfully, managers must choose different leadership styles in different situations.

How does contingency theory work? To illustrate the logic of the contingency approach to leadership, this section reviews two important North American contingency theories of leadership, Fiedler's theory of leadership and path-goal theory. For additional reviews of other similar contingency theories of leadership, students should consult standard organizational-behavior textbooks. The contingency theories discussed next identify several factors that influence the effectiveness of different leadership styles in different situations. They also provide the basic framework that multinational managers can use to adapt their leadership styles to work in different national contexts.

FIEDLER ON LEADERSHIP EFFECTIVENESS

Fred Fiedler, an expert on leadership, developed one of the most popular early contingency views of leadership (Fiedler and Garcia 1987). **Fiedler's theory of leadership** proposed that managers tend to be either task- or person-centered leaders.

Exhibit 14.2

Predictions of Leader Effectiveness under Different Conditions

Leadership Style	Leader Effectiveness		
Person-Centered	Ineffective	Effective	Ineffective
Task-Centered	Effective	Ineffective	Effective
Contingency Conditions	• good relations between leader and group • structured tasks • low power in leader's position (generally favorable for the leader)	Mixed	• poor relations between leader and group • unclear job requirements • low power in leader's position (generally unfavorable for the leader)

Source: Adapted from Fiedler 1978.

The success of these leadership styles depends on three contingencies or characteristics of the work situation: the relationships between the leader and his or her subordinates (e.g., the degree to which the subordinates trust the leader); the degree to which subordinates' tasks are easily and clearly defined (e.g., tasks for assembly-line work usually are clearly defined); and the officially granted organizational power of the leader (e.g., the formal power of a position such as a ship's captain).

As with all contingency theories, effective leadership occurs when the leadership style matches the situation. What situations suggest a task- or person-centered leadership? Exhibit 14.2 shows predicted effectiveness of task- and person-centered leadership in different conditions. Task-centered leadership works best when the work situation includes a positive relationship between the leader and subordinates, highly structured tasks, and higher levels of organizational power. It also works best in just the opposite conditions, such as when the job requirements are unclear. Person-centered leadership is required in mixed conditions, such as when a leader has low formal power but has good relationships with subordinates.

The theory's logic suggests that task-centered leadership works best in situations that are favorable or unfavorable for a leader. In favorable situations, the leader does not need to worry about the psychological needs of subordinates. They already feel positive about their work, the tasks are clear, and the leader is powerful. The leader just tells people what to do and they do it willingly. In unfavorable situations, such as when job requirements are unclear or subordinates are uncooperative, the leader must just focus on getting subordinates to complete the job. In mixed situations, however, employee commitment and satisfaction become more important, and a successful leader must focus more time on people rather than on just getting tasks done.

PATH–GOAL THEORY

Path-goal theory

Four types of leadership styles that a manager might choose depending on the situation.

Another popular contingency theory, **path–goal theory**, identifies four types of leadership styles that a manager might choose depending on the situation. These styles include:

- *Directive style:* Give subordinates specific goals, schedules, and procedures.
- *Supportive style:* Show a concern for satisfying subordinates' needs and establishing good relationships.
- *Participative style:* Consult with subordinates; ask for suggestions; encourage participation in decision making.
- *Achievement-oriented style:* Set goals; reward goal accomplishment.

Exhibit 14.3 A Simplified Model of Path–Goal Theory

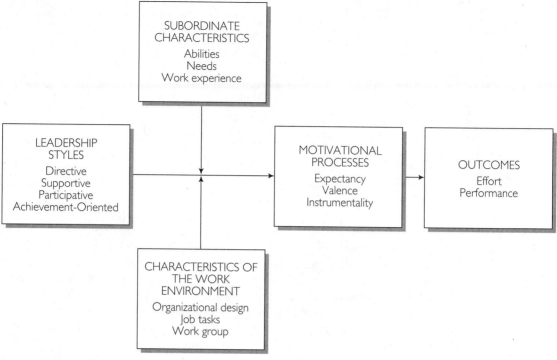

Source: Adapted from Hellriegel, Slocum, and Woodman 2001.

In path–goal theory, the key contingency or situational factors that determine the choice of the best leadership styles are the nature of the subordinates and the characteristics of the subordinates' tasks. Exhibit 14.3 presents a simplified overview of path–goal theory.

What can we learn from path–goal theory? The theory proposes many outcomes regarding the complex interactions between leadership and the contingency factors. As such, a complete review of path–goal theory is beyond the scope of this chapter. However, some key leadership suggestions based on path–goal theory include the following (House and Baetz 1979):

- When subordinates have high achievement needs, successful leaders adopt the achievement-oriented style.
- Subordinates with high social needs respond best to the supportive leadership style.
- When the subordinates' job is unstructured, the theory suggests using a directive style (the leader details very specific job tasks and requirements) or an achievement-oriented style (the leader gives subordinates responsibility to discover solutions).

TRAITS, BEHAVIORS, AND CONTINGENCIES

So far, this chapter has reviewed basic North American and Japanese views of leadership based on leadership traits, leadership behaviors, and contingency theory. We know that leaders have different characteristics than their subordinates. However, it seems that leaders can develop these characteristics if they do not come naturally.

Leaders have a variety of behaviors that they can use to get the job done. These range from a task- to a person-centered style and include decision-making styles from autocratic to democratic.

Most experts now believe that there is no consistent leadership trait or behavior that works in all situations. The contingency theory of leadership suggests that a successful leader must diagnosis the situation and pick the behaviors and/or develop the leadership traits that fit best. The next sections will build on your knowledge of leadership concepts and contingency theory to help you understand how national culture and social institutions such as the educational system affect the choice of an appropriate leadership style for a multinational manager.

NATIONAL CONTEXT AS A CONTINGENCY FOR LEADERSHIP BEHAVIORS

Most experts on leadership in multinational companies argue that a contingency perspective is required (House, Wright, and Aditya 1997; Rodrigues 1990)—that is, successful leadership in multinational companies requires that managers adjust their leadership styles to fit different situations. This adjustment must occur not only in response to traditional contingency factors, such as subordinates' characteristics, but also in response to the cultural and institutional contexts of the multinational's country locations.

The following Case in Point illustrates the effects of culturally contingent management behavior by showing how one U.S. company had equally successful plants in Mexico and the United States, using two different management styles.

The first step in understanding how to adjust one's leadership to a multinational situation comes from understanding what local managers do to lead successfully in their own country. The second step is using this knowledge to modify one's leadership style appropriately to fit a particular national context. That is, although it is unlikely that an expatriate manager can ever lead in exactly the same way as local managers, knowledge of how successful local leaders behave can be highly useful to suggest necessary modifications in a multinational leader's behavior.

National-context contingency model of leadership

Shows how culture and related social institutions affect leadership practices.

As a guide both for understanding leadership behaviors in different national contexts and for modifying one's own leadership behaviors in different cultural contexts, the next section presents a **national-context contingency model of leadership**. This model shows how culture and related social institutions affect leadership practices. Exhibit 14.5 presents a summary of this model.

THE NATIONAL-CONTEXT CONTINGENCY MODEL OF LEADERSHIP: AN OVERVIEW

Similar to the classic contingency theories of leadership discussed earlier, the model shown in Exhibit 14.5 begins with the basic contingency assumption that to be successful, leaders must modify their behaviors or develop particular leadership traits, depending on two key contingencies. The first contingency is the characteristics of their subordinates. The second contingency is the nature of their work setting.

However, in the multinational setting, the basic components of the contingency leadership model (leader behavior and traits, subordinates' characteristics, and the work setting) are affected by the national context. As you remember, the national context includes the national culture, business culture, and social institutions. For additional descriptions of the national context, see Chapters 12, 13, and 15.

Do the same leadership styles produce the same results in different cultures? One study suggests that effective leadership may require different styles in different cultures. Using two plants of a U.S. manufacturer, one in the United States and the other in Mexico, two researchers from the University of San Diego found that different leadership styles produced the same level of success.

Exhibit 14.4 shows their results based on the classification of management styles developed by Likert and discussed earlier. Neither plant used a participative management style. The U.S. plant achieved success with a consultative management style. The Mexican plant succeeded by using a management style falling into the authoritative range on all of Likert's management behaviors. That both plants performed equally well suggests that national culture may be an important contingency factor in choosing a leadership or management style.

Exhibit 14.4 Likert's Management Styles in Mexican and U.S. Plants

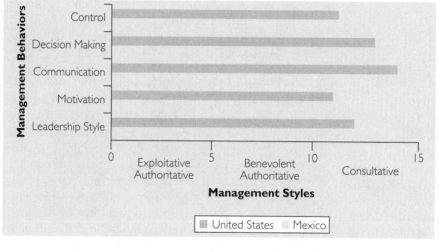

Source: Adapted from Morris and Pavett 1992.

The following points briefly outline how leadership behaviors, traits, and contingencies are affected by the national context:

- *Leader behaviors and traits:* National culture, business culture, and social institutions define the array of preferred and acceptable leader behaviors and traits for managers. Consider the following examples. In high power-distance countries, leaders and subordinates expect the manager to act with authority. Educational systems like the French *grandes écoles* train managers to believe that they should act as an elite social class. If the host country's legal system gives power to unions to participate in management decisions, then managers must adjust their leadership behaviors to this situation (see Chapter 12).
- *Subordinates' characteristics:* As discussed in detail in Chapter 13, national and business cultures influence workers' needs and levels of achievement motivation. Additionally, a country's socioeconomic development and institutional support for education affect the quality and availability of training and educa-

Exhibit 14.5 A National-Context Contingency Model of Leadership

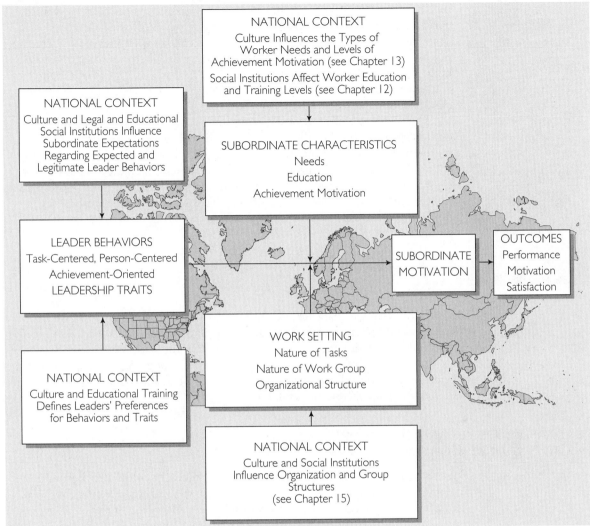

tion for workers (see Chapter 12). Consequently, a leader must modify his or her style to fit the types of workers available in a particular nation.

- *Work setting:* As shown in Chapter 12, culture and social institutions affect the choices managers make in designing organizations and subunits. These organizational characteristics in turn affect the leader's options in the work setting: that is, task characteristics, such as routine work, and organizational characteristics, such as formalized jobs, constrain leadership options. In fact, the organizational context can be so powerful that, in some situations, certain leader behaviors may not even be necessary (Kerr and Jermier 1978). For example, a highly formalized organization may not require much direct leader supervision.

The next sections expand on the cultural-contingency model of leadership. They provide you with more examples and detail on how national culture, business culture, and social institutions affect the choice of leader behaviors or traits in different countries. In addition to this discussion, your previous readings provide you with a knowledge of how the national context affects the two leadership-contingency

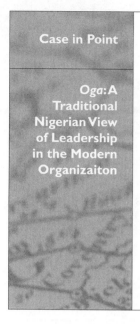

In Nigerian society, the concept of *oga* means master. It is broadly used in superior-subordinate relationships in all phases of life. Bosses are called *oga*. Teachers are called *oga*. Domestic employees call their employers *oga*. Traditionally, *oga* connoted a status with divine or ascribed authority. Royalty, kings, heads of the family, and religious leaders had *oga*. *Oga* also included a concept of reciprocity. The *oga* was also obligated to provide for the well-being of subordinates.

The concept of *oga* evolved during the British colonial period. European expatriates took on the title of *oga*. With this adaptation, the concept lost its more spiritual connotations. In modern organizations, managers are still called *oga*. It shows deference and respect. Thus, it remains a concept of authority. However, the use of *oga* as a title communicates to superior and subordinate to activate the traditional view that they have reciprocal relationship obligations. The deference of the subordinate has the cultural expectation of a paternalistic caring from the superior.

Source: Based on Ogbor 2000.

factors of subordinate characteristics and the work situation. Chapter 12 on national differences and human resource management practices and Chapter 13 on motivation in the multinational organization discuss how the national context influences the nature of subordinates' characteristics. Later, in Chapter 15, on comparative strategy and organization design, you will see how the national context affects another major contingency factor, the work setting.

LEADERSHIP TRAITS AND BEHAVIORS IN THE NATIONAL CONTEXT

There is considerable evidence that people from different cultural backgrounds prefer certain traits and behaviors in their leaders. That is, different cultures have different images of what distinguishes successful leaders. However, there is also evidence that some leader behaviors and traits are cultural universals. That is, they are endorsed or accepted by almost all people. The following section provides more detail on cross-national differences in leadership. Following that presentation, you will see some of the traits and behaviors that seem successful in numerous national contexts.

Geert Hofstede (1993) points out that conceptions of management and leadership do not necessarily translate well into other national contexts. In Germany, for example, it is the engineer and not the manager who is the cultural hero. Ph.D. degrees are more important than business degrees. In France, the distinction between management and worker reflects social class distinctions between *cadres* and *non-cadres*. Becoming a member of the *cadre* requires graduating from one of the *grandes écoles*, and, most often, coming from the correct social-class background. In Holland, a desired leadership trait is modesty, in contrast to the trait of assertiveness usually valued in the United States. In the Chinese family business, the leader is the patriarch, the oldest male head of the family. Consider the evolution of the traditional Nigeria view of leadership discussed in the preceding Case in Point.

The very latest research on cross-national differences in leadership is a project called GLOBE (Global Leadership and Organizational Behavior Effectiveness). The GLOBE study contains insights regarding leadership that can help the multina-

Exhibit 14.6
Culture Contingent
Leadership Traits and
Behaviors

Large Range of Cultural Differences	Moderate Range of Cultural Differences	Small Range of Cultural Differences
Cunning	Class conscious	Self-sacrificing
	Autonomous	
Subdued	Ruler	Compassionate
	Domineering	
Provocateur	Group competitor	Intuitive
	Habitual	
Sensitive	Individualistic	Enthusiastic
	Willful	
Evasive	Micro-manager	Worldly
	Elitist	
Ambitious	Self-effacing	Logical
	Formal	
Group conflict avoider	Procedural	Able to anticipate
	Self-sacrificing	
Status-conscious	Compassionate	Unique
	Intuitive	
Risk taker	Enthusiastic	Sincere
	Worldly	
Independent	Logical	Orderly
	Able to anticipate	
Cautious	Unique	Indirect
	Sincere	
	Orderly	

Source: Adapted from House et al. 1999.

tional manager develop a leadership style to navigate successfully through a maze of cultural settings. Led by Robert House, nearly 200 researchers from 60 countries are looking at what makes a leader successful and to what extent leader behaviors and traits are contingent on the national context (House et al. 1999; Brodbeck et al. 2000). Prior to this comprehensive study, we had studies that only considered leadership in a few countries at one time.

The GLOBE research team assembled a list of over 100 leader behaviors and traits. They asked people from countries representing the majority of the world's population and from every continent whether these traits or behaviors inhibit a person's leadership or contribute to their leadership success. The first task of the team was to see which leadership traits/behaviors are "culturally endorsed." By culturally endorsed they mean which traits/behaviors are considered best for a leader in a particular national context.

The GLOBE team found that numerous leader behaviors and traits are culturally endorsed in some societies but not others. These are the culturally contingent aspects of leadership and vary by the national context. Exhibit 14.6 shows a listing

Exhibit 14.7
Culture Free Positively
and Negatively
Regarded Leadership
Traits and Behaviors
from 60 Countries

Positively Regarded Traits and Behaviors		Negatively Regarded Traits and Behaviors
Trustworthy	Dependable	Loner
Just	Intelligent	Asocial
Honest	Decisive	Not cooperative
Plans ahead	Effective bargainer	Non-explicit
Encouraging	Win–win problem solver	Egocentric
Positive	Skilled administrator	Ruthless
Dynamic	Communicator	Dictatorial
Motivator	Informed	
Confidence builder	Team Builder	

Source: Adapted from Den Hartog et al. 1999.

of these leader characteristics separated into three groups. The groups divide the traits and behaviors by the range of variance across cultures. The greater the differences among cultures, the more the culturally accepted leadership is contingent on the national context. In turn, larger variations among countries means it is more likely that successful multinational managers must moderate their leadership styles to succeed in different national contexts.

The GLOBE team also found that most people, regardless of cultural background, believe that some traits and behaviors lead to outstanding leadership, while other traits and behaviors prevent managers from leading successfully. We consider these traits and behaviors cultural universals because they seem to work for everyone regardless of cultural or national background. Exhibit 14.7 shows a list of the universally acceptable or disliked behaviors and traits identified by the GLOBE study. The implication for the multinational manager is that one can adopt these traits or behaviors and behave within cultural expectations almost anywhere in the world.

Another way of looking at the leadership traits and behaviors is to consider groups of traits/behaviors that represent different leadership styles. Earlier in the chapter you saw the classic distinctions among leadership styles focusing on the person versus the task leader and the degree of participation. The GLOBE research team also identified leadership styles that are particularly relevant for looking at leadership in different cultural settings. Some are similar to the classic leadership style distinctions. We consider five here: team-oriented, self-protective, participative, humane, and charismatic.

The team-oriented style characterizes a leader who is an integrator, diplomatic, benevolent, and has a collaborative attitude about the team. The self-protective leader is self-centered, status conscious, conflictual, procedural, and a face saver. The participative leader is a delegator and encourages subordinate participation in decisions. The human style characterizes leaders who have modesty and a compassionate orientation. Finally, as you will see in more detail below, the charismatic leader is decisive, performance-oriented, a visionary, an inspiration to subordinates, and is willing to sacrifice for the organization.

Exhibit 14.8 Culturally-Contingent Beliefs Regarding Effective Leadership Styles

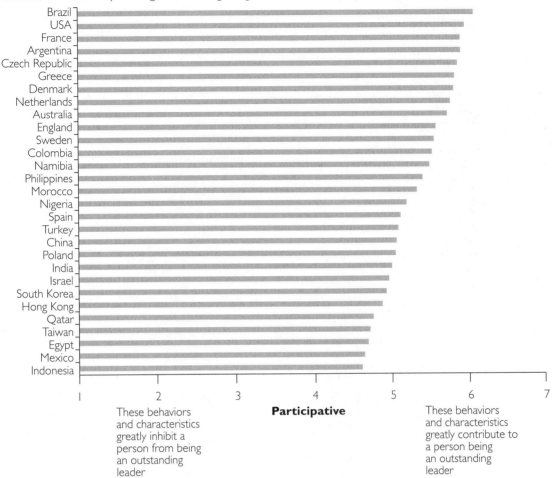

Exhibit 14.8 shows how each of these styles varies across a large sample of nations representing Africa, Europe, the Middle East, South America, and North America. Note that the charismatic leader is generally favored in all countries and the self-protective leader is generally viewed as less successful. However, all of these styles have significant variations across countries (House et al. 1999).

Why do leaders from different countries have different characteristics and use different behaviors to achieve the same organizational ends? These differences occur because the national context produces differences in the repertoire of behaviors and traits available to managers to express their leadership styles. Both superiors and subordinates see the leader's task or person orientation based on culturally and institutionally defined sets of leader behaviors; that is, each national context has its own acceptable ways to communicate a leader's concerns for tasks or people. As such, to lead successfully in multicultural companies, managers must be particularly sensitive in using locally appropriate leadership behaviors to communicate their intended leadership styles.

The next section shows that even the basic tactics leaders use to manage subordinates vary by the national context.

Exhibit 14.8 Culturally-Contingent Beliefs Regarding Effective Leadership Styles *(continued)*

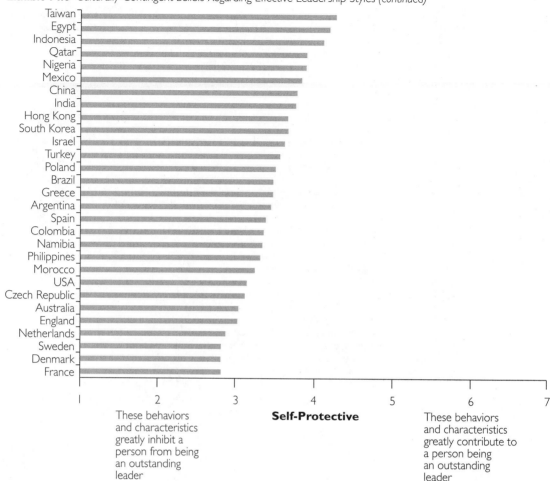

NATIONAL CONTEXT AND PREFERRED LEADER-INFLUENCE TACTICS

Influence tactics

Tactical behaviors leaders use to influence subordinates.

Beyond broad approaches to leadership behaviors, one can look more specifically at the tactical behaviors leaders use to influence subordinates. U.S. managers favor seven major **influence tactics** (Kipnis, Schmidt, and Wilkinson 1980). These include the following:

- *Assertiveness:* Example behaviors include being forceful, directive, and demanding.
- *Friendliness:* Example behaviors include being friendly, being humble, and being receptive.
- *Reasoning:* Example behaviors include using logical arguments, providing reasons, and using plans.
- *Bargaining:* Example behaviors include offering favors and exchanges.
- *Sanctioning:* Example behaviors include using threats, rewards, and punishments.
- *Appeals to a higher authority:* Example behaviors include appeals for help to higher authorities and sending problems to higher authorities.

Exhibit 14.8 Culturally-Contingent Beliefs Regarding Effective Leadership Styles *(continued)*

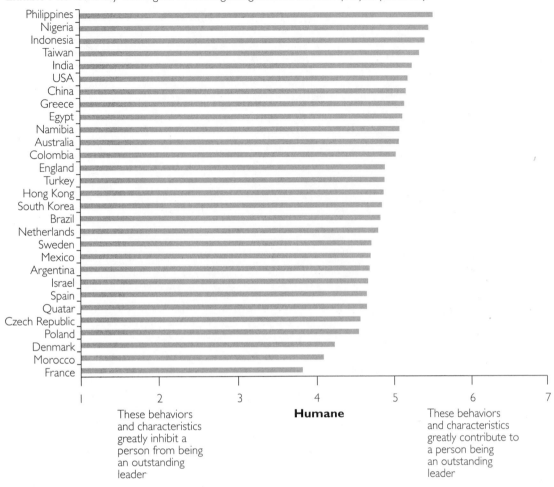

- *Coalitions:* Example behaviors include building support for ideas by networking and using friendships.

What influence tactics are used in other national contexts? One research study found that most managers, regardless of cultural background, use the same general types of influence tactics. However, different nationalities favor specific influence tactics (Schmidt and Yeh 1992). For example, the British prefer bargaining, while the Japanese favor reasoning. Exhibit 14.9 on page 552 shows the favored types of tactics for Taiwanese, Japanese, Australian, and British managers.

NATIONAL CONTEXT AND SUBORDINATES' EXPECTATIONS

Subordinates' expectations

Expectations regarding what leaders "should" do and what they may or may not do.

Leaders cannot lead without the cooperation of subordinates. In addition to influencing the expected leader traits and the range of legitimate leader behaviors, the national context also affects **subordinates' expectations** regarding who can be a leader and what a leader "should" do and what a leader may or may not do. All levels of culture—national, business, occupational, and organizational—influence the types of leader behaviors considered appropriate or fair by subordinates. For

Exhibit 14.8 Culturally-Contingent Beliefs Regarding Effective Leadership Styles *(continued)*

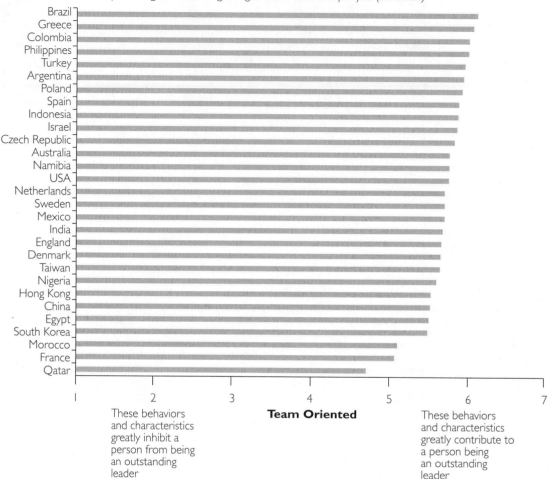

These behaviors and characteristics greatly inhibit a person from being an outstanding leader	These behaviors and characteristics greatly contribute to a person being an outstanding leader

Team Oriented

example, at the level of organizational culture, even universities differ in the range of leader behaviors students perceive as acceptable for professors. At some universities, two 25-page papers for a semester class represent a "fair" expectation. At other universities, students would resent this assignment and perceive it as "unfair."

We saw earlier that subordinates of different nationalities classify certain behaviors differently, as different leader behaviors communicate the leader's person or task orientation. Subordinates also accept or reject certain behaviors as legitimate prerogatives of leadership. For example, North American workers consider leadership behaviors associated with applying pressure to work, considered normal in Japan, as harsh or punitive (Peterson, Brannen, and Smith 1994).

What makes different behaviors acceptable in one country but not in another? The cultural and institutional settings provide a framework for people to interpret leader behaviors. For example, as you saw in Chapter 12 on national differences in human resource management, labor-relations laws in some European countries mandate that managers consult with workers regarding key strategic issues, such as plant closures. At the level of national culture, Geert Hofstede (1984) suggests that the cultural value of power distance has profound effects on subordinates' expectations regarding leaders.

Exhibit 14.8 Culturally-Contingent Beliefs Regarding Effective Leadership Styles *(continued)*

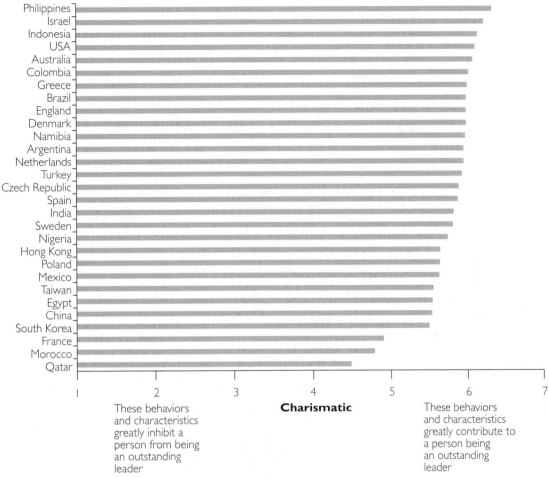

Sources: Adapted from Den Hartog et al. 1999 and House et al. 1999.

Exhibit 14.10 on page 553 shows Hofstede's ideas regarding how subordinates from countries with three different levels of power distance respond to different leadership issues. In countries with high power-distance values, including many of the Latin and Asian countries, subordinates expect autocratic leadership. The leader often assumes the status of a father figure and acts as a caring but authoritarian master. A leader is different and is expected to show visible signs of status (e.g., a chauffeur-driven car). In low power-distance countries, such as Sweden and Norway, subordinates expect the leader to be more like them. Good leaders should involve subordinates in decision making and should forgo excessive symbols of status.

Besides power distance, other cultural values likely affect subordinates' expectations regarding leadership styles and behaviors. Hofstede's work suggests that strong masculinity norms often lead to the acceptance of more authoritarian leadership, although perhaps this is a paternalistic authoritarianism in the case of the Japanese. Strong uncertainty-avoidance norms may cause subordinates to expect the leader to provide more detail in directions. For example, workers may expect the leader to "tell us exactly what you want, how, and when" (Hofstede 1984).

Exhibit 14.9 Preferred Leader Influence Tactics in Four Countries

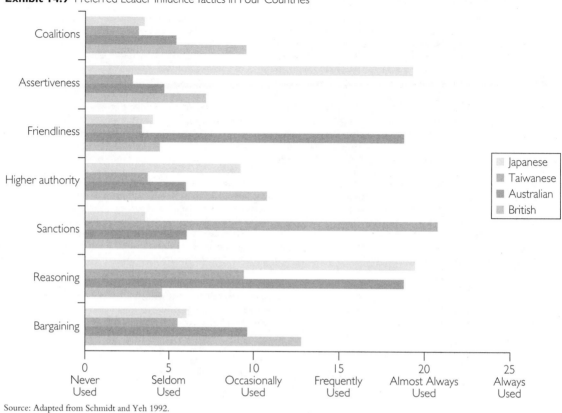

Source: Adapted from Schmidt and Yeh 1992.

The Multinational Management Brief on page 554 gives more examples of international differences in subordinates' preferences for leadership behaviors.

The classic contingency view of leadership and the national-context contingency model of leadership can provide multinational managers a guide as to when and how to adapt leadership styles to different national contexts. We now extend our discussion to consider additional contemporary views of leadership and their applications to multinational settings.

CONTEMPORARY LEADERSHIP PERSPECTIVES: MULTINATIONAL IMPLICATIONS

The next section of the chapter reviews two contemporary approaches to leadership: transformational leadership and the attribution approach to leadership. It considers how these views of leadership apply in multinational settings.

TRANSFORMATIONAL LEADERSHIP

Transactional leadership

One where managers use rewards or punishments to influence their subordinates.

In asking the question what makes some leaders truly great and different, some leadership experts have concluded that there are two basic forms of leadership. Most ordinary leaders use **transactional leadership**. Transactional leadership means that managers use rewards or punishments to influence their subordinates—that is, if you do what the manager wants, he or she rewards you. If you fail do to

Exhibit 14.10 Subordinates' Expectations under Three Levels of Power Distance

Leadership Issue	Low Power Distance (Great Britain)	Medium Power Distance (United States)	High Power Distance (Mexico)
Subordinates' Dependence Needs	Weak dependence on superiors	Moderate dependence on superiors	Heavy dependence on superiors
Consultation	Strongly expected as part of superior's role	Expect consultation but will accept autocratic leadership	Expect autocratic leadership
Ideal Superior	A democrat	A moderate democrat	A benevolent autocratic or a paternalistic father figure
Laws and Rules	Apply to superiors and subordinates	Apply to all, but superiors have some privileges	Superiors are above the law and take advantage of privileges
Status Symbols	Viewed as not appropriate	Accepted as symbolic of authority	Very important contributions to the authority of superiors

Source: Adapted from Hofstede 1980 and 1984.

what she or he wishes, the manager punishes you. According to the leadership experts, transactional leadership does work. However, it does not lead to truly great organizations (Bass and Avolio 1994).

To achieve a really great organization, argue some experts, managers must adopt a higher form of leadership known as **transformational leadership**. Of importance to the multinational manger is the finding by the GLOBE researchers that transformational leadership is considered superior in almost all societies. What makes a transformational leader? What do transformational leaders do that separates them from ordinary leaders?

Studies identify several behaviors and characteristics of transformational leaders (Bass and Avolio 1994; Conger and Hunt 1999; Conger 1991). The transformational leader:

Transformational leadership

One where managers go beyond transactional leadership by articulating a vision, breaking from the status quo, providing goals and a plan, giving meaning or a purpose to goals, taking risks, being motivated to lead, building a power base, and demonstrating high ethical and moral standards.

- *Articulates a vision:* Presents in vivid and emotional terms an idealized vision of the future for the organization—what it can and should become—and makes this vision clear to followers.
- *Breaks from the status quo:* Has a strong desire to break from tradition and do things differently; is an expert in finding ways to do things differently; challenges subordinates to find new solutions to old problems.
- *Provides goals and a plan:* Has a vision that is future oriented, and provides clear steps for followers to transform the company.
- *Gives meaning or a purpose to goals:* Places the goals in emotionally laden stories or a cultural context so that subordinates see the need to follow the leader's ideals and to share a commitment to radical change; helps subordinates envision a future state of a better organization.
- *Takes risks:* Is willing to take more risks with the organization than the average leader.

Multinational Management Brief
National Differences in Leadership Preferences

Workers from thirteen countries were given two descriptions of the ideal manager. These descriptions represented cultural norms and values that contrast styles of analysis. In some cultures, the "best" way to analyze a complex phenomenon is to dissect it into specifics. This means that the phenomenon should be broken down into parts, units, facts, etc. In other cultures, the "best" way to analyze a complex phenomenon is to see patterns and relationships in the whole—not the parts that make up the whole.

The two descriptions of the ideal leaders were:

The specifics leader:
- Gets the job done
- Gets the information, people, and equipment to accomplish tasks
- Gives subordinates autonomy to accomplish tasks
- Intervenes only as necessary

The integrated-whole leader:
- Gets subordinates working well together
- Knows the answers to most questions at work
- Guides subordinates continuously
- Helps subordinates solve work and nonwork problems
- Acts as a father figure

Which type of leader is preferred where? Exhibit 14.11 shows the percentage of people from thirteen countries who preferred the specifics-oriented leader.

Exhibit 14.11 Preferences for the "Specifics" Leader in Thirteen Countries

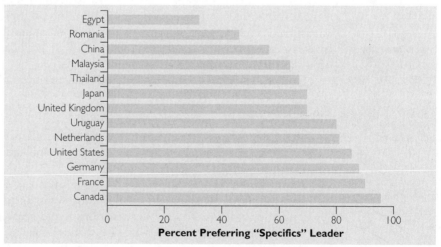

The information in Exhibit 14.11 suggests that employees in most Western nations prefer leaders with the behaviors described as the specifics leader. This leader deals with specific job-related tasks rather than a broad approach to the worker and the work situation.

Sources: Based on Hampden-Turner and Trompenaars 1996 and Trompenaars and Hampden-Turner 1998.

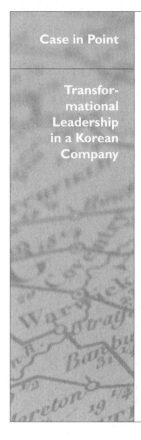

Case in Point

Transformational Leadership in a Korean Company

Fortune's Asia's Businessman [sic] of the Year is Yun Jong Yong of Samsung Electronics. He was selected for his transformational leadership qualities of a clear vision of the future, skill in leading people, a penchant for risk, and a feel for new technology. A reader of everything from astrophysics to Asian novels, Yun says "I'm often bored with routine work, very curious, and always looking for new ways of thinking and doing."

What did Yun do? Charged with turning around a company slumping in the Asian crises of the mid-1990s, Yun had Samsung Electronics' stock up 214 percent with a tenfold increase in revenues between 1997 and 1999.

How did he do it? This transformational leader launched new cutting-edge products such as sophisticated cell phones that compete with Sony and Nokia. He shook up the corporate culture. In a national culture where lifetime employment and the respect for seniority is paramount, Yun cut one-third of the payroll and one-half of the senior managers. He also introduced performance-based pay, a HRM practice common only among the newest Korean companies and used by less than 20 percent of Korean companies overall.

Yun's transformational leadership rests on his philosophy of the "cycle of change." First comes chaos to shake up old traditions. Second comes criticism of past success—a tactic designed to eliminate complacency. Third comes building a new corporate value system. Fourth, and finally, comes a return to stability.

Sources: Based on Kraar 2000 and *Economist* 2000.

- *Is motivated to lead:* Seeks leadership positions and displays strong enthusiasm for the leadership role; acts as a role model.
- *Builds a power base:* Uses personal power based on expertise, respect, and the admiration of followers.
- *Demonstrates high ethical and moral standards:* Behaves consistently and fairly with a known ethical standard.

Although the detailed study of transformational leadership is new, the German sociologist Max Weber recognized the existence of transformational leadership throughout history (Weber 1947). This type of transformational leadership he called "charisma," and he noted that it existed in all cultures. According to Weber, Jesus Christ and Muhammad were among the first transformational leaders. Most people also consider leaders such as Martin Luther King, Adolf Hitler, Mao Zedong, and Lee Iacocca as representative of transformational leaders—regardless of whether they accept the goals and behaviors of these leaders as ethical.

Transformational leaders succeed because subordinates respond to them with high levels of performance, personal devotion, reverence, excitement regarding the leader's ideas, and a willingness to sacrifice for the good of the company (Greenberg and Baron 1995). However, true transformational leaders are rare. They seem to arise when organizations need change or face a crisis. In the preceding Case in Point, you can see how Yun Jong Yong of Samsung Electronics is trying to act as a transformational leader and move his company into new levels of competition.

Although transformational leaders exist in all countries, the same leadership traits and behaviors may not lead to successful transformational leadership in all countries.

The charisma of transformational leadership requires tapping into basic cultural values and evoking national cultural myths and heroic deeds (Kets de Vries 1988). For example, Hitler built part of his charisma by tapping into the heroic myths and symbols of German culture, while Gandhi capitalized on Indian culture in his struggles with the British (Erez and Earley 1993). In addition, traits associated with charisma—such as risk-taking—and behaviors necessary to communicate a transformational vision may have different consequences in different national settings.

Next, we will examine one final perspective on leadership and its application to multinational operations.

ATTRIBUTIONS AND LEADERSHIP

Attributional approach to leadership

Emphasis on what leaders believe causes subordinates' behaviors.

The **attributional approach to leadership** emphasizes the leader's attributions regarding the causes of subordinates' behaviors. We all make attributions when we observe someone's behavior and attach a reason or motivation to that behavior. For example, when a student walks quickly across campus, we may assume (correctly or incorrectly) that she is late for class, or we might believe that the student is hungry and going to lunch.

The most important attribution for leaders concerns the attribution of responsibility for work performance. In determining how to respond to subordinates' behaviors, leaders make two key distinctions in attributions: the external attribution and the internal attribution. The external attribution explains a person's behavior based on factors outside the person and beyond the person's control (e.g., natural disasters, illness, faulty equipment, etc.). For example, a leader uses an external attribution when she assumes an employee was late because of a severe storm. The internal attribution explains a person's behavior based on the characteristics of the person (e.g., personality, motivation, low ability, etc.). For example, a leader makes an internal attribution when he assumes an employee was late because he is lazy.

Once a leader makes an attributional decision regarding a subordinate, the leader responds to the subordinate based on that assumption. If the leader perceives the cause of a subordinate's behavior to be based on an internal attribution, he or she tends to correct or reward the worker. If, on the other hand, the leader perceives the cause of a subordinate's behavior to be based on an external attribution, the leader modifies the work environment. Consequently, according to this view, successful leadership requires making the correct attributions regarding subordinates' behavior (Heneman, Greenberger, and Anonyuo 1989).

In most Western nations, people have a greater tendency to assume an internal attribution. That is, managers more often believe that people behave in certain ways because of internal motivations, such as laziness or ambition, and not because of outside factors, such as poor working conditions. This assumption is so strong in Western culture, it is called the **fundamental attribution error** (Mullen and Riordan 1988).

Fundamental attribution error

Assumption by managers that people behave in certain ways because of internal motivations, rather than outside factors.

Similar to the problem faced in international negotiation, where mistakes in attribution represent a major source of misunderstanding, the challenge for the multinational leader is to understand the cultures of subordinates sufficiently well to avoid serious attribution errors. The following Multinational Management Challenge shows how a U.S. manager working in Mexico and his Mexican subordinate imposed their own culturally biased attributions regarding the use of time, authority, and interpersonal relations. This illustration shows what can happen when superiors and subordinates attach the wrong motivations to each other's behaviors. How would you advise these managers?

Multinational Management Challenge
Getting Attributions Right

Paul Jones makes some observations regarding his leadership challenges during his first year as a manager in Mexico. Jones's observations are countered by the perceptions and attributions of Sr. González, a subordinate manager at Jones's plant.

Paul Jones:	Sr. González:
First day: "It is well past 9:00 A.M. and the office staff just arrived. I must emphasize punctuality at the next staff meeting."	"Mr. Jones wants us to behave as if we were robots. He seems crazy about the clock. Doesn't he realize that there are legitimate reasons to be late?"
"I just toured the plant and González pointed out various problems. He really pressed me to meet all the supervisory staff, but there are many more pressing problems."	"Mr. Jones did not take the time or make the effort to meet the supervisors. Doesn't he realize that this neglect really hurt their feelings?"
Second month: "My managers keep asking me for advice, or, worse, asking me to solve their problems. Don't they realize that this lack of taking responsibility reflects poorly on their performance?"	"Mr. Jones does not seem to realize that many managers feel he is the boss and he must make the decisions."
"I had to correct a first-line supervisor today when he was incorrect in teaching a worker how to operate a machine. The whole plant seemed to stop and listen. These people need to get over their fear of criticism."	"Mr. Jones's actions today created an extreme embarrassment for one of my supervisors. Jones criticized him in public! Now all the supervisors are afraid to do anything, for fear of a public reprimand."
"I thought things were looking up. My managers recently produced a beautiful document on how to improve procedures. Three weeks later, much to my astonishment, only one manager had made any attempt at implementation."	"Doesn't Mr. Jones realize that the managers were waiting for him to tell them when to begin?"
"I figured, maybe I should try a 'U.S. style' meeting—shirt sleeves, feet up on the desk, and open communication. However, the managers just stood around looking embarrassed. I don't understand."	"Mr. Jones did not act like a plant manager at all. Can you imagine a plant manager putting his feet up on the desk? How uncivilized!"

Source: Based on Kras 1995.

GETTING RESULTS: SHOULD YOU DO WHAT WORKS AT HOME?

Most of what we have discussed so far in this chapter suggests that leadership works differently in different national contexts. Accordingly, this contingency view of leadership suggests that managers cannot assume that the leadership styles or traits that worked successfully in their home country will result in equally successful leadership in a foreign country.

Exhibit 14.12 Leadership Behaviors and Job Performance of U.S. Managers in the United States and in Hong Kong

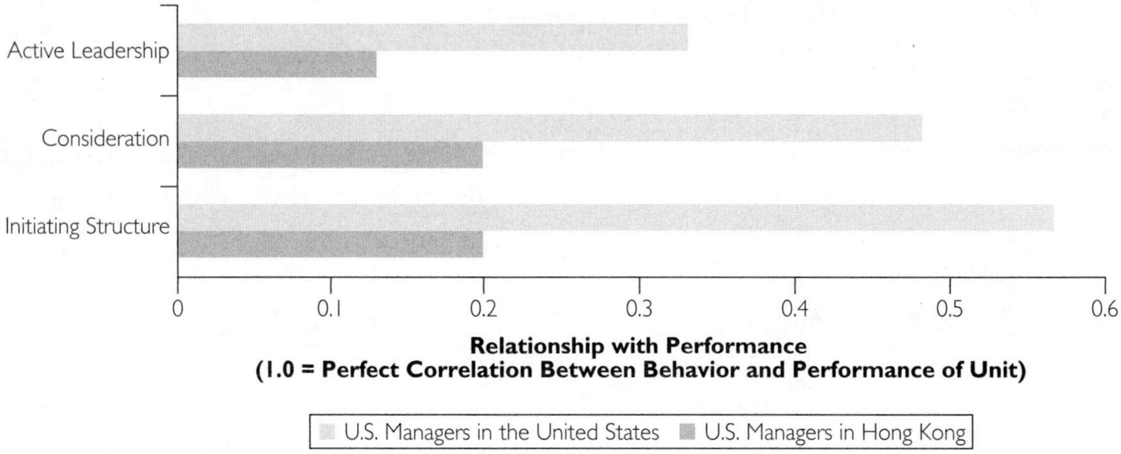

Relationship with Performance
(1.0 = Perfect Correlation Between Behavior and Performance of Unit)

☐ U.S. Managers in the United States   ☐ U.S. Managers in Hong Kong

Source: Adapted from Black and Porter 1991.

What happens if leaders do not adapt to local conditions? The results of at least one study suggest that home-based leadership styles do not work very well in other cultural settings (Black and Porter 1991). Based on this study, Exhibit 14.12 shows the correlation between managerial performance and leadership behaviors for two groups of U.S. managers, one working in the United States and one working as expatriates in Hong Kong. A +1.0 indicates a perfect correspondence between the leadership behavior and the performance of the leader's unit; a 0 indicates no relationship; and a negative number indicates that leader's behavior reduced performance levels. As you can see from the example, typical U.S. leadership behaviors did not work as well in Hong Kong as in the United States. In particular, the highly involved "hands-on" leadership style that worked very well in the United States had little impact on the performance of Hong Kong workers.

One potential reason that many managers (especially from the United States) fail in international assignments may be their inability to modify their behavior and adopt leadership styles congruent with the cultural setting. This difficulty in adaptation is not surprising. As noted in Chapter 11, on international human resource management, selection for an expatriate assignment usually requires prior success as a manager in the home country. Thus, before getting an international assignment, most expatriate managers likely demonstrated successful leadership in their home country. As a result, without adequate cross-cultural training and awareness, many previously successful managers will continue to use in their international assignments the same leadership behaviors that worked well at home.

THE CULTURAL CONTEXT AND SUGGESTED LEADERSHIP STYLES

Probably because of the extreme variability among cultures and nations, there are few prescriptive theories of multicultural leadership; that is, there is no simple formula identifying how to lead in every national context. However, some writings by Geert Hofstede and Carl Rodrigues do suggest some general recommendations (Hofstede 1991; Rodrigues 1990). Using the dimensions of national culture considered most important by Hofstede for organizations—power distance and uncer-

Exhibit 14.13
National Culture and
Recommended
Leadership Styles

Cultural Context: Low Power
Distance and Low Uncertainty
Avoidance
Leader Type: "The Democrat"
**Recommended Leadership
Styles:** Supportive,
Participative, and Achievement
Example Country: Great Britain

Cultural Context: High Power
Distance and Low Uncertainty
Avoidance
Leader Type: "The Master"
**Recommended Leadership
Styles:** Directive and Supportive
Example Country: China

Cultural Context: Low Power
Distance and High Uncertainty
Avoidance
Leader Type: "The Professional"
**Recommended Leadership
Styles:** Directive, Supportive,
and Participative
Example Country: Germany

Cultural Context: High Power
Distance and High Uncertainty
Avoidance
Leader Type: "The Boss"
**Recommended Leadership
Style:** Directive
Example Country: France

Sources: Adapted from Hofstede 1991 and Rodrigues 1990.

tainty avoidance—Exhibit 14.13 shows these experts' recommended leadership styles for different cultural settings. Chapter 15, which compares organizational designs in different nations, also shows that these same dimensions of national culture have affected the nature of organizational designs.

Power distance is important for leadership because it affects both subordinates' and superiors' expectations regarding the leader's degree of directiveness or task orientation. In high power-distance countries, leaders generally behave more autocratically. Subordinates also feel, "You are the boss, tell us what to do." Hofstede (1991) suggests that managers from low power-distance countries can usually adjust a high power-distance country without much difficulty. They must develop a more authoritarian leadership style. However, he suggests that it is more difficult for managers from high power-distance countries to become less authoritarian and more participative or person-centered.

The uncertainty-avoidance norm also affects the range of acceptable leadership styles (Hofstede 1991). In high uncertainty-avoidance national cultures, both leaders and subordinates often feel more comfortable when the leader removes ambiguity from the work setting. In countries such as France, this may take the form of *le directeur* telling subordinates exactly what to do. In countries such as Germany, substitutes for leadership such as professional training may make the work setting predictable and allow leaders more discretion for participation.

Ultimately, each multinational manager must diagnose the institutional, organizational, and cultural situations that may affect the success of his or her leadership style. Too many contingencies exist to predict what may work in all situations faced by multinational managers. However, successful global leaders remain flexible and highly sensitive to the national context.

Summary and Conclusions

All managers who work for multinational companies should strive to become global leaders, unconstrained by national or cultural limitations and able to adjust to any national context. Toward this goal, this chapter has provided background information on the nature of leadership, information crucial to understanding leadership options in a multinational setting.

First the chapter defined leadership and introduced the concept of the global leader. The chapter then reviewed three classic North American views of leadership based on leadership traits, leadership behaviors, and contingency theory. Trait theories identify the personal qualities of leaders. Leadership-behavior theories identify the behaviors that signify certain leadership styles; these styles are usually considered person-centered or task-centered. Contingency theories identify characteristics of the supervisor, organization, and subordinates that determine the appropriate leadership style in a given situation. The chapter also showed that the Japanese have similar views of leadership.

The national-context contingency model of leadership extended traditional contingency theories to show how culture and social institutions affect the leadership process. Culture affects the preferences that leaders have for certain leadership styles. Culture and the nation's social institutions affect subordinates' expectations regarding the leadership behaviors considered fair or appropriate. Using the most recent findings from the GLOBE study, you saw numerous examples of national differences in preferred leadership traits and behaviors.

The national context also affects leadership contingencies indirectly. Culture and social institutions, such as a nation's educational system or economic system, influence the characteristics of the workforce available in a country and the nature of typical companies there. In turn, the types of workers available in a country and the typical designs of organizations and jobs limit the successful leadership options for the multinational manager. In addition to developing a national-context contingency view of leadership, the chapter reviewed the international implications of contemporary views of leadership, focusing on the transformational leader and leadership attributions.

Finally, the chapter applied elements of the national-context contingency model of leadership to suggest leadership styles for expatriate managers in selected countries. Specifically, we showed that the power-distance norm and the uncertainty-avoidance norm suggest different choices in leadership styles. Although it is impossible to identify all cultural and situational factors that affect the choice of leadership style, a careful reading of this chapter should sensitize the multinational manager to the array of complex cultural issues facing the global leader of today.

Discussion Questions

1. Define leadership. How might people from different national cultures define leadership? What are the implications of these definitions for multinational leaders working in these countries?

2. Discuss how the cultural norms of power distance and uncertainty avoidance affect the preferred leadership styles in different nations.

3. Pick a national culture with which you are familiar and identify leadership traits and behaviors that would be detrimental to organizational effectiveness.

4. From the perspective of the subordinates, discuss why culturally inappropriate leadership behaviors might be de-motivating.

5. Discuss whether transformation leadership qualities are culture free. That is, are transformational leaders similar regardless of cultural background, or are there different types of transformational leaders for each cultural group?

Chapter Internet Activity

The Academy of Leadership provides a centralized source for leadership information on the Internet. Go to their site at: http://www.academy.umd.edu/ILA/links.htm and discover what is new in leadership.

For the latest research on cross-national differences in leadership go to the GLOBE (Global Leadership and Organizational Behavior Effectiveness) site at: http://mgmt3.ucalgary.ca/web/globe.nsf/index.

Internet sites

Selected Companies in the Chapter

AT&T   http://www.att.com

British Telecommunications   http://www.groupbt.com/about/index.htm

Deutsche Telekom   http://www.dtag.de/english

McKinsey and Co.   http://www.mckinsey.com

Samsung   http://www.samsung.com

Sony   http://www.sony.com

Some General Views on Leadership

http://www.leader-values.com/   *Links to many sources on leadership—mostly U.S. views.*

http://www.academy.umd.edu/ILA/links.htm   *Presents a variety of views on leadership.*

Check Country Background Information for Hints on Leadership Strategies

http://www.odci.gov/cia/publications/factbook/index.html   *The CIA's World Factbook Master Home Page— includes background information on country geography, people, government, economy, communications, and defense forces.*

http://www.cultures.com/welcome.html   *The Web of Culture—articles on cultural differences.*

http://dir.yahoo.com/Society_and_Culture/ *Cultural information from Yahoo.*

http://www.craighead.com/country_rep_ind.html *Cultural background relevant to business for numerous countries—hard copy is in most university libraries— Internet site has limited country information, free.*

http://www.imd.ch/   *The Institute for Management Development publishes a home page with extensive summaries of cross-national economic and trade data, as well as survey data on cross-national management and HRM issues.*

http://www.towers.com/   *An international consulting firm with many downloadable articles on management.*

Chapter Case: Grupo UNIKO

In March of 1995, Rubén Galván, director of Grupo UNIKO (UNIKO), faced a threatening competitive and economic environment. The Mexican auto parts industry faced increasing competition due to a shrinking economy and the passage of the North American Free Trade Agreement (NAFTA). The massive devaluation of the Mexican peso spurred a financial crisis that negatively impacted most of Mexican industry. Most importantly, the economic crisis resulted in the contraction of the market for vehicles and conse-

quently in the demand for auto parts. UNIKO had to implement a strategy that would assure the group's survival and continued performance in Mexican and international markets. Galván had to decide how to position UNIKO for global competitiveness.

Grupo UNIKO has chosen to focus on achieving long-term fundamental competitiveness through a focused corporate vision: "becoming a group of companies deploying a service spirit in an environment of continuous development and

Source: Stephen M. Hills, G. Keong Leong, and P. Roberto Garcia, *Cases in International Business: A Focus on Emerging Markets*. St. Paul, MN: West Publishing Co., 1996. Copyright © 1996 by West Publishing Co. Used with permission of the authors.

Exhibit I   UNIKO's Vision

- To become a group of companies deploying a customer service spirit in an environment of continuous development and creativity.

- Our customers' perception of the quality and competitiveness of the company will be forged with the honesty, congruency, and enthusiasm of the leaders.

- The processes of any kind, applied to satisfy our customers' expectations will be reliably structured and systemized to guarantee success.

creativity." (Exhibit 1). Galván broadly defines fundamental competitiveness as the ability to satisfy and exceed customer expectations while maintaining high levels of quality and technological competence. UNIKO's customer focus, however, encompasses more than simply catering to its clients. In fact, UNIKO defines its customers as its clients, shareholders, personnel, and community (Exhibit 2). UNIKO's management believes that the group as a whole will attain fundamental competitiveness by meeting the needs of all its customers. Therefore, UNIKO's goal is to optimize critical processes across functional areas, identified according to all of its customers' demands and needs, while maintaining high quality products and levels of technology. UNIKO must foster an environment that is conducive to change and to the implementation of its "customer focus."

COMPANY BACKGROUND

Grupo UNIKO is a collection of companies in the manufacture of auto-parts for both Mexican and international original equipment manufacturers (OEMs) and distributors (aftermarket). As of 1994, exports accounted for only 20 percent of sales while the OEMs and aftermarket accounted for 50 percent and 30 percent, respectively. UNIKO's principal products include Constant Velocity (CV) crankshafts, pistons and related parts, pick-up boxes, valves, and valve lifters. UNIKO is composed of a number of manufacturing subsidiaries (Pistones Moresa, Vel-con, Fomasa, Morestana, Alfisa, Copresa, and Morinsa) and Tecnysia, a systems automation firm. These companies are owned by UNIK, a holding group and subsidiary of DESC, one of the largest Mexican business conglomerates (Exhibit 3).

Grupo UNIKO resulted from the restructuring of SPICER S.A. in January 1994. Before the 1994 restructuring, SPICER was a collection of auto parts companies similar to Grupo UNIKO but with a much larger product base. SPICER was a partnership between DESC and the U.S.-based DANA Corporation. The partnership's history traces back to the 1960s, when DANA Corporation joined the Senderos Trouyet Group (now DESC) in a joint venture. In January 1994, DANA Corporation decided to dilute and re-focus its investment to concentrate on its primary fields of interest. This resulted in the formation of unik, Grupo UNIKO's parent company, and SPICER S.A. SPICER S.A. manufactures universal joints, axles, drive-shafts, transmissions, and clutches. DANA retained 49 percent ownership of SPICER, and gave up its interest in all but one (Vel-con) of the companies under UNIK.

A critical feature of Grupo UNIKO is its strategic alliance and partnership with several foreign firms. UNIKO is supported by technical agreements with world leaders in the automotive industry. Its foreign technology partners include:

- TRW, U.S.A.: Shareholders of MORESA and provider of technical assistance for Valves,
- GKN, Europe: Shareholder of Vel-con and provider of technical assistance for CV joints,
- UNISIA-JECS, Japan: Provider of technical assistance for Pistons,
- FANUC, THK, and PHD, U.S.A.: Provider of technical assistance on Automation, and
- AERCOLOGY, U.S.A.: Provider of technical assistance on Environmental Control Systems.

Aside from this technical support, each of Grupo UNIKO's companies has fully developed its own technological capacity in order to provide the best combination of local resources to achieve competitive potential.

UNIKO'S TOTAL QUALITY PHILOSOPHY

UNIKO's total quality philosophy (Exhibit 4), shared with the parent company UNIK, dictates that the group must be committed to exceeding the expectations of its four customers (clients, shareholders, personnel, and community), and must emphasize the projection of a consistent

Exhibit 2 UNIKO's Customers

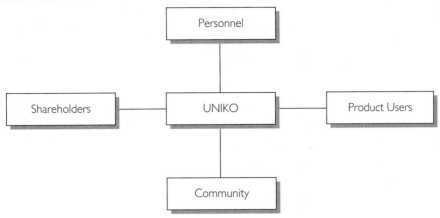

Exhibit 3 Mexican Business Conglomerate DESC

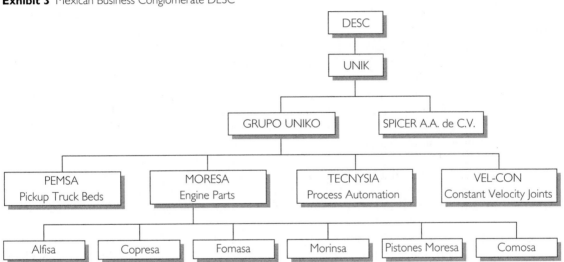

company "image" and strategy. Total quality is related to UNIKO's vision (Exhibit 1). In addition, UNIKO's vision involves using customer perception as a platform for the improvement of plans and products and implementing processes in a reliable, structured, and systematized manner. Galván believes that enforcing UNIKO's total quality philosophy will guarantee customer satisfaction and future competitiveness.

The total quality philosophy is ingrained in the company's strategic objectives which include:

- Participation
- Productivity
- Zero downtime or unscheduled stops
- Zero unrecycled scrap and rework
- Zero inventory
- Zero changeover time

Specifically, the total quality philosophy dictates the following strategies for meeting the needs of each of its customers:

Clients

Total quality demands that UNIKO provide clients with competent service, competitive price, quality, and technological creativity in manufacturing processes, product design and development.

Exhibit 4 UNIKO's Quality Policy

- To serve our customers is the only reason for existence of the company.

- Our customers' perception must be the platform to design improved plans.

- The expectation of our customers must be exceeded.

- It is the leader's task to establish the conditions, plans, structure, and system to assure customer satisfaction.

- It is everyone's task to apply our best effort as individuals and through teamwork to achieve the goals.

- The key processes shall be robust and continuously updated to optimize response time and value to our customers.

Shareholders

UNIKO aims to meet shareholders' demands for profitability, sales growth, and image. UNIKO's management hopes to achieve a return on investment greater than 15 percent through long-term planning and careful preparation of investment strategies. Similarly, UNIKO hopes to increase sales by creating and implementing an integrated marketing strategy. The projection of a consistent corporate image is a critical aspect of UNIKO's competitive strategy. Ruben Galván has emphasized the importance of maintaining an image of high quality and technological competence. He has admitted that some investments in technology were made mainly to meet customers' wants and expectations, not to satisfy any overriding technical requirement. However, UNIKO also views its investments in technology and automation as a way to achieve discipline and consistency in its processes and quality.

Personnel

Because personnel are also customers, UNIKO has both a short-term and long-term vision on people development. Special emphasis is placed on building a satisfied, productive, and skilled workforce because UNIKO considers it to be the source of current and future competitive advantage. Consequently, UNIKO strives to meet the current and future needs of its workforce, emphasizing long-term people development. Long-term people development involves the use of continuous in-house training. Moreover, UNIKO makes an effort to improve the working environment in its plants, as well as to provide competitive income commensurate with skill levels. Management prefers to increase skills and consequently wages in order to improve the quality of its workforce and reduce turnover. Similarly, UNIKO provides subsidized services such as cafeterias, medical care, and safety.

Community

Ruben Galván states that UNIKO seeks to "establish roots" in the communities in which it operates. Community activities are aimed at creating a "family" environment with the families of its workers as well as other people in the community. Their "community focus" emphasizes active participation, family programs, respect for the environment, and good citizenship. Active participation entails attention to visitors, support to charities, and promotion of symposiums. Family programs include ceremonies, weekend workshops where employees' families obtain handicraft-making skills, as well as the distribution of a company newsletter, "Communiko." UNIKO places strong emphasis on preserving and protecting the environment. Its main concerns involve noise emissions, waste in the plants, and hazardous waste. The firm follows all Mexican, and most U.S., environmental standards and regulations.

Leadership

Effective leadership is a "key issue, a pivot" on which the success of these policies depends, argues Galván. UNIKO stresses leadership in its managers. A "genuine leader" (Exhibit 5) is defined as honest, forward looking (able to conceptualize the vision as shown in Exhibit 1), inspiring (able to explain and energize others with that vision), and competent, both as an individual, and within teams. UNIKO's corporate culture stresses an atmosphere of trust and teamwork, and managers are urged to advance it through respect for employees and with a hands-on egalitarian supervisory style.

The Mexican Auto Parts Industry

The performance of the Mexican auto parts industry has long been tied to that of the Mexican

Exhibit 5 UNIKO's Leadership

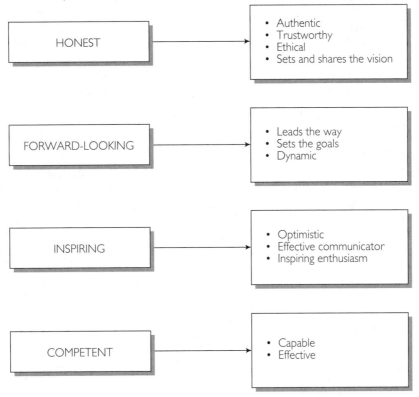

HONEST
- Authentic
- Trustworthy
- Ethical
- Sets and shares the vision

FORWARD-LOOKING
- Leads the way
- Sets the goals
- Dynamic

INSPIRING
- Optimistic
- Effective communicator
- Inspiring enthusiasm

COMPETENT
- Capable
- Effective

auto industry as a whole. From 1962 to 1983, the industry was heavily restricted to promote domestic production (import-substitution strategy). For example, required local content level for domestic market vehicles was 60 percent. These local content restrictions, coupled with domestic ownership restrictions (majority Mexican capital), created an industry that was quite small and (by world standards), parochial and inefficient.

The industry is currently in a transitional phase characterized by a trend towards deregulation and liberalization. Beginning in 1989, automotive imports were finally allowed and many domestic content and ownership restrictions were lifted. Local content requirements in terms of value-added in Mexico were reduced to 36 percent. Auto imports were allowed to rise to 15 percent of the market in 1991, with an increase to 20 percent in 1993. With the passage of NAFTA, the 49 percent foreign ownership restriction was lifted in 1999 and all tariffs on imports will be gradually eliminated by 2005.

NAFTA and the Mexican Peso Devaluation

NAFTA and the December 1994 Mexican peso devaluation caused UNIKO to speed up the integration and implementation of its competitive strategy. NAFTA will put added pressure on auto parts suppliers who lack adequate investment in plant, equipment, and technology and who are unable to serve all the needs of assemblers in Mexico. First, NAFTA will further liberalize the auto parts industry by reducing local content requirements, making Mexican firms vulnerable to increasing imports from foreign suppliers possessing competitively priced, higher quality products. Second, national suppliers may experience higher competition from new entrants to the industry as ownership restrictions are removed.

UNIKO's strategy to meet the challenges of NAFTA is to implement its total quality philosophy with a long-term focus. With respect to NAFTA, total quality involves maintaining UNIKO's competitive advantage and redirecting UNIKO's efforts towards export-oriented production. According to Galván, the Mexican auto part suppliers' critical short-term competitive advantage (relative to foreign competition) is low labor costs. NAFTA will open the doors for foreign investors seeking to take advantage of low Mexican labor costs. However, Galván and UNIKO's management believe that entering Mexico solely on the basis of lower labor costs is a myopic strategy. In the short run, these companies will have to cope with inadequate infrastructure, volatile political and economic conditions, and inadequate service from suppliers not up to par with world standards. Because UNIKO expects labor costs to increase in the future, it will attempt to maintain its competitive advantage by developing and modifying the talent of its people. UNIKO stresses in-house development of personnel through educational training programs.

The second tier of UNIKO's strategy is to increase export sales. The peso devaluation and its impact on the Mexican economy has underscored the importance of export sales as a hedge against currency fluctuations. In 1994, Galván recognized that UNIKO's exposure to peso fluctuations, due to its U.S. dollar denominated debt, would be offset by UNIKO's export sales. However, UNIKO cannot rely on short-term beneficial exchange rates to support sales, as this would create an unhealthy dependence on volatile currency markets.

UNIKO's export strategy targets aftermarket parts supply in the United States, Latin America, and Europe. UNIKO is seeking to establish a niche in the aftermarket because of the transportation difficulties associated with meeting OEM needs. Most importantly, serving the aftermarket requires lower lead times and greater production flexibility. In the future, UNIKO must become fundamentally competitive, providing world class products at competitive prices.

UNIKO'S MANUFACTURING FACILITIES AND CORPORATE PHILOSOPHY

UNIKO's plants follow the focused factory design concept. Each plant is relatively small and produces an individual product line. The average workforce is around 400, and no plant has more than 1,000 employees. The relatively small size of these plants is designed to promote close, cooper-

ative working environments and to take advantage of efficiencies of scale. A smaller workforce is more easily monitored by management. Because the company's workers are located in different facilities, instead of housed in one large plant, the strength of the workers' union is minimized. The focused factory concept is carried even further in the manufacture of pistons. Aftermarket production is located at the Morinsa factory, which is separate from OEM production at Pistones Moresa.

Rubén Galván admits that not all of UNIKO's plants have equal quality standards or similar levels of modern technology investment, that is, the same level of competitiveness. He estimates that 80 percent of UNIKO's plants are not up to world standards for competitiveness and that 60 percent are not as modern as Pistones Moresa and Vel-con (UNIKO's two most modern plants). Galván recognizes that in order for UNIKO's plants to become fundamentally competitive, they must be willing to restructure in a way that permits the implementation of the UNIKO vision. Galván believes that it is not the lag in technology that puts the less competitive plants in danger, but the inability or unwillingness of the people in the plants to accept change and adopt the total quality philosophy.

TECHNOLOGY AND PEOPLE: FINDING THE APPROPRIATE MIX

Grupo UNIKO has implemented in its organization a mix of technological and human assets that it feels are appropriate for Mexico.

Technology
In the field of high-precision parts manufacturing, technology means automated machining and Computerized Numerical Control (CNC) equipment. UNIKO has an in-house division, Tecnysia, that custom develops such systems for the firm. Tecnysia upgrades and adapts second-hand U.S. and European robotics with custom electronic control systems. This approach is more cost effective than buying new systems and paying outside vendors to adapt them to UNIKO's purposes. It also allows for the development of special-use tools and machinery proprietary to the firm, an advantage not easily duplicated by its competition.

The use of an inside vendor to design systems is as much a part of UNIKO's technology development strategy as any other cost factor. UNIKO is trying to build a capability for technology. "We're trying to grow roots, not just be a low-cost opportunity," says Rubén Galván.

UNIKO needs to use automated manufacturing systems. Automated systems create quality and, when properly designed and configured, can perform complex machining operations at high speed without error. However, the "atmosphere of discipline" that automation creates for the customer is equally important. Many customers demand a high level of automation, because automation is perceived as a hallmark of quality. Customer perceptions and needs must drive improvements. This is part of UNIKO's quality policy. The use of in-house technology also develops workforce skills.

People

UNIKO believes in investing in its workforce. Training is a primary component of this policy. At the firm's Cedei training centers, workers receive basic theory training in pneumatics, hydraulics, electronics, and electrical and mechanical systems. This training starts before they ever step on to the factory floor. They also receive instruction on how to operate machinery and controls. Most employees also receive extensive diagnostic and preventative maintenance training. Such training in both theory and systems avoids the information obsolescence which is common in machine-specific instruction programs.

Tecnysia works with line employees to design and install new equipment and systems. This process requires knowledgeable employees with broad-based skills. Workers are encouraged to redesign their own jobs, in order to increase both efficiency and quality. This demands high skill levels. Furthermore, implementing the firm's quality philosophy requires that key processes be continuously updated. Continuous upgrading of manufacturing, design, and development processes are required to satisfy the needs of UNIKO's clients.

Outside observers still might wonder why UNIKO has invested so much in its workers, given the low Mexican wage rates and huge labor pool. Labor costs are a big advantage for UNIKO (vis-à-vis U.S. and European competitors). But the firm's leadership has realized that this advantage is not a long-term one. As the Mexican economy develops, Mexican labor rates will eventually rise to parity with those in the industrialized world. In line with the firm's ambition to become a long-term leader, it must develop labor as a resource and not as a commodity. "Training is the key to our development," says Galván.

In order to retain skilled workers, UNIKO realizes that compensation is an important factor. Employees are rewarded through initial hourly pay of over three times the national minimum wage, with a regular series of increases, a program of subsidized meals through the company cafeteria, free comprehensive health care, family education, and limited profit sharing.

Highly trained workers are valuable. Good benefits help keep them. UNIKO has largely succeeded in its goal to retain its human investments. Company-wide, UNIKO's employees stay an average of 8–10 years.

Plant working environment is also an important factor in employee retention and motivation. The firm does not use any type of time-based supervision. Management has discovered that the timecard system, formerly used throughout the firm, cost more to implement than the absenteeism it was designed to curtail. Current absenteeism levels are below industry standards.

UNIKO has discovered that its employees are concerned about the safety and environment of their working area. The company uses sensor technology and extensive training to avoid on-the-job accidents. Working areas are kept clean, are well lit by natural and artificial light, and are decorated with plants and artwork created by employees and their families at the company-run continuing education facilities. Managers make themselves approachable to line employees by involving themselves in day-to-day plant floor operations. Galván espouses management by "walking around." He believes that his managers must maintain regular contact with operations to detect problems as soon as they occur. A good manager must, in Galván's words, develop "a sense of smell" for trouble.

A CLOSER LOOK: PISTONES MORESA AND VEL-CON

Pistones Moresa and Vel-con are two of UNIKO's most modern, technologically advanced plants.

PISTONES MORESA

"The Pistones Moresa plant is located in Celaya, about 260 kilometers from Mexico City. It is a modern facility that produces aluminum pistons for original equipment manufacturers. Most of the automotive companies in Mexico, including Chrysler, Nissan, GM, Ford, and Volkswagen are customers of Pistones Moresa.

The plant is maintained as a clean, open, well-lit facility. Artwork from employees is displayed in offices and on various walls throughout the factory. Clean, lively fish tanks can be seen from many of the offices. The plant atmosphere helps to maintain positive employee morale and provides an impression of quality and professionalism to both employees and visitors.

Piston Manufacturing Press

The piston manufacturing process consists of 1) production of piston castings and 2) machining of the castings.

1) Production of piston castings

Pistons are cast from aluminum alloy of specified composition. Currently, castings used are produced at the plant or are shipped from UNIKO's Alfisa plant in Huehuetoca. Management plans to eventually produce all of the required castings on site.

The castings made at the plant are produced in one of two automated cellular stations. Each station contains three large vats of liquid aluminum alloy mounted on a rotating platform. A pair of robotic arms alternately removes liquid from one of the vats while the others are refilled and tested for proper aluminum alloy composition. Testing is performed in a nearby room with state of the art chemical and optical analysis. Each robotic arm pours liquid alloy into a casting mold. Two molds, each with four cavities, are alternately filled by a single robotic arm. This alternate filling speeds up the manufacturing process since one mold can be filled while the other cools to the proper temperature. Once a mold has cooled to the proper temperature, the castings are automatically removed.

2) Machining of the castings

The majority of the plant's operations are concentrated on machining the rough castings to specified dimensions. The plant contains a total of 12 machining lines: six manual, four semi-automatic, and two recently installed fully-automatic lines. The semi-automatic lines are set up in a U-shaped structure that allows individual workers to perform more than one operation.

Two technicians are required to maintain the operation of the automatic lines. Each of the machine stations has its own control panel and lights to indicate if the machine is running properly (green) or if there is some sort of problem (red). If a problem develops in one of the machines, the entire line is shut down until it can be resolved by one of the technicians.

To maintain tight tolerances in the final product, and to avoid any expansion or contraction of the metal, the pistons must be kept at a constant temperature of 20°C throughout the milling process. The pistons are bathed in a solvent solution prior to each stage in the machining process, and held in the solution until they reach the exact temperature for machining. The solution is also used to cool the cutting heads.

Once the machining is completed, workers check each of the pistons to ensure they are within the required weight tolerances. If the weight is too great, small amounts of material are machined from the piston in order to reduce its weight to a specified level.

Workers at the end of the lines insert offset pins (produced at UNIKO's Copresa plant near Mexico City) into the pistons and then package them for shipping.

Additional Characteristics of the Plant

The automated machining lines are not dedicated to individual customers. In fact, minimal changeover time on these lines allows several models to be produced during a given shift. Changeover time for the manual lines is much greater, which results in more dedication of these lines to specific products. Pistones Moresa is continuing to work towards a goal of 100 percent flexibility in all of its lines.

To maintain levels of product quality on the manual lines comparable to that of the automated lines, the manual lines are operated at a slower production rate. The manual lines run at about half of the speed of the fully automated line. By operating at a level lower than the maximum possible rate, workers are able to maintain required levels of product quality.

Pistones practices predictive (not preventive) maintenance to keep machines up and running. Engineers chart equipment performance to head off the kind of irregular or atypical failures that preventive maintenance is able to forestall.

Vel-con

The Vel-con plant is located near Pistones Moresa and produces Constant Velocity (CV) joints for front-wheel-drive and four-wheel-drive vehicles. Unlike pistons, CV joints are composed of a number of different components assembled at the plant. The facility produces in excess of 120 different product assemblies. Vel-con has an information center inside the main factory floor entrance where employees can peruse sales, quality, and product charts, along with other displays and reviews. The facility has a similar environment to that of Pistones, with extensive natural lighting and a large amount of greenery.

Market Information

Vel-con produces 55 percent of its products for the original equipment manufacturer market and 45 percent for the aftermarket. They have a 97 percent OEM market share, and control 87 percent of the aftermarket. Aftermarket parts are manufactured to the same exacting quality standards demanded by OEM consumers. Price is the primary selling point in the aftermarket.

In general, domestic (Mexican) steel quality is lower than that of other countries, so most steel bar stock is imported. The plant has almost 60 suppliers and over 153 distributors for its finished products. Average inventory for finished goods is 30 days.

Production Techniques

Production is not labor intensive, but instead relies heavily on automation. Emphasis is placed on having one interrelated and flexible production line rather than separate stations. Each line can handle components for up to four different types of joints at a time. Components are tracked through a system of magnetically coded assembly platforms, each of which carries four units. Vel-con is currently working on the development and installation of parallel assembly lines to increase the flexibility of this process.

Vel-con conducts most of its development work separate from Tecnysia. The in-house engineering staff allows the division to move from idea to finished process in about two months. Velcon also charts each employee's skill level, and encourages them to learn as many skills as possible. This allows management to move workers from one task to another in response to changes in production volume or special setup needs.

Environmental Issues

All of the plant's waste products are thoroughly treated. The machine tools are constantly bathed in a solution of water and a chemical solvent that carries away heat and metal shavings. At a plant facility, the shavings are collected for recycling and the solvent is extracted for reuse. Oil, which is washed from the tools, is removed in a bacterial holding tank. The remaining wastewater is settled out and chemically purified. The facility's power plant meets EPA emissions standards.

A COMPETITIVE BALANCE

UNIKO has adopted a mixture of high technology and human skill in its production processes. Advanced technology is essential to survival in the newly globalized auto parts market. Skilled personnel give the firm flexibility and allow it to constantly update and improve its processes. Through a combination of strategic alliances, export-derived capital, and forward focused leadership, UNIKO is reinventing itself. It is in transition from being a fairly typical producer of highly technical products in a parochial market to becoming a world-class fabricator of competitive parts for global assemblers. UNIKO is adapting to the changing needs and faces of its customers, becoming, in the process, a customer-driven company. UNIKO's leadership realizes the promise and perils posed by NAFTA and it's making the investments necessary to weather these and other uncertainties of the Mexican economy. The ultimate challenge, however, is for all of UNIKO's plants to complete the transition and become globally competitive.

CASE QUESTIONS FOR DISCUSSION

1. The director of Grupo UNIKO, Rubén Galván, does not believe that new technology and its financing are the main problems confronting the Mexican auto-parts industry. In contrast, he believes that the most important problem is human resources. Show how the case reflects Galván's belief.

2. Previous policies of import substitution in Mexico allowed auto-parts firms to develop in an environment in which they did not have to be terribly sensitive to their customers. Firms were relatively paternalistic, and the workforce was not presumed to have much interest in managerial decisions. Show how UNIKO has departed from these old assumptions in some instances but in others reflects past practices.

References

Bass, Bernard M., and Bruce J. Avolio. 1994. *Improving Organizational Effectiveness through Transformational Leadership.* Thousand Oaks, Calif.: Sage.

Black, J. Stewart, and Lyman W. Porter. 1991. "Managerial behaviors and job performance: A successful manager in Los Angeles may not succeed in Hong Kong." *Journal of International Business Studies,* First Quarter, 99–113.

Brodbeck, Felix, and 44 associates. 2000. "Cultural variation of leadership prototypes across 22 European countries." *Journal of Occupational and Organizational Psychology* 23, 1–29.

Byrne, John A. 1994. "A global citizen for a global McKinsey: Rajat Gupta will be the consulting giant's first non-Western leader." *Business Week,* April 11.

Conger, J. A. 1991. "Inspiring others: The language of leadership." *Academy of Management Executive* 5, 31–45.

———, and James G. Hunt. 1999. "Overview—Charismatic and transformational leadership: Taking stock of the present and future (Part I)." *Leadership Quarterly* 10, 112–7.

Den Hartog, Deanne N., Robert J. House, Paul J. Hanges, Peter W. Dorfman, S. Antonio Ruiz-Quintanna, and 170 associates. 1999. "Culture specific and cross-culturally generalizable implicit leadership theories: Are attributes of charismatic/transformational leadership universally endorsed?" *Leadership Quarterly* 10, 219–56.

Deutsche Telekom AG. 2000. "Deutsche Telekom expands position on key markets around the world." *Press Release* August 29, http://www.Telekom.de.

———. 2001. "Preliminary key figures for the 2000 financial year." *Press Release* January 23, http://www.Telekom.de.

Doktor, Robert H. 1990. "Asian and American CEOs: A comparative study." *Organizational Dynamics,* Winter, 46–56.

Economist. 2000. "Business in South Korea: Career path." March 30, http://www.economist.com.

Erez, Miriam P., and Christopher Earley. 1993. *Culture, Self Identity and Work.* Oxford: Oxford University Press.

Fiedler, F. E. 1978. "Contingency model and the leadership process." In *Advances in Experimental Social Psychology,* vol. 11, edited by L. Berkowitz, 60–112. New York: Academic Press.

———, and J. E. Garcia. 1987. *New Approaches to Effective Leadership.* New York: Wiley.

Greenberg, Jerald, and Robert A. Baron. 1995. *Behavior in Organizations.* Englewood Cliffs, N.J.: Prentice-Hall.

Hampden-Turner, Charles M., and Fons Trompenaars. 1996. "A world turned upside down: Doing business in Asia." In *Managing across Cultures,* edited by Pat Joynt and Malcolm Warner, 275–305. London: International Thomson Business Press.

Harris, Philip R., and Robert T. Moran. 2000. *Managing Cultural Differences.* Woburn, MA: Gulf Professional Publishing.

Hellriegel, Don, John W. Slocum, Jr., and Richard W. Woodman. 1989. *Organizational Behavior,* ninth edition. Cincinnati, OH: South-Western.

Heneman, R. L., D. B. Greenberger, and C. Anonyuo. 1989. "Attributions and exchanges: The effects of interpersonal factors on the diagnosis of employee performance." *Academy of Management Journal* 32, 466–76.

Hofstede, Geert. 1980. "Motivation, leadership, and organization: Do American theories apply abroad?" *Organizational Dynamics,* Summer, 42–63.

———. 1984. *Culture's Consequences.* Newbury Park, Calif.: Sage.

———. 1991. *Cultures and Organizations.* London: McGraw-Hill.

———. 1993. "Cultural constraints in management theories." *Academy of Management Executive* 7, 81–93.

House, R. J., and M. L. Baetz. 1979. "Leadership: Some empirical generalizations and new research directions." *Research in Organizational Behavior* 1, 341–424.

———, N. S. Wright, and R. N. Aditya. 1997. "Cross-cultural research on organizational leadership: A critical analysis and a proposed theory." In P.C. Earley and M. Erez (Eds.), *New Perspectives in International Industrial Organizational Psychology.* San Francisco: New Lexington, 536–625.

———, Paul J. Hanges, S. Antonio Ruiz-Quintanilla, Peter W. Dorfman, Mansour Javidan, Marcus Dickson, Vipin Gupta, and 170 GLOBE Country Co-Investigators. 1999. "Cultural influences on leadership and organizations: Project GLOBE." *Advances in Global Leadership* 1, 171–233.

Kerr, S., and J. M. Jermier. 1978. "Substitutes for leadership: Their meaning and measurement." *Organizational Behavior and Human Performance* 22, 375–404.

Kets de Vries, M. F. R. 1988. "Origins of charisma: Ties that bind the leader to the led." In *Charismatic Leadership,* edited by J. A. Conger and R. N. Kanungo, 237–52. San Francisco: Jossey-Bass.

Kipnis, D. S. M. Schmidt, and I. Wilkinson. 1980. "Intraorganizational influence tactics: Explorations in getting one's way." *Journal of Applied Psychology* 65, 440–52.

Kraar, Louis. 2000. "Asia's businessman of the year." *Fortune,* January 24, http://www.fortune.com.

Kras, Eva S. 1995. *Management in Two Cultures.* Yarmouth, Maine: Intercultural Press.

Likert, R. 1961. *New Patterns of Management.* New York: McGraw-Hill.

———. 1967. *Human Organization: Its Management and Value.* New York: McGraw-Hill.

———, and Jane G. Likert. 1976. *New Ways of Managing Conflict.* New York: McGraw-Hill.

Miller, Karen Lowry, Gail Edmondson, Larry Armstrong, and Christopher Power. 1995. "The toughest job in Europe: Can Ron Sommer transform bloated Deutsche Telekom in time?" *Business Week,* October 9.

Misumi, J., and M. F. Peterson. 1985. "The performance-maintenance theory of leadership: Review of a Japanese research program." *Administrative Science Quarterly* 30, 198–223.

Morris, Tom, and Cynthia M. Pavett. 1992. "Management style and productivity in two cultures." *Journal of International Business Studies*, First Quarter, 169–79.

Mullen, B., and C. A. Riordan. 1988. "Self-serving attributions for performance in naturalistic settings: A meta-analytic review." *Journal of Applied Social Psychology* 18, 3–22.

Ogbor, John O. 2000. "Organizational leadership and authority relations across cultures: Beyond divergence and convergence." *International Journal of Commerce & Management* 10, 48–73.

Peterson, Mark F. 1988. "PM theory in Japan and China: What's in it for the United States." *Organizational Dynamics*, Spring, 22–38.

———, Mary Yoko Brannen, and Peter B. Smith. 1994. "Japanese and U.S. leadership: Issues in current research." *Advances in International and Comparative Management* 9, 57–82.

Rodrigues, Carl A. 1990. "The situation and national culture as contingencies for leadership behavior: Two conceptual models." *Advances in International Comparative Management* 5, 51–68.

Rosen, Robert, Patricia Digh, Marshall Singer, and Carl Phillips. 2000. *Global Literacies: Lessons on Business Leadership and National Cultures*. New York: Simon & Schuster.

Schmidt, Stuart M., and Ryh-Song Yeh. 1992. "The structure of leader influence: A cross-national comparison." *Journal of Cross-Cultural Psychology* 23, 251–64.

Stogdill, Ralf M., and Alvin E. Coons. 1957. *Leader Behavior: Its description and Measurement*. Columbus: Bureau of Business Research, Ohio State University.

Tannenbaum, R., and W. H. Schmidt. 1958. "How to choose a leadership pattern." *Harvard Business Review,* March-April, 95–102.

Trompenaars, Fons, and Charles Hampden-Turner. 1998. *Riding the Waves of Culture*. New York: McGraw-Hill.

Weber, M. 1947. *The Theory of Social and Economic Organization*. New York: Oxford University Press.

Yukl, Gary. 1998. *Leadership in Organizations*. Englewood Cliffs, N.J.: Prentice Hall.

Part 5 Integrating Case

Chiba International, Inc.

Ken Morikawa, the general manager for administration of a Japanese manufacturing plant under construction in rural Georgia, was troubled. This morning his American personnel manager, John Sinclair, had walked eagerly across the temporary open-plan office and announced: "I've found a professor of Japanese at Georgia State University who is willing to help translate our corporate philosophy. I would like to hire him for the job."

Ken felt pressured. He thought that John Sinclair, like many Americans, was expecting too much of Japanese companies. The company philosophy that he, Ken, had learned to live by in Tokyo would continue to guide him, but he did not feel that Americans would welcome or even understand a Japanese company philosophy.

Ken had a very large task to do in supervising the building of a plant that might ultimately provide jobs for up to 2,000 employees in the area where very few workers had had any industrial experience. He wished to show that his was a company that cared about the welfare of its workers and their job security and could be trusted to treat them fairly and not to lay them off. He believed that such a philosophy, if it could be properly explained to workers and carefully implemented, would help to build a high morale among the employees and consequently improve productivity.

Ken also wanted to ensure that high morale would be maintained as the workforce expanded to full capacity. Indeed, aside from issues of ease of transportation and distribution, the characteristics of the local workforce, their "Japanese" work ethic, had been one of the primary reasons for establishing the plant here. He believed that the training costs involved in transforming very "green" workers were well worth it to avoid people who had picked up "bad habits" or had had their morale lowered in prior industrial jobs. In Japan, teaching company philosophy is an important part of the company's introductory training program. But will it work here?

Ken wondered if his new administrative duties were lowering his concern for personnel matters. Ever since he had had to read Alfred Sloan's *My Years with General Motors* during the company training program and had written a review that fo-

Source: This case was written by Nina Hatvany and Vladimir Pucik for class discussion only. Used with permission of the authors. None of this material is to be quoted or reproduced without the permission of the authors.

cused on human resource issues, he had held positions related to his field. Even though he had majored in mathematical economics in college, his first assignment had been in the personnel "design center," which controlled training and salary administration for white-collar employees. After two years he was sent to a district office as a salesman. He returned after 13 months to the employee welfare section of the personnel department at the head office, administering such programs as house loans and recreational activities. Eight years with the company had passed by the time he was sent to an American college to study personnel-related subjects and improve his English.

After receiving his MBA, he returned to the head office. His most recent assignment before coming to Georgia was in personnel development research, planning new wage systems. It was expected that in his new job in Georgia he would eventually hand the reins over to an American general manager and remain only in an advisory capacity. However, he felt that it was at this vital stage that the corporation depended on his human relations expertise to set the scene for future success. Was he neglecting an area in which he had been trained to be sensitive?

He brought the subject up at lunch with John Sinclair. "Let me tell you something, John. I have a hunch why the Japanese are more successful in achieving high quality and productivity than Americans have been recently. It has to do with application, rather than ideas. Many great ideas have come from the United States, but the Japanese concentrate on applying them very carefully. Americans emphasize creating something new and then moving on. The Japanese meticulously analyze a problem from all angles and see how a solution might be implemented.

"As they say, Rome wasn't built in a day. I'm not sure our American workers will understand what it really means to have a company philosophy. Let's take it slowly and see what kind of people we hire and then see what best meets their needs."

John, who had worked at a rather traditional U.S. company for 11 years and had become increasingly interested in how Japanese companies managed their U.S. employees, had been eager to join a Japanese company. He wanted to see in action such "Japanese" strategies as long-term employment, the expression of a company philosophy and careful attention to integrating the employees into the company. He answered comfortingly, "Ken, I know you hate conflict. But I also know that you think it is important to gather information. One of our purchasing agents, Billy, told me about a Japanese company that he recently visited, Chiba International. Apparently, they already have a fully developed company philosophy and I understand that they're doing very well with it. Why don't we go out to California and talk with their management and try and understand how and why they concentrated on communicating their philosophy."

"And soak up some sun, too," beamed Ken. "You're on!"

THE COMPANY

Chiba International, Inc., in San Jose, California, makes high-precision, sophisticated electronics parts used in the final assembly of customized and semi-customized integrated circuits-particularly the expensive memory chips used in computers and military hardware. In such products, reliability is everything, price a lesser consideration. The similar but cheaper parts that manufacturers use once a product reaches a high volume are left for others to make.

Chiba International is a subsidiary of Chiba Electronics Company. *Nihon Keizai Shimbun,* Japan's preeminent business paper, recently ranked Chiba Electronics as one of the foremost companies in Japan on the basis of its management earnings stability and performance, ahead of such better-known giants as Sony, Matshushita Electric and Toyota Motor. Chiba Electronics Co. has 70 percent of the $250-million-a-year world market for its products. Chiba International likewise has a 70 percent share of the $250-million-a-year U.S. market.

Chiba International started in the United States 12 years ago, with a small sales office. A manufacturing plant that had been losing $100,000 to $200,000 a month was acquired from an American competitor. The American management was terminated, and a team of Japanese, headed by a Canadian-born Japanese-reared executive, succeeded in turning it around within two years.

Today 14 of the 24 top executives and 65 of 70 salesmen at Chiba are Americans. All the employees in other categories are also American.

CHIBA'S PHILOSOPHY

"As the sun rises brilliantly in the sky,
Revealing the size of the mountain, the market,
Oh this is our goal.
With the highest degree of mission in our heart we serve our industry,
Meeting the strictest degree of customer requirement.
We are the leader in this industry and our future path
Is ever so bright and satisfying."

"That's a translation of our company song," said a high-ranking Japanese executive, one of the group of Japanese and American managers who had agreed to meet with Ken and John. "But we haven't introduced it to our employees yet. That's typical of the way we brought the company philosophy to our employees—slowly and carefully. Every line worker gets a leaflet explaining our company philosophy when he or she starts work. We don't have a specific training session on it, and we don't force them to swallow it. It's up to them to digest and understand it."

"What about when you acquire a company as you have done over the past few years?" asked John.

"The same thing. It's very gradual. If we force it, it causes nothing but indigestion. Here it has been easy; the work is very labor intensive, repetitive, tedious assembly. In other places the soil is different. At one, for example, almost all the employees are exempts. They understand the philosophy but won't necessarily go by it. Engineers and technical people also seem to be less receptive than people in sales, personnel, and administration. In other sites, though, where the technology is more similar to this, we have had no problem at all."

One of the other managers present in the group, this one American, interrupted to show Ken and John a copy of the leaflet. It was quite rhetorical in tone, and a few paragraphs struck them as particularly interesting.

Management Philosophy
Our goal is to strive toward both the material and spiritual fulfillment of all employees in the Company, and through this successful fulfillment, serve mankind in its progress and prosperity.

Management Policy
(. . .) Our purpose is to fully satisfy the needs of our customers and in return gain a just profit for ourselves. We are a family united in common bonds and singular goals. One of these bonds is the respect and support we feel for our fellow family coworkers.

Also, the following exhortation:

When there is a need, we all rally to meet it and consider no task too menial or demeaning; all that matters is that it should be done! We are all ready to sweep floors, sort parts, take inventory, clean machines, inspect parts, load trucks, carry boxes, wash windows, file papers, run furnaces, and do just about anything that has to be done.

MEETINGS

"Daily meetings at the beginning of each shift are held in the courtyard," explained the group. "All the workers stand in lines (indicated by metal dots in the asphalt). Each day, a different member of management speaks for about five minutes. On Mondays executives speak, on Tuesdays, personnel and administration are represented, Wednesdays are about safety concerns, and on Thursdays and Fridays, members of production and sales speak. They are all free to say whatever they like. The shift workers tend to develop favorites, especially among the more extroverted sales managers.

"Then a personnel coordinator delivers news about sports events and so on, and perhaps a motivational message, and goes on to lead the group in exercises for one minute. These calisthenics are voluntary, but most of the employees join in. After that, the large group breaks up for brief departmental meetings.

"Again, in the departmental meetings, a speaker is chosen for the day and speaks for about five minutes. Even people at the lowest exempt level find themselves speaking. Then the department manager discusses yesterday's performance, today's schedule and any other messages, such as that housekeeping is inadequate or that certain raw materials are in short supply.

"Once a month, there is an announcement of total company performance versus plans. This is important, as all company employees share at the same rate in the annual company bonus, which is based on profitability and usually equals about one month's salary or wages."

Another Japanese manager continued, "Years ago, there were complaints about having so many meetings, but I haven't heard any for a long time now. The employees like to hear important announcements and even less important ones, such as who is selling theater tickets, bowling league reports, and tennis match dates."

The American personnel manager chimed in: "I was the one who came up with the idea of exercises. I saw it on my visit to Japan. They are just a part of the rituals and symbols that you need in order to get better mutual understanding. The atmosphere was right and the timing was good. Even so, because they weren't mandatory, it took about one-and-a-half years until everyone joined in. Now most people understand the meaning behind it. If we were to stop it now, we'd get complaints.

"Besides the morning meeting, we have several other meetings. On Mondays, we have a very large liaison meeting for information sharing. All the executives attend: sales managers and staff managers, the plant manager and the assistant plant manager. On Tuesdays, we have a production meeting attended by the production managers and any staff involved with their problems. On Monday at four o'clock every second week we have a supervisors' meeting, mainly for one-way communication to them. On the alternating weeks we have a training meeting. The whole personnel department also meets every week.

"Less formally, we have many sales meetings about, for example, new products. We have combination sales and production meetings, which are called on an as-needed basis. Team meetings on the production line are also called whenever needed.

"All these formal meetings are supplemented by many company-sponsored activities. We have a company bowling league, tennis matches, softball, fishing, and skiing. We often organize discount tickets. We're planning the Christmas party. Each employee can bring a guest, so it costs us about $40,000. Our company picnic costs $29,000."

"It sounds very well worked out for the non-exempts," commented John. "How about for the exempts?"

SALES FORCE

They started with the largely American sales force.

"They're a very different species. They have tremendous professional pride. Most American sales engineers have a very arrogant take-it-or-leave-it attitude. Our attitude is almost the complete opposite. We try to serve our customers' needs, almost like a geisha girl, who makes her customer feel that he is the only one served by her.

"We try to communicate the following motto to them:

S	incerity
A	bility
L	ove
E	nergy
S	ervice

Sincerity is the basic attitude you need to have, as well as the ability to convince the customer. You must love the products that you sell or you can't convince the customer. You must have energy because at the end of the day it's always the case that you could have done one more thing or made one more sales call. Finally, the mentality of serving the customer is the most important.

"We communicate that to our sales force and they like it, especially when they don't have to tell white lies to customers or put up with harassment from customers. We also want them to be honest with us, even about their mistakes. Quite often we depend on the salesmen's input for our understanding of customers, so an objective daily report by fax or phone is very important to us.

"No one in our company works on a commission basis, not even salesmen. We would lose market share for products that are difficult to promote. Also, the nature of different sales territories would make commissions unfair.

"Although we pay on straight salary only, we don't just have a unilateral sales quota. The salesman discusses his targets with his boss. They are purposely set high, so good performance against goals is grounds for a merit increase the next year.

"We don't really have a marketing department. We feel that it is an expensive luxury and while we have a vice president in charge of marketing, his is almost a corporate sales staff function."

U.S. MANAGEMENT

John was curious about how American line managers reacted to working in a Japanese company.

A Japanese manager explained: "When Americans join us, they expect the usual great deal of internal politicking. They scan people in meetings, looking for those with real power, looking, to use our expression, for whose apple they should polish. It takes time for them to realize that it's unnecessary.

"When we interview American executives for a job, we do it collectively so five to ten interviewers are present. This usually puzzles the interviewee. He wonders whom he will report to. We reply that he will be hired by the company, although he may report to one individual. As in Japan, the company will take care of him, so it does not depend on his loyalty to one individual."

What about your company criteria for hiring managers?

"His way of thinking, not necessarily his ability. Although a Harvard MBA is welcomed, it is not essential. In fact, no one here has one. We don't provide an elegant fit to his social elite. There are no private offices. Salary and benefits are up to par for the location (and industry) but not especially high. We work long hours.

"We're looking for devotion and dedication as well as an aggressive attitude. We conduct two or three long interviews for an important position. We ask questions like 'What is your shortcoming?' We're interested not in the answer itself but in the kind of thinking behind it. We do make mistakes sometimes, but our batting average is good.

"Sometimes there's a very deep communication gap between Japanese management and U.S. management because we believe in dedication and devotion to the company. They do, too, but only to a certain point. We often tell them that the joy of working for the company can be identical to personal happiness with the family. I ask my wife for her understanding of that, and I work six days a week, from seven o'clock to ten o'clock. Their wives place demands on them to come home at six o'clock. U.S. executives put personal and family happiness first. I'm not telling you which is right. But it is second nature for me to think about the future of the company. So long as I have challenging assignments and job opportunities, I will put the company before my personal happiness."

What do American interviewees feel about all this?

"One problem is that they ask, 'What's my real future? Can I be considered for president?' There's no real answer because it probably will be a Japanese. However, we don't like to close those doors to a really capable American.

"The issue of communication between Japanese and Americans is still a problem. After the Americans go home, the Japanese get together at seven or eight o'-clock and talk in Japanese about problems and make decisions without the Americans present. Naturally this makes the Americans feel very apprehensive. We're trying to rectify it by asking the Japanese managers not to make decisions alone and asking the Americans to stay as late as possible.

"More important, if we could really have our philosophy permeate the American managers, we Japanese could all go back to Japan and not worry about it. Our mission is to expedite that day by education and training.

"So far, however, there is a gap. Americans are more interested in individual accomplishment, remuneration and power. When they are given more responsibility, they don't feel its heavy weight, rather they feel that it extends their sovereign area so that they have more of a whip. That creates power conflicts among U.S. managers."

"Let me tell you, though," summarized the American personnel manager, "I like it. I was recruited by a headhunter. Now, I've been with the company five years and the difference from my former employer is astounding. I don't have to get out there and be two-faced, fudging to keep the union out, hedging for the buck. In general, it's hard to find an American employer that really sincerely cares for the welfare of the low-level employee. This company went almost too far in the opposite direction at first. They wanted to do too much for the employees too quickly, without their earning it. That way, you don't get their respect."

FINANCIAL PEOPLE

"Our financial people throughout the company are proud because of our impressive company performance. Only 20% of our financing is through debt, in contrast to many Japanese companies. We also have a rather unique way of treating some of our raw materials internally. We try to expense everything out. It's derived from our founder's very conservative management. We ask the question: 'If we closed down tomorrow, what would our liquid assets be?' In line with that, for example, internally we put our inventory at zero.

"We follow the 'noodle peddler theory.' The noodle peddler is an entrepreneur. He has to borrow his cart, his serving dishes and his pan to make ramen. He has to be a good marketer to know where to sell. He has to be a good purchasing director and not overbuy noodles, in case it rains. He could buy a fridge but he would need a lot of capital, the taste of noodles would deteriorate, and he would need additional manpower to keep an inventory of the contents of the fridge. The successful noodle peddler puts dollars aside at the end of the day for depreciation and raw materials for tomorrow. Only then does he count profits. That's also why we don't have a marketing department. The successful peddler doesn't have time to examine opportunities in the next town.

"This is the way a division manager has to operate. In order to maximize output with minimum expenditure, every effort is made to keep track on a daily basis of sales, returns, net shipment costs and expenses."

OPEN COMMUNICATIONS

"I understand all that you've said so far," mused John, "but how exactly do you take all these abstract philosophical ideas and make them real?"

"Oh, open communications is the key. We have a fairly homogeneous workforce. Most are intelligent, some are even college graduates. Most are also very stable types with dependents or elderly parents they send money to.

"We're lucky, but of course it's not as homogeneous as in Japan, where everyone has experienced one culture. So here, the philosophy has to be backed up by a great deal of communication.

"We mentioned the meetings. We also have a suggestion box and we answer all the suggestions in print in the company newspaper. Also, one person from personnel tours the plant all day, for all three shifts, once a week, just chatting and getting in touch with any potential problems as they arise. It's kind of a secondary grievance system. We're not unionized and I guess we'd rather stay that way as it helps us so much with flexibility and job changes among our workforce.

"In the fall, when work is slow, we have many *kompas*. You may not know about this, John. A *kompa* is a small gathering off-premises after work. Eight to eighteen people participate, and the company pays for their time and refreshments. They're rarely social, they have an objective. For example, if two departments don't get along and yet they need to work together, they might hold a *kompa*. A *kompa* can take place at all levels of the company. Those groups that do it more frequently tend to move on from talking about production problems to more philosophical issues."

APPRAISAL AND REWARD SYSTEMS

"It all sounds great," sighed Ken, "just as good as Japan. But tell me, how does it tie in with wages and salaries, because people here are used to such different systems."

"Well, we don't have lifetime employment, but we do have an explicit no-layoff commitment. We are responsible for our employees. This means that employees also have to take responsibility and have broad job categories so we don't have to redo paperwork all the time. We have tried to reduce the number of job classifications to the raw minimum, so we have two pay grades covering 700 workers. At the higher levels, we have three pay grades for craftsmen and two for technicians."

John ventured, "I guess an example of your job flexibility in action is the mechanic you mentioned when we toured the plant."

"Yes, the person you spoke with was a dry press mechanic. He's doing menial labor this week, but his pay hasn't been cut, and he knows he wouldn't be taken off his job if it weren't important."

"We don't hire outside, if we can avoid it," added the personnel manager. "Only if the skill is not available in-house. The bulk of our training is on-the-job. We don't utilize job postings. We promote when a person's skills are ripe or when there is a need.

"The job of a 'lead' or team leader is the stepping-stone to supervisor. It's not a separate job status within our system, but the lead is given a few cents an hour extra and wears a pink, not a yellow, smock. The lead is carefully groomed for his or her position, and although a lead might be demoted because a specific need for them no longer existed, a lead would rarely be demoted for lack of skills or leadership ability.

"Rewards are for service and performance. Plant workers, unskilled and semi-skilled, are reviewed every six months. The lead completes the evaluation form (see Exhibit 1). This is checked or confirmed by the supervisor and the overall point score translates into cents per hour. There are two copies, one for the supervisor and one for the employee. Depending on the supervisor, some employees get a copy, some don't.

"The office clerical staff are all reviewed on April 1st and October 1st. A similar review form for managers is used to determine overall letter scores. All the scores are posted on a spread sheet and compared across departments, through numerous meetings of managers and personnel people, until the scores are consistent with one another. Then the scores are tied to dollars. Some managers feed back, some don't.

"Exempt staff are reviewed on April 1st, and as a separate process, the spreadsheet procedure just outlined is carried out. At least two managers review any exempt employee, but feedback is usually minimal. The reason is that we encourage feedback all year. If there are no surprises for your subordinate at review time, then you've managed well.

"Agreements on reviews for exempt personnel take place in many meetings at various levels. The process is very thorough and exceptionally fair, and contributes to the levels of performance we get."

Exhibit I

Employee's Name	Clock No.	Dept.	Shift	Over Last 6 Month Period			
				Days Absent	Number Tardies	Number Early Exit	Work Days Leave of Absences
Employee's Job Title	Anniversary						

Rate on Factors Below:		Numerical Score			
		L	S	M	F
1. LOYALTY/EDUCATION	Faithful to the company cause, ideals, philosophy, & customers; a devoting or setting aside for company purposes.				
2. SPIRIT/ZEAL	Amount of interest & enthusiasm shown in work; full of energy, animation & courage; eagerness & ardent interest in the pursuit of company goals.				
3. COOPERATION	A willingness & ability to work with leaders & fellow employees toward company goals.				
4. QUANTITY OF WORK	Volume of work regularly produced; speed & consistency of output.				
5. QUALITY OF WORK	Extent to which work produced meets quality requirements of accuracy, thoroughness & effectiveness.				
6. JOB KNOWLEDGE	The fact or condition of knowing the job with familiarity gained through experience, association & training.				
7. SAFETY ATTITUDE	The willingness & ability to perform work safely.				
8. CREATIVENESS	The ability to produce through imaginitive skill.				
9. ATTENDANCE	Includes all types of absence (excused or unexcused), tardies, early exits, L.O.A.'s from scheduled work.				
10. LEADERSHIP	The ability to provide direction, guidance & training to others.				

OVERALL EVALUATION OF EMPLOYEE PERFORMANCE:

Supervisor's Approval		Personnel Dept. Approval

Do Not Write Below This Line—For Human Resource Department Use Only

Present Base Rate	New Base Rate	Effective Date of Increase	Refer to instructions on the back side of this paper

QUALITY AND SERVICE

A question from John as to how Chiba International was doing as a result of all this elicited much pride.

"Turnover is 2½ percent a month, which is very satisfactory for our kind of labor, given a transient society. We rarely have to advertise for new employees now. The community knows about us. But we do select carefully. The personnel department does the initial screening, and then the production managers and supervisors get together and interview people.

"The lack of available technically trained people used to be a big problem, but over the years we've developed the expertise internally. Our productivity is now almost as high as in Japan."

Ken and John asked what other aspects of the company they had not yet discussed. They were told that quality, and, hence, customer service, was another central part of the philosophy.

"Our founder, Mr. Amano, firmly believes in zero defect theory. Doctor Deming taught us the concept of quality control. Unfortunately, many American companies did not emphasize this. During World War II, the concept of acceptable quality level was developed in the United States. The idea was that with mass production there will be some defects. Rather than paying for more inspectors on the production line, real problems, for example, with cars, could be identified by the consumer in the field and repaired in the field.

"We don't allow that. We have 100 percent visual inspection of all our tiny parts. They only cost $50 per 1,000 units. We inspect every finished package under a microscope, so we have 130 inspectors, which is about one-sixth of our production staff.

"The company's founder, Amano, has said to us, 'We try to develop every item our customers want. Being latecomers, we never say no, we never say we can't.' Older ceramic manufacturers would evaluate a proposal on a cost basis and say no. Yet we have been profitable from the start."

As the interview drew to a close, one Japanese manager reflected that Mr. Suzuki has a saying:

$$\text{Ability} \times \text{philosophy} \times \text{zeal} = \text{performance.}$$

If the philosophy is negative, performance is negative because it's a multiplicative relationship.

"But in our company, which now numbers 2,000, we must also start to have different kinds of thinking. The Japanese sword is strong because it is made of all different kinds of steel wrapped around one another. The Chinese sword is also very strong, but because it's all one material, it's vulnerable to a certain kind of shock. We must bear that in mind so that we have differences within a shared philosophy.

"We're thinking of writing a book on our philosophy, addressing such issues as what loyalty is, by piecing together events and stories from our company history. This would be a book that would assist us in training."

Ken and John walked out into the parking lot. "Whew!" sighed John. "It's more complicated than I had thought."

"Oh, yes! You need a great deal of patience," responded Ken paternally.

"So we'd better get started quickly," enthused John. "Where shall we begin? Perhaps I should call the translator."

CASE QUESTIONS FOR DISCUSSION

1. Can Japanese motivation practices work in the U.S. without being adapted? Why or why not?
2. How should Ken and John adapt Chiba's California practices to their own situation in Georgia? What problems might they run into?
3. What aspects of the Japanese management approach used by Chiba are the most interesting or unusual?

Part 6

Understanding Collaborators and Competitors: Comparative Strategic Management and Organizational Design

CHAPTER 15
Comparative Strategic Management and Organizational Design

Chapter 15

Comparative Strategic Management and Organizational Design

LEARNING OBJECTIVES
After reading this chapter you should
be able to:

- Understand how the forces of
  globalization lead to convergence
  among nations in strategic
  management practices and
  organizational design.

- Know how the elements of the national
  context (social institutions, national
  and business culture, resource pool)
  affect a firm's choices regarding
  strategy formulation and content and
  organizational design.

- See how mission statements are used
  in different nations.

- Understand national differences in how
  companies assess their strategic
  situations.

- Appreciate how national cultures lead
  to basic differences in organizational
  design preferences.

- Understand the uniqueness of the
  Japanese consensus bureaucracy and
  the *ringi* decision-making process.

- Understand how social institutions
  support organizational designs.

Preview Case in Point	Banco Comercial Portugues (BCP) is the biggest private sector bank in Portugal. However, it ranks only 63rd in Europe and is one of only three Portuguese companies in the Eurotop-300, an index of market capitalization size for the EU. Why are Portuguese companies so small?
Institutional and Resource Constraints on Portuguese Companies	In spite of Portugal's membership in the EU and the potential of its companies to compete anywhere in Europe, the small domestic market limits the base from which Portuguese companies can expand. Unlike Swiss companies, they also lack experience in building multinational operations. BCP, for example, was founded only 15 years ago.

Three typical strategies for growth have emerged in this small country. First, many companies form alliances with larger foreign companies. For example, fearing the loss of local companies to the larger European stock exchanges, the Portuguese stock exchange is looking to joint Euronext, the merged exchanges of Amsterdam, Brussels, and Paris. Second, Portuguese companies target foreign markets where they have a unique advantage, namely Portuguese-speaking Brazil. For example, the cement company Cimpor is the third largest supplier in Brazil. Third, to offset the small size of the Portuguese economy, some companies used unrelated diversification to grow by being in many markets. Sonae, for example, is Portugal's largest producer of wood panels, but it is best known as the country's leading retailer and the first to open a hypermarket. Other activities range from mobile phones to venture capital.

Source: Adapted from *Economist* 2000b.

The Preview Case in Point shows how the characteristics of a nation state can influence the strategies and designs of local organizations. It also shows how globalization trends such as international competition and regional trade agreements can affect the actions of companies. This chapter considers both of these issues: how companies respond to the unique characteristics of the national locations and how companies respond to the pressures of globalization.

There are two key questions to consider when you look at the organizational strategies and design of companies from other nations. What makes organizations from different societies alike? What makes them different? The following sections describe the pressures that lead organizations from all societies to be similar and the pressures that lead organizations from different nations to be different. Later in the chapter you will see specific examples of how these processes work.

ORGANIZATIONS ALIKE: GLOBALIZATION AND CONVERGENCE

Convergence

Increasing similarity of management practices in different nations.

Some experts believe that many management practices, especially those related to strategy and structure, are becoming more similar. This increasing similarity of management practices is called **convergence**. In fact, many of the multinational management examples given in this book show the effects of convergence. The examples come from organizations throughout the world and illustrate management practices readily copied and used by managers of all nationalities.

Exhibit 15.1 The Effects of Globalization on the Convergence of Strategy and Structure

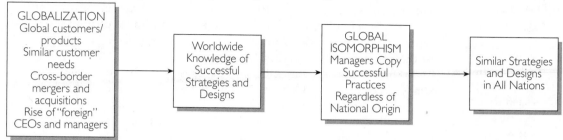

Convergence is most apparent with transnational firms. Transnationals competing in the same industry tend to have similar structures and strategies regardless of the location of the company's headquarters. They use what they see as most effective. In addition, because they compete in worldwide markets, transnationals not only seek uniform products and strategies but also seek strategies and ways of organizing that need not differ by national boundaries. Transnational managers also often lack deep-seated national cultural or societal identification. Their companies, not their nations, are more important to them.

The same forces that lead companies to become transnational in strategy and structure also encourage organizations from different nations to become more alike. Coercive, mimic, and normative isomorphic pressures for similarity (see Chapter 12 for definitions) not only work within countries but are also beginning to work cross-nationally. For example, agreements among countries such as regional trade agreements and membership in the WTO provide supranational regulatory environments that affect management practices. Cross-border competition, trade, mergers, and acquisitions provide more opportunities to learn about and copy successful managerial practices from anywhere in the world. Normative pressures for similarity come from the internationalization of business education and the movement of managers across borders. Exhibit 15.1 shows visually how these processes work.

The points below show in more detail how globalization pushes organizations to be more similar.

- *Global customers and products:* The similarity of customer demands and the increased likelihood that companies and people shop worldwide limits the options managers have in strategy and structure. This results in managers creating similar organizations with similar capabilities to serve similar customers.
- *Growing levels of industrialization and economic development:* This results in convergence because more organizations have the technical and financial capability to use similar technologies. In turn, the technologies used by organizations limit the strategy and design options available to managers.
- *Global competition and global trade:* International competition raises managerial awareness of what people in other countries are doing. The growth of U.S. managers' interest in Japanese management, for example, occurred because of increasing Japanese competition with U.S. companies. Increased trade means that managers interact more with each other and learn more about the strategies and structures of organizations from different societies. Both competition and trade encourage managers to mimic or copy what works in other nations.
- *Cross-border mergers, acquisitions, and alliances:* As with cross-border trade when companies from different nations combine, such as the recent merger of

Exhibit 15.2 Migrating CEOs

Company Location	Company Name	CEO Name	CEO's Nation of Origin
Australia	CSR Ltd.	Peter Kirby	South Africa
	McPhersons Ltd.	David Aikman	UK
Canada	BC Telecom	David A. Carter	Scotland
	Chartwood Pacific Group	U. Gary Chartwood	Germany
France	Eridania Beglin-Say	Sefano Meloni	Italy
	L'Oréal	Lindsay Owen-Jones	UK
Germany	Deutsche Telekom	Ron Sommer	Israel
Hong Kong	China Light & Power	Ross Sayers	New Zealand
	Sino Land	Robert Ng	Singapore
Italy	Dulma	Michael Davies	UK
	Agnesi	Francis Glaizal	France
Japan	Nissan	Carlos Ghosn	France
	Mazda	Mark Fields	USA
Mexico	Chase	John Donnelly	Panama
	Citibank	Julio de Quezada	Cuba
The Netherlands	Baan	Pierre J. Everaert	Belgium
	Grolsch Brewery	J. Troch	Belgium
South Africa	South African Airways	Coleman Andrews	USA
Spain	HN Hoteles	Gabrielle Burgie	Italy
	Pryca	Georges Plassat	France
Switzerland	ABB	Goran Lindahl	Sweden
	Nestlé	Peter Brageck-Letmathe	Austria

Sources: Adapted from Lyons and Stuart 2000 and Sprague 2000.

Chrysler and Daimler Benz, managers combine the strategies and organizational designs from both nationalities. These combined organizations provide a wealth of information on the organizational practices of other societies. Later, parent organizations use this knowledge to change and improve their own organizations. They must find strategies and structures that work for all of the participating companies regardless of nationality.

- *Cross-national mobility of managers:* Increasingly, organizations are looking for CEOs, managers, and technical experts from any country that can provide the highest level of talent. When managers cross borders, they bring with them the technical and managerial knowledge from their country of origin. This migratory knowledge increases mimic isomorphism or the ability of managers to copy strategies and designs from other countries. Exhibit 15.2 shows examples of foreign CEOs who now run companies in different nations.
- *Internationalization of business education:* Business education also serves to homogenize organizational practices. In particular, the large number of international

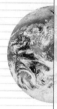

Multinational Management Brief
Management Transfer

Many of the high-tech firms in Korea, India, and Taiwan are staffed with top executives who were educated in the United States and stayed on to work for a decade or more. Now they are returning to their homelands armed with technical and managerial expertise. John Gage, an executive at Sun Microsystems, estimates that half of the vice presidents of engineering in Taiwanese electronics companies originally worked for U.S. companies such as Hewlett-Packard or Sun. Former expatriates such as Hong Kong's Allan Wong are borrowing management systems learned from their former U.S. companies and adapting them to local needs. Wong, for example, is following his former company's (NCR) example by investing in continuing education for his managers as a technique for sustaining long-term growth.

In China, approximately 25 universities have joint MBA programs with U.S. universities. The China Europe International Business School is financed jointly by the Shanghai Municipal Government and the EU. The first graduating class from an international collaboration was in July 1999 from a program between Beijing's Qinghua University and MIT's Sloan School of Management. Expectation is that the demand of MBAs in China will soar as local companies go international and more multinationals enter China.

Sources: Based on *East Asian Executive Reports* 1999 and Engardia et al. 1994.

students in U.S. and European MBA programs helps spread common business techniques. Many students return to their home countries with the intent of adopting management practices that best fit their national cultures. Cooperative MBA programs between universities in developing nations and partner universities in the United States and Europe also transfer management practices. Consider the preceding Multinational Management Brief, which shows examples of the transfer of management knowledge.

In spite of the trend toward convergence, national differences still affect the way many firms compete via their choices of strategies and designs. Savvy multinational managers must understand these differences for three important reasons. First, managers in successful multinational firms must understand and anticipate the strategies of rivals from other countries. Second, managers in successful multinational firms must understand the strategies and preferences for organizational designs of potential business partners, since cross-national partnerships often exist for any value-chain activity, from raw-material suppliers to downstream distribution. Third, strategies and designs developed in one national context might be copied and modified to fit another national context.

To provide a better understanding of international rivals and collaborators, three sections follow. First, the chapter presents an overview of how the national context leads to national differences in strategic management practices and organizational design. Second, using this overview as background, the chapter presents a more detailed explanation of the national differences in strategic management practices. Third, the chapter discusses national differences in organizational design.

THE NATIONAL CONTEXT AND ORGANIZATIONAL STRATEGY AND DESIGN: OVERVIEW AND OBSERVATIONS

The national context has been discussed at length throughout this text. Following is a brief summary of the effect of the national context on organizational strategy and design. The national context represents the immediate environment where firms compete. These environments provide firms with nation-specific opportunities and threats; that is, there are specific combinations of opportunities and threats in a nation that are different from those in other nations. As a result, the varieties of national contexts lead to the flourishing of different industries and the prospering of different strategies and designs.

More specifically, the national context affects organizational design and strategy formulation and content through the following processes (Li 1993):

- The social institutions and national and business cultures encourage or discourage certain forms of businesses and strategies in each nation. There are generally acceptable and unacceptable ways of conducting business. For example, isomorphic forces that encourage copying successful firms and responding to government policies create national similarities in strategy.
- Social institutions and national culture serve as barriers to the easy transfer of competitive advantages among countries (Kogut 1985)—that is, the culture and social institutions prevent or inhibit the easy copying of management practices from other countries.
- Each nation must rely on its available factor conditions for developing industries and the firms within industries. Factor conditions lead to the existence of each country's unique resource base. Local firms have the easiest access to local resources. Consequently, firms in a nation are most likely to favor similar strategies and organizational designs that take advantage of their unique bundle of local resources.
- Social institutions and culture determine which resources are used, how they are used, and which resources are developed. The resource base limits the strategic and design options available to firms in any nation.

The points just discussed give you a general picture of the processes by which national context affects strategic management and organizational design. Multinational managers can generalize and apply these ideas to understand the actions of rivals or alliance partners in any country where their firm does business. The following sections of the chapter use this general model as background first to look at strategy formulation and content and second to look at organizational design in specific nations.

COMPARATIVE STRATEGY FORMULATION AND CONTENT: EXAMPLES FROM AROUND THE WORLD

THE U.S. MODEL OF STRATEGY FORMULATION AND CONTENT: A BASIS OF COMPARISON

To compare different strategic management systems from different countries requires some starting point as a basis of comparison. This section describes the strategy-formulation process from a U.S. management perspective. British, Canadian, and Australian views on strategic management are similar to those in the United States, so this perspective might also be considered the "Anglo" view of strategic management.

U.S. strategic management process

Assumption that managers can accurately analyze the competitive environment in which the company operates and logically craft strategies that maximize competitive strengths and avoid competitive weaknesses.

The steps in the **U.S. strategic management process** represent the ideal of a rational decision-making process. The model assumes that managers can accurately analyze the competitive environment in which the company operates. In turn, from this environmental analysis, managers logically craft the strategy content that maximizes competitive strengths and avoids competitive weaknesses.

The remainder of this section uses the steps in the U.S. model of the strategic management process as a means for comparison among the company strategies common in several different countries. You will see that the meaning and consequences attached to each step and the sequence of steps differ widely among firms of different nationalities.

The U.S. strategy management process has four tasks, each arising from a basic assumption. The tasks and assumptions are as follows:

1. *Define the business and its mission.* Each company, no matter how small or large, must have a clear-cut definition of its business. It is essential for a company to identify clearly who its customers are and what the products or services are that it provides to its customers. To provide general direction and guidance for a company, top management must develop a mission statement.
2. *Define objectives that target performance.* To put a mission statement into action, managers and workers need specific goals or targets that guide their efforts in the organization.
3. *Assess the company's situation for opportunities and threats in the environment and to understand competitors' actions.* To accomplish this task, managers must study general environmental trends (e.g., interest rates), industry trends (e.g., technological innovation), and competitors' actions (e.g., offering new products) (Pearce and Robinson 1994).
4. *Craft strategy content.* Using a detailed analysis of the environment and the company's strengths and weaknesses, managers develop game plans that allow the company to achieve its mission and objectives. Managers look for competitive advantages that build on the company's strengths, avoid the company's weaknesses, and exploit domestic and global opportunities.

The following sections give examples from various nations showing the effects of national context on the strategic tasks of defining the business and its mission, setting objectives, assessing the company's situation, and crafting a strategy content.

DEFINING THE BUSINESS AND ITS MISSION

The first question organizational leaders must ask is, what business are we in? Definitions of the business tie directly into the types of business that are possible in any country, as the pool of resources available to the firms in a country limit and encourage certain types of businesses.

Factor conditions, both natural and induced, provide the most basic constraints. For example, if firms want to compete in high-tech industries, they must have the necessary engineering and scientific talent. Cultural and institutional constraints encourage the development of some businesses and restrict the development of others. For example, Muslim prohibitions against usury (strictly interpreted as receiving any interest from loans) restrict the development of the financial industry in many Arab states.

Mission statement

Tells the organizational members and outsiders what the company does and why it exists.

The mission defines the domain of the organization. That is, the **mission statement** tells organizational members and outsiders what the company does and why it exists.

Exhibit 15.3

French and British
Mission Statements

Components	British	French
Time Orientation	Short (less than a year)	Longer (more than a year)
Focus	Strategic	General values
Priority Stakeholders and Issues	Shareholders and investors Customers Employees Service	Clients and employees Value to society Service Shared destiny
Participation and Ownership	Mostly senior management	Management and workers

Source: Adapted from Brabet and Klemm 1994.

U.S. MISSION STATEMENTS

According to conventional wisdom, at least as stated in U.S. management text-books, a good mission statement meets several criteria. It helps focus efforts, provides a rationale for resource allocation, establishes broad job responsibilities, and leads to more specific organizational objectives (Certo and Peter 1990). U.S. mission statements favor an emphasis on target customer, products, services, or market segments (David 2001).

MISSION STATEMENTS IN BRITAIN AND FRANCE

Exhibit 15.3 contrasts mission statements from British and French companies. The cultural and institutional differences between these European countries, while quite distinct, are not as wide as those between the United States and China, for example. Will their views on mission statements be different? The insights of two scholars writing in the British journal *Long Range Planning* (Brabet and Klemm 1994) suggest so. British and French mission statements reflect the particular characteristics of their national contexts.

Probably because of similar philosophical approaches to strategic management, British mission statements resemble those of U.S. companies. The most common mission statement in British companies focuses on strategic issues, especially emphasizing the role of shareholder returns. Unlike the British approach, French mission statements reflect a national context with cultural values and social institutions rooted in a social democracy. As a result, participation by lower levels in the organization is more common than in Britain. Mission statements also often mention benefits for employees and social priorities, along with the service and success goals more common in British and U.S. statements. Such mission statements result from the close relationship of government and business, which fosters a paternalistic relationship among management and workers. References to profit and shareholders remain vague, if they are present at all. The open pursuit of financial goals is considered vulgar.

The differences in these statements arise from differences in the business cultures and institutional environments of the two countries. The French government takes a more active role in industry. The state directs investment priorities and maintains a high level of state ownership in key industries, such as the railroad. As such, social priorities dominate management concerns. In addition, by law, management must consult workers on matters that affect the workforce. In contrast, capitalism in the United Kingdom as in the United States, is more laissez-faire. State ownership is minimal and decreasing rapidly. Serving the investor now dominates management's interests.

DEFINING OBJECTIVES

Objectives support the mission of the company. Good objectives are measurable, challenging, and achievable. "Measurable" means that managers can assess whether objectives are achieved or exceeded. Objectives that are "challenging but achievable" require that meeting an objective stretches the organization members but is still within reach with reasonable effort.

There are two general classes of objectives, financial and strategic. **Strategic objectives** often focus on beating competitors. **Financial objectives** generally focus on stockholder returns or financial-performance ratios.

The major cross-national difference in objectives occurs when companies choose which class of objective is more important, the financial or the strategic. Some nations have national contexts that favor choosing financial objectives. Other nations have national contexts that support the choice of strategic objectives. Differences in the priorities given to various objectives arise mostly from cultural differences in time orientations and institutional differences in economic systems. Next, we compare U.S., Japanese, and British choices regarding objectives.

Strategic objectives

Those that focus on beating competitors.

Financial objectives

Those that focus on achieving stockholder returns or financial performance ratios.

HEAD TO HEAD IN INTERNATIONAL COMPETITION: OBJECTIVES OF U.S., JAPANESE, AND BRITISH FIRMS IN THE UNITED KINGDOM

What happens when U.S. and Japanese companies compete in the same market? The differences in the strategic postures of Japanese companies and their competitors become apparent.

A study by British scholars looked at how major Japanese, British, and U.S. firms compete in the United Kingdom. Examples of firms in the study included Hewlett-Packard and IBM from the United States, Canon and Sony from Japan, and GEC Telecommunications and Jaguar from Britain (Doyle et al. 1992). The study revealed two distinct views of strategy held by the Japanese and their Western competitors. Exhibit 15.4 summarizes the results of this study.

British and U.S. companies were dominated by financial and efficiency objectives. Japanese firms based their objectives on the market and the competition. Consistent with their financial orientation, British and U.S. companies emphasized short-term profits. As compared to less than a third of the Japanese managers, nearly 90 percent of the British and 70 percent of the U.S. managers responded that short-term profit is the most important objective of the company.

Situational assessment

Determining the internal strengths and weaknesses of the company and external opportunities and threats to the company.

The Japanese firms took a very aggressive stance in the strategic focus of their objectives. Their dominant objectives were to enter new and growing market segments and to win "by beating the competition" (Doyle et al. 1992). In contrast, British firms were defensive and focused on cost reduction and improving efficiency. U.S. companies fell between their British and Japanese competitors on these objectives. Next we see how the national context affects how companies assess their strategic situation.

ASSESSING THE COMPANY'S SITUATION

A key step in strategy formulation is a firm's managers' assessment of the situation faced by their company. In **situational assessment**, managers seek to understand

Exhibit 15.4 Financial and Strategic Objectives of U.S., Japanese, and British Subsidiaries in Britain (by percent reporting)

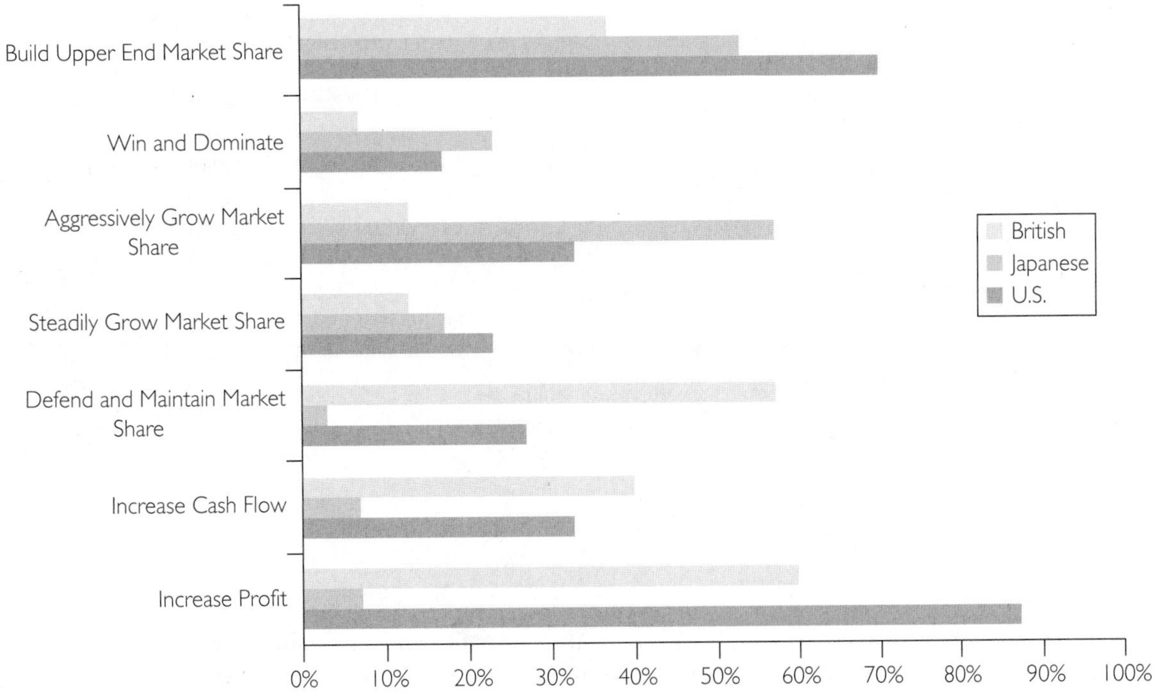

Source: Adapted from Doyle et al. 1992.

issues such as: what the internal strengths and weaknesses of their company are; what the opportunities and threats that their company faces in the environment are; and how the company is doing in comparison to its competitors (Thompson and Strickland 1999).

In the highly rationalistic view of strategic management, which characterizes the U.S. system, the analysis of the company's situation serves as a diagnostic tool for managers. First they seek to understand the environment faced by their company, and then they select a strategy that best fits their company's strengths, avoids exposing weaknesses, and takes advantage of opportunities while avoiding environmental threats.

ASSESSING INTERNAL STRENGTHS AND WEAKNESSES: GERMAN AND BRITISH EXAMPLES

All companies have different strengths and weaknesses. However, the national context influences beliefs regarding which organizational characteristics managers consider important and necessary for success.

A recent survey of high-growth companies in the United Kingdom and Germany provides a good example of how this works. The study showed that successful companies from both countries identified the same key success factors that were needed to succeed in their industry. However, there were differences between the countries in the organizational characteristics that managers believed most necessary to achieve the key success factors. Exhibit 15.5 presents some of this material.

Why did the two sets of managers make such different assessments? The U.K. and German companies drew from different resource pools, used different cultural values and norms, and applied different institutional biases to their strategic

Exhibit 15.5 Responding to Key Success Factors in Medium-Sized German and British Firms

Key Success Factor	German Response	British Response
Flexible Production and Operations	Employ multiskilled workers	Use project teams and autonomous units
Diversification	Vertically integrate with suppliers and distributors	Acquire high growth business
Select and Retain Quality Employees	Provide job security and profit sharing	Build incentive systems
Serve Market Niches	Work with customers to develop specialized skills	Enter niches with low entry barriers
Information Systems	Use for production control	Use for financial control
Enter Growth Markets	Be first to enter with customized product	Focus on mature markets
Build Organizational Culture	Establish a formal value system based on family ownership	Emphasize leader's view of business

Source: Adapted from Taylor et al. 1990.

thinking regarding organizational strengths. As Exhibit 15.5 shows, German firms emphasized technical solutions for quality and innovation. This reflects the values of German managers, who often have technical backgrounds and hold Ph.D.s. It also reflects the availability of the German labor pool with its high degree of technical and vocational training. British firms, in contrast, emphasized their organizational and leadership skills as most important for building organizational strengths. British managers usually have an elite liberal arts education. The tradition of this education assumes that the broadly educated person can build an organization for success in any venture.

The final step of strategic management process is crafting the strategy content. The next section gives a brief example of Japanese strategies to show national differences in strategy content.

NATIONAL DIFFERENCES IN STRATEGY CONTENT: AN EXAMPLE

Three general strategic orientations, individually or in combination are commonly used by Japanese companies. These strategic orientations fit the national context of Japan and are part of the strategic game plans of many successful Japanese *kaisha*. *Kaisha* is the Japanese word for "corporation." They include:

- *Compete with a high ratio of products where the company can add value with knowledge rather than some other factor.* Examples include cameras and consumer electronics. Since Japan is a country with limited physical resources, Japanese companies use the major asset available—workers and managers with good education and high motivation.
- *Emphasize the production side of the organizations to improve productivity.* Examples include just-in-time inventory systems, quality circles, and total quality control. Japanese companies use these techniques to improve the quality of their products and to make their production more efficient. Companies attempt to use the Japanese national assets of high quality and loyal workers.

Keiretsu

Japanese conglomerate such as Mitsubishi.

- *Use the resources of networks.* The large Japanese conglomerates, called *keiretsu*, interlock banks and other industries. **Keiretsu** such as Mitsubishi provide member companies (e.g., Kirin Brewery) several benefits: access to long-term capital, the leverage to engage in long-term competitive attacks, and often-friendly outlets in other industries to experiment with products (Ross 1991). In addition, to a degree that would be illegal in the United States, Japanese competitors often collaborate in areas where the risk is high or the capital requirements are great. Recently, however, government policies have changed in response to the Japanese recession of the late 1990s. The number of *keiretsu* is declining. Originally, there were six major *keiretsu*. By the year 2000, only four remained. Still, some doubt whether the *keiretsu* system will die entirely (*Economist* 2000a).

COMPARATIVE STRATEGY FORMULATION AND CONTENT: SUMMARY OBSERVATIONS

The forgoing sections gave examples of how the national context led to different strategy-formulation techniques and strategy content in a variety of countries. Comparing and contrasting the U.S. approaches to strategy formulation versus the approaches used in other countries provide examples of different techniques and philosophies. Country-level differences in strategy formulation and content arise from different resource pools, institutional pressures, and cultural values and norms. The examples highlight the differences among only a few countries to show key issues that managers should consider when assessing national effects on the strategies of competitors or collaborators. Next you will see how the national context affects the major component of strategy implementation: organizational design.

COMPARATIVE ORGANIZATIONAL DESIGN

BASIC CONCEPTS

To provide a common terminology to view organizational design comparatively, this section adds to the primer on organizational structure presented in Chapter 7. Specifically, this section reviews basic ideas related to organizational control and introduces the concepts of vertical differentiation, horizontal differentiation, span of control, integration, standardization, formalization, and mutual adjustment.

Vertical differentiation

Number of levels in the organization.

Horizontal differentiation

Number of subunits in the organization.

An organizational chart shows how companies handle the problem of dividing work both vertically, into managerial positions, and horizontally, into subunits. **Vertical differentiation** represents the number of levels in the organization. Levels in the organizational chart show the formal reporting relationships among managers and workers. Vertical differentiation is also called the hierarchy of authority.

Horizontal differentiation represents the number of subunits in the organization. The organizational charts shown in Chapter 7 show some of the generic and multinational options for allocating tasks among organizational subunits. Organizations have subunits with functional, product, geographic, or a hybrid mixture. A flat organizational pyramid has many subunits relative to its number of vertical levels. A tall organizational pyramid has fewer subunits relative to its number of vertical levels. The nature of the organizational hierarchy created by differentiation affects the span of control. The span of control is the number of people who report to each manager. A flat organizational pyramid has a wide span of control. That is, many people report to one manager. Exhibit 15.6 shows preferred organizational hierarchies for several countries.

Differentiation creates the need for integration—that is, the second major problem for organizational design: how to integrate or pull together the components of

Exhibit 15.6 Preferred Organizational Hierarchies for Selected Countries

Turkey	Nigeria	Japan	Germany	Norway
Pakistan	Spain	Portugal	Switzerland	Denmark
China	Belgium	Italy	Australia	Canada
India	Thailand	Finland	Sweden	USA
Austria	France	Ireland		
Ethiopia	Greece	UK		
Mexico	Argentina			

Source: Adapted from Trompenaars and Hampden-Turner 1998.

**Control
mechanisms**

*Control mechanisms
link the organization
vertically.*

an organization with coordination and control mechanisms. Chapter 7 summarizes the basic mechanisms for coordination and control used in multinational companies. The next section reviews and extends some of these points.

Control mechanisms link the organization vertically. There are five broad types of control: personal control, output control, bureaucratic control, decision-making control, and cultural control (Daft 1995). Organizational control mechanisms formalize how leaders and subordinates interact. As such, since control mechanisms deal with social relationships, they may be among the most susceptible to cultural and institutional influences.

Personal control or direct supervision means that the immediate supervisor directs the actions of subordinates face to face. Output-control systems assess the performance of a unit based on results, usually profit, and not on the processes used to achieve those results. Companies using output control may have similar goals for all units or managers may negotiate goals unique to each unit.

Bureaucratic control focuses on managing behaviors and processes within the organization. Managers implement bureaucratic control by standardization and formalization. Standardization specifies the exact behaviors workers and managers must use in specific organizational activities. For example, in Disneyland, operators of amusement rides must follow standardized scripts that allow very little deviation. Standardization results in predictable behavior of workers and units. Formalization represents the number of written rules and regulations in the organization. Usually these rules and regulations pertain to behaviors and actions over which managers wish to exercise strict control. Low levels of standardization and formalization result in mutual adjustment. Mutual adjustment means that people in organizations do not follow standardized procedures or written rules for all situations. Rather, through informal communication and personal judgments, managers and workers react to each situation uniquely. Usually organizations that face complex or rapidly changing environments favor mutual adjustment over standardization and formalization.

Decision-making control represents the level in the organizational hierarchy where managers have the authority to make decisions. All organizations use some form of decision-making control, and this is a key issue for cross-cultural comparisons. In decentralized organizations, lower-level managers make a larger number of more important decisions. In centralized organizations, higher-level managers make most of the important decisions. Centralization usually works best when top managers can deal easily with organizational problems. Small size, few products, and a stable environment favor centralization. Decentralization usually works best in complex situations that make it impossible for top managers to deal adequately with all organizational issues. Decentralization favors flexibility and allows lower-level managers to react more quickly to any situation.

Cultural control systems use the organizational culture (see Chapter 2 for a review) to control behaviors and attitudes of employees. Organizational cultures represent shared norms, values, beliefs, and traditions among workers. Organizations that use cultural control usually have selection and socialization systems that emphasize learning and fitting in with the culture. Selection systems, such as choosing only family members, attempt to recruit people who already have the organization's norms, values, and beliefs. Socialization systems use education and psychological pressures to have workers adopt the company's culture as their own.

NATIONAL CULTURE AND ORGANIZATIONS

Hofstede argues that the cultural norms of power distance and uncertainty avoidance (defined in Chapter 2) are the most important for understanding how people deal with the basic problems of organizational design—differentiation and integration (Hofstede 1991); cultural expectations associated with power distance and uncertainty determine the implicit models of what people believe an organization should look like.

To illustrate his point, Hofstede (1991) divided national cultures into four groups based on a two-by-two matrix of high and low power distance and high and low uncertainty avoidance. The four groups included countries high on power distance and uncertainty avoidance, countries low on both, and two low and high combinations. Exhibit 15.7 shows these combinations with representative countries and describes the preferred organizational designs favored by people from these cultures. The aspects of design considered include vertical and horizontal differentiation, control and coordination mechanisms, and decision-making processes.

These preferred organizational designs represent only examples of "typical" organizations in a national culture. Although nations tend to differ on their typical or average designs for organizations, individual organizations vary from the "standard" types. Understanding the design of the typical organization, however, provides a starting point to aid managers in understanding how national culture affects the choices of organizational designs. Students of multinational management must remember that people in the different cultures described have only a tendency to prefer certain organizational designs. Within every country, there is a wide variety of organizations. In particular, the characteristics of industries may make some organizations more similar to those from different societies. In addition, within any of these broad groups defined by power distance and uncertainty, some countries fall closer to the borders than do others. As with all broad characterizations of cultural effects on management practices, multinational managers must use caution in applying this knowledge to specific organizations.

With this caution in mind, what types of organizational designs emerge from societies with different levels of uncertainty avoidance and power distance? Exhibit 15.7 shows four types of organizations: adhocracy, professional bureaucracy, full bureaucracy, and family bureaucracy. In addition, because of the importance and

Exhibit 15.7
National Culture and
Preferred Organiza-
tional Designs

	Low Power Distance	**High Power Distance**
Low Uncertainty Avoidance	*Cultural context:* Low Power Distance and Low Uncertainty Avoidance *Preferred design:* **Adhocracy** *Representative country:* Great Britain	*Cultural context:* High Power Distance and Low Uncertainty Avoidance *Preferred design:* **Family bureaucracy** *Representative country:* China
High Uncertainty Avoidance	*Cultural context:* Low Power Distance and High Uncertainty Avoidance *Preferred design:* **Professional bureaucracy** *Representative country:* Germany	*Cultural context:* High Power Distance and High Uncertainty Avoidance *Preferred design:* **Full bureaucracy** *Representative country:* France

Source: Adapted from Hofstede 1991.

competitive success of Japanese organizations, this section looks at the unique case of the Japanese consensus bureaucracy.

ADHOCRACY

Adhocracy

Flat organizational pyramid, mutual-adjustment control mechanisms, and participative or consultative decision making.

Countries low on power distance and uncertainty avoidance favor the organizational design called adhocracy. The **adhocracy** fits cultures where people can tolerate ambiguity in organizational roles and have less need for formalized rules and regulations. The perceived distance between management and workers tends to be small.

The typical adhocracy includes the following organizational-design characteristics:

- *Vertical and horizontal differentiation:* Fewer levels and wider spans of control result in flat organizational pyramids.
- *Control mechanisms:* The preferred control mechanism is mutual adjustment. The tolerance for ambiguous situations results in lower standardization and formalization. Managers make adjustments in organizational procedures as the situation demands. They rely on the organizational culture to ensure commitment and reliability.
- *Decision making:* Decision making is participative or consultative. Managers include subordinates in the decision-making process or at least ask subordinates' opinions before making decisions.

Hofstede (1991) considers Great Britain as typical of the national culture that favors adhocracy as an organizational design. However, most other Anglo countries also fall into this cluster. In spite of Great Britain's highly developed social-class system and the formality of interpersonal relationships, organizations there are surprisingly free from rules and have low formalization. Instead, the British prefer to "muddle through" organizational decision making and develop commonsense solutions to problems. In many ways, this parallels the British common-law tradition, in which legal decision making comes from precedent (the history of past decisions) rather than from codified laws based on detailed, written rules (as is true in France).

In the mutual-adjustment system, meetings are important because managers typically make decisions jointly. However, junior managers often participate only by asking questions (Gannon 1994). Consistent with these organizational styles, comparative research shows that U.K. multinationals do not emphasize the standardized output controls common in U.S. companies. Although similar on most dimensions of organizational structure, U.K. companies tend to have less formalization of rules and procedures than do U.S. and Canadian companies (Egelhoff 1984; McMillan et al. 1973).

PROFESSIONAL BUREAUCRACY

Professional bureaucracy

Has moderate levels of vertical and horizontal differentiation, uses standardization of skills as the preferred control mechanism, and may also centralize decision making.

The **professional bureaucracy** is the preferred organizational form for cultures with small power distance and high uncertainty-avoidance norms. Hofstede (1991) suggests that the ideal for these organizations is to work like a well-oiled machine with management influence only in exceptional cases.

The typical professional bureaucracy includes:

- *Vertical and horizontal differentiation:* This organization has moderate levels of vertical and horizontal differentiation. In some cases, the organizational pyramid can be flat, and subunits may act quite independently from headquarters.
- *Control mechanisms:* The preferred control mechanism is the standardization of skills. Standardized skills mean that people have very predictable behaviors, in the sense that managers know exactly what jobs people are qualified to perform.
- *Decision making:* In spite of the predictability of worker skills, the professional bureaucracy often has centralized decision making. Decisions made at the top help reduce uncertainty about what happens in the organization.

Hofstede (1991) identified Germany as the country most likely to produce professional bureaucracies. Anthropologists note that the need for order and compartmentalization are the dominant themes in German organizations (Hall and Hall 1990). Compartmentalization and the need for order help define the German professional bureaucracy.

Compartmentalization dominates many phases of German life. In the organization, compartmentalization occurs with time (there are strict schedules), with offices (there are clear barriers and closed doors), and between departments. The compartmentalization of departments often limits information flow and results in slower decision making and less flexible organizations. However, compartmentalization also leads to decentralized decision making. German superiors expect subordinate department managers to solve their own problems and generate profits without much involvement by senior management (Hall and Hall 1990).

German organizations build a hierarchy of authority based on technical competence. Top managers often have a technical Ph.D. It is often paradoxical to people from other cultures that while Germans pay strict attention to formal rank and the symbols of rank (title, office size, etc.), decision making is not only decentralized but also largely lateral. Consensus decision making occurs within departments and at the highest levels of the organization. Even a CEO's power is often limited by an executive board of three to fifteen people, the *Vorstand,* which must agree on important operational decisions (Hall and Hall 1990).

Germans have a need for control but prefer standardization and formalized rules and procedures rather than personal control through centralized decision making. In practice, when there is an organizational problem, Germans assume it lies with faulty procedures. The British, on the other hand, assume an organizational problem lies with a breakdown of relationships among people (Hall and Hall 1990).

FULL BUREAUCRACY

Full bureaucracy

Rules, procedures, and hierarchical relationships dominate the organization.

The **full bureaucracy** occurs in countries high on both power distance and the need to avoid uncertainty. The full bureaucracy is the most formalized of the typical organizations discussed by Hofstede (1991). Rules, procedures, and hierarchical relationships dominate the organizations. Formalized organizational roles and relationships serve to support the authority of managers and to reduce uncertainty.

The typical full bureaucracy includes the following organizational design characteristics:

- *Vertical and horizontal differentiation:* Tall pyramids and narrow spans of control keep managers informed of all major activities by their subordinates.
- *Control mechanisms:* Standardization of the work processes (everyone should do the task the same way) and a high degree of formalized rules and regulations bring predictability and control to the full bureaucracy.
- *Decision making:* Decision making is highly centralized. Clear barriers exist between members of the elite (called the *cadre* in France) and the workers.

Hofstede identified France as the country that best typifies the use of the full bureaucracy. French organizations are rigid and hierarchical and follow a model reminiscent of the Roman military. Superiors seldom share vital information with subordinates regarding what is going on within the organization. Decision making is highly centralized, with the expectation that managers have and should exercise extensive control. Reflecting social class and education, there are large class distinctions between management (the *cadre*) and the workers. Consequently, French leaders are usually formal, impersonal, and authoritarian (Gannon 1994; Amado et al. 1991). Classical French management theorists call for a unity of command, which means a person can only report to one boss. The concept of a matrix structure with its dual reporting system is inconceivable to many French managers (Laurent 1983; Amado et al. 1991).

Rules, regulations, and procedures proliferate in the French organization much like the German organization. However, their use is quite different. Whereas the Germans use standardization and formalization to deal with the detail of organizational functioning, the French see perfection in *savoir faire,* or a certain way to do something regardless of the situation. Cultural expectations say German managers should stay on schedule, keep commitments, and generally deal with problems sequentially. The highly individualistic French are more concerned with an ultimate goal of following proper protocol. However, they will ignore the details of rules when they get in the way of an overall goal (Hall and Hall 1990). Exhibit 15.8 gives a more detailed view of the French organization in contrast to the U.S. organizational design.

Family bureaucracy

Similar to an extended family, with a dominant patriarch or father figure.

FAMILY BUREAUCRACY

The **family bureaucracy** occurs in countries with large power distance norms and low uncertainty avoidance norms. This structure is called "family" because it most parallels an extended family with a dominant patriarch or father figure.

Exhibit 15.8 U.S. and French Views of Organizational Design

Design Issue	U.S. View	French View
The nature of the organization	A system to achieve objectives Based on order and rational decision making	A social system of people Based on hierarchical relationships among people
The main reason structures exist	To complete activities To solve problems To define responsibilities	To define authority To identify hierarchy of people to be managed To identify status differences
Organizing principle of units	Based on functions or activities	Based on degree of authority and status
Duties of management	Coordinate tasks and assign responsibilities	Define legitimate authority for people in organization
The nature of authority	Specific to organizational position Limited in scope to defined authority Impersonal	Specific to the person Diffuse to all situations in personal encounters Personal between people
The need for coordination and control	Decentralize responsibility and decision making	Centralize responsibility and decision making
Reporting to two bosses	Possible in some situations	Should be avoided at all times
The chain of command	Can be bypassed if necessary	Should be followed most of the time

Sources: Adapted from Amado et al. 1991 and Inzerilli and Laurent 1983.

Hofstede selected China as the most likely country to produce family organizations. However, the family organization is also prevalent in Chinese companies located outside of China, organizations in other Asian societies, and in the companies of some Latin American countries.

The typical family organization includes the following organizational design characteristics:

- *Vertical and horizontal differentiation:* Family organizations tend to be small and have less specialization of roles. As a result, horizontal differentiation is often minimal. The organizational pyramid is flat and broad with all reporting to the leader.
- *Control mechanisms:* The favored control mechanism is direct control by personal supervision. That is, the leader deals directly with subordinates rather than using intermediate managers.
- *Coordination mechanisms:* Because the organization is small, direct contact predominates as the method of coordination.
- *Decision making:* Decision making is highly centralized. However, collective norms in some societies may require consultation with key senior family members before the leader (usually the senior man) makes a decision.

The following Multinational Management Brief gives more detail on the role expectations in a Chinese family company.

THE JAPANESE CONSENSUS BUREAUCRACY: A SPECIAL CASE?

The power distance and uncertainty avoidance norms of Japanese society suggest that Japanese organizations should favor the full bureaucracy. However, because of

Multinational Management Brief
Wu Lun and the Chinese Family Company

In Taiwan and for many of the overseas Chinese, the dominant organization is the family firm. Taiwanese family companies employ the most people and contribute most to Taiwan's national production. Most of these family companies are small, father dominated, and nepotistic. Only relatives or friends of the family work for the company.

The culture of the family firm reflects Confucian values regarding family relationships and superior–subordinate relationships. The Confucian philosophy regarding relationships among family members is called *Wu Lun*. *Lun* is the "way" of getting along with others. *Wu* represents the relationships of master/follower, father/son, older brother/younger brother, husband/wife, and friends. Each relationship has a specific behavior expectation regarding how each side should behave toward the other.

Wu Lun is a paternalistic system, highly centralized, with the father being the dominant force. In an organization, all relationships among family members and other subordinates define a hierarchy with the father figure at the center. The *Wu Lun* chart in Exhibit 15.9 shows these relationships.

The Chinese family business seems best adapted for smaller organizations where centralized decision making is most effective. However, Chinese companies are very successful in areas where speed and flexibility in technology changes are important and where speed and flexibility in making a deal are important.

Exhibit 15.9 *Wu Lun:* The Five Basic Human Relationships and Their Obligations

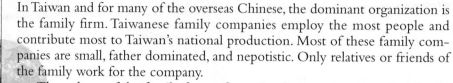

Father	← RESPECT AND OBEY / PROTECT AND CONSIDER →	Son
Brother (Older)	← FOLLOW AND MODEL / TAKE CARE OF →	Brother (Younger)
Master	← BE LOYAL / BE COURTEOUS →	Follower
Friend	← TRUST / TRUST →	Friend
Husband	← SUBMIT / MEET OBLIGATIONS →	Wife

Sources: Based on Syu 1994 and Montagu-Pollock 1991.

Consensus bureaucracy

Has little job specialization for individuals, an age seniority system, close personal bonding among section members, functional organizational structures, and strong cultural control mechanisms.

the unique style of group orientation in Japanese organizations, some experts believe the Japanese have developed a unique type called **consensus bureaucracy** (Rieger and Wong-Rieger 1990).

The typical Japanese consensus bureaucracy includes the following organizational design characteristics:

- *Vertical differentiation:* Japanese organizations have little job specialization for individuals. Instead, whole sections, which are usually the lowest operating subunits in the company, take on specific functional roles. Individuals within a section have very general jobs determined largely by their section chief (*kacho*). Closely linked to the age hierarchy of Japanese society, Japanese organizations have tall organizational hierarchies. The span of control is seldom greater than five. Even within a section, the organization emphasizes hierarchy. There are seldom people of exactly the same rank within a section. Virtually all relationships follow an age seniority system. Individuals refer to their "forward companion" (*sempai*) or "follower companion" (*kohai*). Some analysts claim that the vertical hierarchy is easier for Japanese to deal with than horizontal relationships. Japanese language and culture reinforce the nature of hierarchy. Vertical relationships remove competition and allow close personal bonding among section members (Yoshino and Lifson 1986).
- *Horizontal differentiation:* Above the level of the section, departmentalization about equals that in the United States. However, when compared to similar U.S. companies, Japanese companies prefer functional organizational structures to product divisions (Lincoln and Kalleberg 1990; Kagono et al. 1985).
- *Control mechanisms:* Most Japanese organizations favor cultural control over bureaucratic control mechanisms. Studies suggest that Japanese companies control unit and individual behavior by the cultural mechanism of sharing information and values. Cultural control also builds on basic national cultural values supporting self-discipline (Kagono et al. 1985). In spite of having a relatively high need for uncertainty avoidance, the Japanese use less formalization and standardization than do comparable U.S. companies (Eveleth et al. 1995; Kagono et al. 1985).
- *Decision making:* Decision making in the Japanese firm is neither centralized nor decentralized in the sense used in most Western companies. The broad strategic orientation of the company usually follows the general framework set by top management or the founder's philosophy. However, within a very broad framework, decision making becomes more decentralized, with middle levels of management having a strong influence. Consensual decision making, for which the Japanese are famous, may include both broad participation and strong conformity pressures.

Ringi system

Formal decision-making procedure used in Japanese organizations.

Before a decision enters the formal decision-making system, called the ***ringi system***, there is considerable informal discussion, called *nemawashi* (Gannon 1994; Sekaran and Snodgrass 1986). The next Multinational Management Brief describes procedures used in the classical style of Japanese organizational decision making.

As with strategic management processes, organizational design is also affected by social institutions. The section below gives an example of the changing institutional context of Korea and its dominant organization form, the *chaebol*.

SOCIAL INSTITUTIONS AND THE KOREAN CHAEBOL

The Korean *chaebol* are family dominated, multi-industry conglomerates that dominate much of Korean business. For example, the Samsung Group has over

Multinational Management Brief
The *Ringi* System and Japanese Decision Making

Japanese organizations have a clear hierarchy for age and status. Great respect must be shown to those senior, even if only a year apart. In the modern and complex business world, however, there are pressures to decentralize decision making to lower levels. Large size and diversified products and markets pressure Japanese organizations to give lower-level managers more autonomy. In addition, within the age hierarchy of the management structure, managerial talent may not always be at the key decision-making points. To adapt to these constraints of culture and organization, many Japanese organizations use a form of decentralized decision making called the *ringi* system. However, it is a type of decentralization quite different from Western counterparts.

The ringi system is a formal decision-making procedure in Japanese organizations. *"Ringi"* means that subordinates submit a proposal to superiors and superiors grant their approval. In the *ringi* system, managers circulate a formal document, called the *ringisho,* for approval. All departments affected by the decision must be involved. Gradually, the *ringisho* works its way up the organizational hierarchy. Along the way, each manager stamps the document with his seal (a stamp having the Japanese characters of his name) and notes any comments on the document. When the *ringisho* finally reaches top management, it has had a wide circulation among the management group. At this point, top management's approval is often a formality.

Extensive discussion and politicking occur before circulating a formal proposal. Since it would be bad form to argue against a proposal once it is in a *ringisho,* these early discussions allow managers to disagree in informal ways. The real decision making takes place at this step. Even proposals made by top management often never reach the formal proposal stage because they fail in this informal negotiating stage. This preproposal consensus building is called *nemawashi.*

Most proposals originate from mid levels of management. However, ultimately, top management retains responsibility for decisions. When something goes bad the chief must take the blame. However, this upper-level management responsibility is often symbolic since the entire management group shares ownership of the decision. The person or persons who actually made the proposal are not accountable.

(continued)

Chaebol

Family-dominated multi-industry conglomerate, such as Daewoo, dominant in Korean business.

twenty businesses in industries including electronics, heavy industry and chemicals, precision instruments, food processing, textiles, insurance, hotel, retail sales, natural-resource development, and newspapers and magazines.

Even more than for the Japanese version of the networked conglomerate (*keiretsu*), coercive isomorphism from government sources dominated the founding and growth of the Korean *chaebol*. During the 1960s and 1970s, the Korean government favored the development of large-scale family-owned businesses. Low-interest loans, tax rebates, and access to foreign currency allowed these companies to compete worldwide in industries identified by the government as strategic. Al-

Multinational Management Brief
The *Ringi* System and Japanese Decision Making *(continued)*

Will the *ringi* system survive the electronic age? Tokai Bank thinks so. They filed a patent application for an electronic *ringi* system that reduces circulation time from one week to two days for loan applications.

Exhibit 15.10 shows the steps taken in a typical *ringi* decision-making system.

Exhibit 15.10 Steps in the *Ringi* Decision-Making Process

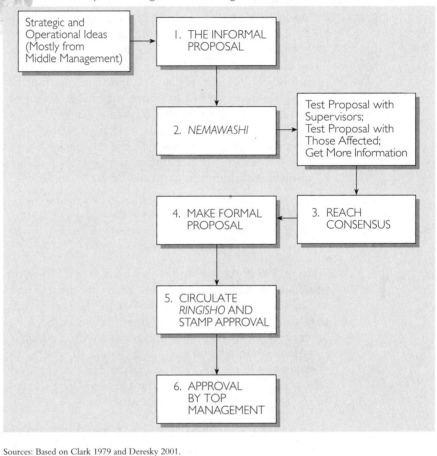

Sources: Based on Clark 1979 and Deresky 2001.

though the government relaxed many of these policies by the mid-1980s to aid the development of small businesses, the impact of coercive isomorphism on the *chaebol* was already in place (Steers et al. 1989). They became the dominant organizational form in Korea.

However, the Asian economic crises and failure of several *chaebol* in late 1997 caused the Korean government to rethink its institutional support for *chaebol*. To solve their fiscal crisis, the Korean government is yielding to pressures from international investment banks and the IMF to restructure the Korean economy

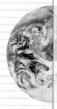

Multinational Management Brief
Korea's New Institutional Context

A recent survey of 21 countries including the United States, Norway, India, and Germany, found that Korea had almost twice as many workers in new firms than any other country in the world. How is this possible in a country dominated by large businesses committed to lifetime employment?

There is a new entrepreneurship in Korea and the number of workers in companies less than four years old is booming. Unlike the *chaebol*, these new companies are profit rather than growth oriented and are more transparent to investors. Workers are evaluated on performance rather than age.

The changing national context that favors entrepreneurship includes several factors. The demise of government support for the dozens of failing *chaebol* has created new niches for start-ups in the Korean economy. The cadre of laid off *chaebol* workers have abandoned the hope of lifetime employment. They are now part of a flexible labor market willing to change jobs and motivated by financial incentives. Consider that in 1997, only two Korean companies listed on the Korean stock exchange offered stock options to employees. Now there are over 100 including some *chaebol*. Investors are abandoning debt laden banks and are flocking to start-ups. The cultural criticism of failure is waning and failure is no longer a deterrent to starting one's own business.

Source: Based on *Economist* 2001.

(Ihlwan 1998). As a condition of loans, the IMF demanded reduced economic growth rates, higher interest rates, and restructuring, downsizing, or closing of failing *chaebol*. To restructure the *chaebol*, the Korean government also mandated that they reduce the interlocking of their businesses (i.e., cross-business unit debt guarantees and between business unit trading with the *chaebol* [*Business Korea* 2000]).

Although the *chaebol* may resist change, the restructuring of the Korean institutional environment has created a fertile environment for new organizational forms. The preceding Multinational Management Brief shows how these conditions lead to the rise of entrepreneurial organizations.

NATIONAL CULTURE, SOCIAL INSTITUTIONS, AND ORGANIZATIONAL DESIGN: SUMMARY OBSERVATIONS

Clearly, national culture permeates the boundaries of organizations. However, the brief survey presented here does not cover adequately all the subtleties of how national cultures affect design. The preceding section provided only an illustration of some general trends in the cultural effects on organizations for selected countries. Countries used for examples were chosen because they receive the most attention from experts in international business. As such, there is more information available on their organizational designs. In multinational business practice, managers must deal with many different nations, and, within nations, with many different organizations. Understanding possible effects on organizational design of general cultural values serves only as a beginning point for successfully designing organizations for local operations or for understanding how competitors or collaborators organize.

Perspectives on national culture, such as Hofstede's, provide a basis to anticipate preferred forms of organizations in different cultures. However, even under the broad umbrella of cultural effects on organizations, regional, industry, and local organizational cultures also affect design choices.

The creation of the Korean *chaebol* shows how the government can make an institutional environment that encourages the development of large-scale organizations. The Korean *chaebol* provide an example of how the state, in particular, can provide a coercive institutional environment for the creation of certain organizational forms. In the push to industrialize, the Korean government directly and indirectly helped to build the large financial-industrial groups that dominate the Korean economy. In Korea's more contemporary economy, the organizational design of the *chaebol* is losing favor and the support of the Korean national context.

Summary and Conclusions

Understanding how firms from different countries approach strategy and organizational design allows managers to compete more successfully in the international arena and to collaborate more successfully with partners and customers from other nations. This chapter first discussed the forces that lead organizations in different nations to be similar in management practices. Convergence in organizational design and strategy occur because of globalization pressures to produce similar products with similar technologies that serve similar customer needs.

Although there are strong pressures for convergence, organizations do differ by nation in terms of their strategies and designs. Differences among countries' social institutions and national cultures result in different orientations toward key business practices. Combined with variations in the resources available to a country's businesses, these conditions make up the national context. In turn, a country's national context produces similarities in the formulation and content of strategy and in organizational design by limiting the options available to companies located in the country.

There are differences in the way managers from different countries define their companies' missions and objectives. There are differences in the way managers from different countries assess their international strengths and weaknesses and environmental threats and opportunities. Even using the same data, there are national differences in the way managers arrive at the content of their strategies. These

national tendencies to use different strategies show up even when companies from different nations compete in the same markets.

To illustrate the effect of national culture on organizational design, the chapter used Hofstede's model of national cultures to show how "typical" organizational forms arise in different cultural settings. The adhocracy has few formal rules and little hierarchy. The professional bureaucracy has centralized decision making and standardized worker skills. Full bureaucracies are highly centralized and have tall organizational hierarchies. Family bureaucracies model a paternalistic family with a central leader. The Japanese consensus bureaucracy is unique in that it has some family traits and a hierarchy based on age, but with departmentalization like U.S. organizations.

The Korean *chaebol* provide examples of strong institutional forces at work. Born with the strong support of the Korean government, the *chaebol,* or networks, evolved into multinational conglomerates. Changes in the economic environment, however, have caused the Korean government to withdraw this support and challenge the continued existence of this organizational design.

Multinational managers will collaborate and compete with many organizations from different countries. An understanding of the inner workings of the organizations from other societies—how strategies are formulated and their resulting content, how decisions are made, how work is controlled, and where and how things are done in the organization—will benefit multinational managers on two major fronts. The knowledgeable multinational manager will be able to spot international competitors' competitive moves and organizational strengths and weaknesses more easily. The knowledgeable multinational manager will be better able to mesh the workings of organizations representing different nationalities into successful multinational collaborations.

Discussion Questions

1. Pick a country different from the examples in the book and discuss how natural- and induced-factor conditions lead to national tendencies in strategic-management practices or organizational design.

2. Find examples of how isomorphic processes affect a company's choices of strategy in the United States and Germany.

3. Discuss how the mission statement is linked to cultural values.

4. Discuss how social institutions such as the family and education influence the types of organizations in your country.

5. Discuss the advantages and disadvantages of other countries copying the Korean *chaebol*.

6. How would you design a foreign subsidiary for Germany? Assume most of the managers are German and the parent company is French.

7. How does the family bureaucracy compare with family-run companies in your country?

8. Discuss some costs and benefits of the Japanese *ringi* system of decision making. How could it be adapted to work in the full bureaucracy, professional bureaucracy, and the adhocracy?

Chapter Internet Activity

Explore the Web sites for companies discussed in the chapter. Read the background information on the company and annual reports (often in the investor sections). Find the mission statements for as many companies as possible—about half the companies include their mission statement on the corporate Web sites. Select companies based on different cultural characteristics as defined in Chapter 1. See if you find any differences in mission statements for companies located in countries with different cultural characteristics. Can you see any differences?

Internet Sites

Selected Companies in the Chapter
Banco Comercial Portugues   http://www.bcp.pt
Canon   http://www.canon.com
Hewlett-Packard   http://www.hewlett-packard.com
IBM   http://www.ibm.com
Jaguar   http://www.jaguarvehicles.com
Mitsubishi   http://www.mitsubishi.com/index_e.html
NCR   http://www.ncr.com
Samsung   http://www.samsung.com
Sony   http://www.sony.com

Sumitomo   http://www.sumitomocorp.co.jp/
Sun Microsystems   http://www.sun.com

Check Out Company Home Pages for Companies from Around the World
http://www.lycos.com/business/cch/guidebook.
   html?lpv=1&docNumber=P03_4001
   http://www.businessplans.org/Mission.html   *Build a mission statement using these sites for companies in different nations.*

http://www.ciber.bus.msu.edu/busres/Static/
  Company-Directories-Yellow-Pages.htm
  *Locations of company home pages, many of which describe
  organizational strategy.*
http://www.internationalist.com   *Publicly traded
  companies throughout the world.*

http://www.yahoo.com/Business_and_Economy/
  Companies/   *Find a company on the search engine
  Yahoo!*

Hint: Many company home pages have information on
missions and strategies.

Chapter Case: Královopolská: The Search for Strategy

*Management intends to concentrate its efforts on the
long-term development of the company, to increase productivity to a level that is five times its current status by
1997, to increase the value of the company by 30 percent every year, and to pay dividends to its shareholders
starting in 1994.*

These words, from the Královopolská Annual
Report for 1992, reflected the optimism felt by
many Czech managers soon after the "Velvet
Revolution" of 1989.[1] Goals to become more
productive and pay dividends were typical for
many Czech companies. Královopolská was one
of the companies that appeared in the early years
to be making the transition from central planning
to market economy fairly successfully. It was
among the top third of large Czech companies in
business performance in 1992, according to
Zdeněk Pánek, the general director. But the company reported losses in 1993 and 1994. Profits returned in 1995 and 1996, but they were small and
the company's gross margin from production was
negative. None of the goals in the 1992 Annual
Report had been achieved. Pánek knew that
Královopolská had to focus its business strategy,
but he was not sure how. It was critical to answer
this question because the management team he
headed had purchased 51 percent of Královopolská via a leveraged buyout. Pánek was not only
the president, but also an owner.

THE COMPANY AND ITS BUSINESS

Královopolská was a medium-sized producer of
industrial equipment for a diverse range of end
users. The company was located in Brno, the sec-

ond largest city in the Czech Republic (population 400,000 in 1990), about 200 km (120 miles)
southeast of Prague. Sales revenue in 1995 was Kč
4,184 million (about $160 million), and employ-
ment was 3,200.

Královopolská was established in 1889 at
Královo Pole (King's Field) on a greenfield site as
a machinery works, first making railway carriages
and storage tanks, and soon adding steam boilers,
woodworking machinery and cranes. Employment
was 300 to 400 people in the 19th century. The
company's production program did not change
throughout the World War I and II periods.
Czechoslovakia's post-World War II government
nationalized Královopolská in 1945 and enlarged
it by combining six facilities in addition to the
original plant in 1948. The company stopped producing railway carriages but added chemical plant
equipment during the first five-year plan imposed
by the communist government beginning in 1949.
The company's product lines were expanded in
1958 with the addition of steel structures and in
1961 with water treatment plant equipment.

In 1958, the Czechoslovak government consolidated the country's chemical and food processing industries. Královopolská manufactured equipment for the industries, and in addition was given
responsibility for directing and controlling the activities of other enterprises in the industries, including two research and development institutes, a
design engineering firm, and a construction firm.
Seven years later, in 1965, Královopolská lost its
central role and its independent status when the
government reorganized the chemical and food
equipment industries and placed the enterprises

Source: This case was prepared by Karen L. Newman and Stanley D. Nollen of the School of Business of Georgetown University. Their research was supported
by the Pew Foundation and Georgetown University's Center for International Business Education and Research, School of Business, and Graduate School. The
authors are indebted to Vladimír Relich and the managers of Královopolská for their informative cooperation. Copyright © 1996 by the *Case Research Journal*
and Karen L. Newman and Stanley D. Nollen.

Exhibit I Business Under Central Planning

The Czechoslovak economy was nearly totally state-owned, and mostly closed to trade and investment with the West from 1946 until the end of 1989. Most industries had only a few large enterprises, and in many instances they were monopoly producers of individual products. This meant that enterprises were typically very big (relative to the size of the market) and specialized in the production of just one product or a narrow product line. Enterprises in an industry were typically combined under a single "konzern" such as CHEPOS. The needs of the Soviet Union shaped the production program of many enterprises.

Producers in centrally planned economies typically were only manufacturing plants (an enterprise was termed a "statni podnik" or state plant). They were producers, but they did not do other business functions such as marketing and finance. Distribution and sales were handled by separate state-owned trading companies, research and development was either centralized or assigned to a separate enterprise, and capital investment decisions were made by the state. Banks disbursed funds and collected "profits" but did not make lending decisions. There were no capital markets.

The goal of the firm that all managers understood was to meet the production plan set by the central ministry. Successful managers were those who could skillfully negotiate a favorable plan and who knew how to produce the required quantity. Another goal imposed on firms by the state was to provide employment for everyone. There was little concern about costs, prices, money, or profits.

Most managers were technically trained, and all top managers were necessarily members of the Communist Party; selection depended on political as well as business considerations.

Enterprises were centralized and hierarchical, and typically had a functional organizational structure in which the production function was the biggest and most important. Other functions usually included a technical function, a commercial function (this was mainly order-filling and shipping), an economy function (mainly financial record-keeping), a personnel function, and others depending on the company's type of business.

Large enterprises during the socialist era typically provided a wide range of housing, recreation, education, and medical services to their employees. For example, Královopolská had 579 flats (apartments) for workers and a "staff quarters building" with 478 beds (later to become the company hotel); four recreation centers, a youth pioneer camp, and a heated swimming pool near the factory (open to townspeople as well); three kindergartens and one nursery that could accommodate all employees' children; a clinic located within the plant area staffed by 13 full-time and five part-time medical doctors; and two kitchens that prepared hot meals for all three shifts, served in 10 dining rooms on the grounds.

under the control of CHEPOS [a type of holding company whose acronym comes from the Czech words for chemical (chemicky), food (potrava), and machinery (strojirna)]. Královopolská regained its independence from CHEPOS in 1988 but remained primarily an equipment manufacturer.

During 1958–1965, as the head of the Czechoslovak chemical and food equipment industries, Královopolská developed the capability to manage turnkey projects—to design, engineer, manufacture, deliver, install, and service entire water treatment and chemical manufacturing facilities in cooperation with other enterprises. The turnkey business diminished substantially in 1965. A small turnkey operation, later known as the RIA Division survived. (RIA stands for Realizace Investičních Akcí, translated literally as "Realization of Investment Activities," but more meaningfully rendered in the company's reports as Comprehensive Plant Equipment Delivery.)

At the time of the Velvet Revolution, Královopolská primarily manufactured equipment for the chemical industry, which accounted

for half its production volume. Nuclear power stations purchased about another quarter of its output, and water treatment plant equipment and cranes and steel structures each accounted for less than 10 percent of Královopolská's production.

PRIVATIZATION

Centrally planned economies in eastern and central Europe with communist governments functioned very differently from market economies. Central planning business methods may have been well-adapted to that system, but were not suitable for firms in market economies. Companies in eastern and central Europe had to adjust when central planning ended, and Královopolská was no exception. (Features of business under central planning are detailed in Exhibit 1.) The first order of business after the Velvet Revolution was to privatize the economy.[2]

Královopolská's management urged the Ministry of Privatization to support early privatization of the company because, "we wanted to be free of

Exhibit 2 Economic Conditions in Czechoslovakia, 1989–1996

Variable	1989	1990	1991	1992	1993	1994	1995	1996
Gross domestic product, real % change	0.7[a]	−3.5	−15.0	−7.1	−0.9	2.6	4.8	4.4
Industrial production, real % change	0.9	−3.7	−23.1	−12.4	−5.3	2.3	8.8	6.7
Consumer price inflation, %	1.4	10.0	57.8	11.5	20.8	10.0	9.1	8.9
Interest rate, % lending rate	5.5	6.2	15.4	13.9	14.1	13.1	12.8	12.5
Exchange rate, Kč/$, annual average	15.1	18.0	29.5	28.3	29.3	28.8	26.5	27.0
Current account balance, % of gdp	0.9[b]	−1.8[b]	−1.0[b]	−0.0[b]	2.2	0.0	−2.9	−8.2
Unemployment rate, % at year-end	na	0.3	6.8	7.7	3.5	3.2	2.9	3.5

Notes: 1989–1992 data refer to Czechoslovakia; 1993–1996 data refer to Czech Republic only. [a]Net material product. [b]Hard currency trade.

Sources: Economist Intelligence Unit, *Country Report: Czech Republic and Slovakia*, 2nd quarter 1997, 1st quarter 1996; 2nd quarter 1994; 2nd quarter 1993, 2nd quarter 1990. London, 1997, 1996, 1994, 1993, 1990; and International Monetary Fund, *International Financial Statistics*, May 1997, March 1996, January 1994, March 1994. Washington, D.C. 1997, 1996, 1994.

the state method of management as soon as possible," according to one manager. Initial privatization for Královopolská occurred in May 1992 during the first wave of voucher privatization. About 30 percent of the company's 1,004,000 shares were sold to individuals and investment funds (the shares began trading one year later). The National Property Fund (NPF), the state agency that held shares pending the completion of privatization, retained 66 percent of the shares. The legal status of the company changed from that of state plant (s.p.) to joint stock company (a.s.).

In March 1995 a partnership called KENOP, created by Pánek and six other managers from Královopolská, bought shares from the NPF to create a 51 percent stake to complete privatization. (Individuals held 22 percent and investment funds held the remaining 27 percent of the company's shares.)

BUSINESS CONDITIONS DURING THE TRANSITION

The transition from central planning to a market economy caused many hardships and brought severe challenges to all Czech companies. Macro-economic conditions made business difficult. Real gross domestic product in Czechoslovakia dropped by 26 percent between the Velvet Revolution and 1993, and industrial production fell by 44 percent, thus reducing demand for the company's products from the domestic market. In 1991, the government allowed the market to set prices, and inflation soared to 58 percent. Short-term financing was scarce and nominal interest rates were around 14–15 percent in 1991–93. The government devalued the currency from Kč 15 per U.S. dollar to about Kč 29 per U.S. dollar in 1991 and pegged the exchange rate to the German mark and U.S. dollar with 60–40 weights (see Exhibit 2).

Export Markets

Královopolská was a relatively low-cost producer. Low labor wages outweighed low labor productivity. At the same time, Královopolská had a reputation as a manufacturer of good, serviceable products. The company won medals at industry fairs in Brno despite the fact that the central planners had authorized no significant investment in technology or equipment during the twenty years prior to the Velvet Revolution. Královopolská produced equipment that met the prevailing specifications in the East. Nevertheless, the combination of price and quality gave Královopolská a potential advantage in international markets because it could underprice western producers (by about 10–15 percent, some managers estimated), and make affordable products for developing countries.

In 1989, Královopolská earned three-quarters of its revenue from exports, and of that total, about 70 percent came from business with the Soviet Union and Iraq. In August 1990, the United Nations embargo against Iraq stopped those exports; and, in August 1991, the Soviet Union collapsed and went into a steep economic decline. Královopolská's exports dropped sharply to 9 percent of sales in 1991 and 16 percent in 1992. A recovery to 48 percent of sales in 1993 was partly illusory because Slovakia became a separate country in January 1993 so that formerly domestic sales became export sales.

Through this period, some of Královopolská's exports to Russia continued, despite that country's economic hardship, because the products were furnaces and replacement parts for oil refineries, which Russia needed to generate its own hard currency exports. Russia continued to buy these products from Královopolská and paid for them in U.S. dollars. Exports to Russia accounted for about 10 percent of Královopolská's production volume in 1993.

The company found it difficult to develop new export business. Like many Czech firms, Královopolská did not own or control its distribution channels so it had few direct relationships with customers. Fifty percent of its exports were handled through one state trading company, Technoexport, before the Revolution. The other half was exported indirectly via the engineering firms that actually constructed power plants, chemical plants, and water treatment facilities.

Other factors made export development difficult as well. Much of western Europe was in the midst of recession in the early 1990s and west European technical standards were different from those that Královopolská followed. In some cases, price was less important than established relationships with customers, where Královopolská was at a disadvantage because it had very little western business experience. In some developing countries, on the other hand, the problem was national

political and economic instability. Královopolská developed new export business in Iran, accounting for about a quarter of all exports in 1993, but this business encountered its own problems—the Iranian government defaulted on payments in 1994. Other business was developed in Syria, Egypt, and Iraq.

Domestic Market

Similar to other Czech firms, Královopolská had been a monopoly producer in most of its domestic businesses, including chemical equipment, industrial cranes, and water treatment plant equipment. However, its domestic monopoly in water treatment facilities eroded after the Revolution as new privatized firms entered the business. In addition, water treatment equipment was readily available outside the Czech Republic and could be imported after the Revolution.

Nevertheless, the water treatment plant business was of special interest to Královopolská. During the previous 40 years, municipal and industrial water treatment systems were seldom improved. Roughly half of all city water supplies were below standard in water quality, according to a government study. A new effort to reduce environmental pollution and improve water quality led to government regulations and investments in water purification and sewage treatment facilities, effectively expanding one of Královopolská's markets. Growth in this business helped to counter declines from the depressed chemical and nuclear power industries and contributed to increased revenues for the RIA Division especially.

Financial Results

Královopolská posted better financial results than many other companies in the early (1991–1993) transition years, though the firm was not without its troubles. (See Exhibits 3 and 4.) Revenue decreased in 1990 and 1991, and the high rate of price inflation in 1991 meant that revenue in real terms declined about 40 percent in that year. However, revenue went up both in nominal and real terms in 1992 and 1993, counter to the trend in the economy as a whole. Královopolská was profitable throughout the transition period until 1993, when it incurred a loss of Kč 103 million (about $3.5 million). This loss was largely a result of a first-time charge for reserves of Kč 180 mil-

Exhibit 3 Královopolská's Selected Income Statement Data for 1989 to 1995 (Kč million current)

	1989	1990	1991	1992	1993	1994	1995
Revenue							
Sales of products and services to external customers	1826	1737	1560	1915	2430	2304[a]	3143
Other revenue	1	8	82	114	155	1204	1041
Total revenue	1827	1745	1642	2029	2585	3508[a]	4184
Costs							
Cost of purchased inputs and services	na	na	1145	1360	994	1987[a]	2105
Labor, depreciation, reserves	448		459	461	731	1018	1072
Of which: wages		244	263	261	322	327	311
Change in inventory and work in process	−132	153	−438	−97	710	−169	617
Total costs of production	na	na	1166	1724	2435	2836[a]	3794
Other costs	na	na	270	104	253	723	226
Total costs	1788	1625	1436	1828	2688	3559[a]	4022
Profits							
Gross margin from production (Sales of products less costs of production)	na	na	394	191	−5	−532	−651
Profits before taxes (total revenue less total costs)	39	120	204	201	−103	−51	162
Employment (year end)			5469	4652	4000	3250	3000

Notes: [a]Data for 1994 internal sales of one division to another, and costs of purchased inputs by one division from another; therefore these figures cannot be compared to 1993 or earlier data. However, profit figures are comparable.

Other revenue includes sale of fixed assets, penalties received, and interest from financial investments. Reserves were first set aside in 1993 for plant and equipment repair and upgrades in the amount of Kč 180 million. Change in inventory and work-in-process appears in the revenue section of the income statement in the company's annual reports as is the German custom; we have moved it to the costs section. Other costs include costs of selling fixed assets, penalties paid, gifts, write-off of accounts receivable, interest paid on loans, and exchange rate losses.

Source: Královopolská *Annual Reports* for 1992–1995 and personal interviews with managers.

lion. Its loss of Kč 54 million in 1994 was partly the result of little new business booked in 1992 and 1993 and partly due to more changes in financial reporting to bring accounting standards in line with western financial reporting methods. Sales were up substantially in 1995, with a small profit of Kč 162 million.

Czech companies faced a serious financial threat during the transition due to the lack of trade credit. The Czech government followed a conservative fiscal and monetary policy from 1991 onward, resulting in tight credit and high nominal interest rates. In the absence of a functioning banking system, and lacking trade credit from banks, firms financed sales to customers by simply not paying their bills from suppliers, creating huge balances of both accounts payable and receivable. The sum of all receivables in the Czech Republic was Kč 200 billion ($7 billion) in 1993.

Královopolská was in relatively good shape during this period because it managed to keep its receivables under control (which also helped its position with banks). Receivables exceeded payables in 1989 and 1990, but not after that. Královopolská managers attacked the receivables problem vigorously, sending its sales force to customers to work out swaps of receivables, sometimes in three-way trades facilitated by the Ministry of Finance or assisted by consultants from Brno Technical University, who provided

Exhibit 4 Královopolská's Selected Balance Sheet Data for 1989 to 1995 (Kč million current)

	1989	1990	1991	1992	1993	1994	1995
Assets							
Accounts receivable	485	781	717	1008	796	697	779
Inventories	2698	2942	1471	832	1567	1515	1747
Total current assets	3287	3741	4797	5244	4323	4336	3914
Total fixed assets	640	654	1114	1105	1130	1098	1116
Total assets	3927	4394	5910	6349	5453	5435	5054
Liabilities							
Accounts payable	133	456	941	1050	1041	1223	1424
Bank loans	1605	1284	1016	972	1167	371	224
Total liabilities		3689	4409	5185	4180	4202	3672
Equity Capital		705	1501	1164	1273	1232	1378
Total liabilities and equity		4394	5910	6349	5453	5435	5054

Notes: Changes in accounting systems from the central-planning era to western concepts require some balance sheet data to be interpreted with care.

Source: Královopolská *Annual Reports* for 1992–1995.

computer tracking. As a result, Královopolská's receivables were less than payables in the critical years 1991–1993, thus easing its cash flow problem and reducing its need for bank credit to cover receivables.

It was almost impossible for firms to obtain long-term loans. Komerčni Banka (Commercial Bank), Královopolská's bank, "is very good if we don't ask for anything," said finance director, Jiří Cupák, in 1993. "Getting credit is very difficult. We need 100 percent collateral for loans. This is new for us. It is uncomfortable. Before the Revolution it was no problem to pay off loans. Now we have trouble. Sometimes we are late. We only get one-year loans now."

However, Královopolská was more fortunate than other companies. It was able to obtain short-term credit because, according to one manager, "We pay our interest." The Czech government was cooperating with Královopolská in long-term financing and trade credit for major export business, notably equipment for the aluminum refinery on which Iran later defaulted.

When asked about the effect of his country's economic condition on Královopolská in 1993, Zdeněk Pánek said, "I cannot change the economic conditions. If I want to cross a dirty river I

either have to build a bridge or jump in and swim." He knew he could not "clean the river" himself, so he had to find another way to the other side and was likely to get a bit muddied in the process.

MANAGEMENT'S ACTIONS DURING THE TRANSITION

After initial privatization in 1992 (see Exhibit 5), Královopolská changed its top management, which acted quickly to reorganize the company, to try to instill a new corporate culture, to improve technology and quality, and to develop new markets.

The Managers

Královopolská managers reported that even before the Velvet Revolution, people were promoted more on the basis of merit than Party membership. Technical qualifications were always more important than political favor. In this way Královopolská was different from the central planning norm. After the Revolution, political history was not a major factor in top management succession. Former Communist Party officials left the company, but technically qualified rank and file Party members stayed. None of the new top man-

Exhibit 5 Organization Chart for 1992 after Initial Privatization

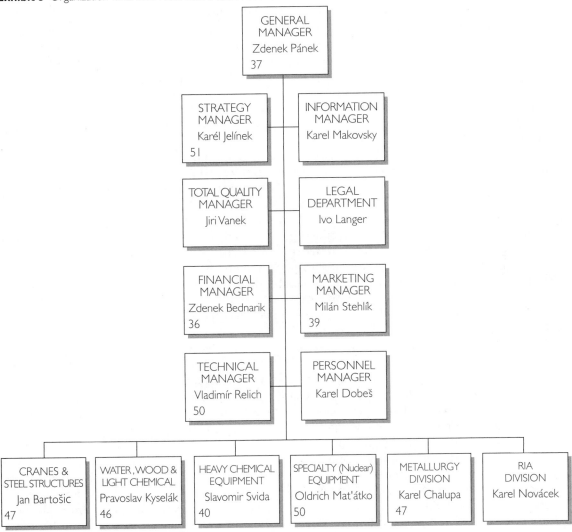

Incumbents' ages shown in bottom left area of box, when known.

agers was old enough to have been deeply involved in the failed Prague Spring of 1968 or the reprisals that followed it. The average age of the 11 top managers was only 43.

Karel Jelínek was Chairman of the Board, a position the company established in 1992. He simultaneously served as the company's strategy director. Jelínek was the only top manager after privatization who was also a top manager in 1989, when he was production director (before that he was the company's technical director). He was also unusual by being just over 50 years old in 1993. Together, Pánek and Jelínek, who was technically educated, ran Královopolská.

The board appointed Zdeněk Pánek to be the new general manager in July 1992 after initial privatization (his predecessor had served just 1½ years and then left the company). Pánek, 37, was the director of the RIA Division at the time, but was not in top management of the company when the Velvet Revolution occurred. Pánek was unusual because he was trained in economics rather than engineering. Before he headed the RIA Division, he was a field sales engineer. Pánek had no western-style management training, and spoke neither German nor English. However, he mandated that all top managers learn English in company-provided classes (although he himself did not do so). Pánek had a keen sense of the importance of customers' needs and of the necessity to change the corporate culture to one that rewarded quality, customer orientation, financial performance, and initiative rather than longevity or Party membership.

The rest of the management team was composed of engineers who had devoted their entire working life to Královopolská. Vladimír Relich was typical. He was educated at Brno Technical University in engineering. He started at Královopolská as a designer, then became head of a department (chemical equipment), then head of all design, then head of central product development, and finally technical director and a member of top management in 1992. Relich retained this position until April 1996 when KENOP reorganized the company, and the technical director position was taken inside the marketing department.

Královopolská's marketing director in 1991 was Milan Stehlík, who had spent some time in Belgium and Britain before the Velvet Revolution. He was succeeded as marketing director in 1995 by Karel Ziemba at the age of only 28. Ziemba joined the company in 1989 after his engineering education at Brno Technical University and worked on new technologies, both their technical and commercial aspects. He joined the RIA Division in 1992 as a foreign trade manager just as Pánek left this division to become general director. Nevertheless, Ziemba became Pánek's assistant in 1994, and Pánek appointed him marketing director in 1995.

Organizational Structure

Královopolská was organized by function until 1991, like most Czech firms. The functional departments were production, technical, economy, commercial, personnel, and training. The economy function under central planning involved record-keeping for cash, production, and wages. Královopolská eliminated this function in 1991 and created instead a finance function. The former commercial function was remade and renamed as the strategy function (headed by Jelínek), and a marketing function, for which there was no need before, was added.

The company reorganized in 1991 into six product divisions: (1) Water, Wood, and Light Chemical Equipment, (2) Heavy Chemical Equipment, (3) Specialty (Nuclear) Chemical

Equipment, (4) Cranes and Steel Structures, (5) Metallurgy, and (6) RIA. The first three of these divisions manufactured tanks and pipes for sale to engineering and construction firms. RIA was a small engineering and construction firm for water treatment plants, purchasing some of its product from the Water, Wood, and Light Chemical Equipment Division.

In 1992, three more functions were added to the organization: quality assurance, information systems, and legal. Also in 1992 after initial privatization, Královopolská created an inside board of directors to whom the general manager was responsible, and an outside advisory board, consistent with Czech law.

The RIA Division became the largest division in terms of revenue generated from external customers by 1993 [other divisions sold some of their output to RIA so that the reckoning of division size in terms of revenue understates the size of the other divisions in terms of volume (Exhibit 6)].

In 1994, the first three product divisions, distinguished primarily by the technical aspects of their products (e.g., size and specifications) and their end use (e.g., petrochemical plants, water treatment plants, or nuclear power stations) were combined into one division. The intent was to eliminate unproductive interdivisional competition, combine similar technologies and production processes, make all divisions into strategic business units with decentralized profit responsibility, and move further away from technologically determined collections of products to a customer focus. (Exhibit 7 shows the company's organizational chart in 1995.)

Further organizational changes were made in April 1996. A small chemical engineering unit, created in 1994 to try to develop business in the sale of scientific services separate from the manufacture of products, and initially attached to Jelínek's strategy department, was moved inside the RIA Division, where it was expected to land its first contract in 1997. Another change was the incorporation of the technical director position, held by Relich since 1992, into the marketing department.

New Market Development

Královopolská made progress in new market development and marketing after 1991. The com-

Exhibit 6 Revenues of Královoplská Divisions (Kč million current)

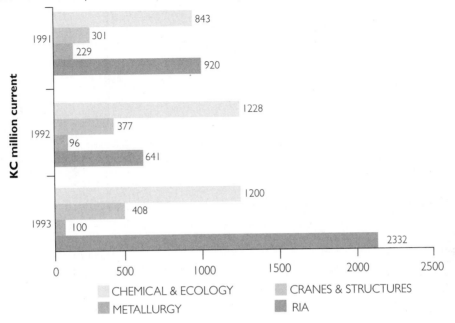

CHEMICAL AND ECOLOGY DIVISION (formed in 1994 by consolidation of three former divisions)

Water, Wood, and Light Chemical Division: Tank, tubes, filters, pumps, evaporators, agitators, furnaces, and other small equipment for water treatment plants, wood-working machinery, and light chemical industries.

Heavy Chemical Division: Tanks, towers, reactors, heat exchangers, hydrogenerators, extractors, autoclaves, steam reformers, and other large scale equipment for the chemical and petrochemical industries.

Special Chemical (Nuclear) Division: Special purpose, highly engineered steel, alloy, and plastic equipment for nuclear power stations and water treatment plants.

CRANES AND STEEL STRUCTURES DIVISION

Bridge cranes, gantry cranes, special cranes, steel buildings, and road and railway bridges for industrial and commercial applications designed in accordance with customers' requirements and erected on-site.

METALLURGY DIVISION

Production of tubes, elbows, castings, forgings, steel and alloy ingots, and annealing, tempering, and surface treatment of metallurgic products for the chemical and other industries.

RIA DIVISION

Design, engineering, production, delivery, installation, commissioning, and maintenance of complete water treatment, chemical, and nuclear plants as turnkey jobs.

Source: Královopolská *Annual Reports*. Division-level data not available after 1993.

pany's objectives were to build business relationships with large Czech chemical and construction companies, to create new distribution channels for export business independent of its former export trading company, and to focus on West European markets for both export and joint venture opportunities while also maintaining its trade links with Russia.

The company succeeded in setting up a joint venture with seven other Czech companies for trading with Russia, and it established country-level trading entities in Slovakia, Poland, and Italy. By 1997, Královopolská had established some cooperative business with west European companies (e.g., Thyssen, the German steel company), and some business in the former Soviet Republics was returning. However, gaining new customers, especially in new markets, was difficult in this industry because most relationships between equipment makers and customers were

Exhibit 7 Organization Chart for 1995 after Final Privatization

```
┌─────────────────────────────────┐          ┌──────────────────────────┐
│      BOARD OF DIRECTORS:         │          │    ADVISORY BOARD:       │
│      Karel Jelínek, Chair        │- - - - - │ Jaroslav Kadmožka, Chair │
│   Jaroslav Soja, Vice-Chair      │          │   Ivo Samek, Vice-Chair  │
│        Jiři Langer               │          │     Anna Fedorová        │
│       Icarel Maksvský            │          │      Karel Klíma         │
│        Zdeněk Pánek              │          │    Miroslav Herzán       │
│     Dagmar Šamaliková            │          │     Jiři Vodička         │
│     Stanislav Žalmánek           │          └──────────────────────────┘
└─────────────────────────────────┘

        ┌─────────────────────────┐
        │    GENERAL DIRECTOR     │
        │      Zdeněk Pánek        │
        └─────────────────────────┘

┌──────────────┐  ┌──────────────┐              ┌──────────────┐
│  CHEMICAL    │--│  STRATEGY    │              │  COMMERCIAL  │
│ ENGINEERING  │  │  MANAGER     │              │   MANAGER    │
│              │  │ Karel Jelínek│              │ Karel Ziemba │
└──────────────┘  └──────────────┘              └──────────────┘
```

INFORMATION MANAGER	TOTAL QUALITY MANAGER	LEGAL DEPARTMENT	FINANCIAL MANAGER	TECHNICAL MANAGER	PERSONNEL MANAGER
Karel Makovsky	Jiři Vaněk	Ivo Langer	Jan Špondr	Vladimír Relich	Karel Dobeš

CRANE DIVISION	CHEMICAL & ECOLOGICAL DIVISION	METALLURGY DIVISION	RIA DIVISION
Josef Ambrož	Zdeněk Žanřel	Pavel Kovařil	Karel Nováček

Sources: 1995 Annual Report and company officials.

Quality Initiatives and Competitiveness

Quality, customer orientation, and competitiveness became the mantra of top management. Královopolská started a company-wide quality assurance program in 1992, and obtained ISO 9000 and other relevant certifications by the end of 1994. The technical director, Vladimír Relich, said, "Our products were always high quality, but they did not meet West European standards. Now we have certificates of quality according to West European standards. Our products are higher in quality than Italian products." The company pro-duced glossy brochures with eye-catching graphics that illustrated Královopolská's commitment to quality, including language about the firm's trust in its employees to demonstrate Královopolská's commitment to quality in every interaction with customers.

Relich conducted an international competitive analysis of every Královopolská product in 1993 and 1994, including the products' technical specifications, quality, price, and perceptions of customer service. Competitors included companies from France, Italy, and Germany. The competitive analysis yielded six categories of products: those that were excellent (7 percent), competitive (44 percent), needed innovation (11 percent),

long-standing. Technoexport remained the main distribution channel.

needed a price decrease (21 percent), needed marketing support (7 percent), and those that were not competitive (11 percent). The competitive analysis served as an important guide for investment and divestment decisions during 1994 and 1995.

Although product quality was satisfactory, delivery time still was not. In 1997, Relich said,

Delivery time is a problem. It is better than two years ago, but it is still a problem. It used to take us a year from design to delivery on the average, and now it is four months. But it has to get down to 2½ months. It is hard to reduce the time without better controls. We need an information system to connect design and commercial functions. We lose business sometimes because of delivery problems. We are working on it, but maybe we need a strategic investor.

Research and Technology

Before the change in governments, Královopolská obtained research and development services centrally from the CHEPOS organization, as was usual in centrally planned economies. However, the breakup of CHEPOS during privatization meant that its R&D unit began competing with Královopolská, so Královopolská began to build its own R&D capability through alliances with universities and technical colleges and through a newly created internal R&D group. This was inevitably going to be a slow process, according to Relich.

"We need to buy or license technology," said Relich in 1994. "It is an acute problem. We need a partner who does not need a return right away." While no such licensing deal occurred immediately, Královopolská did make commercial agreements with firms in Austria and Finland for long term purchases of high-technology components by Královopolská that would enable it to make, sell, and deliver new products.

Ziemba repeated the need in 1997. "We still need technology updates. It is hard to meet this need. We are trying to find a foreign partner. It is a big effort to do our own R&D. We are also trying to get support from the Ministry of Industry."

Corporate Culture

Královopolská's managers identified the company's culture as a persistent challenge. The history of the firm favored manufacturing. "Production was king," said one manager. "Management

tries now to put sales on top and production next. We are still learning to make what the customer wants." He went on to say, "Our main problem is not on-time delivery. The problems are inside the company—deciding that one contract is more important than another and writing a contract that we can fulfill."

Karel Jelínek, speaking in 1994, discussed the difficulty Královopolská was having in changing the corporate culture from one that focused on following orders to one that focused on customers, quality, and initiative.

We are trying to change the corporate culture, and have been trying hard for three years. The easy thing is to write it down. The hard thing is to persuade the people so that they are convinced about the company. We want our customers to feel the corporate culture from every employee. This is the basis of a market-based approach. . . . We introduced a motivation system. It is too early to show results. People don't like to take responsibility for their own decisions. They expect other signatures on decisions [an attitude left over from the Communist era]. We are trying to find people who are not afraid of big decisions. I like people who make me lose sleep because of the possible bad results of their decisions. I prefer these people to those who wait for my approval.

Královopolská was attempting to create a new corporate culture in several ways. In addition to public statements by the general manager and the chairman of the board, Královopolská used management training, competitive analyses, merit-based performance appraisal, and incentive pay (with "disappointing results so far," said one manager in 1994) to create a more customer-, quality-, and performance-oriented climate. Pánek's observations in 1993 illustrate the challenge.

All of top management went through training to use human and democratic elements of management. But these management techniques can't be applied completely. We need order. To make order we use a direct system which is supported by control. The old system was disorder.

We want a new organizational culture in our new company. The new culture is presented on video. Each meeting of managers begins with the video. They see the video until order is there. In the worst cases they work on Saturdays seeing the video. After three Saturdays it is okay because even the worst cases don't want to come in for a fourth Saturday.

Pánek's frustration with the pace of change echoed Jelínek's:

The hardest problem is changing the people. In one year we worked out all of our quality control manuals with detailed descriptions about quality and activities. Now we fight the human factor. Even though we describe the changes in detail, people don't behave that way. They go back to the old system in which they were raised. We change people with pressure.

Královopolská also needed to create an awareness of costs, prices, profits, and financial discipline. Cupák noted, "We have a problem with management internally—with financial controls. They [financial controls] are good discipline but managers don't like them." Královopolská created a company bank to stimulate accountability and competition among divisions for corporate resources. Each division was required to show a profit or run the risk of being sold.

Královopolská steadily reduced its employment during the five years after the Velvet Revolution, from 5,469 in 1991 to about 3,000 at the end of 1995. Top management planned to reduce employment by about 400 people per year through 1997.

STRATEGIC OPTIONS

During the transition, Královopolská top management sought to determine "a clear strategy of development for the company with the objective of creating an added value very close to the value usual in the prosperous companies in the developed European countries" (*Královopolská* 1992, a company document). When Pánek became general manager in 1992, his first effort was to create a genuine business plan. Working with people from the Consulting Institute of the Prague School of Economics, top managers addressed a number of key issues, among them the objectives of the company, its strategy, and its structure. At this early stage, top management agreed to focus on quality, customer orientation, and improved discipline and motivation among employees. "We will increase productivity by 15 percent, decrease costs by 10 percent, increase efficiency by 10 percent, and extend our business into new markets," said Pánek.

Královopolská managers remembered and used a gem of Czech management wisdom from the 1930s that predated the central planning era. It is written in *Královopolská Strojírna Brno 1992*, a company document, and it refers to the famous Czech industrialist, Tomas Bat'a:

We follow the well-known—and nearly forgotten, but today often repeated—Czech saying: "Our customer, our master."

Pánek's emphasis on "order" and incentive pay was also part of the Bat'a philosophy.

The Role of Consultants

Královopolská undertook business transformation largely without the help of western consultants. Pánek believed that western consultants were too interested in the consultant's way of doing things and not familiar enough with Czech business practices, circumstances, and culture to be of much use. One bad early experience with a German consulting firm that delivered a product (for DM 38,000) that was little more than copies of publicly available documents supported his point of view. "Consultants," he said, "don't respect Czech management. They forget that we did not just jump down from the trees." He added, "We think, therefore we are." His allusion to philosophy in this statement was his way of emphasizing the cultural sophistication and intellect of Czech managers.

Pánek elaborated his view of consultants. While admitting that Královopolská needed help with financial management and business strategy, he did not want to hire consultants. "I would prefer that no one give us company-to-company advice. If someone wants to share the risk with us they should become our employee and solve problems together."

Nevertheless, the company did employ Arthur D. Little to provide management consulting in 1996. New cost accounting and management information systems were purchased from outside suppliers as a package.

Pánek also was determined not to use foreign trade companies as had been the practice prior to the Revolution. Instead, he wanted his own sales people.

The goal of the new business policy is to build up a high quality sales network of our own people in the Czech Republic. Also outside the Czech Republic. In this region [western Europe] we don't know the markets and don't have enough qualified people. Our philosophy is our employees will become qualified. We will hire people from abroad rather than consultants. We will pay them in their currency.

What Lines of Business?

Exactly how Královopolská could best achieve its business objectives was yet to be determined. Two questions needed to be resolved: What should the company's main business be? On what basis could the company best compete?

The company's long history, pride in Czech management, and skepticism of western advice indicated that it should try to remain independent and evolve its current lines of business. Exports to Russia could be expected to continue, although they were not very large. Progress was being made in developing new business in the Middle East, where Královopolská's products and prices were well-suited, and where it had some experience from central planning times, although this business was unstable.

Domestically, Královopolská was lucky that one of its businesses, water treatment plant equipment, was in a growth industry after the Revolution. The Czech government adopted a policy of extending long-term, low-interest loans to municipalities to help them finance improved water treatment facilities. Laws passed in 1992 mandated ecologically conscious water systems that adhered to environmental regulations, and required Czech company participation. Company managers projected an expenditure of Kč 16 billion (about $575 million) on municipal water treatment projects in the Czech and Slovak Republics over the five-year period 1993–98. However, Pánek believed that Czech investment in water treatment facilities would decrease after that.

Already by 1996 it had become clear that most of the big water treatment projects were finished, and that the small town water treatment projects yet to come would attract many competitors, including former state-owned enterprises that now also were privatized and restructured. One of the competitors was Sigma Engineering in Olomouc (a large town near Brno), which was strong in industrial waste water treatment, the forecasted fastest growing market segment. Sigma also posed a threat to RIA internationally because it had a good foreign sales unit and an international network left over from its role as a hard currency earner before 1989. Another competitor

was Vitkovice in Ostrava (a steel town near Poland), which was expert in small water treatment plant projects for villages of 1,200 or fewer inhabitants, a segment in which Královopolská acknowledged it was less efficient and less experienced. However, Vitkovice relied on outside installers and thus did not do complete turnkey projects. Three other potential competitors, Kunst, Eko, and Fontana, were created in 1992 out of a larger former state plant but they were hampered by quality problems with their biological water treatment products. Because they were new, they did not have the name recognition and reputation that Královopolská had.

Numerous engineering and manufacturing firms were potential competitors in western Europe. For example, Královopolská benchmarked itself against forty firms that manufactured equipment for water treatment plants, among them English firms (A.G. Tapsell, Ltd., Contra-Shear Development, Ltd., Jones Attwood Ltd., Kee Services Ltd., and Three Star Environmental Engineering Ltd.), German firms (Durr GmbH, Eisenbau Heilbronn GmbH, Fischtechnik GmbH, Handke Stengelin GmbH, Kary GmbH, Preussag Hoell GmbH, and Windolf ag, among others), and Dutch firms (Hubert Stavoren BV, Kopcke Industrie BV, and Landustrie Maschinenfabrik BV).

One of the options that especially interested Pánek and Jelínek was to develop vigorously the RIA Division and become a full-service engineering company that would design, engineer, manufacture, and build complete projects, such as the water treatment projects with which RIA already had some experience. Both industrial waste water treatment and purification of drinking water would be included. The RIA Division was small in employment (only 215 employees in 1995) and marginally profitable (Kč 43 million 1995, amounting to less than 2 percent of its sales), but fast-growing. Pánek thought a reasonable goal for the RIA Division was that it should account for 70 percent of total company revenue by 1997; in 1995 it was well over half.

The RIA Division purchased some of its components from the other divisions. About 30 percent of the Chemical and Ecological Division's output went to RIA. In early 1995 the RIA Division opened every job to outside suppliers for bids. "Every RIA job is contested for suppliers.

When the internal price is competitive, our division will get the job. Now RIA buys more products from other companies than from our division," said one manager.

Pánek recognized value in turnkey capability for chemical plants, nuclear power plants, and steel construction also. To this end, Královopolská established a small chemical engineering group reporting directly to Jelínek in 1994 and a small engineering capability in the cranes division at the same time. This group had grown to 15 people plus support staff by 1996 and was moved into the RIA Division. However, except for a controversial new plant at Temelín in Bohemia in which Královopolská was involved, the nuclear power business was on hold.

The company's formerly biggest line of business, which was chemical and petrochemical plant equipment, began to look more attractive in 1996 when the Czech government privatized the nation's oil refining and petrochemical industries. The oil refining business became 49 percent owned by a foreign consortium consisting of Shell, Conoco, and Agip. These companies were to invest $480 million within five years, and there were some provisions favoring Czech suppliers in the deal. However, this investment was slow in coming and had produced no new business for Královopolská yet by mid-1997.

Relich, when asked about the company of the future, said,

We will be in all our businesses [in the next five years] but we must change the base of our divisions. I hope the new chemical engineering department will support production in the shops by getting orders and work in the field [within five years]. We will operate as an engineering company with a majority of the company moving toward turnkey projects in cranes, water, and chemical plants. We will start with small projects and learn for bigger projects, step by step. Technology know-how has to be purchased because it is owned by big American and German companies.

Královopolská needed newer technology than it had if it was to be up to world standards, and like all Czech companies, it needed capital for plant modernization. For these reasons Královopolská explored a foreign partnership. A joint venture between the RIA Division and a West European partner was sought to improve access to West European markets that otherwise were proving difficult to enter.

Discussions took place in 1993 with a French firm in which the RIA Division was especially interested. The business of the proposed joint venture would be to build water treatment facilities in the Czech Republic. The French company was interested in the venture because it needed a Czech partner to satisfy government requirements for domestic participation. Královopolská saw the joint venture as a means for obtaining technology—the French firm would license its technology to the joint venture—and capital. Technology included not only physical processes and hardware, but also management techniques such as cost accounting. Capital was needed for investment in new plant and equipment. In addition, Královopolská's Chemical and Ecological division might be able to sell its products to the French parent. The risk of doing business with the French was that it allowed easy access to the potentially large Czech and Slovak markets—possibly trading away future business for current business. In the end, the two firms failed to reach an agreement. Though revenue for the joint venture was projected to grow rapidly, profits were expected to be too small and too far in the future for the French firm.

Another new business prospect, which was to manufacture brake shoes for motor vehicles, was not developed once the future chemical plant equipment brightened in 1996.

Decision Questions

When the management buyout occurred in January 1995, the company's financial situation captured more of Pánek's attention than ever before. Cash flow and debt repayment had to become priorities. The company was the collateral for the bank loan used for the purchase. More profitable business was needed soon. When asked about the future, one top manager said,

Královopolská is among the top third of all Czech companies. Our products are competitive. We have good equipment and well-trained people. . . . The future looks relatively good for us, but the next few years are important for us. It is necessary to change people's minds. The highest level people have changed but it is necessary to go to the lowest level. . . . We will change the base of our business. We want to become an engineering company. Results from turnkey projects will be two times higher in five years. We will buy parts from outside Královopolská. The result will be a more competitive environment within our own divisions.

Pánek reviewed Královopolská's position in mid-1995. He knew he would have to harness Královopolská's resources quickly to improve profitability, but he was not sure what his priorities should be. The industries on which the company's business depended were changing. New competition, inside and outside the Czech Republic, was becoming a factor. Pánek's managers wanted him to spend money on new technology, but KENOP, like most leveraged buyouts, was burdened with debt. Would the company's attempt to become an engineering and turnkey business instead of a tanks-and-pipes maker succeed? It was time for a new business plan.

CASE ASSOCIATED READINGS

Associated readings are given below. These are not required to analyze the case. They provide a useful context for discussion.

Fogel, D. S. (ed.). 1994. Managing in Emerging Market Economies: *Cases from the Czech and Slovak Republics*. Boulder, Colo.: Westview Press. See especially Chapters 1 and 2.

———. 1995. *Firm Behavior in Emerging Market Economies: Cases from the Private and Public Sectors in Central and Eastern Europe*. Aldershot, U.K.: Avebury.

Journal of Economic Perspectives. 1991. Special section on privatization in Eastern Europe. Vol. 5, No. 4.

Mann, C. L. 1991. "Industry restructuring in East-Central Europe: The challenge and the role for foreign investment." *American Economic Review* 81:2, 181–84.

Maruyama, M. 1990. "Some management considerations in the economic reorganization of Eastern Europe." *Academy of Management Executive* 4:2, 90–91.

Matesova, J. 1993. "Country overview study: Czech and Slovak Republics. Will the manufacturing heart beat again? *Eastern*

European Economics 31:6, 3–35.

Newman, Karen L., and Stanley D. Nollen. 1995. "Zetor tractors (A) and (B)." *Case Research Journal* 15:1, 10–33.

———. 1996. "Managerial challenges during organizational re-creation: Industrial companies in the Czech Republic." In *Privatization and Entrepreneurship: The Managerial Challenge in Central and Eastern Europe*, edited by A. A. Ullman and A. Lewis. Binghamton, N.Y.: Haworth Press. (This chapter contains a brief analysis of Královopolská as a case in discontinuous change.)

Sacks, P. M. 1993. "Privatization in the Czech Republic." *Columbia Journal of World Business* 28:1, 189–94.

Shama, A. 1993. "Management under fire: The transformation of managers in the Soviet Union and Eastern Europe." *Academy of Management Executive* 7:1, 22–35.

Svejnar, J. (ed.). 1995. *The Czech Republic and Economic Transition in Eastern Europe*. San Diego: Academic Press.

Williams, C. 1993. "New rules for a new world: Privatization of the Czech cement industry." *Columbia Journal of World Business* 28:1, 62–68.

World Bank. 1993. *Enterprise behavior and economic reforms: A comparative study in Central and Eastern Europe*. Washington, D.C.: World Bank.

CASE NOTES

1. The Velvet Revolution occurred in late November and early December of 1989 in Czechoslovakia, a few months after the fall of the Berlin wall. The name, "Velvet Revolution," comes from the fact that the existing communist government resigned without bloodshed, after massive peaceful demonstrations in Prague, giving way to a democracy almost overnight. The first post-communist government was led by Václav Havel, a playwright who had been imprisoned under the former regime for his political views. Havel, though inexperienced in government, was a strong symbol of the moral underpinnings of the Velvet Revolution and the future for Czechoslovakia.

2. The Czech economy was the most state-owned of all Soviet bloc countries (97 percent of industry was state-owned). However, the Czech Republic had a history of capitalism. Between World Wars I and II it was among the ten largest economies in the world. Privatization of large state-owned enterprises began in 1992. In some cases, foreign companies bought Czech firms in deals brokered by the government (e.g., Volkswagen bought Skoda), or foreign companies established joint ventures with Czech companies [e.g., ABB, the Swiss-Swedish multinational, and První Brněnska Strojirna (PBS) created a new 67%–33% joint venture company from part of the formerly state-owned PBS]. However, the largest share of Czech industry was privatized by vouchers. Because the government wanted to privatize industry quickly but Czech citizens had insufficient funds to buy companies, enterprises were practically given away. Each citizen could buy a voucher book for Kč 1,000, which was about one week's pay for the average industrial worker at that time. Vouchers could be spent on shares of stock in companies or sold to investment funds that purchased shares. The vast majority of large firms were privatized via this voucher method between 1992 and 1995.

References

Amado, Gilles, Claude Faucheux, and André Laurent. 1991. "Organizational change and cultural realities: Franco-American contrasts." *International Studies of Management and Organization* 21:62–91.

Brabet, Julienne, and Mary Klemm. 1994. "Sharing the vision: Company mission statements in Britain and France." *Long Range Planning* 27:84–94.

Business Korea. 2000. "Economic crisis and chaebol reform in Korea." 17, 28–30.

Certo, Samuel C., and J. Paul Peter. 1990. *Strategic Management*. New York: McGraw-Hill.

Child, J. 1981. "Culture, contingency, and capitalism in the cross-national study of organizations." *Research in Organizational Behavior* 3:303–56.

Clark, Rodney. 1979. *The Japanese Company*. Tokyo: Charles E. Tuttle Company.

Daft, Richard L. 1995. *Organization Theory and Design*. Minneapolis/St. Paul: West.

David, Fred R. 2001. *Strategic Management*. Upper Saddle River, NJ: Prentice Hall.

Deresky, Helen. 2001. *International Management*. New York: HarperCollins.

Doyle, Peter, John Saunders, and Veronica Wong. 1992. "Competition in global markets: A case study of American and Japanese competition in the British market." *Journal of International Business Studies* 23:419–42.

East Asian Executive Reports. 1999. "China: Joint MBA programs." 21, 15–16.

Economist. 2001. "Entrepreneurial fresh air." January 11, http://www.economist.com.

Economist. 2000a. "Japan's *keiretsu:* Regrouping." November 23, http://www.economist.com.

Economist. 2000b. "Big fish in small ponds." November 30, http://www.economist.com.

Egelhoff, William G. 1984. "Patterns of control in U.S., U.K., and European multinational corporations." *Journal of International Business Studies,* Fall, 73–83.

Engardia, Pete, Peter Galuska, Shekhar Hattangadi, and Neil Gross. 1994. "Have skills, will travel—homeward." *Business Week Online,* November 18.

Eveleth, D. M., J. B. Cullen, B. Victor, and T. Sakano. 1995. "Patterns of control: a cross-culture comparison of formalized, professional, and clan control of Japanese and U.S. accountants." *Advances in International Comparative Management* 10:127–43.

Gannon, Martin J. 1994. *Understanding Global Cultures.* Thousand Oaks, Calif.: Sage.

Hall, Edward T., and Mildred Reed Hall. 1990. *Understanding Cultural Differences.* Yarmouth, Maine: Intercultural Press.

Hofstede, Geert. 1991. *Cultures and Organizations.* London: McGraw Hill.

Ihlwan, Moon. 1998. "Can Kim get Koreans to swallow this medicine?" *Business Week Online,* International Edition, January 12.

Inzerilli, Giorgio, and André Laurent. 1983. "Managerial views of organization structure in France and the U.S.A." *International Studies of Management and Organization* 13:1–2, 97–118.

Jiji Press Ticker Service. 2000. "Tokai Bank seeks patent on electronic 'ringi' system." August 17.

Kagono, Tadao, Ikujiro Nonaka, Kiyonori Sakakibara, and Akihiro Okumura. 1985. *Strategic vs. Evolutionary Management.* Amsterdam: North-Holland.

Kogut, Bruce. 1985. "Designing global strategies: Comparative and competitive value-added chains." *Sloan Management Review,* Summer, 15–28.

Laurent, André. 1983. "The cultural diversity of Western conceptions of management." *International Studies of Management and Organization* 13:75–96.

Li, Peter Ping. 1993. "How national context influences corporate strategy: A comparison of South Korea and Taiwan." *Advances in International Comparative Management* 8:55–78.

Lincoln, J., and A. Kalleberg. 1990. *Culture, Control, and Commitment.* New York: Cambridge University Press.

Lyons, Denis B. K. and Spencer Stuart. 2000. "International CEOs on the rise." *Chief Executive,* February, 51–53.

McMillan, Charles J., David J. Hickson, Christopher R. Hinings, and Rodney E. Schneck. 1973. "The structure of work organizations across societies." *Academy of Management Journal* 16:555–69.

Montagu-Pollock, Matthew. 1991. "All the right connections." *Asian Business,* January, 19–24.

Pearce, John A. II, and Richard B. Robinson, Jr. 1994. *Strategic Management: Formulation, Implementation, and Control.* Burr Ridge, Ill.: Irwin.

Rieger, Fritz, and Durhane Wong-Rieger. 1990. "The development of culturally-based organizational configurations." *Advances in International Comparative Management* 5:21–49.

Ross, Douglas N. 1991. "Keiretsu: Global managers' unseen rivals." *Advances in International Comparative Management* 6:205–23.

Sekaran, Uma, and Coral R. Snodgrass. 1986. "A model for examining organizational effectiveness cross-culturally." *Advances in International Comparative Management* 2:211–32.

Sprague, Jonathan. 2000. "Foreigners at the wheel: A new boss at scandel-hit Mitsubishi Motors." *Asia Week,* September 19, 1.

Steers, Richard M., Yoo Keun Shin, and Gerardo R. Ungson. 1989. *The Chaebol.* New York: HarperBusiness.

Syu, Agnes. 1994. "A linkage between Confucianism and the Chinese family firm in the Republic of China." In *Management International,* edited by Dorothy Marcic and Sheila Puffer, 78–83. St. Paul, Minn.: West.

Taylor, Bernard, Armand Gilinsky, Adrian Hilmi, Dietger Hahn, and Ulrich Grab. 1990. "Strategy and leadership in growth companies." *Long Range Planning* 23:66–75.

Thompson, Arthur A. Jr., and A. J. Strickland III. 1999. *Strategy Formulation and Implementation.* Homewood, Ill.: Irwin.

Yoshino, M. Y., and Thomas B. Lifson. 1986. *The Invisible Link.* Cambridge, Mass.: MIT Press.

Part 6 Integrating Case

Café MAM and ISMAM

INTRODUCTION

The ISMAM (Indigenous Peoples of the Sierra Madre of Motozintla) cooperative grows and markets organic coffee, Café Mam (sounds like "mom"). This cooperative of native Mayan farmers lives in the highlands of Chiapas, Mexico. Emphasizing responsibility to the coop, hard work and standards of excellence, ISMAM built its cooperative on a foundation of egalitarian democratic ideals. Within a period of less than 10 years, the cooperative became a world exporter of gourmet coffee and is currently diversifying into other food processing ventures and ecotourism. Unlike some other groups, ISMAM did not succumb to the "postmodern condition" characterized by homogenization of culture and domination by big capital (Jameson 1990). Instead ISMAM sought specific markets for their products. In these markets they have been able to capitalize on their cultural identity and maintain a competitive advantage.

MAM MAYA

The members of ISMAM, who live in Chiapas, are part of the Mam Tzetal and Moche peoples. The ethnic group's demographic center is in Guatemala and is home to approximately half a million Guatemalan Mames. The Mames inhabit traditional communities established in colonial times. The Chiapas Mam also date back to the colonial period; however, in the 16th century they migrated to join the workforce of the Spanish cacao plantations. The current Mam population in Chiapas (estimated at around 8,000) came later toward the end of the 19th century. They were fleeing from the policies of the Guatemalan government, which was passing laws to expropriate communal lands and forcing Indians to work for ladino land owners (Hernandez 1995).

After migrating to Chiapas, the Mam experienced more repression. Around the turn of the century, many Mames were forced to serve as laborers on coffee plantations owned by Germans and foreign investors. Much of the best coffee lands were

Source: Case prepared by Ronald Nigh, Ph.D., Co-founder of Dana Association, a Mexican nongovernmental organization formed in 1987 to promote sustainable practices of forestry and agriculture; Ann D. Walsh, Ph.D., Assistant Professor of Marketing, Western Illinois University; and Dahinda Meda, Partner of Royal Blue Organics. Used with permission of the authors.

taken from the natives before the Mexican Revolution of 1910. What was left was *ejido* (common community) land or private land, both of which were divided into small parcels. Even though the Mam gained control of small parcels of poor land, their marketing outlets were still controlled by middlemen or "coyotes." The prices that they received for their coffee were kept low.

During the past two decades, the Mam society experienced further disruption as Guatemalan *braceros,* those who work far below the Mexican minimum wage, flooded local labor markets. These and other economic trends stimulated large migrations to other lands and various social changes such as widespread conversion to Protestantism (Hernandez 1994). But since the 1970s the Mexican government has reversed some of its policies in favor of Mam ethnic identity and has developed programs that support the recovery of Mam culture and language. Also, during this period the government has opened alternative coffee markets for the small producers.

Coinciding with these developments, the Catholic Church reoriented its policies toward indigenous people in this area. Historically, the Catholic Church in Mexico has been much further to the left than its counterpart in Rome. In the Revolution, the Roman Church backed the wrong side and subsequently lost much of its land and many of its churches. Under the distrustful eye of the government, the Mexican Catholic Church adapted its symbolism to the natives and directed its efforts to the indigenous people. As political advocates of the oppressed native American classes, many bishops promoted liberation by economic, political and theological means. In this context, some church sectors began to look more sympathetically on Mam culture and ethnic identity. In attempts to address the needs of the poor, the local priest of Motozintla, Father Jorge Aguilar, assumed a social activist role and greatly influenced the formation of the ISMAM cooperative. Father Aguilar literally went from community to community to convince farmers that with cooperation and hard work they could free themselves from the downward spiral that was threatening their culture and their ability to support themselves.

THE ORGANIC COFFEE MARKET

The organic food market appears to be growing due to the changes in consumer behavior in developed countries. Between 1994 and 1995, total sales of organic foods grew from $2.31 billion to $2.8 billion. This 20 percent increase surpassed that of other food categories (Mergintine and Emerich 1994). Sloan (1994) estimated that U.S. sales of organic food will increase nine times in the next ten years.

Organic coffee contributes to this growth. According to 1994 estimates, 71 million sacks of coffee were produced worldwide. Of the total, nearly 500,000 sacks of organic coffee were produced by 20 countries. Mexico's share of the organic coffee market was about 20 percent, which is less than Peru's, but twice that of Guatemala and Kenya. Demand for organically grown coffee is a relatively recent phenomenon with the first exportation of organic coffee from the Finca Irlanda Plantation in Chiapas in 1967. Recently, Lucas (1997) reported that modest sales interest in organic coffee is noted in a study by the Specialty Coffee Association of America.

Meeting the needs of this market poses a number of challenges. On the market side, the world consumers of organic coffee seek much more than a commodity. They want a product that is produced according to internationally established methods and free of chemicals, in a "socially responsible" manner, and one that meets their taste expectations. On the production side, farmers must have access to the information and possess the skills to produce coffee that meets the strict standards of organic certification. As Santoyo et al. (1995, 133) point out:

> . . . it should be emphasized that the production of organic coffee requires impeccable discipline in cultivation and marketing, which is not easy for an organization that only seeks economic benefit. For this reason, the organizations that have been successful in this market establish rules that go beyond mere production and commerce, orienting organic production to an entire way of life.

Thus, the argument evolves, if neither the consumer market nor the production process lends itself to commodity production, organic coffee production may be a viable option for only those who are willing to make it a way of life.

ASSOCIATIVE CORPORATIONS

In Mexico, as elsewhere, populations divide themselves on a number of different lines such as religions, political parties, and organizational lines, as well as on typical territorial-based communities. Some organizations operate on regional levels, often cutting across ethnic and religious ties. Agriculture coops like ISMAM are examples of regional organizations. To describe this type of regional organization, Batra (1991) coined the term "associative corporations." On the surface, associative corporations resemble traditional cooperatives. They base their collective organizations on Indian concepts of communitarian democracy and reciprocity, yet, they share commonalties with modern corporations with clearly defined administrative structures and well-established financial controls. While they practice voluntary working relations, common property management, and horizontal decision-making processes, they focus on making a profit. Overall, associative corporations reflect "hybrid" cultural institutions, which Garcia Canclini (1991) claimed are typical for postmodern Latin America.

THE MAM ORGANIC COFFEE COOPERATIVE ISMAM

From its humble beginnings with 59 members in 1979–80, ISMAM has grown to its current size of over 1,300 members from 34 regions. Most of the members are Mames, though not exclusively. The cooperative's present-day structure grew out of reorganization and extensive discussion and workshops conducted over a two-year period in 1986–87. In the reorganized structure, farmers elect officers and members to nine standing committees: executive-administration, finance, education, vigilance, solidarity, technical, advisory, membership admission, and the representative congress. Officers and committee members are elected for two-year terms and in accordance with Mayan tradition they cannot be reelected. The two-year rule places emphasis on process and cooperation rather than on personal power and personalities. Even though the transition of officers and committee members temporarily weakens the cooperative, it also strengthens it. Rotation of officers and committee members increases the depth of talent and knowledge.

Communication among members is carried out by monthly representative assemblies and a general assembly of all members. At the general assemblies, members make major decisions and elect officers and heads of committees in charge of coop business. In addition, assemblies serve as a vehicle for conveying and getting information, especially information of a technical nature. At times the current structure, which is highly dynamic, appears somewhat random. For instance, if the members dislike leaders, they oust them and elect others.

In the field, members work together in groups of ten *socios* (there are no hired laborers). Each group selects one representative who coordinates with ISMAM's nine-person technical staff and serves in the coop congress. Often the groups function as teams farming the combined land of all ten owners. However, each farmer must provide an equal work-share and insure that his own farm meets all standards of fertilization, pruning, harvesting, and postharvest treatment of the crop. Equality of human work over the randomness of parcel size and distribution are emphasized. Cash prizes are awarded for highest production per acre and highest quality grown in each district. Working together results in higher yields and sharing of knowledge.

ISMAM'S STRATEGY

The cooperative based its strategy on the assumption that with cooperative effort ISMAM could achieve a high enough volume of coffee production, which would permit direct export without intermediaries. The elimination of intermediaries would generate greater return for the small growers. From the start, the coop was determined to produce high-quality gourmet coffee for an exclusive, upscale market, even though the market potential for organic coffee was unknown at the time.

In the first workshops, ISMAM's founding members faced a gloomy situation. Small farmer production was much lower relative to that of the larger private growers. In addition, production costs were rising due to increasing costs of agrochemicals, while profits were being absorbed by ladino intermediaries who controlled the market channels and forced the farmers to accept low prices. ISMAM members realized that they had to do something about the low levels of production and the channels of distribution.

Eliminating the intermediaries proved to be a difficult task. The political mechanism of expropriating the peasants' products and transferring the value to the regional and extraregional economy was a traditional feature of the Chiapas regional economy. Intermediaries, who enjoyed the full repressive support of regional, oligarchic political structures, were not about to turn over their lucrative businesses to peasant farmers. As a result, farmers' initial attempts to assume more control of the marketing channels were met with repression from local and state governments. Repression was further compounded by the imposition of a military man as state governor. Policies aimed at neutralizing agrarian claims and obstructing independent farmer organizations resulted in systematic violation of human rights.

Apart from the political difficulties associated with "appropriation of the productive process," the new cooperative encountered a number of technical and economic problems. To address these challenges, the coop turned to outsider advisors and financial support of several kinds. Two key people in the field were Robert Soto, an agronomist and organic specialist, and Jose Caballero, a specialist in composting, erosion, and annual crops for higher altitudes. Also, Guatemalan agronomists, who were fleeing their country's repression of Indian coops, brought technical expertise and workshop methodology experience to the ISMAM cooperative. Together, these advisors and ISMAM members developed a methodology for collective analysis and problem solving. The methodology evolved into a group discussion workshop called *trabajo comun organizado* (TCO), "organized work together." Now, all new ISMAM members are required to participate. In these workshops, members continue to analyze their socioeconomic situation, its causes, and the possible solution to their severe problems of poverty and social marginality.

THE IMPORTANCE OF ORGANIC FARMING

ISMAM's decision to adopt organic farming methods proved to be a critical element in production and marketing strategies. But, before the collective decision was made, ISMAM members carefully weighed the pros and cons of organic methods. In their discussions, members noted that organic methods were more harmonious with Indian traditional agriculture. For centuries the Mayan people of Chiapas and Guatemala practiced polycultural farming on loosely scattered farms in the jungles. They also experimented with canals and terraces. Their methods were sustainable and organic, and so effective that Pre-Columbian Mexican agriculture has been cited as a model of sustainability, the most productive and least erosive in the world. Not until they abandoned their native ways did they encounter the problem of massive erosion caused by mismanagement and use of large machinery on environmentally sensitive lands. Therefore, when the concept of organic farming was discussed as a possible alternative, ISMAM members were already favorably disposed toward it.

Besides being more harmonious with Indian traditional agriculture, organic farming opened the door to a highly specialized market in Europe, the type that ISMAM was seeking. At that time the Western European market was supported by a network of 300 "social solidarity" shops that carried products from indigenous communities and cooperatives of the Third World. To help consolidate indigenous organizations, the shops collected a surcharge of around 10 percent on all products sold. In turn, the surcharge was returned to the producers. For ISMAM the surcharge from the sales of organic coffee provided critical support during the years of development and allowed the cooperative to circumvent the trading monopolies of conventional products. Today, the direct solidarity market accounts for a little over 15 percent of ISMAM's annual sales.

Transition to organic methods profoundly affected ISMAM's internal organization and the technological development of coffee production among the growers. To enter the organic market, ISMAM had to insure that all phases of their coffee production (i.e., growing, cleaning, drying, milling, bagging, shipping import customs, transporting, warehousing, and roasting) met the guidelines for "organic labeling." The label not only meant that no synthetic chemicals were used in growing or processing but that a long-term fertility management system had to be put into place. In the case of Mexican organic coffee, fertility management involved maintenance of a diversified population of shade trees, the terracing of inclined fields, production and application of composts, ecological pest control, and crop diversification. Organic products are certified by recognized certification organizations who carry out yearly inspections in the fields and who may contract laboratory analyses to determine levels of pesticide residues in products, all at the growers' expense. National and state legislation in the United States, the EC and in many other countries including Mexico currently regulate organic food production.

ISMAM had to implement strict internal controls on all phases of their coffee production: postharvest processing (carried out by each grower on his farm), transportation of dried coffee to the final processing plant, and selection of lots for export. To insure that all farmers would comply, ISMAM's agronomists had to establish an inspection plan. They set up monthly visits with each grower to check on progress in fertility management and to provide advice and assistance. All visits were recorded and entered into a computer bank in the central office in Motozintla. The coop also established a system for labeling bags of coffee so that any single bag could be traced to its origin.

Switching to organic farming also helped solve the technical problems identified by ISMAM members in their early workshops. First, productivity increased as much as fivefold or more in three to five years as a direct result of the long-term fertility program required for certification. Second, organic methods such as production of compost and biological controls eliminated the need for agrochemicals, thereby significantly lowering the production costs. Third, organic methods resulted in a much higher quality product, which could be exported directly to European and U.S. gourmet markets. Furthermore, organic methods helped insulate ISMAM from fluctuations in the commodity coffee market. For instance, in 1989 when the price of coffee collapsed on the international market, ISMAM's organic strategy paid off. While many other Mexican producers, large and small, left their coffee crops unharvested in the fields, ISMAM members received premium prices for their organic coffee. To further stabilize their position, coop members agreed to retain profits to contract their own agronomists and for harvest-time credit to members. Retaining profits helped strengthen ISMAM's independence from government, banks, and middlemen in matters of technology and marketing.

THE POLICY CONTEXT OF THE NEW AGRARIAN MOVEMENT

Traditionally, peasants have been expected to assume the roles of providers of raw materials and/or cheap labor. Political force has been used to insure that other sectors of regional society can appropriate the value added by marketing peasant products or exploiting peasant labor. The "appropriation of the productive process" (including marketing) by intermediaries has been one of the cornerstones of the political economy systems related to peasants. Without access to global information and communication structures, peasants remain captured in this traditional structure.

In contrast with the ISMAM Mam, most rural Mexican societies are unable to access new information and communication structures. Social disorganization and anomie tend to prevail. ISMAM's ability to utilize global structures to create alliances outside the region help explain why the coop has been able to successfully consolidate; whereas, Indian members of many sister organizations in the Selva Lacandona have not been successful and have had to seek other options to solve their political problems.

Thus, while the ISMAM experience is atypical of Indian and peasant organizations in Mexico, it is not unique. ISMAM's organizational structure reflects a general process that is taking place in Mexican rural society. The traditional communities and the political and economic organizations associated with those identities are giving way to new organizations based on cross-community and cross-ethnic ties. The new organizations promote Indian identity in a regional, national, and even transnational context. These organizations demand more than land, technical assistance, and credit; they expect cultural and political autonomy, and multilingual and intercultural education as well. As demonstrated in the political program of the Zapatista movement in Chiapas today, political freedom, democracy, and local autonomy are fundamental demands of the new peasant organizations. Land reform is simply not enough.

Overall, the new organizational structures can be seen as a response of Indian communities to changes in three fundamental links between global and local processes: (1) changes in national government policies as versions of a neoliberal ideology promoted by global financial brokers, (2) changes in the relations of power within regional society, in this case in Chiapas, and (3) new relationships between local Indian societies and other global forces, such as the growing demand for organic foods and Indian solidarity movements in the First World.

ISMAM DIVERSIFICATION

ISMAM recently won a multimillion dollar grant to develop an ecotourism model coffee farm. The 700-acre farm will be located in the Sierra Madre mountains at an altitude of 1,300 meters and will be large enough for mountain biking, hiking, bird watching, and organic farmwork. With its own electrical system, the farm will become the new home of 120 native families. All visitors and inhabitants will find themselves in a lush, tropical, chemical-free environment.

Other coop projects include a new cultural center in Tapachula. The center, a gift of a German church group, is in the final stages of construction. ISMAM has also entered into a joint venture with a fishing cooperative on an island surrounded by a 4,700-square-mile ecological preserve. In addition, ISMAM has expanded its product lines, adding organic honey and cacao (chocolate), and it will soon add cinnamon and hibiscus tea. Other projects under consideration involve a joint venture with U.S. partners to form a company that will market all ISMAM products and tourism options.

ISMAM's current products and most recent undertakings can be found on the Internet, at http://mmink.com/mmink/dossiers/cafemam.html.

CASE QUESTIONS FOR DISCUSSION

1. How is the ISMAM cooperative similar to a U.S. corporation? How is it dissimilar?
2. Describe the roles that technology and social institutions have played in the development of ISMAM.
3. How has the Maya Indian culture influenced the organizational structure of ISMAM?
4. Would the management style and organizational structure of ISMAM work for a U.S. corporation?
   Explain.
5. Find CAFEMAM on the Internet. What products besides coffee does ISMAM market? Are these suitable extensions for ISMAM? What challenges will diversification create for ISMAM?

CASE REFERENCES

Batra, Armando. 1991. Pros, contras y asegunes de la "appropiacion del proceso productivo." *Cuadernos desarrollo de base* 2:5–22.

García Canclini, Nestor. 1991. *Culturás híbrídas. Estrategías para entrar y salír de la modernídad*, Los noventa #50. Editorial Grijalbo, Mexico City.

Hernandez Castillo, Rosalva Aida. 1994. Identidades colectivas en los márgenes de la nación: etnicidad y cambio religioso entre los mames de Chiapas. *Nueva Antropología*, No. 45.

———. 1995. Inventando tradiciones: encuentros y desencuentros de los mames con el indigenismo mexicano. *América Indígena* (special volume on Chiapas).

Jameson, Frederic. 1990. *Post-modernism or the Cultural Logic of Late Capitalism*. Durham: Duke University Press.

Lucas, Eric. 1997. "Socially responsible coffee." Downloaded from http://www.coffeetalk.com/html/current_issue.html.

Mergintine, K., and M. Emerich. 1994. NFM's organic market overview, 1993. *Natural Food Merchandiser,* 15, No. 6: 48–50.

Santoyo, Cortés, V. Horacio, Salvador Díaz Cardenas, and Benigno Rodríguez Padrón. 1995. *Sístema Agroíndustrial Café en Mexico: Díagnóstico, Problemática y Alternativas*. Universidad Autónoma Chapingo, Mexico.

Sloan, A. E. 1994. Top ten trends to watch and work on, *Food Technology,* July: 89–100.

7d culture model A seven dimension cultural model based on beliefs regarding how people relate to each other, how people manage time, and how people deal with nature.

A

Achievement versus ascription How a society grants or gives status.

Achievement-motivation theory Suggestion that only some people have the need to win in competitive situations or to exceed a standard of excellence.

Adhocracy Flat organizational pyramid, mutual-adjustment control mechanisms, and participative or consultative decision making.

Anchor partner A partner that holds back the development of a successful strategic alliance because it cannot or will not provide its share of the funding.

Asia-Pacific Economic Cooperation (APEC) A confederation of 19 nations with less specific agreements on trade facilitation in the Pacific region.

Attitudinal commitment The willingness to dedicate resources and efforts and face risks to make the alliance work.

Attribution Process by which people interpret the meaning and intent of spoken words or nonverbal exchanges.

Attributional approach to leadership Emphasis on what leaders believe causes subordinates' behaviors.

Autocratic leadership Leaders make all major decisions themselves.

Autonomous work group Team or unit that has nearly complete responsibility for a particular task.

B

B2B Business-to-business transactions.

B2C Business-to-consumer transactions.

Back stage of culture Aspects of culture that are understood only by insiders or members of the culture.

Backdoor recruitment Prospective employees are friends or relatives of those already employed.

Balance-sheet method Attempts to equate purchasing power in the host country with the expatriate's purchasing power in his or her home country.

Benevolent trust The confidence that the partner will behave with good will and with fair exchange.

Bonus system In Japan, employees often receive up to 30 percent of their base salary, usually given twice a year during traditional gift-giving seasons.

Brick-and-mortar The traditional or non-virtual business operation.

Building a relationship The first stage of the actual negotiation process, when negotiators concentrate on social and interpersonal matters.

Bureaucratic control system Focuses on managing organizational processes through budgets, statistical reports, standard operations procedures, and centralization of decision making.

Business culture Norms, values, and beliefs that pertain to all aspects of doing business in a culture.

Business-level strategies Those for a single business operation.

C

C2B Consumer-to-business transactions.

C2C Consumer-to-consumer transactions.

Calculative commitment Alliance partner evaluations, expectations, and concerns regarding potential rewards from the relationship.

Capabilities The ability to assemble and coordinate resources effectively.

Chaebol Family-dominated multi-industry conglomerate, such as Daewoo, dominant in Korean business.

Co-determination Surrender by management to workers of a share of control of the organization, traditionally reserved for management and owners.

Coercive isomorphism The force or power of social institutions to make organizations adopt certain practices.

Collectivism A set of cultural values that views people largely in terms of the groups to which they belong.

Commitment In a strategic alliance, occurs when partners take care of each other and put forth extra effort to make the venture work.

Comparative advantage That arising from cost, quality, or resource advantages associated with a particular nation.

Compensation Organization's entire reward package, including not only financial rewards and benefits but nontangible rewards, such as job security.

Competitive advantage When a company can outmatch its rivals in attracting and maintaining its targeted customers.

Competitive negotiation Each side tries to give as little as possible and tries to "win" for its side.

Competitive scope How broadly a firm targets its products or services.

Competitive strategies Moves multinationals use to defeat competitors.

Competitor analysis Profiles of your competitor's strategies and objectives.

Complementary skill One that enhances but does not necessarily duplicate an alliance partner's skills.

Concession making Process requiring each side to relax some of its demands to meet the other party's needs.

Consensus bureaucracy Has little job specialization for individuals, an age seniority system, close personal bonding among section members, functional organizational structures, and strong cultural control mechanisms.

Consultative or participative leadership Leader's style falls midway between autocratic and democratic styles.

Contingency theory Assumption that different styles and different leaders are more appropriate for different situations.

Contract manufacturers Produce products for foreign companies following the foreign companies' specifications.

Control mechanisms Control mechanisms link the organization vertically.

Control system Vertical organizational links, up and down the organizational hierarchy.

Convenient relativism What occurs when companies use the logic of ethical relativism to behave any way they please, using the excuse of differences in cultures.

Convergence Increasing similarity of management practices in different nations.

Coordination system Horizontal organizational links.

Copycat businesses Those following the "Me too" strategy, whereby they adopt existing strategies for providing products or services.

Corporate-level strategies How companies choose their mixture of different businesses.

Counter-parry Fending off a competitor's attack in one country by attacking in another country, usually the competitor's home country.

Country clusters Groups of countries with similar cultural patterns.

Craft union Represents people from one occupational group, such as plumbers.

Credibility trust The confidence that the partner has the intent and ability to meet promised obligations and commitments.

Cross-cultural training Increases the relational abilities of future expatriates and, in some cases, their spouses and families.

Cultural beliefs Our understandings about what is true.

Cultural control system Uses organizational culture to control behaviors and attitudes of employees.

Cultural norms Prescribed and proscribed behaviors, telling us what we can do and what we cannot do.

Cultural relativism A philosophical position arguing that all cultures, no matter how different, are correct and moral for the people of those cultures.

Cultural rituals Ceremonies such as baptism, graduation, or the tricks played on a new worker, or the pledge to a sorority or fraternity.

Cultural stories These include such things as nursery rhymes and traditional legends.

Cultural symbols These may be physical, such as national flags or holy artifacts. In the workplace, office size and location can serve as cultural symbols.

Cultural values Values that tell us such things as what is good, what is beautiful, what is holy, and what are legitimate goals for life.

Culture The pervasive and shared beliefs, norms, and values that guide the everyday life of a group.

Customer contact techniques Trade shows, catalog expositions, international advertising agencies and consulting firms, government-sponsored trade missions, and direct contact.

D

Decision-making control Level in the organizational hierarchy where managers have the authority to make decisions.

Defensive competitive strategies Attempts to reduce the risks of being attacked, convince an attacking firm to seek other targets, or blunt the impacts of any attack.

Democratic leadership Leader includes subordinates in decision making.

Deontological ethical theory Focus on actions that, by themselves, have a good or bad morality regardless of the outcomes they produce.

Differentiation strategy Strategy based on finding ways to provide superior value to customers.

Direct communication Communication that comes to the point and lacks ambiguity.

Direct contact Face-to-face interaction of employees.

Direct exporting More aggressive exporting strategy, where exporters take on the duties of intermediaries and make direct contact with customers in the foreign market.

Dirty tricks Negotiation tactics that pressure opponents to accept unfair or undesirable agreements or concessions.

Dispersed subunits Subsidiaries located anywhere in the world where they can most benefit the company.

Distinctive competencies Strengths that allow companies to outperform rivals.

Dominant partner The partner that controls or dominates strategic and operational decision making.

Dual system Form of vocational education in Germany that combines in-house apprenticeship training with part-time vocational-school training, and leads to a skilled certificate.

E

E-commerce The selling of goods or services over the Internet.

E-commerce enablers Fulfillment specialists that provide other companies with services such as Web site translation.

Economic analysis Of an ethical problem, focuses on what is the best decision for a company's profits.

Elephant-and-ant complex Occurs in strategic alliances when two companies are greatly unequal in size.

Enterprise union Represents all people in one organization, regardless of occupation or location.

Entrepreneur Person who creates new ventures that seek profit and growth.

Entry wedge Company's competitive advantage for breaking into the established pattern of commercial activity.

Equity theory Proposal that people perceive the fairness of their rewards vis-à-vis their inputs based on how they compare themselves to others.

ERG theory Simplified hierarchy of needs, including growth needs, relatedness needs, and existence needs.

Escalation of commitment Companies continue in an alliance relationship longer than necessary because of past financial and emotional investments.

Ethical analysis One that goes beyond focusing on profit goals and legal regulations.

Ethical convergence Refers to the growing pressures for multinational companies to follow the same rules in managing ethical behavior and social responsibility.

Ethical relativism Theory that each society's view of ethics must be considered legitimate and ethical.

Ethical universalism Theory that there are basic moral principles that transcend cultural and national boundaries.

Ethics gap Idea that U.S. political and legal social institutions create greater coercive and normative pressures for U.S. businesses to follow ethical standards.

Ethnocentric HRM All aspects of HRM for managers and technical workers tend to follow the parent organization's home-country HRM practices.

Ethnocentrism When people from one culture believe that theirs are the only correct norms, values, and beliefs.

European Union (EU) Austria, Belgium, Britain, Denmark, Finland, France, Germany, Greece, Ireland, Italy, Luxembourg, the Netherlands, Portugal, Spain, and Sweden, plus Norway and Switzerland in the related European Free Trade Area.

Expatriate Employee who comes from a different country from where he or she is working.

Expectancy theory Assumption that motivation includes an individual's desire to satisfy his or her needs and their beliefs regarding how much their efforts at work will eventually satisfy their needs.

Export department Coordinates and controls a company's export operations.

Export Management Company (EMC) Intermediary specializing in particular types of products or particular countries or regions.

Export Trading Company (ETC) Intermediary similar to EMC, but it usually takes title to the product before exporting.

F

Fair exchange In a strategic alliance, occurs when partners believe that they receive benefits from the relationship equal to their contributions.

Family bureaucracy Similar to an extended family, with a dominant patriarch or father figure.

Fiedler's theory of leadership Proposal that success of task- or person-centered leader depends on relationships between the leader and his or her subordinates; the degree that subordinates' tasks are easily and clearly defined; and the officially granted organizational power of the leader.

Final agreement Signed contract, agreeable to all sides.

Financial objectives Those that focus on achieving stockholder returns or financial performance ratios.

First offer First proposal by parties of what they expect from the agreement.

First-mover advantage That of the entrepreneur who moves quickly into a new venture and establishes the business before other companies can react to the opportunity.

Foreign Corrupt Practices Act (FCPA) Forbids U.S. companies to make or offer illegal payments or gifts to officials of foreign governments for the sake of getting or retaining business.

Foreign direct investment (FDI) Multinational firm's ownership, in part or in whole, of an operation in another country.

Foreign subsidiary Subunit of the multinational company that is located in another country.

Formal communication Communication that acknowledges rank, titles, and ceremony in prescribed social interaction.

Formal international cooperative alliance A nonequity alliance with formal contracts specifying what each company must contribute to the relationship.

Four tigers The newly industrialized countries (NICs), including Hong Kong, Singapore, South Korea, and Taiwan.

Front stage of culture The easily observable aspect of culture.

Full bureaucracy Rules, procedures, and hierarchical relationships dominate the organization.

Full-time integrator Cross-unit coordination is the main job responsibility.

Functional structure Has departments or subunits based on separate business functions, such as marketing or manufacturing.

Functions of work Outcomes such as providing necessary income and providing satisfactory experiences.

Fundamental attribution error Assumption by managers that people behave in certain ways because of internal motivations, rather than outside factors.

G

General Agreement on Tariffs and Trade (GATT) Tariff negotiations between several nations that reduced the average worldwide tariff on manufactured goods.

Generic strategies Basic ways that both domestic and multinational companies keep and achieve competitive advantage.

Geographic structure Has departments or subunits based on geographical regions.

Global culture Managerial and worker values that view strategic opportunities as global and not just domestic.

Global IHRM Recruiting and selecting worldwide, and assigning the best managers to international assignments regardless of nationality.

Global integration solution Conducting business similarly throughout the world, and locating company units wherever there is high quality and low cost.

Global leader One who has the skills and abilities to interact with and manage people from diverse cultural backgrounds.

Global mindset One that requires managers to "think globally, but act locally."

Global pay system Worldwide job evaluations, performance appraisal methods, and salary scales are used.

Global platform Country location where a firm can best perform some, but not necessarily all, of its value-chain activities.

Global start-up Company that begins as a multinational company.

Globalization The worldwide trend of businesses expanding beyond their domestic boundaries.

Globalization drivers Conditions in an industry that favor transnational or international strategies over multilocal or regional strategies.

Global–local dilemma Choice between a local-responsiveness or global approach to a multinational's strategies.

Goal-directed behavior One that people use with the intention of satisfying a need.

Goal-setting theory Assumption that the mere existence of a goal is motivating.

Great-person theory Idea that leaders are born with unique characteristics that make them quite different from ordinary people.

Greenfield investments Starting foreign operations from scratch.

H

Headquarters-based compensation system Paying home country wages regardless of location.

Hierarchy of needs theory States that people have five basic types of needs: physiological, security, affiliation, esteem, and self-actualization.

High-context language One in which people state things indirectly and implicitly.

Hofstede model of national culture A cultural model mainly based on differences in values and beliefs regarding work goals.

Holistic approach Each side makes very few, if any, concessions until the end of the negotiation.

Home country nationals Expatriate employees who come from the parent firm's home country.

Horizontal differentiation Number of subunits in the organization.

Host country nationals Local workers who come from the host country where the unit (plant, sales unit, etc.) is located.

Host-based compensation system Adjusting wages to local lifestyles and costs of living.

Human resource management (HRM) Functions are recruitment, selection, training and development, performance appraisal, compensation, and labor relations.

Hybrid structure Mixes functional, geographic, and product units.

I

ICA International cooperative alliance.

Ideological union Represents all types of workers based on some particular ideology (e.g., communism) or religious orientation.

IHRM orientation Company's basic tactics and philosophy for coordinating IHRM activities for managerial and technical workers.

IJV and ICA performance criteria Often must include criteria other than financial, such as organizational learning.

IJV International joint venture.

IJV negotiation issues Include points such as equity contributions, management structure, and "prenuptial" agreements regarding dissolution of the relationship.

Importance of work Goals that people hope to achieve from working.

Independent management structure Alliance managers act more like managers from a separate company.

Indirect exporter Uses intermediaries or go-between firms to provide the knowledge and contacts necessary to sell overseas.

Individualism The relationship between the individual and the group in society.

Induced-factor conditions National resources created by a nation, such as a superior educational system.

Industrial union Represents all people in a particular industry, regardless of occupational type.

Influence tactics Tactical behaviors leaders use to influence subordinates.

Informal international cooperative alliance An agreement not legally binding between companies to cooperate on any value-chain activity.

Inpatriate Employees from foreign countries who work in the country where the parent company is located.

Interdependent relationships Continuous sharing of information and resources by dispersed and specialized subunits.

Internal versus external control Beliefs regarding whether one controls their own fate.

International business ethics Those unique ethical problems faced by managers conducting business operations across national boundaries.

International cadre Separate group of expatriate managers who specialize in a career of international assignments.

International cooperative alliance (ICA) An agreement for cooperation between two or more companies from different nations that does not set up a legally separate company.

International division Responsible for managing exports, international sales, and foreign subsidiaries.

International franchising Comprehensive licensing agreement where the franchisor grants to the franchisee the use of a whole business operation.

International human-resource management (IHRM) All HRM functions, adapted to the international setting.

International joint venture (IJV) A separate legal entity in which two or more companies from different nations have ownership positions.

International sales intensity Amount of international sales divided by total sales of the company.

International strategic alliance Agreement between two or more firms from different countries to cooperate in any value-chain activity from r&d to sales.

International strategies Selling global products and using similar marketing techniques worldwide.

Internet hosts Computers connected to the Internet with its own IP address.

Interpreter's role To ensure the accuracy and common understanding of written and oral agreements.

ISO 9000:2000 The current name for the technical and quality standards of the International Organization for Standardization.

J

Job-characteristics model Suggests that work is more motivating when managers enrich core job characteristics, such as by increasing number of skills a job requires.

K

Keiretsu Japanese conglomerate such as Mitsubishi.

Key success factors (KSFs) Important characteristics of a company or its product that lead to success in an industry.

Key success factors for expatriate assignments Motivation, relational abilities, family situation, and language skills.

Kinesics Communication through body movements.

L

Labor relations Ongoing relationship between an employer and those employees represented by labor organizations.

Leadership Process of influencing group members to achieve organizational goals.

Legal analysis Of an ethical problem, focuses on only meeting legal requirements of host and parent countries.

Less developed countries (LDCs) The poorest nations, often plagued with unstable political regimes, high unemployment, and low worker skills.

Levels of culture These include national, business, and occupational and organizational culture.

Liability of newness A large percentage of new businesses fail within a year.

Liability of size Being small often makes business failure more probable, because small size usually means limited resources.

Liaison role Part of a person's job in one department to communicate with people in another department.

Licensing Contractual agreement between a domestic licenser and a foreign licensee (licenser usually has a valuable patent, technological know-how, trademark, or company name that it provides to the foreign licensee).

Local union Represents one occupational group in one company.

Local-responsiveness solution Responding to differences in the markets in all the countries in which a company operates.

Location advantages Dispersing value-chain activities anywhere in the world where the company can do them best or cheapest.

Long-term orientation A basic orientation toward time that values patience.

Low-context language One in which people state things directly and explicitly.

Low-cost strategy Producing products or services equal to those of competitors at a lower cost than competitors.

M

Masculinity Tendency of a society to emphasize traditional gender roles.

Meister In Germany, a master technician.

Mimetic isomorphism Voluntary imitation by managers of strategies of the most successful organizations.

Minireplica subsidiary Smaller version of the parent company, using the same technology and producing the same products as the parent company.

Mission statement Tells the organizational members and outsiders what the company does and why it exists.

Moral languages Description of the basic ways that people use to think about ethical decisions and to explain their ethical choices.

Motivation A psychological process resulting in goal-directed behavior that satisfies human needs.

Motivator-hygiene theory Assumption that a job has two basic characteristics, motivators and hygiene factors.

Multidomestic strategy Emphasizing local-responsiveness issues.

Multinational company Any company that engages in business functions beyond its domestic borders.

Multinational management The formulation of strategies and the design of management systems that successfully take advantage of international opportunities and respond to international threats.

N

National context National culture and social institutions that influence how managers make decisions regarding the strategies of their organizations.

National culture The dominant culture within the political boundaries of the nation-state.

National-context contingency model of leadership Shows how culture and related social institutions affect leadership practices.

Natural-factor conditions National resources that occur naturally, such as abundant water supply.

Need Feeling of deficit or lacking that all people experience at some time.

Need theory Of motivation, assumes that people can satisfy basic human needs in the work setting.

Negotiation steps Preparation, building the relationship, exchanging information, first offer, persuasion, concessions, and agreement.

Nenpo **System** New Japanese compensation system based on yearly performance evaluations that emphasize goals—although goals are not always the same as in Western companies.

Neutral versus affective The acceptability of expressing emotions.

New ventures Entering a new market; offering a new product or service; or introducing a new method, technology, or innovative use of raw materials.

Nonverbal communication Face-to-face communication that is not oral.

Normative isomorphism Imitation by organizations of designs, cultures, and strategies of other organizations, without the conscious effort of mimetic isomorphism.

North American Free Trade Agreement (NAFTA) A multilateral treaty that links the United States, Canada, and Mexico in an economic bloc that allows freer exchange of goods and services.

O

Occupational cultures Distinct cultures of occupational groups such as physicians, lawyers, accountants, and craftspeople.

Offensive competitive strategies Direct attacks, end-run offensives, pre-emptive strategies, and acquisitions.

Operant conditioning Model proposes that, if a pleasurable consequence follows a behavior, the behavior will continue, whereas if an unpleasant consequence follows a behavior, the behavior will stop.

Organizational culture The norms, values, and beliefs concerning the organization shared by members of the organization.

Organizational design How organizations structure subunits and use coordination and control mechanisms to achieve their strategic goals.

Organizational isomorphism Pressure from social institutions to follow similar paths in strategy and other management practices.

Output control system Assesses the performance of a unit based on results, not on the processes used to achieve those results.

P

Participation strategies Options multinational companies have to enter foreign markets and countries.

Particularism Dealing with other people based on personal relationships.

Passive exporter Company that treats and fills overseas orders like domestic orders.

Path-goal theory Four types of leadership styles that a manager might choose depending on the situation.

Performance appraisal System to measure and assess employees' work performance.

Performance-maintenance (PM) theory Japanese perspective on balancing task- and person-centered leader behaviors.

Permanent employment In Japan, continuous employment, often to the age of 55.

Personal success characteristics Ability to tolerate ambiguous situations, flexibility, creativity, humor, stamina, empathy, and knowledge of a foreign language.

Person-centered leader One who focuses on meeting employees' social and emotional needs.

Persuasion Stage when each side in the negotiation attempts to get the other side to agree to its position.

Pervasive The idea that culture affects almost everything we do, everything we see, and everything we feel and believe.

Polycentric IHRM Firm treats each country-level organization separately for HRM purposes.

Power distance Expectations regarding equality among people.

Prescriptive ethics for multinationals Suggested guidelines for the ethical behavior of multinational companies.

Privatization The sale of government-owned businesses to private investors.

Problem-solving negotiation Negotiators seek out mutually satisfactory ground that is beneficial to both companies' interests.

Process theories Of motivation, arising from needs and values combined with an individual's beliefs regarding the work environment.

Product structure Has departments or subunits based on different product groups.

Professional bureaucracy Has moderate levels of vertical and horizontal differentiation, uses standardization of skills as the preferred control mechanism, and may also centralize decision making.

Profit center Unit controlled by its profit or loss performance.

Proxemics The use of space to communicate.

Punishment Consequences of a person's behavior that discourage the behavior.

R

Recruitment Process of identifying and attracting qualified people to apply for vacant positions in an organization.

Regiocentric IHRM Regionwide HRM policies are adopted.

Regional strategy Managing raw-material sourcing, production, marketing, and support activities within a particular region.

Regional trade agreements Agreements among nations in a particular region to reduce tariffs and develop similar technical and economic standards.

Reinforcement Reactions to a person's behavior that encourage the person to continue the behavior.

Repatriation problem Difficulties that managers face in coming back to their home countries and reconnecting with their home organizations.

Resource pool All the human and physical resources available in a country.

Resources Inputs into the production or service processes.

***Ringi* system** Formal decision-making procedure used in Japanese organizations.

S

Secure server An Internet host that allows users to send and receive encrypted data.

Selection Process by which companies fill vacant positions in the organization.

Sequential approach Each side reciprocates concessions made by the other side.

Shared cultural values, norms, and beliefs The idea that people in different cultural groups have similar views of the world.

Shared management structure Occurs when both parent companies contribute approximately the same number of managers to the alliance organization.

Situational assessment Determining the internal strengths and weaknesses of the company and external opportunities and threats to the company.

Size barrier to internationalization It is often more difficult for small businesses to take the first step in internationalizing their organization.

"Small" business UN definition: less than 500 employees. Popular press definition: less than 100 employees. U.S. Small Business Administration's definition: varies by industry and uses both sales revenue and the number of employees.

Small-business advantage Fast-moving entrepreneurs can use their competitive advantage of speed. Being first to market, they can capture significant sales before larger competitors react.

Small-business stage model Process of internationalization followed by many small businesses.

Social institution Enduring system of relationships among people, such as an educational or political system.

Social loafing Term used when people put out less effort when they work in groups.

Social responsibility Idea that businesses have a responsibility to society beyond making profits.

Sociotechnical systems approach Focuses on designing motivating jobs by blending the social system (i.e., organizational structure, culture) with different technologies.

Specialized operations Subunits specializing in particular product lines, different research areas, or different marketing areas.

Specific versus diffuse The extent to which all aspects of an individual's life is involved in their work relationships.

Split-control management structure Partners usually share strategic decision making but split functional-level decision making.

Stereotyping When one assumes that all people within a culture behave, believe, feel, and act the same.

Strategic complementarity One that complements the alliance partner's.

Strategic objectives Those that focus on beating competitors.

Strategy formulation Process by which managers select the strategies to be used by their company.

Subordinates' expectations Expectations regarding what leaders "should" do and what they may or may not do.

Sustainable Strategies not easily defeated by competitors.

Switching costs Expenses involved when a customer switches to a competitor's products.

SWOT The analysis of an organization's internal *strengths* and *weaknesses,* and the *opportunities* or *threats* from the environment.

T

Task force Temporary team created to solve a particular organizational problem.

Task-centered leader One who gives subordinates specific standards, schedules, and tasks.

Task-related information Actual details of the proposed agreement.

Team Permanent unit of the organization designed to focus the efforts of different subunits on particular problems.

Technological leadership Being first to use or introduce a new technology.

Teleological ethical theory One that suggests that the morality of an act or practice comes from its consequences.

Third country nationals Expatriate workers who come from neither the host nor home country.

Time horizon The way cultures deal with the past, present, and future.

Touching Basic form of human interaction, including shaking hands, embracing, or kissing when greeting one another.

Training and development Giving employees the knowledge, skills, and abilities to perform successfully both in current jobs and in future jobs.

Training rigor Extent of effort by both trainees and trainers required to prepare the trainees for expatriate positions.

Transactional leadership One where managers use rewards or punishments to influence their subordinates.

Transformational leadership One where managers go beyond transactional leadership by articulating a vision, breaking from the status quo, providing goals and a plan, giving meaning or a purpose to goals, taking risks, being motivated to lead, building a power base, and demonstrating high ethical and moral standards.

Transition economies Countries in the process of changing from government-controlled economic systems to capitalistic systems.

Transnational strategy Two goals get top priority: seeking location advantages and gaining economic efficiencies from operating worldwide.

Transnational subsidiary Has no companywide form or function—each subsidiary does what it does best or most efficiently anywhere in the world.

Transnational-network structure Network of functional, product, and geographic subsidiaries dispersed throughout the world, based on the subsidiaries' location advantages.

TRIAD The world's dominant trading partners: European Union, United States, and Japan.

Turnkey operation Multinational company makes a project fully operational and trains local managers and workers before the foreign owner takes control.

U

U.S. legal requirements for appraisals Regulating performance-evaluation practices to ensure their fairness.

U.S. strategic management process Assumption that managers can accurately analyze the competitive environment in which the company operates and logically craft strategies that maximize competitive strengths and avoid competitive weaknesses.

Uncertainty avoidance How people react to what is different and dangerous.

Union membership density Proportion of workers in a country who belong to unions.

Universalism Dealing with other people based on rules.

Utilitarianism Argument that what is good and moral comes from acts that produce the greatest good for the greatest number of people.

V

Value chain All the activities that a firm uses to design, produce, market, deliver, and support its product.

Verbal negotiation tactics Promises, threats, recommendations, warnings, rewards, punishments, normative appeals, commitments, self-disclosures, questions, commands, "No" (refusals), interruptions.

Vertical differentiation Number of levels in the organization.

W

White-collar or professional union Represents particular occupational group, similar to craft union.

Whorf hypothesis Theory that language determines the nature of culture.

Work centrality Overall value of work in a person's life.

Works council In Germany, employee group that shares plant-level responsibility with managers over issues such as working conditions.

World Trade Organization (WTO) A formal structure for continued negotiations to reduce trade barriers and a mechanism for settling trade disputes.

Worldwide geographic structure Has geographical units representing regions of the world.

Worldwide matrix structure Symmetrical organization, usually with equal emphasis on worldwide product groups and regional geographical divisions.

Worldwide product structure Gives product divisions responsibility to produce and sell their products or services throughout the world.

NAME INDEX

COMPANY INDEX